Single Season Sitcoms
of the 1980s

ALSO BY BOB LESZCZAK

The Odd Couple *on Stage and Screen:*
A History with Cast and Crew Profiles
and an Episode Guide (McFarland, 2014)

Single Season Sitcoms, 1948–1979:
A Complete Guide (McFarland, 2012)

Single Season Sitcoms of the 1980s
A Complete Guide

Bob Leszczak

McFarland & Company, Inc., Publishers
Jefferson, North Carolina

LIBRARY OF CONGRESS CATALOGUING-IN-PUBLICATION DATA

Names: Leszczak, Bob, 1959– author.
Title: Single season sitcoms of the 1980s : a complete guide / Bob Leszczak.
Description: Jefferson, North Carolina : McFarland & Company, Inc., Publishers, 2016 | Includes index.
Identifiers: LCCN 2016015439 | ISBN 9780786499588 (softcover : acid free paper) ∞
Subjects: LCSH: Situation comedies (Television programs)—United States. | Television serials—United States.
Classification: LCC PN1992.8.C66 L475 2016 | DDC 791.45/617—dc23
LC record available at https://lccn.loc.gov/2016015439

BRITISH LIBRARY CATALOGUING DATA ARE AVAILABLE

ISBN (print) 978-0-7864-9958-8
ISBN (ebook) 978-1-4766-2384-9

© 2016 Bob Leszczak. All rights reserved

No part of this book may be reproduced or transmitted in any form or by any means, electronic or mechanical, including photocopying or recording, or by any information storage and retrieval system, without permission in writing from the publisher.

Front cover image of TV set and remote © 2016 dumayne/iStock

Printed in the United States of America

*McFarland & Company, Inc., Publishers
Box 611, Jefferson, North Carolina 28640
www.mcfarlandpub.com*

To the memory of my mom, Margaret,
whose unconditional love I miss
more and more with each passing day.

Table of Contents

Acknowledgments xi

Preface 1

Single Season Sitcoms of the 1980s 3

Ace Crawford, Private Eye	3	The Duck Factory	31
a.k.a. Pablo	4	The Dukes (animated)	33
All Is Forgiven	5	Easy Street	33
Aloha Paradise	7	Eisenhower and Lutz	35
Amanda's	9	The Ellen Burstyn Show	36
Ann Jillian	10	Empire	37
Annie McGuire	11	Enos	38
At Ease	11	E/R	38
Baby Boom	12	Everything's Relative	40
Baby Makes Five	13	Family Man	41
Baker's Dozen	14	The Famous Teddy Z	41
Best of the West	14	Fast Times	42
Better Days	15	Fathers and Sons	44
Beverly Hills Buntz	16	A Fine Romance	44
Blue Skies	17	First Impressions	45
The Boys	18	Fitz and Bones	45
Boys Will Be Boys	18	Foley Square	46
The Brady Brides	18	Foot in the Door	47
Brand New Life	19	Foul Play	49
Breaking Away	20	The Four Seasons	49
Bustin' Loose	20	Frank's Place	50
The California Raisin Show (animated)	22	Free Spirit	51
Charlie and Company	22	Freebie and the Bean	51
Checking In	24	Galaxy High (animated)	52
Chicken Soup	24	The Gary Coleman Show (animated)	52
The Completely Mental Misadventures of Ed Grimley (partially animated)	25	George Burns Comedy Week	53
		Gilligan's Planet (animated)	54
Condo	26	Gloria	55
Dads	26	Good Time Harry	56
Dirty Dancing	27	Goodtime Girls	56
The Dom DeLuise Show	28	Gun Shy	58
Domestic Life	28	Gung Ho	58
Down and Out in Beverly Hills	29	Hail to the Chief	60
The Drak Pack (animated)	30	Half Nelson	61
Dreams	31	Hard Knocks	61

Harry	62
Have Faith	63
Heartland	65
Herbie the Love Bug	65
He's the Mayor	66
Homeroom	67
I Had Three Wives	68
I Married Dora	68
I'm a Big Girl Now	70
Isabel Sanford's Honeymoon Hotel	71
It Takes Two	72
It's Not Easy	73
It's Your Move	73
Jack and Mike	75
Jennifer Slept Here	75
Joe Bash	76
Just in Time	76
Just Our Luck	77
Karen's Song	78
Knight and Daye	78
Ladies' Man	79
The Last Precinct	81
Learning the Ropes	82
Legmen	83
Leo and Liz in Beverly Hills	84
Lewis and Clark	84
Life and Times of Eddie Roberts (L. A. T. E. R.)	86
Life with Lucy	87
Live-In	88
Living Dolls	89
Lobo	91
The Lucie Arnaz Show	91
Madame's Place	92
Maggie	93
Making the Grade	94
Mama Malone	95
Mama's Boy	95
Marblehead Manor	96
Mary	97
Me and Maxx	98
Me and Mom	98
Meatballs and Spaghetti (animated)	99
Melba	99
Misfits of Science	100
Mr. Merlin	101
Mr. Smith	102
Mr. Sunshine	102
Mork and Mindy (animated)	104
Nearly Departed	104
The New Adventures of Beans Baxter	106
The New Love American Style	109
The New Monkees	110
The New Odd Couple	111
Nick and Hillary	113
No Soap Radio	113
Nobody's Perfect	114
Nothing in Common	114
Nothing Is Easy	115
The Nutt House	115
Off the Rack	117
Oh, Madeline	118
Once a Hero	119
One Big Family	119
One in a Million	120
One of the Boys (1982)	121
One of the Boys (1989)	122
Open All Night	123
Open House	124
Park Place	125
Partners in Crime	126
The People Next Door	126
Phyl and Mikhy	127
Police Squad	129
The Popcorn Kid	130
Probe	131
Pursuit of Happiness	132
Raising Miranda	134
The Redd Foxx Show	135
Reggie	137
Report to Murphy	137
The Robert Guillaume Show	138
Roomies	139
The Rousters	140
Roxie	140
Sanchez of Bel Air	142
Sara	143
Second Chance	144
Semi-Tough	145
Seven Brides for Seven Brothers	145
Shadow Chasers	146
Shaping Up	147
Shell Game	147
Shirley	148
Sister Kate	149
Six O'Clock Follies	150

The Slap Maxwell Story	151	The Thorns	168
Small and Frye	152	Three's a Crowd	169
Snoops	153	Together We Stand	170
Spencer	154	The Tortellis	171
Square Pegs	156	Tough Cookies	172
Star of the Family	158	Trial and Error	173
Starting from Scratch	159	Tucker's Witch	175
Steambath	160	Under One Roof	176
Stir Crazy	160	United States	176
The Stockard Channing Show	161	The Van Dyke Show	176
Suzanne Pleshette Is Maggie Briggs	163	Washingtoon	177
Sweet Surrender	164	What a Country	177
Take Five	164	When the Whistle Blows	178
Tanner '88	165	Women in Prison	180
Tattingers	166	You Can't Take It with You	181
Tenspeed and Brown Shoe	167	Zorro and Son	182

Appendix A: Shows Invited Back for a Truncated or Vastly Different Second Season   183

Aftermash	183	Joanie Loves Chachi	209
Angie	184	Laverne and Shirley (animated)	211
The Bad News Bears	185	Me and Mrs. C.	211
The Baxters	188	The Misadventures of Sheriff Lobo	212
Buffalo Bill	188	Mr. President	214
The Cavanaughs	190	My Sister Sam	215
Charles in Charge	192	The New Leave It to Beaver	217
The Charmings	193	Rags to Riches	217
Coming of Age	195	The Ropers	218
Day by Day	196	Sanford	219
Double Trouble	197	Sledge Hammer	220
Filthy Rich	198	Still the Beaver	221
Flo	199	Teachers Only	223
FM	201	13 East	225
Good Morning, Miss Bliss	202	Trying Times	227
Goodnight, Beantown	203	The Two of Us	228
Harper Valley	205	We Got It Made	228
Harper Valley P.T.A.	205	You Again?	230
Hello, Larry	206		

Appendix B: The Sitcom Topical Index   232

Index   235

Acknowledgments

My most sincere, heartfelt thanks go out to all of the talented TV performers, writers, producers, directors, showrunners, and musicians who took time out of their own hectic schedules to supply their quotes, memories, insight, kindness, and even some photographs for this volume. Many have become cherished friends.

This TV Hall of Fame list of interviewees is in alphabetical order—Nick Abdo, Lucie Arnaz, Cindy Begel, Jack Blessing, John Boni, Joyce Bulifant, Dean Cameron, Randall Carver, Robert Clohessy, Julie Cobb, R. J. Colleary, Murphy Cross, Elinor Donahue, Christine Ebersole, John Femia, Lucy Lee Flippin, Teresa Ganzel, Dave Hackel, Molly Hagan, James Hampton, Clint Howard, Bruce Jarchow, Israel Juarbe, Bo Kaprall, Caren Kaye, Bill Kirchenbauer, Dennis Klein, Audrey Landers, Michael Leeson, Rick Lenz, Rick Lohman, Philip Charles MacKenzie, Wendel Meldrum, Caitlin O'Heaney, Stuart Pankin, Jerry Perzegian, David Pollock, Wayne Powers, Michael Preece, Lawrence Pressman, Paul Provenza, John Rappaport, Martin Rips, Mark Rothman, Jennifer Runyon, Ed Scharlach, Jack Seifert, Ralph Senensky, Charles Shyer, Joseph Staretski, Renny Temple, Alicia Ulrich, Billy Vera, and Joel Zwick. Those not quoted (but very important to this book's completion) include Mark Arnold, Robert Fox, Tom Kleinschmidt, Jim MacKrell, Dennis Ostrom, Richard Sackley, David Schwartz, Rob Sinclair, Vincent Terrace, Mark Topaz, Carl Weintraub, and Mitch Weisberg.

Preface

The prime-time lineup landscape of the 1980s was chock full of situation comedies. In fact, sitcoms enjoyed quite a resurgence at this time. *Amen, Cheers, The Cosby Show, A Different World, Empty Nest, Family Ties, The Golden Girls, Growing Pains, Kate and Allie, Newhart, Night Court, Roseanne,* and *227* were all big hits.

This book is *not* about these shows, although some of them receive a mention or two where relevant. As a sequel to my first book, *Single Season Sitcoms, 1948–1979: A Complete Guide*, this volume focuses upon short-lived situation comedies from the totally awesome and most excellent '80s—the decade that gave us Rubik's Cube, Ms. Pac Man, video cassette recorders, boom boxes, the Swatch Watch, the mullet, and Cabbage Patch Dolls. While certainly not as significant as the shows listed above, many covered here did serve as a springboard to fame for the likes of Julia Louis-Dreyfus (*Day by Day*), Jason Alexander (*Everything's Relative*), George Clooney (*E/R*), Katey Sagal (*Mary*), Patrick Dempsey (*Fast Times*), Jason Bateman (*It's Your Move*), Jim Carrey (*The Duck Factory*), Megan Mullally (*The Ellen Burstyn Show*), Teri Hatcher (*Karen's Song*), Jon Cryer (*The Famous Teddy Z*), George Wendt (*Making the Grade*), Michael Richards (*Marblehead Manor*), Sarah Jessica Parker (*Square Pegs*), Jason Priestly (*Sister Kate*), Ellen DeGeneres (*Open House*), Bryan Cranston (*Raising Miranda*), David Hasselhoff (*Semi-Tough*), Courteney Cox (*Misfits of Science*), Nell Carter (*Lobo*), Cynthia Nixon (*Tanner '88*), and John Stamos (*Dreams* and *You Again?*).

And even though the programs listed here are considered "flops," it should not be forgotten—they still had millions of weekly viewers or were important "must see TV" for a select few. A surprising number have surfaced as DVD box sets: *Angie, Buffalo Bill, Flo, Joanie Loves Chachi, Rags to Riches, Sledge Hammer, Square Pegs, The Stockard Channing Show, Tanner '88,* and *Tenspeed and Brown Shoe*, to name a few.

Because cable television channels and the new FOX TV Network flourished in the 1980s, the amount of original programming increased exponentially. This explains the large number of failed sitcoms included in this new volume. Between 1948 and 1979, there were only three, and very briefly four, TV networks (remember the DuMont Network?) and a little more than 300 short-lived sitcoms of that era. But in the 1980s, there were cable channels such as Nick at Nite, The USA Network, HBO, Showtime, The Disney Channel, and A&E producing some of their own programming, some of which included situation comedies. Well over 200 sitcoms from the decade lasted only a single TV season (or less). A few others were renewed for what became a truncated second season before being canceled. These are included in Appendix A, as are such series as *Charles in Charge*, and *Still the Beaver/The New Leave It to Beaver*, which enjoyed several successful seasons, but differed greatly from their freshman year. Single season programs that debuted in 1979 and had aired episodes in 1980 are excluded if they were written about in the first volume. Those programs include *Joe's World*, and *The Associates*. Programs such as *Love, Sidney; She's the Sheriff; The New Gidget;* and *Hooperman* enjoyed two full seasons in prime-time, and are thus excluded. Obviously, those programs that lasted for slightly more than two full seasons, such as *Doctor, Doctor; The Righteous Apples;* and *Crazy like a Fox*, are also excluded from this volume.

Information has been extracted from my large collection of classic TV programs, while others were viewed at the Paley Centers for Media in New York City and Los Angeles, as well as the UCLA TV Archives in Los Angeles. A large number were viewed on YouTube. For many of these programs, quotes from the cast and/or crew take us behind the scenes for some enlightening revelations and never-before-published information, hilarious anecdotes, and amazing stories about these short-lived sitcoms.

For each of the sitcoms contained in this volume, there is an overview of what the program was about, where it took place, its time slot, the network affiliation, the cast and crew, the duration, the production studio, the episode titles, and where available, the sponsor. Cast photos are also provided for many of the shows. Appendix B provides numerous, interesting topical lists, breaking these sitcoms down into informative subsets. You will also notice the frequent use of a couple of terms—*dramedy* and *crimedy*. Dramedy is an oft-used term for a program with both dramatic and comedic elements, recorded without a live audience or laugh track. Crimedy is my own term for crime shows that combine action with lighter, often very funny moments (and I use the term liberally).

So, whether you're skimming through the book seeking out your own favorite short-lived situation comedy of the 1980s, or combing the book from cover-to-cover, thank you for a *continued* interest in *Single Season Sitcoms*. Rest assured the 1990s and the new millennium will be addressed in future volumes.

The Single Season Sitcoms of the 1980s

Ace Crawford, Private **Eye** Conway Enterprises. CBS. Tuesday nights 8:00 (March 15, 1983–April 12, 1983). Five episodes were filmed with a laugh track.

At one time, the license plate on Tim Conway's car read "13 WKS." It was there for a good reason—every TV vehicle in which he starred was gone in thirteen weeks (at least he had a sense of humor about it). Of course, he had long runs as a co-star on *McHale's Navy* and *The Carol Burnett Show*, but his starring vehicles, *Rango*, *The Tim Conway Show* (two different shows with that title), *The Tim Conway Comedy Hour*, *Turn On*, and *Ace Crawford, Private Eye*, were less than successful.

As Ace Crawford, a bumbling gumshoe in a trench coat and a fedora (channeling Craig Stevens as Peter Gunn), Conway got to replay many of the zany characters from Burnett's show (including the hard-of-hearing, slow-walking old man). In the debut episode, one of the characters was named Mrs. Wiggins (a nod to Carol Burnett's hilariously inefficient secretary to Conway's Mr. Tudball). Here, Tim portrayed a lone wolf running the Ace Detective Agency. Joe Regalbuto (later of *Murphy Brown*) played his accountant, Toomey (and also served as the narrator); diminutive Billy Barty played Inch, the owner and bartender at The Shanty—a wharfside watering hole (Barty, coincidentally, had the similar role of Babby, the snitch in the aforementioned *Peter Gunn* series); Shera Danese (Mrs. Peter Falk in real life) was Luana, the hot lounge singer (à la Lola Albright on *Peter Gunn*) who was "warm for Ace's form" (always heard belting out the same song, "A Bicycle Built for Two"); Bill Henderson was her blind accompanist, Mello; and Dick Christie was Detective Lieutenant Fanning, who was always surprised at Ace's crime-solving abilities.

Yes, abilities. Despite all of the bumbling and fumbling, Ace somehow managed to "ace" each and every case. Well, five cases—then the show was canceled. In those five episodes, however, Ace has a reputation as a sleuthing superstar, and is occasionally asked for his autograph. Director Michael Preece recalled, "I had worked with Tim previously on the film *The Prizefighter*, in which he co-starred with Don Knotts. Tim and I became quite good friends. He is very outgoing and an amazing talent. One

Tim Conway starred in this sendup of *Peter Gunn*—*Ace Crawford, Private Eye*—on CBS. After five aces, it folded its hand.

episode of this series was about four minutes short, and Tim asked for a few props—Scotch Tape, a feather duster, a typewriter and some paper—and filled more than those four minutes brilliantly, in one take." Preece added, "He's also a kind and generous man. In one scene set in a laundry, I was attempting to show Tim how to do the scene without getting hurt. It involved a falling laundry sack, and wouldn't you know it, that laundry sack knocked me down. I was fine, but I scraped an elbow and tore my sweater. Tim felt so bad about me hurting myself and tearing my sweater, he replaced it with a very expensive brand new sweater."

For the nightclub scenes, Preece added, "Tim had all the stuffing taken out of his seat in the booth in which he always sat so that he would always sit much lower than everyone else, for comic effect." Every episode ended the same way, with Ace walking off into the fog while the narrator describes Ace as "the peeping Tom of justice, and two steps ahead of everyone else," followed by a big splash as Ace falls into an unseen body of water. Preece said, "Even though this series lasted only five episodes, it was one of my highlights. I had so much fun, I couldn't wait to get to work each day. However, we were up against an instant hit on NBC called *The A-Team*, and couldn't compete. I got to do another pilot called *Great Day* with Tim a while later, after Dick Van Dyke backed out of the project. It was set in a sporting goods store and was quite good, but it didn't sell. Too bad—I think it would have been a hit."

Episodes of *Ace Crawford, Private Eye* were titled "Murder at Restful Hills," "Bull Bates," "Inch in a Pinch," "The Microchip Caper," and "The Gentleman Bandit." The executive producer was Philip Weltman; the producer was Ron Clark; the writers included Ron Friedman and Mickey Rose; the director was Michael Preece. Music was provided by Hughie Cannon and Peter Matz.

a.k.a. Pablo Embassy Television. ABC. Tuesday nights 8:30 (March 6, 1984–April 17, 1984). Six episodes were videotaped before a live audience.

Latino comedian Paul Rodriguez went into this project knowing it would be a big flop, but took his $18,000.00 a week and ran—for a total of six episodes. The program wanted us to believe the entire large cast was Mexican, but several were Puerto Rican, and Joe Santos, who portrayed Paul's Latino father on the show, was of Italian heritage. Rodriguez places some of the blame for the program's failure on that fact. Even with veteran producer Norman Lear behind it, *a.k.a. Pablo* failed to find an audience and was gone in a month and a half.

It told the story of Paul (a.k.a. Pablo) Rivera, a stand-up comic who still lives at home (a house with number 2435 on the front door) with his mom and dad. Working at nightclubs until the wee hours of the morning, his schedule differs greatly from that of his extremely large family, and getting sleep during the day with their coming, going, yelling, and fighting is almost impossible. Paul's parents were born in Mexico, but now reside in east Los Angeles. His father, Domingo Rivera (Joe Santos), is a hard-working gardener/landscaper who is very stubborn, set in his ways, and disapproving of son Paul's chosen career path (he doesn't want his son to be another Freddie Prinze, the well-known Puerto Rican comedian who battled drug abuse and committed suicide in 1977, at the age of twenty-two). He also detests the fact that a large percentage of Paul's act consists of jokes about Latinos. Paul's mother, Rosa Maria (Katy Jurado), is a great cook and an impeccable housekeeper (who even irons her son's socks) and tries to keep peace in that noisy and hot-tempered household. Paul has two sisters—the somewhat butch Sylvia (Alma Cuervo), who works at K-Mart, and Lucia (Martha Velez), who cleans houses in Beverly Hills. Lucia is married to the swaggering Hector Del Gado (Arnaldo Santana), often seen flexing his muscles. Paul also has a brother, Manuel (Bert Rosario), a bricklayer, who is Paul's complete opposite. Manuel takes after his father and is serious-minded and, often, very combative. An extremely young Mario Lopez had his first recurring role in this show, albeit a very small one, as Tomas Del

Latino comic Paul Rodriguez starred in the ABC sitcom *a.k.a. Pablo*. It was given the axe—a.k.a. canceled—after only six episodes. Pictured are guest star Bea Arthur and Rodriguez.

Gado—one of Paul's innumerable nieces and nephews. The ubiquitous Héctor Elizondo portrayed Paul's bad toupee-wearing agent Jose Shapiro (his actual surname is Sanchez). There was another member of the family, Ramon, a parrot who resided in a large cage in the living room.

Episodes were titled "The Pilot," "The Big Mouth" (with guest star Merv Griffin), "My Son the Gringo" (with guest star Beatrice Arthur), "The Presidential Joke Teller," "The Whole Enchilada," and "The Woman Who Came to Dinner." The executive producer was Norman Lear; the producer was Rick Mitz; the writers included Norman Lear, Rick Mitz, Jack Elinson, Jose Rivera, Steven Kunes, and Seth Greenland; the directors included Héctor Elizondo, Joan Darling, and Thomas McConnell. The creators were Norman Lear and Rick Mitz. Music was provided by the Latino vocal group Tierra, most famous for the song "Together."

All Is Forgiven Charles-Burrows-Charles Productions/Paramount Television. NBC. Thursday nights 9:30 (March 20, 1986–March 27, 1986), Saturday nights 9:30 (March 29, 1986–April 19, 1986), and Thursday nights 9:30 (May 29, 1986–June 12, 1986). Nine episodes were filmed in front of a live audience.

Pretty and perky Bess Armstrong didn't have the best luck with TV sitcoms. In the 1970s, she starred in the short-lived *On Our Own*. In the 1990s, it was *Married People*. In between those came *All Is Forgiven*. The title of this sitcom was also the title of the show-within-a-show, on which Bess's character, Paula Winters Russell, served as producer. To backtrack a bit, in the debut episode, Paula hadn't yet tacked on the surname of Russell.

There was an abundance of expository information in that first episode—here's the "CliffsNotes" version. Year after year, March 29th is the date on which good things happen to Paula Winters. For example, she got her first kiss from a guy and her first charge card at

All Is Forgiven (on NBC) was a show within a show. All was forgotten after only nine episodes. Pictured at top is David Alan Grier; the next row has (left to right) Judith-Marie Bergan, Terence Knox, and Bill Wiley; in the row after that are Shawnee Smith, Bess Armstrong, and Carol Kane; the bottom row includes Debi Richter and Valerie Landsburg.

Bloomingdales on that day. She then opted to schedule her wedding and apply for a new job on March 29th—both on the very same March 29th. At the job interview she is initially granted the title of associate producer of a troubled TV soap opera called *All Is Forgiven*, but when Paula's new immediate superior is let go for defying the big boss, the clueless and impetuous Mrs. Fontaine (voiced by Doris Grau, who was heard, but never seen; behind the scenes, Grau was also the sitcom's script supervisor), Paula is hastily named producer. Paula's fiancé, Matt Russell (Terence Knox), is forced to delay the wedding for a few hours because his bride-to-be is immersed in her new role and has fires to put out. Try as they might to tie the knot on Paula's lucky day, their impromptu wedding occurs just minutes after midnight. Said wedding was conducted by the director of the soap opera, white-haired Wendell (Bill Wiley). Wendell was ordained during a lull in his directing career. The couple's honeymoon plans in Cancun, however, are disrupted. Matt was divorced, and from his first marriage he has a very difficult, vocal and sarcastic teenage daughter named Sonia (Shawnee Smith pre–*Becker*), who was totally unaware until that moment that she had a stepmother. The relationship between Paula and Sonia is initially very strained, and plunges downhill when Sonia is forced to move into her father's big New York apartment (with the number 32 on the door). She had been ousted from college for being a no-show, and couldn't move in with her natural mother because they didn't get along. Her last resort is to live with her father, the donut executive. One of his career objectives is to create healthier donuts, but his family eschews the free samples of the unsavory new flavors (such as rhubarb) that are foisted upon them. Paula is an ex-smoker, but takes up the bad habit anew after being confronted with Matt's daughter's new living arrangement (plans to stay with them forever), as well as with all the crazies at her overwhelming new job. On the staff of writers for the soap opera is Nicolette "Nick" Bingham (Carol Kane)—an airy Southern belle with a Southern drawl, a love for reading, and a saccharin eagerness to become Paula's best friend from day one. She and Paula, along with her receptionist/secretary Lorraine Elder (Valerie Landsburg) are forced to pull several "all-nighters" to keep the short-staffed show on schedule. In episode two of the sitcom (titled "With Child"), it is discovered that Mrs. Fontaine has hired a completely inexperienced African-American writer named Oliver Royce (pre–*In Living Color* David Alan Grier). He is actually a TV repairman, and Fontaine finds his everyman qualities and knowledge of "what the public really wants to see" refreshing. Royce has, in fact, never seen *All Is Forgiven*. All of the writers, producers, and directors have to kowtow to the mercurial and demanding star of the soap, Cecile Porter-Lindsey (Judith-Marie Bergan), without whom there would be no ratings.

The show's nine episodes revolved around Paula's delicate and unnerving balancing act between newlywed stepmom and inundated producer of a doomed serial. It's interesting to note that, upon its move to Saturday nights on NBC, an episode of *All Is Forgiven* actually aired on March 29th, but it wasn't a very lucky time slot, and the program went on hiatus after four weeks there.

Episodes were titled "On-Air Commitment," "With Child," "And Sonia Makes Three," "Part Perfect" (with guest star Adam Arkin), "Mother's Day" (with guest stars Jake Steinfeld and Christina Applegate), "And Justice for Ollie," "I Can't Say No" (with guest star Gwen Verdon), "Paula Russell II," and "Matt at the Barricades" (with guest star Joe Regalbuto). The creators and executive producers were Howard Gewirtz and Ian Praiser; the producers were Kimberly Hill and Tim Berry; the writers included Kimberly Hill, Tim Berry, Miriam Trogdon, Glen and Les Charles, Tom Seeley, Joe Fisch, Howard Gewirtz, Norm Gunzenhauser, Janet Leahy, Ian Praiser, and Bob Rosenfarb; the directors included James Burrows, Jeff Chambers, Barnet Kellman, and Jim Drake. Music was provided by Robert Kraft.

Aloha Paradise Aaron Spelling Productions/Universal Television. ABC. Wednesday nights 9:00 (February 25, 1981–April 29, 1981). Eight hour-long episodes were filmed with a laugh track.

This was Debbie Reynolds's second attempt at TV success—a dozen years after *The Debbie Reynolds Show* on NBC. *Aloha Paradise* was, for all intents and purposes, *The Love Boat* for landlubbers (the theme song was similar, it was

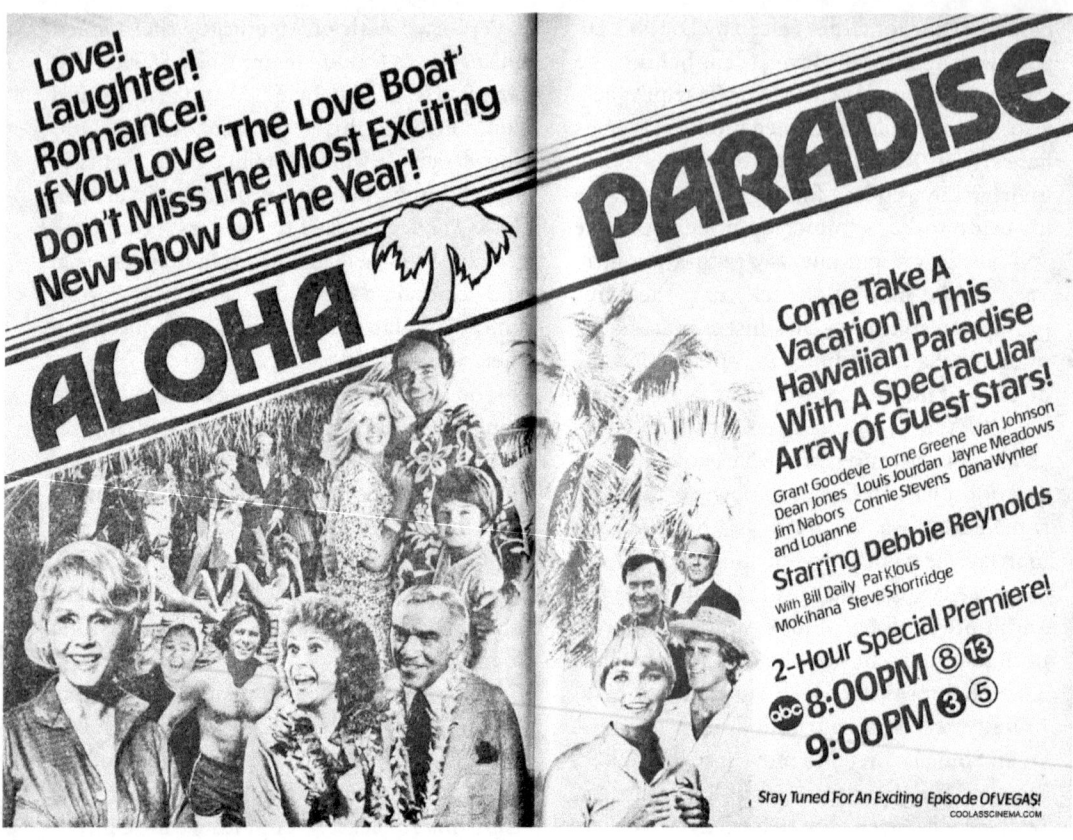

Aloha Paradise, ABC's attempt at a second *Love Boat*, was Debbie Reynolds's second shot at TV sitcom success. Low ratings caused the network to say aloha after only eight weeks. Pictured (lower left to right) are Debbie Reynolds, Jayne Meadows, and Lorne Greene.

an Aaron Spelling Production, and it was on ABC). Or, as episode three's guest star Audrey Landers recalled, "It was closer to being a *Fantasy Island*. I had the pleasure of working on almost all of Aaron Spelling's shows. He was kind of a quiet man—not imposing. He would pop in and out at will. He didn't like to fly, so whenever an episode of any of his shows was done out of the country, he didn't go with it."

Debbie Reynolds played Sydney Chase, the lovely manager of the equally lovely Paradise Village Resort in Hawaii. About Reynolds, Landers shared, "Debbie is amazingly talented, so professional, and couldn't have been nicer." Sydney's (Debbie's) assistant was Curtis Shea, played by sitcom veteran Bill Daily; overly friendly Fran (Pat Klous) was the social director; Evelyn Pahinui (Mokihana) was the em-

pathetic and helpful bartender; Richard Bean (Stephen Shortridge) was the good-looking lifeguard; and Charles Fleischer was Everett. Landers said, "I remember Charles being in one particular scene with me. I was asked if I was afraid of spiders and I said no. Well, the memorable scene had me covered in spiders. I was reassured by the spider handler that they were harmless. Viewers were probably more freaked out by it than I."

Each episode had at least three intertwining plots/storylines, and each focused upon love or its absence. It was rumored that Debbie Reynolds was unhappy with the show's scripts, and somewhat relieved when the program ended. Even with a bevy of celebrity guests, including Red Buttons, Jonathan Winters, Ray Bolger, Van Johnson, Gene Barry, Jim Nabors,

Joan Fontaine, Connie Stevens, Lorne Greene, Gene Rayburn, and Audrey Landers, the program failed to find an audience. After only eight episodes had aired, ABC said *aloha* to the entire project.

Episodes were titled "Alex and Annie/Blue Honeymoon/Another Thing," "The Star/The Trouble with Chester/Fran's Worst Friend," "Sydney's First Love/The Swingers/The King of Gardens," "Turn Me On/Treasure Hunt/A Child Will become Father," "Best of Friends/Success/Nine Karats," "Love Teacher/The Actress/Prodigy," and "Catching Up/Warbling a Letter from Broadway/Bad Day at Black Rock." The executive producers were Douglas S. Cramer and Aaron Spelling; the producers were Lew Gallo and Michael Norell; the writers included Tom Greene and Michael Norell. The theme song was provided by Charles Fox and Norman Gimbel.

Amanda's E & L Productions/CBS Viacom Productions. ABC. Thursday nights 8:30 (February 10, 1983–March 24, 1983) and Thursday nights 9:30 (May 5, 1983–May 26, 1983). Thirteen episodes were filmed before a live audience, but only ten aired.

Amanda's (sometimes referred to as *Amanda's by the Sea*) was an attempt at a U.S. version of the wildly popular Britcom called *Fawlty Towers*, starring John Cleese. Actually, the first attempt, a pilot titled *Snavely's* with Harvey Korman and Betty White, aired on ABC quite a bit earlier (June 24, 1978), but did not become a series.

Amanda's starred Bea Arthur, in between her successes in *Maude* and *The Golden Girls*. Amanda Cartwright was a sarcastic widow with a grown married son named Marty (Fred McCarren), whose birth, Amanda liked to remind him, had her in labor for eighteen agonizing hours. Marty is a graduate with a degree in hotel management (it doesn't help much), and his bride is Arlene (Simone Griffeth)—a spoiled, wealthy, self-centered brat from Boston. Instead of *Fawlty Towers*, the establishment is known as Amanda's by the Sea—a small, cozy hotel on the Pacific Ocean, in the shadow of the much larger and more successful Casa Krinsky, formerly The Daisy Inn (the owner, Mr. Krinsky, was played by sitcom veteran Michael Constantine). Also in the cast were Tony Rosato as Aldo, the inept bellhop who speaks very little English; Rick Hurst as Earl Nash, the rather daft long-winded hotel chef who had been orphaned as a child; and Keene Curtis as Clifford Mundy, the banker who is always threatening foreclosure.

This sitcom earned two different times slots to find an audience, but after ten episodes had aired, ABC beat Mundy to the punch and foreclosed on *Amanda's* before the last three episodes aired. Stories revolve around broken

In between successes on *Maude* and *The Golden Girls*, Bea Arthur spent a few not-so-golden moments running a hotel on ABC's *Amanda's*.

ovens, the menu, overbookings, surly guests, birthday parties, hotel reviewers, a gun-toting robber, local golf tournaments, and competition from Casa Krinsky. Yet another attempt at a successful U.S. version of *Fawlty Towers* was called *Payne*, starring John Larroquette. This one aired on CBS in 1999, and like *Amanda's*, the audience checked out very quickly and it was gone in a couple of months.

Episodes of *Amanda's* were titled "All in a Day's Work," "You Were Meant for Me" (with guest stars Jerry Stiller and Leonard Stone), "The Man Who Came on Wednesday," "I Ain't Got Nobody," "My Cheatin' Staff," "Aunt Sonia," "Last of the Red Hot Brothers," "I'm Dancing as Close as I Can," "One Passionate Night, Part One," "One Passionate Night, Part Two," "Amanda's Number One Son," "I Was Wild about Harry," and "Oh, Promise Me." The last three didn't air. The executive producer was Len Rosenberg; the creator and producer was Elliot Shoenman; the writers included Elliot Shoenman, Sam Greenbaum, Clayton Baxter, Bill Davenport, John Markus, Neal Marlens, Karyl Miller, Richard Raskin, Harvey Silberman, Susan Stevenson, Diane Wilk, and Michael Loman; the directors included John Rich, Marc Daniels, Howard Storm, Charles S. Dubin, and J. D. Lobue. Music was provided by Peter Matz.

Ann Jillian Castlerock Entertainment. NBC. Thursday night 8:30 (November 30, 1989), Sunday nights 8:00 (December 3, 1989–January 20, 1990), and Sunday nights 7:00 (August 5, 1990–August 19, 1990). Thirteen episodes were videotaped in front of a live audience, but only ten aired.

Prior to this venture, Ann had years of success as Cassie—part of the ensemble on *It's a Living* (originally titled *Making a Living*), but her first solo venture, *Jennifer Slept Here*, was short-lived (see entry). In 1989, Jillian landed another starring role, this time in the eponymously titled *Ann Jillian*. This program just made it into this '80s book—it debuted on the final day of November in 1989 right after *The Cosby Show*, before settling into its regular Sunday nighttime slot.

Here, Jillian portrayed Ann McNeil, an unemployed widow (her fireman husband was killed on duty) with bad credit. Ann and her husband had honeymooned in the small Northern California town of Marvel years earlier, and years later found a house there with a porch swing they loved and opted to buy it. Despite her husband's untimely passing, Ann decides to go ahead with the plans to move cross-country, and her daughter, the sarcastic, cynical, Whitesnake-loving Lucy (Lisa Rieffel), unwillingly tags along. They are met immediately by Kaz (Zachary Rosencrantz), an insecure young boy who lives next-door. Kaz is shorter than most members of his family, even his sister, a basketball player; he is teased by his classmates as a result). Kaz lives with his grandfather Duke Sumner (Noble Willingham). In the debut episode, "California Dreaming," we discover that Ann experienced numerous rejections when she attempted to finance her new home. Despite her straitened circumstances, Ann inexplicably purchases bicycles for herself and her daughter. With virtually no work experience, she still manages to land a job at Aunt Betty's Coffee Bean, run by a stern woman named Sheila Hufnagel (Cynthia Harris). Aunt Betty's Coffee Bean had a nicer ring to it than Sheila Hufnagel's Coffee Bean. She had a chain of twelve of these stores to run and needed someone she could trust to assist her in the Marvel store, and that person was definitely *not* her current employee, the timid and rather inept Robin Winkle (Amy Lynne). As mother and daughter adjust to their new life, many episodes feature serious and emotional moments, taking on more of the feel of a dramedy.

On its own without Bill Cosby's strong lead-in, *Ann Jillian* failed to find an audience on Sunday nights and it was placed on hiatus early in 1990. Several previously unaired episodes were burned off during August of that year, including an alternate format episode that featured only Ann and Lisa. While delivering products from the coffee shop to Marsh Pearson (Bruce Kirby), president of the Marvel Mall, Ann makes a few suggestions to him about improvements. Marsh loves her ideas and hires her away from her current job. The changes came too late to save the ailing series, and no other episodes were aired. Had the new format been successful, the title would have likely been changed to *The Ann Jillian Show*.

Episodes were titled "California Dreaming," "Interrupted Melody," "Love: 15," "Since I Don't Have You," "Buddy System" (with guest star Dabbs Greer), "Career Week," "The Crush," "Run for the Roses," "Old Friends," "Good Citizen Ann," "A Housewarming" (with guest stars Jane Kean and David Doyle), and "It's a Mall World After All." The creators and executive producers were Deidre Fay and Stuart Wolpert; the producer was Rita Dillon; writers included Shelley Zellman, Tom Straw, Steve Hattman, Barbara Hall, Deidre Fay, Stuart Wolpert, Jack Elinson, Dick Bensfield, Efrem Seeger, Lyla Oliver, Stephen Neigher, and Patrick Cleary; the director was John Bowab. Music was provided by Ray Colcord; the theme song was written by Joey Murcia and performed by Sam Harris and Ann Jillian. Ms. Jillian is now a popular motivational speaker, often discussing her battle with and much-publicized triumph over breast cancer. Her website is www.AnnJillian.com.

Annie McGuire MTM Productions. CBS. Wednesday nights 8:30 (October 26, 1988–December 28, 1988). Eleven episodes were filmed single-camera style without a laugh track; only eight aired.

Annie McGuire was Mary Tyler Moore's fourth consecutive unsuccessful attempt at TV success after the legendary *Mary Tyler Moore Show* left the airwaves in 1977. The 1980s also marked the decline of MTM Productions, which was wildly and consistently successful in the 1970s. This series, filmed *sans* audience or laugh track, aired on Wednesday nights at 8:30, immediately following Mary's old sitcom partner Dick Van Dyke is his equally unsuccessful new venture called *The Van Dyke Show* (see entry). Both were gone after two months on the air.

Annie McGuire is the Deputy Coordinator of Community Relations in New York City, whose office number is 805. McGuire (née Block) lives in Bayonne, New Jersey, and takes the ferry to and from work every weekday. She is a newlywed (married only five weeks), and her new husband, Nick (Denis Arndt), an engineer who is working on the Brooklyn Bridge. Both Annie and Nick have kids from former marriages. She has a son, Lewis Block (Bradley Warden); he has a son, Lenny (played by future Oscar winner Adrien Brody), and a daughter, Debbie (Cynthia Marie King). Like her mother, Emma (Eileen Heckart, who had portrayed Mary Richard's aunt Flo on *The Mary Tyler Moore Show*), Annie is a Democrat; Nick is a Republican. Their politics were vastly different, but somehow they make it all work. Nick's father, Red (John Randolph), owns Red's All-American Grill, and Nick often calls him for advice. In the debut episode, Annie is held up and robbed by a man in a wheelchair on the streets of New York. She takes matters into her own hands by hitting him over the head and wheeling him to the police station. She later rues her actions and she and the down-on-his-luck perpetrator eventually become friends.

Episodes were titled "Hold Up," "Emma's Eviction," "Annie and The Brooklyn Bridge," "Fried Shoe," "Legend of the Bad Fish," "Ferry," "Lewis in Love," "The Journey," "The Computer," "The Honeymoon," and "Soft-Hearted Annie." The program was canceled before the latter three aired. The creators/executive producers were Elliot Shoenman and Paul Wolff; the writers included Lisa Albert, Stuart Silverman, Josh Goldstein, Jonathan Prince, Anne Convy, Paul Wolff, and Elliot Shoenman; the directors included Arlene Sanford, Helaine Head, Tom Cherones, and David Steinberg (Steinberg, a comedian from Canada, directed most of the eleven episodes). Music was provided by J. A. C. Redford.

At Ease Aaron Spelling Productions/Paramount Studios. ABC. Friday nights 8:30 (March 4, 1983–July 15, 1983). Fourteen episodes were filmed single-camera style, with a laugh track. The sponsors were Post cereals and Cheer laundry detergent.

In the opening credits, the "A" in *At Ease* was made to look like (if you can envision it) the lower half of a recruit in camouflage pants holding his rifle in a horizontal position. This military sitcom joined the ranks of numerous other short-lived, service sitcoms, such as *Ensign O'Toole*, *Broadside*, *Roll Out*, *Mister Roberts*, *No Time for Sergeants*, and *The Wackiest Ship in the Army*. Even with the seasoned Aaron Spelling and Hy Averback at the helm, this program failed to find an audience. Apparently, viewers already had their fill of the armed-forces hijinks on *McHale's Navy*, *M*A*S*H*, and *The Phil Silvers Show* (originally titled *You'll Never Get Rich*). In fact, this show was touted as an updated *Phil Silvers Show* (wherein Silvers played the scheming Master Sergeant Ernie Bilko), but without the savvy Nat Hiken behind it, it broke no new ground and *At Ease* disappeared after fourteen episodes. Oh, like "Bilko," there were money-making schemes and there was a substantial amount of gambling, but without the panache, aplomb, and comic timing of the original.

The action takes place in the 5033rd Personnel Actions Command, Company J at Camp Tar Creek in Texas, during peacetime. *Good Times* veteran Jimmie Walker portrayed the Bilko-esque Sergeant Val Valentine, and Roger Bowen (from the sitcoms *Arnie* and *The Brian Keith Show*) played Colonel Clapp—far from the sharpest bayonet in the arsenal. The tomfoolery concocted by Val and his best buddy, PFC Tony Baker, portrayed by David Naughton (the singer/dancer who wanted to be a pepper in the late 1970s Dr. Pepper TV ads) is continually thwarted by the strict and staid Major Hawkins (Richard Jaeckel) and/or his informant Corporal Wessel (nicknamed "Weasel") played by George Wyner. Wessel continually corrects those who use the nickname, to no avail. The comely Corporal Lola Grey, played by Jourdan Fremin, goes on romantic maneuvers with PFC Baker; John Vargas played Cardinel, a Latino recruit with a thick accent; and portly Joshua Mostel (the son of Broadway legend Zero Mostel, he had been billed as Josh Mostel on *Delta House*) portrayed Maxwell (he also has a dog named Ace) and possesses an appetite that is never fully sated. Speaking of appetites, the mess hall door has the number 932 on it.

Episodes were titled "A Tankful of Dollars," "Chariots of Fear," "Computer Dating," "Prairie Moon Over Texas," "Murder on the Tar Creek Express," "Love Sick," "The Marriage of the Figaros," "The Ballad of Lucinda Ballard," "The Great Computer Robbery," "A PFC and a Gentleman," "A Tar Creek Sting," "Valentine's Day," "Maxwell's People," and "The Tar Creek Chronicles." The executive producers were Aaron Spelling and Douglas S. Cramer; the producers included Hy Averback and Jim Mulligan; the writers included Tom Biener, Arthur Julian, Ron Landry, Stephanie Garman, and Hollace White; the directors included Hy Averback, Edward H. Feldman, and Bob Sweeney. The creator was John Hughes. Music was provided by Jack Elliott.

Baby Boom A Nancy Meyers/Charles Shyer Production/Finnegan-Pinchuk/MGM/United Artists Television. NBC. Saturday night 9:30 (September 10, 1988), Wednesday nights 9:30 (November 2, 1988–December 21, 1988, and July 13, 1989–September 10, 1989). Thirteen episodes were filmed single-camera style without a laugh track, but only ten aired.

The percentage of hit motion pictures that later became hit TV shows is small, indeed. Diane Keaton starred as the upwardly mobile J. C. Wiatt in the motion picture version of *Baby Boom* in 1987, but the TV version had former *Charlie's Angels* star Kate Jackson in that lead role (Jill Whitlow and Nikki Feemster portrayed a younger Wiatt in flashbacks).

Wiatt works as a high-level management consultant for the Sloane-Curtis Company on Manhattan's Upper East Side. Her busy life is buzzing along pretty much as planned until a distant cousin died unexpectedly—naming J.C. the guardian of the deceased's three year-old child. Although J.C. struggles mightily to be a good mom, this new wrinkle in her life quickly stalls her rise up the corporate ladder. Wiatt's new young ward, Elizabeth, was portrayed by twins (a common practice for sitcoms), in this case the Kennedy twins, Michelle and Kristina (often seen asleep at the bottom of the huge staircase, awaiting her new mom's return from a long day at work); her demanding and often clueless boss was Fritz Curtis (Sam Wanamaker, reprising his film role); her secretary was Charlotte (Susie Essman); and her back-stabbing assistant was Ken Arrenberg (Daniel Bardol). Others in the cast included a fellow attorney named Arlene Mandell (Robyn Peterson); and an überstrict nanny, Helga Von Haupt (Joy Behar, using a German accent). Helga was replaced with Ofelia (Camille Saviola) in episode ten. Making the transition from writing the screen version to executive producing the TV series were Nancy Meyers and Charles Shyer. Unfortunately, as Shyer shared, "The TV version of *Baby Boom* was not a great experience. Nancy and I were never in sync with Kate, and because of that, everyone ended up pretty miserable. Very early on, things got so tense that Kate quit and flew to Aspen. The studio begged us to cajole her back with balloons and flowers, but we weren't going for it ... feeling instead [that] Kate owed us the apology. Kate was eventually lured back—but Nancy and I left the series after eight episodes. We should've split after the pilot—slipping into the night—the way Robert Irsay and the Colts ducked out of Baltimore." The program's on-again/off-again erratic schedule proved to be its undoing and it was gone from prime-time very quickly. Remaining episodes were burned off during the summer of 1989.

Episodes were titled "The Pilot," "Guilt" (with guest stars Jane Wyatt [*Father Knows Best*] as Margaret Anderson, and Barbara Billingsley [*Leave It to Beaver*] as June Cleaver), "The Right School for Elizabeth," "Stress," "Saturday," "The He-Man Woman Hater's Club," "Christmas '88" (with guest star Tippi Hedren), "One Wednesday in July," "Xylophone" (with guest star Ed Marinaro), "When It Rains," "A Fine Romance," "Charlotte's Secret," and "J. C. the Man." The executive producers were Charles Shyer and Nancy Meyers; the producers were Bruce A. Block and Winifred Hervey-Stallworth; the writers included Charles Shyer, Nancy Meyers, Carrie Honigblum, Nat Bernstein, Winifred Hervey-Stallworth, Wayne Terwilliger, Mitchel Katlin, Donald Marguiles, Patricia Irving, J. W. Melville, and Renee Phillips; the directors included Charles Shyer, Ron Lagomarsino, Steve Robman, Bruce A. Block, Alan Mandel, Mary Kay Place, Tom Schiller, Jeffrey Brown, Max Tash, James Gardner, John Whitesell, and Gino Tanasescu. Music was written and produced by Steve Tyrell.

Baby Makes Five Mort Lachman and Associates/Alan Landsburg Productions. ABC. Friday nights 8:00 (April 1, 1983–April 29, 1983). Five episodes were videotaped in front of a live audience. Sponsors included Post Cereals.

In the business, it is often said only fools work with children and animals. Well, this sitcom debuted on April Fools Day 1983, and revolved around The Riddle Family with five young kids. Jennie (Louise Williams) has just added a set of twins to the brood, adding up to five (shouldn't the title have been '*Babies' Make Five*?). The other three kids were Annie (Brandy Gold), Laura (Emily Moultrie) and Michael (Andre Gower). The father of this large group was a hard-working accountant named Eddie (Peter Scolari, in between *Bosom Buddies* and *Newhart*). Jennie and Ed were very lucky—their in-laws loved to babysit for the little ones. Jennie's mother, Edna Kearney (Priscilla Morrill), is rather old-fashioned, stubborn, and set in her ways, while Ed's mother, Blanche Riddle (Janis Paige), is a real free spirit with many suitors. She is constantly attempting to get Edna to loosen up, and even manages to make some headway in that area. Coincidentally, *Baby Makes Five* disappeared forever after only *five* episodes.

Episodes were titled "The Pilot," "Eddie's Night Out," "Jennie Gets a Job," "Matchmakers," and "Jennie's Old Flame." The executive producer was Mort Lachman; the producers included Douglas Arango, Phil Doran, and Michael Mount; the writers included Robert Van Scoyk, Phil Doran, Douglas Arango, Sy Rosen, Harriet Weiss, E. Michael Weinstein, Hank Bradford, and Bill Larkin; the directors included Tom Trbovich, Jim Drake, Lila Garrett, and Russ Petranto; the creator was Sy Rosen. Music was provided by Harriet Schock and Misha Segal.

Baker's Dozen Grosso-Jacobson Productions. CBS. Wednesday nights 9:30 (March 17, 1982–April 21, 1982). Six episodes were filmed in New York City with a laugh track.

Like *Barney Miller*, *Baker's Dozen* was a somewhat comical look at life as a cop. It also had an in-office romance. Terry Munson (Cindy Weintraub) and Mike Locasale (the ubiquitous Ron Silver) are undercover officers and undercover lovers. Their attempts to keep the lover part of that equation a secret from their demanding commanding officer Captain Florence Baker (Doris Belack), provides the fodder for most of the program's humor. The program's title refers to the anti-crime unit, of which Baker is in charge. Others in the dozen included Alan Weeks as "OK" Otis Kelly and Sam McMurray as Harve Schoendorf. John Del Regno played Jeff Diggins, a con man in the area who sometimes provided the dozen with valuable crime-solving information. Thomas Quinn appeared on occasion as Desk Sergeant Martin, the building's philosopher.

Episodes were titled "The Pilot," "A Class by Himself," "Dear John" (with guest star Estelle Getty), "What a Difference a Cop Makes," "I Was Told You Were a Racetrack" (with guest star Carol Lynley), and "Sauce for the Goose." The executive producers were Sonny Grosso and Larry Jacobson; the producer was Kenneth Utt; the writers included Nick Arnold, Gary Gilbert, and Phil and Stuart Rosenberg; the directors included Bill Persky, Tony Mordente, and Edward H. Feldman. The creator was Sonny Grosso.

Best of the West Weinberger-Daniels Productions/Paramount Television. ABC. Thursday nights 8:00 (September 10, 1981–September 17, 1981), Thursday nights 8:30 (September 24, 1981–January 21, 1982), Friday nights at 9:00 (February 12, 1981–February 26, 1981), and Monday nights 8:00 (June 7, 1982–June 21, 1982). Twenty-two episodes were filmed in front of a live audience.

This unique period parody—often guffaw-out-loud funny—was set in the post–Civil War South, circa 1865. Originally from Philadelphia, Sam Best (Joel Higgins, later of *Silver Spoons*) opts to go west (young man) with his new bride, Elvira (Carlene Watkins of other short-lived sitcoms *Mary*, *Bob*, *It's Not Easy*, and *The Tortellis*) and a son from his first marriage, Daniel (Meeno Peluce), in tow. Sam buys the old general store in Copper Creek, and he and his family move into the rooms in the rear of the building. Sam is a Yankee, but his new wife is a Rebel. They met while he was torching her father's plantation (her father, Lamont Devereaux, was portrayed by Andy Griffith). Neither Elvira nor Daniel are very keen on their new life and locale, but they both love Sam and make the *best* of the situation (although young Daniel's comments are consistently dripping with sarcasm). Sam is named the town marshal after chasing away an outlaw nicknamed "The Calico Kid"—a recurring role portrayed with much flair by Christopher Lloyd.

Producer Dennis Klein recalled, "Lee Van Cleef was the original choice for the role, but fled Paramount after the first reading of the script, and Lloyd came to the rescue within an hour of being called." Sam was constantly at odds with the devious and conniving keeper of the Square Deal Saloon, Parker Tillman (Leonard Frey). Tillman's toady is the inept, gullible, gray matter–challenged, kindly, and flat-out hilarious Frog Rothchild, Jr. (Tracey Walter). About the funny Frog character, writer Michael Leeson said, "I remember the night we had to come up with a name for Tracey Walter's character who had only a first name, Frog. I'd like to think I was the one who suggested Frog Rothschild Junior. I remember everyone in the room laughed for a long time about that. Fellow writer Ed. Weinberger got a wife out of the show—he married Carlene Watkins." Copper Creek's "tough-as-nails" own version of Annie Oakley was Laney Gibbs (Valri Bromfield), and the inebriated, impoverished and unkempt town physician, Dr. Jerome Kullens, was brilliantly portrayed by big-screen great Tom Ewell.

After several ill-fated time slot changes, ABC put *Best of the West* on hiatus at the end of February. The rest of the unaired but uproariously funny episodes were burned off in June of 1982. About the program's failure to catch on, Leeson pondered, "Why something works or doesn't work is inexplicable. Someone, I'm sure, could analyze what made something like *Three's Company* a hit, while *Taxi* was canceled and picked up by another network. Casting is the reason for the success or failure of most half-hour series. And comedy is subjective, so at a particular time in history or on a program schedule, an audience may judge a genre or style of comedy to be worth watching if they like the characters. Would *Hogan's Heroes* have worked if it appeared at the same time *M*A*S*H* did? Now *Transparent* [an Amazon show concerning a transgendered father, played by Jeffrey Tambor] is considered comedy, so I guess *someone* is laughing. I think that's the essential element—Does it make you laugh?"

The show's failure must have come as a blow to the cast and crew, or at least the majority of them. On this point, Leeson said, "Well, I suppose a few people stopped looking for houses." Producer/writer Dennis Klein added, "Earl Pomerantz is the best writer in TV, but this was an odd period piece. If you think about it, this was the only period piece done with multiple cameras. *M*A*S*H*, *Hogan's Heroes*, and *F Troop* were done single camera. Also, there was inconsistency—was this a show about the west or was it a spoof of westerns? That line was never clearly defined. I think this may have been confusing for the audience."

Episodes were titled "The Pilot," "The Prisoner" (with guest star Richard Moll), "Mail Order Bride" (with guest star Betty White as ex-hooker Amanda Tremaine), "The Calico Kid Returns," "The Reunion" (with guest star Andy Griffith), "They're Hanging Parker Tillman, Parts One and Two" (with guest star Al Lewis), "The New Marshal," "Daniel's First Love," "Laney in Love," "The Railroad," "The New Jail," "A Man a Woman and a Horse," "Frog's First Gunfight" (with guest stars Chuck Connors and Barbara Babcock), "The Calico Kid Goes to School," "Tillman Held for Ransom," "The Cave-In," "Daniel Fights a Bully," "The Pretty Prisoner" (with guest star Dixie Carter), "Elvira's Old Beau," "Sam's Life Is Threatened" (with guest star Joe Regalbuto), and "The Funeral." The executive producer and creator was Earl Pomerantz; the producers were Ronald E. Frazier, David Lloyd, Dennis Klein, and Greg Nierman; the writers included Earl Pomerantz, David Lloyd, Mitch Markowitz, Chip and Doug Keyes, Sam Simon, Sy Rosen, and Michael Leeson.

About the entire experience, Leeson added, "It was a very pleasant writers' room." The directors were James Burrows, Howard Storm, Stan Daniels, Ed. Weinberger, Jeff Chambers, Michael Lessac, Will Mackenzie, Doug Rogers, and Tom Trbovich. The music was by Roger Steinman, and the theme song was written by Earl Pomerantz and performed by Rex Allen. About Pomerantz, Leeson shared, "He did the warm-up and would sing sitcom theme songs. He knew thousands of them." Although there were only twenty-two episodes filmed, reruns of the series aired on the Ha! cable channel in 1990. This is a series that needs to be on DVD.

Better Days Magnum/Thunder Road Productions/Lorimar Television. CBS. Wednesday nights 8:30 (October 1, 1986–October 15, 1986) and Wednesday night 8:00 (October 29, 1986). Eleven episodes were filmed (some scenes with a laugh track and some before a live audience), but only four aired.

Young, blonde California surfer dude Brian McGuire (Raphael Sbarge) experiences culture shock when his parents suddenly suffer serious financial woes, and he is forced to move from Beverly Hills to Brooklyn. As he says in the opening credits, "At least they both begin with the letter *B*."

It was almost a *Beverly Hillbillies* in reverse. He moves in with his grandfather, Harry Clooney (Dick O'Neill), who runs a fruit stand on the streets of New York. Director Joel Zwick shared, "This show was based upon the executive producer Jeff Freilich's real-life story. *Better Days* is the story of a white basketball player's attempts to adjust and fit in at Braxton High School in Brooklyn, which was 65 percent African American. Liberties were taken, however, as Freilich's story actually occurred at DeWitt Clinton High School in the South Bronx, but the series mirrored the same issues he encountered." Despite his prowess on the basketball court, McGuire is never given the ball and is ridiculed by his classmates Anthony "The Snake" Johnson (Guy Killum) and Luther Cain (Chip McAllister, who resurfaced in 2004 as the winner on *The Amazing Race*). Brian's grandfather recommends that his grandson "do something big" to gain their respect, trust, and friendship. Opportunity knocks when Luther finds himself unprepared for an oral report, and Brian attempts to keep him from getting a zero for the day by concocting a wild story for Miss Harriet Winners (Randee Heller), the substitute teacher. Brian explains that Luther is from Africa and that only he can only converse with him, using the "click click" language. As sitcoms are wont to do, all works out in the end, as Brian bonds with Luther and "The Snake." Director Joel Zwick added, "The outdoor scenes at the grandfather's fruit stand were done single-camera style with a laugh track, but many of the indoor scenes, including Brian's bedroom, were filmed in front of a live audience. It was a mix and match. Chip McAllister and Guy Killum were very fine actors; I really thought they'd become big stars. Raphael Sbarge, however, was out of his element on TV. He wasn't at ease there. However, I've seen him on stage and he was absolutely brilliant in that venue."

Episodes were titled "Squad R," "Cheaters Never Win," "Wendell and the Three Sure Things," "Double-D," "Never Blow Up the World," "A Car Is Not a Home," "Ground Rules," "West Coast Girl," "Wooly Bully" (with guest star Cuba Gooding, Jr.), "29 Minutes," and "All Rapped Up." The executive producers were Jeff Freilich and Stuart Sheslow; the writers included Jeff Freilich, Ralph Farquhar, Eric Blakeney, Phil Kellard, Rob Edwards, Tom Moore, Gene Miller, David Nichols, Marty Nadler, Ronald Rubin, Arthur Silver, and Stuart Sheslow; the directors included Bill Bixby, Stan Lathan, Mel Ferber, Howard Storm, and Joel Zwick. Music was provided by Jesse Frederick and Bennett Salvay, who also wrote the theme song for the long-running *Family Matters*. The unit production manager/first assistant director was Bruce Chevillat, about which Zwick said, "He was part of the old guard and his expertise came in very handy. He was peppered with questions."

Beverly Hills Buntz MTM Productions. NBC. Ran on various days—Thursday night 9:30 (November 5, 1987), Sunday night 9:30 (November 29, 1987), Thursday night 9:30 (December 24, 1987), and Wednesday night 9:30 (January 27, 1988), and Friday nights 9:30 (March 25, 1988–April 22, 1988). Thirteen episodes were filmed without a laugh track, but only nine aired.

Beverly Hills Buntz was a crimedy—part sitcom, part private-eye drama. The main character, Norman Buntz (Dennis Franz), had previously been seen as part of the ensemble cast of *Hill Street Blues* on NBC. In this humorous spinoff, Buntz resigns from the police force and, with his equally unethical friend Sid "The Snitch" Thurston (Peter Jurasik) in tow, drive cross-country in his weather-beaten vehicle (with the license plate number 593 763), with designs on setting up a private detective office in beautiful Beverly Hills, California. Thurston only intends to stay for a short time, and becomes a window washer to make ends meet, but is eventually made a partner in Buntz's new business venture (in office number 233). Their office is across the hall from that of a very attractive young writer named Rebecca Griswold (Dana Wheeler-Nicholson); she also works part-time for the Fun-O-Gram Messenger Service. The initial animosity she harbors for her new neighbors thaws considerably when they rescue her from an abusive business relationship. With shades of *The Beverly Hillbillies'* "fish out of water" premise, Buntz and Thurston attempt to fit in in their new digs. Episodes were few in number, but most involve the not-so-dynamic duo going undercover to nab perps and thugs. NBC's Brandon Tartikoff considered this series one of his "designated hitters" and ran episodes once a month in slots after *Cheers* and *Night Court*. However, the erratic scheduling likely led to its early demise after only nine of the thirteen episodes filmed had aired.

Episodes were titled "The Pilot," "Fit to Be Tied," "Sid and Randy," "Duck L'Orange," "Umbrella in the Water," "Brief Encounter," "El Norte by Norte West," "Buntz of the Desert," "A Christmas Carol," "Ad Astra Per Peoria," "A Falcone in the Hand," "Cannon-Aid," and "Terry and the Pirates." The producers were Jessie Ward Dugan and Christian Williams; the writers included Peter Silverman, Jeffrey Lewis, Christian Williams, David Milch, Barry Jay Kaplan, and Mark St. Germaine; the directors included Barnet Kellman, John Patterson, Michael Vittes, Eric Laneuville, Hal Ashby, Paul Lynch, Ray Danton, and Gabrielle Beaumont. The program was created by David Milch and Jeffrey Lewis. As with *Hill Street Blues*, music was supplied by Mike Post.

Blue Skies McKeand Productions. CBS. Monday nights 8:00 (June 13, 1988–August 1, 1988). Eight hour-long episodes were filmed single-camera style, without a laugh track.

Not to be confused with the 1994 sitcom of the same name, this *Blue Skies* was a weekly 60-minute dramedy series that starred Tom Wopat as Frank Cobb, a widowed advertising executive who makes a fresh start at life, with a new home, a new job, and a new location. The new location is Eagle Falls, Oregon, and the new job involves running his family business, Cobb's Mill. His biological children are twelve-year-old Sarah (Alyson Croft) nicknamed "Scout," and eleven-year-old Charley (Danny Gerard). Director Ralph Senesky shared, "I fondly remember eleven-year-old Danny Gerard—very bright and very precocious. He told me he was writing a script for the series. I remember doing a scene with him and Pat Hingle. I was doing his close-up and during a break between setups Danny said something to the effect of 'This is a very good scene.'" Frank Cobb's new bride on the program, Annie Pfeiffer (Season Hubley), was a divorcee (divorced from Alan, played by Vincent Baggetta) from New York, with a daughter of her own, twelve-year-old Zoe (Kim Hauser). During the show's run Annie learns that she is pregnant. About Hubley, Senensky recalled, "I remember Season fondly, of course. We had done the *Westside Medical* series for ABC together in 1977. Season was one of those actresses who was able to bring up tears very readily. I remember she had an emotional scene coming up and sensational writer Carol McKeand asked me to get her *not* to cry in the scene. I'm not sure how I broached that to Season, but whatever I did, it worked." Others in the cast included Pat Hingle as Frank's newly engaged father, Henry, and Lois Foraker as Claire Ordway. Episodes deal with the family's adjustments to life in a small town (imagine a more serious version of *Green Acres*). The program's original working title was *Fresher Pastures*, but it was too close to *Green Acres* and therefore changed at the last minute. Under any title, sadly, the program failed to find an audience and was put out to pasture after only eight episodes had aired.

Episodes were titled "A Bend in the River," "I Am the Moon," "The Visitor," "Something Old Something New," "White Horse," "Fathers," "Written in the Stars," and "Changes." The producer was Robert Hamner; the writers included Linda Salzman, Peter Orton, John Gray, Ann Hamilton, Valerie West, and Carol and Nigel Evan McKeand.

About the latter, Senesky reflected, "I had done some very fine work with both Carol and Nigel. I worked with Nigel as an actor in *The Greatest Show on Earth* and *12 O'Clock High*; as a writer he wrote one of my favorite shows 'The Marathon' episode of *The Waltons*; and as a producer on *Family*—I directed an episode called 'Lovers and Strangers.' Carol I worked with even more. She was story editor on *The Waltons*—the rewrite lady, and I directed the first script of hers to be produced, 'The Gift' on *The Waltons*. *Blue Skies*, unfortunately, was following in that long trail of family shows the network tried for in the wake of the success of *The Waltons*, which had come thirteen years earlier so it was a very long wake!" *Blue Skies'* directors included Ralph Senensky, Lee Philips, Gwen Arner, Peter Crane, Charlie Correll, and Alexander Singer.

The Boys Bernie Brillstein Productions/Silly Robin Productions. Showtime. Saturday nights 10:00 (September 10, 1988–September 28, 1989). Eight episodes were videotaped but only five aired, and were very erratically scheduled.

This extremely short-lived sitcom aired with no consistency on the Showtime cable channel between the fall of 1988 and the fall of 1989. It was an ensemble comedy that takes place in a faded and very private New York City men's club with a group of elderly card players who attempt to stay in touch with modern times, but fail miserably. The cast consisted of the king of malapropisms, Norm Crosby as Norm, *Three's Company*'s Norman Fell as Dave, Jackie Gayle as Mel, Allen Garfield as Arnie, and *Hart to Hart*'s Lionel Stander as Gene. Others in the cast included Janet Carroll as Marjorie and Tom La Grua as Fredo. This series is not to be confused with the 1993 sitcom titled *The Boys* starring Christopher Meloni.

The five aired episodes were titled "Gene's Problem," "Some Don't like It Hot" (with guest star Tommy Lasorda), "The Apartment," "Friar's Club," and "Labor Day." The executive producer was Brad Grey; the producer and creator was Alan Zweibel; the writers included Alan Zweibel, Larry Levin, Bob Schiller, and Norma Safford Vela; the director was Alan Rafkin.

Boys Will Be Boys *see* **Second Chance**

The Brady Brides Redwood Productions/ Paramount Television. NBC. Friday nights 8:30 (February 6, 1981–April 17, 1981). The first three episodes were filmed with a laugh track, the latter seven were filmed before a live audience.

Here's the story of the family Brady—and the numerous attempts to recapture the magic of the original *Brady Bunch* series that ran from 1969 to 1974 on ABC, all of which fell flat. There was a variety series called *The Brady Bunch Hour* in 1977; there was an attempt at a drama series simply called *The Bradys* in 1990; and in between there was *The Brady Brides* (with the famous theme song reworded to rhyme with "brides" instead of "bunch") in 1981. The *Brady Brides* was originally intended as a 90-minute TV movie called *The Brady Girls Get Married* on NBC, and the entire cast of characters reunited for this event—Florence Henderson as Carol (now in real estate), Robert Reed as Mike (still an architect), Ann B. Davis as Alice (married to Sam for four years), Barry Williams as Greg (now a doctor), Christopher Knight as Peter (in the air force), Mike Lookinland as Bobby (away at college), and Cindy (Susan Olsen, also in college). The two other Brady girls, Eve Plumb as Jan (now an architect) and Maureen McCormick as Marcia, (now a designer for Casual Clothes) were in the spotlight—they were *The Brady Brides*, and were married on the same day at the same ceremony.

Originally there were issues about the kind of wedding they would have—Jan and her intended, the perpetually serious science teacher Phillip (always Phillip, never Phil or Philly) Covington III (Ron Kuhlman), wanted a very old-fashioned ceremony with classical music. Marcia and her free-spirited fiancé Wally Logan (Jerry Houser) wanted a less formal and more laid-back wedding. Jan and Phillip had been dating for a long time, but Marcia and Wally enjoyed a whirlwind courtship of seven days. The two couples eventually compromise on the big event, and to cut down on expenses, opt to share a home—the four of them under one roof.

These living arrangements were fodder for many a quarrel between the two couples. For example, Wally likes to walk around the house naked, much to the chagrin of the others. In fact, as of episode four, when the program began filming before a live audience, it was obvious that big laughs were much more important than in the original *Brady Bunch* series. Some of the humor was now PG-rated (stuck zipper jokes, chicken breast and thigh jokes among them). It was the '80s after all. Carol Brady is very happy with the situation—the girls' purchase of that house is her first sale as a realtor. A wee bit of diversity also enters the picture in the form of a wisecracking African American youth named Harry (Keland Love), who pops in on *The Brady Brides* in a few episodes.

Actor Stuart Pankin, who portrayed one of their moving men, Frank, in the 90-minute movie pilot, recalled, "This TV movie had an unusual shooting schedule. We worked on Christmas Eve of 1980, and the actress who was to share the scene with us took ill. I was then asked to come back on Christmas Day, for an additional paycheck, to finish the scene. I had to say no because I didn't want to ruin my wife's plans to be with her family in New York for the holiday. No amount of money was worth that. That brought about cheers from backstage, because the crew wanted to be off on Christmas, too."

That 90-minute TV movie was later edited into the first three episodes of what became the sitcom called *The Brady Brides*. Ten total episodes were filmed, but low ratings led to the entire premise being shattered like Marcia's nose (remember the football episode). This program was gone from NBC's schedule by the middle of April. It's interesting to note that, in the debut episode, Carol and Mike Brady are watching *Gilligan's Island* on TV in the living room. *Gilligan's Island* and *The Brady Bunch* were both Sherwood Schwartz shows. After the third episode, only Florence Henderson and Ann B. Davis make occasional appearances, but Cindy, Mike, and the three sons are not seen again. *The Brady Brides*, Jan and Marcia, were now really on their own.

Episodes were titled "The Brady Girls Get Married, Parts One, Two, and Three," "Living Together," "Gorilla of My Dreams," "The Newlywed Game" (with guest star Bob Eubanks), "The Mom Who Came to Dinner," "The Siege," "Cool Hand Phil" (with guest star Alan Sues), and "A Pretty Boy Is Like a Melody." The executive producers were Sherwood and Lloyd J. Schwartz; the producer was John Thomas Lenox; the writers included Sherwood and Lloyd J. Schwartz, Mark Essinger, Hope Juber, Richard Gurman, Mara Lideks, Philip John Taylor, and Warren S. Murray; the directors included Peter Baldwin, Alan Myerson, Tony Mordente, and Herbert Kenwith. Music was provided by Frank DeVol.

Brand New Life Walt Disney Television/Buena Vista Productions/NBC Entertainment. NBC. Sunday nights 7:00 (aired erratically between October 1, 1989, and April 15, 1990). Five hour-long episodes and a two-hour pilot movie were filmed without a laugh track.

This hour-long dramedy had an erratic run on NBC's *The Magical World of Disney* between October of 1989 and April of 1990. Only five episodes were filmed and aired after a two-hour pilot movie (the pilot aired on Monday night, September 18, 1989, as an *NBC Monday Night Movie*). The series starred Barbara Eden as Barbara McCray Gibbons, a divorcee who is raising her three teenagers (Ericka, played by Jennie Garth; Chris, played by Allison Sweeney; and Bart, played by David Tom) and seeking a fresh start and a new love. She finds her new soul mate in Roger Gibbons (Don Murray), and they marry. He has three teens of his own (Amanda, played by Shawnee Smith; Laird, played by Byron Thames; and Barlow played by Eric Foster). Not unlike *The Brady Bunch*, they all live under one very large roof (this time in luxurious Bel Air, California) and attempt to become a family, as their "brand new life" unfolds. Much like Eden's previous series, *Harper Valley*, the pilot film did very well in the ratings, but the resulting series did not hold onto those impressive Nielsen numbers.

Episodes were titled "Brand New Life: The Honeymooners" (two-hour pilot film), "Above and Beyond Therapy," "I Fought the Law," "Private School," "Children of a Legal Mom," and "Even Housekeepers Sing the Blues." The executive producer was Chris Carter; the directors included Eric Laneuville, Don Weis, and

Steve Robman. The creator was Chris Carter. The theme song was composed by Steve and Stephanie Tyrell, and performed by Jill Colucci.

Breaking Away 20th Century-Fox. ABC. Saturday nights 8:00 (November 29, 1980–January 10, 1981). Eight hour-long episodes were filmed single-camera style without a laugh track, but only seven aired.

Dennis Christopher played the main character, Dave Stohler (a boy obsessed with bike races, opera, and Italian heritage) in the 1979 motion picture version, but teen idol Shaun Cassidy took the reins in the short-lived TV version in 1980. The program, what we now call a dramedy, was a victim of that season's writers' strike, and it debuted two months late (in between Thanksgiving and Christmas). Thus, it was almost totally ignored by the TV viewing public, even with Academy Award nominee Barbara Barrie reprising her role as Dave's supportive mom, Evelyn.

As the program progresses, she attempts to broaden her horizons with a real estate license. John Ashton (reprising his role from the film as well) played Dave's campus policeman brother Roy, and Vincent Gardenia portrayed Dave's calorically challenged borderline-diabetic dad—the emotionally impaired, old-fashioned, retired quarry worker (who was now a used car dealer) Ray Stohler. Because their fathers were stone cutters, Dave and his friends are looked down upon by the local frat boys and nicknamed "cutters." To get even, Dave and the fellow cutters play harmless-but-effective pranks on those who mock them. The debut episode has two separate plots—a bicycle race in which the prize is a treasured $1,295 La Strada bicycle, and the high school graduation of Dave and his buddies Moocher (Jackie Earle Haley, reprising his role from the film); Cyril (Thom Bray), the Chicago Cubs fan; and Mike (Tom Wiggin), the jock, chick magnet, and occasional drag racer. Dave not only wins the bike race after a rough start, but is also the only member of his clique accepted into college (although he remains uncertain as to whether he wants to pursue higher education). Lest his friends be envious, he chooses not to share the news of his acceptance.

Recurring roles included Moocher's live-in girlfriend and eventual fiancée, Nancy (Shelby Brammer), and Dave's girlfriend, of course with an Italian name, Paulina (Dominique Dunne). The program was very typical of the early 1980s—Shaun Cassidy's Dave character and his buddies were frequently seen donning "Daisy Duke" jean shorts—a sight that strikes one as odd when seen with modern eyes.

Episodes were titled "The Cutter," "The American Dream," "Knowing Her," "King of the Quarry," "Heart Like a Wheel," "Rainy Night in Georgia" (even though set in Bloomington, Indiana, the program was actually filmed in Athens, Georgia), "La Strada," and "Grand Illusion." The program was canceled after the "La Strada," episode and "Grand Illusion" remained unaired until the A&E cable network reran the series in the middle 1980s. The executive producer was Peter Yates (he also directed the movie); the producer was Herbert B. Leonard; the writers included Charles Rosin, Jerry McNeely, Steve Pritzker, Caroline Elias, Glenn Gordon Caron, and the writer of the motion picture Steve Tesich; the directors included Joe Ruben, Kim Friedman, Stan Lathan, Jack Bender, Victor Lobl, Ralph Rosenblum, and Jeff Bleckner. Music was by Dominic Frontiere and supervised by Lionel Newman.

Bustin' Loose Golden Groove Productions/Universal Television. Syndicated. Saturday nights 7:30 (September 19, 1987–May 28, 1988). Twenty-six episodes were videotaped in front of a live audience.

Set in Philadelphia (numerous Phillies baseball banners adorn the walls of the sets), this sitcom is not to be confused with the 1977 series *Busting Loose*, starring Adam Arkin. This one dropped the *G* from its title and was loosely based upon the 1981 Richard Pryor movie of the same name. The TV version featured *Good Times* star Jimmie Walker as Sonny Barnes—a former con artist sentenced to five years of community service. His penance is to

The syndicated TV version of the 1981 Richard Pryor motion picture *Bustin' Loose* was a bust. Pictured (left to right) are Tyren Perry, Jimmie Walker, and Marie Cole.

live in the home of social worker (and sports fan) Mimi Shaw (Vonetta McGee).

Writer Cindy Begel recalled, "We were hired by the executive producer, Topper Carew. The character Richard Pryor played in the movie version was a pretty bad dude, but Jimmie Walker organized a meeting with us writers and gave us his vision of the character he wanted to portray—a much softer, tamer, more lovable guy. There was also a mandate that the character of Rudey couldn't be totally blind, as he was in the film, but rather only vision-impaired. These changes were limiting enough, but also because the show aired in most markets at 7:30 on Saturday nights, the subject matter from the R-rated film had to be watered down considerably."

Sharing the same digs with Sonny were four orphaned children whom Mimi took in—the aforementioned vision-impaired (eldest) Rudey Butler (Larry O. Williams, Jr.); the immensely mature Trish Reagan (Tyren Perry); streetwise Nikky Robinson (Aaron Lohr); and Sue Anne (Marie Cole, a.k.a. Marie Lynn Wise). Sonny lives in the basement, and is assigned many odd jobs around the house. He is also required to help out with the kids (although he usually has a myriad of excuses for not completing his assignments). Sonny tells those impressionable youngsters many a tall tale, and has them hanging on his every word. Mimi has misgivings about the young waifs buying into Sonny's extraordinary adventures of climbing Mount Everest, having dinner with kings, and meeting big-name celebrities, but puts off doing anything about it. Rock and Roll Hall of Famer Little Richard played P. J. Pinkston in three episodes.

Episodes were titled "The First Day of the Rest of My Life," "The Baby," "Turn Around," "Cold Water Blues, "Homeless Sweet Homeless," "Sisters," "Go for the Gold" (with guest star Kareem Abdul-Jabbar), "Wet Weather Ahead," "I Paint What I See" (on which Jimmie Walker was reunited with BernNadette Stanis, his *Good Times* co-star), "Rain Rain Go Away" (with guest stars Patti Deutsch, Ron Masak and Dody Goodman), "Seems Like Old Times,"

"Words of Wisdom," "The Kindest Cut," "Doo Wop," "Oh Big Brother" (with guest star Ted Lange), "Scammed Straight," "The Grass Isn't Greener," "Snow Place like Home," "The Parent Trap," "The Gang's All Here," "I Am Woman," "Nostalgia Ain't What It Used to Be," "Rodeo and Tricia-ette," "It's a Great Big Wonderful World," "What's a Nice Girl like You?," and "It's a Pizza Cake" (with guest star Liz Torres). The executive producer was Topper Carew; the producers included Linda Nieber, Alyce S. Carew, Allan Manings, and Alan Myerson; the writers included Lisa Medway, Kevin White, Allan Manings, Chuck Tately, Lesa Kite, and Cindy Begel; the directors included Marlene Laird, Bob Lally, George Tyne, and Alan Myerson. Music was provided by Greg Poree and Ron Boustead, and the theme was performed by the Four Tops.

The California Raisin Show Murakami Wolf Swenson Films/Will Vinton Productions. CBS. Saturday mornings 10:00 (September 16, 1989–December 9, 1989). Thirteen episodes were filmed without a laugh track.

Based on the singing Claymation figures used in the TV commercials touting California Raisins (from the California Raisin Growers) and a popular TV special called *Meet the Raisins*, *The California Raisin Show* was an animated Saturday morning cartoon series that lasted for thirteen episodes very late in 1989. The group even charted one single in *Billboard Magazine*'s Hot 100—"I Heard It through the Grapevine" (Priority no. 9719) in 1988. Their music was produced by Ross Vannelli, a producer for the rock group Earth, Wind and Fire. The characters in the group were A. C. (Dorian Harewood), Beebop (Cam Clarke), Stretch (Brian Stokes Mitchell), and Red (Willard E. Pugh). After the thirteen animated episodes aired, another Claymation special, *Raisins: Sold Out—The California Raisins II*, was produced. All thirteen episodes, the two specials, and four commercials were included on the DVD box set from Hen's Tooth Video in 2011.

Episodes were titled "The Apple Raisin Style," "No Business like Shoe Business," "School Is Cool," "A Royal Mess," "Lights Camera Disaster," "The Good the Bad and the Broccoli," "Abracadabra Beebop," "The Grape Outdoors," "Rocket and Rollin' Raisins," "Hold that Jungle," "Olivera Street," "Picture-Perfect Shirelle," and "You Can't Grow Home Again." The executive producer was Will Vinton; the producer was Walt Kubiak, the writers included Barry Bruce, Lawrence G. DiTillio, Rowby Goren, Mark Gustafson, and Ryan Holznagel; the directors included Kent Butterworth, Ron Myrick, Walt Kubiak, and Vincent Davis. Music was provided by Dennis C. Brown and Chuck Lorre.

Charlie and Company 20th Century Fox. CBS. Wednesday nights 9:00 (September 18, 1985–December 25, 1985), Tuesday night 8:30 (January 28, 1986), Friday nights 8:00 (April 25, 1986–May 9, 1985). Eighteen episodes were videotaped in front of a live audience, but only seventeen aired.

Charlie and Company was CBS's attempt to mimic *The Cosby Show*, but fell rather short. This was also Flip Wilson's attempt at a TV comeback following a great run on *The Flip Wilson Show* (1970–1974). Here, as blue collar worker Charlie Richmond, he is employed by the Southside of Chicago's Department of Roads, Highways and Maintenance. He often tries to be more of a friend to his kids than a father, but his attempts usually backfire. R&B diva Gladys Knight portrayed his wife of twenty years, schoolteacher Diana Richmond. They have three outgoing, extroverted children—sixteen-year-old Charlie, Jr. (Kristoff St. John), fifteen-year-old Lauren (Fran Robinson), and nine-year-old Robert Richmond (a very young, pre–*Family Matters* Jaleel White). The recurring role of Diana's acerbic aunt Rachel was played by fellow diva Della Reese (in four episodes). Charlie's co-workers are all male and racially diverse. There is the boss, Walter Simpson (Ray Girardin); the pudgy, mustachioed and easily confused Milton Bieberman (Richard Karron); Ronald Sandler, who always dons a bowtie (Kip King); the smart aleck Jim Coyle (Terry McGovern); and the suave ladies' man Miguel Santana (Eddie Velez).

Viewers didn't flip over the CBS sitcom *Charlie and Company*, Flip Wilson's TV comeback attempt. Pictured (top left to right) are Kristoff St. John, Gladys Knight, and Flip Wilson; the bottom row includes Jaleel White and Fran Robinson.

The debut episode has Charlie standing up in front of Charlie, Jr.'s high school class on career day, and stumbling through a description of his chosen occupation (but he returns the next day with a different and better approach, leading his son to beam with pride). Other episodes remain focused more on Charlie's family than his workplace. Over a quarter of a century after the program was canceled, Gladys Knight and Jaleel White were reunited on ABC's *Dancing with the Stars*.

Episodes were titled "The Pilot," "Easy for You to Say," "Muggers or Us," "Buddy Can You Spare a Dime?," "The World According to Jim," "Like Father Like Son," "Will Be Around," "Operation Richmond," "Happy Anniversary … Sort of," "For the Love of Lauren," "Who's Watching the Roads?," "Silent Knight," "Beaus and Arrows," "Here's Rachel," "Rachel and the Stranger," "When You Least Expect It," "Don't Take My Son Please," and "Rent and Rave." The executive producers were Allan Katz and Bob Henry; the producers were Alan Rafkin, Bill Richmond, and Gary Gilbert; writers included

Gary Gilbert, Allan Katz, Bill Richmond, Mike Kagan, Aubrey Tadman, Liz Sage, Gary Murphy, Monty Aidem, and Gerry Ferrier; the director was Alan Rafkin. The creator was Allan Katz. Music was provided by Lionel Newman and Perry Botkin. The theme song was written and performed by Gladys Knight.

Checking In TAT Communications, Inc/Ragamuffin Productions. CBS. Thursday nights 8:00 (April 9, 1981–April 30, 1981). Four episodes were videotaped in front of a live audience.

It's rare for a spinoff of a spinoff to succeed. *Checking In*—a spinoff of *The Jeffersons*, which itself was a spinoff of *All in the Family*—starred Marla Gibbs as Florence Johnston, who opts to leave domestic housekeeping behind for a job as an executive housekeeper in New York City's St. Frederick Hotel. Her assistant is Elena Beltran, played by Liz Torres, who previously had a recurring role on *All in the Family*. Others in the cast include Patrick Collins as the rather inept house detective Earl Bellamy; Robert Costanzo as the handyman Hank Sabatino; R&B singer Ruth Brown as Betty, the floor supervisor; and Jordan Gibbs (Marla's ex-husband) as Dennis the bellboy. Larry Linville played Lyle Block, Florence's stuffy boss—a character rather similar to the Frank Burns character he played on *M*A*S*H*. *Checking In* checked out after only four episodes, and luckily for Marla Gibbs, she was able to return to *The Jeffersons* with the explanation that the St. Frederick had burned down.

In truth, Marla Gibbs did not want to do this series. She was quite happy being part of a major hit and had a stipulation in her contract allowing her to return to *The Jeffersons* if *Checking In* failed. That proved a wise move. As writer Cindy Begel recalled, "I also worked with Marla on *The Jeffersons* early in its run, and she kept her job taking reservations for a major airline for quite a while until she was certain *The Jeffersons* was a bona fide hit and her job was secure—a very savvy lady." To prepare for the new position for Florence on *Checking In*, Gibbs observed the duties of the executive housekeeper at a major hotel chain, but was then disappointed when none of what she had learned was used in the show. One episode of this series was used as a bonus, or "Easter Egg" as they're called, on *The Jeffersons* DVD box set from Shout Factory.

Gibbs achieved sitcom success on her own years later with *227*, and Ruth Brown surfaced in *Hello, Larry* (see entry). Speculating about the show's lack of success, Begel opined, "With the character of Florence in charge on the new show, there was no space for her to be funny. It was a much more serious role, and there was very little room for her great comic timing and abilities. The whole concept was very limiting." Begel added, "We were new writers at the time without a lot of experience, but because of the upcoming Writers Guild strike at that time, we had to turn out scripts very quickly—time was of the essence. In fact, one team of writers got to write act one while another team did act two. The clock was ticking, and the odds of act one matching up perfectly with act two were very small, but we got really lucky. They did match."

Episodes were titled "Boo Who?," "Block's Party," "Whose Side Are You On?," and "Florence and the Salesman." The executive producer was Norman Lear; the producer was Patricia Fass Palmer; the writers included Bob Schiller, Bob Weiskopf, Michael G. Moye, Bob and Howard Bendetson, Jay Moriarty, Mike Milligan, Lesa Kite, and Cindy Begel; the director was Jack Shea. The theme song was provided by David Talisman.

Chicken Soup Carsey/Werner Productions. ABC. Tuesday nights 9:30 (September 12, 1989–November 7, 1989). Twelve episodes were videotaped in front of a live audience, but only eight aired.

When the pilot for this series was videotaped in front of a live audience, the show didn't yet have a name. Tickets for that May 5, 1989, performance merely read "A New Situation Comedy Starring Lynn Redgrave and Jackie Mason." Seventeen years earlier, a high-rated sitcom about an interfaith marriage between a Jewish man and a Catholic girl called *Bridget Loves Bernie* was canceled because of pressure from religious groups. *Chicken Soup* was also canceled, but it was because of low ratings, and brouhaha incited by series star Jackie Mason over incendiary comments about New York City's mayoral race.

Even with a cushy lead-in from *Roseanne*, *Chicken Soup* never did come to a boil and the show was gone after only eight of the twelve videotaped episodes aired. *Chicken Soup* just wasn't "Mm Mm good." The show's failure surprised many—it was projected to be one of the biggest hits of the season. Each episode opens and closes with a Jackie Mason monologue, delivered from the roof of his apartment building. In the debut episode, fifty-two-year-old Jackie Fisher (Mason) shakes up his stagnant life by both quitting his sales job (he sold pajamas for the Sleep Soft Company), and revealing his relationship with "the widowed shiksa next door" Maddie Peerce (Redgrave) to his mother, Bea (Rita Karin). He'd kept the affair from her because Maddie was Catholic, and the news would surely have made his mom *plotz*. In the interim, because she didn't see him with any girls in his life, she began thinking he was gay. True to form, his mom did indeed disapprove of the relationship, at least initially, but she likes Maddie and her three kids (and even babysits for them on occasion)—Patricia (Kathryn Erbe), Donnie (Johnny Pinto), and Molly (Alisan Porter). Her chilly reaction eventually thaws considerably. Mike and Barbara Donovan (Brandon Maggart and Cathy Lind Hayes, respectively) are Maddie's brother and sister-in-law. (Cathy Lind Hayes was the daughter of early TV stars Peter Lind Hayes and Mary Healy.) Maddie works as a teacher for the Henry Street Settlement, and occasionally Jackie sits in to instruct the class about his area of expertise—sales. Episodes revolve around the couple's struggles to stay together despite so many attempts by others to break them up, and with being a single parent with a daughter who wants to move in with her boyfriend.

Episodes were titled "The Pilot," "The Dinner," "The Bartender," "The Reservation," "Double Date," "Take My Kids, Please," "Bea Moves Out," "Almost Father Jackie," "The Ralph Hearns Story," "Operation: Jackie," "Bea's Night Out," and "Community Service." The executive producers were Bernie Orenstein and Saul Turteltaub; the producer was Paul Perlove; the writers included Paul Perlove, Bernie Orenstein, Saul Turteltaub, and Manny Basanese; the directors included Terry Hughes and Alan Rafkin. Music was provided by Howard Pearl and Gordon Lustig.

The Completely Mental Misadventures of Ed Grimley Hanna Barbera Productions/Sepp International. NBC. Saturday mornings 11:30 (September 10, 1988–December 3, 1988). Thirteen episodes were videotaped without a laugh track.

Martin Short originated this cowlicked character during his *Second City* days. The nerdy and oblivious Ed Grimley then made the transition to *Saturday Night Live*, and eventually to Saturday mornings in animated form on *The Completely Mental Misadventures of Ed Grimley*.

Ed lives at 11 Wooden Road, and in each episode finds himself in some very unusual, almost surreal situations. The program wasn't entirely animated. There was a live action segment with Count Floyd (Joe Flaherty, reprising one of his *Second City* characters) featuring a spooky story. Other animated characters include Ed's landlord, Leo Freebus, and his wife, Deidre (Jonathan Winters and Andrea Martin, respectively), wannabe actress and neighbor Belinda (Catherine O'Hara) and her younger brother, Wendell (Danny Cooksey). This series ran only one season and thirteen episodes on NBC, but was later seen in reruns on Cartoon Network. All thirteen episodes were released in a DVD set from Warner Bros. in 2013.

Episodes were titled "Tall Dark and Hansom," "Ed's Debut," "E. G., Go Home," "Ed's in Hot Water," "Crate Expectations," "Grimley, P. F. C.," "Moby Is Lost," "Good Neighbor Ed," "Driver Ed," "Blowin' in the Wind," "Eyewitness Ed," "Eddie, We Hardly Knew Ye," and "The Irving Who Came to Dinner." The executive producers were Martin Short, William Hanna, Joseph Barbera, and Freddy Monnickendam; the producers were John Hays, Scott Shaw, and Mark Young;

the writers included Martin Short, Michael Short, Mark Young, Kelly Ward, John Loy, John Ludin, Ali Marie Matheson, and Wayne Kaatz; the directors included Jim Drake, Bob Goe, Paul Sommer, and Don Lusk. Music was provided by Michael Tavera and Joanne Miller.

Condo Witt-Thomas Productions. ABC. Thursday nights 8:00 (February 10, 1983–March 10, 1983), Thursday nights 8:30 (February 24, 1983–April 28, 1983), and Thursday nights 8:00 (May 26, 1983–June 9, 1983). Thirteen episodes were videotaped in front of a live audience.

This was McLean Stevenson's next-to-last shot at a successful post–*M*A*S*H* TV series. He did everything he could to make this one click, but it wasn't meant to be. *Condo* joined earlier attempts *The McLean Stevenson Show*, *In the Beginning*, and *Hello, Larry* (only the latter made it past thirteen weeks).

The program is set in Los Angeles and McLean's character is James Kirkridge, an insurance salesman who has recently suffered a reversal of fortune, necessitating a move from a large, expensive house into a much more compact, cost-efficient condo. Sharing the condo are his high-strung, daft, golf-loving wife, Kiki Kirkridge (Brooke Alderson), and their two sons, Billy (Marc Price, pre-Skippy on *Family Ties*), and the elder Scott (Mark Schubb), who is dating the neighbor's daughter, Linda (Julie Carmen). In fact, early in the program's short run they announced their intentions to marry, and that a baby, Joselito, was on the way. There's the rub—the young boys got along swimmingly with their Latino neighbors, but James and the head of the Rodriguez household, successful landscaper Jessie (Luis Avalos), came to immediate loggerheads and maintained a strained and contentious relationship. Jessie was short for Jesus, and he was married to Maria (Yvonne Wilder). Her father, the bearded Jose Montoya (James Victor), also lives with them. Jose arranges for one wall between the two condos to be torn down and replaced with sliding-glass doors to improve relations between the two families, but it doesn't work. Like *All in the Family*, *Condo* was rife with ethnic humor but it just wasn't done with as much savvy. After thirteen weeks and three different Thursday nightime slots, *Condo* was razed by ABC. McLean got one more shot five years later, in the TV version of the 1987 motion picture *Dirty Dancing* (see entry).

Episodes were titled "The Neighbors" (with guest star Florence Halop), "The Announcement," "The Wedding," "The Baby," "The Babysitters," "The First Fight," "That's Entertainment," "The Franchise," "The Dog," "Condomania" (with guest star Peter Tomarken), "The Affair," "Nouveau Poor," and "Members Only" (with guest star Jack Riley). The program was created by Sheldon Bull; the executive producers were Paul Junger Witt, Tony Thomas, and John Rich; the producers included Saul Turteltaub and Bernie Orenstein; the writers included George Bloom, Alan Uger, Kathy Speer, Mike Kagan, Barbara Benedek, Deborah Leschin, Bob Fraser, Barbara Hall, Richard Baer, Ron Dames, and David Angell; the director for all thirteen episodes was the prolific John Rich. Music was provided by George Aliceson Tipton, and the theme song's lyrics ("Live and Love It Up") were written by Paul Williams (and performed by Drake Frye). Being a Witt-Thomas Production, much of the same and/or similar between scenes transition music used in *The Golden Girls*, *Empty Nest*, *Soap*, and *Benson* was used on *Condo*.

Dads Victoria Productions/Summa Enterprises/Four for a Quarter Productions/Columbia Pictures Television. ABC. Friday nights 9:00 (December 5, 1986–January 9, 1987), and Friday nights 9:30 (January 16–February 6, 1987). Nine episodes were videotaped in front of a live audience.

All of the images of the cast in both the opening and closing credits for this series are pencil sketches. Not to be confused with the 2013 *Dads*, this one was yet another spin on *The Odd Couple* premise (although *everyone* in the household is an Oscar Madison—very sloppy) as two newly single dads from Philadelphia (friends since high school) share a house and the expenses as they raised their kids.

Rick Armstrong, played by Barry Bostwick (Sam McMurray in the unaired pilot) is an up-and-coming reporter (currently writing the newspaper obituaries) with a thirteen-year-old daughter named Kelly (Skye Bassett), to whom he tries to be both a father and mother (divorced from Karen); Louie Mangiotti (Carl Weintraub in a very stereotypical über-macho Italian-American role) works with his hands as a mason, and those hands are full with two sons—sixteen-year-old Allan (Eddie Castrodad, in the series; Danny Nucci, in the unaired pilot) and twelve-year-old Kenny (Jason Naylor). His late wife was named Louise. Comedy is mined from the kids and their problems, as well as the oil-and-water relationship of the upwardly mobile Rick (a smoker), and the non-smoking, carefree, streetwise, old school "Joe six-pack" Louie (usually donning a tank top). There was very little on-screen chemistry and, as a result, the series fell flat. The sitcom only lasted for nine episodes before the dads were evicted by ABC.

Episodes were titled "The Doing of the Dishes and the Cleaning of the Room," "On Changing the Status Quo," "The Thing on Allan's Nose," "Why Algebra?," "The Shadow of Pompasso," "Especially Thy Father," "Of Mice and Dirty Jokes," "The Rivals," and "Waiting." The executive producers were Jeff Harris and Mark Waxman; the producer was Al Lowenstein; the writers included Mark Waxman, Lindsay Harrison and Jeff Harris; the directors were John Pasquin and Zane Buzby. The creator was Lindsay Harrison. Music was provided by Jeff Harris and Alf Clausen.

Dirty Dancing The Steve Tisch Company/Vestron Television. CBS. Saturday nights 8:00 (October 29, 1988–December 31, 1988), and Saturday nights 9:30 (January 7, 1989–January 21, 1989). Eleven episodes were filmed single-camera style without a laugh track.

Yet another failed attempt at bringing a hit major motion picture from the silver screen to the small screen. This one might be called a "musical dramedy." Based on those same characters created by Eleanor Bergstein, the action took place at Kellerman's, a summer resort in the Catskills, in 1963.

Frances "Baby" Kellerman, played by Melora Hardin (her surname had been Houseman in the movie), the very attractive seventeen-year-old daughter of Max Kellerman (McLean Stevenson), a student at the Holyoke School, gets a summer job at her father's resort. She would have been quite satisfied with a waitressing gig, but her father makes her the talent coordinator (because she had studied dancing as a child). This ruffles the feathers of the club's handsome and talented young dance instructor, Johnny Castle (Patrick Cassidy, in the role made famous by another Patrick named Swayze). Castle has a reputation as a lothario, and Max views him as one of the great unwashed (he works as a garage mechanic in the off-season). When it becomes obvious that Baby is under-qualified, she becomes a waitress, and Johnny gets his job back. However, a love affair between the two is brewing. Even though Baby is no longer directing the talent, Johnny still wants her to be in the show and practices a few dance routines with her to work off the rust. Because of Johnny's reputation and the suggestive dance routines, Max forbids Baby from being in the show and from having anything to do with Johnny. She heeds Daddy's wishes for a time, but the chemistry and attraction between the two is so strong it drives her to be disobedient. This greatly displeases Johnny's current girlfriend and dance partner, Penny Rivera (Constance Marie), but her attempts to keep Johnny for herself prove unsuccessful. Johnny and Baby were meant to be together. Others in the cast included wannabe comedian Norman Bryant (played by Paul Feig, who has a mad crush on Baby); Robin Kellerman (Mandy Ingber), Baby's cousin, best friend, and confidant; an African American pianist named Sweets Walker (John Wesley); and Neil Mumford (Charles Stratton), the resort's lifeguard, the guy with whom Max wanted Baby to be.

The show failed to catch on, even though the dance routines were quite well executed, the characters were very likeable, and the soundtrack was flawless. The debut episode was an hour long (all subsequent episodes were only thirty minutes in length) and it featured pre-Beatles pop classics such as "Just One Look" by Doris Troy, "Pride and Joy" by Marvin Gaye, "The Locomotion" by Little Eva," "Heat Wave" by Martha and the Vandellas, "Gee Whiz" by Carla Thomas," "Tossin' and Turnin'" by Bobby Lewis, and the song for which the episode was titled, "Baby, It's You," by the Shirelles. This show was McLean Stevenson's fifth (and final) shot at a hit series after unwisely exiting *M*A*S*H*, and once again he was issued a pink slip. Baby was quickly put in the corner.

Episodes were all titles of late 1950s/early 1960s major hit records, "Baby, It's You," "Heat Wave," "Save the Last Dance for Me," "Walk Like a Man," "Breaking Up Is Hard to Do," "Poetry in Motion," "Book of Love," "Turn Me Loose," "Our Day Will Come," "Hit the Road, Jack," and "Don't Make Me Over." The producers were Robert Lovenheim, Steve Tisch, Mireille Soria, and Christopher Morgan; the writers included Robert Rabinowitz and Barra Grant; the directors included Kenny Ortega, Tony Bill, Jan Eliasberg, Michael Fresco, Ed Kaplan, Michael Peters, Oz Scott, Barra Grant, Steve Tisch, and Gabrielle Beaumont. Music was provided by Michael Lloyd and Michel Rubini. *Dirty Dancing* was also the title of a 2006 reality show hosted by Chris Judd on the WE cable TV channel.

The Dom DeLuise Show Multimedia Productions. Syndicated. Air dates and times varied. September 1987–March 1988. Twenty-four episodes were videotaped in front of a live audience.

Not to be confused with *The Dom DeLuise Show* of 1968—a summer variety series—this *Dom DeLuise Show* was syndicated and came twenty years later. Mostly a sitcom, it did have a few elements of variety in its fabric, and characters frequently addressed the audience directly. Dom portrayed a widower named Dom DeLuca. He owns Dom's Barber Shop, and is the father of a teenage girl named Rosa (Lauren Woodland). They both live behind the shop, and Dom, true to form, does a lot of cooking and eating. Dom's partner in the shop is an African American named George (comedian George Wallace). Others in the cast included Maureen (Maureen Murphy), the airheaded manicurist; Charlie Tyde (comedian Charlie Callas), the skittish trench-coat-donning private eye; Penny (Angela Aames), the hot aerobics instructor; Billy (Billy Scudder), who wears a sandwich board to advertise the barber shop; pizza delivery guy/dancer Michael (Michael Chambers); and Dom's on-again/off-again girlfriend, Blanche Maxwell (Lois Foraker), who runs a nearby pet shop and gives Dom a pet chimpanzee as a holiday gift. She is a widow, whose late husband was named Monty. Because Dom's tonsorial parlor is based in Hollywood, it is frequented by many celebrity guests from movies, television, and music. Among the guest stars were Zsa Zsa Gabor, Dean Martin, John Forsythe, and Dom's real-life friend Burt Reynolds. Said guests didn't help the ratings any, and after twenty-four episodes, Dom had to hang up his scissors.

The program's episodes don't appear to have been assigned titles. The executive producer was Greg Garrison; the writers included Howard Albrecht, Sol Weinstein, Karin Babbitt, Monty Aidem, Stan Burns, Jack LoGuidice, Jeff Zimmer, and Rod Burton.

Domestic Life 40 Share Productions/Universal Television. CBS. Wednesday nights 8:00 (January 4, 1984–February 1, 1984), Sunday nights 8:00 (March 18, 1984–April 15, 1984), and Tuesday nights 8:30 (July 17, 1984–July 24, 1984). Ten episodes were videotaped in front of a live audience. Sponsors included Pepto Bismol.

On *Domestic Life*, a character named Martin Crane was portrayed by Martin Mull. Coincidentally, both Martin Cranes lived in Seattle (Mull's character at 106 Liberty Lane). A decade later, a character named Martin Crane, played by John Mahoney, began a long run on NBC's *Frasier*. On *Frasier*, Martin Crane was a retired cop and his son was a radio psychologist. But on this show, Martin was a commentator for KMRT-TV Channel 8. His segment on *The Ac-*

tive 8 News is called "Domestic Life," and focuses upon the humorous situations that crop up when one has a home, a wife, and a family. However, the stories he conjures up for the newscast are far more joyful than the real ones he encounters in his own kooky family. His wife has the adorable name of Candy Crane (Judith-Marie Bergan) and she often whines about their finances; his fifteen-year-old daughter, Didi (Megan Follows), experiences one teen crisis after another; and his ten-year-old son, Harold (Christian Brackett-Zika), wears husky-sized clothing and becomes the real breadwinner in the household with his many savvy investments (in fact, the family frequently has to borrow money from him). Harold is the only member of the family with an IRA account. A very young Tina Yothers, later of *Family Ties*, had the recurring role of Sally—Harold's girlfriend (she called him Doughboy, and he called her Sookie). Martin's life at work is no picnic either—he has to deal with sarcastic, opinionated, egotistical co-anchors Jane Funakubo (Mie Hunt) and Cliff Hamilton (Robert Ridgely). The floor manager is named Jeff (J. Alan Thomas), and the owner of the station is a former movie cowboy named Rip Steele (singer/songwriter Hoyt Axton). Despite having Axton in the cast, Martin Mull performed the show's theme song, "God Bless the Domestic Life," which he co-wrote with Wendy Haas-Mull and Ian Praiser. Said theme started and ended with "Be it ever so humble, there's no place like home." The surname of one of the show's writers, Howard Gewirtz, was worked into the opening credits—seen on the side of a van as Gewirtz Diaper Service.

Episodes were titled "Harold in Love," "Small Cranes Court" (with guest star Sylvia Sidney), "Good Neighbor Cliff," "He Ain't Heavy He's My Dentist" (with guest star Paul Sand), "Harold Can You Spare $4,000?," "Cooking with Candy," "Rip Rides Again," "The Candidates" (with guest star Jack Riley), "Showdown at Walla Walla," and "Harold at the Bat." The executive producers were Steve Martin and John Whitman; the writers included Steve Martin, Martin Mull, Howard Gewirtz, Ian Praiser, David Angell, Jack Carrerow, Lisa A. Bannick, and Craig Kellem; the directors included Jim Drake, Will Mackenzie, Michael Lessac, and Sam Weisman. Music was provided by David Michael Frank.

Down and Out in Beverly Hills Touchstone Television. FOX. Sunday night 9:00 (April 26, 1987), Saturday nights 8:00 (July 25, 1987–August 8, 1987), and Saturday nights 9:00 (August 15, 1987–September 12, 1987). Thirteen episodes were filmed with a laugh track, but only eight aired. Sponsors included Bartles and James wine coolers and Pledge furniture polish.

This show has the distinction of being the first prime-time series canceled by the new Fox TV Network. Based on the popular 1986 motion picture with Richard Dreyfuss, Nick Nolte, and Bette Midler, the only holdover from the film was the Border collie named Matisse (Mike, the dog). The film and the TV series tell the story of the nouveau riche Whiteman family, whose clothes hanger business has afforded them the opportunity to move into a Beverly Hills mansion. Héctor Elizondo assumed the Dreyfuss role of Dave Whiteman; Anita Morris, the Midler role of his wife, Barbara; and the ubiquitous Tim Thomerson the Nolte role of Jerry Baskin—the spacey, down-on-his-luck former flower child who attempts suicide in the Whitemans' pool, only to be rescued and taken in by Dave, Barbara, and the kids—goody-goody twenty-year-old Jenny (Eileen Seely), and cunning and mischievous seventeen-year-old Max (Evan Richards). Other characters include Carmen, the maid (April Ortiz), and Barbara's mother, Vickie (Jo de Winter). Episodes revolve around the family's adjustment to Beverly Hills life, and Jerry's philosophies and attempts to teach the Whitemans what life is really all about. The program debuted in April of 1987 with very little audience reaction, and *Down and Out in Beverly Hills* wasn't seen again until July, when seven more of the thirteen produced episodes aired. The last five never saw the light of day.

Episodes were titled "Jerry's Mission," "Something Mild," "Skin Tight," "Max Bedroom," "Altared States," "Shapiro's Carmen," "Dancing in the Dark," "You Ought to Be in Pictures," "Fistful of Dollars," "For a Few Dollars More," "Jerry Jumps Right In," "The Legend that Is Barbara," and "Jerry Strikes Out." The executive producers were Howard Gewirtz and Richard Rosenstock; the writers included Howard Gewirtz, Robert Bruce, Martin Weiss, Cindy Begel, and Lesa Kite; the directors included Bill Foster. Music was provided by David Michael Frank.

The Drak Pack Hanna-Barbera Productions/Southern Star Productions. CBS. Saturday mornings 11:30 (September 8, 1980–December 20, 1980). Sixteen animated episodes were filmed without a laugh track.

The Drak Pack was an animated Saturday morning series featuring a trio of unusual teenagers who were the offspring of famous monsters (Frankie from Frankenstein, Howler from a werewolf, and Drak from Dracula) who were headed by Dracula himself—often called "Big D" (Alan Oppenheimer). They attempt to do good to atone for their ancestors' misdeeds. Frankie and Howler were voiced by William Callaway, and Drak by Jerry Dexler. They all appear to be normal teenagers, at least until trouble ensues. They are then able to morph into superheroes with super powers by doing "the Drak Whack"—slapping their palms together—at which time they all jump into their airborne car, the Drakster. They are constantly at odds with OGRE—an acronym for the Organization of Generally Rotten Enterprises. Its leader is the evil Doctor Dred (Hans Conried). Dred's lackeys include Vampira (Julie McWhirter-Dees), The Mummyman (Chuck McCann), Fly, and Toad (both Don Messick). Toad greatly resembles actor Peter Lorre, and saves Dred the trouble of slapping him around when he does wrong—he does it himself, with a flyswatter. They all get around in a blimp called the Dredgible. Scenes change with the help of a big red cartoon curtain. The same sixteen episodes ran over and over again for two seasons on CBS's Saturday morning schedule. A DVD box set from VEI and Millennium Entertainment was released in 2008 and contained all sixteen episodes.

Episodes were titled "Color Me Dredful," "Mind Your Manners, Doctor Dred," "Happy Birthday, Doctor Dred," "Dredful Weather We're Having," "The Perilous Plunder of Pirate Park," "Night of the Terbites," "Time Out for Doctor Dred," "Hideout Hotel," "Dred Goes Hollywood," "Dred's Photo Finish," "Doctor Dred Is a Shrinker," "A Dire Day at Dredfuland," "Package Deal," "The Grimmest Book of Records," "International Graffiti," and "It's in the Bag, Doctor Dred." The executive producers were William Hanna and Joseph Barbera; the producers were Doug Paterson and Art Scott; the writers included Doug Booth, Larz Bourne, Cliff Roberts, and Glenn Leopold; the director was Chris Cuddington. Music was provided by Hoyt Curtin.

Dreams The Guber-Peters Entertainment Company/Centerpoint Productions. CBS. Wednesday nights 8:30 (October 3, 1984–October 31, 1984). Twelve episodes were filmed with a laugh track, but only five aired.

It seemed like a great idea at the time—combining situation comedy with the flourishing popularity of music videos. The result was an expensive and ambitious flop called *Dreams*. The series starred twenty-two-year-old John Stamos (pre–*Full House* and Oikos Yogurt ads) as Gino Minnelli. His day job is that of a welder, but at night he attempts to be a rock star, something he dreams about often. He has a great record collection, too. *Dreams* was the name of the series and also the name of Gino's music group, and his dreams involve leaving Philadelphia and his blue collar job behind.

Gino not only sings and plays guitar, he is also a chick magnet. His backup singer is Martha Spino (Jami Gertz, pre–*Still Standing* and *The Neighbors*). Phil Taylor (Cain Devore) wrote most of the band's music, and Morris Weiner (Albert Macklin) was the band's zany keyboard player. Lisa Copley (Valerie Stevenson) was named a member of the band mostly because of her father's clout and money (he is a U.S. Senator) needed to buy new amplifiers to replace the old ones that had been stolen, and also because she is a pretty decent vocalist who provides the band with that certain something they had been missing. The band often performs at Frank (Ron Karabatsos) and Louise Franconi's (Sandy Freeman) nightclub, Club Frank. The Franconis are Gino's aunt and uncle, and they occasionally use another band, Acid Rain. Videos by the band and lots of breakdancing are interwoven into the fabric of each episode. Twelve episodes were produced, but the program performed so poorly in the ratings, it was yanked after the fifth episode aired, resulting in many broken *Dreams*.

Episodes were titled "Kiss Me Red," "Friends," "Boys Are the Best," "Working Life," "Fortune and Fame," "Head Over Heels," "Alone," "Rusted Dreams," "Stuttering," "Suspicion," "Tears in the Night," and "Birthday Party." The producers were Bill Bixby, Alan Collis, Ronald E. Frazier, Peter Guber, and Jon Peters; the writers included Andy Borowitz, Alan Collis, Susan Stevenson, Richard Raskin, Chris Lucky, Janis Hirsch, Barbara Hall, Nancy Steen, David Chambers, and Neil Thompson; the directors included Bill Bixby, Tom Trbovich, Will Mackenzie, and Mark Rezyka. The creator was Andy Borowitz. Music was provided by Jon Wolff, Trevor Veitch, and John E. Oliver.

The Duck Factory MTM Productions. NBC. Thursday nights 9:30 (April 12, 1984–May 24, 1984), and Wednesday nights 9:30 (June 6, 1984–July 11, 1984). Thirteen episodes were filmed single-camera style with a laugh track.

The Duck Factory never did become a "duck dynasty." Skip Tarkenton (a young Jim Carrey) had been adopted as a young child. In an effort to "find himself," he travels by bus halfway across the country to start work at his dream job as an animator on *The Dippy Duck Show* for his lifelong idol, Herman "Buddy" Winkler's tiny, way-past-its-heyday cartoon studio. Skip's wide-eyed wonder and youthful exuberance are dashed when, just as he arrives at the rodent-infested studio, with the huge Dippy Duck on its edifice, Winkler's employees are toting his coffin down the alley.

The Duck Factory on NBC was one of few "fowls" from MTM Productions. Pictured are two of the show's stars, Jim Carrey and Teresa Ganzel.

His employees aren't exactly crestfallen—he wasn't very well liked. Sheree (Teresa Ganzel), Winkler's young trophy wife of three weeks, then takes over the reins of the business. The problem: she has absolutely no experience in running an animation studio. Ganzel said, "Let's face it, Sheree Winkler was another dumb blonde role. But I think what gave her a bit more depth was that she was in mourning. She was lonely living in her mansion by herself. We shot it in Bugsy Siegel's Spanish estate that Madonna later bought. I think there was a sadness about the character that made her endearing. It was this show I was most excited to get cast in. The producers were from *The Mary Tyler Moore Show*, *M*A*S*H*, and *WKRP in Cincinnati*. It was *the* pilot to get that year, and MTM was my favorite lot. I was heartbroken when those thirteen weeks were up. I wanted to go to work there for years and years. My audition for the show was good, but it was not a done deal. It was really the producers seeing me as a panel guest on Johnny Carson's *Tonight Show* that got me the role."

Luckily for young Skip, his pilgrimage from the Midwest was not in vain—the cartoon studio is extremely short-handed and he is immediately hired. He even gets to stay in a spare room in the building (it came with a leaky waterbed). When that waterbed springs a massive leak, Buddy moves into a spare room at Casa Contento with Sheree. Had the show continued, would there have been a romance between Skip and Sheree? Ganzel says, "My guess is actually no. I think it would have taken things in a more limiting direction." The circumstances are totally innocent, but when the other co-workers get wind of the living arrangement, they give Skip a lot of flak. Things get even worse for the newbie Skip when Sheree promotes him to the position of producer, over the other long-term employees, such as elderly grunion hunter Brooks Carmichael (Jack Gilford), who has a pet chicken named Elliott; the pushy, jealous of her co-workers, and self-serving Aggie Aylesworth (Julie Payne), who was briefly stationed in Vietnam and had served in the navy; sassy Andrea Lewin (Nancy Lane), a fan of doo wop vocal group Frankie Lymon and the Teenagers; Winkler's only African American employee Roland Culp (Clarence Gilyard, Jr.); Marty Fenneman (Jay Tarses), who has a mad crush on Sheree; and Waldorf "Wally" Wooster (cartoon voice-over legend Don Messick)—the voice of Dippy Duck. About the latter two, Ganzel recalled, "Jay Tarses was happy to be acting instead of writing for a change and he was great. Don Messick was happy to be doing on-camera work as opposed to voice-overs. We were all thrilled to be there—we thought we had landed in a pot of gold. I remember telling friends that I was working with the funniest guy ever, Jim Carrey. I was reacting to Jim Carrey at lunch, however. On the show he was playing straight man to all of our characters, but when Jim was Jim he was a scream. I loved seeing him succeed as the guy I knew as Jim. Truly hilarious."

The cartoon studio was in deep financial straits and, to save money, the employees take turns being the office receptionist. Much like *My World and Welcome to It* (but to a lesser degree), the opening credits and some scenes featured animation. Instead of the usual "Meow," the cat at the end of this MTM Production's credits quacked. With MTM's amazing track record of consistent successes, why did this show fail? Ganzel recalled, "The show was Grant Tinker's baby. When he was out, we were out. I think that had a lot to do with it—a new regime. Also, we were way ahead of our time. A single-camera half-hour comedy with location work and no studio audience just wasn't done at that time." Does Ganzel prefer the single-camera method, or the multi-camera with a live audience? She says, "I prefer single camera only because your acting seems more real for the small screen. Much harder to not get *big* when there is an audience out there, like for a stage play. But when it comes to just having fun, multi-camera is hard to beat. It's 'showtime!'"

Episodes were titled "Goodbye Buddy, Hello Skip," "Filling Buddy's Shoes," "The Annies," "No Good Deed," "The Way We Weren't," "Can We Talk?," "The Education of Mrs. Winkler,"

"Ordinary People Too," "It Didn't Happen One Night," "The Duck Stops Here," "The Children's Half Hour," "You Always Love the One You Hurt," and "Call Me Responsible." The executive producer was Allan Burns; the producers included Dan Wilcox, Thad Mumford, and Rod Daniel; the writers included Allan Burns, Barbara Hall, John Steven Owen, Katherine Green, Steve Kline, Bob Stevens, Jordan Moffet, Stuart Silverman, Dan Wilcox, and Thad Mumford; the directors included Gene Reynolds, Jim Drake, Rod Daniel, Burt Brinckerhoff, Kim Friedman, Victor Lobl, Harry Winer, and Peter Baldwin. The program was created by Allan Burns and Herbert Klynn. Music was provided by Tom Wells and the theme song was by Mark Vieha.

The Dukes Hanna-Barbera Productions/ Warner Bros. Television. CBS. Saturday mornings 10:00 (February 5, 1983–October 29, 1983). Twenty animated episodes were filmed without a laugh track.

The Dukes was a short-lived animated Saturday morning series based upon the popular live-action show *The Dukes of Hazzard*. In the animated version, the short first season (started midseason) utilized replacements as similar lead characters because Tom Wopat (Luke) and John Schneider (Bo) were in the throes of a salary dispute, thus Byron Cherry voiced Coy Duke, and Christopher Mayer was Vance Duke. The Duke boys are in a race around the world with Boss Hogg, and have an adventure in a different country each week. When the series was renewed for a second season (beginning with episode fourteen) the dispute had been ironed out and Wopat and Schneider were on board. During both short seasons, Catherine Bach provided the voice for Daisy, Denver Pyle for Uncle Jesse, James Best for Sheriff Rosco P. Coltrane, and Sorrell Brooke for Boss Hogg. Frank Welker "voiced" the General Lee, Flash, and Smokey. A DVD box set was released by Warner Bros. as part of their Hanna-Barbera Collection late in 2010.

Episodes were titled (*Season One*) "Put Up Your Dukes," "Jungle Jitters," "Dukes of Venice," "Morocco Bound," "Secret Satellite," "Dukes of London," "Greece Fleece," "Dukes in India," "Dukes in Uzbekistan," "Dukes in Hong Kong," "Dukes in Scotland," "Dukes Do Paris," "Dukes in Switzerland"; (*Season Two*) "Boss O'Hogg and the Little People," "Tales of the Vienna Hoods," "The Kid from Madrid," "A Dickens of a Christmas," "The Canadian Caper," "Dukes in Hollywood," and "A Hogg in the Foggy Bogg." The executive producers were William Hanna and Joseph Barbera; the producer was Kay Wright; the writers included John Bradford, Benny and Clive Ferman, O. Gordy, John T. Graham, David R. Toddman, and Tom Ruegger; the directors included Rudy Zamora, John Walker, Oscar Dufau, Ray Patterson, George Gordon, and Carl Urbano. The creators were Gy Waldron and Jerry Rushing. Music was provided by Hoyt Curtin, Cecil Broughton, Terry Moore, and Paul DeKorte.

Easy Street Viacom Productions. NBC. Saturday nights 9:30 (September 13, 1986–September 20, 1986), Sunday nights 8:00 (September 28, 1986–November 9, 1986), Sunday nights 8:30 (November 16, 1986–March 1, 1987), Tuesday night 9:30 (March 31, 1987), and Wednesday night 9:30 (April 29, 1987). Twenty-two episodes were filmed in front of a live audience.

Much like *Leo and Liz in Beverly Hills, Easy Street* was a sitcom about fitting in. In its debut episode, clam juice–loving Alvin "Bully" Stevenson (Jack Elam) and his African American roommate, Ricardo Williams (Lee Weaver), are seated at the tiny kitchen table in their ramshackle lean-to (in the Shady Grove Retirement Village), contemplating life and death. Bully opts to off himself by drowning in the bathtub, when some truly divine intervention in the form of the divine L. K. McGuire (Loni Anderson) knocks on his weather-beaten door. It turns out that she is Bully's only surviving relative (he hasn't seen her since she was a child—his late sister Lucinda's daughter).

She invites both Bully and Ricardo to spend a weekend at her seventeen-room, four-bathroom mansion at 4163 Hillcrest Drive. Her chauffeur is waiting outside to escort them.

L. K. is a beautiful former Las Vegas card dealer and exotic dancer who inherited the mansion after the sudden death of her beloved husband, Ned, in a private plane crash. The inheritance had a stipulation, however—she has to share it with her snooty, ultra-conservative sister-in-law Eleanor and effete investment broker brother-in-law Quentin Standard (Dana Ivey

(Left to right) Loni Anderson, Jack Elam, and Lee Weaver briefly lived on NBC's *Easy Street*.

and James Cromwell, respectively). L. K. is indeed a sweet, kind soul, but has an ulterior motive for bringing the two members of the great unwashed home with her—getting the goat of her in-laws (and she succeeds with flying colors). The modern-day Beverly Hillbillies are then invited to stay on at the mansion full-time, and a sitcom rife with family strife is born. L. K. was not a gold-digger as most would assume—she truly loved Ned, is still attempting to cope with his sudden loss, and now finally feels at home with these unkempt-but-kindly additions.

Episodes were titled "The Pilot," "Pride Goeth Before a Cheap Hotel," "Two Party System," "Comes a Horse," "Man Overboard," "Spoonlighting," "Are We Not Men?," "Be Bop Man," "Charity Begins at Home," "Like That Brave Little Gal in the Philipines," "My Dinner with L. K.," "Demon Child '86," "Friends for Life," "Frames and Dames," "The Check Is in the Mail," "The Mad Gardener" (with guest star Richard Sanders), "Will Power," "Too Many Cooks" (with guest star Dom DeLuise), "Our Kind of People" (with guest star Peter Noone of Herman's Hermits), "The Country Club," "Maid in Italy," and "Spring Fever." The executive producer was Hugh Wilson; the producer was Max Tash; the writers included Hugh Wilson, Andy Borowitz, Bruce Rasmussen, Sheldon Bull, Richard Dubin, and Janis Hirsch; the directors included Hugh Wilson, Tony Mordente, Sam Weisman, Tony Singletary, J. D. Lobue, Bill Foster, Alan Bergmann, and Peter Baldwin. The creator was Hugh Wilson. Music was provided by Parmer Fuller, and the *Easy Street* theme song was performed by Loni Anderson.

Eisenhower and Lutz MTM Productions/ 20th Century Television. CBS. Monday nights 9:30 (March 14, 1988–June 20, 1988). Thirteen episodes were filmed in front of a live audience.

Initially, this series showed great promise and a funny premise. Barnett "Bud" Lutz, Jr. (Scott Bakula), graduated from the Las Vegas School of Law and Acupuncture (but left off the last two words on his résumé). While still in Sin City, Lutz lucks into a $5,000 windfall at one of the local casinos. Sensing a great opportunity, he packs up and moves back to his native Palm Springs, California, and sets up his "ambulance chasing" law practice in an abandoned hot tub store (one working hot tub remains in the showroom and clients are told that this is because Mr. Lutz lives in an apartment complex without a pool). It is located in a high-traffic area where car crashes are common, and those involved are always presented with one of Bud's business cards (he also coaches his few clients on the fine art of milking the most from their injuries).

It should be noted that there was no Eisenhower in *Eisenhower and Lutz*—the name was only used to add some class to the practice. Bud's curmudgeonly sign-making father, Barnett Lutz, Sr. (Henderson Forsythe), painted one for the business on the cheap with several words misspelled (it reads "Attorny at Laws"). Rose Portillo portrayed Millie Zamora, Bud's sarcastic and yet-to-be-paid receptionist; Leo Geter played Dwayne Spitler, Bud's young and geeky assistant who is studying pre-law at Joshua Tree University (while delivering sushi for Tanaka's, the restaurant next door); DeLane Matthews was Bud's cute blonde girlfriend Megan O'Malley; and Patricia Richardson was Kay ("Kay Kay") Dunne, Bud's former girlfriend—an attorney-at-law for the respected Griffith, McKendrick, and Dunne firm. Bud and Kay are reunited at what Bud thought was a job interview, but which turns out to be merely a referral. He was previously unaware that she was the Dunne in their company name, and discovers that they both still had some feelings for each other. Episodes revolved around Bud's struggling law practice, and the delicate balance between his current and past love. The debut episode is quite funny, but, unfortunately, the quality of some of the later episodes pale in comparison. Bud closed up the shop and drained the hot tub after just thirteen weeks.

Episodes were titled "The Whiplash Kid Returns, Parts One and Two," "The Hernia Chronicles," "Take My Ex-Wife, Please," "Blast from the Past," "Bud Junior Junior, Parts One and Two," "Don't Change a Hair for Me," "Petrified Forest," "Bud's Birthday," "Pride and Prejudice," "Play It Again, Bud," and "The Devil Wears a Toupee." The executive producer was Dan Wilcox; the producers were Shelley Zellman, Gareth Davies, Mark Egan, and Mark Soloman; the writers included Cheryl Blythe, Mark Egan, Allan Burns, David Nichols, Gina Goldman, Dava Savel, Burt Prelutsky, Dan Wilcox, Mark Solomon, and Shelley Zellman; the directors included Peter Burns, Allan Burns, Beth Hillshafer, Andy Cadiff, Dan Wilcox, David Steinberg, and Arlene Sanford. The program was created by Allan Burns. The theme song, "Boys Like You," was by Patrick Williams and performed by Amanda McBroom. Additional music was provided by Eddie Karam.

The Ellen Burstyn Show Ellen Burstyn Productions/P. S. 235 Productions/Touchstone Television. ABC. Saturday nights 8:30 (September 20, 1986–November 15, 1986, and August 8, 1987–September 5, 1987). Thirteen episodes were videotaped in front of a live audience.

Ellen Burstyn began her acting career as Ellen McRae, and was best known for her work on the silver screen in *The Last Picture Show* (1971), *The Exorcist* (1973), and *Alice Doesn't Live Here Anymore* (1974). *The Ellen Burstyn Show* was an attempt at success on the small screen, and was a true rarity in that it was filmed in New York City (Ellen lived in Nyack, New York), and also that the program was sold to ABC on just its premise and star power alone. There was no pilot, only a debut episode.

Writer Bo Kaprall said, "Ellen was not really excited about doing television, and with three very headstrong women on the show, Ellen Burstyn, Elaine Stritch, and Megan Mullally, it was far from TV's happiest set. My good friend, executive producer Norman Steinberg liked happy sets and this was not one of them. I was also writing for *What a Country* at the time and was flying back and forth between Los Angeles and New York every week. I had recently moved my family to Minnesota to escape the madness of Los Angeles for a while, but I was called back into it. One of my jobs on the Burstyn show was to try to keep the peace, and I even wrote myself into one episode titled 'Sydney's Night Out.' There were also problems with a very demanding head writer named Howard Gewirtz. It eventually just became too taxing, and I thought about just doing *What a Country*, but, fortunately, the Burstyn show was canceled after thirteen weeks."

Burstyn portrayed Professor Ellen Brewer, a writer who lives under the same roof with four generations of family members—her mother, the sarcastic Sydney Brewer (Elaine Stritch), whose favorite phrase is "duly noted"; her daughter, the newly divorced (from Mark Ross) wannabe writer Molly Brewer Ross (a young, almost unrecognizable Megan Mullally, pre–*Will and Grace* and *The Megan Mullally Show*); Molly's five-and-a-half-year-old son, Nick (Jesse Tendler); a financially strapped writing student named Tom Hines (Barry Sobel); and a pet dog named Angie, who gave birth to a large litter of puppies. Most episodes kicked off with Burstyn's Ellen Brewer character offering up reminiscences of her two marriages ("one marriage ended in her husband's *d*eath, the other in *d*ivorce, leading to yet another *d* word, *d*ating"), along with reflections of her early days as a writer, all presented in monologue form. Her character's biggest claim to literary fame was a novel titled *A Woman on Top*—a best-seller. She held writing classes in her very spacious-yet-frenetic home.

One of the latter episodes of the series, "The Box," was most unusual and memorable. Sitcom episodes normally wrap up all the loose ends after thirty minutes (minus commercials) have elapsed, but this one offered no closure. It revolved around a package with no return address that Ellen received in the mail. Everyone in the Brewer household fantasized about what might be in the box and questioned whether it should even be opened. It wasn't.

Episodes were titled "The Debut Episode," "Monkey Business," "Where There's a Will" "Guest Lecturer" (with guest star Eileen Heckart), "Crime and Punishment" (with guest star Jack Gilford), "Sydney's Night Out" (with guest star Bo Kaprall), "Reading Between the

Lines," "Family Affair," "Molly Sings the Blues," "Writer Wronger," "The Box," "Writes of Passage," and "I'm Dancing Faster Than I Can." The executive producer was Norman Steinberg; the producer was Ronald E. Frazier; the writers included Bo Kaprall, Jim Mulligan, Holly Nadler, Robert Bruce, Martin Weiss, Howard Gewirtz, David Frankel, Cheryl Gard, Pamela Norris, Tom Walla, Dave Wollert, David Steven Cohen, Roger S. H. Schulman, Norman Steinberg, and Bob Rosenfarb; the directors included Dolores Ferraro, Norman Steinberg, David Steinberg, John Tracy, Arlene Sanford, and Sam Weisman. The program was created by David Frankel. Music was provided by Artie Butler, and the theme song titled "Nothing in the World Like Love" was written by Artie Butler and John Bettis, and performed by Rita Coolidge.

Empire Humble Productions, Inc./MGM-United Artists Television. CBS. Wednesday nights 8:30 (January 4, 1984–February 1, 1984). Six episodes were videotaped with a laugh track.

Empire has been utilized for the title of three very different TV shows in three different decades. In 1962, *Empire* was a western drama series starring Richard Egan and Ryan O'Neal (a.k.a. *Redigo*). In 2015, it was a FOX Network musical drama series starring Terrence Howard. And, in 1984, it was the title of a sitcom parody of corporate America (and perhaps prime-time soap operas such as *Dallas* and *Dynasty*). The large cast's many winks at the camera were not only visible but also very audible.

The action took place at Empire Industries, and *Avengers* star Patrick Macnee portrayed the ruthless board chairman Calvin Cromwell. The lovely Caren Kaye played Meredith, the unrelatable director of public relations. As Kaye recalls, "This was a great, wonderful show—way ahead of its time. It's interesting to note that, in an odd coincidence, my best friend, who shall remain nameless, was cast for a part in the show. However, she called me crying that she'd just been fired. While I was on the phone with her, my other phone rang and it was my manager telling me to get to the set because an actress had just been fired, and they needed me right away. Luckily, we stayed friends—she understood that it was just the nature of the business." Others in the cast included Richard Masur as the spineless (despite his years of assertiveness training) Jack Willow, vice-president of sales (often requiring an oxygen mask and tank during tense corporate meetings); Christine Belford as Jack's ballsy and controlling wife, Jackie Willow; Dick O'Neill as the past-his-prime marketing manager Arthur Broderick (an alcoholic who was married five times—currently to Dotty, dyed his gray hair jet black to appear younger, and was fired for embezzlement but then rehired in the debut episode); a pre–*L.A. Law* Susan Ruttan as his sympathetic secretary, Marge; Edward Winter as the skittish security chief T. Howard Daniels (who gave each of his co-workers pistols for Christmas); Howard Platt as the unethical chief counsel (and admitted murderer) Tom Martinson; Michael McGuire as Everett Roland—a married board member (to the ailing Virginia) who is having a fling with his secretary, Renee (Patricia Elliott); Maureen Arthur as Peg; and Dennis Dugan as Ben Christian—a neophyte appointed to the position of vice-president of development and research (he frequently calls his mother in Ohio on the company dime).

Caren Kaye said, "Because my deal with the William Morris Agency specified that I would always get dressing rooms close to the set, I shared one with Dennis Dugan, which led to rumors of us being an item. Of course, none of it was true—I had already been with Renny Temple for many, many years, and we're still happily married today." Episodes deal with one-upmanship, backstabbing, and cooking the books. Every member of the board wants to take the reins of Empire Industries, and no one can be trusted. About the cancellation, Kaye stated, "It was a very expensive show to produce. We had quite a large and seasoned cast, and the show was done single-camera style with a laugh track, so it took a lot longer, too. I was very proud of this show. It was brilliantly written in an almost Broadway style by Fred Freeman. My character was not a really important member of the ensemble initially, but was about to climb the corporate ladder. I had great optimism about where my character would be going in the future, had the show continued."

Empire episodes don't appear to have been assigned actual titles, only Episode 1 through Episode 6. The executive producers were Lawrence J. Cohen and Fred Freeman; the producer and director was Terry Hughes; the writers included Lawrence J. Cohen, Fred Freeman, Jim Geoghan, Dennis Danzinger, George Zateslo, and Ellen Sandler. Music was provided by Patrick Williams. Patrick Macnee died June 25, 2015 at the age of 93.

Enos A Lou Step Production/Gy Waldron Productions/Warner Bros. Television. CBS. Wednesday night 8:00 (November 5, 1980–May 20, 1981), and Saturday nights 8:00 (May 30, 1981–September 19, 1981). Eighteen episodes were filmed without a laugh track.

A *Dukes of Hazzard* spinoff, *Enos* might be categorized as an action sitcom—lots of comedy and lots of action in an hour-long format. Car chases made up a substantial amount of that action. After all, Enos was a cop, and with a name like Enos, it's likely he was teased as a child.

Enos Strate (Sonny Shroyer) is promoted to the Los Angeles Police Department (Metro Squad, Division Eight) after solving a tough murder case while a deputy sheriff for Hazzard County, Georgia. Now on his own show, he is paired with a streetwise African American policeman named Turk Adams (Samuel E. Wright). Turk is soon in therapy because of Enos's daredevil driving feats and near misses. Enos is almost always smiling, and usually calls Turk "Buddyroo." He has a Gomer Pyle–like quality, and numerous catchphrases, like "Sure as a bump on a warthog's nose." Enos and Turk share an odd handshake, and despite countless mishaps and a litany of reprimands from beleaguered Lieutenant Joseph Broggi (sitcom veteran John Dehner), and Captain Dempsey (John Milford), Strate and Adams always manage to solve crimes. Because of Enos's Southern roots, banjo and/or fiddle music plays throughout most of each hour. The show's announcer was prolific actor William Schallert, who died at the age of 93 on May 8, 2016.

Episodes were titled "Enos," "Uncle Jerry's Visit," "Where's the Corpus?," "Blu Flu" (with guest star Beverly Garland), "Grits and Greens Strike Again," "Snow Job," "House Cleaners," "One Daisy Per Summer," "Horse Cops," "The Head Hunter," "The Hostage," "Now You See Him Now You Don't," "Once and Fur All," "Cops at Sea," "Moonshiners," "Shaming of the Shrew," "Pistol Packing Enos," and "Forever Blowing Baubles." The executive producer was Paul R. Picard; the producers were James Heinz and B. W. Sandefur; the writers included Simon Muntner, A. J. Christopher, Robert J. Holt, Leonard B. Kaufman, Leo Gordon, Elroy Schwartz, Rick Mittleman, William Kelley, William Raynor, Myles Wilder, Richard Christian Matheson, Jim Rogers, Stephen Thornley, Ray Brenner, B. W. Sandefur, Milt Rosen, Gerald Sanford, Thomas E. Szollosi, and Gy Waldron; the directors included Donald McDougall, Rod Amateau, Michael Caffrey, Dennis Donnelly, Hollingsworth Morse, Bruce Kessler, Richard C. Bennett, Robert Totten, and Bernard McEveety. The show was created by Gy Waldron. Music was supplied by Dennis McCarthy.

E/R Embassy Television. CBS. Sunday night 8:00 (September 16, 1984), Tuesday nights 8:30 (September 18, 1984–October 30, 1984), Wednesday nights 8:30 (November 7, 1984–February 27, 1985). Twenty-two episodes were videotaped in front of a live audience.

Based upon the popular play of the same name from Chicago's Organic Theater, *E/R* stood for emergency room—a CBS sitcom set in Chicago's Clark Street Hospital. A Band-Aid served as the backslash in the program's title. The lead role portrayed by Elliott Gould was Dr. Howard Sheinfeld—an ear, nose, and throat specialist who works marathon hours at the hospital to help with his alimony payments and child support for his fifteen-year-old son. Howard has two ex-wives, and the most recent one, Phyllis (Patch MacKenzie), who got the car, the house, and even the dog (Godiva) in the settlement, regularly calls him at work, much to his dismay.

Sheinfeld smokes cigars, naps often while on duty, and hits on anything in a skirt. During the run of the show, he becomes a full-time hospital employee. His superior is Dr. Eve Sheridan, the supervisor of all emergency room activities. Sheridan was played by the late Marcia Strassman in the pilot, but rather by Mary McDonnell in the rest of the episodes. Despite her position at the hospital, few employees heed her constant critiques. She has a lot on her mind—her elderly father recently suffered a stroke, and her only option was to place him in a nursing home. Under her very stern façade is a good and caring person. Other hospital staff members included Conchata Ferrell (pre–*Two-and-a-Half Men*) as Nurse Joan Thor (usually just called Thor), a hard-working, fun-loving presence who can be tough-as-nails when necessary, and who experiences health issues in later episodes. Her shift was from 5 p.m. to 1 a.m. She is married to a freeloader named Bud (she is the breadwinner, while he sits at home, watching soap operas); Lynne Moody portrayed African American nurse Julie Williams. We learn in the pilot episode that Julie is the niece of George Jefferson (Sherman Hemsley). Hemsley guest starred in the two-part pilot episode, and while visiting the hospital is shot (however, the gift in his pocket for Julie deflected the bullet). The bossy and frightfully honest Filipino-American receptionist, who has a pet peeve about patients waiting behind the white line surrounding her desk, is Maria Amardo (Shuko Akune). To save money, she shares an apartment with Julie Williams, and is very upset about getting the smaller of the two bedrooms. Maria is dating a highly possessive black cop named Fred Burdock (Bruce A. Young), who frequently visits the emergency room lobby. A perky young blonde pediatric nurse named Cory Smith (Corinne Bohrer) is very uncomfortable in the emergency room and has a thing for Dr. Sheinfeld. Other recurring characters included (Sheinfeld sounds like Seinfeld and coincidentally) Jason Alexander (with hair) as hospital administrator Harold Stickley (a babe repellent); George Clooney (who, coincidentally, was later cast in another series titled *ER*) played the newbie emergency room doctor nicknamed Ace (a.k.a. Mark Kolmar, Thor's nephew), who is usually seen in a leather vest; the follically challenged Dr. Thomas Esquivel, played by Luis Avalos; William G. Schilling as the often disgruntled orderly named Richard; Jeff Doucette as a paramedic named Bert; and Shirley Prestia as a hypochondriac named Irene who is constantly being ousted from the emergency room due to her perfect health. Much in the same manner of *M*A*S*H*, *E/R* was a comedy with some occasional serious moments and unfortunate, unavoidable losses in the operating room. The crew's favorite after-hours hangout is a dive called Houlihan's. Reruns were briefly aired on the Lifetime cable network.

Episodes were titled "Pilot, Part One," "Pilot, Part Two" (both with guest star Sherman Hemsley), "The Sister" (with guest star Dennis Franz), "My Way," "Son of Sheinfeld" (with guest star Jonathan Silverman), "Save the Last Dance for Me" (with guest stars David Faustino and Don Galloway), "Say It Isn't So," "Growing Pains," "All's Well That Ends," "Only a Nurse," "Sentimental Journey," "Mr. Fix-It" (with guest star Ron Masak), "A Cold Night in Chicago," "Both Sides Now" (with guest stars Candice Azzara and John Schuck), "The Storm," "Enter Romance," "Brotherly Love," "I Raise You," "Merry Wives of Sheinfeld, Part One," "Merry Wives of Sheinfeld, Part Two" (with guest star Karen Black), "All Tied Up," and "A Change in Policy" (with guest star Ron Cey of the Los Angeles Dodgers). The creators and executive producers were Saul Turteltaub and Bernie Orenstein; the producer was Eve Brandstein; the writers included Saul Turteltaub, Bernie Orenstein, Sally Wade, Bruce A. Young, Susan Stevenson, Mark Schaefer, Milt Rosen, Richard Raskin, Carolyn Purdy-Gordon, Mark Masuoka, Joe Martin, Sherwood Kiraly, J. Kahn, Gary Houston, Stuart Gordon, Gary Gilbert, Zaid Farid, Ron Clark, Eve Brandstein, Ron Berman, Tom Towles (who also appeared in the "Save the Last Dance for Me" episode), and Richard Fire (who also appeared in the episode titled "All's Well That Ends"); the director for all twenty-two episodes was Peter Bonerz (dentist Jerry Robinson on *The Bob Newhart Show*). Music was provided by the prolific Jimmy Webb, and the theme song was performed by soul music great Lou Rawls.

Everything's Relative Fredde Productions, Inc./Embassy Television. CBS. Saturday nights 8:30 (October 3, 1987–November 7, 1987). Ten episodes were videotaped in front of a live audience, but only six aired.

There have been numerous TV shows titled *Everything's Relative* over the years—a 1965 Nicholson and Muir game show, a 1999 NBC sitcom with Jeffrey Tambor, and, in between, a very short-lived 1987 CBS program. The latter starred Jason Alexander (with hair, pre–*Seinfeld*) as Julian Beeby, a sensible, divorced (his wife cheated on him with a talk show host), hard-working thirty-three-year-old businessman (he is a consumer product tester), who shares a loft apartment in New York's SoHo region with his twenty-five-year-old babe magnet, construction worker brother Scott (John Bolger). Scott's way with women evokes hero worship from the Beeby Brothers' errand boy, Mickey Murphy (Tony Deacon Nittoli), and much envy from Julian. Even though they are brothers, the Beebys were very much like *The Odd Couple*—differing lifestyles, values, careers (white collar vs. blue collar), and friends. The door to their loft reads "Tutto E Possibile" (Everything Is Possible), and Julian's business partner of five years, Emily Cabot (Gina Hecht), attempts a seemingly impossible task—bringing the brothers closer together. She also wants to marry Julian, but he wants their relationship to remain platonic. Anne Jackson had a recurring role as the boys' meddling, opinionated mother, Rae.

Episodes were titled "Meet the Beeby Brothers," "Taking Stock," "Post Graduate," "The Mom Who Came to Dinner" (with guest star Rob Morrow), "Hit the Road Jack" (with guest star Peggy Cass), "It's a Business Doing Pleasure with You," "Forgotten but Not Gone," "It Had to Be You and You," "Brother's Keeper," and "Emily's Turn." The executive producer was Maurice Duke; the producers were David Debin, Richard Heller, Ellen Falcon, George Barimo, and Marshall Karp; the writers included Marshall Karp, Trish Vrandenburg, Larry Levin, Alan Kirschenbaum, David Crane and Marta

John Bolger, Jason Alexander, and Anne Jackson (clockwise, from top) starred in one of several TV shows bearing the title *Everything's Relative*; this one aired briefly on CBS in 1987.

Kauffman; the directors included John Bowab, Valentine Mayer, Andrew D. Weyman, Matthew Diamond, Ellen Falcon, Steve Robman, and David Trainer. The creator was Marshall Karp. Music was provided by David Horowitz. Anne Jackson died on April 12, 2016 at the age of 90.

Family Man S. B. B. Productions/Universal Television. ABC. Friday nights 9:30 (March 18, 1988–April 29, 1988). Seven episodes were filmed with a laugh track.

This show is not to be confused with the 1990 Gregory Harrison sitcom of the same name, nor is it to be mistaken for the animated series *Family Guy*. This *Family Man* was an ABC series starring Richard Libertini as a comedy writer named Shelly Tobin (who still uses a typewriter). Except for the fact that his TV wife is quite a bit younger than he, any other resemblances to *The Dick Van Dyke Show* end there. Said TV wife, Andrea (Mimi Kennedy), had been married once before and had two children from that marriage—ten-year-old Rosie (Alison Sweeney), who has the word "Knock!" on the outside of her bedroom door, and seven-year-old Josh (Whitby Hertford). Together, Shelly and Andrea have one child, three-year-old Sara (Keeley Mari Gallagher). This show was originally intended to be a FOX Network show, but landed instead on ABC. *Family Man* was also the title of a 2000 Nicolas Cage motion picture, and a 1983 Top Ten hit by Hall and Oates.

Episodes were titled "A Night Out," "Dad," "Above the Fruited Plain," "Valentine's Day," "Hmmm," "Preferred List," and "Weekend." The producer was Peter V. Ware; the creator and writer was Earl Pomerantz, and the directors included David Steinberg and James Gardner. Music was provided by Roger Steinman. The theme song was written by Roger Steinman and Earl Pomerantz, and performed by Kipp Lennon. Richard Libertini died on January 7, 2016 at the age of 82.

Richard Libertini portrayed a comedy writer, and Mimi Kennedy played his wife, in one of a couple of unsuccessful sitcoms called *Family Man*. **This one could be seen on ABC in 1988.**

The Famous Teddy Z Hugh Wilson Productions. CBS. Monday nights 9:30 (September 18, 1969–October 30, 1989), Monday nights 8:30 (November 13, 1989–January 22, 1990), and Saturday night 9:00 (May 12, 1990). Twenty episodes were videotaped in front of a live audience, but only fifteen aired.

Teddy Zakalokis (Jon Cryer, pre–*Two-And-A-Half-Men*) was supposed to work in the family bakery, but joined the army and was a paratrooper (but made only one jump) in an attempt to delay that fate. He was torn between pursuing his dream gig, and pleasing his grandmother Deena (Erica Yohn) by taking the bakery job. In the interim, he accepted a temporary position in the mailroom of the Unlimited Talent Agency (U. T. A.).

Jon Cryer as *The Famous Teddy Z*, long before he was the even more famous Alan Harper on another CBS show, *Two and a Half Men*.

Teddy immediately falls for a young, blonde co-worker named Laurie Parr (Jane Sibbett), but she spurns his advances, saying she'd rather eat paint off of a stucco house than date him. Against his wishes, his immediate supervisor, Richie Herby (Tom La Grua), sends him out to escort a temperamental movie star named Harland Keyvo (Dennis Lipscomb) from the airport to his hotel. Keyvo is the agency's biggest cash cow, and everyone kowtows to him—everyone except Teddy, that is. Teddy's no-nonsense approach impresses the mercurial star so much that he is asked to become his agent. Teddy has managed the impossible—he soared from the mailroom to one of the highest-paid agents in a single day, much to the chagrin of his new boss (and the actor's former agent), Al Floss.

The impatient Floss, with an automatic door closer on his desk and a passion for popcorn, was portrayed brilliantly by Alex Rocco. In fact, despite the single-season status of the program, he garnered a "Best Supporting Actor" Emmy for the role. Besides a nice salary and his own office, Teddy also gets to hire his own secretary and, of course, he requests Laurie Parr from the mailroom. Another of Teddy's superiors, Abe Werkfinder (Milton Selzer), suggests that Teddy Zakalokis adopt the professional name of Teddy Z, and an agent is born. However, Teddy has absolutely no experience, thus the title of the program's second episode, "What's an Agent to Do?" Grandmother Deena was upset about Teddy's new career (making a lot of money for doing nothing), but his high school–aged brother, Aristotle (Josh Blake), is quite impressed.

Episodes were titled "The Pilot," "What's an Agent to Do?," "Bobby the Chimp" (with guest star Mary Hart), "A Day at the Beach," "The Dark Closet," "Mr. Zakalokis Goes to Washington," "Baking with Esther Luna," "Teddy Sells the House," "A Case of Murder," "Teddy Gets a House Guest," "Seasons Greeting from Al Floss" (with guest star Bill Macy), "Grandpa Goes to Work," "Engineer Bob," "Loyalty," "Agent of the Year" (with guest star Sid Melton), "Teddy Goes to the Awards," "Pitching the Net," "Al Tells the Truth" (with guest star Robert Culp), "Teddy's Big Date," and "Teddy Gets a Guru" (with guest star Bebe Neuwirth). The creator and executive producer was Hugh Wilson; the writers included Hugh Wilson, Robert Wilcox, Wayne Lemon, Sid O. Smith, Craig Nelson, Richard Dubin, Chuck Ross, Marilynn Marko-Sanders, Richard Sanders; the directors included Max Tash, Richard Dubin, Hugh Wilson, Frank Bonner, and Ginger Gregg. Music was provided by Guy Moon, Stephanie Tyrell, and Steve Tyrell. Hugh Wilson was also the creator of *WKRP in Cincinnati*, and had cast members Frank Bonner (Herb Tarlek) and Richard Sanders (Les Nessman) appear on *The Famous Teddy Z* as well. The program's concept was allegedly inspired by the real-life events of talent agent Jay Kantor who shared a limousine with Marlon Brando and then quickly ascended to the stratosphere of the talent agent industry. Alex Rocco died on July 18, 2015 at the age of 79.

Fast Times Universal Studios. CBS. Wednesday nights 8:00 (March 5, 1986–April 23, 1986).

Seven episodes were videotaped single-camera style without a laugh track.

Right from the get-go, the big problem with the TV version of the 1982 motion picture *Fast Times at Ridgemont High* was that it was scheduled in the 8 p.m. hour on CBS (the family hour), thus the R-rated elements of the memorable motion picture had to be tamed considerably (much as ABC's *Delta House* lost the edge that made *National Lampoon's Animal House* a runaway hit in 1978).

Dean Cameron, who portrayed Jeff Spicoli, said, "Because of the time slot, there was also no mention of drugs of any kind in the series. Also, the title was shortened from *Fast Times at Ridgemont High* to simply *Fast Times*. The network was afraid of alienating adults with the *Ridgemont High* part of the title. They wanted the show to be about students and the adults in their lives."

Ray Walston reprised his role as Ridgemont's no-nonsense, taciturn Mr. Arnold Hand (and was promoted to vice principal in the episode titled "My New Best Friend"). Cameron said, "That was the real Ray Walston. He was a classic—a cool, funny, foul-mouthed presence (I learned the word cockerlocker from him, and still use it today) and he didn't take shit from anyone. One of my fondest memories of Ray—I went on a press junket to New York City with him to promote the series. In those days, stars flew only first class. It's not well known, but many of them, Ray included, would then sell their first class ticket, pocket the considerable difference, and fly coach. So there was this very familiar face sitting in coach—and wouldn't you know a stewardess found it unacceptable that the great Ray Walston was in coach. She had him bumped up to first class. Long story short, Ray not only kept the change, but got to fly first class anyway. He was awesome."

According to Cameron, taking on the role of Jeff Spicoli—the spacey, mullet-wearing beach bum student with the IQ of plankton—was terrifying: "I had originally read for the part of Mike Damone in the film, but I didn't get it," he explained. "It's interesting that I was studying at the same acting studio as Sean Penn. Allegedly, Penn was so into the role he had all of his friends call him Jeff during the shoot. Anyway, when it came time for the TV version, everyone was wondering what loser would get the role of Spicoli. Those were big flip-flops to fill. I read for all of the parts on the show, but kept getting callbacks for the role of Spicoli. Even Keanu Reeves read for the part (I think he was K. C. Reeves at the time). It took a long time, but I got the part and, like the Spicoli in the film, my hair was dyed blonde. Well, after the first day of filming, the network saw the 'dailies' and took issue with my hair color. They wanted a dark-haired Spicoli. Eventually, I got to keep the blonde hair, but it was a battle for a while."

Jeff's younger brother, skateboard-savvy Curtis Spicoli, was portrayed by future *Wonder Years* co-star Jason Hervey. Cameron added, "Hervey's mother was my agent for a brief time." The popular lothario named Brad Hamilton (James Nardini), who worked at the Cattle Burger fast food restaurant, drove a classic convertible he called "the cruising vessel." Because of the 8 p.m. time slot, Brad was watered down considerably, thus rendering him a rather dull main character. Brad's insecure but very pretty sister, Stacey, was played by future *According to Jim* co-star Courtney Thorne-Smith (her character had a crush on singer Corey Hart and loved mocha almond crunch ice cream). Cameron recalled, "I got to work with Courtney again a while later in the motion picture called *Summer School* [1987]." Brad had a "thing" for Stacey's best friend, Linda Barrett (Claudia Wells). In one episode, Linda agreed to go out on a date with Brad if no one else found out about it. The cocky, overtly confident, sly, and conniving Mike Damone was portrayed by the future Dr. McDreamy on *Grey's Anatomy*, Patrick Dempsey. Other faculty members included the eternally positive, emotional, and overly concerned life studies teacher Ms. Leslie Melon (Kit McDonough); and the eccentric science teacher with the hangdog expression, Mr. Hector Vargas (Vincent Schiavelli, reprising his role in the film). Schiavelli later embodied a similar presence on *Scrubs*. Summing it up,

Cameron stated, "What a great cast. I had a great time doing *Fast Times*. If only it had lasted."

Episodes were titled "The Pilot," "Last Laugh," "The Engagement," "What Is Life?" (with guest star Martin Mull), "My Brother the Car," "My New Best Friend," and "Secret Romance" (with guest star Fred Willard). Dean Cameron recalled, "On one episode, we were running really late. We needed to get a scene in a phone booth very quickly. Because of union demands, we had to do it in one take. Wouldn't you know, we almost got through the scene, but some asshole driving by messed up the shoot by laying on his horn." The executive producer was Allen Rucker; the producers included Amy Heckerling, Jonathan Roberts, and John Whitman; the writers included Amy Heckerling, Dennis Rinsler, Marc Warren, Kevin Parent, Myles Berkowitz, Roger S. H. Schulman, Allen Rucker, David Steven Cohen, and Jonathan Roberts.

About the writers, Cameron said, "I hear they had pictures of the cast of *Square Pegs* in the writers' room with the caption 'Remember, we are not doing this show.'" The directors included Amy Heckerling, Neil Israel, Daniel Attias, and Claudia Weill. Creative consultants for the program were Cameron Crowe (who inspired the original novel and screenplay), and Moon Unit Zappa (for input about teenage lingo). Zappa also had a recurring role on the sitcom as Barbara DeVilbiss. Music was provided by Barry Goldberg. The "Fast Times" theme song was written by Danny Elfman; it was performed by Oingo Boingo. Many pop hits of the day, such as "Straight from the Heart," by Bryan Adams, and "Freeway of Love," by Aretha Franklin, were used as transitional music between scenes.

Fathers and Sons American Flyer Television, Ltd./20th Century Television. NBC. Sunday nights 7:30 (April 6, 1986–May 4, 1986). Four episodes were filmed with a laugh track.

Fathers and Sons was an extremely short-lived sitcom that aired during the Sunday "family viewing time." The series starred former Los Angeles Rams "fearsome foursome" great Merlin Olsen as Buddy Landau, an athlete turned elementary school coach. He and his family were the focus of the show. Buddy's wife is named Ellen (Kelly Sanders) and his son, Lanny (Jason Late), is a bit on the pudgy side, likes the Los Angeles Lakers, but only participates in sports because it is expected of him (he joined the wrestling team). Other students at Charles Lindbergh Elementary School included Sean Flynn (Andre Gower), an up-and-coming Romeo; Matty Bolen (Ian Fried), the smart kid; and Brandon Russo (Hakeem Abdul-Samad), the energetic, vertically challenged ball of fire. Others on the faculty are assistant coach Tony Salvadore (Bert Rosario) and science teacher Mr. Belnap (Sal Viscuso). School was out forever after only four episodes. Merlin Olsen had more success in an earlier series with "Father" in its title—*Father Murphy*.

Episodes were titled "The Ironman," "We'll Always Have the Mall," "Desperately Seeking Einstein," and "Which Championship Season?" The executive producer was Michael Zinberg; the producer was Joseph M. Ellis; the writers included Nick Arnold, Michael Zinberg, and Randall Zisk; and the directors included Will Mackenzie, Peter Baldwin, Michael Zinberg, and Robert McCullough. Music was provided by Patrick Williams.

A Fine Romance Indie Production Company/Phoenix Entertainment Group. ABC. Wednesday night 10:00 (January 18, 1989), and Thursday nights 8:00 (January 26, 1989–March 16, 1989). Twelve hour-long episodes were filmed without a laugh track, but only seven aired.

This romantic dramedy was filmed in a myriad of locations in Europe. A free spirit named Louisa Phillips (Margaret Whitton), and Michael Trent (Christopher Cazenove), a Cambridge professor, are a divorced couple who host a travel show on television called *Ticket to Ride* (in fact, when this series was aired in the UK it was retitled *Ticket to Ride* to avoid confusion with an earlier British Judi Dench series called *A Fine Romance*). While bouncing around exotic locations, they continually happen upon murders that needed solving. *A Fine Romance* was set to debut in the fall of 1988, but because of that season's Writers Guild of America strike, it didn't make its bow until early in 1989. Others in the cast included Ernie Sabella as George Shipman, the travel show's producer, Dinah Lenney as Friday, George's assistant; and Xavier Kuentz as Francois Boyer. Only seven of the twelve filmed episodes aired, and, appropriately, the final unaired entry was titled "Th-Th-That's all, Folks." Many of the episode titles shared names with motion pictures, and were indeed mild spoofs of said films.

Episodes were titled "Desperately Seeking Louisa," "A Horse Is a Horse of Course of Course" (with guest star Barbara Barrie), "Below Suspicion," "The Day of the Third Thin Wrong Woman Who Knew All too Much about Eve," "A Yank and the RAF," "South by Southeast," "Double Indignity," "School Daze," "The Thomas Crown Affair," and "Th-Th-That's All, Folks" (with guest star Jack Riley). The executive producers were Charlotte Brown, Nick Elliott, Bruce J. Sallan; the producers were Barrie Melrose, Kevin Inch, Tony Bishop, Courtney Pledger, and James C. Hart; the writers included Ian Gurvitz, Michael Aitkens, Kathy McCormick, John Amodeo, Thomas J. Wright, Gabrielle Beaumont, Terry Nation, Mark Lisson, Charlotte Bingham, Sally Robinson, Peter Spencer, Terence Brady, and Andy Schatzberg; the directors included Reza Badiyi, Ray Austin, Richard Franklin, Peachy Markowitz, Jane Petteway, Harry Harris, David Tucker, Thomas J. Wright, Gene Reynolds, Stan Lathan, Kevin Hooks, and Bill Froelich.

First Impressions The Greif-Dore Company/Humble Productions/Orion Television. CBS. Saturday nights 8:00 (August 27, 1988–October 1, 1988). Eight episodes were videotaped in front of a live audience, but only five aired.

Sitcoms about advertising agencies don't fare well in prime-time (e.g., *Nothing in Common*, *The Crazy Ones*). This one starred Brad Garrett, pre–*Everybody Loves Raymond*. Coincidentally, this show also had a character named Raymond (James Noble, of *Benson*), a studio sound engineer with a gambling problem and designs on attaining public office. Garrett portrayed Frank Dutton—a recently divorced father of nine-year-old Lindsay (Brandy Gold). The program was titled *First Impressions* because of Dutton's proficiency with voice impressions. His ad agency is called Media of Omaha (an obvious play on Mutual of Omaha) and his impersonations of celebrity voices get him clients who want those voices in their commercials. Others in the cast included Dutton's self-aggrandizing partner, Dave (Thom Sharp), and their naïve receptionist, Donna Patterson (Sarah Abrell). After a year as a single dad, Dutton begins dating again, but finds that he is sorely out of practice. Keeping an eye on the small family's comings and goings is Mrs. Madison (Ruth Kobart), the Duttons' nosy neighbor. Singer/songwriter Harry Nilsson performed the theme song, titled "First Impressions," but it was his theme song from *The Courtship of Eddie's Father* ("Best Friend") for which he is best known. The original working title for the show was "Just You and Me," but under any title it wasn't a ratings winner and disappeared quickly.

Episodes were titled "The Pilot" (with guest star Dabbs Greer), "Frank's Date," "Raymond vs. the Computer," "Public Trust," "On His Own," "Poor Clara," "The Audition," and "The Selling of Frank." The executive producer was Bonny Dore; the producers were Leslie Greif and Gordon Hunt; the writers included Lawrence J. Cohen, Fred Freeman, and Richard Marcus; the directors included Phil Ramuno, Terry Hughes, Alan Rafkin, Jack Shea, and Howard Storm. Music was provided by Joey Carbone, George Doering, and Leslie Greif. The theme song was written by Joey Carbone, George Doering, Leslie Greif, and Harry Nilsson. James Noble died on March 28, 2016 at the age of 94.

Fitz and Bones Glen A. Larson Productions/Universal Television/NBC. Saturday nights 10:00 (October 24, 1981–November 14, 1981). Five hour-long episodes were filmed without a laugh track.

This was an attempted comeback vehicle for The Smothers Brothers. It's surprising they agreed to a scripted series, as they absolutely hated their experience with a 1965 CBS sitcom called *The Smothers Brothers Show*, on which Tom Smothers portrayed an angel.

Fitz and Bones was a weekly sixty-minute dramedy series (the opening credits were rather ambiguous—is this a comedy or drama?) on which Dick Smothers (Mom always liked him best) played Ryan "Fitz" Fitzpatrick, a pushy investigative reporter for a San Francisco TV station and Newsline 3. "Bones" Howard (Dick's brother, Tom Smothers, portraying a non-brother) is his clumsy and clueless cameraman. As a team, they follow stories and news leads within their city limits—some stories are light and fun features, and others are serious and filled with peril. Fitz is obsessed with getting the story before his rival and nemesis, Lawrence Brody (*The Mothers-in-Law*'s Roger C. Carmel), from another station in the San Francisco market. Fitz and Bones have their problems with the intense station staff, namely program director Robert Whitmore (sitcom veteran Mike Kellin) and news editor Terri Seymour (Diana Muldaur). Fitz often gets leads from Bones's ex-wife, Lt. Rosie Cochran (Lynette Mettey), of the San Francisco police department (they are still on somewhat friendly terms after the divorce). Much like their earlier scripted sitcom, *Fitz and Bones* failed to find and audience and disappeared quickly after only four sixty-minute episodes had aired. Although there were numerous light moments in each episode, the dramatic scenes featuring Tom and Dick proved unpopular with viewers. (Even the Smothers Brothers' mother didn't like the show.) The brothers took one more shot at a variety series on CBS in 1988, but it failed to recapture the magic of the legendary *Smothers Brothers Comedy Hour* that ran on the Tiffany network from 1967–1970.

Episodes were titled "Terror at Newsline 3," "Blue Pigeon Blues," "To Kill a Ghost," "A Difficult Lesson," and "Terror at Alcatraz." The executive producers were James D. Parriott, Lou Shaw and Glen A. Larson; the producers were Dean Zanetos and Ben Kadish; the writers included Lou Shaw; the directors included Nicholas Colasanto, Donald A. Baer, and Jeff Gold. The creator was Glen A. Larson. Music was provided by Stu Phillips.

Foley Square CBS Entertainment Productions. CBS. Wednesday nights 8:30 (December 11, 1985–February 26, 1986), Tuesday nights 9:30 (March 25, 1986–April 8, 1986). Fourteen episodes were filmed in front of a live audience.

Up against the popular *Highway to Heaven* on NBC, CBS debuted two new sitcoms on December 11, 1985. Mary Tyler Moore's newest attempt at a TV comeback, *Mary*, kicked off the evening at 8 p.m., followed by *Foley Square* at 8:30. Both programs focused on a female lead character in a mostly male-dominated office. Both women lived alone, but their co-workers and neighbors become like family. Mary, on *Mary*, worked for a newspaper, while tall, leggy Margaret Colin portrayed single, perky, hardworking, dependable Assistant District Attorney Alex Harrigan on *Foley Square*.

Alex was an expert on 1960s girl groups such as The Shirelles, The Supremes, and The Velvelettes. New York City's Foley Square and the Criminal Courts Building were seen in the opening credits. Alex worked for gruff District Attorney Jesse Steinberg (Héctor Elizondo). Like Lou Grant of the original *Mary Tyler Moore Show*, Jesse had a gentle side, and was very protective of Alex. Assistant District Attorney Carter DeVries (Sanford Jensen) was, for all intents and purposes, the office's Ted Baxter—pompous, egotistical, self-serving, and quite funny. Alex's two best friends in the office were newbie Assistant District Attorney Molly Dobbs (Cathy Silvers) and Denise Willums (Vernee Watson-Johnson). The girls in the office are always attempting to hook Alex up with Mr. Right. They even talk her into using the personal ads to find a mate in the debut episode, but their efforts are mostly in vain. Denise isn't the only minority working in the building—there is also Angel Gomez (Israel Juarbe), a Latino former gang-banger who has gone straight and was given the opportunity to

Paired on CBS with the ill-fated *Mary*, *Foley Square* was a pleasant, if short-lived, show starring Margaret Colin and Hector Elizondo.

be a runner for the workers in the Criminal Courts Building (although he had a brush with the law again in the episode titled "Where Angel Goes").

About his time on the series, Juarbe said, "I auditioned for the role several times, and I made a sound when I entered the room that floored them. Diane English loved it, and I got the role. I also had this whistle I would blow, then I'd toss it up and catch it behind my back, but they told me not to use it because if I dropped it during filming it would cause too much disruption. I really wanted to keep the whistle in the show, so I made them a deal—if I could do the whistle thing three consecutive times without dropping it, they would keep it in the show. Well, luckily I never did drop the whistle, so it stayed in."

After hours, those in the office love to hang out at a small restaurant/bar called Spiro's Coffee Shop. The owner, Spiro Papadapolis, was played by Richard C. Serafian. At home, Alex's best friend was her single upstairs neighbor, hirsute schoolteacher Peter Newman (Michael Lembeck). They truly were just friends, but they made the ideal couple. For some reason neither could see the forest for the trees. If the program had a longer run, one can be certain Alex and Peter would have become romantically involved.

Jon Lovitz very briefly portrayed a character named Mole. Juarbe elaborated, "He played a photographer for the prosecutor. His character was very funny, and whenever he was on screen, he just nailed it. Unfortunately for us, he was snatched up by *Saturday Night Live* after a few episodes and he had to be written out of our show. He was (and still is) a super nice and funny guy."

It's interesting to note that Cathy Silvers's father, Phil, and Michael Lembeck's father, Harvey, had worked together on *The Phil Silvers Show* from 1955–1959. In fact, Juarbe recalled, "Cathy brought her dad to one of the filmings. One could tell he wasn't in the best of health, but he paid me a huge compliment that night and it's something I'll never forget."

Juarbe shared two memorable things about being young (twenty-five) and a regular on a TV series—"The poor assistant director always had a hard time finding me. I wasn't a troublemaker, but I wandered around the studio lot a lot. I was a wide-eyed kid in awe of the whole thing. People were always asking, 'Where's Izzy?' Then there was the time I was flown to New York City to be interviewed at the legendary Russian Tea Room. I got to stay at the swanky Regency Hotel, and CBS said that I should take advantage of the opportunity and charge what I wanted to them. Well, I went a bit overboard. Being from New York originally, I invited all my friends and relatives to the hotel room, and we had Dom Perignon champagne. I went overboard, and that prompted a call from CBS telling me to continue enjoying myself ... but in moderation."

Despite having above-average writers, *Mary* and *Foley Square* both failed to find an audience and were pulled from CBS's Wednesday night lineup on February 26, 1986. Had CBS then separated the two similar programs and placed them on different nights, *Foley Square* might have been saved. That was not meant to be, and CBS then moved *Mary* to 9 p.m. on Tuesday nights in late March, backed again with *Foley Square* at 9:30. The result was the same, and both were canceled after three weeks in the new time slot. Juarbe recalled, "CBS put us up against *Moonlighting* in our new time slot, and we were crushed in the ratings. It's really too bad—it was such a good and unique show, with limitless possibilities. I remember when we got the call during rehearsals that we would only be filming three more episodes. We were canceled. I just thought it was so unfair." About his cast, Juarbe said, "Several of us are still in touch. Thanks to Facebook, I've reconnected with Cathy Silvers. For several years I was on the same celebrity softball team with Michael Lembeck. I've stayed in contact with Héctor Elizondo and Vernee Watson-Johnson—wonderful people."

Episodes were titled "Personals," "Make My Day," "Hey, Landlord," "Court-ship," "The Star" (with guest star Andy Garcia), "The Longest Weekend," "The Prosecution Never Rests," "Nobody's Perfect," "Where Angel Goes" (with guest star Paul Sylvan), "Kid Stuff," "Jack's Back," "Judgment Call," "24 Hours," and "Someone to Watch over Me." The executive producers were Saul Turteltaub, Bernie Orenstein, and Diane English, about whom Juarbe stated, "They made it feel like a family, and as the showrunners they worked extremely long and hard hours. I wish it [the show] could have lasted a lot longer." The writers included Turteltaub and Orenstein, Diane English, Dennis Danzinger, Ellen Sandler, Korby Siamis, and Karyl Geld Miller; the directors included Ellen Falcon, Peter Baldwin, and Peter Bonerz. About the latter, Juarbe said, "Bonerz is an amazing guy—a great actor and director, and so friendly and easygoing. He 'let me go' to create my character and made a lot of great suggestions about honing my skills. He was a pleasure to work with."

Foot in the Door D. L. Taffner, Ltd. CBS. Monday nights 8:30 (March 28, 1983–May 2, 1983). Six episodes were videotaped in front of a live audience.

After forty years of safe, unadventurous marriage, Jonah Foot's (Harold Gould) wife, Agnes, dies. Callous Jonah was not exactly in mourning over her passing—she was an extreme prude, and now that she is gone, Jonah vows to add more pizazz to his life (including smoking cigars and drinking). He leaves his sedate existence in Pitts Valley, New Hampshire, behind and relocated to Manhattan and the co-op apartment (number 6) inhabited by his conservative advertising agency copywriter son, Jim (Kenneth Gilman), and Jim's wife, the kindly Harriet (Diana Canova)—a buyer for a famous department store. Jonah constantly nags Harriet about giving him a grandchild. Jim, Harriet, and especially Mrs. Griffin (Marian Mercer), the apartment building manager, all disapprove of Jonah's new swinging-single lifestyle. The program was loosely based upon the British sitcom *Tom, Dick, and Harriet*, but was far less successful. In fact, *Foot in the Door* lost its footing after only six episodes had aired.

Episodes were titled "The Pilot," "Jonah Moves Out," "If the Suit Fits," "The Big Breakthrough," "Jonah the Babysitter," and "Jonah Takes a Job." The executive producers were Jay Folb, Don Taffner, and Robert F. Stolfi; the producer was Irma Kalish; the writers included Brian Cooke, Jay Folb, Alan Eisenstock, Bryan Joseph, Gary Jacobs, Larry Mintz, and Irma Kalish; the directors included John Bowab, Mel Ferber and J. D. Lobue.

Foul Play Miller-Milkis-Boyett Productions/ Myrt-Hal Productions/Paramount Television. ABC. Monday nights 10:00 (January 26, 1981– February 23, 1981), and Sunday night 8:00 (August 23, 1981). Six episodes were filmed without a laugh track, but only five aired.

Foul Play, the TV series, was based somewhat upon *Foul Play* the 1978 motion picture that starred Goldie Hawn and Chevy Chase. However, the wonderful comedic moments of the film were inexplicably toned down for the small screen, likely leading to its quick demise. Set in San Francisco, the late Deborah Raffin portrayed Gloria Munday—a TV talk show hostess, and Barry Bostwick was former concert violinist Detective Tucker Pendleton. In tandem, they solve crimes and caught bad guys. Tucker's superior is Captain Vito Lombardi (Richard Romanus), and the diminutive Beau and Ben (Greg and John Rice) were both their landlords and helpful informants. Also in the cast was Mary Jo Catlett as Gloria's coworker Stella at the TV station. After only four episodes aired during the early part of 1981, the program was yanked from ABC's prime-time schedule due to foul ratings. One of the two remaining unaired episodes aired late in the summer of 1981.

Episodes were titled "The Big Bang," "Sins of the Father," "Double Play" (with guest star Corey Feldman), "Play It Again, Tuck" (with guest star William Windom), "Hit and Run," and "Exit the Dragon." The executive producer was Hal Sitowitz; the producers were Roy Irving, Thomas L. Miller, and Robert L. Boyett; the writers included Bob Shayne, Parke Perine, Jimmy Huston, Steven E. DeSouza, Hal Sitowitz, and Irving Pearlberg. The theme song, "Ready to Take a Chance Again," was composed by Charles Fox and Norman Gimbel. The TV series utilized an instrumental version of that song, made famous by Barry Manilow.

The Four Seasons Mayflower and Mayfair Productions/Universal Television. CBS. Sunday nights 8:00 (January 29, 1984–February 12, 1984) and Sunday nights 8:30 (March 4, 1984– July 29, 1984). Thirteen episodes were filmed. The hour-long pilot movie did not have a laugh track, but the series did.

The Four Seasons TV sitcom was inspired by the hit 1981 motion picture of the same name. Jack Weston and Alan Alda's daughters (Elizabeth and Beatrice) reprised their roles in the TV version, and Alan appeared in the pilot episode (as Jack Burroughs). For the rest of the episodes, he worked behind the camera. The opening credits were true to the motion picture, with Danny's beloved Mercedes Benz falling into the frozen pond with Vivaldi's violin concerto "The Four Seasons" in the background. Weston was Danny Zimmer—a hypochondriacal, insecure, self-centered dentist, and a Manhattanite through and through. Eschewing change, Danny and his family move to Los Angeles and the series revolves around the big adjustments the Zimmer family has to make (earthquakes, houses on stilts, etc.). Zimmer's wife, Claudia, was played by sitcom veteran Marcia Rodd (Rita Moreno had played the role in the movie). Their transition was made easier by being reunited with their New York friends who had made the trek to California before them. There was realtor Ted Bolen (Tony Roberts) and his significant other (they weren't married), stuntperson Pat Devon (Joanna Kerns). The Zimmers were also friendly with the Elliots—Boris (Allan Arbus) and Lorraine (Barbara Babcock). Boris surrenders his law practice after a "heart event" necessitating a pacemaker. He then opens a much less stressful bicycle shop (and takes long rides on a regular basis); Lorraine is a professor at the UCLA School of Medicine. Alda's real life daughters Beatrice and Elizabeth portrayed roommates Lisa Callan and Beth Burroughs, who moved to The Golden State to make it big in show business (Lisa was an actress, and Beth was a writer). Reruns of the short-lived series were briefly shown on BBC 1.

Episodes were titled "Pilot, Parts One and Two," "Backseat Drivers," "A Call from the Wild," "The Loan," "Living Dangerously," "The Kiss," "Cabin Fever, Parts One and Two," "The Matchbreaker," "Head-to-Head," "The Doctor Is Out," and "Back in Business." The executive producers were Alan Alda and Martin Bregman; the producer was Stefanie Staffin Kowal; the writers included Alan Alda, Phil Margo, Paul Robinson Hunter, Don Segall, Richard Baer, Ellen Guylas, Marshall Goldberg, John Kostmayer, Rick Sultan, Gary Ress; the directors were Hy Averback, Charles S. Dubin, and Jay Sandrich. Music was provided by John Cacavas.

Frank's Place Viacom. CBS. Monday nights 8:00 (September 14, 1987–November 30, 1987), Monday nights 8:30 (December 7, 1987–February 3, 1988), Monday nights 9:30 (February 17, 1988–March 7, 1988), Tuesday nights 8:00 (March 15, 1988–March 22, 1988). Twenty-two episodes were filmed single-camera style without a laugh track.

Frank Parrish (Tim Reid) is a professor of Renaissance history in Boston. He studied classical piano as a child and was raised well by his mother. Both were abandoned by Frank's father, Ennis, when Frank was only two. Frank never saw his father again. As Ennis's only son, however, Frank was named in his daddy's will and inherits some rental property, a small nest egg, and a restaurant—an old but successful creole restaurant called Chez Louisiane, rife with a cast of most unusual characters, such as Big Arthur (Tony Burton), the head cook who doesn't like to be addressed as "Chef"; Shorty (Don Yesso), the assistant chef who doesn't like to be called a cook); Anna-May (Francesca P. Roberts), the main waitress; Miss Marie (Francis E. Williams), the elderly, impatient, and very surly "waitress emeritus" who only waits on longtime customers; Tiger Shepin (Charles Lampkin), the elderly bartender; and Cool Charles (William Thomas, Jr.), the extremely handy handyman. Frank has a few quirks of his own: he was afraid to fly and takes the train down to New Orleans to inspect the restaurant (which he intends to sell off), and he is also very superstitious. Other eccentric entities in the cast (regular customers) include Sy "Bubba" Weisberger (Robert Harper), a seemingly honest attorney, always clad in pastel-colored suits; the right Reverend Tyrone Deal (Lincoln Kilpatrick), more shady than holy; Mrs. Bertha Griffin-Lamour (Virginia Capers), the very controlling owner of the Griffin-Lamour Funeral Home; and her extremely attractive mortician daughter, Hanna (played by Tim Reid's wife in real life, Daphne Maxwell Reid). Frank finds Hanna to be visually pleasing, but her profession proves to be a real turn-off (although they do date on occasion). Initially, Frank was gung-ho on selling the restaurant and being done with it. He has two options—sell to the employees who took out a loan specifically for said purchase, or buckle under the pressure from a competing area restaurant and sell the business to them to avoid broken kneecaps. A third option, to keep and manage the restaurant himself, wins out after wise old Miss Marie informs Frank of a spell placed upon him that would render him unable to leave New Orleans. Miss Marie was quite aware of the fact that the other two options would bring an end to Chez Louisiane. The program features a wonderful soundtrack of blues and jazz, and its theme song is the Louis Armstrong classic, "Do You Know What It Means to Miss New Orleans?" It was another one of those shows lauded by the critics, and eschewed by the masses. Frank never really did find his place, and after twenty-two high-quality episodes and three Emmy Awards, the Chez Louisiane closed its doors for good. Because of music clearance issues and the expense involved, *Frank's Place* has yet to be made available on DVD. When it does it will likely have a new musical score (much in the manner of the DVD release of *WKRP in Cincinnati*). The program was very briefly rerun on the BET cable TV network in the early 1990s.

Episodes were titled "The Pilot," "Frank Returns" (with guest stars Joe Frazier and Don King), "Frank Takes Charge," "The Bridge" (with guest star Conchata Ferrell), "Frank Joins the Club," "Eligible Bachelor," "Disengaged," "Cool and the Gang, Parts One and Two," "The Reverend Gets a Flock," "I. O. U.," "Food Fight," "Season's Greetings," "The Bum Out Front," "Dueling Voodoo," "Where's Ed?" (with guest star, co-creator Hugh Wilson), "Night Business," "Shorty's Belle," "Frank's Place: The Movie," "Cultural Exchange" (with guest star Dizzy Gillespie), "Recruiting Game," and "King of Wall Street." The executive producers were Tim Reid and Hugh Wilson; the producers were Max Tash and David Chambers; the writers included Hugh Wilson, David Chambers, Samm-Art Williams, Pamela Douglas, Tim Reid, Craig Nelson, Don Yesso, and Richard Dubin; the directors included Asaad Kelada, Richard Dubin, Kevin Rodney Sullivan, Max Tash, Hugh Wilson, Frank Bonner, Roy Campanella II, Neema Barnette, and Stan Lathan. The creator was Hugh Wilson. Music was provided by Sam Winans.

Free Spirit ELP Communications/Columbia Pictures Television. ABC. Friday night 9:30 (September 22, 1989), Sunday nights 8:00 (September 24, 1989–January 7, 1990) and Sunday night 8:30 (January 14, 1990). Fourteen episodes were videotaped with a laugh track, but only thirteen aired.

Ten-year-old Gene Harper (Edan Gross) makes a wish for someone to have time for him—everybody around him is always too busy. His dad, Thomas J. "T. J." Harper (Frank Luz, in the series; Christopher Rich, in the first pilot), is a divorced single father (his ex-wife's name was Annie) and attorney who recently moved his practice to Connecticut. He has custody of his three kids—sixteen-year-old girl-crazy Robb (Paul Scherrer), thirteen-year-old Jessie (played by Alyson Hannigan in the series; Shonda Whipple, in the first pilot), and Gene. Gene makes his wish at the perfect time—a witch named Winnie Goodwin appears magically before him. The kids take to Winnie immediately, but urge her not to tell their dad about her special powers—he would likely ask her to leave if he found out she was a witch. Much like on *Bewitched*, the special powers are occasionally more troublesome than helpful. It becomes obvious in the second pilot (the one that aired) that T. J. and Winnie are attracted to one another. Had the program been successful, that storyline would no doubt have been explored. However, the show received scathing reviews, and did poorly in the ratings. After thirteen of the fourteen videotaped episodes had aired, Winnie hopped on her broomstick and took off for parts unknown.

Episodes were titled "The Pilot," "The Bosses Are Coming," "Wedding Bell Blues," "Too Much of a Good Thing," "Guess Who's Staying for Dinner," "Hallowinnie," "Two for the Road," "Not with My Sister You Don't," "Love that Winnie," "The New Secretary" (with guest stars Florence Henderson and Robert Reed), "Radio Nights," "We Gotta Be Me," "Blast from the Past" (with guest stars Michael Constantine and Dave Coulier), and "Love and Death." The executive producers were Richard Gurman and Phil Doran; the producer was Mark Fink; the writers included Kevin Abbott, Phil Doran, Mark Fink, Rebecca Parr Cioffi, Howard and Susan Meyers, Bob Rosenfarb, Leslie Ray, April Kelly, Ellen Guylas, and Martin Pasko; the directors included Art Dielhenn and Phil Squyres. The creators were Leslie Ray and Steven A. Vail. Music was provided by David Michael Frank, and the theme song, "She's a Free Spirit," was by Steve Dorff and John Bettis.

Freebie and the Bean Hyjack Productions/Jay Folb, Inc./Warner Bros. Television. CBS. Saturday nights 9:00 (December 6, 1980–January 17, 1981). Nine hour-long episodes were filmed single-camera style without a laugh track. Sponsors included High Point decaffeinated coffee.

The hit 1974 motion picture starred Alan Arkin, James Caan, and Loretta Swit. Six years had elapsed before *Freebie and the Bean* was attempted as a TV series. This crimedy series did have a great cast—Tom Mason took Arkin's role of Freebie (Detective Sergeant Tim Walker), and Héctor Elizondo assumed the Caan part of the Bean (Detective Sergeant Dan Delgado).

They were a plainclothes police *Odd Couple* of sorts. Freebie doesn't play by the rules, but the Bean does. Bean is usually cajoled into Freebie's methodology, only to be burned by his decision in the end. Their immediate supervisor is District Attorney Walter W. Cruikshank (William Daniels). Poor Rodney "Axle" Blake (Mel Stewart) has the unenviable task of repairing the wrecks from their many automobile chases. Carmen Filipi played Wally the Wino, their informant. Although there are several moments of inspired slapstick on this series, up against *The Love Boat* without a paddle, it capsized quickly. Director Michael Preece said, "Yes, likely *The Love Boat* did us in. That, and the fact that there was almost a generation between the film and TV series. The actors were wonderful, however. The premise was similar to a series I directed in 1977 with Lou Antonio and Kim Basinger titled *Dog and Cat*. Well, they can't all be hit series—there are always a few flops along the way."

Episodes were titled "The Pilot," "Freebie and the Bean," "Health Nuts," "Flying Aces," "Highway Robbery," "Tee-Off for Two," "Lover Come Back," "A Pair of Pirates," and "Follow the Leader." The writers included Donald R. Boyle, Jay Folb, Bill Taub, Dick Nelson, Rick Mittleman, and Robert W. Lenski; the directors included Lawrence Dobkin, Hy Averback, Bruce Kessler, Alex March, Arnold Laven, Michael Caffrey, and Michael Preece. Music was provided by Dominic Frontiere, and the theme song "You and Me, Babe" was performed by singer/songwriter Bobby Hart.

Galaxy High TMS Entertainment, Ltd. CBS. Saturday mornings 10:00 (September 13, 1986– December 6, 1986). Thirteen animated episodes were filmed without a laugh track.

Two teenagers, Doyle Cleverlobe (Hal Rayle), the popular jock, and Aimee Brighttower (Susan Blu), a bright but unpopular teenage girl, are sent to represent Earth at Galaxy High School, an interplanetary learning facility with classmates from every planet in the universe. The faculty consisted of Miss Biddy McBrain (Pat Carroll), Professor McGreed (Howard Morris), and Coach Frogface (Pat Fraley). Fraley also provided the voice for the janitor/dog named Sludge. Classmates included Gilda Gossip (Nancy Cartwright) with multiple lips that told secrets all at one time; the portly bespectacled Milo De-Venus (David L. Lander) with multiple arms; and The Creep (Danny Mann), who became attached to anyone who was nice to him. Even the lockers talked, and Aimee's was voiced by Henry Gibson. A single season of thirteen episodes was filmed and shown on CBS Saturday mornings. All thirteen episodes were released on DVD (in two volumes) in 2006, from Media Blasters.

Episodes were titled "Welcome to Galaxy High," "Pizza's Honor," "The Beef Who Would Be King," "Where's Milo?," "Those Eyes Those Lips," "Doyle's New Friend," "Dollars and Sense," "Beach Blanket Blow-up," "Brain Blaster," "Brat Pack," "Founders Day," "Martian Mumps," and "It Came from Earth." The executive producer was Yutaka Fujioka; the producers were Barry Glasser and Gerard Baldwin; the writers included Chris Columbus, Laurence G. DiTillio, Ken Koonce, Chris Weber, David Weimers, Jina Bacarr, Karen Willson, Marc Scott Zicree, and Eric Lewald; the directors included David Hilberman, Sam Nicholson, Toshiyuki Hiruma, Hiroshi Ishiodori, Kaziyuki Hirokawa, Saburo Hashimoto, Keiko Namba, and Nobuo Tomizawa. Music was provided by Danny Goldberg and Ron Stone, and the theme song was by Don Felder of the Eagles.

The Gary Coleman Show Hanna-Barbera Productions. NBC. Saturday mornings 10:30 (September 18, 1982–December 11, 1982). Twenty-six twelve-minute cartoons were filmed without a laugh track.

Based upon the live action Gary Coleman TV movie *The Kid with the Broken Halo* (original air date: April 5, 1982), this animated series was created for and ran for one season on the peacock network. Voiced by Coleman, an apprentice angel named Andy LeBeau is sent back to earth (and the town of Oakville) to earn his wings by helping those in need. He is guided by Angelica (Jennifer Darling). The evil Hornswoggle (Sidney Miller), greatly resembling Dick Dastardly, constantly throws a wrench into LeBeau's good deeds, keeping him from getting those prestigious wings he desires. Other regulars included snooty limo driver Lydia (Julie McWhirter-Dees); close friend Tina (LaShana Dendy, who usually called Andy "Cupcake"); the very pretty Chris (Lauren Anders); bookish Spence (Calvin Mason); and cool guy Haggle (Geoffrey Gordon). Andy keeps his trusty halo in his pocket, and uses it only when in a real jam. His friends are not aware of his heavenly connection. Reruns of this short-lived cartoon series were later shown on the Adult Swim cable channel.

Episodes were titled "Fouled Up Fossils," "Going Going Gone," "You Oughta Be in Pictures," "Derby Daze," "Hornswoggle's Hoax," "Calamity Canine," "Cupid Andy," "Space Odd-Essey," "Hornswoggle's New Leaf," "Keep on Moving On," "Mansion Madness," "Wuthering Kites," "In the Swim," "Put Up or Fix Up," "Haggle and Double Haggle," "The Royal Visitor," "The Future Tense," "Dr. Livingston, I Presume," "Haggle's Luck," "Head in the Clouds," "Teacher's Pest," "Andy Sings the Blues," "Easy Money," "Take My Tonsils, Please," "The Prettiest Girl in Oakville," and "Mack's Snow Job." The executive producers were William Hanna and Joseph Barbera; the producer was Art Scott; the writers included Sandy Fries, Mark Shiney, Bob Langhams, Tom Ruegger, John T. Graham, Dianne Dixon, Janis Diamond, Allan Helford, Larry Parr, David Villaire, Paul Dini, John Bates, Peter L. Dixon, Robert Jayson, Martin Werner, and Cliff Roberts; the directors included George Gordon, Bob Hathcock, Rudy Zamora, Ray Patterson, and Carl Urbano. Music was provided by Hoyt Curtin.

George Burns Comedy Week 40 Share Productions/Universal Television. CBS. Wednesday nights 9:30 (September 18, 1985–December 25, 1985). Thirteen episodes were filmed with a laugh track.

After Gracie Allen retired, George Burns found it hard going it alone on television. Even surrounded by the supporting cast of *The George Burns and Gracie Allen Show* in 1958's *George Burns Show*, a major element was missing—Gracie. In 1964, George found a capable surrogate Gracie in Connie Stevens for ABC's *Wendy and Me*—a very funny show that failed to gain an audience up against CBS's Monday night comedy juggernaut and lasted only a season. He tried once more in 1985 with a comedy anthology series. His job was an easy one—he hosted the show and was part of the opening and closing, providing the setup and closing for each episode. *George Burns Comedy Week* was much like a series of comedy pilots with a

Many found the comedy weak on *George Burns Comedy Week*, and the anthology series was gone after just thirteen weeks on CBS.

totally different cast and storyline each week. Among the celebrities who performed in these episodes were Harvey Korman, Ruth Buzzi, Howard Hesseman, Geena Davis, Fred Willard, Patrick Duffy, Casey Kasem, Don Knotts, James Whitmore, Telly Savalas, Eugene Levy, Martin Mull, Paul Reiser, Jack Blessing, and Don Rickles. The series had some rather anemic lead-ins on its Wednesday nightime slot— *Stir Crazy* and *Charlie and Company*, and after thirteen weeks *George Burns Comedy Week* was pulled from the CBS prime-time schedule. However, one of the more popular episodes of the series, "The Couch" with Harvey Korman and Valerie Perrine, was spun off into a series of its own and retitled *Leo and Liz in Beverly Hills*. Sadly, it too failed to find an audience and lasted only six episodes (see entry). Steve Martin was the executive producer for both shows. Despite a dearth of TV success, George Burns enjoyed great motion picture success in classics such as *The Sunshine Boys* (for which he won a Best Supporting Actor Academy Award) and *Oh, God* in the 1970s, and even scored a hit country-western record, "I Wish I Was Eighteen Again," (Burns actually lived to be 100). Was Burns immersed in the production of this series? Jack Blessing of the "Disaster at Buzz Creek" episode said, "Unfortunately, no. He did show up to do his thing and I said, 'Hi,' but that was it."

Episodes were titled "The Dynamite Girl," "Home for Dinner," "Death Benefits," "The Smiths," "The Couch," "The Assignment," "Dream Dream Dream," "Boris and Ivan Visit Las Vegas," "The Honeybunnies," "The Funniest Guy in the World," "A Christmas Carol II: The Sequel," "The Borrowing," and "Disaster at Buzz Creek." About guest starring in the latter episode, Jack Blessing shared, "That was with Stephen Collins, Paul Brinegar, Don Rickles, and Lana Clarkson (the poor girl who died at hands of Phil Spector, so sad). I will say that Lana was one of the most naïve actors I have ever met. Rickles was a revelation. Truly one of the kindest men I have ever met. Sure, quick with the cut and the one-liner, as you would expect, but also very warm and generous. His jokes, even if they were at your expense, were always just too damn funny. [He was] a little insecure in his acting abilities, which made him all the more endearing." The executive producers were Steve Martin and Carl Gottlieb; the producers were Paul Perlove and George E. Crosby; the writers included Steve Martin, David Steven Cohen, David Axelrod, Roger S. H. Schulman, and Carl Gottlieb; the directors included Steve Martin, Carl Gottlieb, Phil Alden Robinson, Peter Bonerz, John Fox, Alan Myerson, John Korty, Neal Israel, and John Landis. Blessing said, "I must say that this was as much fun as I have ever had on a television shoot. The cast was amazing, but the real reason was John Landis. Never, ever have I worked with a director who had so much energy, creativity, and fun on a set. He was like a kid in a candy shop. He was like a film student on his first big-league set. Every time we would wrap a scene he would, literally, go running down the street to the next set with the cast huffing and puffing behind screaming at the top of his lungs how great this was going to be. It was truly hysterical. And Steve Martin producing the show brought a lot of people in— folks who didn't usually do television." Music was provided by David Michael Frank, and the theme song was by Claude Debussy.

Gilligan's Planet Sherwood Schwartz Productions/Filmation/MGM/UA. CBS. Saturday mornings 10:30 (September 18, 1982–December 11, 1982). Thirteen animated episodes were filmed with a laugh track.

Fifteen years after *Gilligan's Island* was canceled by CBS, most of the original castaways were back, in animated form (Bob Denver, Alan Hale, Jr., Russell Johnson, Jim Backus, Natalie Schafer, and Dawn Wells). The only exception was Tina Louise, who didn't take part in this new series, and so Dawn Wells took up the slack and provided voices for both Ginger and Mary Ann.

In this redux, the professor has built a functional spaceship after years of work, (like their original vessel, it is called the S. S. *Minnow*) to get the castaways off the island, but it misfires and crash lands on an unknown planet capable of supporting human life. This becomes known as Gilligan's Planet, and the new predicaments for the spaceshipmates now has an interplanetary bent. A new character, Gilligan's reptilian pet Bumper, was added to the fray. Thirteen episodes were filmed, and if not the last, this was among the last Saturday morning cartoon shows to employ a laugh track. All thirteen episodes were released on DVD by Warner Bros. during the summer of 2014.

Episodes were titled "I Dream of Genie," "Turnabout Is Fair Play," "Let Sleeping Minnows Lie," "Journey to the Center of Gilligan's Planet," "Amazing Colossal Gilligan," "Bumper to Bumper," "Road to Boom," "Too Many Gilligans," "Space Pirates," "Invaders of the Lost Barque," "Wings," "Super Gilligan," and "Gilligan's Army." The executive producer was Lou Scheimer; the writers included Tom Ruegger, Marc Richards, and Robby London; the director was Hal Sutherland.

Gloria Tandem Productions/Embassy Television. CBS. Sunday nights 8:30 (September 26, 1982–April 10, 1983) and Wednesday nights 8:30 (June 22, 1983–September 21, 1983). Twenty-one episodes were videotaped in front a live audience.

Although much anticipated, *Gloria* was an ill-conceived spinoff of *All in the Family* and *Archie Bunker's Place*. The aired pilot episode was an actual episode of *Archie Bunker's Place* titled "Gloria Comes Home" that ran on Groundhog Day of 1982. Actor Rick Lohman, who co-starred in the unaired *Gloria* pilot, "Gloria, the First Day" said, "That was quite a heartbreaker. Carroll O'Connor pulled the whole deal together for Sally Struthers. I got to know Sally, one of the sweetest people on the planet, and Burgess Meredith. I was in heaven working with these two brilliant actors. We recorded the very good and very funny pilot. Immediately after wrapping up, I had to fly back to New York for a commercial. I then started to get some really weird vibes that something was wrong because I hadn't yet received a final letter of commitment. I told my agent about my feelings, but he told me I was imagining things. Well, a short time later, my manager called and told me that I was right. Norman Lear's Tandem Communications was being taken over by Embassy Television, and they wanted to put their own imprint on the show. Carroll O'Connor was no longer involved, either. Sally was just too nice to put her foot down and demand changes, and the program that CBS eventually got just wasn't as funny and fun as our pilot. This was a real blow for me."

What may have looked good on paper just didn't translate well to videotape. Unlike the original program from which it was spun, *Gloria* was never "ha ha" funny. The show's opening credits told the story pretty well—there were X's through the names Gloria Bunker and Gloria Stivic on screen. After twelve years of marriage, she was newly separated from Michael. She and he had grown apart, and each came to the realization that they would be happier on opposite sides of the country—she in upstate New York and he in San Francisco (in a commune with fifty naked people). She got custody of eight-year-old Joey Stivic (Christian Jacobs) and his canine friend, Archie (named for his maternal "grandfather"). Gloria finds work with a kindly old veterinarian named Dr. Willard Adams (the brilliant Burgess Meredith). The new job is just one of the many big adjustments she has to make in her life. She is also coping with single parenthood, single life, a new place of residence, and the dating scene. Her co-workers included a new best friend, Dr. Maggie Lawrence (Jo de Winter), who wants to get Gloria back into circulation; and the horn dog male receptionist, Clark V. Uhley, Jr. (Lou Richards). Episodes focus upon visitation rights, casting a positive light on Michael for Joey's sake, and maintaining a merry Christmas tradition. Those opening credits alluded to earlier in this paragraph ended each week with Gloria reassuring her son with the words, "But you know what, Joey? We'll be OK." She was right—albeit briefly.

Episodes were titled "The First Day," "First Date," "Bully for You," "If At First You Don't Succeed," "Pig in a Blanket," "Teacher's Pet," "Malpractice," "F-F-Father's Day," "The Taxman Cometh," "Still Life with Cat," "Miracle at Fox Ridge," "Visitation," "Gloria on the Couch" (with guest star Jeffrey Tambor), "Love in the Past Tents" (with guest star Paul Sand), "Truth or Consequences," "Let's Call the Whole Thing Off" (with guest star Eileen Heckart), "Death Row Dog" (with guest star Gregory Sierra), "Coming Apart," "It Almost Happened One Night," "Class Struggle," and "An Uncredited Woman" (with guest star Paul Rodriguez). The executive producers were Steve Marshall and Dan Guntzelman; the producers were Joe Gannon and Lissa Levin; the writers included Rich Reinhart, Tim O'Donnell, Joe Gannon, Patt Shea, Harriet Weiss, Dan Guntzelman, Steve Marshall, Michael Cassutt, Lew Levy, Frederick Hoffman, Max Tash, Melody Rowland, Jurgen Wolff, and Lissa Levin; the directors included Bob Claver and Paul Bogart. Jo de Winter died on February 17, 2016 at the age of 94.

Good Time Harry Rollins/Joffe/Bessell (RJB) Productions/Universal Television. NBC. Saturday night 10:00 (July 19, 1980, hour debut), and Saturday nights 10:30 (July 26, 1980–September 13, 1980). Seven episodes were filmed with a laugh track.

Me and the Chimp was a setback for Ted Bessell's career and *Good Time Harry* was an attempt to get him back on track. Unfortunately, audiences didn't go ape for this NBC sitcom either. On this series, Bessell played Harry Jenkins—the vain sportswriter for the *San Francisco Sentinel* (it changed to the *San Francisco Journal* during the show's short run), who is very fond of hugging, is a pathological liar, and has the nerve of a jewel thief. He had previously been fired from the *Boston Globe* and the *Detroit Free Press*. He also has quite a reputation as a playboy. Said reputation often gets in the way of Harry's work, much to the chagrin of the newspaper's sports editor, Jimmy Hughes (Eugene Roche). In fact, Harry's dalliances once got him fired from the *San Francisco Sentinel* (only to be rehired years later in the debut episode against Hughes's better judgment). Others in the cast included Carol (Marcia Strassman)—another reporter for the paper (her attempts to dislike Harry are in vain); Sally (Ruth Manning), Jimmy's harried secretary; Martin Springer (Steve Peterman), the eager-beaver copy boy and wannabe writer; Billie (Jesse Welles), a waitress at the local hangout, Danny's Bar (Billie is an old flame of Harry's; she has a daughter named Debbie and a mob-connected ex-husband named Carmine [Dan Hedaya]); Lenny (Richard Karron), the bartender at Danny's, he knows all of Harry's deepest, darkest secrets; and Stan (Barry Gordon), a next-door neighbor (Stan lives in apartment 4, Harry in 3), he sells insurance and idolizes Harry because of his luck with the ladies. Harry has a huge poster of W. C. Fields (one of whose onscreen guises was that of an inveterate con man) on his living room wall. *Good Time Harry* did not have such a good time with the Nielsen families, and, after a short summer tryout, was never seen again.

Episodes were titled "Harry, Parts One and Two," "The Wally Smith Story," "Audrey Simpson," "Play It Again, Sam," "Harry Kisses Death on the Mouth," and "Ben Younger" (with guest star Tom Poston). The executive producers were Larry Brezner and Charles H. Joffe; the producer was Gareth Davies; the writers included Steve Gordon, Glenn Gordon Caron, Stephen Nathan, and Mickey Rose; the directors were Steve Gordon, Jeff Chambers, James Burrows, Tony Mordente and Mark Gordon. The creator was Steve Gordon. Music was provided by Peter Matz. The theme song, "Wild about Harry," was performed by Norman Brooks in a vaudevillian manner, and harkened back to the sound of 1950s sitcom themes.

Goodtime Girls Paramount Studios. ABC. Tuesday nights 8:30 (January 22, 1980–February 12, 1980), Saturday nights 8:30 (April 12, 1980–April 26, 1980), and Friday nights 8:30 (August 1, 1980–August 29, 1980). Twelve episodes were filmed in front of a studio audience, but only eleven aired.

Garry Marshall had such whopping success with his 1950s period pieces *Happy Days* and *Laverne and Shirley*, he went to the well again, but back even further—to the 1940s—in *The Goodtime Girls*. This time, however, the results were less than spectacular. Was it too far back for audiences to relate? Joel Zwick, who directed the debut episode, said, "Maybe. This show was also less raucous and more character-driven than *Happy Days* or *Laverne and Shirley*. The original working title was 'On the Homefront,' but that didn't test well. *Goodtime Girls*, however, tested off the charts. We had some rather complicated scenes, too, for example, a ladder balanced on a taxicab on which Loretta's husband climbs to sneak into the window."

Instead of Milwaukee, Wisconsin, this one was set in a boarding house in Washington, D.C., during World War II. Sharing the attic apartment are four females—Edith Bedelmyer (Annie Potts), who works every night for the U.S.O; Betty Crandall (Lorna Patterson) of Sioux City, Iowa, who works at a defense plant in Baltimore; timid war bride Loretta Smoot (Georgia Engel), who works for General Culpepper (Richard Stahl) at the Pentagon; and snooty magazine writer Camille Rittenhouse (Francine Tacker), who is forced to move into the cramped space after losing her classier and more spacious apartment after a reversal of fortune. The boarding house is run by George and Irma Coolidge (Merwin Goldsmith and Marcia Lewis, respectively). The Coolidges also look after a young boy named Skeeter (Sparky Marcus). Marcia Lewis had previously co-starred in another short-lived Paramount sitcom, *Who's Watching the Kids?* A handsome young cabbie named Frankie Millardo (Adrian Zmed), who loves to sing and dance, lives downstairs. Frankie and Edith have a brief tryst in the episode titled "Frankie and Edith Were Lovers," but find that their relationship works better as just good friends. Frankie tries to join the military, but is rejected because of flat feet. He shares his apartment with a pre–*Bosom Buddies* and *Newhart* Peter Scolari, who had the recurring role of Benny Loman, a street performer who performs pantomime, juggling, and magic for tips.

Speaking of Scolari, Zwick recalled, "He helped me save *Bosom Buddies*. The original actor slated to work alongside Tom Hanks just wasn't working out and ABC was about to scrap the whole thing. I had the brainstorm of bringing in Peter Scolari after *Goodtime Girls* was canceled, and told ABC that I had the answer. I got them to hold off putting the kibosh on the project, and the rest is history."

After a slow start on Tuesday nights in January and February of 1980, *Goodtime Girls* was placed on hiatus until April when it was given another shot on Saturday nights, but also foundered there. A few remaining unaired episodes were shown during August of that year. World War II—era concerns, such as rationing and a shortage of rubber, were addressed during the show's short run. There were great period costumes and lots of jitterbug dancing. Is it difficult to do such period pieces? Zwick shared, "Not really. There are research people. As long as wardrobe people and set designers are on the same page, and the scripts echo the values of today and are based on relationships and/or family, period pieces can work just fine."

About the show, Zwick reflected, "The program should have succeeded. We had some sharp writing and an amazing cast—Adrian Zmed, Annie Potts, Georgia Engel, Marcia Lewis, Peter Scolari, Lorna Patterson. Speaking of Lorna, she later dated and married actor Michael Lembeck. One day when I was going to temple for a bat mitzvah, I was so surprised to see that she was the cantor. Because of her new husband, she had converted to Judaism and went to school to become a cantor. She had a wonderful singing voice. Who knew?"

Actor Jack Blessing, who guest starred in the debut episode, described the experience as "great fun. Maybe the first show I did after I arrived in L.A. I learned later that debut or pilot episodes are fraught with tension and stress. Not this one. Annie Potts and I became lifelong friends. And I stayed very friendly with Francine Tacker, Peter Scolari, and Lorna Patterson. Great memories. I honestly don't remember Garry [Marshall] ever coming around, though I am sure he did. Having gotten to know him in later years, you would think that with his giant personality, I would remember him, but I don't. I think that they pretty much trusted Joel [Zwick] and left it in his hands."

Episodes were titled "George Gets Drafted," "Too Many Fiancés," "Frankie and Edith Were Lovers," "Growing Pains" (with guest star Scott Baio), "Loose Lips," "Edith Dates a War Hero," "Loretta's Dilemma," "Internal Injury" (with guest star Michael McKean), "The Show Must Go On," "Who's Benny?," "Sing 'Til It Hurts," and the unaired "Night and Day." The executive producer was Garry Marshall; the producers were Thomas L. Miller, Edward K. Milkis, and Robert L. Boyett; the writers included Mark Rothman, Lowell Ganz, Robert L. Boyett, Thomas L. Miller, Sheldon Bull, E. J. Purdum, Leonard Ripps, Leonora Thuna, William Bickley, Michael Warren, and Chris Thompson; the directors included Howard Storm, Tony Mordente, and Joel Zwick. The program was created by Leonora Thuna. Music was provided by John Beal, and the theme song titled "When Everyone Cared" was written by Charles Fox and Norman Gimbel. The pilot used "Don't Sit Under the Apple Tree," sung by the Andrews Sisters, as its theme song.

Gun Shy Walt Disney Productions. CBS. Tuesday nights 8:30 (March 15, 1983–April 5, 1983) and Tuesday nights 8:00 (April 12, 1983–April 19, 1983). Six episodes were filmed with a laugh track, but only four aired.

Set in California in 1869, *Gun Shy* was based upon the antics in Walt Disney's *The Apple Dumpling Gang*, and *The Apple Dumpling Gang Rides Again*. The pilot was titled "Tales of the Apple Dumpling Gang" and it aired on January 16, 1982. John Bennett Perry (Matthew Perry's father) had the lead role in the pilot, but as *Gun Shy* developed, the star was Barry Van Dyke (Dick's son) as Quake City's friendly neighborhood gambler, Russell Donovan (played by Bill Bixby in the films).

Speaking of gambling, Donovan was also the caretaker for two "young'uns" he won in a card game—their names were Celia (Bridgette Andersen) and Clovis (played first by Adam Rich and then Keith Mitchell). Adam Rich was replaced after two episodes had been filmed, and only the four with Keith Mitchell in the Clovis role were aired. Clovis loves having pets but doesn't have the best of luck with their longevity (a large area is set aside for the burial of a series of goldfish, frogs, and even one oblong site for a pet snake). Clovis is seemingly always competing for attention with Quake City's "boy braggadocio" named Little Jim (Jason Hervey, pre–*The Wonder Years*), and usually prevailed. The town's unkempt desperadoes are Theodore Ogilvie (Don Knotts, in the movies) played by Tim Thomerson, and Amos Tucker (Tim Conway, in the movies) played by the late Geoffrey Lewis of *Flo*. This dastardly duo attempts to get a reputation as outlaws, and although somewhat menacing, they aren't such bad guys when it comes right down to it. Homer McCoy (Henry Jones) wears many hats in Quake City—sheriff, justice of the peace, and barber. His ex-wife, Nettie (Janis Paige), runs the Parker Hotel (the only hotel in town), and Colonel Mound (Pat McCormick) owns the local stagecoach. McCormick also worked behind the scenes on the show as executive story consultant. Had CBS called the show *The Apple Dumpling Gang* it might have been more successful, but the ratings were abysmal and CBS placed a silencer on *Gun Shy* after only a month. While it was never as laugh-out-loud funny as *Best of the West*, it still had some merit and deserved more of a chance to catch on.

Episodes were titled "Western Velvet," "Pardon Me Boy Is That the Quake City Choo Choo?," "What Do You Mean *We*, Amigo?" (with guest star Lyle Waggoner), "You Gotta Know When to Hold 'Em," "Reading, Whining and Robbing" (with guest star Ruth Buzzi), and "Mail Order Mommy" (with guest star Delta Burke). The executive producer was William Robert Yates; the producers were Tom Leetch and Eric Cohen; the writers included Eric Cohen and Farnsworth Gallagher; the directors included Peter Baldwin. Music was provided by Dennis McCarthy.

Gung Ho Imagine/Four Way Productions/ Paramount Television. ABC. Friday nights 9:30

(December 5, 1986–January 9, 1987), Friday nights 9:00 (January 16, 1987–February 6, 1987). Nine episodes were filmed in front of a live audience.

Based on the hit motion picture of the same name, *Gung Ho* the TV series utilized many of the Japanese actors used in the film. Among the multi-taskers was Gedde Watanabe, who played Kaz Kazuhiro, the new plant manager who is consistently between a rock and a hard place as his U.S. employees and his company's Japanese bosses have diametrically opposing points of view and customs. Also returning was Clint Howard (he was Paul in the movie) now known as Googie, the character Rick Overton portrayed in the film. Clint's brother, Ron Howard, directed the film and his Imagine Entertainment Company produced both versions.

The setting was Hadleyville, Pennsylvania, where the Assan Motors Company has taken over an American automotive assembly plant. Most of the former U.S. employees are kept on, but the clash in cultures was fodder for much of the show's humor. About the show's tone, Clint Howard recalled, "I think one of the problems with the TV show was that it was more of a sitcom than the motion picture. Sure, the movie had some humor, but it wasn't a sitcom. The sitcom had a tricky tone, and the transition was not an easy one. Also, the film was shot on location in Buenos Aires, Argentina, for the most part, and also Pittsburgh. The series was filmed on the Paramount Studios lot. When the idea for the TV series came about, my brother asked if I'd be interested in doing the series, and of course I jumped at the opportunity."

How involved was Ron Howard on the TV version? Clint Howard said, "Not very. He wasn't part of the daily routine. He would read the scripts, but was never really hands-on for the TV arm of Imagine Entertainment—he left that to others." The shop steward, or liaison between management and the workers, is Hunt Stevenson, played by Scott Bakula (Michael Keaton, in the film version), but Howard shared, "The Hunt character was played by Ned Eisenberg in the pilot, and he was good, but a change was made for the series and Bakula was brought in. Scott was also very good in the role and a good guy. He was still very young, and has had quite a career." About that change, John Rappaport added, "I came on as executive producer of *Gung Ho* after the pilot was made and ABC had picked it up. Ned was no longer in the show and it was left to me to find the replacement. We looked for a long time because Michael Keaton was great as Hunt in the feature. We finally discovered a very good and funny and real nice guy in Scott Bakula, who was pretty new to the scene."

The Japanese cast included Patti Yasutake as Kaz's wife, Umeki (who liked American customs and the new freedoms afforded her in the U. S); Sab Shimono, whom Rappaport felt was hilarious, was another member of management—the stern Mr. Saito (his wife, Yukiko, played by Emily K. Kuroda, still followed all of the old Japanese traditions and customs); and Scott Atari, who played the spelling-challenged Kenji (Kaz's son). About the Japanese cast, Howard reflected, "We had some really nice bonding going on and this show was a really nice opportunity for them. Sab was really good in his role—he knew how to play that guy, and Gedde was very funny. The attempt was made to establish a solid family bond for the Japanese characters, and I think that was among the show's strongest points." Rappaport added, "It was very difficult keeping the scripts politically correct."

The cast included Stephen Lee as Buster the welder (who was fired in the debut episode, but was later reinstated with the help of Hunt). Howard recalled, "George Wendt was the original choice to play Buster, but he was still involved with *Cheers* at that time, and Stephen did a fine job in the role."

Yet again, a blockbuster hit on the silver screen failed to catch on as a TV series. This rather funny show deserved better, but when scheduled up against the juggernaut *Dallas* on CBS just could not compete. Rappaport added, "ABC gave us a terrible time slot and a totally humorless crank as the show's liaison. Nevertheless, we had a real good time in our short stay on the air. Clint Howard was a doll to work with. And Patti [Yasutake], who was charming and sweet, also owned a terrific Asian restaurant, so we had two really delicious wrap parties." About cancellation, Howard said, "One can sense when the axe is about to fall on a TV show. It all has to do with the number of network executives milling about, and their attitudes. The signs are pretty obvious. It's a shame, too, because working on this show was a very enjoyable experience. I wish we'd had more time to develop it."

Episodes were titled "The Pilot," "Line of Credit," "Talk of the Town," "Sick and Tired," "Love Me Tender," "Help Wanted," "Kaz Over Easy," "Where the Boys Are," and "Brother, Can You Spare a Dollar?" The executive producer and head writer was John Rappaport; the other writers included James Berg, Stan Zimmerman, Dennis Klein, Babaloo Mandel, Lowell Ganz, and Bruce Ferber; the directors were Jeff Chambers, John Bowab, George Sunga, Art Dielhenn, Randy Carter, Art Dielhenn, Thomas Lofaro, and Dick Martin (half of the comedy team Rowan & Martin of *Laugh-In*). Howard shared, "Dick was such a nice man, and quite a trouper. During one of the weeks he directed the show he came down with shingles, but still got the job done. He was amazing." Music was provided by David Michael Frank, and the theme song was penned by both Fran and Robert Jason.

Hail to the Chief Witt/Thomas Productions. ABC. Tuesday nights 9:30 (April 9, 1985–July 20, 1985). Seven episodes were videotaped in front of a live audience.

Viewers will never see the likes of *Hail to the Chief* again. This irreverent sitcom took no prisoners—fun was poked at every group imaginable and racial, gay, religious, and socioeconomic slurs were abundant. The action revolves around the United States' first female president (still a far-fetched topic in 1985), Julia Mansfield (Patty Duke). The opening credits run through an array of humorous black-and-white drawings of several recent Presidents, in order, leading up to Mansfield.

Her husband, "the first man," General Oliver Mansfield (Ted Bessell) experiences difficulty "performing" in the bedroom (the thought of making love to the president seems to him like a "Capitol" offense), so he strays countless times, becoming quite the philanderer. His indiscretions with a sexy Russian spy named Darlene (Alexa Hamilton) lead to blackmail and marital problems. His getting shot in the chest and having a near-death experience in one episode was also fodder for quite a few jokes and more unfaithfulness right there in his hospital bed.

The Mansfields' three children also caused them great consternation. Their tennis pro son, Doug (Ricky Paul Goldin), has a history of impregnating the daughters of important political and military figures. Daughter Lucy (Quinn Cummings) is "horny" for the butler, Raoul (Chick Vennera). And little Willy (Taliesin Jaffe) is frequently bullied and constantly attempting to skip school. Julia's alcoholic mother, Lenore (Maxine Stuart), also resides in the White House, and wanders in at all hours of the night (but remains a great source for helpful advice and strength).

The president has a lot on her plate: a lunatic major is threatening World War III; the equally unstable Russian Premier, Dmitri Zolotov (played brilliantly by Dick Shawn) is constantly on the hot line threatening a preemptive strike; and a religious zealot named Reverend Billy Joe Bickerstaff (Richard Paul) is attempting to have Madame President impeached because he believes Satan was behind her presidential victory. As if this weren't enough, her impetuous cabinet of zanies—Helmut Luger (Herschel Bernardi), Senator Sam Cotton (Murray Hamilton), and General Hannibal Stryker (John Vernon) all threaten the future of mankind. The only seemingly sane cabinet voice is the lone African American member, Secretary of State LaRue Hawkes (Glynn Turman). Amid all of the frenetic goings-on, Julia's rock, best friend, and confidant is her gay chief of staff, Randy (Joel Brooks). Despite a great production crew and a great cast with an incredible sitcom pedigree, *Hail to the Chief* failed to find an audience and was impeached from 1600 Pennsylvania Avenue after only seven episodes had aired. Guest stars included Rose Marie, Morey Amsterdam, George Wyner, and Pat Hingle.

The episodes do not appear to have been assigned titles. The executive producers were Paul Junger Witt and Tony Thomas; the producer was Marsha Posner Williams; the writers included Susan Harris, Mort Nathan, Barry Fanaro, Terry Grossman, Kathy Speer, Tony Thomas, and Paul Junger Witt; the lone director was J. D. Lobue. The creator was Susan Harris. Music was provided by George Aliceson Tipton and Scott Gale. Patty Duke died on March 29, 2016 at the age of 69.

Half Nelson Glen Larson Productions/20th Century Fox Television. NBC. Sunday night 9:00 (March 24, 1985), Friday nights 9:00 (March 29, 1985–May 10, 1985). One two-hour TV movie and seven hour-long episodes were filmed without a laugh track.

Pint-sized Rocky Nelson (Joe Pesci) is a decorated and dedicated New York undercover cop who often uses unconventional and unscrupulous methods to solve crimes—a diminutive Columbo, if you will. He is noticeably shorter than everyone else in the cast (even the ladies)—a subject addressed in several episodes. Nelson's dream is to become an actor, but when his heroic story is sold to Hollywood, he is denied the opportunity to portray himself because he is too short. In his spare time, he auditions for other acting roles, mostly in commercials (he is dressed as a hot dog in one episode and smeared with various condiments, much to his annoyance).

Nelson is mainly a private detective with the Beverly Hills Patrol for celebrities who wish to stay safe from crazed fans. He is immediately hired by Dean Martin (portraying himself) as his part-time security guard. Because of his lack of stature, he is also good at solving crimes because he can get into places that others couldn't. Nelson is a thorn in the side of others on the police force, namely Chester Long (Fred "the hammer" Williamson), Kurt (Bubba Smith), and Beau (Dick Butkus). Yes, the cast was indeed overladen with former stars of the NFL. Earlier, Smith and Butkus had co-starred in another short-lived series, *Blue Thunder*. Others in the cast included switchboard operator Annie O'Hara (Victoria Jackson), Detective Hamill (Gary Grubbs), and Nelson's pet bull terrier Hunk (his real name was Tony). Guest stars were plentiful, and included Cesar Romero, Robert Reed, Julie Newmar, and Donald O'Connor.

Episodes were titled "The Pilot," "Deadly Vase," "Uppers and Downers," "Diplomatic Immunity," "Nose Job," "Chariots for Hire," "Beverly Hills Princess," and "Malibu Colony." The executive producers and creators were Glen A. Larson and Lou Shaw; the producer was Joseph T. Naar; the writers included Glen A. Larson, Lou Shaw, Aubrey Solomon, Simon Muntner, Richard Freiman, and Mark McClafferty; the directors included Bruce Bilson, James Sheldon, Bernard McEveety, Arthur Allan Seidelman, and Alan Cooke. The opening theme song "L. A., You Belong to Me" was written by Stu Phillips and Robert Jason, and performed by Robert Jason. The closing theme, "L. A. Is My Home" was written by Jack Latimer and Jackie Altier, and performed by Dean Martin.

Hard Knocks Chris Thompson/Gary Nardino Productions. Paramount Television. Showtime Productions. Showtime. Friday nights 8:30 (April 20, 1987–August 6, 1987). Thirteen episodes were videotaped in front of a live audience.

The opening credits begin with executive producer Chris Thompson shooting his television set. Not to be confused with the HBO show about the NFL, this *Hard Knocks* featured Bill Maher as Gower Rhodes—a former hippie turned straight arrow. He is teamed with Nick Bronco (Tommy Hinkley), a testosterone-laden tough guy with many prurient needs and urges. He also has a poster of G. Gordon Liddy on his wall. Together, they are oil-and-water private detectives in Manhattan in this "crimedy" that originated on one of cable's premium channels, Showtime, in 1987.

The duo sets up their agency in the back of a restaurant called Maggie's Farm in Beverly Hills in an attempt to lure a wealthy clientele. Maggie (a.k.a. Mags), who has a crush on Jay

Leno, is a sarcastic ex-con and informant played by Judith-Marie Bergan. Bronco's niece, the sweet-but-shrewd Terry (Babette Props) and her husband/cook, Silky (James Vallely), work in the restaurant. Rhodes occasionally dates a shady lady named Sheila Jesswalters (Gracie Harrison), whose parents changed their immigrant surname to honor their favorite actress, Jessica Walter. Our wannabe sleuths frequently cross paths with an unsavory Los Angeles mob man named simply Tony (Tom Spiroff). Some weeks the series almost took on a comic book quality, and in one particular episode, Rhodes and Bronco have to save the world from certain extinction as a killer poison (that also works wonders on cleaning Formica) is accidentally released into the atmosphere. Thirteen half-hour episodes aired as part of Showtime's Friday night comedy lineup. *It's Garry Shandling's Show* also aired in that block and fared much better, enjoying several successful seasons.

Episodes were titled "The Pilot," "Play, Mr. Tambourine Man, for Me," "What Becomes a Legend Least?," "End of the World," "Bronco's Rib," "Fallen Idol," "Luck Be a Gangster Tonight," "If You Knew Nancy," "Highway to Hard Knocks," "The Hits," "Captain Justice," "Sap Cops," and "Hammerhead Is Out." The executive producers were Gary Nardino, Chris Thompson, and Chip Hayes; the producers were Marie Connolly, and Shelley Jensen; the writers included Chris Thompson, Rob Dames, Bob Fraser, Don Reo, Marjorie Gross, Ron Zimmerman, and George Beckerman; the directors included Jules Lichtman, Don Barnhart, Shelley Jensen, Rob Dames, and Chris Thompson. The creator was Chris Thompson. Music was provided by Dan Foliart, Howard Pearl, and Billy Vera.

Harry Walt Disney Studios/Touchstone Television. ABC. Wednesday nights 8:30 (March 4, 1987–March 25, 1987). Seven episodes were filmed in front of a live audience, but only four aired.

Harry Porschak, played by Alan Arkin, was for all intents and purposes Sergeant Ernie Bilko (*The Phil Silvers Show*), with a dash of *M*A*S*H*'s Hawkeye Pierce, set loose in a new environment—the purchasing department of the Ninth Street Community Hospital. Harry was merely a purchaser, but appears to have an amazing amount of clout there. He is always late for work, and travels everywhere by bicycle. He is cunning, scheming, and manipulative. Like Bilko, Harry has a passion for gambling (there are bets on when patients would pass kidney stones, gin rummy games with those just waking up from having been anesthetized, and outpatient poker), and he knows a pigeon when he sees one. However, unlike Bilko, the wheeling and dealing is usually not for selfish reasons. For example, in one episode Harry sells off a bevy of unnecessary excess equipment at the hospital. His superiors think he is pocketing the money, but in reality he is purchasing a sorely needed new X-ray machine (the old one was constantly in a state of disrepair). His methods are questionable at best, but his heart is always in the right place. He is surrounded by a cast of zanies, including Thom Bray as nerdy, bespectacled, by-the-rules Lawrence Pendelton.

Bray's character on this program is the complete antithesis of his Cyril character on the earlier dramedy called *Breaking Away*. Pendelton is in cahoots with dour-faced Nurse Ina Duckett (Holland Taylor), but their attempts to get Harry fired always seem to backfire. Others in the cast included Barbara Dana as Dr. Sandy Clifton, a psychiatrist; Kurt Knudson as the overwhelmed hospital administrator Wyatt Lockhart; comedian Richard Lewis as the neurotic Richard Breskin (who flunked out of medical school in Guatemala, but perpetuates the ruse that he is a medical doctor); and Matt Craven as the math whiz/gofer Bobby Kratz. It's interesting to note that Craven co-starred with Alan Arkin's son Adam in the equally short-lived sitcom *Tough Cookies*. *Harry* was not a bad show by any stretch of the imagination. It was just a bit too familiar—the public had seen this setup before. No new ground was broken here, and *Harry* quickly disappeared from prime-time.

Episodes were titled "Meet Mr. Porschak," "How Do You Solve a Problem Like Nurse Duckett?," "This Is the Army, Mr. Porschak," "The Great Rat Race," "Rebel with Sort of a Cause," "Harry's Big Night," and "Mr. Imperfect." The executive producers were Barry Levinson, Mark Johnson, and Alan Arkin; the producers were Don Van Atta and Shelley Zellman; the writers included Gary Jacobs, Ken Finkelman, and David Axelrod; the directors included Steve Robman. The creator was Susan Kramer. Music was provided by Alf Clausen.

Have Faith Pronoun Trouble, Inc./Adam Productions/20th Century Television. ABC. Tuesday nights 9:30 (April 18, 1989–June 13, 1989). Seven episodes were videotaped in front of a live audience. Sponsors included Clairol Final Net.

Successful sitcoms with a religious bent are *pew* and far between. *The Flying Nun* ran for three seasons, but *In the Beginning* with McLean Stevenson and *Sister Kate* with Stephanie Beacham were short-lived. ABC tried again in the spring of 1989 with some familiar sitcom faces—Joel Higgins of *Silver Spoons* and Ron Carey of *Barney Miller*—but lost faith in *Have Faith* after only seven episodes and then changed its prime-time schedule.

The series was set in the Catholic parish of St. Catherine's Church, in a rough part of Chicago. Higgins portrayed the rather untidy baseball and golf-loving Monsignor Joseph MacKenzie, often called "Mac" (known for his "unorthodox" approach), and Carey played Father Vincent Paglia. Paglia also serves as the parish's accountant, and is notorious for keeping very tight purse strings. About the casting, producer Alicia Ulrich said, "The role that went to Joel Higgins was originally written for an older actor, Jack Warden, and he was interested in doing it. ABC had a deal with Joel Higgins from his time on *Silver Spoons* and the casting changed. Ron Carey was cast, as both Noam Pitlik and Nat Mauldin had worked on *Barney Miller* with Ron. He was a fabulously funny, neurotic, lovely man."

Also in the cast, from *National Lampoon's*

The penance for ABC's *Have Faith* was a quick cancellation. Pictured is the show's star, Joel Higgins, as Monsignor Joseph MacKenzie.

Animal House, Stephen Furst was Father Gabriel Podmaninsky (who played football in his youth), and Frank Hamilton was Father Edgar Tuttle—(an old school traditionalist who eschews change). Francesca P. Roberts portrayed their secretary (the non-Catholic, very organized, and sassy Sally Coleman), and Todd Susman was Arthur Glass.

The program was filled with wacky parishioners and even more wacky confessions. About the show's origins, Ulrich recalled, "I had been a producer for the local Los Angeles CBS station and did a profile on a talented woman artist, named Pascal. Her husband was a former monsignor, ready to become a bishop, when he left the church and married her. We all became friends and I was frequently invited to dinner at their Beverly Hills home, where there was an eclectic mix of guests ranging from Abigail Van Buren [*Dear Abby*] to John Kluge [Metromedia] to members of the Swarovski Crystal family, to members of the clergy. I loved hearing the clergy tales about the behind the scenes world in the church and the rectory. When Pascal created some beautiful stained glass windows for one of her monsignor friends, there was a celebration at the church when they were installed. I attended the 'after party' in the rectory, where I saw up close, once the collars were off, priests were really just normal people. They had a sense of humor, liked to have a cocktail … or two, and talk Notre Dame Football. One priest, with a gleam in his eye, said to me, 'Oh, if I had seen you before the Pope had seen me.' It was a world very unlike what I had imagined. Peeking behind the collar, it was clear these were mortal men—very human and accessible. I could see a TV show in my head. I made arrangements to live in the rectory for a week to take notes. The week I stayed, there was a visiting priest from Our Lady of Las Vegas—you can't make it up! I saw the day-to-day life. I saw things left in the collection basket besides money (a toy G. I. Joe, notes, a dropped pacifier). Then there were the congregation 'groupies' who would drop well intentioned, but inedible, baked goods at the rectory door. The interaction between the different personalities under the rectory roof seemed like a boys club, but with a certain sanctity and class due to the collars. It appeared to be a natural setup to a sitcom—to have a situation where very different personalities were forced to live together and get along. The original title of the show was 'Gents.' That's what the group of priests I knew called themselves. I wanted to take the show out of such a religious context, but Nat [Mauldin] and the network thought *Have Faith* would be better. The pitch was also originally written with a Latin priest and a female secretary. The studio changed it to five white men. After testing, the network decided to add African American actress Francesca Roberts as the secretary."

Asked how the program was received within the religious community, Ulrich said, "One interesting story—the attorney at 20th Century Fox warned us that every time a new sitcom comes out people come out of the woodwork to claim they had a similar idea. Sure enough, we not only had an individual who tried to lay claim, a group of priests from Detroit tried to sue saying they had sent a similar idea to ABC years ago! I wondered why they were working on trying to do a sitcom rather than administering to their flock! Quite often, networks will just pay out a nominal amount to not deal with the hassle and expense for lawyers. 20th Century Fox did not work that way, and fought it, and the case was obviously thrown out."

Regarding the suits' decision to cancel the show, Ulrich said, "We were a mid-season replacement airing after *Roseanne*. They tried three shows in the time slot, including *Coach*. We got a B+ from *People Magazine*, good reviews, and even tested better and rated higher than *Coach*. The first time we aired, we were the third highest-rated show for the week. But Bob Iger had come from sports to the new position of network chief and preferred *Coach*, while we were sent to a non-winnable time slot [Sunday nights at 8:00 for reruns]. Thus, the end of *Have Faith*." Reruns popped up briefly on the now-long-defunct Odyssey Channel and Ulrich added, "I had no idea they were rerunning. A cousin of mine saw them and notified me, which allowed me to cash in on some residuals!"

Episodes were titled "The Teacher," "Holy Smoke," "The Window," "Bingo," "Letters from Home" (with guest star William Windom), "The Confession," and "The Competition." Pronoun Trouble, Inc. was Nat Mauldin's production company, and Adam Productions belonged to John Ritter and his attorney, Bob Myman. Ulrich said, "John was a wonderfully caring and supportive producer. He was hands on and even guest starred in an episode ['The Window']. His wife at the time even played a bit part as a voice in one of the confessionals. He believed in the show. At the time, I believe his production company was also doing another mid-season replacement with Jamie Lee Curtis titled *Anything But Love*, so he had two shows he was hoping to get on the schedule." The executive producers were Nat Mauldin, Robert M. Myman, and John Ritter; the producers were John Ritter, Faye Oshima Belyeu, Alicia Ulrich, and Jerome Lew (sometimes credited as Jeremy Lew); the writers included Nat Mauldin and Tony Sheehan. Sheehan also wrote for *Sister Kate*. The lone director was Noam Pitlik, whom Ulrich recalled as "a big bear of a guy that made the actors feel very secure. A consummate pro. Nat Mauldin and Ron Carey had worked with him on *Barney Miller*." The creators were Nat Mauldin, Jerome Lew, and Alicia Ulrich. The theme song, "Have Faith," was by Gordon Lustig.

Heartland Witt/Thomas Productions/Touchstone Television. CBS. Monday nights 8:30 (March 20, 1989–July 31, 1989). Ten episodes were videotaped in front of a live audience.

After two hit series—*Family Affair* and *Hardcastle and McCormick*—Brian Keith attempted TV success again in this pleasant sitcom set in the mythical heartland town of Pritchard, Nebraska. Keith, sporting gray hair, portrayed B. L. McCutcheon—a very conservative, crusty, opinionated, stubborn old-timer whose farm has just been repossessed, necessitating a move into his daughter Casey's house.

B. L. is totally out of touch with pop culture and unaware of the toll inflation has taken on hotel rates and cab fare. Casey's (Kathleen Layman) husband, Tom (Richard Gilliland), does not get along well with his father-in-law and a continuous stream of barbs are tossed back and forth between the two. Casey and Tom have a large family of their own—elder son, Johnny (Jason Kristofer), who is obsessed with soccer, and especially television, and yearns to live in or near Hollywood; clumsy and plump Gus (Devin Ratray), who loves food and wrestling; and an adopted Asian American daughter named Kim (Daisy Keith, Brian's real-life daughter), who has designs on attending the Julliard School of Music in New York City. In the episode titled "No Place like Home," we discover that both B. L. and Kim are afraid to fly. It's interesting to note that CBS had two sitcoms set in Nebraska in that same TV year (the other being *First Impressions*), and neither one was welcomed back for a second season.

Episodes were titled "The Tornado," "B. L. Moves Out," "Johnny Goes to California," "Gus Sees a Dead Guy," "Girl Wrestler," "Life and Death," "The Sky Is Falling," "The Dog Story," "No Place Like Home," and "The Wild One." The executive producers were Don Reo, Tony Thomas, and Paul Junger Witt; the producers were Judith D. Allison, David Amico, and Mitchell Hurwitz; the writers included Don Reo; the directors were Steve Zuckerman, Andy Cadiff, Terry Hughes and Zane Buzby. The program was created by Don Reo. Music was provided by George Aliceson Tipton, and the theme song was performed by Rock and Roll Hall of Famer Dion Di Muci.

Herbie the Love Bug Walt Disney Productions. CBS. Wednesday nights 8:00 (March 17, 1982–April 14, 1982). Five episodes were filmed single-camera style without a laugh track.

Neither Dean Jones nor Patricia Harty had much luck on the small screen, but each one had their fair share of opportunities. Before this venture, Jones had starred in *Ensign O'Toole*, *What's It All About, World?* and *The Chicago Teddy Bears*. Patricia Harty had co-starred in *Occasional Wife*, *Blondie*, and *The Bob Crane Show* (on the latter she had briefly changed her name to Trisha Hart). Collectively, *Herbie the Love Bug*, the story of a Volkswagen Beetle with a mind of its own, was their biggest flop and was canceled after only five hour-long episodes. Jones had starred as Herbie's original owner in the very successful 1969 film and one of the sequels (*Herbie Goes to Monte Carlo*). Here, he reprises the role of Jim Douglas, and now runs the Famous Driving School (with the phone number 555-7636) and also teaches driver's education in the local high school. Douglas's assistant is Bo Phillips (Richard Paul), who, because the business isn't doing well, isn't always paid on time.

In the debut episode, Herbie takes control of Douglas's car, thwarts a bank robber's escape, and rescues Susan MacLane (Harty), a pretty young lady, whom the thug has been holding hostage. Not knowing that Herbie is the hero, Susan takes an instantaneous liking to Douglas, and vice versa. However, she already has a fiancé, Randy Bigelow (Larry Linville), and three kids—Julie (Claudia Wells), Robbie (Douglas Emerson), and Matthew (Nicky Katt) from her previous marriage to a race-car driver. Susan begins to fall for Douglas and begins questioning her relationship with Bigelow. However, when Douglas appears to be returning to auto racing, she agrees to marry Bigelow in Santa Barbara. Herbie, the buttinski, delivers Douglas to the church in the nick of time to stop the wedding (much to the dismay of Randy's mother, Mrs. Bigelow, played by Natalie Core). Susan decides not to rush into becoming Mrs. Jim Douglas, and the new couple wait until episode 4 of the ill-fated series to march down the aisle (conveniently, Herbie is able to play "Here Comes the Bride" on his horn), despite Bigelow's attempts to break them up and get Herbie on the scrap heap. Because her place is much bigger than Jim's, he opts to move into Susan's place (after the wedding, of course—this is a Disney project after all).

Episodes were titled "Herbie the Matchmaker," "Herbie to the Rescue," "My House Is Your House," "Herbie the Best Man," and "Calling Doctor Herbie" (with guest star George Lindsey). The executive producer was William Robert Yates; the producers were Kevin Corcoran (who had appeared in a few Disney films in his youth), Don Nelson, and Arthur Alsberg; the writers include Arthur Alsberg, Gordon Buford, Don Tait, and Don Nelson; the directors included Bill Bixby, Charles S. Dubin, and Vincent McEveety. Music was provided by Frank DeVol and Tom Worrall. Dean Jones sang the program's theme song, "Herbie, My Best Friend." Reruns of the series briefly ran on the Disney Channel.

He's the Mayor Universal Television. ABC. Friday nights 9:30 (January 10, 1986–March 21, 1986). Thirteen episodes were filmed in front of a loud live audience, but only ten aired.

The credits open with old scrapbook photos showing Mayor Carl Burke (Kevin Hooks) from childhood to the present. The theme song has elements of early rap, and is also used between scenes on occasion. In a landslide victory, the unmarried African American Burke is elected mayor at the age of twenty-five. He is often heard singing the Gene Chandler classic "Duke of Earl." His "kitchen cabinet" consists of his wise but somewhat overbearing City Hall custodian Alvin (Al Fann), who is also his widower father, a Korean War vet who never graduated high school (but gets his G.E.D. in the "My Dad the Grad" episode). Carl often seeks advice from his dad. Carl's best friend/cousin/driver is the ever-tardy Wardell Halsey (Wesley Thompson). Also in the cast were sneaky, smarmy, and well-connected City Council President Harlan Nash (David Graf), who takes over in the mayor's absence; the mayor's secretary, Paula Hendricks (Mari Gorman); next-door neighbor Ivan Bronski (Stanley Brock); and the hangdog Police Chief Walter Padget (Pat Corley, pre–*Murphy Brown*). Stories revolve around the unexpected difficulties that come with the elected office, as well as trying to balance family problems with job requirements and obligations. The debut episode briefly addresses a modern-day problem—chokeholds by the police department (much in the news in 2015). Thirteen episodes were produced, but only ten aired.

Episodes were titled "The Honeymoon's Over," "Take My Father, Please" (with guest star Gail Fisher), "The Mayor's Best Friend," "An Officer and the Mayor" (with guest star Vanessa Williams), "My Dad the Grad," "New and Improved Mayor," "Burke's Acres," "Take This Job and Shove It," "Early Retirement," "Dinner for Two," "Mayors, Don't Let Your Uncles Grow Up to Be Cowboys," "Heart and Soul," and "And That's the Way It Was." The executive producer was Alessandro Vieth; the producers were Fred Rubin, Fred Fox, Jr., Kris Keiser, and John Forbes; the writers included Ilunga Adell, Bill Daley, Bob Weiskopf, Larry Spencer, Ehrich Van Lowe, Bill Boulware, Fred Fox, Jr., Mark Fink, Fred Rubin, Bob Schiller, Jean Johnson, Bob Peete, Shelly Goldstein, and Terry Hart; the director was Oz Scott. The creators were Bob Peete and Winston Moss (should have been called a Peete-Moss Production—a missed opportunity). Music was provided by Glen Ballard and Mark Davis.

The Tiffany network (CBS) attempted to get more mileage out of a 1969 Disney movie classic, but *Herbie, the Love Bug* ran out of gas very quickly. Pictured (clockwise, from top) are Dean Jones, Patricia Harty, Claudia Wells, Douglas Emerson, and Nicky Katt.

The theme song was performed by Thelma Houston and Wesley Thompson.

Homeroom Castle Rock Entertainment/Giggling Goose Productions. ABC. Sunday nights 8:30 (September 16, 1989–December 17, 1989). Thirteen episodes were videotaped in front of a live audience, but only ten aired.

Homeroom is likely the only sitcom developed because of a stand-up routine performed on *The Tonight Show Starring Johnny Carson*. In the series, comedian Darryl Sivad played Darryl Harper—a well-compensated advertising copywriter who opts to make a life change and become a teacher for underprivileged children (he calls them "The Termites") at an inner-city elementary school in New York City. He is usually seen in class wearing cardigan sweaters and items to accompany whatever his topic is that day (a stovepipe hat on the day he covers Abraham Lincoln). At home he sometimes wears his wife's bunny slippers. Darryl's wife, Virginia (Penny Johnson), nicknamed Vicky, a New York Giants fan, offers support for his mission, but his father-in-law, Phil Drexler (Bill Cobbs), does not. Sarcastic Phil (he drove a bus for fifteen years before being named district supervisor for the bus company) voices his displeasure, and feels justified to do so. After all, Darryl and Vicky live in his brownstone rent free (Phil lives upstairs from them), and Darryl used to earn good money writing advertising jingles before changing careers. Darryl's unemployed younger brother is named Anthony (Claude Brooks), and his fourth grade students include Devon (Jahary Bennett), and pianist Donald (Billy Dee Willis). Donald's catch phrase is "Sue me." The program quickly experienced ratings issues up against *Murder She Wrote*, and despite a write-in campaign by the cast and crew in an attempt to save the show, *Homeroom* was expelled after only ten of its thirteen episodes had aired.

Episodes were titled "The Pilot," "The Lookin' for West Coast Travelin' 'Long the Missouri River Blues," "Food for Thought," "It's Not Easy Bein' Green," "Dirty Laundry," "Who Is Captain Fitness?," "Dinner at Fiveish," "Commercial Break," "Mr. Drexler's Neighborhood," "Who'll Be My Role Model after My Role Model Is Gone?," "The Visitor," and "The Mom Who Came to Dinner." The producer was Topper Carew; the writers included Marc Cherry, David Cohen, Roger S. H. Schulman, Gary Gilbert, and Andrew Scheinman; the directors included Linda Day, Arlando Smith, Tony Singletary, and Art Wolff. The creators were Gary Gilbert and Andrew Scheinman.

I Had Three Wives Warner Bros. Television. CBS. Wednesday nights 8:00 (August 14, 1985–September 4, 1985), and Friday night 8:00 (September 13, 1985). Five hour-long episodes were filmed without a laugh track.

This dramedy could have been called "A Nexus with My Exes." Jackson Beaudine (Victor Garber) drives a classic Pontiac GTO convertible, and is a detective with his own agency (at 1163 Vandover Street in Los Angeles). He is adept at solving crimes, but not at staying married. He refers to his situation as having been "thrice blessed." He is still on very friendly terms with all three of his ex-wives, and their areas of expertise come in handy in his sleuthing. There is Mary Parker (Maggie Cooper), his first wife (now remarried), who is an attorney in Brentwood (and maintains custody of their pre-teen son, Andrew—a very young David Faustino), who provides Jackson with great legal advice; Samantha Collins (Teri Copley), his second wife, who is an actress and a master of disguises (and karate); and Liz Bailey (Shanna Reed), his third wife, who is a reporter for the local (fictional) newspaper, the *Los Angeles Chronicle*, and has an unparalleled Rolodex chock full of helpful contacts. Everyone, even the exes, get along extremely well together (that's a stretch), and behave like one big extended family. Although lucky with ex-loves, Jackson Beaudine does not have a lot of luck with automobiles, and is frequently seeking repairs.

Episodes were titled "You and I Know," "'Til Death Do Us Part" (with guest stars Paul Sand and Sela Ward), "Bedtime Stories," "Butterfly Murder," and "Runaround Sue." The executive producers were Nick Thiel, Carla Singer, Peter Lefcourt, and Marc Merson; the producers were Stephen Hattman, Tom Chehak, Michael S. McLean, Donald A. Baer, and Jan Worthington; the writers included Ron Osborn, Tom Chehak, Jan Worthington, A. J. Nathan, Stephen Hattman, and Jeff W. Reno; the directors included Bob Sweeney and John Hancock. The creator was Peter Lefcourt. Music was provided by Bill Conti, Sylvester Levay, and Udi Harpaz.

I Married Dora Reeves Entertainment Group/Welladay, Inc. ABC. Tuesday night 9:30 (September 22, 1987), Friday nights 8:30 (September 25, 1987–January 8, 1988). Thirteen episodes were videotaped in front of a live audience.

Not to be confused with *I Married Joan*, *I Married Dora* is the story of a divorced Los Angeles architect, Peter Farrell (Daniel Hugh Kelly), who, along with his family, grows very fond of their housekeeper, Dora Calderon

(Elizabeth Peña). She is great with the kids, and quite adept at video games. However, Dora is an illegal alien, and when her visa expires, in an effort to avoid being deported, she marries her employer. Episodes then revolve around the real possibility that their sham marriage could be discovered by the authorities. Because of the situation, they are both "free agents" and allowed to date other people, even though Dora has grown to really love Peter. The program's creator and executive producer Michael Leeson elaborated, "It seemed at the time that comedy could arise from having a very straight single white guy marry the El Salvadoran nanny who cared for his two kids—not because he loved her but because he needed her and he felt a moral obligation to keep her from being deported back to El Salvador where she was likely, because of her family's political associations, to be murdered by a death squad. She would speak Spanish or heavily accented English, and because of the language and cultural differences, there would be hilarious misunderstandings and conflict and eventually, perhaps, romance and love. Elizabeth Peña, after being cast, decided that she would play the character of Dora Calderon without an accent. Had I considered that Elizabeth was born and raised in New Jersey, and her roots were Cuban and not Central American, I might have cast someone more authentic, but then ABC probably would not have greenlit the series. Daniel Hugh Kelly was a network pick and I went along with casting him despite thinking that he seemed too handsome and heroic and not the image of the character Peter Farrell I had written. Casting is the most important element in half-hour TV. The concept may be weak, the writing may be weak, but if the casting isn't right, the result will likely be a short run."

Farrell's two children are teenaged Kate (Juliette Lewis) and eleven-year-old Will Farrell, played by Jason Horst. "Yes, I must have known in 1987 that big Will Ferrell would emerge as a comedy sensation," Leeson later said. Others in the cast included Henry Jones as Peter's boss, Hughes Whitney Lennox, and Sanford Jensen as Peter's co-worker Dolf Mennenger. About the cast, Leeson recalled, "Juliette Lewis was about sixteen at the time. I thought she was incredibly funny and never could tell if she knew she was being funny or if she was just innately funny. I doubt she remembers doing the series. Henry Jones was a real pleasure to work with. His voice alone was funny. Alley Mills is always great. I worked on a series called *The Associates* [1979] in which she starred with Martin Short, Wilfrid Hyde-White, Joe Regalbuto, Tim Thomerson, and Shelly Smith. Another one-season series."

Didn't the first episode of *I Married Dora* come complete with a disclaimer about marrying someone to keep them in the country? Leeson pondered, "I think it did. The characters of Peter and Dora were committing a crime. I attempted to alert the audience in a funny way. The audience apparently didn't find very much about the show funny." Was there any backlash about the subject matter? Leeson added, "The backlash was that not enough viewers watched the show. The reviews were not good, which probably didn't help keep it afloat. Sometimes you can have a show that's not getting big ratings but the critics love, and the network will keep it on the air for the critical cachet." Because the series had low ratings, the cast was well aware that cancellation was imminent. Said cancellation was addressed in the thirteenth and final episode of the show on January 8, 1988.

About that memorable ending, Leeson shared, "The episode story was that Peter was going off to Saudi Arabia and there was a scene at the airport and he boards the plane then reappears and says something like, 'It's been canceled.' And Dora says, 'Your flight?' And he says, 'No, our series.' Peter Hunt, the director, came up with the Russian circus bow with all the cast members. We shot only one ending, so the network had the choice to air it or eat the cost of the episode—I admire them for airing it. I think I was in an editing room when I got the call from Brandon Stoddard saying he was sorry to have to tell me the show was to be canceled. At the time I thought it would be funny to do the ending we did. Some thought it was the only funny thing in the entire series." When asked about response from the studio audience, Leeson said, "They seemed to find it funnier than the viewing audience. We served tequila between scenes. We didn't—my attempt to be funny, which may explain the plethora of one-season series I've done."

Episodes were titled "I Married Dora" (with guest star Wendel Meldrum), "My Parents Are Coming," "Our Little Girl's Growing Up," "Where There's a Will There's No Way," "God's Waiting Room," "Happy Happy Birthday, Dora," "A Matter of Moulding," "Club Montez," "Dora Steps Out," "West Coast Story," "35-Year Itch," "Guess Who's Coming to Dinner Forever?" and "Millionaire's Club." About her guest shot on the sitcom's debut episode, Wendel Meldrum shared, "The late Elizabeth Peña was a focused, hard-working professional who took her comedy very seriously." The executive producer was Michael Leeson; the producers were Wendy Blair, Vic Rauseo, Linda Morris, and Coleman Mitchell; the writers included Michael Leeson, Frank Mula, Linda Morris, Vic Rauseo, Chris Cluess, Jan Fischer, Stu Kreisman, Russell Marcus, Mark Masuoka, Robert Rabinowitz, Jace Richdale, Patt Shea, and Harriet Weiss; the directors included Lee Shallat, and Peter H. Hunt. The creator was Michael Leeson. Music was provided by Glenn Jordan. About the entire experience, Leeson said, "Being a show runner is sort of like running in front of a train. You're breaking stories, preparing scripts, casting, rehearsing, shooting, editing, dealing with network notes, and you can't slow down or you get destroyed. Probably this train analogy isn't a good one in view of Randall Miller's tragic production, so maybe don't use this. I didn't get much sleep, and the sleep I got was riddled with anxiety. But as my mother once said to me after seeing a pilot I had done, 'Well, they paid you, didn't they, darling?'" Guest star Wendel Meldrum added, "There was a very strong feeling of passion to tell this story, and breaking the rules was an inspired and courageous decision by the creatives whose voice had been silenced too soon."

I'm a Big Girl Now Witt/Thomas Productions. ABC. Friday nights 8:30 (October 31, 1980–July 24, 1981). Nineteen episodes were videotaped in front of a live audience.

Sparked by her popularity as Corinne Tate on *Soap*, Diana Canova (daughter of comedienne Judy Canova) was given her own sitcom by producers Paul Junger Witt, Tony Thomas, and Susan Harris, beginning in the fall of 1980. However, as writer R. J. Colleary recalled, "She

Diana Canova (left) and Sheree North were co-workers and friends on ABC's *I'm a Big Girl Now*.

was a popular secondary character. Placing her in a lead role was quite another story." Canova portrayed Diana Cassidy, a divorcee (from Zach, with custody of a nasal-sounding eight-year-old daughter named Becky [Rori King]). Colleary said, "Yes, Rori tended to mumble her lines and was often hard to understand. She didn't do very much after *I'm a Big Girl Now* was canceled."

The premise has Diana and young Becky moving in with Diana's father, Dr. Benjamin Douglas, a dentist (Danny Thomas), who often treats his daughter as if she were still a little girl (hence the show's title). Benjamin has a lot of room for them in his home as his wife had recently run off with his former dental partner, Ira (Sheldon Leonard). (It should be noted that Sheldon Leonard produced Danny's long-running *Make Room for Daddy/The Danny Thomas Show*, on which he also had a recurring role as Phil Brokaw.) Benjamin also has a son (Diana's brother), the neurotic Walter Douglas (Michael Durrell), who is married to the rarely seen Polly (Joan Welles). Diana works for the Cramer Research Testing Group, a Washington, D.C., think tank, where her boss is the firm-but-fair and rather anal-retentive (all of the shoes in her closet have to be pointing in the exact same direction) Edie McKendrick (Sheree North); the secretary is the daft, animal-loving Nebraska native Karen Hawks (Deborah Baltzell); and her co-worker is the insecure hair-loss-obsessed Neal Stryker (Martin Short). Colleary added, "The show was off balance—Danny Thomas and Martin Short were placed and wasted in secondary roles, and even though the cast looked great on paper, the show just didn't have a lot of chemistry." In the "Shrinking" episode, a mandate is issued that all employees of the think tank have to undergo a psychological assessment because of a company computer breach. Diana is dead set against that policy and opts to leave her job (albeit temporarily) rather than face being analyzed. In an effort to save the program from ABC's axe, the last few episodes show Diana and the same co-workers suddenly (and inexplicably) working for a newspaper. Actor/director Philip Charles MacKenzie, who guest starred in the episode titled "Singles Bar," recalled, "This was historic—it was the first time I was cast as a sleazeball. It became the first of many. By the way, Diana Canova and I became great friends, and we had a nice reunion backstage a few years ago while she was doing *Company* on Broadway and picked up right where we left off."

Episodes were titled "The Pilot," "Daddy's Girl," "Career vs. Kid," "Younger than Springtime," "The Singles Bar," "Walter Comes Home," "First Christmas," "Fear and Loathing in Georgetown," "Best Friends" (with guest star Joe Regalbuto), "Let's Give Ben a Hand," "It's Him or Me" (with guest star Corey Feldman), "Shrinking," "He's Not Heavy He's Neal's Brother," "Ira Returns" (with guest star Sheldon Leonard), "There's No Business Like Joe Business" (with guest star Adrian Zmed), "Cops" (with guest star Dolph Sweet), "With Becky You Get Eggroll," "Hangers No Starch" (with guest star Lyle Alzado), and "S. M. I. L. E. Everybody." The executive producers were Paul Junger Witt and Tony Thomas; the producers were Marc Sotkin and Judy Pioli; the writers included Barbara Benedek, Susan Harris, Judy Pioli, Paula A. Roth, Marc Sotkin, Susan Seeger, Deborah Leschin, and R. J. Colleary; the directors included Jon Sharp, John Bowab, Doug Rogers, Tony Mordente, and Noam Pitlik. The creator was Susan Harris. The theme song was composed by George Aliceson Tipton and Leslie Bricusse, and performed by Diana Canova. Much of the same transitional music later used in *The Golden Girls* and *Benson* (also from Witt/Thomas Productions) was employed in *I'm a Big Girl Now*.

Isabel Sanford's Honeymoon Hotel DeLaurentiis Entertainment Group/Silverman/Farr Productions. Syndicated (by Access Syndication). Weeknights 11:00 (January 5, 1987–January 9, 1987). Five videotaped episodes with a laugh track aired during the first full week of 1987 as a five-part pilot.

This was an extremely short-lived situation comedy series. It starred the former Louise

"Weezy" of *The Jeffersons*. Sometimes referred to as simply *Isabel's Honeymoon Hotel* and *Honeymoon Hotel*, the opening credits do indeed contain the long, full title. Isabel Sanford was Isabel Scott, a divorcee at the helm of a once-profitable but now debt-laden hotel. Ernie Banks played her ex-husband, K. C.—they were married on the unlucky 13th of an unnamed month. He calls her Izzy and still has feelings for her. Isabel stays in suite number 22. Isabel's niece, Jolie, a girl with a passion for pickles, was played by Renee Jones. Isabel's assistants include the very tall Rhonda Bates as Martha, and *Phyllis*'s John Lawlor as Carlton. Earl Boen played Mel the bartender; and Lana Schwab was Agnes the chambermaid. Guest stars included Kelly Monteith, *Laverne and Shirley*'s David L. Lander and *The Bob Newhart Show*'s Marcia Wallace. The title of the series was likely inspired by the "Honeymoon Hotel" episode of *The Jeffersons* that originally aired on April 15, 1984.

The episodes don't appear to have been assigned titles. The executive producers were Gordon Farr and Fred Silverman; the producer was David Yarnell; the writers included Emma Fligg, Richard Albrecht, Simon Muntner, and Casey Keller; the directors included Dennis Steinmetz and Bob Claver. The creators were Gordon Farr, Casey Keller, and Richard Albrecht. Music was provided by David White, Evan Pace, and Steve Diamond. Casey Kasem was the program's announcer.

It Takes Two Witt/Thomas/Harris Productions. ABC. Thursday nights 9:30 (October 14, 1982–September 1, 1983). Twenty-two episodes were videotaped with a laugh track.

Not to be confused with the Vin Scully game show of same name, *It Takes Two* starred two highly successful sitcom veterans—Patty Duke Astin and Richard Crenna as a happily married couple of twenty years. Actually, the working title for the program was "For Better or Worse." Despite a syrupy opening theme, this show was quite well written and often very funny. Sandwiched between an aging *Too Close for Comfort* and *20/20* on Thursday nights, *It Takes Two* failed to catch on, but definitely deserved a second season to prove itself. Duke portrayed Molly Quinn, an assistant D. A. in Chicago. Crenna was her husband, Sam, the chief of surgery at a Windy City hospital. They are constantly forced to cancel plans with each other because of their schedules. As if their lives aren't busy enough, they have two teenage children to mind—eighteen-year-old college student and aspiring musician Andy (Anthony Edwards pre–*ER*), and wisecracking and emotional high school student Lisa (Helen Hunt pre–*Mad about You*). Helping out with the kids and some of the housework is Molly's salty-tongued, dizzy-yet-wise mother, Mama (Billie Bird). Mama gets to deliver many of the program's best one-liners—many of which were reminiscent of those delivered by the late Gracie Allen. Episodes deal with the couple's very busy lives and the lack of quality time spent together, and their opposing political viewpoints—he is a liberal; she, a conservative. Others in the cast included Richard McKenzie as one of Sam's colleagues at the hospital, Dr. Walter Chaiken (a psychiatrist); and Della

After a long run in the "de-luxe apartment in the sky," on CBS's *The Jeffersons*, the show's distaff star had a very brief stay at the syndicated *Isabel Sanford's Honeymoon Hotel*.

Reese as the sassy Judge Caroline Phillips, who adjudicates many of Molly's court cases. Before going to the final commercial, Patty and Richard took turns saying, "You do it this time. *It Takes Two* will return in a moment. I'll do it next time." This quality show, with only twenty-two episodes, did surface briefly in syndicated reruns.

Episodes were titled "Sam and Molly," "Turnabout," "Death Penalty" (with guest star Kim Stanley), "Promises in the Dark," "Heartbreak," "Hello, I Must Be Going," "Andy and the Older Woman," "Healthy Romance," "An Affair to Remember," "Mr. Molly Quinn," "The Anniversary," "The Choice," "Looks Bad Feels Good," "Lying Down on the Job," "Rhythm Blues," "Swan Song," "Inside Lisa Quinn," "Only When You Laugh" (with guest star Charlie Callas), "Molly's Best Friend," "Mother and Child Reunion," "The Suit" (with guest star Florence Halop), and "The Instinct." The executive producers were Paul Junger Witt and Tony Thomas; the producer was Greg Antonacci; the writers included Susan Harris, Nat Mauldin, Jordan Moffet, Greg Antonacci, Richard Freiman, Diane Wilk, and Stephen Neigher; the directors included Jay Sandrich, John Bowab, Greg Antonacci, and Ellen Gittelsohn. Music was provided by George Aliceson Tipton, and Paul Williams and Crystal Gayle performed the theme song called "Love Spends the Night."

It's Not Easy Patricia Nardo Productions/The Konigsberg Company/20th Century Fox Television. ABC. Thursday nights 9:30 (September 29, 1983–October 27, 1983). Nine episodes were videotaped with a laugh track, but only four aired.

Reminiscent of another sitcom flop called *Here We Go Again* from 1973, *It's Not Easy* tried to mine humor from divorce and found that it's not easy. In fact, this show had an even shorter life span—it was canceled after only four of the nine filmed episodes were aired. Nor was it easy getting the series on the air. Gerald McRaney was originally cast to star as Jack Long in 1982, but his *Simon and Simon* series was unexpectedly renewed for another season on CBS and he was suddenly unavailable. After a long delay, Ken Howard was chosen to replace him, and a new pilot was filmed. The program was then beset with tragedy as actor Larry Breeding, who was to play Neal Townsend on the show, was killed in an automobile accident in Los Angeles. After another search, Bert Convy got the nod to take his place. Finally, in the fall of 1983, the program debuted on ABC and instantly experienced yet another blow—bad Nielsen ratings.

The program revolves around a divorced couple—Jack (Ken Howard) and Sharon (Carlene Watkins)—who, for their kids' sake, now live across the street from each other. Those offspring are eleven-year-old Carol (Rachel Jacobs) and eight-year-old Johnny (Evan Cohen, formerly of *The Ropers*). Sharon's new husband is Neal (Convy), and her new stepson is fourteen-year-old Matthew Townsend (Billy Jacoby). Jack and Neal maintain a mutual dislike. Jack's meddlesome mother, Ruth (Jayne Meadows), lives with him and help out with household chores and the kids. Jack also has a girlfriend, Sherry Gabler (Christine Belford), whom Sharon despises. Coincidentally, *It's Not Easy* aired on Thursday nights, and was clobbered by *Simon and Simon*'s ratings.

Episodes were titled "The Pilot," "Jack Kills Sharon's Grandmother," "Betrayal," "Teacher's Pets," "My Dinner with Andrea," "Taking Sides," "All Night Long," "Neal Kills Johnny's Fish," and "You Made Her Love You." The writers included Patricia Nardo, Robert Sternin, Prudence Fraser, Mitzi McCall, Anne Convy, Robert Stevens, Carmen Finestra, Gary Kott, and Michael Cassutt; the directors included Robert Moore, Charlotte Brown, Tony Singletary, and John Tracy. Music was provided by Charles Fox. Jayne Meadows died April 26, 2015 at the age of 95.

It's Your Move Embassy Television. NBC. Wednesday nights 9:30 (September 26, 1984–January 9, 1985) and Saturday nights 9:30 (January 26, 1985–February 23, 1985). 18 episodes were filmed before a live audience.

There was quite a lot of Sergeant Ernie Bilko

(*The Phil Silvers Show*) in the clever young goldbrick Matthew Burton (a young Jason Bateman). However, Matthew finally meets his match (and intellectual equal) in Norman Lamb (David Garrison)—the new neighbor across the hall, in apartment 406. Their constant one-upmanship rendered *It's Your Move* both a sitcom and a chess match. In fact, the opening credits are set on a chess board. Each time one of them was one-upped, the words "You're gonna laugh" were usually part of the equation. Matthew always has a pocketful of paper money, and always gets his way through trickery. He has his classmates (especially the spelling, mathematics and calorically challenged Eli, played by Adam Sadowsky), the landlord Lou Donatelli (Ernie Sabella, with a bad combover), and even his widowed mom, Eileen (pretty Caren Kaye), wrapped around his little finger. Eileen seems oblivious to Matthew's conniving ways and fancies him a good boy. Matthew is ecstatic that his mother is dating the wealthy Mort Stumplerutt—a successful businessman who stars in his own TV commercials. The appearance of Norman Lamb next door throws a wrench into Matthew's plans. Norman is not the sacrificial "Lamb" to which Matthew has grown accustomed. He is a former insurance salesman who is working as a substitute teacher while trying (thus far, unsuccessfully) to make it as a writer. Even though he is extremely bright, he is having great difficulty just making ends meet, and Eileen usually picks up the check on their dates. Every one of Matthew's attempts to keep Norman and his mom apart backfire and only drew the couple closer. Norman and Eileen also share a love for "the oldies but goodies" by recording artists such as the Drifters and Sam Cooke. (Caren Kaye shared an amusing anecdote about the show's premise, "Behind the scenes, we called the show *Don't F*#k My Mother.*") Matthew's cheerleader sister, Julie (Tricia Cast), is wise to her younger brother's chicanery, often serving as his conscience and moral compass.

It's Your Move was well received by critics and earned many diehard fans, but succumbed to competition from ABC's *Dynasty*. (In fact, Matthew give *Dynasty* a dig in the "Pajama Party" episode.) The decision to soften Matthew's character and make him appear "nicer" in the later episodes (under the guise of being placed on probation after Eileen caught on to his hijinks in the "Caught in the Act" episode on which he broke into her workplace—the law office) also led to the program's demise. Too bad—there was some nice chemistry here, especially in the early episodes. About that decision, Caren Kaye said, "Michael G. Moye and Ron Leavitt wanted an edgier show, and later got to do the show they wanted—the wildly successful *Married with Children* on FOX. What I think happened was that NBC presented a mandate that if we wanted to have any chance at renewal for another season, Jason Bateman's character had to be softened somewhat. In the end, it ruined the original chess match premise, and the show suffered as a result. This really should have been a five-season or more show. It was a wonderful cast too—so many great people with lots of talent." Today, Caren Kaye is a well-respected psychologist.

Episodes were titled "The Pilot," "Put to the Test," "Dating Games," "Night Work," "Pajama Party" (with guest star Justine Bateman, Jason's real-life older sister, as shy Debbie), "Love Letters," "Dad and Me," "The Rival," "Top Dog," "Don't Leave Home Without It," "The Christmas Show," "The Dregs of Humanity, Part One," "The Dregs of Humanity, Part Two," "Caught in the Act," "Eli's Song," "A Woman Is Just a Woman," "The Experts," and, appropriately, the final first-run episode was called "Goodbye Farewell Amen" (a cute parody of *Alfred Hitchcock Presents*, with guest star Garrett Morris). The executive producers were Michael G. Moye and Ron Leavitt; producers included John Maxwell Anderson, Fred Fox, Jr., and Katherine Green; the writers included Ron Leavitt, Michael G. Moye, Fred Fox, Jr., Sandy Sprung, Pamela Norris, Marcy Vosburgh, and Al Aidekman; the directors included Linda Day, Jim Drake, John Pasquin, Tony Singletary, Peter Bonerz, John Tracy, Bob

Lally, Thomas McConnell, Herbert Kenwith, and Arlando Smith. The theme song was by Rik Howard and Bob Wirth.

Jack and Mike David Gerber Productions/MGM Television. ABC. Tuesday nights 10:00 (September 16, 1986–March 24, 1987). Eighteen episodes were filmed without a laugh track, but only sixteen aired.

Jack and Mike was ABC's blatant attempt to create another *Moonlighting*. Best described as a dramedy (there were some heavy moments amid the many light and romantic ones), it was set in Chicago (and filmed there, too). Jackie Shea (Shelley Hack) is a beautiful and popular columnist for *The Mirror* (her column is titled "Our Kind of Town"). She is always chasing hot news tips, a pursuit that frequently involves much peril. She kept the name Shea even after her marriage. Her husband, Mike Brennan (Tom Mason, who speaks more like a New Yorker than a Chicagoan), is a chef, restaurateur, and a fair saxophone player. Nicknamed "Restaurant King," he owns two very successful establishments, and has recently opened a third (this one with a 1950s motif). Jackie and Mike have such busy schedules that their plans for quality time together often lead to broken promises. Mike is sometimes embarrassed by what Jackie writes in her columns (including one about busy couples who no longer have any time for sex). Others in the cast included city editor Nora Adler (Jacqueline Brookes); waitress Carol (Holly Fulger); attorney, friend, and confidant Rick Scotti (Vincent Baggetta); Mike's sister Kathleen (Carol Potter); and his parents, Mary (Beatrice Straight), and John (James Green).

Episodes were titled "The Pilot," "Change of Heart," "Personal Foul," "Ready or Not," "High Anxiety," "Cry Uncle," "The Mentor," "Taste of Chicago," "Separate Lives," "Come Together," "Charity Ball," "Till Death Do Us Part," "Fire and Ice," "Light My Fire," "Dreamland," "The Reluctant Hero," "Quality of Mercy," and "Spirits in the Night." The executive producer was David Gerber; the producers included Bill Badalato, Christopher Chulack, and Liz Coe; the writers included Sara Davidson, and Lee David Zlotoff; the directors included Victor Lobl, Paul Stanley, Kim Friedman, Jack Bender, Peter Crane, Harry Winer, Paul Krasny, Jan Eliasberg, Gus Trikonis, and Lee David Zlotoff. Music was provided by Nan Schwartz and Brad Fiedel.

Jennifer Slept Here Larry Larry Productions/Columbia Pictures Television. NBC. Friday nights 8:30 (October 21, 1983–December 16, 1983), Saturday nights 8:30 (April 14, 1984–May 12, 1984). Thirteen episodes were filmed with a laugh track.

Jennifer Slept Here is a fantasy, and one of numerous failed attempts at a *Topper* redux. This time around, Ann Jillian portrayed a beloved deceased actress named Jennifer Farrell (what a wardrobe this ghost had!). Jennifer was best known for her hit musical film *Stairway to Paradise*. Her home at 32 Rexford Drive in Beverly Hills remained on the Hollywood Celebrity Tours route for five years after her demise, even when the house was bought by the Elliot family of New York. The Elliots consist of Susan (Georgia Engel) and successful lawyer George (Brandon Maggart), their young daughter Marilyn (Mya Akerling), and their fourteen-year-old son Joey (John P. Navin, Jr.). Again, harking back to *Topper*, Joey is the only one who can see Jennifer's ghost (because he got her bedroom), and despite his wishes to the contrary, she becomes like a second mother, guiding him along the straight and narrow path (she also helps him meet girls). Because no one else can see Jennifer, Joey is often overheard talking to himself (and to lamps, to doors, to walls, etc.) by his family and his new best friend, Marc (Glenn Scarpelli). Joey greatly misses his New York sports teams and former girlfriend Lindaman, but eventually comes to like the year-round warmth of Southern California.

After the first eight episodes had aired on Friday nights, the program was put on hiatus until spring when the remaining episodes were burned off on Saturday nights. The ratings were not good, and *Jennifer Slept Here* never had a ghost of a chance at a second season.

Episodes were titled "The Pilot," "Jennifer, the Movie," "Not with My Date, You Don't," "Boo" (with guest star Debbie Reynolds), "Calendar Girl" (with guest star Monty Hall), "One of Our Jars is Missing," "Trading Faces," "Rebel with a Cause," "Risky Weekend," "Do You Take This Ghost?," "Life with Grandfather," "The Tutor Who Came to Dinner," and "Take Jennifer, Please." The executive producers were Larry Rosen and Larry Tucker; the producers were Douglas Arango and Phil Doran; the writers included Larry Rosen, Larry Tucker, Nick Arnold, Larry Balmagia, Bruce Ferber, Tom Chehak, David Lerner, Terry Hart, Rick Mittleman, Larry Spencer, and Jurgen Wolff; the directors included Charles S. Dubin and John Bowab. The program's theme song was written by Joey Murcia, Bill Payne, Clint Holmes, and Ann Jillian, and it was performed by Joey Scarbury. Other music was provided by Perry Botkin. The program was nominated for an Emmy Award for its technical direction (for lots of ghostly trickery), but it did not win.

Joe Bash Tetagram, Ltd. ABC. Friday nights 9:30 (March 28, 1986–May 2, 1986), and Saturday night 8:30 (May 10, 1986). Six episodes were videotaped single-camera style without a laugh track.

Much like a cop show from the 1970s called *The Smith Family*, *Joe Bash* was never really certain if it was a sitcom or a drama. The embittered Bash (Peter Boyle, pre–*Everybody Loves Raymond*) has lost his hair and his youth after thirty years on the force and is now nearing retirement age (and playing it safe on the streets so as to reach said retirement). A member of the 33rd Precinct, his beat is in a crime-ridden part of New York City. Bash isn't above unlawful behavior himself—his girlfriend, Lorna (DeLane Matthews) is a hooker, he frequents pornographic movies, he often turns a blind eye to repeat offenders, and he keeps a bag of cash he found at a crime scene. Joe's impressionable young partner, Officer Willie Smith (Andrew Rubin), is supposed to be observing and mimicking his elder but instead spends most of his time trying to keep him in line. Others in the cast included Val Bisoglio as Sergeant Carmine DiSalvo, and Larry Hankin as Stu, the owner of the greasy spoon frequented by Bash and Smith. Despite many rave reviews, ABC una*bash*edly canceled the series after only six episodes.

Episodes were titled "The Pilot," "Tour of Duty," "Feinbaum" (with guest star Jack Gilford), "Janowitz," "Joe's First Partner," and "Cash" (with guest star LaWanda Page). The executive producers were Danny Arnold and Chris Hayward; the producer was Martin J. Gold; the writers included Danny Arnold, Chris Hayward, and Philip Jayson Lasker; the directors included Danny Arnold and John Florea. Music was provided by Jack Elliott.

Just in Time Fat Dog Productions/Pan Productions/Tim Matheson Productions/Warner Bros. Television. ABC. Wednesday nights 9:30 (April 6, 1988–May 18, 1988). Six episodes were filmed without a laugh track.

Just in Time revolves around a once successful magazine (since 1967) that is sorely in need of a jump start. Based at 177 Wilshire Boulevard in Los Angeles, *The West Coast Review* (California's Monthly Magazine) is suddenly being outsold by its more up-to-date competitors. Harry Stadlin (Tim Matheson), who had great success revamping *Chicago Magazine*, is hired to get the periodical back on track within a six-month period. Along the way, this recently divorced man (from a woman named Blair—each one cheated on the other) becomes romantically linked with Joanne Gail Farrell (Patricia Kalember), a very attractive reporter and columnist for the magazine. Unwittingly, they first met in an airport before his first day on the new job. Others in the cast included Nada Despotovich as Isabel Miller, the magazine's art director; and Ronnie Claire Edwards as Carlie Hightower, who airs all of Hollywood's dirty laundry in her gossip column. Episodes focused upon Stadlin's attempts to increase both the circulation of the magazine and the intensity of his fling with Joanna. The show's pilot episode, done in 1987, was titled "It Had to Be You," with Annette Bening in the Joanna role. Despite several good reviews, the sitcom failed to find an audience and was taken out of circulation after only six episodes. Smokey Robinson's Top Ten hit "Just to See Her" was used in ABC promos for the series. An earthquake in the Los Angeles area delayed the shooting of one of the episodes.

Episodes were titled "Nothing Sacred," "All the Editor's Men," "2 Rms No Vu," "Mixed Doubles," "The Boys in the Boardroom," and "Unnatural Phenomena Supernatural Acts." The executive producers were Tim Matheson and Fred Barron; the producers were Bob Comfort, Rick Kellard, and Charles and Lawrence Gordon; the writers included Fred Barron, Judy Toll, Wendy Goldman, and Alan Mandel; the directors included Tom Cherones, Peter Sasdy, and Barnet Kellman. The creator was Fred Barron. Music was provided by Lee Holdridge.

Just Our Luck Lawrence Gordon Productions/Lorimar Productions. ABC. Tuesday nights 8:00 (September 20, 1983–December 27, 1983). Thirteen episodes were filmed single-camera style with a laugh track.

A modern-day *I Dream of Jeannie*, *Just Our Luck* revolves around Keith Barrow (Richard Gilliland), the friendly weatherman for KPOX-TV Channel 6 in Venice, California, and an African American genie named Shabu (T. K. Carter). Their meeting is purely accidental, as Keith breaks a bottle at a souvenir stand and is forced to buy it. The contents are not discovered until the bottle is brought home. Shabu had previously served some of the greats in history, such as Napoleon, King Arthur, and Cleopatra, but this current assignment is a huge comedown for him, and he is not above practical jokes and mischief. Alcohol makes him lose control of his powers and his senses. One of Shabu's first duties is giving the very ordinary and somewhat dull Barrow charisma so that he won't lose his job at the TV station; both the station manager, Nelson Marriott (Rod McCary), and the program director—and his fiancée, Meagan Huxley (Ellen Maxted) claim he lacks it. With Shabu's help, Barrow becomes charismatic—way *too* charismatic, in fact.

One of the episodes, "Engelbert Humpercricket," borrowed a story from a classic Warner Bros. cartoon called *One Froggy Evening* (1955). In the cartoon, a singing frog had a construction worker seeing dollar signs—that is, until it is discovered that the frog's singing follows no particular schedule and proving his amazing find to others proves both frustrating and embarrassing. On the *Just Our Luck* episode, it is a cricket that is given powers by Shabu, and the cricket (actually more of a Bobby Darin than an Engelbert Humperdinck) is discovered by station manager Marriott, who experiences the same frustrations as the construction worker in the cartoon. As one might expect, the NAACP took umbrage with the depiction of the black servant and his white master in this series and a few changes were made (black writers were added, as well as the black character Jim Dexter, played by Leonard Simon). The changes didn't help the low-rated sitcom, and it was placed back into its bottle after only thirteen episodes.

Episodes were titled "The Pilot" (with guest star Tab Hunter), "The Shabelles" (with guest stars Don Cornelius and Wink Martindale), "Transition," "Photo Finish," "Uncle Harry" (with guest star Dody Goodman), "Something Alien This Way Comes" (with guest star Roy Orbison), "Engelbert Humpercricket," "No Holds Barred," "Wedding Bell Shablues," "Ballad of Dead Eye Dick" (with guest star Dr. Joyce Brothers), "King Kahommi's Curse," "Keith's Car Crusade," and "Dr. Jekyll and Mr. Burrows." The executive producers were Charles and Lawrence Gordon, Bob Comfort, and Rick Kellard; the producer was Ronald E. Frazier; the writers included Linda Morris, Vic Rauseo, James Berg, Tony Colvin, Bob Comfort, Scott Spencer Gordon, Rick Kellard, Danny Jacobson, Ria Nepus, Fred Rubin, Barry Vigon, Michael Russnow, and Stan Zimmerman; the directors included Bruce Bilson, Bob Sweeney, John Astin, and Alan Bergmann. Music was provided by Joseph Conlan, and the very Michael Jackson-esque theme song was performed by the group Shalamar.

Karen's Song MGM/United Artists. FOX. Saturday nights 9:30 (July 18, 1987–September 12, 1987). Thirteen episodes were videotaped in front of a live audience, but only nine aired.

Karen's Song was *Cougar Town* long before the term "cougar" was even coined. The unintentional cougar was one Karen Matthews (Patty Duke), born in Yonkers, New York. Suzanne Pleshette played Karen in the original pilot made for CBS. Karen is a diehard Los Angeles Dodgers fan who is about to turn forty. Ten years earlier, her husband, Zach (Granville Van Dusen), left, and she slowly had to piece her life back together. In the debut episode, Karen has just moved into a new condo, and is promoted at her workplace, Dexter's Publishing. Besides an increase in pay, her new position also comes with an admirer twelve years her junior—the building's sandwich salesman, Steven Foreman (Lewis Smith). Foreman owns his own business, A Catered Affair, and traveled extensively as a child (his father was in sales for Coca-Cola). He gives Karen a complimentary sandwich as a gesture of friendship, and a spark is ignited. Fanning the flames is Karen's superior and best friend, Claire Steiner (Lainie Kazan). Karen strongly resists the affair with the caterer (after all, she is the mother of an eighteen-year-old daughter in college named Laura, played by future *Desperate Housewives* co-star Teri Hatcher), but eventually gives in to the mutual attraction. Not seen in the pilot episode was Karen's previous romantic interest, neighbor and real estate broker Michael Brand (Charles Levin). Surprisingly, Brand is extremely supportive of Karen's May/December romance. In fact, everyone was supportive except for the TV viewers. Abysmal ratings led to the airing of only nine of the thirteen videotaped episodes of the program during the summer of 1987. The opening credits feature the show's title on a musical staff. The notes then drop down and, much in the manner of a 1950s game show hosted by Jack Narz called *Dotto*, Patty Duke's face is then drawn onscreen like a "connect the dots" puzzle. Appropriately, all of the episodes of *Karen's Song* shared titles with popular songs. This was Patty Duke's third failed sitcom of the 1980s, following *It Takes Two* and *Hail to the Chief* (see the entries for both).

Episodes were titled "Take Me Out to the Ball Game," "Tonight's the Night," "Happy Birthday," "Do You Want to Know a Secret?," "It Was Fascination," "You've Got a Friend," "Heart Attack," "Seems Like Old Times," "Aloha Oe," "High Noon," "Don't Fence Me In," "My Boy Bill," and "Take this Job and Shove It." The executive producers and creators were Linda Marsh and Margie Peters; the writers were Linda Marsh and Margie Peters; the directors included Bonnie Franklin, Asaad Kelada, Peter Baldwin, J. D. Lobue, Valentine Mayer, Jack Shea, and Allan Smithee. Music was provided by Doug Timm.

Patty Duke and Lewis Smith, the stars of the short-lived FOX sitcom *Karen's Song*, pose for a publicity shot.

Knight and Daye Partner Television Productions/Imagine Television. NBC. Saturday night 9:30 (July 8, 1989), Wednesday nights 9:30 (July

12, 1989–August 9, 1989), and Monday night 9:30 (August 14, 1989). Seven episodes were videotaped in front of a live audience.

By the time *Knight and Daye* debuted in 1989, real live personality radio was, for the most part, just a distant memory or at least on the wane. That may have been the issue for the program's poor showing in the Nielsen Ratings—the younger demographics just couldn't relate. Decades earlier, Hank Knight (Jack Warden) and Everett Daye (Mason Adams) were thrown together (mostly because of their names) to host a morning radio program in New York on fictional radio station WLMM. The program became a huge success—Daye was the straight man, and Knight was the funny one. In real life, they lived up to their names and were like "Night and Day" (that song fittingly used as the program's theme song, performed Frank Sinatra-style). The opening credits show them in their black-and-white heyday. However, in 1989, the once-popular radio team had been estranged for over thirty years because both men had designs on the same woman, Gloria (Hope Lange), who eventually became Daye's bride. Gloria admittedly dated both men, and while Knight was the most fun, Daye was the rock steady choice for a mate with whom she could imagine growing old. She never regretted her decision, but did regret what it did to their respective radio careers. Daye and the family settled in beautiful San Diego and one day, out of the blue, Daye was contacted by the program director (Julia Campbell as Janet Glickman, whom both men refer to as Miss Fortunato—a past mutual acquaintance) of a local radio station with the call letters KLOP (number 15 in the ratings in a sixteen-station radio market) to host a morning radio program that would reunite him with his down-on-his-luck former co-host (Knight now dons a red toupee and dresses in a flashy manner, although he has holes in the soles of his shoes). Knight frequently refers to himself as "The Big Red Machine" (also the nickname for the Cincinnati Reds). Initially, Daye was dead set against the reunion, and Knight opted to host the program alone. Daye eventually acquiesced and the once-great duo find that the chemistry is still there—the old magic still works, and the insults fly. Others in the Daye household included zoologist daughter Ellie, played by Lela Ivey (who said that she had great difficulty getting rid of "gorilla smell" on her person); her Latino husband, Cito Escobar (Joe Lala); and their children, Chris (Emily Schulman), Amy (Shiri Appleby), Dougie (Glenn Walker Harris, Jr.), and Laurie (Brittany Thornton). NBC touted this series as "*The Odd Couple* of the airwaves." Despite the considerable amount of talent in front of and behind the camera, the program survived very few nights and days, and was canceled after only seven episodes and three time slots.

Episodes were titled "Knight and Daye," "Sugar Mama," "New York, New York?," "Still Motile After All These Years," "Stalk Radio," "Goodbye, Mr. Scrimshaw," and "The Last Honest Man in America." The executive producers and creators were Lowell Ganz and Babaloo Mandel; the producer was Jason Shubb; the writers included Lowell Ganz and Babaloo Mandel; the directors included Bill Persky and Jeffrey Ganz. Music was provided by David Michael Frank.

Ladies' Man Herbert B. Leonard Productions/20th Century Fox. CBS. Monday nights 8:30 (October 27, 1980–January 26, 1981) and Saturday nights 9:30 (February 7, 1981–February 21, 1981). Sixteen episodes were videotaped in front of a live audience, but only fifteen aired.

This short-lived sitcom starred Lawrence Pressman as Alan Thackeray, a single dad (divorced from Sheila [Julie Cobb], who cheated on him at her workplace). Alan lives in apartment 305 with an old trunk serving as his living-room coffee table. He scores a job as the only male writer for a ladies' magazine called *Women's Life*, and comedy ensues in his attempts to fit in (in the office with number 212 on the door). Pressman said, "It was like *The Mary Tyler Moore Show* turned inside out. Mary was the only female in the WJM newsroom, and I was the only guy in the offices of

The cast of mostly ladies on CBS's *Ladies' Man* included (clockwise from top) Karen Morrow, Louise Sorel, Lawrence Pressman, Betty Kennedy, Allison Argo, Natasha Ryan, and Simone Griffeth (photograph courtesy Lawrence Pressman).

Women's Life." He added, "It was also a throwback to all of those old Jack Lemmon 'fish-out-of-water' comedies—the last of an era. It was an anomaly—the program possessed a lot of sweetness. CBS loved the show, but unfortunately it never found an audience." A running gag on the show had Alan using the women's room after removing the *wo* from the restroom door (and replacing it afterwards).

Pressman's co-stars were Herb Edelman (listed as Herbert Edelman in the credits) as Reggie Eglash—accountant for the magazine (the only other man occasionally seen in the office), and Louise Sorel as Elaine S. Holstein—the managing editor. Pressman recalled, "Herb and Louise used to be married in real life. They were divorced by the time we did the show, but they parted on good terms and remained friends. The ultimate professionals, they had no problems working together." Others in the cast included Simone Griffeth as Gretchen, in research; Betty Kennedy and Allison Argo as magazine writers airheaded Andrea with a mad crush on Alan, and naïve Susan who has aspirations of becoming a playwright, respectively; Karen Morrow as Thackeray's next-door neighbor and fill-in mom/babysitter Betty Brill with four sons of her own (married nineteen years to the unseen Harry, on whom she considered cheating with Bert the mailman, but couldn't go through with it); and Natasha Ryan as Alan's ten-year-old daughter (an only child), Amy.

Many situations in this situation comedy revolve around Alan's attempts to balance life as a single father and a career man. We get to see Alan's ex, Sheila, in the two-parter called "The Games." Julie Cobb, as a brunette in the role, recalled, "I had sort of a run playing ex-wives in those days on *Hearts Afire* and *Designing Women*. I had fun and became friends with Larry [Pressman] and Louise [Sorel]." Among Alan's assignments for the magazine was an article about "Sexual Harrassment and the Working Woman," and one for which he had to beg, titled "Why Women Pose Nude." In the latter we discovered that researcher Gretchen had posed nude years earlier and threatened to quit the magazine, lest her co-workers find out her little secret. All of the workers had to answer to the demanding, unseen publisher, "Mimsy" Davenport. About his professional name, Pressman shared, "My real name is David Pressman, but Actor's Equity already had a David Pressman, so I became Lawrence Pressman, and a schizoid was born." Pressman also co-starred in *Mulligan's Stew* with Elinor Donahue in 1977, in *Stockard Channing in Just Friends* in 1979, in *Doogie Howser, M. D.* from 1989–1993, and, most recently, in *Hart of Dixie* (as Vernon "Brando" Wilkes) and *Transparent* (as Ed Paskowitz).

Episodes were titled "The Pilot," "Play It Again, Alan," "Gretchen's Problem," "Amy's Fear," "An Obtuse Triangle," "The Mugger," "Holstein's Affair," "Alan's Infidelity Column," "Andrea's Crush," "Alan's Money Problem," "Susan the Playwright," "Think Young, Ladies," "Women Need Not Apply," "Games, Parts One and Two," and the unaired "The Committee." The executive producer was Herbert B. Leonard; the producers were Michael Loman and Lee Miller; the writers included Mitzi McCall, Beverly Bloomberg, Carmen Finestra, John Steven Owen, Deidre Fay, Stuart Wolpert, Michael Weinberger, Doug and Chip Keyes, Michael Loman, and Bert Convy's wife, Anne; the directors were John Tracy, Lee Miller, and Wes Kenney (sometimes credited as H. Wesley Kenney). The creator was David Wiltse. Music was provided by Jack Elliott, with lyrics by Brian Neary.

The Last Precinct Stephen J. Cannell Productions. NBC. Sunday night (January 26, 1986, after Super Bowl XX), Friday nights 9:00 (April 11, 1986–May 30, 1986). Eight episodes were filmed single-camera style without a laugh track.

Similar to, but not as funny as, *Police Squad*, *The Last Precinct* was an hour-long cop spoof that would probably have worked better in a half-hour format. An hour was possibly just too much of an average thing. The action took place in seedy Precinct 56, which was, for all intents and purposes, a dumping ground for misfits and eccentrics within the police department. Whoopie cushions, naps in the morgue drawers, and inappropriate behavior at the office were all commonplace. The program boasted an extremely large cast, consisting of Jonathan Perpich as Sergeant Price Pascall; Ernie Hudson as Night Train; Wings Hauser as the sheriff, the impulsive Lieutenant Hobbs (always attempting to one-up everyone in his path); Randi Brooks as Mel "Melba" Brubaker (a blond transsexual); Rick Ducommon as Raid; Vijay Amritraj as Alphabet (Shivaramanbhai Poonchwalla); Yana Nirvana as Sergeant Haggerty; Pete Willcox as King, the Elvis impersonator; Keenan Wynn as Butch; Hank Rolike as Sundance (the last two being the senior members of the force); a dog named Waldo; Adam West as Captain Wright, and Lucy Lee Flippin as Rina. About her character, Flippin shared, "Rina was very uptight, worked in the basement of the Precinct in the Evidence Department. She had a flirtation with Ric Ducommon's character named Raid in the Halloween episode. We were in a haunted house." About a few of her co-stars on the program, Flippin added, "Adam West was always upbeat, amusing and pleasant. Keenan Wynn was a curmudgeon. As a tennis fan I loved that Vijay was in the cast—he was really nice and eager. Ernie Hudson was a real gentleman and very talented. I always thought Wings Hauser was a quirky and surprising actor whom I lost track of." The program definitely had an "oldies" feel to it with songs such as "Bad, Bad Leroy Brown," "I Fought the Law," "Blue Suede Shoes," and "That's All Right Mama" among the many soundtrack selections. Adam West ended the debut episode with the same words used to end his *Batman* series each week— "Same bat time, same bat channel" (followed by the familiar "Na na na na" of "The Batman Theme"). Flippin's synopsis of working on *The Last Precinct* is, "The whole experience seemed cumbersome. There were too many characters, and the show offended a lot of 'groups.' Even a friend of mine called the network to complain. It was unrelenting lame, locker room humor. It debuted off the charts, after the Super Bowl, but just deteriorated quickly after that." (That, incidentally, was Super Bowl XX, in which the Chicago Bears defeated the New England Patriots 46–10.) Almost three months after that debut episode, *The Last Precinct* became a regular series, but failed to catch on without its strong lead-in. Cast member Rick Ducommun died on June 17, 2015. Some sources say he was fifty-eight; others say sixty-two.

Episodes were titled "The Last Precinct," "The Gorilla-Giant," "Mr. Cool," "I Want My Mummy," "Never Cross a Vampire," "A Ghost of a Chance," "Toehold," and "Three-Ring Circus." The executive producers and creators were Frank Lupo and Stephen J. Cannell. Flippin's memories of working with the late Cannell are, "He was very hands on, hardworking and easy on the eyes. He seemed really grounded. During the run of our show, there was a fancy birthday party for him at the Roosevelt Hotel in Hollywood." The producers were Jim Mulligan, William F. Phillips, and Jo Swerling, Jr.; the writers included Frank Lupo and Stephen J. Cannell, and the directors included Hy Averback and Michael Lange. Music was provided by John Caper, Jr.

Learning the Ropes Cineplex Odeon Television. CTV. Syndicated. Air dates and times varied. (September 18, 1988–March 31, 1989). Twenty-six episodes were filmed in front of a live audience.

Prior to his scoring the lead role in this syndicated sitcom, Lyle Alzado was a defensive end for eleven seasons in the NFL (Denver Broncos, Cleveland Browns, Los Angeles Raiders). He was nicknamed Mr. Mean and left only after being sidelined by a career-ending Achilles tendon injury. He then moved on to a career in professional wrestling and did some occasional acting on episodic TV shows and films. A company called Producers Group International, headed by Dennis O'Neill and his wife, Jill, spearheaded a project to bring Alzado and wrestling to a new audience. A vehicle to be titled *Learning the Ropes* was then created by Ed Self. Alzado was to play a single father of two, whose wife had left to study law in London. This left him to fend for himself and raise their two teenagers—fifteen-year-old daughter Ellen (Nicole Stoffman, who had previously appeared in *Degrassi Junior High*) and seventeen-year-old son Mark (Yannick Bisson, later of *Sue Thomas, F. B. Eye*). Ellen had a friend named Beth (Jacqueline Mahon) who was obsessed with the opposite sex, and Mark had a timid best friend named Brad (Gordon Woolvett). Alzado's character was named Robert Randall, and he and his wards reside at 34 Hampton Street. Robert is a teacher and vice principal at the exclusive Ridgedale Valley Preparatory School (Ellen and Mark were students there). To make ends meet, Robert moonlights as a professional wrestler named "The Masked Maniac" (portrayed by Steve "Dr. Death" Williams, who was injured numerous times while working on the show). Because he is masked, he is able to keep this part of his life a secret from everyone except his kids. Each episode contains at least one filmed wrestling segment with NWA (National Wrestling Alliance) stars, such as Jimmy Garvin, Lex Luger, Tully Blanchard, and Ric Flair. French and English teacher Carol Dixon (Cheryl Wilson) has a thing for Robert and continually tries to get him to take her out on a date. In the original unaired pilot episode, they were an item, but those scenes were edited and plans for a romance between Robert and Carol were nixed. Barry Stevens played Dr. Jerry Larson, the psychiatrist who lives next door. Carol's father is Principal Whitcomb Mallory (Richard Farrell), Robert's superior. The program ran in Canada on CTV, and in the U.S. in syndication. Episodes were filmed in an abandoned tire plant in Toronto. Reviews for Alzado's acting ability (along with the other wrestlers) were not kind, and after twenty-six episodes had been produced, the series experienced a tapout.

Episode titles for *Learning the Ropes* don't appear to exist, but situations included having Robert fill in for son Mark's regular biology teacher. Mark then thinks he'll have a cakewalk to a good grade, but is sadly mistaken. In another episode, Carol Dixon attends a wake held for a fellow wrestler at Robert's home. The problem—keeping the other wrestlers in attendance from revealing Robert's alter ego. The executive producer was Robert Halmi, Jr.; the producers were Michael W. Hadley, David J. Patterson, and Charles Falzon; the writers included Terry Saltzan and Neil Rosen; the directors included Alan Ehrlich. The creator was Ed Self. Music was provided by David Roberts (he also sang the theme song called "Learning the Ropes").

Legmen Universal Television. NBC. Friday nights 8:00 (January 20, 1984–February 3, 1984) and Friday nights 9:00 (February 17, 1984–March 16, 1984). Eight hour-long episodes were filmed without a laugh track.

Two college men, sharing an apartment, find work as the legmen for the Tri-Star Bail Bonds Agency (with the number 14425 on the door, open 24 hours) to pay their bills. David Taylor (J. T. Terlesky) is studying law (his dad owned Taylor's TV and Appliance store in Van Nuys), and Jack Gage (Bruce Greenwood) wants to be an engineer (and plays a very decent rock and roll guitar, speaks fluent Swedish, and mixes drinks with a hand drill). Their first bail bondsmen boss was Oscar Amismedi (Don Calfa), who often had difficulty paying the boys, but he was replaced by the much more stern and gruff Tom Bannon (Claude Akins) in later episodes, under the guise that Amismedi couldn't take the pressure of the business anymore and moved in with his sister in Lake Havasu, Arizona. Bannon doesn't want to keep the boys on as employees, but they are contracted for three more cases. Also in the cast were Bannon's (and Amismedi's) secretary, the dour, cigar-smoking Mrs. Yehudi (Connie Sawyer), and Police Lieutenant Tedisco (Robert DoQui). The program's title was most fitting, as David and Jack find themselves consistently surrounded by beautiful young women. Guest stars included Jan Smithers, Janine Turner, Frank Bonner, Richard Erdman, Mickey Gilley, Bernie Kopell, Jan Murray, Dick Shawn, Tim Robbins, and Rita Wilson.

Episodes were titled "Take the Credit and Run," "Knight at Casanova's," "The Return of Apple Dan Bonny," "I Shall Be Re-Released,"

"Poseidon Indenture," "Still Alive at Five," "How the Other Half Dies," and "A Woman's Work." The executive producers were Richard Chapman, Bill Dial, and Andrew Mirisch; the producers were Alex Beaton, April Kelly, and Robert Bennett Steinhauer; the writers included Richard Chapman, Bill Dial, Joel Surnow, and Andrew Mirisch; the directors included Jeffrey Hayden, John Llewellyn Moxey, Allen Reisner, Roger Young, and Corey Allen. Music was provided by John Beal, Howard Pearl, Paul Chihara, and Dan Foliart. The theme song was a rock and roll number called "Squeezy Easy." The episode credits for this short-lived series are unique in that they move around on the screen, never standing still.

Leo and Liz in Beverly Hills 40 Share Productions/Universal Television. CBS. Friday nights 8:30 (April 25, 1986–June 6, 1986). Six episodes and a pilot (the pilot as part of *George Burns Comedy Week*) for a total of seven were filmed single-camera style with a laugh track.

On October 16, 1985, *George Burns Comedy Week* (see entry) featured an episode titled "The Couch" (the most popular episode of that comedy anthology series). Liz (Valerie Perrine) and her husband, Leo Green (Harvey Korman), leave New Jersey behind when his cup runneth over with success in the brassiere-manufacturing business. Their destination: Beverly Hills (specifically, the house at 105 North Bevon Drive). To paraphrase the old adage: "You can take the Greens out of Jersey, but you can't take the Jersey out of the Greens." Unlike the stars of *The Beverly Hillbillies* and *Easy Street* who were genuinely oblivious to the fact that they didn't fit in with their new surroundings, the Greens are painfully aware of it and make every attempt to rectify the situation, including attempting to have an A-List celebrity at their party. In the episode called "The Couch" that served as the pilot for what became known as *Leo and Liz in Beverly Hills*, the Greens purchase a rare, 1921 art deco Fermier sofa at auction (for the hefty price of $20,350) as a gift for their daughter Mitzi's wedding (Mitzi was played by Carrie Fisher in the pilot, and Sue Ball in the series). It is just one more failed attempt to impress the neighbors and the parents of their future son-in-law, Bunky Winthrop (Mark Steen). When the pilot became a series, the surname of Winthrop was changed to Fedderson, and Bunky was now played by Peter Aykroyd, and his parents, Diane and Jerry, by Deborah Harmon and Ken Kimmons, respectively. (Incidentally, Jerry is also Leo's accountant.) Other series regulars included Michael J. Pollard as Leonard the handyman, and Julie Payne as housekeeper Lucille Trumbley. Despite having the immensely popular and talented Steve Martin on the producing, writing, and directing staff, the program failed to find an audience and was gone from prime-time after only six regular season episodes.

Episodes were titled were "The Couch" (pilot), "The A List" (with guest star Liberace), "Perfect Days Sleepless Nights," "In the Beginning," "Unaccustomed as I Am to Public Speaking," "Chapter Eleven," and "Remodeling." The executive producer was Steve Martin; the producers were Paul Perlove and Carl Gottlieb; the writers included Steve Martin, Paul Perlove, Carl Gottlieb and Neil Cox; the directors included Steve Martin, Paul Perlove, Pamela Pettler, and David Axelrod. Music was provided by James Burt, Charles Fox, and David Michael Frank. The opening theme song was "Mister Sandman."

Lewis and Clark Carson Productions. NBC. Thursday nights 8:30 (October 29, 1981–November 19, 1981), Saturdays night 8:30 (December 12, 1981–January 2, 1982), and Friday nights 8:00 (July 2, 1982–July 30, 1982). Thirteen episodes were videotaped in front of a live audience.

Sharing a name with the explorers named (Meriwether) Lewis and (William) Clark, Stu Lewis and Roscoe Clark are in business together. About the program's title, producer and writer Ed Scharlach shared, "NBC, in its comedic wisdom, thought it would be cute to name Gabe and Guich's characters 'Lewis' and 'Clark,' and call the series *Lewis and Clark*. We objected (fruitlessly), saying that people are going to think it's a show about explorers—and the furthest thing from a comedy series. And few would even watch it once. Which is essentially what happened." Much in the manner of earlier sitcoms *Guestward Ho* and *Green Acres*, Stu Lewis (Gabe Kaplan) decided to leave the big city to fulfill a lifelong dream—owning a country-and-western nightclub. His wife of fifteen years, Alicia (Ilene Graff), whom he affectionately refers to as "my precious little Bambi nose," and two kids—Kelly (Amy Linker) and Keith (David Hollander)—were very happy in New York, but they all love Stu very much and went along for the ride (not quietly, of course) to tiny Luckenback, in the Texas panhandle. There, the Lewises buy a house (with the number 825 on the door) and a nightclub. Said club, with the humorous sign "Always under new management," had numerous previous owners (nine in just the past six years), but is now known as The Nassau County Café. Comedy and situations were derived from the Lewis's attempts to adjust to a slower pace. Fulfilling the program's title, the café comes with a manager named Roscoe Clark, played by Guich Koock (formerly of *Carter Country*). Clark is not as much of a backwoods hayseed as he appears in the mirror. About Kaplan and Koock, Scharlach shared, "Guich Koock was charming, and had a nice comedy chemistry and an entertaining working relationship with Gabe. He was very professional. The whole cast was terrific. Gabe also had an engaging rapport with Ilene Graff, who played his wife." Others in the cast included Big John, the bartender (Michael McManus); Wendy, the banjo-playing waitress (Wendy Holcombe); beer distributor and fix-it man Silas Jones (Clifton James); and Lester, a bearded drunk (Aaron Fletcher). The sitcom was from Carson Productions, but as Scharlach recalled, "Johnny Carson was not 'hands on' with this series. His company TV executive, John McMahon, a former NBC executive, was the liaison between Carson Productions and us. However, Johnny's son Ricky worked on our staff as a production aide. Our executive producers were George Shapiro and Howard West, managers of Gabe Kaplan (also of me and my writing partner Tom Tenowich). Though this show didn't succeed, the next series they executive produced, starring one of their comedian clients, worked fine—*Seinfeld*." The nightclub's armadillo races were the biggest draw, and armadillo was often on the club's menu as well (perhaps the losers of the races?). One episode, "A Family Affair," takes an interesting dramatic turn in which Roscoe discovers that his real mother is the woman his father is about to marry. About that episode, Scharlach added, "The mom episode was a good premise for our show, which worked better when it got a little deeper than comedy banter, as did the *Mork and Mindy* episodes that Tom [Tenowich] and I wrote and produced. Also, it provided us with a chance to have a talented guest star. As a Broadway fan, it was exciting to write for *Pajama Game*'s Janis Paige." One episode titled "The Uptight End" reunited Kaplan with a few of his former *Kotter* co-stars, about which Scharlach reflected, "I vaguely remember the *Kotter* reunion episode. I think it was fun, and comfortable for Gabe to have the boys in our show. Probably was Gabe's idea to do this. It also could have been the network's as a possible PR boost to our ratings." When asked why Gabe Kaplan occasionally spoke directly to the audience to set up a particular episode, Scharlach stated, "I believe that the forum for Gabe to work his comedy to a live audience was built into the basic structure of the series. As a stand-up, he was most effective and comfortable doing jokes directly to the audience—more comfortable as a comedian than as an actor. Our series had a deeper level than *Welcome Back, Kotter*, and that presented more of an acting challenge to Gabe." This was supposed to be Kaplan's big TV comeback, but up against *Magnum, P. I.*, it failed to find an audience. A move to Saturday nights in December of 1981 didn't help much, and *Lewis and Clark* was gone from NBC's prime-time lineup by early 1982. The remaining episodes were burned off in July of that year.

Episodes were titled "Welcome to Luckenbach," "Opposites Attract," "The Horse's Tale," "Alicia's New York Night," "The Uptight End" (with former *Welcome Back, Kotter* co-stars Robert Hegyes and Lawrence Hilton-Jacobs), "The Family Affair" (with guest star Janis Paige as Rose Wagner, Roscoe Clark's biological mother), "Oil," "Dear John," "Friends," "Yellow Stu of Texas," "In Charm's Way," and "Tex Hex." The executive producers were George Shapiro and Howard West; the producers were Tom Tenowich and Ed Scharlach; the writers included Tom Tenowich, Ed Scharlach, Gabe Kaplan, Richard Gurman, Hank Bradford, Laura Levine, Jerry Ross, Bob Baublitz, and Alan Myerson; the directors included Will Mackenzie and Alan Myerson. About the directors, Scharlach stated, "Loved working with those directors—who added much to the series. Will MacKenzie had been a comedy actor I admired, and I crossed paths with him several times as a director of shows I wrote. When I was in college at Berkeley in the 1960s, I spent as much time as I could in San Francisco seeing the iconic improv group The Committee. Many of its members wound up in TV and movies—and Alan Myerson was The Committee's director—so a thrill for me to work with." The creator was Gabe Kaplan. The theme song was written and performed by Bob Duncan.

Life and Times of Eddie Roberts (L. A. T. E. R.) Columbia Pictures Television. Syndicated. Air times varied. (January 7, 1980–April 4, 1980). Sixty-four episodes were videotaped (five episodes aired each week for thirteen weeks—"Take Me Out to the Ballgame" was the lone repeat).

Much in the same manner as *Mary Hartman, Mary Hartman*, *The Life and Times of Eddie Roberts (L. A. T. E. R.)* was a soap spoof. There were interwoven elements of drama and comedy, rendering this daily program a dramedy. The action revolves around a college professor named Eddie Roberts (Renny Temple) at mythical Cranepool University. About his character, Renny Temple recalled, "He was a little bit of a simpleton—a white collar guy. Our show was a white collar version of *Mary Hartman, Mary Hartman*. Eddie really had little depth. The entire process was very quick. There was no pilot for the series. The show was bought for syndication because of the reputation of Ellis and Ann Marcus. We were hired and on the set within three weeks. Because the program was syndicated, there was no network red tape, and things happened fast." Eddie's athletic wife, Dolores (Udana Power), has aspirations of becoming a major league baseball player. With the University's name being Cranepool, and the running baseball theme, it's likely someone on the creative staff was a New York Mets fan. The Robertses have one daughter, Chrissy (Allison Balson). One of the Cranepools, for whom the university was named, is a professor and colleague of Eddie's (Stephen Parr as Tony Cranepool). Temple said, "To the best of my recollection, the outdoor scenes for the opening credits were videotaped at Claremont University in Claremont, California." Others in the cast included Joan Hotchkis as Lydia, and Allen Case as Dean Knitzer. The favorite eatery is the Kluck O'Rama. Many controversial topics were addressed during the program's short run, with race, child custody, sexual dysfunction, homosexuality, strikes, courtroom battles, and paternity suits among them. About the topics, Temple shared, "One of the problems with the show was that these subjects came and went at a very rapid pace. They all could have lasted longer and milked for more episodes. We'd barely scratch the surface of one topic, and already be on to the next. In fact, my wife in real life, actress Caren Kaye, played my mistress in a couple of episodes, but once again the subject was not fully explored. We moved on to the next subject, and it was forgotten—something that would never happen in real life." It should be noted that Kaye and Temple had a long run together (fourteen years) as part of the creative improv group called War Babies. Was it tough doing five shows a week? Temple said, "Not really. It actually became easy as the scripts had a certain rhythm to them. Because we did five shows a week, there were no cue cards, and our episodes were not word perfect as a result. There were very, very few retakes because of the time restraints, and because editing was expensive. Some flubs and stumbles were left in.

We had many great directors, however, who were used to working at a quick pace." Temple added, "I rarely watch myself on TV. It's one thing to look in a mirror, but I don't like seeing myself from all of those different camera angles. However, after our show had been on a few weeks, I asked my manager to show me a tape of the show. I was very upset by my own performance—it was so over the top. I asked my manager why she never told me, but she said that she was so engrossed in and enthralled by the whole process, she didn't really notice. I immediately harnessed my performance, but it came too late. The program was already experiencing ratings trouble, and we'd been moved to the wee hours of the morning in some markets. After thirteen weeks and over sixty episodes, we were canceled." Temple shared a couple of anecdotes about the show, "The funny, offbeat lady who played my wife, Udana Power, and I are still friends. We really didn't know one another very well, but after a few weeks we loosened up considerably. In fact, in our first bedroom scene together, we were both under the covers and I had shorts on, but I noticed that Udana was totally naked. She really wanted to get into the moment, and boy did she ever. Also, these were very different times. There was a certain coolness associated with drug use, and I vividly recall that in some dressing rooms on some shows there were little packets of cocaine available in the ceiling panels. This was shocking to me, but it was rather commonplace back in the day."

Episodes were titled "Coming to Grips with One's Sexual Problems," "Love Me or Leave Me," "Those Were the Days," "Roses Are Red Violets Are Blue How About TSU?," "Dolores and Chrissy Return," "Stress Is As Stress Does," "School Busing Program Begins," "Racial Warfare Film at 11," "Contraception with Exception," "Cranepool U Gets Ping-Ponged," "Trying to Get the Feelings Again," "Lots of Secrets," "Take Me Out to the Ball Game," "The Truth and Nothing but the Truth," "Tell Me Where It Hurts," "A Remedy for Sexual Dysfunction," "Will the Real Samantha Higgins Please Stand Up," "It's So Nice to Have a Man Around the House," "Getting to Know You," "And in this Corner," "Cranepool U Announces Tenure Recipient," "Monkey Business at Cranepool U," "Wait 'Til the Guinness People Find Out," "Trying to Solve Problems," "There's Definitely a Foul at the Kluck O'Rama," "Guess Who's Coming to Dinner," "Eddie and Dolores and Herb and Marcia," "Do Unto Others as They May Do Unto You," "Pass the Aspirin, Please," "Trying to Deal with a Kidnapping," "Trying to Outkid a Kidnapper," "How Do You Spell Relief?," "Playing the Waiting Game," "Getting Beneath the Surface," "Time to Go to Confession," "True Confessions," "A Senatorial Hearing of a Lesser Degree," "Everybody's Got a Problem," "The Ups and Downs of a Relationship," "Some Good News and Some Bad News," "Child Custody and TSU Side Effects Are Issues of the Day," "An End to the Gay Old Life?," "Hot News for Everyone—Film at 11," "Winging It at the Kluck O'Rama," "Home Sweet Home," "There's No Business like Porn Business," "Trying to Understand the Legalese," "Gertrude's Day in Court," "The Press Is after Gertrude," "Absence Makes the Heart Grow Fonder," "Nervous about a Once-in-a-Lifetime Opportunity," "Getting to Know You Getting to Know all about You," "A Gay Experience in Television," "Do You Promise to Tell the Truth the Whole Truth?," "Perry Mason Would Have Been Proud," "A Paternity Suit for Eddie," "All in the Family," "An Encounter Session for Eddie's Parents," "A Request to Call off the Strike," "Confession Time at Cranepool U," "Here Comes the Bride," "Love Conquers All," "Telling It like It Is," and "One Shocking Revelation after Another." The producer was Leonard Friedlander; the writers and creators were Ellis and Ann Marcus; the director was Tracey Roberts. Music was provided by Peter Kimmel.

Life with Lucy Aaron Spelling Productions/Lucille Ball Productions. ABC. Saturday nights 8:00 (September 20, 1986–November 15, 1986). Fourteen episodes were filmed in front of a live audience, but only eight aired.

After a twelve-year absence from series television, seventy-five-year-old Lucille Ball agreed to do another sitcom if she had full content control. Thus, no pilot episode was necessary for *Life with Lucy* to get onto ABC's prime-time Saturday night schedule. Many of the old writers from *I Love Lucy* and *The Lucy Show* were back again for this venture. The problem with this new Lucy show was that it was almost identical to the other Lucy shows. The audience had seen it all before—no new territory was covered here. The names were different—she was now Lucy Baxter, and her co-star Gale Gordon who was now called Curtis McGibbon, but the situations were unchanged. Lucy was a meddler and a menace, and Gale her blustery foil. Lucy played an energetic, health-crazed grandmother to Becky (Jenny Lewis) and Kevin (Philip J. Amelio II). Lucy moves into a third-floor bedroom in her daughter and son-in-law's house in an attempt to help them with their finances (they weren't quite making ends meet) and assist with the kids. A widow, she inherits half interest in the M&B Hardware store in South Pasadena, California. Curtis and Lucy's late husband were business partners in that store. Lucy is Margo's (Ann Dusenberry) mother, and Curtis was Margo's husband Ted's father. Because Lucy forgets to pick up the grandkids from school one day, and accidentally starts a fire at the store, Curtis decides to move in as well (he wants a more dependable person than Lucy looking after the kids). The sitcom's second episode is likely the most memorable for this forgettable series because of a guest appearance by John Ritter as himself (in real life, Lucy was a big fan of his physical comedy prowess). When he visits the hardware store, seeking crystal doorknobs, he is injured several times as a result of Lucy's mayhem, and has to stay with Lucy and the McGibbon family while he recuperates. In other episodes, Lucy relies on that old chestnut of playing the saxophone badly; she becomes glued to Curtis while he is appearing on a Mr. Fix-It TV show; she has people believing that Curtis had died; she has a cake fight with her sister Audrey (Audrey Meadows); and she accidentally sells her grandson's teddy bear at a garage sale.

This program was the most eagerly anticipated of the 1986 fall season, but soon became its most disappointing. Ratings the first week were decent because a lot of viewers were curious, but by week two the show totally fell off the ratings radar. It was gone from ABC's prime-time lineup after only eight of the fourteen filmed episodes had aired. If only Lucy had gone in a different direction, the program might have caught on, but it wasn't meant to be. Sadly, slightly more than two years later, Lucy passed away following complications from heart surgery.

Episodes were titled "One Good Grandparent Deserves Another," "Lucy Makes a Hit with John Ritter" (with guest stars John Ritter, Greg Mullavey, and Ruth Buzzi), "Lucy Among the Two-by-Fours" (with guest star Peter Graves), "Lucy Gets Her Wires Crossed" (with guest star Dick Gautier), "Lucy Is a Sax Symbol," "Lucy Makes Curtis Byte the Dust" (with guest star Dave Madden), "Lucy Legal Beagle" (with guest star Dena Dietrich), "Mother of the Bride" (with guest star Audrey Meadows), "Lucy and the Guard Goose," "Lucy and Curtis Up a Tree," "Lucy's Green Thumb," "Breaking Up Is Hard to Do," "The World's Greatest Grandma," and "'Twas the Flight by Christmas." The producers were Douglas S. Cramer, Gary Morton, Aaron Spelling, Linda Morris, Vic Rauseo, E. Duke Vincent, Bob Carroll, Jr., and Madelyn Davis; the writers included Bob Carroll, Jr., Madelyn Davis, Bob Fisher, Arthur Marx, Casey Keller, Linda Morris, Vic Rauseo, Steve Granat, Laura Levine, Mel Sherer, and Mark Tuttle; the directors included Marc Daniels, Peter Baldwin, and Bruce Bilson. Music was provided by Joel Higgins, Martin Silvestri, Jeremy Stone, and Rocky Moriana. Eydie Gorme performed the theme song.

Live-In Sternin and Fraser Ink, Inc/Columbia Television. CBS. Monday nights 8:00 (March 20, 1989–June 5, 1989). Nine episodes were videotaped in front of a live audience.

The title card for this short-lived sitcom included a picture of a kangaroo. It was an American sitcom with an Australian star—Lisa

Danny Mathews, played by Chris Young, was hot for the new live-in au pair, Lisa Wells, played by Lisa Patrick (left), on the short-lived CBS program *Live-In*.

Patrick as Lisa Wells. Wells grew up as part of a huge family in the Australian outback. The action centers on the Mathews Family, who reside in Northern New Jersey, and hires her as a nanny (or au pair), through a company called the Broder Agency. A live-in au pair is needed because Sarah Mathews (Kimberly Farr) is heading back to work at her managerial job at Macy's Department Store in Manhattan after giving birth to a girl they named Melissa (played by twins Melissa and Allison Lindsay) a short time earlier. Sarah often breastfeeds the baby at the dinner table, much to the discomfort and embarrassment of her teenage sons. The beautiful new addition to the Mathews household (the au pair, not the baby), gets the attention of the eldest son—a seventeen-year-old girl-crazy high school sophomore and Jason Bateman clone named Danny (Chris Young). Danny wants to date her, but she wants none of it (he is too young and she doesn't wish to jeopardize her new job). It doesn't help matters that their bedrooms are adjacent to one another. Danny's best friend, Gator (Lightfield Lewis), is equally infatuated with the new arrival and, in one episode, drills a hole through Danny's bedroom wall to see into Lisa's shower (but gets caught). Danny's younger brother, Peter (David Moscow), is an awkward, clarinet-playing fourteen-year-old whose hormones haven't yet fully engaged. Hugh Maguire played their dad, Ed, who works in a sporting goods store, and Jenny O'Hara is Muriel Spiegelman, the Mathews' nosy neighbor with a very distinct New York accent. The program's theme song was a reworking of the Turtles' classic, "Happy Together." Paired with the equally unsuccessful *Heartland* with Brian Keith on Monday nights (see entry), both were gone from the CBS lineup in nine weeks. The song "Oh, Yeah" by Yello, from *Ferris Bueller's Day Off*, was used in the debut episode when Danny and Gator are drilling a hole through the wall into Lisa's shower.

Episodes were titled "The Pilot," "The Coupe The Group and Everything," "Dan the Man B-Ball Scam," "Peter's I-dented-it Crisis," "Les Liaisons," "Harmless," "Mommy and Me and Au Pair Makes Three," "Kissing Cousin," "Daddy's Girl," and "It Takes Two to Tutor." The executive producers were Robert Sternin and Prudence Fraser; the producers were Jan Siegelman and David Nichols; the writers included Robert Sternin, Prudence Fraser, Ellen Guylas, David Nichols, and Trish Soodik; the directors included Will Mackenzie, Valentine Mayer, and Andrew D. Wayman. The creators were Robert Sternin and Prudence Fraser. Music was provided by Ray Colcord.

Living Dolls ELP Communications/Columbia Television. ABC. Tuesday night 8:30 (September 26, 1989), and Saturday nights 8:30 (September 30, 1989–December 30, 1989). Twelve episodes were videotaped in front of a live audience.

Living Dolls was a short-lived spinoff of *Who's the Boss?* In fact, Alyssa Milano guest starred in two episodes, and Tony Danza in one, but producer R. J. Colleary clarified things saying, "Because *Who's The Boss?* was still popular at the time, it made for a savvy tie-in, but *Living Dolls* wasn't a true spinoff. This is something they refer to as 'back door pilots.' The real goal of our show was re-creating '*The Facts of Life* with prettier girls.' They did the pilot before I came on board. I joined the fray between two stints with *Saved by the Bell*, so my guess as to why Vivica Fox was replaced by Halle Berry, Jonathan Ward by David Moscow, and Melissa Willis by Deborah Tucker is the response of test audiences." The show was chock full of stars—Leah Remini (later of *King of Queens*), future Oscar winner Halle Berry, and Michael Learned (*The Waltons*), and still it failed to click. Jack Blessing, who guest starred in the "Not So Sweet Smell of Success" episode, shared, "I remember thinking that Halle Berry, who was very young at the time, was one of the most beautiful humans I had ever seen. There was lots of friction between the girls, all bidding for super stardom. I thought it was pretty funny." About the show's ratings issues, Colleary opined, "The program did have a couple of problems. The writing wasn't great. Don't get me wrong, there were many writers on staff who went on to great things, but as a team for our show, they never jelled, and that's too bad because the series had a lot of potential. Remini was really the star of the show—Halle Berry up to then had been a model and had very little acting experience, so the cast was never a true ensemble. Also, Michael Learned, who was terrific on *The Waltons*, was out of her element on our sitcom. She was having a tough time making the transition to comedy, and was eventually let go. Secretly, I think she was very relieved. Additionally, this was Ross Brown's first shot at being a showrunner, and he had his hands full trying to keep the network and Tony Danza happy, with mixed results." Learned portrayed Trish Carlin, owner of the Carlin Agency (working extensively with teenagers)—a friend of the Micellis on *Who's the Boss?* Remini portrayed a rather irresponsible friend of Milano's Samantha character named Charlie Briscoe, who has been disowned by her mother. Berry played Emily, who wants to become a doctor, and works as a model to earn some money to pursue that dream. Martha (Alison Elliott) is the naïve member of the group, and is taken advantage of by vain, red-headed Caroline (former figure skater Deborah Tucker), who is never far from a mirror, and always "me-deep" in conversation. Trish's sixteen-year-old son, Rick, was portrayed by David Moscow. (When he misbehaves, his mother sternly calls him by his full name: Richard T. Carlin.) Rick is living a dream surrounded by these gorgeous young girls. The teenage girls are allowed to stay in Carlin's spacious home as long as they remain on the straight and narrow, work hard, attend all of the classes, and keep up with the exercise regimen. Near the end of the show's short run, Learned's character was "replaced" by her sister, Marion (Marion Ross) and Trish was said to be "away." About Ross, Colleary shared, "When she came on board, the whole dynamic of the show changed dramatically for the better. She was superb, very funny, the captain of the team, a great leader—it all came together quickly. If only the network had given us more time. We were so disappointed the suits let it die too soon." In the debut episode, Charlie is fed up with all of the rules and regulations imposed upon her and opts to leave the agency, but eventually comes to her senses once she realizes that opportunities outside of Trish's home are few and far between. After only twelve episodes and two different people running it, the modeling agency was closed for good.

Episodes were titled "It's All Done with Mirrors" (with guest star Alyssa Milano), "It's My Party" (with guest stars Alyssa Milano and Tony Danza), "Martha Means Well," "Seeing is Believing," "Guess Who's Not Coming to Dinner," "Rick's Model Girlfriend," "The Not So Sweet Smell of Success," "The Flash Is Always Greener," "He's Baaack," "C Is for Model," "And I Thought Modeling Was Hard," and "Beauty and the Beat." The executive producers were Ross Brown, Martin Cohan, Phyllis Glick, and Blake Hunter; the producers were R. J. Colleary, Valri Bromfield, Martha Williamson, and Michael Greenspan; the writers included Ross Brown, Eric Gilliland, Mark C. Miller, and Martha Williamson; and the directors included John Sgueglia, Andy Cadiff, Lee Bernhardi, James Widdoes, Valentine Mayer, and Jonathan Weiss. The creator was Ross Brown. Music was provided by Jonathan Wolff, John Beasley, and John Vester.

Lobo (see *The Misadventures of Sheriff Lobo* in Appendix A)

The Lucie Arnaz Show Taft Entertainment Group/Sam Denoff Productions. CBS. Tuesday nights 8:00 (April 2, 1985–April 23, 1985, and June 4, 1985–June 11, 1985). Six episodes were filmed in New York City with a laugh track.

Lucie Arnaz's first opportunity to "go it alone" came with an episode of *Here's Lucy* titled "Kim Cuts the Apron Strings," designed as a possible spinoff for her own series, but Lucie shared, "I think it tried too hard. I saw it again recently, and I'm rather glad it didn't become a series. It was cute at the time, but looking back, the other characters were just too extreme and not real." Over a decade after the end of her run as Kim Carter on *Here's Lucy*, Lucie did get a chance to do a series of her own that was to be called *Agony* (by Len Richmond and Anna Raeburn) in the role of Jane Lucas. Writer R. J. Colleary shared, "An agony aunt in Great Britain is an advice columnist. The original British version was much edgier, had a gay couple, and was very topical. America was just not ready for the British version, and the concept was watered down too much." Lucie recalled, "It was presented to me by producer David Kennedy, and was based on the very popular British series of that name. Right up until the last minute, it was to be called *Agony*. I even had giant clothespins with the show's title on them made up as gifts for the crew. However, the powers-that-be at the network thought the title was too short, and would be overlooked when one was looking through their *TV Guide*. The title was too short? That didn't hurt *M*A*S*H* or *Alice*, but the title suddenly became *The Lucie Arnaz Show*." That wasn't the only change the network made, as Lucie added, "They were very excited about the show and told me how much they loved it, only to change everyone in the cast except for Karen, who played my daffy secretary Loretta, and me. The original guy chosen to play my radio co-host on the show was brilliant. His name was Chip Zien, but I was told they had found someone much funnier. The guy they did select, Todd Waring, auditioned for the suits at CBS and they thought he was hilarious. Then there was the role of my boss on the show. Terrence Mann was up for the part, and Rod McLarty was brilliant in that role for the pilot, but Tony Roberts replaced him in the series. Now, I love Tony—we worked together in *They're Playing Our Song*, but Ron would have been just as great. Then, after all these changes they all wondered why the show wasn't a hit.

Lucie Arnaz portrayed the multi-tasking Dr. Jane Lucas—psychologist, talk show host, and newspaper columnist—on CBS's *The Lucie Arnaz Show*.

Don't get me wrong, minus the network intrusions, the show was a joy to do, and that was because of Sam Denoff—a brilliant and hilarious producer and head writer. A similar thing happened to me with a 1991 series titled *Sons and Daughters*, and a wonderful pilot I did with my husband, Laurence Luckinbill, called *One More Try* that aired but wasn't picked up as a series. On that pilot, the network didn't want to use my real-life friend, Judy Gibson, for the role of my on-screen friend saying, 'It's not funny her being a little older and heavier—it won't make a good comedy team.' I then came back with, 'You mean like Lucy and Ethel?' The network executive didn't like that and made a very unsavory comment, to which I replied, 'Go f*#k yourself.' By the way, Judy did eventually get the part anyway. At that point I decided that I wanted to do primarily concerts and stage work. I was frankly fed up with the suits running television at that time." *The Lucie Arnaz Show* was filmed in New York City at Fox studios at 54th and 10th because Lucie didn't want to leave Manhattan due to family commitments there, and agreed to do the series if she could remain. Writer R. J. Colleary added, "Also, executive producer Sam Denoff was a Brooklyn boy, and was very comfortable and happy doing a show in New York." It was done single-camera style with a laugh track. About that, Lucie stated, "That was before the networks trusted people to know when to laugh on their own. Shows like *Modern Family* today do just fine without laugh tracks, but this was an entirely different era. I do prefer the multi-camera live audience method—that's a totally different world, although on the single-camera shows, you can hear the timing in your head." Lucie portrayed Dr. Jane Lucas, a psychologist with a busy schedule. She sees patients, writes a column for *Gotham Magazine*, and co-hosts *The Love and Lucas Show*, on radio station WPLE. She was a multi-tasker even before the term existed. The magazine and the radio station are both conveniently located in the same building, directly across the street from New York's Ed Sullivan Theater. Her radio co-host is Larry Love (Todd Waring), and she dispenses advice to the lovelorn who call and/or write in to the program with their problems. Love often imitates a mythical barking dog named Tippie on the show (for no apparent reason). Jane's boss is the demanding and sometimes sneaky Jim Gordon (Tony Roberts), who has a wife named Peggy and a couple of kids. He is also the pitcher on the company's softball team (Jane is the shortstop). Jane's David Bowie–loving secretary is named Loretta (Karen Jablons-Alexander), and her meddling older sister who spells things out when she is upset is named Jill (Lee Bryant). Jane occasionally receives a telephone call from her mom (who is never seen on camera). Lucie added, "One thing only the cast and crew knew at the time was that I was pregnant (with my daughter Kate). I broke the news to Sam Denoff and he got some of the production dates pushed up, but I was already starting to show, and so you'll notice I was always seen wearing big coats, busy sweaters, holding briefcases, packages, pillows, anything to hide the fact that I was expecting. My character was single and, unlike my mom's series, it couldn't become part of the storyline." Before going to the final commercial each week, Jane would say, "Hold your problems for a moment—we'll be right back." Only six episodes were produced, and after four were aired in April of 1985, the program was placed on a temporary hiatus. The remaining two episodes were burned off during the summer of that year.

Episodes were titled "The Old Boyfriend," "Sisters," "Good Sports" (with guest star Danny Aiello), "Larry Writes the Songs," "Jane's Desperate Hour," and "Birthday Blues." The executive producer was Sam Denoff; the producers were Susan Seeger, Kathy Speer, and Terry Grossman; the writers included Susan Seeger, R. J. Colleary, and Laura Levine; the directors included Edward H. Feldman, Peter Baldwin, and Allen Baron. Music was provided by Jack Elliott.

Madame's Place Brad Lachman Productions, Inc./Madame Inc./Paramount Television. Syndicated. Weeknights at 7:30 (September 20 1982–February 23, 1983). Fifty-one episodes were videotaped with a laugh track.

Madame's Place was a syndicated sitcom that starred Wayland Flowers's Madame puppet, with a supporting cast of human co-stars. Pictured are a young Corey Feldman and a not-so-young Madame.

Madame's Place aired five nights a week in syndication. The star of the show was Madame—Wayland Flowers's feisty, saucy, bawdy, horny, elderly, demanding diva talk show hostess puppet. She'd been married and divorced six times, and was constantly seeking her seventh victim, er, husband. Madame was supposed to have been a celebrity ever since vaudeville, and the star of countless films. Her nightly talk show originated from her mansion in Hollywood. Madame is the only puppet on the show—all other cast members are of the human variety; they included Susan Tolsky as her frazzled secretary, Bernadette Van Gilder; Johnny Haymer as Walter Pinkerton, the butler (he was a former welterweight boxer, and was once engaged to Madame); beautiful Judy Landers was aspiring actress Sara Joy Pitts, Madame's often scantily clad niece; Ty Henderson played Barney, her producer; and future star Corey Feldman was eleven-year-old Buzzy, the neighbor kid. Madame doesn't get along well with her neighbors, but Buzzy is an exception. E. J. Peaker played Buzzy's mom Carla St. James, and John Reilly his dad, Max. Despite its short run, *Madame's Place* boasted many big-name guest stars, such as Debbie Reynolds, George Gobel, William Shatner, Phyllis Diller, Tab Hunter, Betty White, Jay Leno, Frankie Avalon, and Dr. Joyce Brothers.

The program's episodes were merely numbered and not given titles. Many were two-part episodes. The executive producer was Brad Lachman; the producers were Bob Sand and Don Van Atta; the writers included Bob Sand, Frank Mula, Tony Garofalo, Greg Fields, Tom Moore, Bob Howard, Marc Warren, Dennis Rinsler, and Wayland Flowers; the directors included Don Barnhart and Paul Miller. Music was provided by Michael K. Miller and Monica Riordan, and the theme song "Here at Madame's Place" was performed by Denise DeCaro. The orchestra was humorously called "The Madame's Place All-Divorced Orchestra," and was conducted by Rollin Espinoza.

Maggie Ermar Productions/Marble Arch Productions. ABC. Saturday nights 8:00 (October 24, 1981–November 7, 1981). Eight episodes were videotaped in front of a live audience.

Not to be confused with the British series of same name, this *Maggie* was created by humor columnist and author Erma Bombeck. Maggie (maiden name Sullivan) Weston (played by Miriam Flynn) was a frazzled and rather inefficient housewife (and part-time babysitter) in Dayton, Ohio, with a working husband and three children. The eldest of these children,

16-year-old L. J. was mentioned often but never seen (he was always in the bathroom, or blasting music by the Go-Gos in his room). The other two children (all boys) were twelve-year-old dark-haired Mark and eight-year-old towhead Bruce (played by Billy Jacoby and Christian Jacobs, respectively)—fans of Froot Loops and Captain Sugar cereal (there always seemed to be a box on the kitchen table). In the pilot episode, Mark and Bruce were played by Garin Bougie and Robert Kiger, respectively. Maggie's husband, Len (James Hampton), was Franklin High School's vice-principal. Hampton shared, "It was a fun show. Just wish it would have lasted longer. Erma Bombeck was a doll." The ubiquitous Doris Roberts played Loretta Davenport, Maggie's gossipy hairdresser at Loretta's House of Coiffures (portrayed in the pilot by Conchata Ferrell). Loretta was not a blood relative although the kids referred to her as Aunt Loretta. Maggie was at the salon to have her hair done in each and every episode. Chris (Margie Impert) was Loretta's rather daft manicurist/assistant; Buffy Croft (Judith-Marie Bergan) was a snooty and seemingly perfect housewife/mother/realtor (and one of Maggie's best friends and rivals) who frequented the salon; and saccharine sweet Tiffany (Rachel Jacobs, Christian Jacobs' real-life older sister) was an acquaintance of young Bruce. Len and the boys were able to see through Tiffany's guise, but Maggie was often taken in by Tiffany's ploys and phony flattery. The late Betsy Palmer portrayed Maggie's mother, Virginia Sullivan. Virginia had no filter, and let Maggie know that she was much more proud of her other daughter, Diane (never seen) who had her own TV show. Bombeck's stories and anecdotes worked so well in her column and her books, but somehow just didn't translate as well to the small screen, and *Maggie* was put out of circulation after only a few of the eight videotaped episodes had aired. The others were burned off in the spring of 1982.

Episodes were titled "The School Conference" (with guest star Marcia Rodd), "A Tooth for a Tooth," "Career," "Bruce's Birthday Party," "Marriage Encounter (with guest star Michael Pataki)," "Alienation of Affection," "Mark's Shrink," and "Maggie the Poet." The executive producer was Erma Bombeck; the producers were Charlie Hauck and Tom Whedon; writers included Erma Bombeck, Bill Davenport, Tom Whedon, Korby Siamis, and Karyl Geld Miller; the director was John Tracy. The theme song was a simple, almost Vaudevillian number played over slapstick clips from the series.

Making the Grade Ubu Productions/Paramount Television. CBS. Monday nights 9:30 (April 5, 1982–May 10, 1982). Six episodes were filmed single-camera style with a laugh track.

This short-lived sitcom from Gary David Goldberg was set in St. Louis at mythical Franklin High—an inner-city school fraught with problems. Many cast members used this series as a springboard to bigger things. George Wendt (pre–*Cheers*) played the über-macho physical education teacher Gus Bertoia; Alley Mills (pre–*The Wonder Years*) portrayed Sara Conover, the drama teacher (whose favorite film is *Casablanca*); Philip Charles MacKenzie (pre–*Brothers*) essayed the role of chemistry teacher/playboy David Wasserman. MacKenzie said, "That was me, playing the creep, the sleazeball again. I must have sleazy genes because I got to play that kind of character quite often." Wasserman was married, but was still constantly making a play for Sara Conover, who continually spurned his advances. The series starred James Naughton as the empathetic dean of boys, Harry Barnes (he has a knack for setting former gang members on the straight and narrow). Others in the cast included Graham Jarvis as Jack Felspar, the clueless and totally out-of-touch assistant principal; and Steve Peterman as Jeffrey Kelton, the overwhelmed, rather nerdy twenty-eight-year-old University of Illinois graduate. Kelton has two years of law school under his belt, but puts that pursuit on the back burner in favor of becoming a substitute teacher. He becomes a regular member of the faculty when the unseen Miss Shoyer suffers a nervous breakdown. MacKenzie added, "Steve Peterman later became a highly successful executive producer, and we were reunited on Brooke Shields' show, *Suddenly Susan*." Even placed on CBS's cushy Monday night schedule, this rather well-written show failed to find an audience and was expelled after only six episodes had aired. MacKenzie opined, "Perhaps the audience was more interested in the students than the teachers, thus the success of *Welcome Back, Kotter* and *Head of the Class*. George Wendt certainly benefitted from *Making the Grade* being short-lived. If our show had been renewed, he would have missed out on *Cheers*."

Episodes were titled "The Pilot," "Marriage, Dave Style" (with guest star Forest Whitaker), "Teach Me Tonight," "Shepherd's Pie Syndrome," "Guess Who's Coming to Class," and "Enter Miss Right." The executive producer was Gary David Goldberg; the producer was Jeffrey L. Melman; the writers included Gary David Goldberg, Lloyd Garver, Michael J. Weithorn, Richard Orloff, Merrill Markoe, and Steve Kline; the directors included Gary David Goldberg, Mark Tinker, Mel Damski, and Jeffrey L. Melman. The creator was Gary David Goldberg. About Goldberg, MacKenzie stated, "He was a terrific talent, and I think this was the first show on which he was the executive producer—the showrunner. Only a very short time later, he hit it big with *Family Ties*." Music was provided by Tom Scott.

Mama Malone Richard Lewis Productions/Barry and Enright Productions/Columbia Pictures Television. CBS. Wednesday nights 8:30 (March 7, 1984–April 25, 1984), and Saturday nights 8:00 (June 9, 1984–July 21, 1984). Thirteen episodes were videotaped with a laugh track.

Jack Barry and Dan Enright were much more famous for their game shows (and Enright was infamous for the part he played in the quiz show scandal of the late '50s). They stepped out of their comfort zone with this unusual sitcom about a cooking show that airs live from Mama Renate Malone's (Lila Kaye) fourth-floor apartment in Brooklyn. This program was originally intended to air in 1982, but the project was tabled for a year and a half. Mama is Italian, but kept the surname of her very Irish deceased husband, police lieutenant Kevin Malone. Her maiden name was Forresti, and her program, *Cooking with Mama Malone*, is carried by a local New York TV station. Unlike other cooking shows, this one is not solely about the culinary arts. Mama's large family and close friends wander in and out during each broadcast and share the latest goings-on in their lives, and episodes deal with family issues as well as moral values. Regulars included her daughter Connie Karamakopoulos (Randee Heller), who is divorced from a Greek husband and works at Paolo's Pizza Patio; Connie's son, New York Mets fan Frankie (Evan Richards), who shares information on his grandmother's program about the lunch money he's stolen; Mama's younger brother, Dino (Don Amendolia), a singer and swinger named Dino; Padre Guardiano (Ralph Manza), the elderly parish priest who has trouble negotiating the four flights of stairs to Mama's apartment; Father Jose Silva (Richard Yniguez), the padre's attractive young assistant; Stanley (Sam Anderson), the announcer on *Cooking with Mama Malone*; Austin (Raymond Singer), the stage manager; Jackie (Joey Jupiter), the script girl; and Ken and Harry (Pendleton Brown and Mitchell Group, respectively), the cooking show's directors.

Episodes were titled "The Pilot," "The Commitment," "Connie's Old Flame," "Father Romeo," "The Education of Frankie," "Karamakopolous and Son," "A New Neighbor," "Shall We Dance?" (with guest star Alice Ghostley), "Even Dino Gets the Blues," "Connie's Move," "Dino's Fan," "A Call from the Vatican," and "Back to Basics." The executive producer was Richard Lewis; the producers were Terrence McNally and Paul Bogart; the writers included Bernard Dilbert, Sid Dorfman, Richard Freiman, Lynn Marie Latham, Bernard Lechowick, Leonard Melfi, Patt Shea, Robert Van Scoyk, Harriet Weiss, and Harvey Weitzman; the lone director was Paul Bogart. *Mama Malone's* rather grating and repetitive theme song was written by John Kander, Fred Ebb, and Andrew Billing.

Mama's Boy Witt/Thomas Productions/Touchstone Television. NBC. Air dates and times varied. (September 19, 1987–August 6, 1988). Seven episodes were videotaped in front of a live audience, but only six aired.

The promos for this show said, "Jake McCaskey is a sportsman, a man's man, a lady's man and his own man, but his mother's moving in and he's about to become a *Mama's Boy*." Jake McCaskey (Bruce Weitz, post *Hill Street Blues*) has the perfect bachelor pad and the ideal bachelor life. He makes a decent living writing a popular regular column called "McCaskey" for the mythical *Manhattan Examiner*. Life is good—and then, all mom breaks loose. His domineering, buttinski mother, Molly (Nancy Walker), suffers a reversal of fortune, and has to return from Florida to share his New York apartment. Can two blood relatives share an apartment without driving each other crazy? The answer is a definite *no*, but only a choice few knew the answer to that question. Like *Beverly Hills Buntz*, with fellow *Hill Street Blues* alum Dennis Franz, *Mama's Boy* was designed to be a "designated hitter" for the peacock network by Brandon Tartikoff—shows that could be plugged in on a monthly basis where needed. Ratings, however, for the debut episode on Saturday, September 19, 1987, were abysmal, and after only three episodes had aired, the program was placed on hiatus until spring and summer of 1988 when three of the remaining four episodes were burned off. Others in the cast included Grace Zabriskie as Molly's sister, Agnes; Dan Hedaya as Jake's friend Mickey Ryan, and James Cromwell as another of his buddies, Lucky. *Mama's Boy* joined Walker's other sitcom disasters, *Blansky's Beauties* and *The Nancy Walker Show*. NBC soon abandoned its "designated hitter" programming idea. For some reason, NBC ran the pilot episode as the third aired episode. Said pilot contains a few characters that didn't make it into the series—David Leisure as the landlord; Susan Blakely as Victoria (whom Jake once left waiting at the altar); and Harold Sylvester as Jake's best friend.

Episodes were titled "The Pilot," "Bachelor of the Year," "Molly's Night Out," "Mickey's Song," "Remembrance of Things Past," "Hamlet," and "Scared Straight." The program was produced by Don Reo and Bill Levinson; the writers included Don Reo, Bob Schiller, Bill Levinson, and Bob Weiskopf; the directors included J. D. Lobue and Greg Antonacci. Music was provided by George Aliceson Tipton. Music was provided by Scott Gale. The theme song, "Mother," was performed by an uncredited a cappella vocal group.

Marblehead Manor Dames/Fraser Productions/Paramount Television. Syndicated. Saturday nights 7:30 (September 19, 1987–May 28, 1988). Twenty-four episodes were videotaped in front of a live audience.

Part of the brief "Prime-time begins at 7:30" campaign, *Marblehead Manor* aired on Saturday nights in that early time slot for a single season. Although not a runaway success, the program did have a few moments of inspired, old-fashioned slapstick (the newly waxed kitchen floor scene in the debut episode is executed quite well). *Marblehead Manor* is owned by Randolf Stonehill (played by Bob Fraser, who also served as executive producer and frequent writer for the series), who had struck oil a few years earlier—corn oil, that is. He amassed a sizeable fortune in that business venture (he had Wessonality), and he and his kindly-but-materialistic wife, Hilary, played by Linda Thorson (formerly Tara King on *The Avengers*), who wants more than anything to have a baby, hires a staff of servants—and rather inept ones at that. Randolf's childhood friend, Albert Dudley (Paxton Whitehead), is the butler. The rest of the zanies included the African American Stockton brothers—fitness-conscious chauffeur Jerry (Phil Morris), and gay handyman Dwayne (Rodney Scott-Hudson); the klutzy gardener Rick (Michael Richards, previewing the future Cosmo Kramer on *Seinfeld*); and Lupe (Dyana Ortelli), the daffy maid/cook, and her eight-year-old mischievous son, Elvis (Humberto Ortiz). Charo played a maid named Cookie in the pilot, which was shown out of order as the final episode of the series. Carol Bruce portrayed Randolf's mother, Margaret Stonehill.

Episodes were cleverly titled "Diamond in the Roughage," "Puppy Love," "Madame Butterfat," "Safe at Home," "Good Impressions,"

"The Fondle Workout," "Full Dress," "I Led Three Wives," "All in a Knight's Work," "Egg McGruffin," "An Aunt Hill for Hilary" "Ballet Ruse," "Tea for Tuba," "Star Struck," "The Lady's Not for Spurning," "Baby on Board," "Now for a Re-butle," "Chinny Chin Chin," "Randolf's Mom," "Come Flu with Me," "Amazing Grace," "Button Your Beau," "Gorilla My Dreams," and "If You Knew Sushi." The executive producers were Bob Fraser, Gary Nardino, and Rob Dames; the writers included Paul K. Taylor, Steven Kunes, Ken Eulo, Barbara Azrialy, Don Hart, Chip Hayes, Florence Peluso, Patt Shea, Harriet Weiss, Ronald J. Fields, Courtney Burr, Frank Rehwaldt, Nick Gore, and Jerry Jacobius; the directors included Shelley Jensen, Rob Dames, Rene Auberjonois, Bill Foster, Whitney J. LeBlanc, and Lee Shallat. The catchy theme song, "It's a Grand Life" was by Judy Hart Angelo and Gary Portnoy (most famous for the *Cheers* theme), and other music was provided by Dan Foliart and Howard Pearl.

Mary MTM Productions. CBS. Wednesday nights 8:00 (December 11, 1985–February 19, 1986), and Tuesday nights at 9:00 (March 25, 1986–April 8, 1986). Thirteen episodes were videotaped in front of a live audience.

After a failed variety show with the same name, Mary was back with another show called *Mary* and met with a similar fate. The gripe most critics had about *Mary* was that it was too much like *The Mary Tyler Moore Show* (she went from a TV newsroom to a newspaper office). Here, instead of having experienced a recent breakup with a boyfriend, Mary Brenner is a recent divorcee (her ex's name was Ken, but he is never seen) with no children. In the pilot episode ("From Pillar to Post"), Mary loses her job at *Women's Digest Magazine* (it folded without warning) and, wanting to stay in Chicago, lands a job (a temporary one, she hopes) at the Windy City's fictional tabloid newspaper the *Chicago Eagle* (owned by media mogul Malcolm Burke, played by Patrick Macnee), where she is given a "consumer helpline" column to expose substandard business practices. The *Eagle* is not a well-respected newspaper, much as WJM Channel 12 on *The Mary Tyler Moore Show* was the joke of Minneapolis/St. Paul. In reality, she only gets this job because her gruff boss, Frank DeMarco (James Farentino), finds her attractive and wants to sleep with her. Frank possesses many of the same characteristics as Lou Grant (including a penchant for gambling), and was hired only three months earlier to "shake things up" at the paper and get it back on the right track. Instead of an incompetent news anchor, Mary has to deal with a legally blind copy editor named Vincent Tully (David Byrd). Because he is differently abled, he constantly utters the words, "You can't fire me," even though his work is shoddy (numbers are accidentally typed inside by-lines, the letter *s* appears three times in the word "disappear,", etc). Sitting across from Mary in the office is the chain-smoking, tough-as-nails, acerbic Jo Tucker (Katey Sagal, pre–*Married with Children*). Her "Mainline Chicago" column is an accurate representation of her bitter personality (although she doesn't like the word "bitter"), and, in fact, Mary thinks Jo Tucker is a man until she meets her in the office. Rounding out the personnel is the smarmy, egotistical playboy theatre critic Ed LaSalle (John Astin, formerly Gomez Addams), who consistently makes a play for Mary's affections, despite repeated rejections. Despite her encounters with her quirky co-workers, Mary Brenner's life at the office seems to flow much better than her life at home. Her relationship with her needy, impulsive neighbor Susan Wilcox (Carlene Watkins) and Susan's new husband, Lester Mintz (James Tolkan), is the program's weakest link. Susan had met Lester only twenty-four hours before she began making wedding plans. Lester's occupation is a big mystery, and likely unlawful (it never is revealed). As a couple, they greatly resemble political pundits Mary Matalin and James Carville. The characters of Susan and Lester were downplayed considerably as the program progressed.

Episodes were titled "From Pillar to Post," "Make My Day," "Chicago Hi-Lo," "Everyone's a Critic," "The Death Threat," "Forest for the Trees," "Same Old Song," "Beans" (with guest star Patrick Macnee) "Table for Two," "Mr. Lucky" (with guest star Robert Pastorelli), "And the Winner Is" (with guest stars Bubba Smith and Barbara Babcock), "Little Jo," and "Steppin' Out with Mary Brenner." The creators and executive producers were David Isaacs and Ken Levine; the writers included David Isaacs, Ken Levine, Dennis Koenig, Emily Marshall, Merrill Markoe, Tom Straw, and Douglas Wyman; the directors included Danny DeVito (the pilot), Rod Daniel, Peter Baldwin, Jeff Chambers, Ellen Falcon, Dolores Ferraro, Nick Havinga, and Will Mackenzie. The theme song was by Dan Foliart and Howard Pearl.

Me and Maxx The Komack Company. NBC. Saturday nights 9:30 (March 22, 1980–April 5, 1980), Friday nights 8:30 (May 30, 1980–July 25, 1980). Ten episodes were videotaped in front of a live audience.

Producer/writer/director/actor James Komack had his share of hit shows—*Welcome Back, Kotter*, *Chico and the Man*, and *The Courtship of Eddie's Father*. He also had quite a few flops—*Mr. T. and Tina*, *Sugartime*, *Another Day*, and *Mister Roberts*. Add *Me and Maxx* to the latter category. Maxx is the name of Komack's own daughter, and inspired the title of this short-lived sitcom in 1980. *Me and Maxx* tells the story of eleven-year-old soap opera–loving Maxx Davis (Melissa Michaelsen), who avers that the *xx* in her name was placed there because she was double crossed. She unexpectedly shows up one day, suitcase in hand, at the door of her deadbeat dad's swinging bachelor pad in Manhattan. Her dad is Norman Davis (Joe Santos), who skipped out when she was a newborn. Maxx's mother felt that it was now her turn to "find herself," and she left the child at Norman's doorstep under the guise that she was taking a two-week vacation. However, in the sealed note she had Maxx deliver to Norman, it was discovered that Maxx is now *his* responsibility—she has no plans to return. Upon watching the pilot, it boggles the mind that this program was ever green lighted by NBC because the viewer can't help but feel an immediate and insurmountable amount of dislike for Norman, the main character, even though he eventually begins to exhibit some loving and nurturing qualities. He gripes about the inconvenient new wrinkle in his life and how it is cramping his style. He had previously only seen his daughter four times and, had his ex-wife not skipped town, would probably never have made the transition to responsible fatherhood. Others in the cast included Mitch (Jim Weston), a fellow swinging bachelor and good friend; Gary (Denny Evans), the elevator operator; and Barbara (Jenny Sullivan), Norman's business partner and occasional romantic interest. Much like Komack's *Courtship of Eddie's Father* TV series a decade earlier, the final scene usually occurs out of doors, with father and daughter chatting, bonding, and walking around Manhattan or on a beach. *Me and Maxx*, however, lasted only ten episodes, thus the bonding of this father and daughter duo never had enough time to jell. A very similar series pilot was nixed by ABC in 1979, featuring a Manhattan bachelor (played by Tim Thomerson) who was named guardian of his ten-year-old daughter, Maxx (also with Melissa Michaelsen).

Episodes were titled "The Pilot," "Lunch at the Plaza," "Maxx's Friend," "Sparrow," "Robert," "The Negotiation," "4," "The Commitment," "Dad's Day," and "Some Are Savers." The executive producer was James Komack; the producers were Neil Rosen, George Tricker and Stan Cutler; the writers included James Komack, Neil Rosen, George Tricker, Stan Cutler, Terry Hart, Mike Marmer, and Steve Kreinberg; the directors included Herbert Kenwith and James Komack. Music was provided by Michael Lloyd and arranged by John D'Andrea. The theme song, "Is It Because of Love?" was performed by Leonore O'Malley. Joe Santos died on March 16, 2016 at the age of 84.

Me and Mom Hal Sitowitz Productions/Viacom. ABC. Friday nights 10:00 (April 5, 1985–May 17, 1985). Six hour-long episodes were filmed single-camera style without a laugh track.

It is said that getting married is an occupation for thrice-divorced Zena Hunnicutt (Holland Taylor). She has it all—money, furs, social status, and yet she is bored with her life. She needs excitement—a challenge. That challenge comes when she joins her young criminologist daughter, Kate Morgan's (Lisa Eilbacher), private-investigation agency. It is just the jolt her life needed, and the agency altered its name to Morgan, Garfield and Hunnicutt, located at 2936 Hampton Boulevard in San Francisco. The "Garfield" in the name of the business is Lou Garfield (James Earl Jones), a former homicide detective. He is also a former co-worker and friend of Zena's late husband, so this marks a reunion of sorts. Lieutenant Rojas, their connection at the police department, was played by Henry Darrow, and Bruce Jenner was the limo driver, Vince Galadon. Only six hour-long episodes of this crimedy aired because too few private eyes—or *any* eyes, for that matter—were watching this series on Friday nights, and The Morgan, Garfield and Hunnicutt Agency was forced to close its doors for good.

Episodes were titled "The Pilot," "A Flawed Affair," "The Murder Game," and "Davie" (two others were not assigned titles). The executive producers were Dean Hargrave and Hal Sitowitz; the producers were S. Bryan Hickox, Joel Steiger, and Bruce Hendricks; the writers included Hal Sitowitz and Marsha Miller; the directors included Bernard L. Kowalski and Jeff Bleckner. The creator was Hal Sitowitz. Music was provided by Richard DeBenedictis. The theme song was composed by Douglas Brayfield, Miles Goodman, and Amy Holland.

Meatballs and Spaghetti Pan Sang East Company/Intermedia Entertainment Company/Marvel Productions, Ltd., MGM. CBS. Saturday mornings 11:30 (September 18, 1982–March 5, 1983). Twenty-five animated episodes were filmed.

Meatballs and Spaghetti was an animated sitcom about a rock group consisting of Meatball (Ron Masak), the rather rotund leader of the band; Spaghetti (Sally Julian), his svelt blonde wife; their pet pooch named, appropriately, Woofer (voiced by Frank Welker)—he plays drums; and their assistant and bass player, Clyde (voiced by former child star Barry Gordon). Episodes revolve around the band, their fans, life on the road, and all the mishaps along the way.

Episodes were titled "Woofer the Wonder Dog," "Mixed Up Medical Reports," "Once Upon a Farm," "Spaghetti's Old Boyfriend," "Space Aliens," "Come Back, Little Woofer," "Monkey Doodle Dandies," "Going to the Dogs," "Piracy on the High C's," "Kid Sitters," "Foreign Legion Air Heads," "Woofer Meets Tweeter," "Christmas Tale," "Jazz Meets Jaws," "Werewolf Story," "The Big Shrink," "Watch the Birdie," "Sunken Treasure Cruise," "Throwing the Bull," "Caveman Story," "Robot Roadie," "Double or Nothing," "Magical Moments," "Flying Carpet Caper," and "Beach Peaches." The executive producers were Fred Silverman and David H. DePatie; the producer was Bob Richardson; the writers included Alex Lovy, Lew Marshall, Jack Mendelsohn, and Michael Joens. The creators were Fred Silverman and Jerry Eisenberg. The theme was composed by Steven DePatie.

Melba Saul Ilson Productions/Columbia Pictures Television. CBS. Tuesday night 8:00 (January 28, 1986), and Saturday nights 8:00 (August 2, 1986–September 13, 1986). Six episodes were videotaped in front of a live audience.

Actress/singer Melba Moore starred in this extremely short-lived sitcom as Melba Patterson, the director of the Manhattan Visitors Center. Her co-workers are Gil (Evan Mirand) and Jack (Lou Jacobi). Recently divorced, Melba is coping with life as a single mother with her nine-year-old child Tracy (Jamilla Perry); actually, she shares custody with her ex, Carl, who has a new girlfriend named Valerie. Melba's mother, Mama Rose (Barbara Meek), lives with her at 623 Bleeker Street in Greenwich Village, and helps out with the rambunctious youngster. Melba had been raised in a white family's home (Mama Rose was housekeeper for the Slater family), and the Slaters' daughter, Susan (Gracie Harrison), and she became as close as sisters (especially after Susan's mother died). Susan works in advertising for the Furth and Preston Agency. This sitcom debuted on the day of the Space Shuttle Challenger disaster and ratings were abysmal. It likely wasn't the fault of the program—everyone was watching the news that evening, but the program was yanked off the schedule after that lone episode had aired. The other five left in the can were burned off during the summer of 1986, and then *Melba* was toast.

Episodes were titled "Manhunt," "Mothers and Other Strangers," "The Triangle," "Mother Knows Best," "My Shadow and Me," and "The Girls Are Back in Town." The executive producers were Michael S. Baser, Kim Weiskopf, and Saul Ilson; the producers were Larry Balmagia and Bob Peete; the writers included Larry Balmagia, Dennis Danzinger, Marcy Vosburgh, Sandy Sprung, Laurie Gelman, Marshall Karp, Ellen Sandler, Jay Moriarty, and Mike Milligan; the directors included Mel Ferber, Linda Day, and Doug Rogers. The creators were Barry Harman and Marshall Karp. Melba Moore performed the theme song, "We're Sisters"—written by Joe Curiale and Barbara Rothstein.

Misfits of Science James D. Parriott Productions/Universal Television. NBC. Friday nights 9:00 (October 4, 1985–December 13, 1985), and Friday nights 8:00 (December 27, 1985–February 21, 1986). Sixteen hour-long episodes were filmed without a laugh track, but only fifteen aired.

Misfits of Science was a fantasy-sci-fi-adventure series with many sitcom elements. Yes, it was all that. In fact, it was too many things. It was also NBC Entertainment President Brandon Tartikoff's baby, and had the unenviable task of going head-to-head on Friday nights against CBS's juggernaut *Dallas*. The series starred Dean Martin's son Dean Paul Martin (who died tragically only a year later) as Dr. Billy Hayes—a research scientist at the Humanidyne Institute (observing human anomalies—freaks of nature, if you will), often referred to as Indiana Hayes because of his adventurous spirit and curiosity. Unlike others in the cast, Hayes has no special powers except for his own gray matter, and his adventures take him in search of Mayan ruins, Martians, a lost tribe in New Guinea, beneath the ocean, into the wrestling ring, and onto the basketball court. Among the "anomalies" in his circle (The Human Investigative Team, or H. I. T. for short) are Dr. Elvin Lincoln (Kevin Peter Hall)—a treetop-tall African American man with the ability to shrink to a mere eleven inches for fourteen minutes at a time. Because his clothing doesn't shrink along with him, special suits are made for the diminutive version of "El," as he was nicknamed. Also in the fray is Johnny Bukowski (Mark Thomas Miller), who was electrocuted while performing a Chuck Berry song on stage (thus, he was nicknamed "Johnny B" as in "Johnny B. Goode"). His accident left him with the ability to absorb all of the electricity in a room and hurl it where it is needed. He wears sunglasses at all times because his eyeballs glow like high-wattage light bulbs. Water is his kryptonite. One of the misfits is a member of the fair sex. A very young Courteney Cox, almost a decade before *Friends*, played Gloria "Glo" Dinallo—a seventeen-year-old Burger Barn delivery person with telekinetic powers that can be harnessed for lifting and moving extremely heavy items. However, she can only control items in her field of vision, and a blindfold negates her powers. She has numerous brushes with the law on her record, and her parole officer is Jane Miller (Jennifer Holmes).

The debut episode included one more misfit, Arnold "Ice Man" Beifneiter (Mickey Jones), who has the power to freeze whatever he touches. Because of complaints from Marvel Comics, however, that character was immediately frozen out of the series. However, even after the iceman goeth, the misfits continued to drive around in his ice cream truck. The harried director of the Institute, Dick Stetmeyer (Max Wright pre–*Alf* and post *Buffalo Bill*), attempts to keep Hayes and the misfits focused on their research, but his attempts are usually in vain as their adventures usually take priority. Miss Nance (Diane Civita) is the institute's cute, self-involved receptionist, who is completely unaware of most of the strange goings-on around her. The late, great Hal Kanter was famous for his innovative opening credits on his shows, but James D. Parriott received a lot of flak from the network about this program's unusual opening, which began with singer Bobby Short performing the theme song cabaret-style on a TV screen. A sneakered foot then kicks over the TV set and a much more up-to-date rendition of the theme song begins to play.

The series is available in a DVD box set in Germany, where it is known as *Die Spezialisten Unterwegs* ("The Specialists Are Coming").

Episodes were titled "Deep Freeze" (with guest star Larry Linville), "Your Place or Mayan," "Guess What's Coming to Dinner," "Lost Link," "Sort of Looking for Gina," "Sonar and Yet So Far," "Steer Crazy," "Fumble on the One," "Twin Engines," "Grand Theft Bunny," "Grand Elusion," "Once Upon a Night," "Center of Attention," "Against All Oz," "Avenging Angel," and "Three Days of the Blender." The executive producer was James D. Parriott; the writers included James D. Parriott, Sara Parriott, Donald Todd, Linda Campanelli, Mark Jones, Michael Cassutt, M. M. Shelly Moore, Morrie Ruvinsky, Pamela Norris, and Blaze Forrester; the directors included James D. Parriott, Alan J. Levi, Barbara Peters, Bernard McEveety, Burt Brinckerhoff, Christopher Leitch, Jeffrey Hayden, John Tracy, Michael Switzer, and Bob Sweeney. Music was provided by Basil Poledouris.

Mr. Merlin Larry Larry Productions/Columbia Pictures Television. CBS. Wednesday nights 8:00 (October 7, 1981–January 6, 1982), and Monday nights 8:00 (January 18, 1982–March 22, 1982). Twenty-two episodes were filmed single-camera style with a laugh track.

Barnard Hughes was a huge, Tony-winning Broadway success in *Da*. He also scored roles in many popular motion pictures, but when it came to television, a hit show proved elusive. There was *Doc* from MTM Productions in the 1970s, and in the 1980s *The Cavanaughs* and *Mr. Merlin*. The latter debuted in the fall of 1981 in the 8 p.m. time slot because it was aimed at a younger audience. Hughes portrayed the title character whose alias was Max Merlin. In reality, he was born in A.D. 381, in Wales (his father was an incubus, his mother a Welsh princess) as Merlin Sylvester. He was a wizard, a sorcerer with magical powers who had provided advice to William the Conquerer, knew King Arthur and his knights of the Round Table, encouraged Attila the Hun to brush his teeth, and dated Marie Antoinette, but, as Max Merlin, he is a mild-mannered garage mechanic in San Francisco. Because he is getting on in years (he was 1,600), it is recommended by his superiors in sorcery that he take on an apprentice. That apprentice makes himself apparent when, as in the tale of "Sword in the Stone," fifteen-year-old Zac Rogers (Clark Brandon) is able to pull a crowbar out of a block of concrete. (It's interesting to note that Clark Brandon had co-starred in an earlier sitcom, *Out of the Blue*, about an angel with magical powers; it also had a very short run in prime-time.) Merlin takes young Zac under his wing, but at first Zac is skeptical of the wizard's claims of superpowers—that is, until said powers are demonstrated. Zac is to work part-time in the garage, and also learn the ways of the sorcerer for fourteen hours a week at Merlin's home (with the address, number 573). Reluctantly, Zac agrees, and very slowly begins to perfect his newfound powers. Zac has to keep his new life a secret from everybody, including his best buddy, Leo Samuels (Jonathan Prince). Between Merlin, Zac, and their superiors in council is a lovely liaison named Alexandra (Elaine Joyce). Each episode contains a moral. In the pilot episode, Zac makes a promise to never use the magical "crystal door," but breaks that promise while Merlin is at a Rams football game. In "The Cloning of the Green," Zac learns not to use his new powers for financial gain.

Episodes were titled were "The Pilot," "The Cloning of the Green," "Starsand," "The Music's in Me," "All about Sheila," "Two Faces of Zac," "A Moment in Camelot" (with guest star Richard Basehart), "A Message from Wallshime," "Take My Tonsils, Please" (with guest star Stacy Keach), "The Ache," "Not so Sweet Sixteen," "Romeo and Dreidelwood," "Getting to Know You," "Alex Goes Popless," "Everything's Coming Up Daisies," "The Egg and Us," "How to Help a Gymnast in a Foreign Country," "Change of Venue, Parts One and Two," "An Absence of Amulets," "Arrivederci Dink," and "I Was a Teenage Loser." The executive producers were Larry Rosen and Larry Tucker; the producer was Joel Rogosin; the writers included Larry Rosen, Larry Tucker, Tom Chehak, Tim Maschler, Jeffrey Scott, Walter J. Keenan, Parke Perine, Hollace White, Stephanie Garman, Ann Woodall, Paula Lintz, George Geiger, Don Tait, Michael Mauer, Paul Haggis, Dinah Kirgo, and Julie Kirgo; the directors included Bill Bixby, John Astin, Harry Winer, Alan Myerson, Leo Penn, Howard Storm, James Frawley, Jeffrey Hayden, Larry Elikann, and Herbert Kenwith. The show's music, with a very classical feel, was provided by Ken Harrison. The program briefly ran in syndication on the USA Network.

Mr. Smith Weinberger/Daniels Productions/Paramount Television. NBC. Friday nights 8:00 (September 23, 1983–December 16, 1983). Thirteen episodes were filmed with a laugh track, but only twelve aired.

Hollywood doesn't always learn its lesson. Even after disastrous sitcom about primates first in the 1960s called *The Hathaways* and then in the 1970s *Me and the Chimp*, another attempt was made in 1983. Oh, but this one had a twist—a talking orangutan. Cha Cha and Bobo were born in a zoo, but became circus performers as members of The Atwood Orangutans of Arizona, owned by the Atwood family—Tommy Atwood (Tim Dunigan), his wisecracking younger sister Ellie (Laura Jacoby), and their late father. After a traffic accident in his van, Tommy was in a coma for several weeks. The orangutans had also been in the van. They were unhurt, but did escape in totally different directions. Cha Cha was taken in by a primate research institute and while there, mistakenly ingested an experimental enzyme that rendered him a genius with an IQ of 256. He was later made a consultant in Washington, working with nuclear energy. Cha Cha can also speak Hebrew, and becomes an expert chess player. His brother, Bobo, however, remains an average orangutan—he did not drink the enzyme. After the pilot episode the brothers were reunited. After initially being confined to the research institute, Cha Cha (renamed Mr. Smith) is finally allowed to leave, although he remains under close supervision so that no one can find out the truth about him. Smith and the Atwood children are placed in a beautiful and secluded house in Washington, D.C., and are constantly under the watchful eye of the fastidious but kindly Raymond Holyoke (Leonard Frey)—secretary to several former presidents and numerous ambassadors. Overseeing everything from afar are Dr. Judy Tyson (Terri Garber), a research scientist, and her boss Dr. Klein (Stuart Margolin). The orangutan had a lot of previous film experience—he had costarred with Clint Eastwood in both *Every Which Way but Loose* and *Any Which Way You Can* in the late 1970s. Co-executive producer Ed. Weinberger provided Mr. Smith's voice. Even though Mr. Smith went to Washington, this program is not to be confused with the motion picture or TV sitcom titled *Mr. Smith Goes to Washington*. After twelve of the thirteen filmed episodes had aired, NBC stopped the monkey business because of poor ratings. Despite being canceled, an episode of the series titled "Mr. Smith Falls in Love" was nominated for an Emmy Award (for best use of music), but did not win.

Episodes were titled "Welcome to Washington, Parts One and Two," "Mr. Smith Finds His Brother," "Mr. Smith Operates," "Mr. Smith Rescues Bobo," "Mr. Smith Falls in Love," "Mr. Smith Gets Physical," "Goodbye, Mr. Smith," "Mr. Smith Loses a Friend," "Mr. Smith Plays Cyrano," "Mr. Smith Makes a Commercial," "Mr. Smith Goes Public" (with guest star Don Ameche), and "Mr. Smith Goes to Court." The executive producers were Ed. Weinberger and Stan Daniels; the producer was Gene Callahan; the writers included Stan Daniels, David Lloyd, Ed. Weinberger, Dari Daniels, George Kirgo, and Douglas Wyman; the directors included Gerald Hirschfeld, Ed. Weinberger, Stan Daniels, and Ralph Heifer. Music was provided by Patrick Williams.

Mr. Sunshine Henry Winkler/John Rich Productions/Paramount Television. ABC. Friday nights 9:00 (March 28, 1986–May 2, 1986), and Saturday nights 8:00 (May 3, 1986–May 24, 1986). Eleven episodes were filmed in front of a live audience.

Mr. Sunshine

Mr. Sunshine is not to be confused with the equally short-lived Matthew Perry sitcom of same name. This one came in 1986, and features Professor Paul Stark (Jeffrey Tambor), who is newly separated from his wife of sixteen years. Stark, who teaches English and creative writing at Kenyon College, is blinded following an accident, but insists that he can manage on his own. He has just moved into an upstairs apartment, and his new landlady, the widowed and self-involved chatterbox June Swinford (Barbara Babcock), is initially oblivious to his condition (she has to be told about it). Swinford is then very uncomfortable with the situation (and comes close to voiding his lease), but eventually warms to the idea of having him around, one flight above her. Paul's typist, Grace D'Angelo (Nan Martin), is even more acerbic than Stark, and she bears a striking resemblance to Madame, Wayland Flowers's most famous marionette. She is constantly attempting to get Stark back into the dating scene. In the pilot, Stark's son, Chris (John P. Navin, Jr., previously the co-star of *Jennifer Slept Here*), looks in on his dad often. Brian Benben portrayed Stark's teaching assistant, the miniskirt-obsessed Gary Franz (in the pilot), but was replaced by David Knell as klutzy and honest Warren Leftwich (for the series). They share classroom number 206. Others in the cast included Cecilia Hart as divorcee and budding romantic interest Janice Hall (she works in a sporting goods store and meets Stark at a singles bar), and Leonard Frey is the annoying, egotistical, and very funny drama professor Leon Walters. Frey was not in the pilot. About her fellow actor, Molly Hagan recalled, "There was no one funnier than Leonard Frey. Sadly, he died only about two years after *Mr. Sunshine*. I followed him around like a puppy."

About her own recurring character, Jane, Hagan said, "She was such a Machiavellian manipulator that she was a joy to play." Because Tambor's character was blind, was it difficult to extract comedy from a series where that's the focus? Hagan replied, "Not if you're Jeffrey Tambor! How brilliant is this actor? He was hilarious on the show. To me the humor came from what he could see that no one else could. Also, watching how characters tried to get away with things around him or their discomfort in dealing with someone with a disability was very funny. It was thrilling being on that set surrounded by these titans. All of them had soooo much experience. Listening to them talk was incredible. I was in my early twenties, had very little experience in Hollywood, and just wanted to absorb everything. They ALL were very kind to me and taught me much. I later studied acting with Jeffrey when he subbed for Milton Katselas." There was no gray area in the public's reaction to this program. A few were incensed because so much of the program's humor was derived from Stark's blindness, but most were impressed by the respect shown for the disability. After eleven episodes, the sun set on the set of *Mr. Sunshine*. The multi-talented Jeffrey Tambor later shone again in *Arrested Development* and *Transparent*.

"John Rich was a tremendous director, personality and story teller," Hagan reflected. "He was effortlessly funny and his laugh was robust and easy. When I made him laugh, it felt like winning the lottery, a gold medal and an Emmy all rolled into one. I adored John. However, he did not suffer fools and you didn't want to piss him off. He loved to talk to the audience during taping. He would use the 'god mic' from the booth to crack jokes or inform the audience what was going on. In fact, I don't remember a warm-up comedian for the show. I feel like John did it. The audiences loved John Rich and were treated to some *real* insight on how sitcoms were made. He liked to make it a seamless experience for them, as if they were going to the theatre. Costume changes were quick. Camera moves to the different sets were well choreographed. If my memory serves me, the audience members even received programs. So if John ever stopped the show you knew something was desperately wrong. During the taping of the episode called 'Leftwich in Love,' John announced from the booth that we were going to take a brief break. I thought to myself, 'Oh, my god, someone must be really screwing up.' Then I saw John round the corner and head towards me. It was *me*! I was screwing up! And I didn't even know it. Again, if my memory serves, all he said was, 'You simply must be better than this.' John had a way of scaring me straight. I think it worked because they asked me back for another episode and if the show had gone on another year they were going to make me a regular (she sighs). Rich and Henry Winkler were producing partners on many projects together. I think one of their projects, *MacGyver*, was only in its second year. So Henry had to divide his time between that and *Mr. Sunshine*. Henry was around for casting, some run-throughs, notes, and I'm pretty sure tape night. John and he were a great team. Henry softened John's edges. Henry had a way of communicating that made you feel like a billion dollars. He's a very kind man and was a terrific cheerleader for me."

Episodes were titled "The Pilot," "Mrs. Swinford Takes the Plunge," "The Evaluation," "Strictly Personal," "Educating Swinford," "The Theater Calls Grace," "Too Many Cooks," "Fear of Falling," "Leftwich in Love," "Great Expectations," and "Take My Ex-Wife, Please." The executive producers were Henry Winkler, John Rich, and Gene Reynolds; the producer was Bob Ellison; the writers included David Lloyd, Bob Ellison, Emily Marshall, Bruce David, Bruce Helford, and Peter Noah; the lone director was John Rich. The creator was David Lloyd. Music was provided by Randy Edelman.

Mork and Mindy (Animated) Hanna-Barbera Productions/Ruby-Spears Productions/Paramount Television. ABC. Saturday mornings 10:00 (September 25, 1982–March 26, 1983). Twenty-six animated episodes were filmed without a laugh track.

This animated version of *Mork and Mindy* went into production as the prime-time series was winding down, and didn't begin airing on Saturday mornings until the original sitcom ended its run. Because of the cancellation of the prime-time version, this new one never ran on its own, but rather as part of *The Mork and Mindy/Laverne and Shirley/Fonz Hour*. Robin Williams provided the voice for Mork, Pam Dawber for Mindy, and Conrad Janis for Mindy's father, Fred McConnell. Orkan leader Orson was voiced by Ralph James. There were, however, a few differences in this cartoon version—Mork was given more magical powers, and he had an unusual Orkan pet—a poodle named Doing that worked just as well in individual segments or all in one (he also ate with his tail). Mork had an ankle alarm set to wake him up in the morning, and Mindy's affections were being pursued constantly by a blond rich guy named Hamilton (voiced by Mark L. Taylor), but Mork always came to the rescue. The animated *Laverne and Shirley* and *Fonz* segments began in 1981. When they returned for a second season in 1982, *Mork and Mindy* was added to the fray. Mork's theme song greatly resembled that of *Sanford and Son*. They all ended their respective runs in 1983.

Episodes were titled "Who's Minding the Brat?," "The Greatest Shmo on Earth," "To Ork or Not to Ork," "Orkan Without a Cause," "Mork Man vs. Ork Man," "Which Witch Is the Witch?," "Every Doing Has His Day," "Beauty or the Beast," "Morkel and Hyde," "The Wimp," "Ride 'em Morkboy," "Meet Mork's Mom," "Muddle in the Huddle," "The Incredible Shrinking Mork," "The Invisible Mork," "The Fluke Spook," "Mayhem for the Mayor," "Coo Coo Caveboy," "A Treasure Ain't No Pleasure," "The Mork with the Midas Touch," "Extra Terrestrial Toddler," "Time Slipper Slip-Up," "Super Mork," "Mork, P. I.," "Monkey on My Back Pack," "On Your Mork, Get Set, Go." The executive producers were William Hanna and Joseph Barbera; the producers were Joe Ruby and Ken Spears; the writers included Norman Maurer; the directors included John Kimball and Rudy Larriva. Among the many celebrity guest star voices were Allan Melvin, Dave Coulier, Stan Freberg, Larry Storch, Alan Young, and Julie McWhirter Dees.

Nearly Departed Baskin/Shulman Productions/Lorimar Television. NBC. Monday nights 8:30 (April 10, 1989–May 1, 1989). Six episodes were filmed, five before a live audience and one with a laugh track. Only four episodes aired.

Nearly *Single Season Sitcoms List* 105

The cast and crew of NBC's soon-to-be-departed *Nearly Departed*: (back row, left to right) executive producers John Baskin and Roger Shulman, director John Rich, and line producer Jack Seifert; (middle row) Eric Idle, Caroline McWilliams, Henderson Forsythe, and Wendy Schaal; (front row) Stuart Pankin and Jay Lambert (photograph courtesy Jack Seifert).

This program's title was a play on the term "dearly departed," and as producer Jack Seifert recalls, "There was a contest at Lorimar Television to come up with a title for the show, and *Nearly Departed* was the winner, hands down. The program had a very clever theme song, written by two very talented songwriters I knew named Randy Petersen and Kevin Quinn, and was performed by Eric Idle. It spelled out the show's premise in the opening credits that I had created, and which were enthusiastically approved by then Lorimar head of production Les Moonves (now head of CBS). In fact, reviewers said things like, 'If only the show was as good as its opening credits theme song.'"

In a nutshell, Grant and Claire Pritchard (*Monty Python*'s Eric Idle and *Benson*'s Caroline McWilliams, respectively) are killed in a rockslide. Regarding McWilliams, Seifert said, "She was married to actor Michael Keaton at the time, and he sometimes dropped by the set on show night." If the program's setup sounds familiar, you've likely seen either the movie or TV series called *Topper*. The only difference in *Topper* was that the ghosts, George and Marian Kerby, were killed in an avalanche, along with their champagne-guzzling St. Bernard named Neil. In *Nearly Departed*, the "departed," Eric and Caroline as the Pritchards, come back to inhabit their old "haunts," including their home, now occupied by the Dooley family—Mike (Stuart Pankin), Liz (Wendy Schaal), their son Derek (Jay Lambert), and Liz's dad, Grandpa Jack Garrett (Henderson Forsythe). For whatever reason, Grandpa is the only one who can see and converse with the spirits. About Forsythe, Seifert said, "For various reasons, he won the role over a lot of heavyweights. Donald O'Connor, Harry Morgan, and Eddie Albert, among others, all auditioned for the role, but just weren't up to it at that stage of their lives." The Pritchards (Eric and Caroline) want the Dooleys to leave the premises, but tolerate their presence after they befriend Grandpa.

Stuart Pankin said, "Our show owes a lot to *Topper*. I'm not certain why only the grandfather on our show could see the Pritchards; I never asked. Perhaps it had something to do with his age." Pankin added, "Five of the six episodes were filmed before a live audience, but the final episode ["Grant's Aunt"] is the exception. Eric Idle portrayed his own aunt who came for a visit, unaware that her nephew had 'departed.' That one was done in the manner of the old *Patty Duke Show*, with Eric in both roles in the same scene" (and naturally relied on special camera effects that were impractical to do in front of a live audience, per Jack Seifert). Pankin went on, "Because three of the four Dooley family members couldn't see the ghosts, this was the only episode in which I got to interact with Eric on camera."

Seifert opined, "The series' premise was ultimately very limiting because only the grandfather could see and communicate with the ghosts. It was like comedy in a straitjacket, and Eric found it especially confining. The necessary comedic chemistry was simply very hard to create under the circumstances. It also became limiting for the writers as the series progressed, as they were rather challenged to invent fresh situations for upcoming episodes."

Topper was quite successful on TV—so why didn't *Nearly Departed* follow in its footsteps? "Who knows why a show fails?" Pankin pondered. "There are so many variables—time slot, lead-in, competition on the other networks. I was just happy to be a working actor working with some terrific people (Caroline became a close friend of my wife and mine) and getting a steady paycheck." Seifert recalled, "Speaking of the competition on the other networks mentioned by Stuart, we were up against *MacGyver*, which also happened to be a show executive produced by our series director, the legendary John Rich. He couldn't help gloating every week, when his other show had beaten us handily, as usual. By the way, *Nearly Departed* was shot on Stage 24, on what was then the Lorimar Studios lot in Culver City, formerly the storied MGM Studios, but which then briefly became Warner Bros., then Columbia, and now is Sony Studios." Several episodes of the series, including "Altared States," in which the ghosts discover that their marriage was not legal because his divorce wasn't yet finalized, and Eric's dual role in "Grant's Aunt," are available for viewing on YouTube.

Episodes were titled "Grant Meets Grandpa," "Adventures in Babysitting," "Altared States," "TV or Not TV," "Grandpa's Date," and "Grant's Aunt." The executive producers were Roger S. H. Shulman and John Baskin (of the Baskin-Robbins family); the producer was Jack Seifert; the (ghost) writers included John Baskin, Roger S. H. Shulman, Sy Dukane, Neil Alan Levy, Denise Moss, Dale McRaven, and Daniel Palladino; the lone director was John Rich, about whom Seifert said, "He could be a bit gruff at first, but actually was very nice once you got to know him and obviously was an excellent director and a true pro. His list of credits, going back to *All in the Family*, is amazing." Music was provided by Richard Berres and Robert Irving, with the theme by Randy Petersen and Kevin Quinn.

The New Adventures of Beans Baxter Fox Square Productions. FOX. Saturday nights 8:30 (July 18, 1987–October 3, 1987) and Saturday nights 9:00 (October 10, 1987–November 28, 1987). Seventeen episodes were filmed in Vancouver, Canada, without a laugh track. Sponsors included Kraft and the U.S. Army.

There never were any *old* adventures of

The cast of FOX's *The New Adventures of Beans Baxter*: (left to right) Jonathan Ward, Elinor Donahue, and Scott Bremner (photograph courtesy Elinor Donahue).

Beans Baxter (except maybe in his native Witches Creek, Kansas), and yet this tongue-in-cheek spy spoof series for the fledgling Fox Network was titled *The New Adventures of Beans Baxter*. Beans is not the only unusual character name in the cast; there is also Cake, Woodshop, Number Two, and Scooter. Beans's real first name is Benjamin (Jonathan Ward), who is seventeen and a junior. Benjamin Baxter, Sr. (Rick Lenz), had been a top-secret spy disguised as a postal carrier, but was kidnapped by UGLI (The Underground Government Liberation Intergroup), an evil group headed by the sinister Mr. Sue (Kurtwood Smith). The kidnapping was made to look like an assassination. Beans's mother, Susan, played by Elinor Donahue (Beans didn't know his mother's first name was Susan until episode number 14), was completely oblivious to her husband's background in espionage, and is equally oblivious to Beans's double life—he is a student at Upper Georgetown High School in Washington, D.C., and (under the direction of Number Two, played by Jerry Wasserman) a messenger for "The Network," in the search for his dad. Beans's mother and much younger brother Scooter (Scott Bremner) believe that the senior Benjamin had died, but Beans knows better—he witnessed the kidnapping.

About earning the role of Susan, Elinor Donahue said, "The odd thing was, I was the only grown woman actress at the audition at 20th Century Fox Studios in Century City, California. After waiting for well over an hour, I met with a large group of executives, sat on a folding chair, and read the script they'd provided. Everyone at the meeting was smiling. By the time I got back home I heard that I had the job—I was the only one up for it."

Cake Lase (Karen Mistal) is one of Beans's best friends at school. She really wants to go steady with Beans, but because finding his old man is his top priority, his personal life is put on the back burner. Beans's best male friend is nicknamed Woodshop (Stuart Fratkin). About the cast, Donahue recalled, "We shot a mini pilot in Moorpark, near Simi Valley. That was the first time I met Jonathan Ward, and I was immediately taken with him. Sweet, smart, polite, easy to work with, very professional. We hit it off right away. Now Scott Bremner was a darling little boy, but every bit of the dickens he played on the show. I'm ashamed to say I was not always patient with him. We never established a rapport, and it was all my fault. However, Karen Mistal, Stuart Fratkin, and I all got on well. However, there was this one time the three of us were all catching the same flight for Los Angeles. Stuart was a budding comic and after going through customs jokingly said, 'Whew, we got away with that.' Well, all hell broke loose, and all of our items were gone over with a fine-tooth comb. We almost missed the plane, but as we boarded I said, 'Well, did we learn anything today?'"

About the launch of the series, Donahue recalled, "There was a big media party at the old KTTV studios in Hollywood. Fox's Barry Diller was brought over to me to say hello, and although our meeting was brief, he said I just lit up the screen. Talk about a thrill!" About the Halloween episode titled "The Nightmare on Beans' Street," Donahue reflected, "For the trick-or-treat scene, Savage Steve asked what would be my heart's desire for a costume, and I said, 'Glinda, the Good Witch' from *The Wizard of Oz*. The costume was gorgeous except that we shot between midnight and 2 or 3 a.m. on a damp, cold night. Stupid me, I could have been a bunny or a clown all covered up, but no, there I was nearly freezing in a sleeveless net ballet dress." She added, "Sometimes we had to shoot no matter what the weather to keep on schedule. Did you know you can't see rain on film unless it's backlit? Well, one night Stuart, Jon, and I were doing our scene and it was misty. We kept going even after it turned to rain until the moisture was running through our hair and down our faces. Then and only then we heard, 'Cut, it's a wrap!'"

Lenz's favorite memory: "In one of the episodes, I shouted, 'Beans! Beans!' And Jonathan hollered back, 'Dad! Dad!' I arrived a few weeks later to shoot another episode and as I got to the set, the crew all hollered, 'Dad! Dad!' It was fun. In fact, I'd say doing *The New Adventures of Beans Baxter* was an absolute blast. I too was disappointed it didn't have a lovely long run. My wife and I flew up three or four times and each time had a nice Vancouver vacation while we were there. The cast was universally swell. I became good friends with Kurtwood Smith and his wife, Joan. I loved working with Elinor, although we didn't have many scenes together—maybe just a series of stills we did as 'the family. We talked about our mutual friend Jane Wyatt. Elinor played Jane's daughter on *Father Knows Best*, and I worked with Jane, also as her child, in a PBS play called *Ladies of the Corridor*. We both had ongoing relationships with her." Lenz shares many more memories of the program in his award-winning memoirs, *North of Hollywood*.

After seventeen fun episodes, the program was canceled by FOX. Donahue recalled, "I was to have more to do on the show in the future, and was looking forward to that. I was on one of my 'home weeks,' enjoying a quiet rest day when the phone rang. I don't even remember who called, but I was told it was over. I loved the people on the set and the Vancouver-ites, my apartment. It was so sad for everyone. The cancelation came directly from Barry Diller, who'd given orders that certain things that were not to be filmed were, and while viewing the dailies in a screening room, ordered that the show be shut down. To this day I really have no idea what caused it."

Episodes were titled "Beans' First Adventure, Parts One and Two," "Beauty and the Beans," "Beans Runs for President," "Beans and the Satanic Backwards Masking Conspiracy" (with guest star Dee Snider of Twisted Sister), "Beans' Wicked and Awesome Adventures at College" (with guest star Jason Priestly), "Beans in Ski Heck," "There's No Place Like Omsk," "Beans Finds His Dad But … Parts One and Two," "Beans' Unpleasant Introduction to Modern Science," "Beans Goes to Camp," "A Nightmare on Beans' Street," "Beans' Home Life Gets UGLI" (with guest star G. Gordon Liddy), "Beans Under the Weather" (with guest star Mike Reno of Loverboy), "Beans Gets His Driver's License," and "Beans in Jungleland." The executive producer was Savage Steve Holland; the producers included Tony Palermo, Giedra Rackauskas, Anthony Eaton, and Douglas C. Forbes; the writers included Martin Olson, Mary Jo Pritchard, Andrew Katz, Rick Overton, Larry Schulze, Bruce Wagner, and Savage Steve Holland. About Holland, Donahue shared, "He wore so many hats on the show that it seems so odd to me I don't recall meeting him until we were in Vancouver, British Columbia, for filming. He'd not be easy to forget—tall, handsome and blond. He was the ski-bum type, full of enthusiasm and fun. Everyone adored him. Wherever he was it was like a party. I gathered he had never directed before, but he was a quick learner and did a very good job. I got to work with Steve again a few years later in his cartoon series, *Eek the Cat*. Of course, I played a mom." Lenz concurred, "Savage Steve was a talented guy. I'm surprised we haven't heard more from him. He was one of those guys with great positivity, always a joy to hang out with." Music was composed by Joseph Vitarelli and performed by jazz great Maynard Ferguson.

The New Love American Style Paramount Television. ABC. Weekday mornings 11:30 (December 23, 1985–May 30, 1986). Eighty-five episodes were videotaped with a laugh track.

The original *Love American Style* enjoyed a five-season run on ABC from 1969–1974 in prime-time. The program consisted of several self-contained sitcom vignettes each week in an anthology format. Each of these vignettes focused on love or the absence thereof, as well as its inherent problems. It boasted a different set of guest stars in every episode—the program didn't have a regular weekly cast or recurring characters, except for those who participated in the blackout segments (very quick romance-related comedy skits in between vignettes).

After more than a decade, ABC opted to resurrect the program and air the episodes five days a week. It was now titled *The New Love American Style*, but very little had changed—the program's format remained intact. The blackout segments returned as well, and regular players in those short comedy skits included Marcia Wallace, Norm Crosby, Arsenio Hall, Barry Pearl, and Amy Yasbeck. About the latter, head writer John Boni shared, "Amy was beautiful, talented, and funny. It's so unusual to find all of that in one person. She was great." And about the title of "head writer," Boni added, "There are a million different titles given in the closing credits—producer, script consultant, story editor. Really, the only difference is the pay scale. The title and the pay changes with your degree of experience."

Airing five half-hour shows a week consisting of two fifteen-minute sitcom segments per show proved to be a very ambitious project. Almost every episode title began with the same three words—"Love and the..." Guest stars included Jamie Farr, Sheila MacRae, Regis Philbin, Fred Willard, Garrett Morris, Marilyn McCoo, Fabian, Gordon Jump, Caren Kaye, and Renny Temple. Temple recalled, "The producers and writers of the show knew that Caren Kaye and I were a couple, and asked if we'd like to do an episode, and we said yes. Much like my *Life and Times of Eddie Roberts* series, *The New Love American Style* aired five times a week, so our episode, 'How to Pick Up a Man/Love and the Mime,' happened very quickly."

Regarding the show's many guest stars, Boni stated, "I didn't get to see many of them. We writers weren't really involved in the tapings for this show. We were busy with writing a five-day-a-week show and not very involved in the actual performances. I do wish I had taken more pictures of the stars I did meet on all of the shows in which I had involvement. The list is staggering." Viewers, apparently, were of the "been there, done that" mindset, and low ratings proved to be *The New Love American Style*'s undoing. After eighty-five episodes and dozens of guest stars, ABC and *The New Love American Style* got a divorce.

The executive producer was Gordon Farr; the producers were Alphy Hoffman, David Yarnell, Linda Morris, and Vic Rauseo; the writers included John Boni, Bob Noonoo, Diane Pershing, John Aylesworth, Ken Kuta, Jonathan Torp, Bruce Trampler, Stephen Sustarsic, and Buddy Atkinson; the directors included Bob Lally and Bob Claver. Music was provided by Howard Pearl, and the theme song was performed by Lou Rawls.

The New Monkees Straybert Productions/Coca-Cola Telecommunications/Colex Enterprises/Columbia Pictures/Warner Bros. Records. Syndicated. Air dates and times varied. Fall 1987. Thirteen episodes were filmed single-camera style with a laugh track.

With few exceptions, the prefix "new" in front of a TV series' title denotes disaster (*The New Andy Griffith Show*, *The New Odd Couple*, *The New Phil Silvers Show*, *The New Loretta Young Show*), and this was certainly no exception. The expensive, ambitious, and exhaustive search for the young men who would portray The New Monkees took longer than the series ran. An unmitigated disaster, this series was concocted to cash in on the popularity surge of the original Monkees as a result of a twentieth anniversary celebration, new album, and reunion tour of 1986. The result was a program with updated music, hairstyles, clothing, and unknown actors placed in a hackneyed 1960s sitcom format (definitely among the last shows to employ a laugh track). The program's tagline was "The fun is back."

The pilot episode even showed some of the audition process and how the final four were selected. They were Larry (Larry Saltis), who donned a blond mullet; Jared (Jared Chandler), who lives to surf; Marty (Marty Ross), who often speaks backwards; and Dino (Dino Kovas), a melding of The Fonz (*Happy Days*) and Stanley Kowalski (*A Streetcar Named Desire*). A bit more high-tech than the original, the boys live and rehearsed their musical selections together in a huge old mansion (in which they often get lost). Their staid butler is named Manford (Gordon Oas-Heim), and a waitress named Rita (Bess Motta) whip up their meals in an in-house diner that serves as their kitchen (both servants came with the house). A bizarre, disembodied set of lips named Helen (Lynne Godfrey) appears on screens throughout the manse expanse and comments on the goings-on (she had previously worked at the Pentagon). There was also a *New Monkees* album (Warner Bros. LP no. 25642) and a single release titled "What I Want" (Warner Bros. no. 28188). The TV-viewing and record-buying public released a loud, collective yawn, and the entire cast soon boarded "The Last Train to

Clarksville," and Columbia Pictures Television was soon out of the Monkee business. It's interesting to note that all four members of The New Monkees reunited for a one-shot twentieth anniversary performance in 2007.

Episodes were titled "Weather the Storm," "All My Martys," "Test Tube Tube," "Minister Bob," "Ruff Day," "Don't Touch that Dial," "Monkee Mall," "Larry Leaves," "King of Space and Time," "Meet the Pope" (with guest star Ray "Boom Boom" Mancini), "Helen Goes Shopping," "The Game of Games Show," and "My Three Sons." The executive producer was Steve Blauner; the producers were Matt Fassberg, and Victor Fresco; the writers included R. B. Armstrong and Jeremy Bate; the directors included Ed Greenberg, Rick Friedberg, George Bloom, Victor Fresco, Rocky Schenck, Robert Radler, and C. D. Taylor. Some of the music was provided by Peter D. Kaye.

The New Odd Couple Henderson Productions/Paramount Television. ABC. Friday nights 8:30 (October 29, 1982–February 25, 1983), Friday nights 8:00 (May 13, 1983–May 20, 1983), and Thursday night (May 26, 1983). Eighteen episodes were filmed in front of a live audience.

The only thing new about *The New Odd Couple* was the cast—finicky photographer Felix Unger (Ron Glass) and sloppy sportswriter Oscar Madison (Demond Wilson) were portrayed by African American actors. This new take on an old chestnut came to be because of how well the original ABC TV version with Tony Randall and Jack Klugman was doing in syndication (much better than it had

The racially diverse cast of ABC's *The New Odd Couple*: (clockwise, from top left) Liz Torres, John Schuck, Bart Braverman, Sheila Anderson, Ronalda Douglas, Demond Wilson, Ron Glass, and Christopher Joy, center.

fared in prime-time). Murray the cop was now portrayed by the very tall John Schuck, and Homer "Speed" Deegan was now played by Christopher Joy (who was originally considered for the part of Oscar). Felix's ex-wife was not named Gloria in this version, but rather reverted to the original Neil Simon play and movie, as she was once again named Frances (Telma Hopkins). Several characters who hadn't been seen since Season One of the old series made triumphant returns—Roy, the card player, was back in the form of Bart Braverman; and the Pigeon Sisters, Cecily and Gwendolyn were now portrayed by Sheila Anderson and Ronalda Douglas, respectively. A couple of new names joined the fray, too—Maria (Liz Torres) and Mona (Jo Marie Payton). Missing in action in this version were card player Vinnie Barella; Oscar's secretary, Myrna Turner; upstairs neighbor Miriam Welby; Dr. Nancy Cunningham; and Oscar's ex-wife, Blanche. Garry Marshall was involved in trying to make a go of this new version, as was former head writer Mark Rothman (from seasons three through five of the original version).

Numerous scripts from the old series were reworked for *The New Odd Couple*, but the magic and chemistry of the original simply wasn't there. Mark Rothman's former writing partner, Lowell Ganz, was not involved in this new take on *The Odd Couple*, but because he co-wrote so many of the reused scripts, his name appeared often in the credits. Ron Glass and Demond Wilson had a good working relationship, but unlike Tony Randall and Jack Klugman they weren't friends and never really socialized together. Rothman shared, "Ron Glass, unlike Tony Randall, was not willing to look foolish on the show, whereas both Randall and Jack Klugman sought out and reveled in the ridiculous nature of their respective characters." Randall, in fact, often requested that the writers make him look as preposterous as possible on a weekly basis, thus the consistent comedic goldmine.

The original version of the episode "That Was No Lady" had Felix unknowingly falling for the opera-loving wife of an extremely jealous and violent football player. In the remake version, Ron Glass was vehemently opposed on moral grounds, and the "wife" had to become merely a "girlfriend" of a famous and violent sports figure (a boxer). The director of most of the episodes, Joel Zwick, also noted, "Instead of the two Jewish forty-year-old men in the original, we had two handsome black men in their thirties. At the time, the term 'metrosexual' didn't exist, and to keep Ron Glass's Felix from being seen as gay, we had to constantly surround him with a lot of women. Also, Jewish men and black men tend to settle arguments differently, so we had to make a lot of dialogue adjustments. Tony Randall and Jack Klugman were quite similar to their roles on the show, while Demond Wilson and Ron Glass were not. Demond always arrived to the studio nattily dressed, while Ron Glass was actually the sloppier dresser. It was their earlier TV characters [Glass on *Barney Miller*, and Wilson on *Sanford and Son*] that typecast them. Also, Ron Glass was miscast as neurotic. Ron was very erudite, sophisticated, and metrosexual, but he was anything but neurotic. I was closer to Ron than Demond during our brief time together. Ron and my daughter really clicked and became buddies."

About Demond Wilson, Rothman recalled, "Week after week I noticed this rather obese, hulking figure of a man hanging around the set. He had a shaggy beard, wore a rumpled raincoat, and resembled a rather seedy homeless guy. I finally asked around to find out who the guy was. Turns out, he was Demond's manager and his name was Roy Radin. I knew the name in an instant—he was a show business promoter and packaged vaudeville-like shows in the 1970s and 1980s, getting work for some long-forgotten talent. Only a very short time after *The New Odd Couple* was canceled, I read that Radin had been murdered. Apparently, he was attempting to get a percentage of the take from *The Cotton Club* motion picture. His involvement led to his being the victim of a murder-for-hire in what became known as 'The Cotton Club Murder.'"

After fifteen episodes had been aired, the program was put on hiatus until May when the final three unaired episodes were burned off. Episodes were titled "The Ides of April" (with guest star Esther Rolle), "The Hustler," "Frances Moves In," "That Was No Lady," "Brother, Can You Spare a Job?," "The New Car," "The Cordon Bleus" (with guest star Gretchen Wyler), "The Odd Triangle," "Opening Night," "Security," "Bachelor of the Year," "A Grave for Felix," "My Strife in Court," "Oscar Dates Felix's Frances," "Murray's Hot Date," "The Perils of Pauline," "The Only Way to Fly," and "The Night Stalker" (with guest star Franklin Ajaye). About the episode titled "Security," Zwick added, "We found out the Demond Wilson had a paralyzing fear of dogs the week we did that episode. We had to shoot around that problem with me playing the dog to get the shot. There are some very funny outtakes from that week." The executive producers were Garry and Anthony W. Marshall; the producers were Norman Barasch, and Bruce Johnson; the writers included Garry Marshall, Mark Rothman, Jeffrey Duteil, Ralph Farquhar, Kurt Taylor, Madeline and Steven Sunshine, Norman Barasch, Lee Kalcheim, Mary Cory Miller, Jerry Ross, Jerry Belson, Dick Bensfield, Perry Grant, Marc C. Miller, Barry O'Brien, Stu Silver, and Millee Taggart; the directors were Joel Zwick and John Tracy. Music was supplied by Dan Foliart and Howard Pearl. The theme song was an updated rendition of the Neal Hefti classic. A still newer and more successful remake version of the series debuted on CBS on February 19, 2015, starring Matthew Perry as Oscar Madison, and Thomas Lennon as Felix Unger.

Nick and Hillary see ***Tattingers***

No Soap Radio Alan Landsburg Productions/Mort Lachman and Associates/Reeves Entertainment Group. ABC. Thursday nights 8:00 (April 15, 1982–May 13, 1982). Five episodes were filmed in front of a live audience.

Prolific actor Stuart Pankin, who portrayed house detective Tuttle on this short-lived sitcom, described the origin of the program's title this way—"It was the answer to a nonsense joke—a gentle prank joke. For example: What do you get when you cross a chicken with a zebra? *No Soap Radio*. The joke teller and his pals would laugh, and the outsider was confused." However, it's likely the show's title caused a lot of confusion for viewers. Was this a program about radio, like *WKRP in Cincinnati*? Was it a spinoff of the sitcom *Soap*? Pankin added, "Perhaps, in the long run, the *No Soap Radio* joke backfired."

No Soap Radio was, for all intents and purposes, American TV's answer to *Monty Python's Flying Circus*, or perhaps it was *Rowan and Martin's Laugh-In* in sitcom form. The program was set in the lobby of the once grand, but now rather seedy and run-down, Pelican Hotel in Atlantic City. Every episode had a storyline, but strayed from that storyline often with a bizarre and zany non sequitur, a bogus newsflash about Mr. Potato Head, a preview for a movie about people named Al, a shoe found in a box of breakfast cereal, a wolf howling in one of the hotel rooms, a boy with a basketball for a head, or the mention of sponsorship by Rico's Boom Boom Room (to name but a select few). The elevator doors and hotel room doors were part of a running gag on the show—they consistently opened up to some outlandish and unexpected goings-on. Steve Guttenberg portrayed Roger, the hotel manager. The hotel is an heirloom, and he is trying to keep the family business going, but is beset by financial woes and expensive-but-necessary repairs. He and his assistant Karen (Hillary Bailey) certainly have their hands full. Because of the hotel's dire financial straits, House Detective Tuttle is constantly attempting to get Roger to sell the building to him so that he can turn it into a profit-making parking lot. About the show, Stuart Pankin said, "It was a lot of silly fun. What a funny cast we had—Steve Guttenberg, Bill Dana [Mr. Plitzky], Edie McClurg [Marion], Fran Ryan [Mrs. Belmont], and Jerry Maren [Morris, the bellboy], one of the last surviving munchkins from *The Wizard of Oz*. I'm grateful to have been part of it—it led to my being cast as anchorman Bob Charles on the long-running and equally irreverent *Not Necessarily the News*."

Episodes were titled "The Pilot," "Carmine the Squealer," "Karen Fools Around," "Miss Pelican," and "The Bum's Rush." The executive producer was Mort Lachman; the producers were Les Alexander and Dick Smith; the writers included Les Alexander, Rich Hall, Ron Richards, Michael Jacobs, and Dick Smith; the directors included Bill Hobin and John Robins. The creators were Michael Jacobs, Dick Smith, Les Alexander, and Ron Richards. Seven years after the cancellation of *No Soap Radio*, Mel Brooks produced a rather similar program called *The Nutt House* (see entry). It was also set in a hotel lobby, there were also countless outrageous occurrences, and, sadly, it was also short-lived.

Nobody's Perfect The Mirisch Corporation/Universal Television. ABC. Thursday nights 9:30 (June 26, 1980–August 28, 1980). Eight episodes were filmed with a laugh track.

Ron Moody and Cassie Yates, the stars of *Nobody's Perfect*, an ABC show that lived up to its name.

This series was aired in the UK as *Hart of the Yard*. It was originally to air in the U.S. as *Hart in San Francisco*, and despite that clever title, ABC thought it would be confused with *Hart to Hart*, also on ABC, so in the U.S. it was known as *Nobody's Perfect*. Much in the manner of The Pink Panther movie series, Ron Moody portrayed a bumbling, accident-prone, pound cake–loving Roger Hart of Scotland Yard, who is transferred to the 22nd Precinct in "the city by the bay" in squad room 202. His new partner, Detective Jennifer Dempsey (Cassie Yates), who is constantly begging to be utilized on more cases, and Hart's immediate superior, Lieutenant Vincent de Gennaro (Michael Durrell), of office 202A, instantly become victims of his clumsiness. Like *The Pink Panther*, this sitcom contains a lot of great slapstick, at which Moody was very adept (along with fun impressions and clever improvisational skills). Other regulars in the cast included Detective Jacoby (Victor Brandt), Detective Ramsey (Renny Roker), and Detective Grauer (Tom Williams). Recurring roles included lab technician Dreyfus (Greg Monaghan), and informant Careful Eddie (Danny Wells). Moody lived to be ninety-one, and died on June 11, 2015.

Episodes were titled "Hart in San Francisco," "The Hart Is Good for Jogging," "What's on Third?," "Return of the Ocelot," "You Gotta Have Hart," "Daddy's Day," "It Was a Very Good Year," and "Hart in Jail." The executive producers were Chris Hayward, Arne Sultan, and Norman Barasch; the producers were Lew Gallo and Edward Montagne; the writers included Ken Hecht, Jordan Moffet, Chris Hayward, Donald Ross, Peter Gallay, Mike Marmer, Arne Sultan, and Bill and Kathy Greer; the directors included Robert Douglas, Norman Abbott, and Tony Mordente. Music was provided by Tom Scott, Allyn Ferguson, and Jack Elliott.

Nothing in Common Rastar Productions/TriStar Television. NBC. Thursday nights 9:30

(April 2, 1987–May 7, 1987) and Wednesday night 9:30 (June 3, 1987). Seven episodes were filmed in front of a live audience. Sponsored by Dodge Trucks.

Inspired by (and loosely based on) the 1986 Tom Hanks/Jackie Gleason film of same name, *Nothing in Common* is the story of the youthful, enthusiastic, and zany head of the David Basner and Associates Advertising Agency in Chicago, and his elderly father. David (Todd Waring) had previously been very successful with another agency, but wants to strike out on his own—a decision he came to rue when his company gets off to an extremely slow start, and his creditors grow very impatient. David certainly does have fun at the workplace; he encourages creativity, and his staff of loonies certainly take full advantage of said opportunity. As director Nick Abdo recalled, the fun was genuine: "The supporting cast consisted of very funny actors/comedians. There was a lot of creative freedom on the set, and we were able to play with the action as well as the words. When actors are allowed to put in their suggestions, it makes for a happy environment. Everyone enjoyed themselves. That is very much a part of all of Garry Marshall's projects. A happy set is reflected on the screen. That's the way he likes to run them."

Under David's employ are the newly hired researcher Jacqueline North (Wendy Kilbourne), who has some difficulty adjusting to the agency's lack of structure; British receptionist/secretary of five years, Victoria Upton-Smythe (Elizabeth Bennett); copywriters Norma Starr (Mona Lyden) and Mark Glick (Bill Applebaum); intern/gofer Myron Nipper (Patrick Richwood); Joey D. (Billy Wirth), the long-haired cameraman who constantly speaks of himself in third person and narrates his every move; and a secret pet tabby cat whose meows are occasionally heard. The onus was also on David to support his recently divorced, unemployed, incorrigible, free-spirited father, Max (Bill Macy, post–*Maude*).

Like many fathers and sons, David and Max have nothing in common, hence the title. Garry Marshall took the reins in bringing the big screen hit to the small screen, but because of his motion picture commitments, his participation lessened as the show progressed. Abdo recalled, "The show was still finding its legs when it was canceled. The numbers weren't bad. I heard the reason it was canceled was because the network wanted to be in business with Garry Marshall. When he left to start a movie, his involvement dwindled, so the network was no longer interested. I don't know if that is true, but that was what I was told." Did he think that the lack of Hanks and Gleason in the lead roles had anything to do with it? Abdo stated, "I don't think so. Todd is a very good actor. Bill Macy was fairly well known from *Maude*. The characters were changed to suit the actors." Sadly, even with *Cheers* as a lead-in, the show was axed after only seven episodes had aired. Had the show survived, would a romance between David and Jacqueline have come about? Abdo said, "There was no long-term Bible that I knew of, but I'm sure it would have eventually gone that route, as most shows do."

Episodes were titled "Dad for Hire," "Kissunderstanding," "Gone Fishing," "Peter Pan Principle," "Best Friends," "A Smile and a Shoeshine," and "Birthday, She Wrote." The producers were Garry Marshall, Alexandra Rose, Ronny Hallin, Millee Taggart, Tom King, and Marty Nadler; the writers included Samuro Mitzubi and Millee Taggart; the directors were Nick Abdo, Howard Shore, and Jules Lichtman. Al Aidekman was a consultant. Music was provided by James P. Dunne. *Nothing in Common* was a Rastar Production. About the origin of the name, Abdo recalled, "That was the name of Ray Stark's Production Company, who also produced the movie."

Nothing Is Easy see ***Together We Stand***

The Nutt House Alan Spencer Productions/Brooksfilms/Touchstone Television. NBC. Wednesday nights 9:30 (September 20, 1989–October 25, 1989). Ten episodes (including an hour-long pilot) were filmed with a laugh track, but only five aired.

This program debuted late in 1989, just

barely making it into this book. *The Nutt House* had a lot in common with a series called *No Soap Radio* from seven years earlier. The action in both take place in a once-grand but now run-down hotel, and most scenes were rife with sight gags, slapstick, incompetent staff members, and an unpredictable elevator. Sadly, both shows were also very short-lived. Molly Hagan, who portrayed hotel secretary Sally Lonnaneck, recalled, "It was a huge soundstage that was also used for a Lily Tomlin and Bette Midler movie called *Big Business*." Set in New York City, *The Nutt House* was a Mel Brooks show, but Hagan shared, "It was really Alan Spencer's, although it had a lot of Mel's sensibility. I remember Mel showed up one day during the filming of the pilot. He was very funny and kind. Alan was always around. He seemed to love the process, and we loved him." Regarding the significance of her character's name, Hagan pondered, "I think Alan was paying homage to Sally Field by naming her Sally [in fact, in the pilot episode, she utters Field's famous 'You like me, you really like me' line]. I have no idea about Lonnaneck … 'long neck?' I think Sally Lonnaneck was a much nicer person than I. I loved her because she always saw the best in people. She was an eternal optimist. All of which made it funny when she lost hope, was angry, or jealous."

The cast was certainly top notch—Harvey Korman played Reginald J. Tarkington, the kindly but incompetent and overwhelmed manager; Cloris Leachman was the dour, clingy, sex-starved, accent-laden head of housekeeping Wanda Frick with a mad crush on Tarkington (Leachman was also the elderly and very pale Mrs. Nutt in the pilot); Mark Blankfield was the bumbling, legally blind, Coke bottle–bespectacled elevator operator Freddy; Brian McNamara was Charles Nutt III, the young, handsome, but clueless ne'er-do-well ["The only thing I do well is ne'er"] son of the owner, Edwina Nutt; and Gregory Itzin was the tidy but scatterbrained desk clerk, Dennis.

About the stellar cast, Hagan said, "I thought I had died and gone to heaven. Every day was like Christmas. No matter how many hours we worked, and we actually worked some long hours, I never wanted to leave the set. I loved that cast and the scripts. We had an unbelievable amount of fun and we were always trying to make each other laugh and be as good as we could be. We would run things by each other and ask each other's advice on how to make it the best. I remember Harvey turning to us and asking, 'So'? This was Harvey Korman, *the king* of comedy, asking Brian, Greg, Mark and myself if what he was doing was any good? We were stunned, we didn't know what to say. He finally shouted, 'My god if it's *awful* you have to tell me!' I remember having a philosophical discussion about comedy with Harvey. He told me comedy couldn't be taught. It was either in your bones or not. He saw the stricken look on my face and said, 'Relax, it's in your bones.' I loved Harvey Korman.

"If I had only seen Cloris as Phyllis Lindstrom it would be enough for me to love her until the end of time. But after seeing her in *The Last Picture Show* [the 1971 Peter Bogdanavich film for which Leachman won a Best Supporting Actress Academy Award], I knew there was nothing this actress could not do. So, needless to say, I was also enamored of her. Cloris loved reading those god-awful rags they used to sell at the grocery checkout line. You know the ones with screaming headlines like: BAT BOY Found Alive and Well Living in New Mexico! or The Statisticians Agree—Sin All you Want, Heaven is Full! One day I was poking fun at her about it and she said, 'Oh you find wonderful things in here. You never know what might inspire you for characters.' Well, that shut me up. Thinking it was the source of her brilliance, I started buying them. I couldn't keep it up, though. They were just too awful. I remember Cloris coming up with really funny ideas at the last minute that drove the prop department crazy. She also liked to learn her lines at the last moment so everything would be fresh. That drove Harvey crazy. I can't remember in what episode it was, but there was one scene where Ms. Frick, in her efforts to cut down on hotel theft, drives a gigantic nail through a bible. Every time we did it I had to keep myself from gasping. Not only did I think it was laugh-out-loud funny, I was convinced we were going to hell.

"Mark Blankfield was so kindhearted and lovable. He was extremely gifted in comedy but I knew he could tear it up in drama too. I think he was working on a one-man show about John Barrymore at the time. I wish I would have seen that. Mark was always so physical in his comedy, I was scared he would hurt himself. Greg Itzin works more than any actor I know. He is an actor's actor who is as comfortable on stage as he is on a set. I loved watching Greg work because Dennis was such a complicated character. Greg would do things I could never have imagined when I read the script. He was always surprising and inspiring. Brian McNamara played Charles Nutt, Sally's love interest in *The Nutt House*. I didn't have a very difficult job. I don't remember any specific thing that is printable, but I know Brian and I were always cracking each other up."

Mrs. Nutt was extremely tight with the purse strings, so episodes of the series revolved around the staff's desperate search for new ways to attract business to keep their many creditors at bay—including staging a visit by the president of the United States (the Presidential Suite hadn't seen a president since Lincoln). The toughest *Nutt* to crack proved to be the ratings, and the program was canceled after only half of its filmed episodes had aired. Hagan said, "We were canceled as we were filming our tenth episode. It was like a murder had taken place on the set. We all felt varying degrees of shock, dismay, horror, sadness, anger, fear, and betrayal. I believe we had to finish shooting that episode, too. Oh, it wasn't fun."

The program was done on film with a laugh track. When asked if it's difficult to know if a bit is working when there's no live audience, Hagan added, "Sometimes I feel like a studio audience can get in the way of knowing whether something is truly funny, so I would say no. But I'm not a fan of laugh tracks either."

Episodes were titled "The Pilot," "The Accidental Groom," "A Frick Called Wanda," "21 Men and a Baby," "Suites Lies and Videotape," "When Charles Met Sally," "A Night at the Reunion," "To Tell the Truth," "My Man Tarkington," and "The Nutt Cracker Suite." The executive producers were Mel Brooks, Alan Spencer, and Bob Brunner; the writers included Mel Brooks, Alan Spencer, Mark Curtiss, Rod Ash, Richard Day, Jim Geoghan, Gerald Gardner, and Alicia Marie Schudt; the directors included Bruce Bilson, Art Wolff, Tom Trbovich, Gary Nelson, Bill Bixby, and Roger Duchowny. About the latter two, Hagan said, "I remember being star struck by Bill Bixby, and Roger Duchowny was another wonderful director. I had crushes on them both." Music was provided by Lance Rubin.

Off the Rack Brownstone and Mugwump Productions/Warner Bros. Television. ABC. Friday nights 9:30 (March 15, 1985–April 19, 1985). Seven episodes were videotaped in front of a live audience.

Off the Rack first appeared in a pilot episode that aired on December 7, 1984. For whatever reason, it didn't become an ABC series until March of 1985 and lasted for only six episodes. The program certainly had star power—Ed Asner was Sam Waltman, the "W" in H & W Garments. The "H" stood for Halloran and the door to their New York City garment district offices clearly states they've been in business together since 1960. Suddenly, in 1984, after twenty-four years of service to the fashion world, Daniel Halloran drops dead, leaving surly Sam in charge of a struggling operation. What isn't previously known by the Halloran family is that Dan had recently cashed in his life insurance policy to meet payroll. To Sam's dismay, Halloran's wife, Kate (Eileen Brennan), opts to take her husband's place. Sam and Kate always had a strained relationship, and Sam continually strives to make enough of a profit to buy her out, but always falls short. The newly widowed Kate has young mouths to feed—sixteen-year-old daughter Shannon (Claudia Wells) and seven-year-old Timothy (R. J. Williams in the pilot, and Corey Yothers in the series). Despite a lack of experience in the field,

Kate is quite adept at the job, much to Sam's chagrin. Pamela Brüll played Sam's devoted busybody secretary, Brenda Patagorski. In the pilot episode, Sam requests that, for the showing of the new clothing line the next day, Brenda wear something to show off her, er, "personalities." For fifty extra dollars, she agrees (a totally inappropriate request by current sensibilities). Besides R. J. Williams, there was one other change from the pilot to the series—William Brian Curran who played the playboy designer named J. P. and wore yellow-colored suits, did not make the cut. Additions for the series were Sandy Simpson as Skip Wagner, and Dennis Haysbert (star of a long series of Allstate TV commercials) as Cletus Maxwell. Likely, one of the program's biggest stumbling blocks was believability. Asner had been typecast as gruff and sloppy newsman Lou Grant in two different series, and transitioning to a role in the world of fashion seemed quite a stretch.

Episodes were titled "The Pilot," "A Date with Kate," "Partners," "Who Do You Trust?," "Here Comes the Bribe," "The Letter," and "Immigration Man." The executive producers were Marc Merson, Steve Marshall, and Dan Guntzelman; the writers included Steve Marshall, Dan Guntzelman, Bob Randall, Lissa Levin, Timothy James, and Larry Balmagia; the directors included Jay Sandrich and Noam Pitlik. Music was provided by Fred Karlin.

Oh, Madeline Carsey Werner Productions. ABC. Tuesday nights 9:30 (September 27, 1983–May 15, 1984). Nineteen episodes were videotaped in front of a live audience.

You have to start somewhere, and *Oh, Madeline* was the first series for Marcy Carsey and Tom Werner. It wasn't a hit, but oh did the hits come a short time later, with *The Cosby Show*, *A Different World*, *Roseanne*, *That 70s Show*, and *Third Rock from the Sun* among the highlights. *Oh, Madeline* starred Madeline Kahn as Madeline Wayne (née Vernon, Class of 1963), a woman experiencing a latent form of the seven-year itch now that she has been married for ten years. Her husband, Charlie (James Sloyan), is a good provider, but rather dull and very square. The only spice in his life occurs in the steamy novels he writes under the pen name of Crystal Love. Madeline still loves Charlie very much, but she is in a rut. Something has to give. Taking matters into her own hands, she opts to broaden her horizons and try every fad, every trend, every newfangled health food item on the market, and, in doing so, finds herself in some wacky predicaments, à la *I Love Lucy*. She attempts skiing, ice skating, bowling, writing, playing the banjo, meat curing, acting, and pottery, but still can't find her niche. Madeline's parents (seen in the "My Mother, the Carnal" episode) were portrayed by Geraldine Fitzgerald (Charlotte) and Ray Walston (Reese).

Writer Cindy Begel recalled, "Without doubt, [Madeline Kahn was] one of the top three people I've ever worked with. My partner Lesa Kite and I wrote the pilot for the show and we got the brilliant Madeline Kahn to read the script both to see if she liked it, and to see if she was right for the part. In both cases, the result was a definite yes."

On some of these new and often madcap ventures, Madeline Wayne is accompanied by her shy, newly divorced neighbor and friend Doris Leone (Jesse Welles), including a first foray to a nightclub that had male strippers. Doris's ex-husband is a free spirit named Bob Leone (Louis Giambalvo)—Charlie's best friend. Annie McIntyre (Francine Tacker) is Charlie's flirty editor who wants *him* more than his manuscript.

The program was based upon a British series titled *Pig in the Middle*, by Charlotte Bingham and Terence Brady. As Begel recalled, "The original British version of the show was quite different—it was about a married man with a girlfriend. Well, a series about that in the U. S. just wouldn't fly, not even today. By the time the show actually aired, it bore very little resemblance to the original. And with the amazing Madeline Kahn as the star, obviously the focus of the show had to be diverted from the husband to her. We wrote the 'To Ski or Not to Ski' episode, on which Madeline had to square dance with a cast on her leg, and the very memorable 'Chances Are' episode with guest star Johnny Mathis. It was originally written for Barry Manilow, but he bowed out because of another commitment and the focus became Johnny Mathis. It was a fun episode to write, but very challenging because we were much more familiar with Manilow's music than Mathis'. It turned out to be a very funny script, on which Madeline promises a performance by Mathis at her high school reunion, but then has difficulty delivering the goods. The funniest scene has her auditioning Mathis look-a-likes, only to send away the real Mathis as not convincing enough."

Occasionally the episode title was even funnier than the episode—"Yes, but I'm Married," "That Was No Lady," "Mummy Dearest," "Portrait of the Artist with a Young Man," "All the World's a Stage," "Book of Love," "To Ski or Not to Ski," "Madeline Acts Forward at the Retreat" (with guest stars Jeffrey Tambor and Jennifer Tilly), "Chances Are," "The Write Stuff," "Sisters," "Ah, Wilderness" (with guest star Joe Regalbuto), "Monday Night Madeline" (with guest star Dennis James), "The Lady and the Lamp," "Things that Go Bump in the Night," "My Mother, the Carnal" (with guest stars Bill Macy and Ray Walston), "Ladies' Night Out," "Play Crystal for Me," and "A Little Fight Music." The executive producers were Marcy Carsey and Tom Werner; the producers were Irma Kalish and Caryn Sneider; writers included Neal Marlens, Lisa A. Bannick, Charlotte Bingham, Terence Brady, Barton Dean, Bruce Ferber, David Lerner, Prudence Fraser, Laurie Gelman, Austin and Irma Kalish, Richard Rosenstock, Robert Sternin, Roy Teicher, Lesa Kite, and Cindy Begel; the director was J. D. Lobue. Music was provided by Dan Foliart and Howard Pearl. Madeline Kahn died much too young, of ovarian cancer, on December 3, 1999, at the age of fifty-seven.

Once a Hero Garden Party Productions. ABC. Saturday nights 8:00 (September 19, 1987–October 3, 1987). Seven hour-long episodes were filmed without a laugh track, but only three aired.

Once a Hero was an ambitious and well-reviewed fantasy-adventure-comedy series with inventive and colorful scenery, and yet was a ratings disaster. A ne'er-do-well comic book artist from Pleasantville named Abner Bevis (sorry, no Butthead), played by Milo O'Shea, creates a character not unlike Captain America called Captain Justice who suddenly, inexplicably comes to life (in a red suit with C. J. emblazoned on his chest). Justice was played by Jeff Lester, and he crossed over into the real world ("The Forbidden Zone") because he was tired of Bevis's hackneyed and repetitive plots and storylines—opting to fight crime as a human being (although, in crossing over, he surrenders his superpowers). Also taking the plunge was a stereotypical private dick named Detective Gumshoe, played by Robert Forster. These strange goings-on pique the interest of snoopy newspaper reporter Emma Greely. Emma's son, Woody, knows about Captain Justice's transformation, but never lets the cat out of the bag. After three imaginative episodes had aired, ABC delivered the "in-Justice" of a cancellation notice. Sadly, episode four with guest star Adam West (TV's *Batman*) never saw the light of day. Marvel also released comic books related to the series, but because of the show's short life only two were issued.

Episodes were titled "Believers" (two-hour debut), "Triangle," "Return of Lazarus," "Things Get Ugly," "Manos Arriba Mrs. Greely," "Remember the Cottonwood," and "Thank You, Captain Justice." The executive producer was Dusty Kay; the producers were Paul Pompian and Ira Steven Behr; the writers included Dusty Kay; the directors included Claudia Weill, Kevin Hooks, Harry Hurwitz, and Kevin Inch. The creator was Dusty Kay. Music was provided by Dennis Dreith.

One Big Family Witt/Thomas Productions/Lorimar Telepictures. Syndicated. Air dates and times varied. (September 27, 1986–May 23, 1987). Twenty-four episodes were videotaped with a laugh track. The sponsor was General Foods.

This one is set in Seattle, and features a

cranky, widowed, cigar-chomping, retired ex-vaudevillian comic named Jake Hatton (Danny Thomas), who is enjoying a nice, quiet existence, until tragedy strikes his family. Jake's brother and sister-in-law are killed in a car crash, and their twenty-three-year-old policeman son (with a penchant for celebrity impressions) Don, played by Anthony Starke (Jake's nephew), then becomes the ward to his four younger brothers and sisters. Jake opts to put his retirement on hold, and moves in to help (sometimes too much), both physically and financially, as Don and his newlywed wife, Jan (Kim Gillingham), raise the four mischievous youngsters, whose ages ranged from eight to nineteen. Marianne (Anastasia Fielding) is the eldest; Brian (Michael DeLuise) is seventeen and quite a handful; Kate (Alison McMillan) is fourteen, and Roger (Gabriel Damon) is eight and quite a scamp. Brian and Kate attend Fillmore High. (A couple of the kids on the show went on to other things. Alison McMillan, who is the daughter of actor Kenneth McMillan, enjoyed a long run on *Days of Our Lives*. Michael DeLuise, Dom's son, had a regular role on *Gilmore Girls*.) Keeping this family unit together is a full-time job, and Jake's sage advice often makes the difference.

The title of this series could also very easily have been *Make Room for Uncle*, but Tony Thomas and Paul Witt were insistent that the series not turn into *The Danny Thomas Show*, although the comedian appeared in twenty-one of the twenty-four episodes, according to co-executive producer David Pollock. But, inevitably, in every scene he was in, his Uncle Jake character always seemed to be the funniest. Aware of Danny's reputation as a scene stealer, Pollock and his partner, Elias Davis, were wary at first, but found the star exceedingly cooperative and easy to work with. One episode, Pollock recounted, that reunited Danny's character with his old vaudevillian partner, portrayed by Bill Macy, evoked such a hilarious on-camera, *Sunshine Boys* chemistry, Macy was invited back for a couple of additional episodes. The opening credits contain a narration by Danny Thomas with a lot of expository information, ending with "It's working out *great*. Alright ... it's working out." A favorite moment from the series, noted Pollock, involved Danny as Uncle Jake giving his youngest nephew comedy lessons for the little boy's third grade Talent Night skit, including mastering the classic "spit take." Sadly, much like Thomas's other post–*Make Room for Daddy* sitcom ventures *Make Room for Granddaddy*, *I'm a Big Girl Now* and the brilliant and very funny *The Practice*, *One Big Family* was short-lived. Reruns were briefly shown on the Goodlife cable channel.

Episodes were titled "Roger Runs Away," "Image Breaker," "Jake's Party," Jake's Commitment," "New House," "Talent Night," "Matchmaker," "Family Vacation," "Kate's Friend," "Charged Battery," "Odd Ball Game," "Stagestruck," "Jake the Beachcomber" (with guest star Barney Martin), "Joy to the Hattons," "Operation: Collins" "Kate's Dates," "Big Bust," "The Essay," "The Tutor," "Dog Daze," "Biting the Hand," "Old Times," "Brian's Law," "The Clip Show," and "The Big Split." The executive producers were Paul Junger Witt, Tony Thomas, David Pollock, and Elias Davis; the producers were Arnold Margolin, Marsha Posner Williams, and Sam Bobrick; the writers included David Pollock, Elias Davis, Daniel Palladino, Arnold Margolin, Jay Folb, Hank Bradford, Sam Bobrick, and Karin Babbitt; the directors included Gary Brown, Jeff Chambers, David Steinberg, Bob Sweeney, Doug Smart, and Terry Hughes. The creators were David Pollock, Elias Davis, and Paul Junger Witt. Music was provided by George Aliceson Tipton.

One in a Million Toy Productions. ABC. Tuesday nights 8:30 (January 8, 1980–January 15, 1980), Saturday nights 8:00 (January 26, 1980–April 5, 1980). Thirteen episodes were videotaped in front of a live audience.

Shirley Hemphill had portrayed Rob's Diner waitress Shirley Wilson for four seasons on the very popular ABC sitcom *What's Happening?* After that show was canceled, ABC and Saul Turteltaub, Bernie Orenstein, and Bud Yorkin's Toy Productions sought a starring vehicle for

Hemphill. They developed a sitcom titled *One in a Million* (not to be confused with the short-lived ABC game show of the same name hosted by Danny O'Neil) on which Hemphill would portray sassy and saucy Shirley Simmons—a cabdriver who, to her great surprise, inherits Grayson Enterprises, a multi-million dollar company from a regular fare, Mr. Grayson himself, with offices in the huge Grayson Building in Manhattan. Her new position within the firm is the one that the hairless and conniving Mr. Roland Cushing (Keene Curtis) had been eyeing. Her concerns for the common man further raises his ire. In the episode titled "Shirley's Prince of a Guy," she is smitten with a wealthy visiting African prince, leading Cushing to hope they will marry and that she would leave the company. Others in the company included Grayson's guileless nephew Barton Stone (Richard Paul post–*Carter Country*); and Shirley's secretary and friend Nancy Boyer (Dorothy Fielding). The wonderful Carl Ballantine portrayed Max, the owner of the deli in which Shirley regularly has lunch; Ralph Wilcox played a street vendor named Duke; and her folks, Raymond and Edna Simmons, were portrayed by Mel Stewart and Ann Weldon (stepmother), respectively.

Episodes were titled "Chairman of the Board," "Executive Dad," "Shirley's Prince of a Guy," "On the Cuff," "Lost Weekend," "Stone vs. Simmons," "The Chairman Babysits," "Suddenly Single," "Cushing Quits," "Max Falls in Love," "Over the Hill," "The Committee," and "The Italian Connection." The executive producer was Bud Yorkin; the producers were Saul Turteltaub, Bernie Orenstein, Arnold Kane, and Sid Dorfman; the writers included Rick Neigher, Chris Cote, Bill Box, Marty Brill, Sid Dorfman, Arnold Kane, Gail Honigberg, Alan Livingston, Barry Meadow, Bernie Orenstein, Donald Ross, Mort Scharfman, Bernie Tanz, Fredi Towbin, Saul Turteltaub, Sally Wade, Sandy Veith, Jerry Winnick, Harvey Weitzman, and Dick Westerschulte; the directors included Peter Baldwin, and Lee Berhardi. Shirley Hemphill performed the theme song.

One of the Boys **(1982)** Toy II Productions/Columbia Pictures Television. NBC. Saturday nights 8:00 (January 23, 1982–March 27, 1982), Saturday nights 8:30 (April 10, 1982–April 24, 1982). Thirteen episodes were videotaped in front of a live audience.

Mickey Rooney was just never able to make the successful transition from the silver screen to the small screen. Taking into consideration his height (or lack thereof), the small screen sounded ideal. He had a failed sitcom in four consecutive decades—*The Mickey Rooney Show/Hey, Mulligan* in the 1950s, *Mickey* in the 1960s, *A Year at the Top* in the 1970s, and this one in the early 1980s. *One of the Boys* tells the tale of Oliver Nugent (Rooney), an energetic geriatric from Rhode Island (a state that was small, like him). He wasn't happy at the Bayview Acres Retirement Home in which he was placed, so he moves in with his grandson, Adam (Dana Carvey), in his small apartment near the college he was attending, Sheffield University in New Jersey. Adam already had a roommate, fellow student Jonathan Burns (Nathan Lane). Burns is less than pleased with the new addition to the apartment. This arrangement also makes it more difficult to get into the bathroom (with the number 1776 and the words "One Way" on the door). Grandpa Oliver is a jogger and has more pep than either of the young students, and he is a noisy early riser. Luckily, he finds a friend in the same boat, Bernard Soloman (Scatman Crothers)—a former cabbie. They are close in age—Oliver is sixty-six, Bernard is sixty-seven, and they both love music. After numerous age-related rejections in their quest for work, they form a combo and perform some one-nighters in area nightclubs. Burns is ecstatic that this new venture keeps Oliver out of the apartment a lot, especially because he has a habit of breaking things while attempting to fix them. Francine Beers portrayed the landlord, Mrs. Green, who has a crush on the old guy, and Meg Ryan played Adam's recurring girlfriend named Jane.

Episodes were titled "The Pilot" (with guest star Wendie Malick), "Too Old or Too Young,"

The amazing (but unsuccessful) cast of the NBC 1982 sitcom *One of the Boys*—(left to right) Nathan Lane, Dana Carvey, and Mickey Rooney.

"Parents Weekend," "Double Trouble," "His Cheatin' Heart" (with guest star Olympia Dukakis), "Too Much to Lose," "Double Date," "The Lass Is Always Greener," "His Old Flame," "Extracurricular Activities," "On the Rebound," and "Don't Bank on It Parts One and Two" (with guest stars Cleavon Little and Barney Martin). The program was produced and created by Saul Turteltaub and Bernie Orenstein; the writers included Saul Turteltaub, Bernie Orenstein, Don Flynn, Norman Barasch, Barry Harman, Dinah and Julie Kirgo, Laurie Newbound, and Suzy Simon; the directors included Peter Baldwin, Lee Bernhardi, and Doug Rogers. Music was provided by Pete Rugolo, and the theme song was by Jonathan Turteltaub and Zina Goldrich. Seven years after this *One of the Boys*, NBC used the title again for another short-lived sitcom (see entry).

***One of the Boys* (1989)** ELP Communications/Stiefel-Phillips Entertainment/the Fred Silverman Company/Hunter-Cohan Productions/Columbia Pictures Television. NBC. Saturday night 9:30 (April 15, 1989), Saturday nights 8:00 (April 22, 1989–April 29, 1989), and Saturday nights 8:30 (May 6, 1989–May 20, 1989). Six episodes were videotaped in front of a live audience.

Not to be confused with the 1982 Mickey Rooney sitcom of the same name. On this one, Maria Conchita Alonso portrayed Maria Navarro—born in Cuba, but raised in Venezuela. She is a former waitress who rides a motorcycle. She takes a job at Lukowski Construction Company as its office manager, and soon becomes romantically involved with the owner, a widowed dad of two years named Mike (Robert Clohessy), who really needs help in the office *and* at home. The company is rife with Lukowski boys, Mike's sons—the chick magnet Luke (Michael DeLuise); Steve, the eldest (Billy Morrissette); and Nick, the youngest (Justin Whalin). About the boys, Clohessy shared, "They were a great bunch of kids. It's interesting to note that Billy Morrissette, who played my son Steve, was only five years younger than I. This was my first series, and the whole cast was great. We had some great chemistry and lots of hilarious fun. I often had a hard time keeping a straight face on camera. It was a blast." Others in the cast included Amy Aquino as Maria's best friend, Bernice DeSalvo, and the ubiquitous Dan Hedaya as Ernie, an employee of the construction company. Things move very quickly in this short-lived series consisting of six episodes—Mike and Maria meet, date, get engaged, and get married. Despite the whirlwind courtship, the series ended abruptly, so we will never know if there were any additions to the already large Lukowski family. Clohessy agreed, "Yes, things did move very quickly on the show. Had it continued, my on-screen relationship with Maria would have kept evolving." About Stiefel-Phillips Entertainment listed in the credits, Clohessy recalled, "I think they were Maria's talent managers, or that was her production company [named for Arnold Stiefel and Randy Phillips]. I'm not exactly sure. Maria was the show's focus—she was the star."

Episodes were titled "The Meeting," "The Dance," "The Date," "The Proposal," "The Wedding," "Maria Conchita Lukowski." The executive producers were Martin Cohan, Blake Hunter, and Fred Silverman; the producers were Lawrence Gay and Michael J. DiGaetano; the writers included Dava Savel, Martin Cohan, Blake Hunter, and Tom Palmer; the directors included Will Mackenzie and John Whitesell. The theme song was by Bob Ezrin and Michael Tavera.

Open All Night Freeway Productions. ABC. Saturday nights at 8:00 (November 28, 1981–January 30, 1982) and Friday nights at 8:30 (February 5, 1982–March 5, 1982). Thirteen episodes were videotaped in front of a live audience. Sponsors included General Foods International Coffees, Head and Shoulders shampoo, and Safeguard soap.

The opening theme to *Open All Night* may have provided more exposition than any other theme song in history. Performed at a very rapid pace, viewers found out that calorically challenged Gordon Feester was born in Ohio on the day before Easter, graduated from Columbus High School in 1962, attended but didn't finish college, and served a two-year army hitch at Fort Hood. A Gordon-of-all-trades, his most recent venture was a 7-Eleven knockoff called "The 364 Store" (closed only on Christmas), a convenience store that is open all night, hence the title. The program was loosely based on a British series called *Open All Hours*. Gordon (George Dzundza) is working a lot of extra hours after getting robbed by his former night manager.

In the debut episode, he hires a new African American night manager—a massive, classical music–loving presence named Robin (former NFL great Bubba Smith). Robin is wrongfully blamed for a robbery in the Carnegie Hall box office, but is cleared of all charges. Gordon's wife is a malcontent named Gretchen (Susan Tyrrell), who had been married three times before and is the former Miss Bandana in a nude magazine photo spread. She is the mother of Gordon's lethargic, dimwitted, ne'er-do-well, rodent-loving stepson Terry (Sam Whipple), whose only redeeming quality is that he speaks fluent Spanish. Terry wants very much to become the new night manager, but he is so inept, careless, and clumsy, said promotion never comes to fruition. His biological father is named Larry "Bud" Hofmeister (James Gallery). The Keystone-calibre cops who patrol the 364 Store beat are humorously named Steve (writer/producer/director/creator Jay Tarses) and Edie (Bever-Leigh Banfield), a nod to married singers Steve and Eydie Gorme. The wild array of miscreants who make up the clientele made for some amusing TV moments, but not for very long. *Open All Night* closed forever after thirteen weeks.

Episodes were titled "Night Moves" (with guest stars Joe Mantegna and Will Mackenzie), "Robin's Return" (with guest star Judge Reinhold), "Centerfold," "Buckaroo Buddies" (with guest star David Letterman), "First Love," "Terry Runs Away," "Sitting Ducks," "Such Good Friends," "Scam," "A Visit from the Folks," "The Chicken Suit," "Death of a Bag Lady," and "Edie's Girl." The producers were Bernie Brillstein, Gayle S. Maffeo, Tom Patchett, and Jay Tarses; the writers included Merrill Markoe, Carol Gary, Ken Levine, Tom Patchett, Jay Tarses, Sy Rosen, Ed Vincent, Dennis Danzinger, Thad Mumford, David Isaacs, Ellen Sandler, and Dan Wilcox; the directors included Will Mackenzie, Tom Patchett, Jay Tarses, Tony Singletary, and Thomas McConnell. Patchett and Tarses also created the show. Music was provided by Tom Wells, and the lyrics for the theme song were written by Patchett and Tarses.

Open House Ubu Productions/Paramount Television. FOX. Sunday nights 9:30 (August 27, 1989–May 6, 1990). Twenty-four episodes were filmed in front of a live audience. Sponsors included Maxwell House Coffee.

Open House was somewhere between a sequel and a spinoff of *Duet*. In fact, it was the replacement for *Duet* and contained several of the same cast members. The final episodes of *Duet* even set up this new series. Its original working title was "Hot Properties," but was renamed *Open House*. Mary Page Keller had the lead role on *Duet*, and Alison LaPlaca a more secondary role, but there is definite role reversal on *Open House* and LaPlaca was now the headliner. She portrayed Linda Phillips, whose job at World Wide Studios has come to an end and she has just started working at the Juan Verde Real Estate Company in Southern California, at 7150 Beverly Glen. Phillips and the obnoxious, persnickety, hyper-aggressive Ted Nichols (Philip Charles MacKenzie) soon become rivals. Both are competitive, a bit snooty, very self-centered (the insults between them are hurled at a fast and furious pace), and secretly attracted to one another. Linda is married to Richard Phillips

An advertisement for the FOX spinoff of *Duet*, called *Open House*. Pictured (left to right) are Danny Gans, Alison LaPlaca, Philip Charles MacKenzie, and Ellen DeGeneres.

(Chris Lemmon), a pianist at Jasper's Bar and Restaurant. The pair separate midseason, and Lemmon's role was eliminated. The daughter they had together, Amanda, appeared only in the first episode.

MacKenzie recalled, "In real life, Alison and I started dating during the run of the show, and we thought we were doing a great job at hiding that fact. All of our efforts to be discreet were for naught because, at a cast party, we discovered that everyone knew we were an item. We also became somewhat involved on the show towards the end of the season. My character, Ted Nichols, was a real schmuck. Ted thought that he was the stud of the century and he was out to conquer the world and become the best real estate agent ever. He met his sarcastic match in Linda Phillips, but kept going back for more. Our two characters became quite flirtatious very late in the season."

Others at the real estate office included Laura Kelly (Mary Page Keller), whose address—13205 Ocean Avenue— is tattooed on her breasts, along with her phone number; she previously owned a catering business, but is now a realtor. She is naïve, separated from her husband, and has a drinking problem. Margo Van Meter (a young Ellen DeGeneres) is the out of step, man-hungry secretary who has a pet cat she named Boris; Scott Babylon (Danny Gans) is one of the more unusual agents—he uses his keen ability to impersonate celebrities, such as George Burns and Sammy Davis, Jr., to sell houses (much in the manner that Brad Garrett's Frank Dutton character got clients on *First Impressions*). Roger McSwain (Nick Tate) was the demanding and overbearing owner of the agency. It's interesting to note that LaPlaca and MacKenzie got married a short time after *Open House* ended its run. So much for the myth about Hollywood marriages—they're still together today. About the show's demise, MacKenzie opined, "Most of the elements came together on this show, with the exception of the writing. We had such a great cast and chemistry—most of us had worked together on *Duet*. All of us, however, became very frustrated about the writing, and it was the writing that was *Open House*'s ultimate downfall. If it's not on the page, it simply can't happen." Several episodes were shown in reruns on the TV Land cable channel.

Episodes were titled "Fish Out of Water," "Scenes from an Office Marriage," "Going for Broker," "Whodunnit?," "Second Honeymoon, Anyone?," "Dome Sweet Dome," "Let's Get Physicals," "Married without Children," "Torn Between Two Houses," "Murder, He Wrote," "In Vegas with Showgirls, Parts One and Two," "Parade of Homes," "Bye Bye, Boris," "Who Framed Roger McSwain?," "An Unmarried Woman," "Bad Seed," "New Kid in Town," "The Real Estate Thing" (with guest star Jay Thomas), "The Roast," and "First Impressions." The executive producers were Susan Seeger, Ruth Bennett, and Bruce Ferber; the producers were Tom Walla, Deborah Leschin, Barry Vigon, and Linda Nieber; the writers included Ruth Bennett, Susan Seeger, Charbie Dahl, Tom Walla, Barry Vigon, and Bruce Ferber; the directors included Arlene Sanford, David Semel, Michael Zinberg, Sam Weisman, Lee Shallat, and Philip Charles MacKenzie. MacKenzie said, "That was part of my contract with the show. I was to direct two of the episodes." The creators were Ruth Bennett and Susan Seeger. Music and the theme song were provided by John Beasley and John Vester.

Park Place Starry Night Productions/Warner Bros. Television. CBS. Thursday nights 8:00 (April 9, 1981–April 30, 1981). Four episodes were filmed in front of a live audience.

Park Place was supposed to become an ensemble workplace sitcom in the same mode as *Taxi* and *Barney Miller*. *Park Place* featured a ragtag cluster of attorneys at the Legal Aid Clinic in Manhattan. Their Park Place Division of the Legal Assistance Bureau is rife with the poor, the downtrodden, and some out-and-out annoying members of society in need of immediate legal help. Sitcom veteran Harold Gould played David Ross, the man who is supposed to be in charge of this band of miscreant mouthpieces. David Clennon played Jeff O'Neill—the newbie; Don Calfa was the attention and photo-op seeking Howard "Howie" Beech; Mary Elaine Monti played the tough-as-nails and often unfeminine Joel "Jo" Keene—a huge advocate for and champion of women's rights; Lionel Smith was Aaron "Mac" MacRae—an African American wheelchair-bound veteran of the Vietnam War; and James Widdoes was Brad Lincoln, the somewhat snooty young know-it-all. Their stereotypical ditzy secretary (who was also devoutly religious), Frances Heine was played by Alice Drummond; and the way-too-cool receptionist, Ernie Rice, was portrayed by Cal Gibson. Unlike the Park Place on the Monopoly board, this one was not a hot property and CBS's verdict was to cancel the show after a *trial* run of only four episodes. The premise did look great on paper, though.

Episodes were titled "Revenge" (with guest star Florence Stanley), "Benign Neglect," "Crazy Judge," and "Marooned" (the latter has the staff and clients trapped in the building and unable to leave). The executive producer was Reinhold Weege; the producer was Tom Blomquist; the writers included Reinhold Weege and Tom Reeder; the directors included Peter Bonerz, Asaad Kelada, and Jeffrey L. Melman. Music was provided by Jack Elliott.

Partners in Crime Carson Productions. NBC. Saturday nights 9:00 (September 22, 1984–November 3, 1984) and Saturday nights 10:00 (November 24, 1984–December 29, 1984). Thirteen hour-long episodes were filmed without a laugh track.

Their names were inspired by movie stars—Carole Stanwyck (Lynda Carter) was a combination of Carole Lombard and Barbara Stanwyck, and Sydney Kovak (Loni Anderson) was Sylvia Sidney and Kim Novak. The very light crimedy had these two lovely ladies teamed to solve murders in San Francisco. Carole, heir to a small fortune, is a photographer and the more staid member of the duo. Sydney, however, is a jazz bassist (she can be seen lugging the instrument in the opening credits) and much more of a free spirit. They were both previously married to a detective named Ray Caulfield, who has passed on, but remain friendly with his mother, Jeanine (Eileen Heckart)—owner of a local mystery bookshop, appropriately called Partners in Crime. Their business was named after the deceased—The Caulfield Detective Agency. Their connection at the local police department is Lieutenant Ed Vronsky (Leo Rossi), who is infatuated with Sydney. Harmon Shain (played by the calorically challenged Walter Olkewicz) is their not-so-bright assistant. The opening credits show the crimefighters at work in a jigsaw puzzle design. After thirteen hour-long episodes had aired, NBC also became a partner in crime and canceled the show because of low ratings.

Episodes were titled "The Pilot" (with guest star John Schuck), "Celebrity," "The Hottest Guy in Town" (with guest star David Soul), "Murder in the Museum" (with guest star Efrem Zimbalist, Jr.), "Duke," "Paddles Up" (with guest star David Carradine), "Is She or Isn't She?," "Fantasyland," "The Set-up," "Fashioned for Murder" (with guest star Patty McCormack), "The Strangler," "Getting in Shape" (with guest star Anne Francis), and "Double Jeopardy." The executive producers were Leonard Stern and William Driskill; the producers were Everett Chambers and Jonathan Bernstein; the writers included James Stark, Leonard Stern, William Driskill, Simon Muntner, Jayne C. Ehrlich, Larry Brody, April Kelly, Janis Hendler, Gina Goldman, Bob Shayne, Harold Livingston, Robert Van Scoyk, Jeffrey Lane, John Stern, Phillip Saltzman, and Donald Ross; the directors included Kevin Connor, James Sheldon, Rod Daniel, Alan Cooke, Harry Falk, Charles S. Dubin, Lee H. Katzin, Sigmund Neufeld, Jr., Guy Magar, Allen Reisner, Don Weis, Leonard Stern, and Sutton Roley. The creators were James Stark and Leonard Stern. Music was provided by Johnny Harris, Ken Heller, Nathan Sassover, Ken Harrison, and Richard Lewis Warren.

The People Next Door The Sunshines, Inc./Wes Craven Films/Lorimar. CBS. Monday nights 8:30 (September 18, 1989–October 9, 1989). Ten episodes were videotaped with a laugh track, but only four aired.

This was a 1960s gimmick show that came twenty-five years too late. Had it been made in 1964 instead of 1989 it might have had a chance to survive. The setting was Covington, Ohio, and the odd gimmick was that cartoonist Walter Kellogg (his strip was called "The People Next Door"), played by Jeffrey Jones (Ed Rooney in *Ferris Bueller's Day Off*), has an extremely vivid imagination—so vivid, in fact, that many of the things he imagines materialize. He tries to keep his mind a total blank, but is never successful. He involuntarily conjures up talking mirrors, mooseheads, and easy chairs. Walter is a widower with two kids from that union—fourteen-year-old Matthew (Chance Quinn) and eleven-year-old Aurora (Jaclyn Bernstein). He is about to get remarried; his fiancée is an attractive psychotherapist named Abigail McIntyre (Mary Gross). Walter's kids know about his condition, but Abby does not. Before strolling down the aisle, he decides to tell her about his unique situation, but initially has difficulty convincing her of his powers. Abby's snooty sister Cissy (Christina Pickles), a beautician, senses that something is amiss with Walter, but just can't put her finger on it. The strange goings-on only exacerbate her disapproval of her sister's pending nuptials. Leslie Jordan played the perplexed postman Truman Fipps, who also senses something peculiar is occurring, but can never get a handle on it. The best and most memorable parts of this bizarre and farfetched series are the cameos by famous people from Walter's imagination—Judge Wapner (*The People's Court*), Henny Youngman, Dick Clark, Steve Allen, Dr. Joyce Brothers, and Casey Kasem. Wes Craven, the hugely successful creator of the *Nightmare on Elm Street* series, found television to be the *real* nightmare and *The People Next Door* was gone from CBS's fall lineup after only four of ten videotaped episodes had aired. Craven died on August 30, 2015 at the age of 76.

Episodes were titled "I Do, I Do," "Town Without Pity," "Dream Date," "You Show Me Yours," "Happy Birthday, Baby," "Halloween," "Make Room for Abby," "The Jealousy Story," "House and Home," and "No ZZZs." The executive producer was Wes Craven; the producers were Bruce Johnson, Joel Simon, Lee Aronsohn, Rod Paul, Bonnie Raskin, and Bill Todman, Jr.; the writers were Wes Craven, Madeline and Steven Sunshine, Bruce Wagner, Bud Wiggins, Dennis Danzinger, Bob Tischler, Lauren Eve Anderson, Lee Aronsohn, Mark Masuoka, and Ellen Sandler; the lone director was J. D. Lobue. Music was provided by Bill Maxwell and Lou Pardini, and the lyrics to the theme song were composed by Madeline Sunshine.

Phyl and Mikhy Elmar Productions. CBS. Monday nights 8:30 (May 26, 1980–June 30, 1980). Six episodes were videotaped in front of a live audience at KTTV Studios in Los Angeles.

Phyl and Mikhy was almost shelved by CBS because of President Jimmy Carter's decision to boycott the Moscow Olympics as a result of Russia's invasion of Afghanistan. It was supposed to run in tandem with the Olympic coverage. Phyllis "Phyl" Wilson (Murphy Cross) and Mikhail "Mikhy" Orlov (Rick Lohman) are track and decathlon stars, respectively, who begin running around together, fall in love, and decide to get married. Because he is Russian, Mikhy had to defect to the United States. Every episode has a quick final scene featuring Phyl and Mikhy in bed.

Lohman recalled, "They were also ready to shelve the show because they couldn't find anyone who could adequately do a Russian accent. Marge Glucksman, who worked in casting for CBS, had seen my audition tape for a show I didn't get, *Trapper John, M. D.*, and called and asked if I could do the accent. I could because I had numerous Ukranian and Russian relatives and I was able to mimic them pretty well. Our show was originally designed to debut in January. William Paley was still working for CBS at the time and loved our show. He intended to use our show to replace *The Jeffersons*, which was on the bubble, but when Jimmy Carter pulled out of the Olympics that year, we were put on the shelf until much later in the season."

Murphy Cross recalled, "I had just come from *A Chorus Line* [on Broadway], and I had a holding deal with CBS. First, I did a TV movie with Lee Remick called *Torn between Two Lovers*, and the casting director for that, Linda Otto, brought me over for this new series to be called *Phyl and Mikhy*. It helped that I was an athlete in real life, because both main characters on the show were athletes. The cast was pretty resilient, and when the tie-in with the Olympics didn't happen, we just kind of shrugged it off, but I think Hal Cooper and Rod Parker were rather disappointed—this show was their first collaboration under their own production company called Elmar."

On the program, Phyl is not much of a cook and only knows how to make toast. The newlyweds have very little income and have to move in with Phyl's father, Max (Larry Haines), a widower who is not exactly enthralled with the situation. Mikhy tries calling Max "Dad," but a running joke on the show has it coming out as "dead" with his thick, Russian accent (also, "Pop" comes out as "Pup," and "Max" sounds like "Mex"). Cross said, "Larry Haines and Rick Lohman had previously worked together on *Search for Tomorrow*, so there was a good chemistry there." Lohman added, "They kept Haines' being cast on the show a secret until the last possible moment. It was a great surprise and a fun reunion. Larry was a very funny guy."

Mikhy is ill at ease with American customs, beliefs, and technology, about which Cross considered, "I think our show was a precursor to *Perfect Strangers*, which dealt with that very same issue a few years later." Numerous attempts are made by Vladimir Gimenko (Michael Pataki) to get Mikhy to return to his native land, but he is unsuccessful. Deborah Pratt was Connie, Phyl's best friend, and Jack Dodson (Howard Sprague from *The Andy Griffith Show*) played Edgar "Truck" Morley, Max's boss. Cross stated, "The cast was full of the sweetest people. I'm still in touch with Rick Lohman today. Jack Dodson was a sweetheart. One day he took me for a ride around town in his beautiful classic old yellow convertible. Michael Pataki, Larry Haines—everyone was just great. We were on after *WKRP in Cincin-*

nati and our ratings were actually pretty good, but we only did those six episodes and that was it." Lohman concurred, "It was a great cast. Jack Dodson and I were close. He introduced the cast to an out-of-the-way old-fashioned tea room where we sometimes had lunch. Of course, Murphy is great. Michael Pataki was great, too, but maybe a bit standoffish. He's probably the only one I never really got close to. And Rae Allen, a great talent, was somewhat unhappy with her role—it was not what she expected and she only did the debut episode before moving on."

Cross related a behind-the-scenes memory: "Since I was a child, my knees cracked a lot—a very audible cracking sound. A few times on the show, if I had to kneel down, the sound could be heard and we'd have to do another take." She added, "Having come from the theater, I was used to projecting my voice, only to be told by the sound man that I didn't need to yell—the microphones would pick up my voice just fine."

About the opening credits, Lohman recalled, "We shot the titles with Murphy running a race in the stadium of a local community college. Then, on the very same day, we drove up to Big Bear, where there was still snow, and shot more scenes for the opening credits, with me running in what was supposed to appear to be Russia. I also got to hear the program's theme song during the ride to Big Bear that same day."

This show about track stars was sadly off CBS's track by the end of June in 1980. Cross said, "In those few short weeks, we also had some great guest stars on the show—Marian Mercer (as a bank teller), Edie McClurg, Charles Lane, Larry Storch, and Mary Waronov. It was great fun while it lasted." Lohman added, "We adopted Larry Storch. Funny guy. I remember that the week he did our show he needed a ride back home each night—I guess he didn't drive. Also, Charles Lane shared the most amazing story about being a child during and experiencing the San Francisco earthquake of 1906."

Episodes were titled "The Meet," "Phyl's Birthday Surprise," "Phyl's Wedding," "Mikhy's Vision," "One Big Happy Family" (with guest star Frank Campanella), and "The Seduction of Mikhail Orlov." The executive producer was Rod Parker; the writers included Madelyn Daley, Mark Solomon, Rob Dames, Tom Reeder, Rod Parker, Mark Egan, Bob Fraser, and Lan O'Kun; the director was Hal Cooper. The creator was Buddy Arnold. The theme song was written by Rod Parker and Hal Cooper. Cross reflected, "Hal Cooper was just a prince among men—I adored him; everyone did. When he passed away last year [2014] the world lost a big piece of television history. He started his career in live TV." Lohman concurred saying, "He was such a sweet guy. We had a great relationship."

Police Squad Paramount Television. ABC. Thursday nights 8:00 (March 4, 1982–March 25, 1982) and Thursday nights 9:30 (July 1, 1982–July 8, 1982). Six episodes were filmed single-camera style without a laugh track.

Influenced by the comedy of The Marx Brothers, Ernie Kovacs, and *Mad Magazine*, the creators of the hit motion picture comedies, 1977's *The Kentucky Fried Movie* and 1980's *Airplane* (Jim Abrahams, David Zucker, and Jerry Zucker) next had designs on a big-screen comedy about a mythical police department. They were so impressed with Leslie Nielsen's comic timing in *Airplane* that they opted to use him for this new project. Michael Eisner suggested that the idea would work better as a TV series, and *Police Squad* was born. ABC bought the show after seeing only the funny opening credits.

The program was patterned after Lee Marvin's TV series *M Squad*, and the Quinn Martin detective shows of the 1960s and '70s, with an Act I, Act II, and an Epilogue. However, in true irreverent *Police Squad* fashion, we would see things such as "Act II, Yankees I," "Act II, Gesundheit," "Act II, Lieber," or "Act II, Ball III" on the screen. They even utilized the talents of Hank Simms, the former announcer for the Quinn Martin shows. Nielsen portrayed bumbling Detective Frank Drebin (although his rank varies from episode to episode). A running gag has Drebin hit something every time he pulls up in his police car. Devotees of the brief series knows the episode number in the sequence of six by the number of items (garbage cans, bicycles, etc.) that Drebin hits when pulling up to the curb (one item in episode one, two items in episode two, and so on).

Drebin lists the criminals apprehended on the show to date in the epilogue of episodes two through six. Drebin's partner, Captain Ed Hocken, was played by Alan North (and by George Kennedy in the film series). Ted Olson, from the police lab, was appropriately played by science teacher-turned-actor Ed Williams. Scenes with Olson were always joined already in progress, in the middle of a very bizarre, inappropriate and/or suggestive conversation. Johnny the Snitch (under the guise of a shoe shiner on the street) was portrayed by William Duell, who always provides tips to Drebin for cash. A running gag has many priests, baseball managers, and other professionals take the same seat after Drebin gets up, also seeking advice for cash. Johnny always has an in-depth answer to every question. *Mission: Impossible*'s Peter Lupus portrayed Officer Norberg in most, but not all, episodes (O. J. Simpson played the character in the film series); Ronald Taylor played Al, a cop so tall that his head is never visible in the camera shot. Several of the one-shot characters in these episodes were named for real people from the show's creators' old neighborhood in their native Milwaukee, Wisconsin, as were the names of streets and local businesses.

Guest stars included Dr. Joyce Brothers, Georg Stanford Brown, Dick Clark, William Conrad (appropriately from Quinn Martin's *Cannon*), Robert Goulet, Lorne Greene, Florence Henderson, Tommy Lasorda, and William Shatner. John Belushi would have been the guest star in the "Testimony of Evil" episode. Eerily mirroring real life, Belushi was killed in the opening of the episode. However, Belushi died before the episode aired and a new opening, with William Conrad, was filmed instead. Strangely, that historic piece of film with Belushi appears to have been destroyed, and no copies have ever surfaced. Goulet was the only *Police Squad* guest star to appear in a *Naked Gun* motion picture (*Naked Gun 2 ½: The Smell of Fear*, in 1991).

Running gags on the show included the announcer saying a different title for that night's episode than was pictured on the screen; in the opening credits, Lee Hamilton is mentioned as portraying Abraham Lincoln (but only appears in the credits); "Satin Doll" was the song of choice for every dance sequence; the names of criminals and victims of their crimes lent themselves to wordplay (Jim Fell, Phil Din, Mr. Once and Mr. Twice); Drebin and Hocken are always oblivious to the elevator stopping on odd floors in which the doors open on stage in a crowded theater or to an Olympic-sized pool; and the cast ends each episode in a mock freeze frame (while a criminal escapes, a chimpanzee ransacks the precinct, etc.).

From the get-go, ABC was certain they had struck gold. They couldn't have been more wrong. Up against *Magnum, P. I.* on CBS and *Fame* on NBC, the ratings were disastrous (Nielsen did poorly in the Nielsens?). Only four of the six filmed episodes aired in March of 1982. The remaining two very funny and silly episodes were burned off during the summer of that year. It was determined by ABC President Tony Thomopoulos that the program required intense concentration to "get" all of the humor, and people just don't watch TV that way—they do other things while watching. In a movie theater, however, people pay for their seat, have very little distraction, and have a much larger screen to command their attention. Thomopoulos was right, and when *Police Squad* was adapted for the big screen in The Naked Gun series (three films), it was a whopping success. *Police Squad* ranks high among the all-time most violent TV programs, with an average of thirty-four instances per episode. Reruns were shown on CBS during the summer of 1991.

Episodes were titled "A Substantial Gift (The Broken Promise)," "Ring of Fear (A Dangerous Assignment)," "The Butler Did It (A Bird in the Hand)," "Revenge and Remorse (The Guilty Alibi)," "Rendezvous at Big Gulch (Terror in the Neighborhood)," and "Testimony of Evil (Dead Men Don't Laugh)." The executive producers were Jim Abrahams, David Zucker and Jerry Zucker; the producer was Robert K. Weiss; the writers included Robert Wuhl, Tino Insana, Pat Profft, Nancy Steen, Neil Thompson, Jim Abrahams, David Zucker and Jerry Zucker; the directors included Jim Abrahams, David Zucker, Jerry Zucker, Reza S. Badiyi, Georg Stanford Brown, Joe Dante, and Paul Krasny.

The Popcorn Kid MTM Productions. CBS. Monday night 8:30 (March 23, 1987) and Friday nights 8:30 (March 27, 1987–April 24, 1987). Six episodes were videotaped in front of a live audience.

Like *Newhart*, *The Popcorn Kid* was a Barry Kemp creation. In fact, Bob Newhart as Dick Loudon was utilized in promotions on CBS (along with Larry, Darryl, and Darryl) to tout this new MTM show. Despite the popularity of *Newhart*, their plugs didn't help much and this new series was gone in a Jiffy Pop. *The Popcorn Kid* told the story of sixteen-year-old Scott Creasman (Bruce Norris), who has a strong desire to be in show business. He decides to get his start in the business by working behind the concession counter in the historic Majestic Theater in Kansas City. He is vastly different from his father, Beryl (James Staley), who works for a business called Patio City. The other high school kids employed at the landmark theater included the lovely Lynn Holly Brickhouse (Faith Ford, pre–*Murphy Brown*) who more than lives up to her surname. Scott has a crush on her, but considers her to be way out of his league (although he *does* ask her out on a date in one episode). Others in the cast included Gwen Stottlemeyer (Penelope Ann Miller), the brains of the bunch, who has a crush on Scott; Willie Dawson (Jeffrey Joseph), the African American athlete of the group; and Marlin Bond (John Christopher Jones), the projectionist who lives in a fantasy world, acting out movie scenes in conversation, and worships Edward Asner. They all have to wear powder blue uniforms, and their immediate supervisor is twelve-year employee Leonard Brown (Raye Birk). Brown and his wife have no children, but he occasionally rues that decision when his young staff achieve something of which he is very proud. He answers to the owner, the never seen "Two-Ton" Tuttle, who has designs on turning the historic Majestic Theater into a multiplex.

Episodes were titled "The Pilot," "There She Is, Vic Damone," "Career Day," "The Break Up," "A Day in the Life of Ed Asner" (with guest star Ed Asner), and "A Car, a House, a Mouse, and a Louse." The producers were Jay Kleckner, Julie Newman, and Emily Marshall; the writers included Mark Ganzel, Barry Kemp, Mark Egan, Irene Mecchi, Mark Solomon, and Jurgen Wolff; the directors included David Steinberg, James Gardner, and Will Mackenzie. The series was created by Barry Kemp. Music was provided by Tim Truman, and the theme was by Judy Hart-Angelo and Gary Portnoy (writers of the *Cheers* theme, "Where Everybody Knows Your Name").

Probe Westland Productions/MCA Universal Television. ABC. Monday night 9:00 (March 7, 1988), Thursday nights 8:00 (March 10, 1988–April 14, 1988). Six hour-long episodes and a two-hour debut movie were filmed single-camera style without a laugh track.

Isaac Asimov, the legendary sci-fi writer, had a hand in creating this hour-long high-tech mystery/comedy series. Austin James (Parker Stevenson), an eccentric, egotistical, and aloof pseudo-genius with a photographic memory, lives in the Batcave—a nickname for his laboratory/home. His work is shared with (and yet, separate from) a company he started called Serendip (where all of the employees walk on eggshells and attend to James's every whim, lest they be fired). While James seeks out clues to crimes, Serendip is run by the jittery Howard Millhouse (Jon Cypher). James is known to sleep in the nude in a cabinet (because of its unique sensory deprivation properties), has tarantulas and rats as pets, is extremely observant with and perceptive about others, but is not adept at making and keeping close friendships or romantic interests. He perfects a prosthetic device for people who have lost limbs, and, despite his rudeness and lackluster people skills, helping mankind is first and foremost in his thoughts. Along with several notable scientific discoveries, James's wall-to-wall gadgetry also assists in piecing together and eventually solving some rather intricate crimes. His world is rocked in the two-hour movie pilot, in which a new employee named Michelle "Mickey" Castle (Ashley Crow), a graduate of the Tidewater Secretarial School, figures out the bizarre code and is able to enter his eerie and massive lair, much to his surprise and chagrin (no other human being has ever accomplished that feat). Mickey is constantly threatening to quit her new job, and yet is intrigued by the adventure and peril that accompanies it. The physical attraction and the chemistry between the two is instantly palpable.

Had this very literate series lasted more than six regular episodes, an eventual romance would likely have been addressed more fully. Together, they are a modern-day Sherlock Holmes and Watson, and there are many light moments blended in with the adventure elements. After the two-hour pilot movie was aired on a Monday night, the regular series moved to Thursday nights at 8:00, up against NBC's juggernaut "Must See TV" lineup that began with *The Cosby Show*. At that time Bill Cosby was like a buzzsaw to his TV competition, and the highly unique and ambitious *Probe* quickly disappeared. The program was filmed in Phoenix, Arizona, and the pilot filmed in Arizona as well as North Carolina.

Episodes were titled "Computer Logic, Parts One and Two" (the two-hour debut movie), "Untouched by Human Hands," "Black Cats Don't Walk Under Ladders, Do They?," "Metamorphic Anthropoidic Prototype Over You," "Now You See It," "Plan Ten from Outer Space" (with guest star Michael Constantine), and "Quit It" (with guest star Darleen Carr). The executive producers were Alan J. Levi and Michael J. Wagner; the producers were Stephen Caldwell and Michael Piller; the writers included William Link, Michael J. Wagner, Isaac Asimov, Lee Sheldon, Robert Bielak, Howard Brookner, Timothy Burns, Colman DeKay, James L. Novack, Philip Reed, and Michael Piller; the directors included Rob Bowman, Kevin Hooks, Robert Iscove, Alan J. Levi, Vincent McEveety, Sandor Stern, and Virgil W. Vogel. The creators were William Link and Isaac Asimov. Music was provided by Sylvester Levay.

Pursuit of Happiness Hanley Productions/ 20th Century Fox. ABC. Friday nights 9:30 (October 30, 1987–January 8, 1988). Ten episodes were videotaped in front of a live audience.

Not to be confused with the short-lived 1995 Brad Garrett sitcom of the same name, this *Pursuit of Happiness* debuted in the fall of 1987 and was set in Philadelphia, at John Marshall University. Roland G. Duncan (Brian Keith), known for a decade-old book about the nation's forefathers, is a renowned history professor teaching there (his office is room 213). He is very set in his ways, curmudgeonly, and eschews change. He had fought in the Korean War, and currently lives in apartment A, just across the hall from his new assistant professor, David Hanley (Paul Provenza), despite being Duncan's complete opposite, idolizes the man. By the way, it was no coincidence that Provenza's character's last name was Hanley—the program was a Hanley Production. David is much more laid-back and freewheeling, and attempts to loosen up his stuffed shirt of a superior. Hanley is attempting to become more of an adult (he's been drifting for years—six months in an Oregon lumber camp, four months on a lobster boat in Maine, a stretch on a turnip farm, a period in Colorado). His best friend is Vernon Morris (Wesley Thompson), who is very much against any kind of romantic commitment. When Vernon is happy, he sings "I Feel Good," James Brown–style. Getting to play the part of David Hanley was quite complicated for Paul—a torturous process.

Provenza recalled, "The show's creator, Michael Weithorn is a great guy—very funny, very skillful. I got to read for the part, we got along like gangbusters, and he liked me for the role and said that I was his guy. That was great because I really liked the innovative fantasy element of the show that involved Magic Johnson as himself, and Kevin Scannell as Thomas Jefferson. I was to play a young, idealistic professor, and my two heroes were Johnson and Jefferson, so whenever I had a conundrum in my life I sought their advice in the fantasy sequence. We did the pilot, but a short time later I got a call from Weithorn. He was very apologetic, but told me the network didn't like me and that they wouldn't do the show unless my part was recast. I was disappointed, but that's the nature of the business. My motto is 'C'est la TV.'

"The very next day, I got a call from director John Bowab, who wanted me for the role of Casey Clark on *The Facts of Life*. I didn't think I was right for that show, but he told me they wanted to go 'edgier,' and really wanted me for the role. I had been doing the warm-up for several shows in which Bowab was involved, and he wanted to find a vehicle for me and thought this was ideal. Just as I was getting started on that show, I got a frenzied call from Weithorn again. The replacement for me on *The Pursuit of Happiness* wasn't working out and I was back in if I wanted the role. Long story short, I wasn't exclusive with *The Facts of Life* and we made arrangements and adjusted schedules so that I could do both shows. By the way, Weithorn and I are still in touch after all these years."

Sara Duncan, Roland's daughter, a very average student, was portrayed by Judie Aronson; and Margaret Callahan, professor of Egyptian history, was played by Wendel Meldrum—a timid, nervous, daffy, A+ student, and Jersey girl who lets her hair down when she drinks (or, more descriptively, slurps) beer. About her character, Meldrum said, "I think of Margaret as someone who is brilliant with limited social skills—quite common in male [TV] characters today. I had a lot of freedom to create her. I owe Michael Weithorn for really pushing for me. Before the network test, he had his dream team in to rehearse and was very helpful with direction. I found out I was pregnant at this same time, and it was a bit of a shock to everyone, myself included. Weithorn called my doctor and asked the last possible date we could shoot before I started showing too much. My skirt was rising by the day. My doctor called it perfectly—they were able to cover me. Margaret is one of my favorite roles. She operated inside her Egyptology passion bubble, and all her quirks came out of that."

The baby came during the show's run. Meldrum said, "I had a newborn at the time and was pumping milk twice a day and keeping it in the small fridge that was just outside my dressing room. One day I went to put in my second milk jar, and saw that the first was gone. I didn't ever say anything, but often wondered if someone used my milk in their coffee or on their cereal." It became quite obvious that Margaret had romantic feelings for David, and to that end Meldrum regretted "getting canceled before I had a chance to unfurl a romance with Paul's character, David. I think that would have been so much fun to explore."

Mrs. Lopez, Roland's sassy receptionist, was played by Wanda DeJesus. She had a genuine aversion to making coffee. In recurring roles, Professor Gruber and Professor Stevens were portrayed by Mary Farrell and John Petlock, respectively. Provenza said, "It was like going home again. I graduated from the University of Pennsylvania in 1979, and some of the exterior scenes for the series were shot on its campus. Even though it was called John Marshall University on the program, it was an Ivy League college in Pennsylvania—it was the University of Pennsylvania. Even my apartment on the show was set up very much like the place I lived in while attending the university." Regarding his co-stars, Provenza recalled, "Brian Keith played a character who was older and rather curmudgeonly. There were similarities between the character and the real Brian Keith, but he loved to laugh, and I developed great affection for him and a great relationship with him. I loved making him crack up. He didn't really like to show it and would sometimes turn his back to me while laughing, but I could still see his shoulders moving."

About Keith, Meldrum added, "He was a crusty softie. He could really sling it and was always cursing out the need for casting people, managers, and agents. In his day, John Huston would call him up and say he had a part for him and would ask if he was interested. Brian had a poetic soft spot for his family that would emerge here and there. He said I was the only truly happy person he knew who wasn't a fool."

About another cast member, Provenza said, "I also loved working with Magic Johnson. I am not now nor have I ever been a sports fan, so I never talked to him about basketball. My friends thought I was nuts because I never took Magic up on his offers for courtside seats to Lakers games. He frequently asked me for suggestions on how to best deliver his lines on the show, and we really bonded. He was also great with kids and very giving when they asked him for autographs. We stayed in touch, and when he got his talk show, he wanted me to be his sidekick, but I was committed to too many things at the time and wasn't able to do it."

Meldrum added, "I never had any scenes with Magic, so we used the same dressing room—we had different schedules. However, once in a while our schedules would cross over and I would go into my room and find that a giant was living there. One shoe was on my dressing table, and it practically took up the whole thing. His shirt was like a blanket. He had a lovely, easy manner and was very sociable."

This show was videotaped multi-camera style in front of a studio audience, but Meldrum said, "I prefer the single camera because I love the feeling of a single intimate focus." Sadly, *Pursuit of Happiness* did not pursue ratings happiness for ABC, and the entire faculty was expelled after only ten episodes. Reruns were shown briefly in the 1990s on the FOX Network.

Episodes were titled "The Arrival," "Put to the Test," "Boys Night Out," "Thirty," "Advice and Consent," "The Defiant Ones," "History Lesson," "Together Again," "Uphill Skiing," and "That Pair of Eyes." The executive producer was Michael J. Weithorn; the writers included Michael J. Weithorn, Anne Kenney, Joelyn

Grippo, John Steven Owen, and Todd W. Langen; the directors included Sam Weisman, Steve Zuckerman, and Art Wolff. About Wolff, Provenza added, "He was fantastic to work with. He later found great success directing my friends Penn and Teller on Broadway." Meldrum added, "Both Art and Steve came from the theatre and understood character. I ran into Steve recently at a small theatre performance, still loving the work. I worked with Sam on a project before doing *Pursuit of Happiness*. I remember one day in the middle of rehearsing Sam got a call, told us he had an emergency at home and would have to leave immediately. It seems his four-year-old son had accidentally closed a drawer on his penis and was very upset. Being a good dad, he dropped everything and went to comfort him." The theme song "Dream On" was written by Gordon Lustig and Mark Mattison, and performed by Mendy Lee. It's interesting to note that credit is given for the use of portraits of Thomas Jefferson to Oppenheimer Publishers, Inc.

Raising Miranda GTG Entertainment. CBS. Saturday nights 8:30 (November 5, 1988–December 31, 1988). Nine episodes were videotaped in front of a live audience, but only seven aired.

The original working title for the series was *My Life Story*. Not to be confused with the sitcom *Raising Hope*, *Raising Miranda* focuses on a construction worker (for Big M Construction) named Donald Marshack (James Naughton)—a newly single dad raising his fourteen-year-old daughter, Miranda (Royana Black). Bonny, Donald's wife and Miranda's mother, abruptly left for Phoenix one day and never returned. For a father and daughter, they get along better than most and became an emotional support system for each other during this trying time in their lives. As they live at 85 Muskeegan Road, in Racine, Wisconsin, it would have been within the producers' Miranda Rights to call this show *Racine Miranda*, but, wisely, they went another way.

The Marshacks' well-meaning, but downright odd, neighbors also had a rather odd surname—Hoodenpyle—Bob Hoodenpyle (Steve Vinovich) and his wife, Joan (Miriam Flynn). The Marshacks found that they could depend upon the Hoodenpyles for help, moral support, and coffee cake. Miranda played the flute, and her best friend is the pushy and mischievous Marcine Lundquist (Amy Lynne). In one episode, Marcine is caught shoplifting. She lives with her mom, Helen (Lee Garlington), at 863 Fairview Lane. Miranda has a male friend named Jack Miller (Michael Manasseri), a new Racine High transfer student; she is selected to help him with his studies.

Also in the cast was Bryan Cranston, pre–*Breaking Bad*, as Miranda's weird burnout Uncle Russell (a maternal relative), who lives in a van in their driveway. He is featured in "Russell's Broken Heart," one of the series' two unaired episodes. Every episode concludes with Miranda writing the day's events in her diary, reminiscent of Sally Field in the TV version of *Gidget*, and prefiguring *Doogie Howser, M.D.* Every diary entry ended with "Confidentially, Miranda." Unfortunately, not very many families listed this program in their Nielsen diary and only seven of the nine videotaped episodes aired. *Raising Miranda* may very well have failed because of its subject matter. A mother abandoning her family just didn't play too well in sitcomland. Writer R. J. Colleary said, "I was brought in to write for the show by *The Facts of Life*'s Martha Williamson. This show was created by Jane Anderson—a really good writer, but not necessarily a sitcom writer. She fared so much better later as a playwright. *Raising Miranda* had kind of a dark premise, what with the mother deserting the family 'to find herself.' It was way ahead of its time, actually. *My Two Dads* was also somewhat dark, but in that case, the moms had died—something that was out their control."

Episodes were titled "Black Monday," "Grounded," "Man in the Middle," "Miranda's Date," "All through the Night," "Home for the Holidays," "Marcine Shoplifts," "Russell's Broken Heart," and "One Night Stand." The executive producers were Jane Anderson, Martha Williamson, and Deborah Aal; the writers included Martha Williamson, July Selbo, Julia Newton, Jane Anderson, and R. J. Colleary; the directors included John Whitesell. The creator was Jane Anderson. The theme song was written by Joel Higgins, Jeremy Stone, and Martin Silvestri.

The Redd Foxx Show Thunder Road Productions/Lorimar Television. ABC. Saturday nights 8:00 (January 18, 1986–April 19, 1986). Thirteen episodes were videotaped in front of a live audience.

In his post–*Sanford and Son* years, Redd Foxx flailed about from *The Redd Foxx Comedy Hour* (a variety series) to *Sanford* (see entry) to *The Royal Family* (his last). In between the latter two came a long-forgotten sitcom called *The Redd Foxx Show* on ABC in 1986. In this one, Foxx portrayed the proprietor of a combination New York City newsstand and coffee shop—Al's Grill. Al is a widower who recently lost his wife, Grace. Together, they set many wayward kids back on the right path. Yes, he is cranky, but Alfonso "Al" Hughes has a compassionate side, proven by his choice to take under his wing a troubled fifteen-year-old girl named Toni Rutledge (Pamela Segall), who seems destined for a juvenile detention center. Toni is a rather "butch" *girl*, an important bit of information that Al doesn't realize until the very end of the debut episode.

It became apparent very early on that this format just wasn't working—a problem about which producer Jack Seifert opined, "It was Redd Foxx playing against type. The pilot was very good, but after that the writers struggled, as did Foxx. He was hamstrung. He was used to being himself—an ornery old guy. When the ratings came in, the first format was quickly canned, Segall and the rest of the original play-

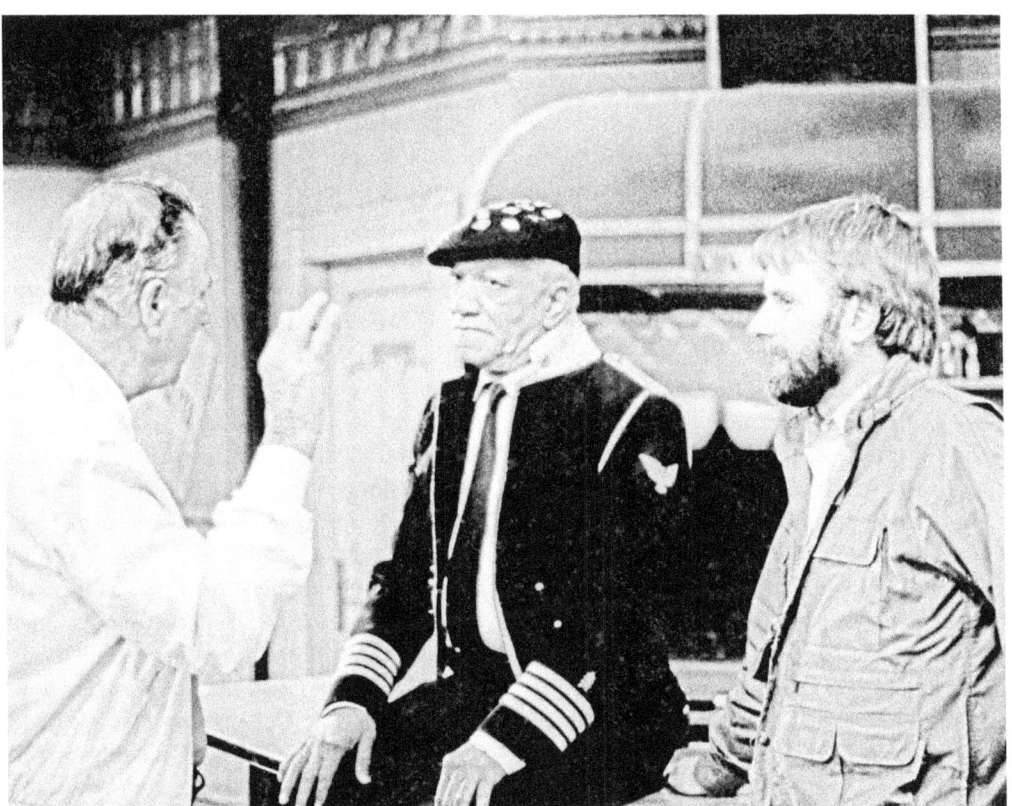

A rare photograph from ABC's *The Redd Foxx Show*; pictured (left to right) are director Dick Martin, Foxx, and line producer Jack Seifert (photograph courtesy Jack Seifert).

ers were dropped from the cast. In a totally unprecedented move, ABC and the executive producers aired a promo for the format change, in effect saying 'We screwed up—we've totally retooled *The Redd Foxx Show*, so please come back and try us again.' It was a public mea culpa."

Al's compassionate side was now lessened greatly, he became newly divorced from a wife named Felicia (Beverly Todd), and he suddenly acquired a foster child named Brian Lightfoot (Sinbad). Al still ran the grill in the new format, and his hired help is waitress Jessica Houston (Vanessa Williams). About the co-stars, Seifert recalled, "Vanessa Williams was very nice and not a bad actress, and Sinbad was good at playing the wise guy to Redd's grumpy old codger persona."

Between the two formats, thirteen episodes were videotaped on stage 4 at Hollywood Center—a stage that Seifert recalled as "old and drafty. The air conditioning as well as the heating units were inefficient. We did *The Redd Foxx Show* in the winter, and Redd caught a bad cold, so production had to shut down for a few days. After a couple of days, panic began to set in due to the cost involved if we could not tape the planned episode that week. I received an okay from the higher-ups to spend about a grand, and my associate producer Judy Zaylor and I went to a ski shop and bought Redd a very expensive and luxurious parka, sheepskin-lined boots, a Russian-style winter hat with flaps, a very handsome scarf, electric hand warmers, long underwear, insulated socks—the whole nine yards, and brought them to him beautifully gift wrapped. We looked like two of the three wise men bearing gifts, and arrived at his office building on LaBrea. Ever the actor, Redd was up in his private suite in a netted and massive four-poster bed, with the light dimmed dramatically, acting as though he would finally be joining Elizabeth in the after-life there on his deathbed. However, he perked up considerably when he saw all the goodies we had brought him, and finally agreed, after much hemming and hawing, interspersed with feigned coughing and wheezing, to come back to the set the next day. When he appeared on set looking like a grizzled, old black Eskimo wearing all of the paraphernalia we had given him, he looked pretty ridiculous since everyone else there was dressed normally and the cold weather had by then subsided. Soon, he had changed into his regular clothing and was back to work much to everyone's relief."

Regarding the thirteen episodes videotaped in front of a live audience, Seifert remembered, "It was sometimes an adventure in diplomacy and downright coercion getting Redd to come to the stage from his double-wide star dressing room trailer parked right outside. He liked to 'get a little buzz on' before coming out to start the show, while a studio audience waited inside on show nights. As I groped through his dimly-lit, smoke-filled trailer searching for him with the stage manager, a contact high was unavoidable. However, we always managed to coax him to take one last puff and then slowly waddle out to the stage in his own inimitable way, grumbling as he went."

Episodes were titled "The Pilot," "High School Blues," "My Funny Valentine," "The Good Samaritan" (with guest star Lawrence Hilton-Jacobs), "Al's First Date" (with guest star Barbara McNair), "Old Buddies" (with guest star Carroll O'Connor), "Prodigal Son," "Lotto Fever," "Mr. Right and Wrong," "A Night to Forget," "The Old and the Restless," and "High Noon." The executive producers were Rick Kellard and Stuart Sheslow. About the latter, Seifert recalled, "Thunder Road Productions was Sheslow's own production company, and after *The Redd Foxx Show*, Stu pursued a dream he had to turn *Star Wars* into a Broadway musical, but unfortunately that never happened." The producer was Jack Seifert (George Sunga produced the pilot); the writers included Bob Comfort, Phil and Rick Kellard, Stuart Sheslow, Tom Moore, Eric Cohen, John Donley, Redd Foxx (contractually), Clay Graham, Carroll O'Connor (contractually, for one episode), Don Seigel, Maiya Williams, and Jerry Perzigian. About the experience, Perzigian shared, "My partner, Don Seigel, and I wrote one episode

["Al's First Date"] as a courtesy, trying to be helpful. Even though I was humble and a pup, I remember that I was appalled at the quality of the rewrite that was eventually used on the air—so much so that I registered for a pseudonym with the Writers Guild. If that episode exists in cyberspace today, it carries the name Rex Beaumont in place of mine. If there really is an actual Mr. Beaumont out there someplace, I should apologize." The directors included Howard Storm, Lee Bernhardi, Stan Lathan, Dick Martin (of *Rowan and Martin's Laugh-In* fame), Tony Singletary, Bill Foster, Dave Powers, and Carroll O'Connor. About O'Connor's directorial debut, Seifert added, "Carroll was a guest star and a guest director on one episode. He really wasn't a director, but he insisted on directing as well as getting writing credits if we wanted him to be a guest star in the episode, and Lorimar agreed just to get him to do the show to help the ratings. His 'directing' was augmented by another more qualified director in the booth." Incidental show music was provided by Sonny Burke, and the theme song called "Heart of the City" was performed by Kool and the Gang (Foxx was seen frequently wearing a Kool and the Gang satin jacket in the early episodes). Seifert said, "Once again, much like *Nearly Departed*, the opening credits got better reviews than the series itself. I won an Art Director's Guild Award for the opening credit sequence of *The Redd Foxx Show*, the Foxx main title, as it's correctly called. It was a unique (at that time) stop action, animated montage and I'm rather proud of it. I think there's an example of it on YouTube."

Reggie Fox Unicorn, Inc./Can't Sing Can't Dance Productions/Columbia Pictures Television. ABC. Tuesday night 9:30 (August 2, 1983), and Thursday nights 9:00 (August 4, 1983–September 1, 1983). Six episodes were videotaped with a laugh track. Sponsors included Crest toothpaste and Zest soap.

The *I* in the opening credits for *Reggie* was an ice cream cone. Even the refrigerator magnets in the kitchen were shaped like ice cream cones. There was a good reason for that—Reggie Potter (Richard Mulligan) works for the Funtime Ice Cream Company on Long Island, but he is not having a fun time. Potter is having a mid-life crisis and is bored with his job, so he fantasizes a lot (à la Walter Mitty) and his fantasies provide fodder for the storylines. In that way, *Reggie* differed from the plot of the British sitcom on which it was based—*The Fall and Rise of Reginald Perrin*, by David Nobbs. In the original British version, Reggie fakes his own suicide (by walking into the ocean) so that he could don countless disguises to spy on his friends and family. Others in the cast included Reggie's demanding boss at the dessert company, C. J. Wilcox (Chip Zien); his pretty secretary, Joan Reynolds (Jean Smart); Reggie's wife, Elizabeth (Barbara Barrie); his son, Mark (Timothy Busfield, pre–*Thirtysomething*), an aspiring actor; his daughter, Linda Potter Lockett (Dianne Kay); his annoying son-in-law, Tom Lockett (Timothy Stack); a cat named Furball; and a stuffed fox named Monty that served as Reggie's teddy bear. Reggie fantasizes most often about his son Mark's girlfriend, and Joan the secretary. Joan also fantasizes about him (she likes older men). After six episodes had aired, Reggie fantasized about still having a series.

Episodes were titled "Mark's Girlfriend," "The Seduction of Reggie," "That's Life," "Reggie's Warning," "It's My Party and I'll Die if I Want To," and "Once a Father." The executive producer was Barbara Corday; the producers were Dinah and Julie Kirgo; the writers included David Nobbs, Dinah and Julie Kirgo, Sylvia Alan, Ken Hecht, Lorin Dreyfuss, David Landsberg, Bernie Kukoff, Harry Lee Scott, Paul B. Price, and Stephen Nathan; the directors included Greg Antonacci, Ellen Gittelsohn, Bernie Kukoff, Ellen Falcon, and John Bowab. The program was developed by Barbara Corday, and Dinah and Julie Kirgo. Richard Mulligan performed the theme song, "The Real Me," written by Roger Kellaway and Morgan Ames.

Report to Murphy Jenro Inc./Roger Gimbel Productions/EMI Television Programs Inc./K C Productions/Jones-Reiker Ink Corp. CBS.

Monday nights 8:30 (April 5, 1982–May 31, 1982). Six episodes were videotaped in front of a live audience.

Michael Keaton portrayed Eddie Murphy (no, not that one) on this short-lived sitcom set in an unnamed metropolis at the Department of Correction and Rehabilitation. Murphy lives at 832 Church Street, and is a parole officer. His methods are often questioned by fellow officers Charlie Dawson (Donnelly Rhodes) and Lucy Webb (Donna Ponterotto). Murphy often finds himself in trouble with his supervisor Blanche Nesbitt (Olivia Cole, of *Szysznyk*), and Internal Affairs Department officer Vernon Culley (Peter Jurasik). Murphy is also involved in a sometimes-turbulent relationship with Assistant District Attorney Joann Baker (Margot Rose). She is taller than he and often has to kick off her high heels to make him feel more comfortable. He constantly parks in her assigned spot and she has his car towed. Among his recurring parolees are Vinnie (Jonathan Banks), Norm (Jack O'Leary), and habitual car thief Big Walter Lewis (Ken Forte). Episodes revolve around the predicaments in which Murphy finds himself because of his psychological approach to his job.

Writer Dennis Klein recalled, "Michael Keaton used to do stand-up comedy. He's a tremendously talented and wildly inventive guy, and during the first full rehearsal performance each week he'd get big laughs with what was written on the page, but he then got bored with the funny lines because he'd already performed them and gotten his laughs, and he'd start changing his delivery because he was driven to explore and not simply repeat. His exploration continued through show night, which as a result presented the least well-performed version of the script. This was the first TV series created and produced by Patricia Jones and Donald Reiker, and I don't think they knew how to handle that." The sitcom failed to find an audience and, like Keaton's earlier ventures in television, *All's Fair* and *Working Stiffs*, *Report to Murphy* experienced a case of Murphy's law and was gone after only six episodes had aired.

Episodes were titled "The Pilot" (with guest star Dan Hedaya), "The Girl Most Likely," "Charlie Goes Awry," "High Noon," "Baker vs. Murphy," and "Papillon." The executive producers were Roger Gimbel and Harry Colomby (Michael Keaton's manager); the producers and creators were Patricia Jones and Donald Reiker; the writers were Mitch Markowitz, Patricia Jones, Joanne Pagliaro, Richard Orloff, Dennis Klein, and Donald Reiker; the directors were Terry Hughes, Asaad Kelada, and Dennis Klein. Music was provided by Jonathan Wolfert and JAM.

The Robert Guillaume Show Guillaume/Margo Productions/New World Television/Universal Television. ABC. Wednesday nights 9:30 (April 5, 1989–August 9, 1989). Thirteen episodes were videotaped in front of a live audience.

Edwin Sawyer (Guillaume) is a divorced father raising two children while conducting his marriage counseling practice out of his home. Even *he* can't save his own marriage. Guillaume conceived the show in an attempt to explore interracial romances, which were still a touchy subject in 1989 (even though the topic had been addressed weekly on shows such as *The Jeffersons*). Guillaume became miffed at ABC very early in the show's run because they aired episodes out of sequence. Guillaume wanted to build up to the first interracial kiss in what was intended to be the eighth episode, but ABC aired said episode in week number two. The kiss was between Edwin and his quirky and chatty new assistant, Ann Sherr (Wendy Phillips). The smooch was too much, too soon, and Guillaume, who had found success on *Soap* and *Benson*, was unable to score a hat trick with this eponymous sitcom. The program failed to find an audience and disappeared after thirteen weeks. Others in the cast included Marc Joseph as Edwin's son, William; Kelsey Scott as his daughter, Pamela; and Hank Rolike as his wise, white-haired father, Henry.

Episodes were titled "The Pilot," "Hello Again," "Together Again," "Drive, He Said," "Guaranteed Not to Shrink" (with guest star

Dennis Haysbert), "Educating Ann," "Fast Friends," "All that Shimmers," "They're Here," "You Win Some You Lose Some," "First Date," "The Day After the Night Before." The executive producers were Sy Rosen, Robert Guillaume, and Phil Margo; the producer was John H. Ward; the writers included Sy Rosen; the directors included Oz Scott. Music was provided by Mitch Margo (of The Tokens) and Kevin Guillaume.

Roomies Swany, Inc/NBC Productions. NBC. Thursday nights 8:00 (March 19, 1987–May 15, 1987). Eight episodes were filmed before a live audience.

Roomies wasn't a bad show, but its premise was extremely far-fetched, improbable, and more than borderline creepy in nature. A fourteen-year-old genius Matthew Wiggins (Corey Haim) with an obsession for sea creatures (and, to a lesser degree, radio broadcasting), and a forty-two-year-old ex-Marine (Burt Young as Nick Chase) who seeks to earn his college degree despite his age, share a dorm room at Saginaw University. The idea of a forty-two-year-old rooming with a fourteen-year-old stranger didn't exactly equate to good Nielsen numbers. Their dorm room (no. 203) is filled with fish tanks (there's even one in the closet). Young Matthew calls shotgun for the upper bunk, by the way. As both are misfits, they bonded quickly and each is able to learn important life lessons from the other (Matthew is very naïve about the opposite sex, and Nick is out of touch with pop culture).

The debut episode takes place on Nick's first day on campus which, coincidentally, is also Matthew's birthday. Matthew is eagerly awaiting a visit from his father on his special day, but is devastated when Dad cancels his plans at the last minute. In an attempt to salvage the young man's birthday, Nick helps him pursue a pretty girl who works in the campus book store, only to show up at her house on her wedding day. In another episode, Nick's appearance in a marine training film titled *Digging a Ditch* comes back to haunt him when it is viewed on campus, and causes a lot of embarrassment. Burt Young is much better known for his role as Paulie, Rocky Balboa's brother-in-law, in the Rocky movie series. Corey Haim is best known for his role alongside Corey Feldman in the vampire movie *The Lost Boys* (1987). Sadly, Haim began using and abusing narcotics at the age of fifteen, and died at the young age of thirty-eight, on March 10, 2010.

Roomies uniquely used a lot of hit songs of the day as transitional music between scenes (songs such as "Walk Like an Egyptian" by the Bangles, "What You Need" by INXS, and "You Might Think" by the Cars), and also featured a group of a cappella singers (performing songs such as "Stand by Me" and "The Lion Sleeps Tonight") heard harmonizing in the hallways and rest room. Billy Vera, singer and co-writer of the show's theme song, recalled, "A producer named Jason Shubb, whom I'd worked for once before on a sitcom, called during the 'At This Moment' run on *Family Ties* and asked if I'd like to write and sing a theme for his new show. My songwriting partner Chip Taylor was already out here, helping me write songs for my follow-up album on Capitol, so I said sure. We knocked the song out in a half hour. I didn't want them to think I'd just taken some old song out of the trunk, so I waited another half hour before calling back to say we had a song. Unlike most TV themes, Chip and I wrote an entire song, rather than the thirty seconds' worth that's usually written. We had to cut it down later to fit. Shubb wanted to hear it, so I said we'd come over to the studio and play it. It was a Ricky Nelson–esque thing, so I told them I wanted to sing it in the men's room, for the echo. Can you imagine, all these studio execs and even secretaries, crowding into the lavatory to hear me sing our song? They all loved it, so I said my only demand was [that] I wanted legendary Rick Nelson guitarist James Burton to play on the session, which he did and was as great as you'd expect. Later, some jackass decided James wasn't enough and overdubbed another guitar and ruined the effect I'd wanted. I loved the song [titled "Answers"] and hoped the show would last, but, like most, it didn't."

Episodes were titled "Pilot," "Wrestling,"

"The One that Got Away," "To Tell the Truth," "The Ditch," "Bobby Midnight," "Obsession," and "Mid Term Fever." The executive producers were Sy Rosen, Coleman "Chick" Mitchell, and Geoff Neigher; the producers were Linda Morris, Vic Rauseo, and Jason Shubb; the writers included Sy Rosen, Chick Mitchell, Geoff Neigher, Linda Morris, Vic Rauseo, Hollis Rich, Richard Marcus, Sybil Adelman, and Martin Sage; and the directors included Jim Drake and John Tracy. The creator was Sy Rosen. Reruns of *Roomies* were briefly shown on NBC's Saturday morning lineup in 1991.

The Rousters Stephen J. Cannell Productions. NBC. Saturday nights 9:00 (October 1, 1983–October 29, 1983, December 20, 1983–December 27, 1983, and June 9, 1984–July 21, 1984). Thirteen episodes were filmed without a laugh track.

For all intents and purposes, this was *The Dukes of Hazzard* with a carnival setting. This program was touted this way on NBC—"*The Rousters* gonna sink *The Love Boat*." However, it quickly fell short of that promise. This show's lead character is constantly teased about his name, and often meets with disbelief about it by the authorities. After all, he is Wyatt Earp III (Chad Everett) and a bouncer and second-in-command for the traveling Sladetown Carnival, run by Cactus Jack Slade (Hoyt Axton, who despite his vast musical background, did not perform the show's theme song). Slade's pistachio-loving lion taming daughter, Ellen (Mimi Rogers), is dating Wyatt (and said lion is almost totally blind in one eye). She also tutors Wyatt's fourteen-year-old son, Michael (Timothy Gibbs). Wyatt's brother, Evan, is not unlike Enos from *The Dukes of Hazzard*, and was played by Jim Varney. Evan thinks of himself as a genius, but experiences extreme delusions of grandeur (none of his inventions ever pan out, including the mousetrap alarm system). He has a good heart, but wreaks havoc wherever he goes. Wyatt and Evan's mother is a no-nonsense, bounty hunting, pistol-packing mama named Amanda (Maxine Stuart)—a tough old girl who lives in a trailer with her sons on the carnival grounds. She shoots first and asks questions later. When she is in a good mood, she sings "Ragtime Cowboy Joe." There were such high hopes for this show, but it quickly had to pack up its tents, and was driven out of town by NBC.

Episodes were titled "The Rousters" (with guest star Fred Dryer), "The Carnival That Ate Sladetown," "Finders Keepers," "A Picture's Worth a Thousand Dollars," "Eye Witness Blues," "Everybody Loves a Clown," "Never Trust a Crystal Ball," "Two-and-a-Half Days of the Condor," "Slade vs. Slade," "Snake Eyes," "Cold Streak," "This Town Ain't Big Enough for the Twelve of Us," "Wyatt Earp to the Rescue." The executive producer was Jo Swerling, Jr.; the producer was Stephen J. Cannell; the writers included Stephen J. Cannell, Terrence McDonnell, Jeff Ray, Mark Jones, Jim Carlson, Babs Greyhosky, and Frank Lupo; the directors included Bruce Kessler, Sigmund Neufeld, Jr., Georg Stanford Brown, Joseph Pevney, Guy Magar, E. W. Swackhamer, Ron Satlof, Barry Crane, and Arnold Laven. The theme song, "Tough Enough," was written by Mike Post and Stephen Geyer, and performed by Ronnie Milsap.

Roxie Reeves Entertainment Group. CBS. Wednesday nights 8:00 (April 1, 1987–April 8, 1987). Six episodes were videotaped in front of a live audience, but only two aired.

Paired on Wednesday nights with *Take Five* at 8:30, *Roxie* had one of the shortest lives ever in prime-time, lasting only two weeks. Technically a spinoff of New York–based *Kate and Allie* (but, unlike that show, videotaped in Hollywood), an episode of *Kate and Allie* titled "Stage Mother" served as the pilot and aired on December 1, 1986. In the pilot, the setting is Cable Channel G, but the series centers on a low-budget Manhattan UHF TV station—WNYV Channel 66 (with the address of 726–730 on the building). Roxie Brinkerhoff (Andrea Martin) is not only the station's program director, but wears many other hats (and, in the debut episode, a fat suit for a news feature about the public's perception of obesity). In an-

Andrea Martin and Mitchell Laurance barely had time for a cup of coffee before CBS canceled their prime-time sitcom, *Roxie*.

other episode, she hosts a talk show and holds an ill-fated on-air group therapy session with the station staff—a session that leads to a lot of hurt feelings. Roxie is married to a sweater-clad schoolteacher named Michael (Mitchell Laurance). Other programs on WNYV include a cooking show called *If You Knew Sushi*, a sportsman show called *Trout Fishing with Earl*, a health and fitness program titled *Exercise with the Plotniks*, and a kids' program called

The Larry the Lizard Show. Larry was played by the dour-faced station manager, Leon Buchanan (Jack Riley). Others in the office include Randy Grant (Jerry Pavlon)—the lowly newbie/gofer/intern; Vito Carteri (Ernie Sabella), the station's chief engineer; and Marcie McKinley (Teresa Ganzel), the beautiful blonde secretary and bookkeeper.

About the program, Ganzel recalled, "We shot six episodes and were given our cancellation notice while shooting number six. I think some of the reason we were not given more of a chance is that Andrea Martin wanted to be funnier, but the network wanted her to be more the leading lady. Similar to what I experienced on *The Duck Factory*, I wish I could have worked with this cast forever. Andrea Martin boggles my mind with her comedy."

How did Ganzel land the role? "I did the Vitametavegimen scene from *I Love Lucy* in Milton Katsella's acting class. Andrea Martin was also in the class, and when I auditioned for her *Roxie* series she told the producers that I did the funniest scene ever from *I Love Lucy* in that class. So my confidence shot up and I nailed it. Andrea read with me for the audition and the next day I had the job. No endless callbacks or network and studio testing. Andrea wanted me, and I was in! My character, Marcie, was the station's accountant and Roxie's best friend." WNYV-TV had two slogans—"Average Programs for Average Viewers," and "WNYV—Pictures that Fly through the Air."

Episodes were titled "You're a Big Girl Now," "Dog Days," "Group Therapy," "Here's Roxie," "It's Not Easy Being Green," and "Professional Courtesy." The executive producer was Allan Katz; the producers were Bill Richmond and Liz Sage; the writers included Allan Katz, Bob Randall, and Bill Richmond; the directors included Sheldon Larry. The program was created by Bob Randall, and music was provided by Perry Botkin.

Sanchez of Bel Air Dog Lips Productions/Paramount Television. USA Network. Friday nights 8:00 (October 3, 1986–December 26, 1986) Thirteen episodes were videotaped in front of a live audience. The sponsors included Pillsbury.

Latino sitcoms fared well in the 1970s, led by *Chico and the Man* and *Que Pasa, USA?* This was not the case in the 1980s, however, and *Trial and Error, a.k.a. Pablo,* and *Sanchez of Bel Air* all failed to make a big splash. The latter tells the tale of an upwardly mobile Latino family named Sanchez. Ricardo Sanchez (Reni Santoni) does extremely well with his clothing business and moves his brood from the barrio in East Los Angeles to California's exclusive Bel Air community. The Sanchezes find their new life to be almost as problematic as their old one. Ricardo had a wife named Rita (Marcia Del Mar) and two teenage children—Gina, whom he nicknamed "Cookie Head" (Alitzah Weiner), who has a habit of saying, "I hate my life," and sixteen-year-old Miguel "Don't call me Mike" Sanchez (Richard Coca). Their new neighbor is a very nice but washed-up pop singer named Frankie Rondell (Bobby Sherman), whose most recent hit was called "Bop Shop" in 1964 (in real life, Sherman's string of hits continued into the early 1970s).

About Sherman's presence on the set, one of the program's executive producers (along with April Kelly) Dave Hackel said, "A number of women—former teenyboppers—came to the show with albums for Bobby to autograph. He was absolutely fabulous, not only as an actor, but as a person. Polite, funny, talented, and, above all, humble. Bobby now devotes his time to various police departments, sharing his passion for helping others. Look him up on the web and you'll learn a lot about the fine work he does. *Sanchez of Bel Air* was one of the first basic cable sitcoms and I like to think it helped pave the way for that particular business model. We were fortunate to have Reni Santoni at the center of the piece." The program was nominated for a "Best New Cable Series" award in 1986, but did not win.

Episodes were titled "Padre Knows Best," "It's My Party and I'll Wear What I Want," "Blind Date," "Spare the Hot Rod and Spoil the Child," "Stolen Moments," "Mi Casa es Everybody's Casa," "My Dinner with Frankie," "Sis

Boom Sanchez," "An Affair to Forget," "The Idolmaker," "Whatever Happened to Baby Jose?," "Chez What?," and "It's Not My Job." The executive producers were Dave Hackel and April Kelly; the producers were Henry J. Lange, Jr., and Larry Spencer; the writers included Ken Kuta, Janette Burleigh, Teena Heim, Larry Spencer, and Barry Gold; the directors included sitcom veteran Bob Claver along with Nancy Heydorn, Gary Shimokawa, Art Dielhenn, and Charles S. Dubin. The creators were April Kelly and Dave Hackel. The music was provided by Michael Scott, and the theme song was a Latin instrumental piece.

Sara Ubu Productions. NBC. Wednesday nights 9:30 (January 23, 1985–May 8, 1985). Thirteen episodes were videotaped in front of a live audience.

Not to be confused with the 1976 short-lived western series of the same name starring Brenda Vaccaro, this *Sara* was a 1985 short-lived sitcom. Sara McKenna (Geena Davis) is an attorney at Bay Area Legal in San Francisco. The program focuses on both her professional and personal life, and her considerable height is fodder for numerous "too tall" jokes (she frequently towers over her dates). A recently divorced single parent in her building named Stuart Webber (Mark Hudson, of The Hudson Brothers) seems like the ideal mate for Sara, and had the series gone beyond thirteen episodes, a romance would likely have bloomed. Stuart also has an adorable four-year-old towheaded son named Jesse (played by a very young Matthew Lawrence), for whom Sara frequently babysits. At the storefront law firm, Sara's diverse co-workers include her best friend, Rozalyn Dupree (Alfre Woodard), an African American attorney who has a penchant for butting into Sara's love life; Dennis Kemper (Bronson Pinchot), an openly gay and uncommonly honest attorney who is often heard asking Rozalyn to introduce him to available men; and pushy, sleazy Marty Lang (Bill Maher), precisely the kind of attorney featured in every lawyer joke ever told. Helen Newcomb (Ronnie Claire Edwards) is the office's secretary whose

The tall and talented Geena Davis briefly starred as a San Francisco attorney in NBC's *Sara*.

motherly instincts somehow keep all of them in line. During June of 1988, NBC reran select episodes of this series in its original Wednesday nightime slot.

A guest star in the "Dueling Lawyers" episode, Murphy Cross, recalled, "Doing that show was so much fun. A great, positive memory for me. Geena Davis, Bronson Pinchot, Alfre Woodard, and Bill Maher—what a powerhouse cast! I remember jumping on either Bronson or Bill's back playing piggy back with him on the set. I remember laughing a lot all week. And I also remember thinking that Bill had an energy about him that said 'independent thinker.'"

Episodes were titled "David Returns," "Sara's Mom," "Dueling Lawyers," "Helen Steps Out," "You Can't Win 'Em All," "A Date with Keith," "Rock and Roll Father," "27 Candles," "Sara's Short Story," "Meet Mr. Cooper," "Girls Just Want to Have Fun," "A Night at the Ballet," and "Brief Encounter." The executive producer was

Gary David Goldberg; the writers included Ruth Bennett; the directors included Will Mackenzie.

Second Chance Lightkeeper Productions/20th Century Television. FOX. Saturday nights 9:00 (September 26, 1987–October 17, 1987), Saturday nights 9:30 (October 24, 1987–November 28, 1987), Saturday nights 8:00 (January 16, 1988–April 9, 1988) and Saturday nights 8:30 (April 16, 1988–July 2, 1988). The latter two time slots were as the revamped *Boys Will Be Boys*. Nine episodes of *Second Chance* were videotaped with a laugh track, and twelve episodes of *Boys Will Be Boys* were videotaped in front of a live audience. Sponsors for *Boys Will Be Boys* included Tilex and Soft Scrub.

Second Chance was one of the upstart FOX Network's early sitcoms in 1987, and it lived up to its title and got a "second chance," as *Boys Will Be Boys*, in 1988. The interesting original premise of the program employed elements of fantasy. Charles Russell dies in a Hovercraft mishap in the futuristic year of 2011. Upon meeting St. Peter, it is determined that, for a time, Russell will remain in purgatory because he is deemed too good for hell, but not good enough for heaven. He is given a chance to redeem himself by being sent back in time as Charles Time to guide his teenage self in the right direction. The adult Charles was played by Kiel Martin, and the teen version, nicknamed "Chazz," was played by an up-and-coming Matthew L. Perry (yes, there used to be an *L* in his professional name). Adult Charles runs a convenience store by day, and rents a spare room in the home shared by Chazz and his divorced mom, Helen (Randee Heller). The extra money from the adult Charles's rent helps pay expenses, as Chazz's deadbeat dad (portrayed by Richard Kline, in the "Life without Father" episode) is months behind on his alimony and child support. Adult Charles is also there for his own benefit to keep his younger self on the straight and narrow, and thus secure entry into heaven. Neither Chazz nor his mom are privy to the facts about adult Charles, but do notice the amazing similarities (they have the same mannerisms, quirks, tastes in food [almond chocolate mint ice cream], eating, and TV viewing habits). At the same time, adult Charles is a friend and father figure to Chazz. Only adult Charles is able to see St. Peter (Joseph Maher) when he visits. Chazz has two teenage friends—the tough "babe magnet" Francis "Booch" Lottabucci (William Gallo) and the nerdy social outcast Eugene Blooberman (Demian Slade). Musclebound "Booch" is rarely seen without a leather vest adorning his tight sleeveless white T-shirt, while ectomorphic Eugene dons a blonde streak in his hair and is usually seen tripping over or bumping into something or someone. His mother is named Bernice. Down deep they are both very decent young men, but not necessarily the greatest influences on Chazz.

Actor Stuart Pankin, who guest starred in the episode titled "Mid-Term Blues," shared, "That was quite a while ago. I recall Joe Maher playing the angel, and I also remember how very friendly Matthew Perry was. We stayed in touch for a long time after that experience. I only made that one appearance on the show, but it was a lot of fun." This format, while intriguing, wore out its welcome very quickly and was scrapped. *Second Chance* was put on hiatus and retooled. When it reemerged in January as *Boys Will Be Boys*, gone was the fantasy element (along with Kiel Martin and Joe Maher). A hipper, more upbeat instrumental version of the "I Gotta Go Back" theme song was employed. The show is still set on Venice Beach, but now Chazz's mom is less dependent upon her ex-husband's alimony. Chazz's friends Booch and Eugene returned, and two new schoolmates were added—Adam Sadowsky as Alex, and Terry Ivens as Debbie Miller (Chazz's girlfriend and next-door neighbor). There is one other format difference—Booch now rents the apartment over the garage (much in the manner of Fonzie on *Happy Days*), and Chazz opts to move in there, too, for a taste of independence (and a little foreshadowing of his later *Odd Couple* redux on CBS in 2015). Even with this "second chance," the program failed to generate enough viewers to warrant a "second season." It should be noted that there was one amazing coincidence in a first format episode in which Muammar Gaddafi was seen being sentenced to spend eternity in hell by St. Peter in the future year 2011. Gaddafi's life, eerily, did in fact end in the year 2011. Whether or not he was issued a pitchfork is another matter entirely.

Episodes were titled (as *Second Chance*) "The End," "Moving In," "Plain Jane," "Life Without Father," "Oedipus Russell," "Handy Boy," "To Have Loved and Lost," "Mid-Term Blues" and "A Hunting We Will Go," (as *Boys Will Be Boys*) "Hot Wheels," "Viva Las Vegas, Parts One and Two," "Changes, Parts One and Two," "The Girl Next Door," "South of the Border," "The Gang," "The Secret of Their Success," "The Front," "Two Men and a Baby," and "The Triangle." The executive producers were David W. Duclon and Gary Menteer; the producer was Mady Julian; the writers included Jim Geoghan, David W. Duclon, Cheryl Alu, Stephen Langford, Gary Menteer, Deborah Serra, Mady Julian, Manny Basanese, Jerry Jacobius, Tom Johnstone, Mike Marmer, Jim Mayer, John Antoniou, Nick Gore, and Lang Elliott; the directors included Jim Drake, Marc Gass, Jack Shea, Gerren Keith, and Jim Cox. The theme song "I Gotta Go Back" and incidental music were written by Rik Howard, Jon Gilutin, Tyrone Johnson, and Robert Wirth.

Semi-Tough Universal Television. ABC. Thursday nights 9:30 (May 29, 1980–June 19, 1980). Four episodes were videotaped with a laugh track.

Semi-Tough was first a popular book by Dan Jenkins, and then a popular 1977 motion picture from United Artists. *Semi-Tough* tells the tale of a hapless New York NFL team called The Bulls, and two of its team members, Billy Clyde Pucket and Marvin "Shake" Tiller, who share an apartment with a lovely young writer named Barbara Jane Bookman. Barbara Jane and "Shake" become something of an item. But things heat up when Billy Clyde tries to make a play for Barbara Jane.

Three years after the film, a pilot was made for a TV version of *Semi-Tough,* but it was entirely recast for the eventual 1980 series. The series starred Bruce McGill, post–*National Lampoon's Animal House*, as Billy Clyde Pucket (Burt Reynolds, in the film; Douglas Barr, in the pilot); David Hasselhoff, pre–*Knight Rider* and *Baywatch*, was Marvin "Shake" Tiller (Kris Kristofferson, in the film; Josh Taylor, in the pilot); Markie Post, pre–*Night Court*, was Barbara Jane (Jill Clayburgh, in the film; Mary Louise Weller, in the pilot); and NFL great Bubba Smith was "Puddin'" (Roger E. Mosely, in the film). Others in the TV cast included Ed Peck as Coach Cooper, Freeman King as "Story Time," Carlos Brown as T. J., and Jim MacKrell as Burt Danby. The set for the series featured a locker room with lockers in the center, making for some very awkward camera shots. Bubba Smith, the only member of the cast who had actually been in an NFL locker room, suggested that the lockers should be along the walls, not only to alleviate the camera issue, but to look more like the real thing. However, the powers-that-be simply wouldn't listen to him. Chuck McCann and Jim McGeorge played sportscasters Pearly and Hal, respectively. Even with a cushy Thursday night slot on ABC's big comedy night, *Semi-Tough* failed to catch on and disappeared after only four episodes.

Episodes were titled "Barbara Jane Moves Out," "One Bad Apple," "That Catch," and "The First Hurrah." The producers were Jerry Davis and David Merrick; the writers included Norman Barasch, Wally Dalton, Howard Gewirtz, John Steven Owen, Ian Praiser, Rich Reinhart, Reinhold Weege, and Shelley Zellman; the directors were all big names—Dick Martin, Richard Benjamin, and John Tracy. Music was provided by Doug Gilmore.

Seven Brides for Seven Brothers David Gerber Productions/MGM Television. CBS. Sunday night 8:00 (September 19, 1982), Wednesday nights 8:00 (September 23, 1982–March 23, 1983). Twenty episodes were filmed without a laugh track.

Seven Brides for Seven Brothers was a 1954

musical dramedy motion picture set in 1850s Oregon. It starred Howard Keel and Jane Powell. In 1982, the show debuted on Broadway, but was not a success. In that same year, the TV series premiered. It was only loosely based upon the original, and, in fact, was set in modern times. This was the tale of seven parentless brothers who opt to live together on the large Circle Bar Seven ranch in Carbon County, Northern California, complete with livestock and horses. The eldest of the seven brothers, twenty-seven-year-old Adam McFadden (Richard Dean Anderson, pre–*MacGyver*) is a former basketball player at Murphy High School, who hastily marries a local waitress named Hannah Moss-McFadden (Terri Treas) without informing her of his living arrangements. Becoming the lone hen in a house overladen with sloppy roosters puts an early strain on the new marriage, especially when she has to clean up after them. Originally, the brothers didn't cotton to her being there, but softened quickly when they noticed how much sunshine she brought into their otherwise dreary existence. Those other brothers were Brian (Drake Hogestyn); Crane (a bearded Peter Horton); Daniel (Roger Wilson); Evan (Tim Topper); Ford (Brian Utman), who had a crush on a local girl named Cleo; and Guthrie (a very young River Phoenix). Israel Juarbe, who guest starred in "The Promised Land" episode, recalled, "River Phoenix and Richard Dean Anderson were both extremely cool guys to work with. I played a character named Guillermo in that episode, and I recall that the other guest stars that week were Theresa Saldana as Angelina, and *Ugly Betty*'s Tony Plana as Carlos. We filmed a lot of that episode in California's beautiful Napa Valley. It was very memorable." The program failed to find an audience, and was canceled after that one ambitious and musical season. As far as we know, the other six brothers are still unmarried. It is alleged that Michael J. Fox auditioned for a role on this series, but was not hired.

Episodes were titled "The Pilot," "The Man in the White Hat," "Challenges," "I Love You, Molly McGraw," "Gold Fever," "Daniel's Song," "A House Divided," "Rodeo," "Catch a Falling Star," "The Election," "Neighbors," "Dreams," "The Christmas Song," "Heritage," "Promised Land," "The Killer," "Deadly High," "The Rescue," "Winter Roses," "Winner," "A Ring for Hannah," and "The Roundup." The executive producer was David Gerber; the producers were Stephen Cragg, Richard Fielder, and James H. Brown; the writers included Josef Anderson, Ira Steven Behr, Michael Brentwood, Leah Appel, Paul L. Ehrmann, Elizabeth Clark, Steve Hayes, Richard Fielder, Marshall Herskovitz, Sue Grafton, Paul Laurence, Steve Hayes, Steven Humphrey, Mitzi Marvin, C. E. Lewis, Earl W. Wallace, Joe Viola, Preston Ransome, Joel Steiger, Jud Scott, Tim Maschler, and Michael Petryni; the directors included Burt Kennedy, Robert C. Thompson, Barry Crane, James Sheldon, John Florea, Michael O'Herlihy, John Patterson, Peter Levin, Gary Nelson, Vincent McEveety, Bernard L. Kowalski, and Harvey S. Laidman. One song each week on this musical dramedy was composed by legendary songwriter Jimmy Webb (famous for "Galveston," "MacArthur Park," "Worst that Could Happen," "Wichita Lineman," "Up, Up and Away," and "By the Time I Get to Phoenix"), who also composed the theme song, performed by Phil Silas.

Shadow Chasers Kenneth Johnson/Brian Grazer Productions/Warner Bros. Television. ABC. Thursday nights 8:00 (November 11, 1985–January 16, 1986). Thirteen episodes were filmed without a laugh track, but only nine aired.

Because of the overwhelming success of the *Ghostbusters* movie in 1984, ABC attempted to jump on the paranormal parkway with *Shadow Chasers* in 1985. It debuted as a two-hour movie, and then settled into its normal time slot on Thursday nights at 8:00. The storyline focuses on Edgar "Benny" Benedek (Dennis Dugan), who writes about the occult for *The National Register* (a takeoff on *The National Inquirer*), a tabloid magazine. He is teamed with staid, stodgy, and proper British anthropologist Jonathan MacKensie (Trevor Eve). They aren't the bravest of ghostbusters (in fact, they are both rather skittish), and their relationship is more adversarial than friendly (à la *The Odd Couple*). Their assignments and eventual comic adventures with the supernatural come with assignments from Dr. Juliana Moorhouse (Nina Foch), who occupies a rather spooky and cave-like office (part of the Georgetown Paranormal Research Unit—P. R. U.). Hermione Baddeley, Mrs. Nell Naugatuck on *Maude*, had the recurring role of Melody Lacey. The program was scheduled in the most dreaded spot on the schedule—against NBC's *The Cosby Show*. Thirteen hour-long episodes were filmed, but only nine aired. The remaining four were only seen on the Armed Forces Network. The two-hour debut movie, however, still surfaces on occasion.

Episodes were titled "Shadow Chasers, Parts One and Two," "The Spirit of St. Louis," "Amazing Grace," "The Middle of Somewhere," "Parts Unknown," "The Many Lives of Jonathan," "The Phantom of the Galleria," "How Green Was My Murder," "Let's Make a Deal," "Cora's Stranger," "Curse of the Full Moon," "Blood and Magnolias," and "Ahead of Time" (with guest star Richard Kline). The executive producers were Brian Grazer and Kenneth Johnson; the producer was Craig Schiller; the writers included Kenneth Johnson, Susan Goldberg, Peggy Goldman, Harry and Renee Longstreet, Craig Buck, Bob Rosenfarb, Brian Grazer, Linda Campanelli, Diane Frolov, Richard Manning, Hans Beimler, M. M. Shelly Moore, Mary Ann Kasica, and Michael Scheff; the directors included Bob Sweeney, Barbara Peters, Alan Myerson, Charles Braverman, Cliff Bole, Chuck Bowman, Victor Lobl, and Kenneth Johnson. Music was provided by Joe Harnell, and the theme song, "Shadow Chasers," was by John Reed and Mark Tanner.

Shaping Up Estin/Simon Productions/Paramount Television. ABC. Tuesday nights 9:30 (March 20, 1984–April 17, 1984). Six episodes were videotaped in front of a live audience, but only five aired.

The original working title for this series was "Welcome to the Club." It was renamed *Shaping Up* before it hit the airwaves. Set in a gymnasium called Buddy Fox's Health Club, in Santa Monica, California, it starred Leslie Nielsen as Buddy—a fit, almost sixty-year-old who has been married and divorced eight times. Even with all of those marriages, Buddy never did manage to have a child of his own. He, in fact, had a vasectomy in the 1970s because one of his wives had a condition in which childbirth had the potential to end her life. Buddy may have been like a father to the young manager of the club, Ben Zachary, played by Michael Fontaine (Tim Robbins, in the unaired pilot), but he badly wants to have a son of his own. The urge for fatherhood is so intense, in fact, that in the debut episode, titled "Baby Be Mine," he opts to buy a baby from a young pregnant woman in dire financial straits. He pursues this option, despite the fact that it is illegal. Luckily, at the last moment, after holding her newborn baby, new mother Vicky's (Allyce Beasley) conscience won't allow her to follow through on the deal. Buddy, however, still gets to visit the baby three or four times a week. Others at the gym include Melissa McDonald (Shawn Weatherly), one of the instructors; Shannon Winters (Jennifer Tilly), who works behind the counter and is studying for her master's degree; and "Body by Jake's" Jake Steinfeld was Jerry, the stereotypical dumb jock. These gym rats really broke a sweat when the Nielsen (no relation to Leslie) Ratings showed very little muscle, and the whole cast was sent to the showers after only five episodes.

Episodes were titled "Baby Be Mine," "Ex Pede Herculem," "Defusing the Muse," "I Should Have Danced All Night," and "Mixed Nuts." The executive producers and creators were Ken Estin and Sam Simon; the producer was Richard Sakai; the writers included Ken Estin, Sam Simon, and Merrill Markoe; the lone director was Michael Lessac. Music was provided by Fletcher Adams.

Shell Game Warner Bros. Television. CBS. Thursday nights 8:00 (January 8, 1987–February 12, 1987). Six hour-long episodes were filmed single-camera style without a laugh track.

Shell Game was a very short-lived hour-long CBS series. Whether one would consider it a dramedy or a crimedy depends upon personal preference. After a con game involving diamond earrings goes sour, Jennie Jerome (*Superman*'s Margot Kidder) contacts her former partner in crime (and ex-husband gone straight) television producer John Reid (James Read) and goes into hiding at his place. For letting her hang out there, she gets him a story for his consumer affairs show, *Solutions*, at KJME Channel Six, in Santa Ana, California. They discover that they haven't missed a beat and can still work together, so she becomes his assistant, much to the chagrin of John's fiancée, the TV station owner's daughter Natalie Thayer (Marg Helgenberger, pre–*CSI*). The duo then utilizes their conning and cunning to solve crimes and acquire stories. Others in the cast included station manager Bert Luna (Chip Zien), and the cocky host of *Solutions*, William Bauer (Rod McCary). The title *Shell Game* refers to the old game involving a ball or a pea placed under a set of cups or shells (a.k.a. "thimblerig"). The shells are then mixed up and, to win a designated prize, one must guess under which shell the ball lies. *Shell Game* usually has a negative connotation, with intentions to commit fraud. Kidder and Read, however, just never clicked and lacked the chemistry of Maddie and David on *Moonlighting* or Kate and Richard on *Castle*, and the program disappeared after only six episodes.

Episodes were titled "The Pilot," "Norman's Parking Ticket," "The Old Team," "The Upstairs Gardener," "Pai Gow," and "Dead Wrong." The executive producer was Michele Rappaport; the producers included Alex Beaton, John Ziffren, and David S. Grant; the writers included Carla Jean Wagner and Nick Thiel, and the directors included Lou Antonio, Paul Krasny, and Christopher Leitch. Music was produced by Richard Lewis Warren, and the theme song was by Michel Colombier.

Shirley Ten Four Productions/Universal Television. NBC. Friday nights 8:00 (October 26, 1979–January 25, 1980). Thirteen hour-long episodes were filmed without a laugh track. The sponsor was Procter and Gamble.

After her success with a family named Partridge, Oscar winner Shirley Jones tried again for TV success in an eponymous hour-long dramedy titled *Shirley*. Jones absolutely loved the pilot—a warm and fuzzy family show that was a mixture of humor and drama. The pilot was sold to NBC and a series was in the works. However, without Shirley's consent, Fred Silverman took hold of the reins and before *Shirley* the pilot became *Shirley* the series, vast changes were made. Because of the success of *Eight Is Enough*, Silverman attempted to pattern *Shirley* after that hit series, with many more laughs and less drama. Shirley was none too pleased, and the show ultimately failed to find an audience, encompassing only thirteen episodes. It was the story of the Miller Family, who, after the death of Jack Miller, the patriarch of the family, decide to follow through with Jack's plans to leave hectic New York City behind for the more serene surroundings of Lake Tahoe, Nevada (they had already put a down payment on a house at 602 Kingsbeach Road; the exterior is actually a cleaned-up version of the Munsters' house, located on the Universal Studios backlot). It isn't an easy transition for Shirley Miller—she has difficulty finding full-time work there and has to support her family with only part-time jobs. Bill Miller (Peter Barton), Shirley's stepson (she was Jack's second wife), has trouble adjusting to his new high school. Her biological children are sixteen-year-old Debra (a young Rosanna Arquette); ten-year-old Hemm (Bret Shryer); and eight-year-old Michelle (a young Tracey Gold). Her bff was named Tracey McCord (Cindy Eilbacher). Even though Shirley's income is sorely lacking, her new home inexplicably comes with a resident housekeeper named Charlotte McHenry (Ann Doran). Charlotte's surly ex, named Dutch, owns a local lunch counter and is a part-time handyman. John Wayne's son Patrick played Lew Armitage, Shirley's brand new beau. He is a ski instructor and the Miller children adore him. The family dog has the unusual name of Oregano.

Episodes were titled "Is This Really What Dad Wanted?," "Hard Hat," "A Gun for Bill/Son of a Gun," "Things Your Mother Forgot to Tell You," "The One that Got Away," "A Play on Words," "Twenty Years to Life," "Separate Agendas," "Visions of Christmas Past," "On the Skids," "Fenced In," "The Three Dates of Shirley Miller," and "Teddy Roosevelt Slept Here." The executive producers were William Hogan and Greg Strangis; the producer was Robert Birnbaum; the writers included Steve Hattman, Gwen Bagni, Paul Dubov, Greg Strangis, Patricia Green, Chris Manheim, Lance Madrid III, Terry Hart, Dusty Kay, Joel Tappis, Jackie McKane, Mary-David Sheiner, Parke Perine, Sandra Kay Siegel, Sheila Judis Weisberg, and Dave Hackel. Hackel shared, "My first staff job ever. On a show like that—a one-hour 'dramedy,' the lowly writers had very little interaction with the cast. My memory is that Shirley Jones was very nice, as was the rest of the cast. We just didn't have much contact. My job was to be wide-eyed and grateful for the gig and I was both." The directors included Robert Birnbaum, Mel Ferber, Alan Myerson, Stan Lathan, Gerald Mayer, William F. Claxton, Gene Nelson, and Michael Preece. Preece shared, "Shirley Jones was absolutely delightful, as was Rosanna Arquette. This was my opportunity to really prove myself as a director—Universal was testing me, and luckily they liked my work and used me a lot as a result. I directed the program's final episode. I vividly recall three guys in suits from Universal visiting Shirley before we started filming. I had the feeling that something was up. After the men left, I asked Shirley what was going on, and she told me the series had been canceled. We finished the episode, but it was definitely the last one. Very memorable." The creator was Lance Madrid III. The theme song, "Here Is Where the Love Is," was performed by Cyndi Grecco, whom the composers Charles Fox and Norman Gimbel discovered performing at Magic Mountain theme park in Southern California.

Sister Kate Lazy B Productions/F. O. B. Productions/Mea Culpa Productions/20th Century Television. NBC. Saturday night 9:30 (September 16, 1989), Sunday nights 8:00 (September 24, 1989–November 26, 1989), Sunday nights 8:30 (December 3, 1989–January 21, 1990), and Monday nights 8:00 (July 16, 1990–July 30, 1990). Nineteen episodes were videotaped in front of a live audience, but only 18 aired.

After her steamy role on *The Colbys*, Stephanie Beacham donned a habit and starred in this short-lived sitcom, as Sister Katherine Lambert. She is reassigned after an archeological dig to run an orphanage (against her will). She makes the most of it, however, and keeps the young waifs in line at Redemption House—a Catholic residence for children. Her wards include an up-and-coming actor, appropriately named (Jason) *Priest*ly as the eldest of her wards, sixteen-year-old girl-crazy Todd Mahaffey (who isn't a bad cook), before his success on *Beverly Hills 90210*; fellow teenagers April Newberry (Erin Reed), a stereotypical blonde; and Frederika Marasco

Stephanie Beacham and Joel Robinson, the stars of NBC's ***Sister Kate***. Viewers didn't find the show habit-forming.

(Hannah Cutrona), who smokes; twelve-year-old wheelchair-bound tomboy Hilary Logan (Penina Segall); eleven-year-old Eugene Colodner (Harley Cross); nine-year-old Violet Johnson (Alexaundria Simmon), who has an imaginary friend named Rachelle; and seven-year-old dreadlocked Neville Williams (Joel Robinson). Yet another orphan, a youngster known as Buster (Miko Hughes), appears in a few of the later episodes. Gordon Jump had a recurring role as Lucas Underwood, the director of Diocesan Service (whom the kids nickname "Spanky"). None of the kids seem as incorrigible or as unadoptable as they are made out to be. Each episode of this show has a moral. Despite several changes in time slot, the program's ratings were very low and it was canceled by NBC in January of 1990. Unaired episodes were burned off during the summer of that year. *Sister Kate* was definitely not "habit-forming" television.

Episodes were titled "The Pilot," "Freddy's Bad Habit," "Eugene's Secret," "Freddy's Date," "Eugene's Model," "Neville's Hired Hand," "Hilary's Date," "Violet's Friend," "Kate's Baby," "Kate's Furnace," "The Nun" (with guest star Marion Ross), "April in Paris," "Father Christmas," "Eugene's Feat" (with guest stars Milli Vanilli), "Kandid Kate," "Sweet Sixteen" (with guest star Sally Struthers), "Bingo," "Todd's Cheap Date," and "Underwood Underfoot." The executive producers were Frank Dungan, Jeff Stein, and Tony Sheehan; the producer was Patricia Rickey; the writers included Brenda Hampton-Cain, William C. Kenny, Frank Dungan, Jeff Stein, and Tony Sheehan; the directors included Jeffrey L. Melman, Phil Ramuno, Noam Pitlik, and John Sgueglia. The creators were Frank Dungan, Jeff Stein, and Tony Sheehan. The theme song, "Maybe an Angel," was written by Mason Cooper and Brian Rawlings, and performed by Amy Grant.

The Six O'Clock Follies P.S. 235 Productions/Ella Productions/Warner Bros. Television. NBC. Aired very erratically (April 24, 1980–April 26, 1980, and August 2, 1980–September 13, 1980). Six episodes were filmed with a laugh track, but only four aired.

Too soon? For *Six O'Clock Follies*, the answer may have been yes. Enough time had elapsed since the Korean war for *M*A*S*H* to flourish, but the conflict in Vietnam was another story. This military comedy was set in 1967 Saigon. The focus was the Armed Forces Vietnam Network—The AFVN News and Sports, patterned after a real nightly six o'clock news program. *Six O'Clock Follies* features GI reporters A. C. Weary (Sam Paige), Don "Robby" Robinson (a very young Laurence Fishburne, credited as Larry Fishburne), and a foxy weather girl named Candi LeRoy (Aarika Wells). Midas Metcovich (Philip Charles MacKenzie) is the news director who also runs the local watering hole called "The Midas Bar"—the favorite hangout for the crew. MacKenzie remembered, "I was the go-to guy on the show. If one of the characters wanted or needed a particular item, I was the one who could get it for them." Also in the cast were sitcom veterans such as Randall Carver (John Burns of *Taxi*) as Lieutenant Beuhler (no relation to Ferris), and Joby Baker of *Good Morning, World* as Colonel Harvey Marvin, as well as extremely well-seasoned sitcom directors Bob Sweeney and Don Weis. George Kee Cheung portrayed Ho, the janitor (and Midas's right-hand man); impressionist Fred Travalena supplied the voice for President Lyndon Baines Johnson, and up-and-coming stars Phil Hartman and Bill Paxton made guest appearances.

MacKenzie added, "As a huge Joe Cocker fan, I'm so proud to say this was the first show for which he performed the theme song." Of course, Cocker's rendition of "With a Little Help from My Friends" was used years later for *The Wonder Years*, but this song was recorded specifically for *Six O'Clock Follies*.

Two episodes aired in the same week at the end of April 1980. Regarding the program's debut, MacKenzie shared, "We had an opening night party for the show with all the cast and crew and lots of great food. However, about five minutes into that debut episode, NBC broke in with a news bulletin about the Iranian hostage crisis and every jaw in the room dropped. I don't know if this was the direct cause of our show's demise, but it certainly didn't help any."

Randall Carver (Buehler) added, "Actually, the debut episode was interrupted by NBC Washington correspondent John Palmer reporting about President Jimmy Carter's failed rescue mission in which U. S. service men were killed and injured when two aircraft collided in the Iranian desert trying to rescue the imprisoned U. S. embassy workers. Less than thirty minutes later the sound stage of about 250 partiers was empty. And it was clear that the timing for a dark comedy about Vietnam wasn't right. The show was good, very good, and it had its heart in the right place, so said the critics. But it was just bad luck and timing that brought about the show's demise. And the magnitude of the loss of eight servicemen and many others injured was significant enough to abandon the series. And we had been picked for seven more shows, but they were canceled immediately."

After two airings, the program didn't surface again until late in the summer of that year when two of the four remaining episodes were burned off. The Vietnam War was addressed again a few years later in the successful dramatic series *Tour of Duty* and *China Beach*, and in the motion picture *Good Morning, Vietnam* (1987).

Episodes were titled "Welcome, Robby," "Ol' Yeller," "Rumors of Peace," "Goodbye, Candi," "Medal Winner," and "Surprise Party." The producers were Marvin Kupfer and Norman Steinberg; the writers included John Steven Owen, Richard Dimitri, Bob Baublitz, and Bo Kaprall; the directors included Bob Sweeney and Don Weis. The creators were Marvin Kupfer and David Steinberg. Music was provided by Harry Betts and Artie Butler. Butler and Cliff Einstein wrote the theme song, "Home" for Joe Cocker.

The Slap Maxwell Story Slap Happy Productions/Warner Bros. Television. ABC. Wednesday nights 9:30 (September 23, 1987–March 16, 1988, and May 6, 1988–May 20, 1988). Twenty-two episodes were filmed single-camera style without a laugh track.

Previously, Dabney Coleman portrayed a totally unlikeable character named Bill Bittinger on *Buffalo Bill*. So many of the same despicable characteristics were present in the form of Slap Maxwell in this venture. Both shows were created by Jay Tarses, and both shows were short-lived. Coleman and Tarses did not get along well in real life, so the fact that they opted to work together a second time is quite astonishing. This time around, however, instead of a TV talk show host, Coleman played an egotistical, stubborn, old-fashioned cigar-chomping fedora-wearing neo-noir fifty-year-old newspaper man, working for a second-rate Southwestern rag known as *The Ledger*. Even though Slap and his wife, Annie (Susan Anspach), parted some fifteen years earlier, he speaks of her as if they were still together. Annie appeared in ten episodes, and their son, Elliott Maxwell (Joseph Brutsman), appeared in four. Viewers never do find out Slap's real first name, but his sports column is called "Slap Shots," and he hunts and pecks it out on his ancient trusty and rusty typewriter. He is most proud of a piece he'd written about Major League Baseball player Al Kaline's final at-bat, and staked claim to a Pulitzer Prize that he should have won (if only he'd remembered to mail in the entry form). Not one to employ tact, his scathing, innuendo-laden columns often get Slap slapped with lawsuits (and/or hit with fists). Said lawsuits draw the ire of the paper's editor, Nelson "Nelly" Kruger (Brian Smiar). Nelly makes use of some of the most peculiar phrases and analogies, such as, "This is as serious as a beaver in the pantry," "Love don't make the buttercup shine," and "Dead as a walnut." He also fires Slap on more than one occasion (including the debut episode), despite the fact that Slap is his son's godfather. They'd worked together for twenty-two years, and had gone trout fishing together numerous times. Slap perpetuates the rumor that Nelly has a glass eye, and is aware of Nelly's fling with a cashier—they had a history. Perhaps the only person who likes Slap (at least some of the time) is his secretary, Judy Ralston (Megan Gallagher)—an on-again/off-again (mostly off) romantic interest. The copyboy, Charlie Wilson, was played by Bill Calvert. When life becomes too stressful and burdensome, Slap finds refuge in a sleazy local establishment run by a slightly more than middle-aged African American gentleman bartender nicknamed The Dutchman (Bill Cobbs).

This well-written sitcom did not employ a laugh track or a studio audience. That practice was a true rarity in 1988, but has become very much the norm in recent years with the success of *The Middle, Modern Family, Community, The Office,* and *Parks and Recreation.* The series went on hiatus in March of 1988 and returned for a few weeks in May to burn off the remaining episodes.

The episodes were not assigned titles, only numbers. The executive producer was Bernie Brillstein; the producer and creator was Jay Tarses; the writers included Jay Tarses and Norma Safford Vela; the directors included Peter Baldwin, Jay Tarses, Steve Dubin, and Gino Tanasescu. The series was developed by Bob Brush. Music was provided by Patrick Williams. It's interesting to note that this series utilized both a Los Angeles and New York casting department.

Small and Frye Walt Disney Company. CBS. Monday nights 8:30 (March 7, 1983–March 21, 1983), and Wednesday nights 8:00 (June 1, 1983–June 15, 1983). Six episodes were filmed with a laugh track.

For all intents and purposes, this was "Honey, I Shrunk the Detective." Former *Mike Hammer* star Darren McGavin is Nick Small—a former cop turned private eye—part owner of Small and Frye Investigations (with the number 206 on their office door). His character is not unlike that of Mike Hammer—a mostly serious-minded, all-business gumshoe of the 1940s (a former Golden Gloves boxer, too). He has a secret safe on his wall that opens when the receiver of his office phone is slammed down on his desk. Even though his name is Small, his partner, Chip Frye (Jack Blessing), has the unique ability to become small because of a laboratory accident. Why wasn't Frye given the name of Small? Blessing said, "Chip Small would have been too precious, even for this show." The situation was similar to the 1970s sitcom *Big John, Little John* with Herb Edelman and Joyce Bulifant.

The opening credits featured the word "Frye" alternating between a large font and a much smaller one. An advantage of the bizarre situation is that Frye, when diminutive, can eavesdrop without being noticed (he is able to see criminals at work, and to hear many confessions and future schemes being planned). By merely twisting his ring, he is usually able to alter his height. His usual hiding place is in a hollowed-out copy of Louisa May Alcott's *Little Men*. About the props, Blessing recalled, "I heard that Disney somehow got a good deal on all of the oversized props left over from Lily Tomlin's *The Incredible Shrinking Woman*, and I think it's possible that this trove led to the series." Temperatures below freezing, fluorescent lights, and ingesting brussels sprouts had an effect on his ability to grow bigger or smaller. Recalling his late co-star, McGavin, Blessing said, "Darren was a terrific guy and I liked him very much. I think he felt like he was slumming a little bit on this, and I suppose he was. He had a million show biz stories and wanted to share them constantly. A little too constantly. Boy, that man could talk. This being my first series and my being so young, I just sat back and listened. Eventually though, it was just to be polite. There were so many older guest stars on the show that every episode was a reunion for someone. So, they gabbed."

Others in the cast included Nick's daughter, Phoebe (Debbie Zipp); Dr. Henry Hanratty (Bill Daily), of the crime lab—a boxing trivia expert; and Eddie Fitzsimmons (Warren Berlinger), the owner of a favorite hangout called Eddie's Bar and Grill (on 210th Street). Eddie's waitress was named Vicki (Victoria Carroll). Regarding his co-stars Blessing said, "Bill Daily was wonderful. I tended to hang out with him the most. A very, very funny man." Guest stars included Rue McClanahan, Kenneth Mars, Larry Storch, and Roddy McDowall. About them, Blessing stated, "It was disappointing to lose Roddy after the pilot episode. He spent all of his down time taking photographs, as he was wont to do. I have always regretted that I did not stay in touch with him and get some of what he shot. Kenneth Mars was every bit as odd as you would expect. Larry Storch was a sweet man. Rue was Rue, what can you say? Exactly as advertised." Was it tough to do a show that utilized a lot of green screen scenes? Blessing said, "We filmed [an episode] in five days. Four for the script and Friday was reserved for me and the green screen. Exhausting. Where do you go when you are small? Bad places. Rat tunnels and bowls of soup. Acting with a piece of paper that had an *x* on it for the eye lines and the script supervisor reading the lines. Twelve to fourteen hour days. You know the thing that made those days so long was not so much my time in bowls of soup and the like, though that was extremely unpleasant. The difficult shots were the shrinking and growing shots. Remember, this was long before CGI and had to be done with conventional film. As I recall, it was a very primitive special effect. They built a ramp for a twenty- or thirty-foot track shot, which was angled about 30 degrees into the air. Somehow, and I don't remember how, they pulled the camera up and away from me for the shrink shots and rolled it back towards me for the growing shots. And for every foot that camera went away from me or approached me, focus had to be maintained. Manually, I assume. How they made it work, I have no idea. What I do know, is that it took endless takes each time to get it right."

After only three episodes had aired in March of 1983, the program was yanked from the CBS schedule. The other three filmed episodes were burned off during the summer of that year. Episodes were titled "The Pilot" (with guest stars Roddy McDowall, Kenneth Mars, Larry Storch, and Rue McClanahan), "Fiddler on the Hoof," "Endangered Detectives" (with guest star Henry Gibson), "The Case of the Street of Silence," "Schlockty Too" (with guest star Barney Martin), and "The Case of the Concerned Husband." The executive producer was Jan Williams; the writers included Nick Arnold, Ron Friedman, George Schenck, Richard Penn, Larry Siegel, and Leonard Ripps; the directors included James Sheldon, Leslie H. Martinson, Mel Ferber, Edward H. Feldman, John Bowab, and Charles S. Dubin.

About the latter two directors, Blessing remembered, "Thrilled to have worked with Charlie Dubin, as he was as hot as they came in those days. To get him for the pilot was a coup. Worked with Bowab a couple of times after that, always fun. He was the youngest of our directors and really the only one that brought any energy or enthusiasm to the show." The creators were George Schenck and Ron Friedman. Music was provided by Dennis McCarthy. What was it like working for Disney? Blessing said, "Disney was a strange place in those days and as I remember, a little rudderless. I remember being taken to meet all of the studio honchos on one of my first days there. Expecting to go to the executive offices, I was instead led to a back room behind the executive dining room where six or seven of the top Disney executives were playing poker, smoking cigars and drinking scotch. It was very odd and felt a little like fiddling while Rome burned."

Snoops Timalove Productions/The Solt Egan Company/Viacom. CBS. Friday nights 8:00 (September 22, 1989–December 8, 1989, and June 22, 1990–July 9, 1990). Thirteen episodes were filmed single-camera style without a laugh track. The sponsor was Luvs Deluxe.

This series should be categorized as a crimedy. Sure, it was a crime drama, but with a lot of very light and, frankly, quite funny moments. It might be considered a modern-day *Thin Man*. Because they were married in real life, the chemistry between the Dennises was strong, but for whatever reason the program was a ratings flop. It is set in Washington, D.C., and Chance Dennis (Tim Reid) is a criminology professor at Georgetown University who hates parties, and despises dancing. His wife, Micki (Daphne Maxwell Reid), works for the state department, and because of that has a driver named Hugo (Troy Curvey, Jr.). She is quite the fashion plate, and loves buying nice, expensive things. The couple resides in a nice home on 30th Street, and they have a penchant for getting involved in solving crimes (usually murders). They often assist third district homicide Lieutenant Carl Akers (John Karlen) in his investigations and very often stumbled upon the answer. Among Chance's students are Yolanda (Tracy Camilla Johns), Doug (Adam Silbar), and—keeping it in the family—Jason, played by Tim Reid II. In flashback scenes, the young Chance Dennis was played by Christopher Babers. After ten episodes had aired, the show was placed on hiatus and the remaining episodes were burned off by NBC during the summer of 1990.

Episodes were titled "Hot Shot," "Close Shave," "The Big Brass Cookie Jar," "Mr. Dennis' Neighborhood," "Remember When," "A Pretty Girl Is like a Malady," "The Sagittarian Candidate," "Photo Opportunity," "Twice Dead," "The Tango Dance of Death," "Someone to Lay Down Beside Me," "Don't Try This at Home," and "Rough Justice." The executive producer was Tim Reid; the producers were David Auerbach and Sascha Schneider; the writers included Sam Egan; the directors included Burt Kennedy. The creators were Sam Egan and Tim Reid. The theme song, "Curiosity," was written by Guy Moon with Steve and Stephanie Tyrell, and performed by Ray Charles. The debut episode featured the classic "I Only Have Eyes for You" by the Flamingos.

Spencer Alan Landsburg Productions/Mort Lachman and Associates. NBC. Saturday nights 9:30 (December 1, 1984–January 12, 1985, as *Spencer*) and Saturday nights 9:30 (March 23, 1985–May 11, 1985, as *Under One Roof*). Thirteen episodes were filmed in front of a live audience (six as *Spencer*; seven as *Under One Roof*).

Not to be confused with *Spenser: For Hire* on ABC, the sitcom *Spencer* was an NBC show. In its first incarnation, Chad Lowe portrayed sixteen-year-old high school student Spencer Winger. He is very shy around girls, but possesses a *Ferris Bueller*–esque flair for mischief and is frequently sent by a frustrated Miss Spier (Beverly Archer) to have a chat with the guidance counselor, Mr. Benjamin Beanley (Richard Sanders). Among the many reasons Spencer is sent to be disciplined include his questioning the existence of God in the classroom, setting all of the white laboratory mice free, accidentally electrocuting the science teacher, passing sex notes in class, and cheating on a test (the latter for which he and his buddies are expelled, causing them to seriously consider joining the army rather than tell their parents). Those best buddies were the very insecure Wayne (Grant Heslov), who is extremely self-conscious about the size of his proboscis (the source of many jokes), and the rather naïve and girl-crazy Bailey (Dean Cameron).

Cameron recalled, "Early on in the series there were concerns about Heslov and I looking too much alike. It was thought we looked like brothers or even twins instead of just buddies. I had concerns that they were going to replace me on the show, but was reassured by the showrunner Mort Lachman that my job was safe."

This trio was not destined to be Rhodes Scholars, but they were very funny—a nice comic chemistry was developing. Despite the need for countless parent-teacher conferences, Spencer's mother, Doris (Mimi Kennedy), continually sees only the good in her son while his dad, George (Ronny Cox), seems fixated on seeing his son with a steady girlfriend. Spencer's younger sister, Andrea (Amy Locane), tends to be the most mature and sensible member of the Winger household. Cameron recalled what happened next: "Chad Lowe was like a rock star. Every taping was like a Beatles concert with girls screaming and wanting autographs between takes. Not only that, but Chad was hearing advice that movies were what he should be pursuing, and that TV was holding him back. The feeling at the time was that 'good actors don't belong on television,' and he wanted to get out of doing the series. I don't think he understood that as the star of a hit series he would have it made, but unfortunately his mind was made up. This was very disappointing and rather heartbreaking because the series was doing well—ratings were good. I think we would have had a ten-season run.

Ronny Cox also decided to leave the show, but that was understandable—his character really didn't have all that much to do. This whole scenario was all part of a very rough time in my life—my very first girlfriend had also just broken up with me and that took a few weeks to get over. A short time later, I was called in to read with some new people—they were retooling the series and adding some new characters."

When the show reemerged as *Under One Roof* on March 23, 1985, Ross Harris was Spencer Winger. Cameron said, "Ross was great and very funny, but his take on Spencer was, obviously, totally different from Chad's. Instead of just two weird teenagers there were now three. It was just too much. There was no balance." To explain Cox's leaving the show, it was said that Spencer's dad had run off with a twenty-three-year-old girl, thus Spencer's maternal grandparents (Ben and Millie Sprague, played by Harold Gould and Frances Sternhagen, respectively) moved in to help Doris (now a single parent) with expenses and child rearing. The elderly couple moved into Spencer's old room and he moved into the attic. The favorite teen hangout was now Polly's Hot Dogs. Cameron said, "While *Spencer*'s ratings kept going up and up each week, it was heartbreaking to see the new version called *Under One Roof*'s ratings go in the opposite direction." After only seven episodes under the new title, Spencer was no longer for hire at NBC.

Although the program was set in the then-current-day 1980s, its soundtrack was consistently late 1950s and early 1960s, with songs such as "Mama Said" by the Shirelles, "Wonderful World" by Sam Cooke, "Problems" by the Everly Brothers, "What's So Good About Goodbye?" by The Miracles, "Let the Good Times Roll" by Shirley and Lee, and "Only the Lonely" by Roy Orbison selected to enhance the action on screen, and transition to the next scene. Cameron said, "That may have been an attempt to keep more senior viewers interested in the show. After all, it was a sitcom focused upon teenagers and high school." The soundtrack was noticeably updated for *Under One Roof*. In fact, in one episode Cameron recalled, "I was supposed to sing a few lines of Rod Stewart's 'Da Ya Think I'm Sexy?,' but they were having great difficulty getting clearance to use the song in the episode, so in front of the first audience I did something else. We did tapings in front of two audiences and the best scenes and audience reactions were used on-air. Truly in the eleventh hour, minutes before the second taping, we got the clearance for me to perform Stewart's tune."

Episodes were titled (as *Spencer*) "The Pilot," "The Divorcee," "Spencer Joins the Army," "Fast Times," "The World's Worst Date," "The Drive-in," (as *Under One Roof*) "The Grandparents Move In" "Millie's Affair," "Voices in the Hall," "Doris and the Tutor," "Crazy Girl," "Wayne's Nose Job," and "Grandpa the Lover." The executive producers were Mort Lachman and Sy Rosen; the writers included Sy Rosen, Chet Dowling, Pamela Chais, Howard and Bob Bendetson, Sandy Krinski, Shelley Zellman, Stan Zimmerman, James Berg, Judy Merl, Sybil Adelman, Martin Sage, Jerry Ross, and George Tricker; the directors included Bill Persky, John Tracy, and Lila Garrett. About the directors, Cameron shared, "Lila Garrett was wonderful. She got the most out of her actors by being very encouraging. She had a way of making one feel safe, and she let you know that she expected greatness. John Tracy is very funny and sharp. His method was more of a dare—he challenged you to be good. I don't think Amy [Locane] liked him very much. He wasn't as patient with her as maybe others were. I think some tears were shed. Fun fact: John Tracy is the reason I gave up red meat. Between *Spencer* and *Under One Roof*, he lost a lot of weight and attributed it to colonics, and giving up red meat. Even though his information was incorrect, to this day I don't touch the stuff." Music was provided by Barry Goldberg. Chad Lowe later went on to win an Emmy for his role as Jesse McKenna on *Life Goes On*. Cameron added, "Chad's also become quite a prolific director for *Bones* and *Pretty Little Liars*."

Square Pegs Embassy Television. CBS. Monday nights 8:00 (September 27, 1982–March 7, 1983), Wednesday nights 8:30 (April 6, 1983–May 4, 1983), and Monday nights 8:00 (May 9, 1983–September 12, 1983). Twenty episodes were filmed single-camera style with a laugh track.

The critically acclaimed *Square Pegs* was all gnarly, rad, and totally awesome all-things 1980s. The action took place in mythical Weemawee High School and, unlike *Welcome Back, Kotter*, the kids were portrayed by kids, not young adults. About the name Weemawee, actor/stand-up comic John Femia shared, "There's no question the 'wee-mo-weh' chorus of 'The Lion Sleeps Tonight' was the direct inspiration for the school name. My guess is Anne [Beatts] had trouble coming up with a name and she had CBS-FM playing in the background. Or K-Earth if she was in L. A." Femia's character, Marshall Blechtman, was that of the class clown. Did that lead him down the path to stand-up comedy? Femia recalled, "I became a comedian because, let's face it, I just can't get enough rejection in my life. My version of the Marshall character was original, taken from the deep recesses of my brain's inner need to belong. The show's brilliant creator, executive producer, and writer Anne Beatts once said in a *Rolling Stone* interview that Marshall was the 'squarest peg of all,' and she was spot-on." He added, "The original version of Marshall was your typical 'pocket calculator nerd.' That just didn't work for me. The writers were going to write him out entirely, and would have, had I not convinced them to make him a class clown instead." Marshall's best friend was the tow-headed (with the braided rat tail), tall, lanky, punk music-loving Jonny "Slash" Ulasewicz (Merritt Butrick) who frequently uttered, "That's a totally different head, man." Sadly, Butrick passed away, at the young age of twenty-nine, on March 17, 1989.

The program opened each week with a monologue about fitting in and conquering all of the high school cliques. Were there cliques among the *Square Pegs*' large cast? Femia recalled, "Absolutely. There's a lot I can say about this, but it's best I save that for my own book. I will say there were a few dividing lines within the group. The major cliques were among the writers and Anne mostly, who were opposed to any outside interference, especially from the network. It was an all-woman writing staff, except for Andy Borowitz. The only outsiders who were accepted were Sarah Jessica Parker and Jami Gertz. Two other girls in the cast, Tracy Nelson and Claudette Wells, became friends and remain best friends to this day. All the boys in the cast were loners, especially me. I have never been one that's of the L. A. mentality, and when I left New York City for L. A. to do *Square Pegs*, I felt like an exchange student who couldn't speak one word of English. It was a terribly lonely period for me."

The large cast consisted of Sarah Jessica

Two of the stars of *Square Pegs*—John Caliri and Tracy Nelson. Despite its short run, the CBS show (now available on DVD) has gained something of a cult following.

Parker as bespectacled Patty Greene—girl nerd (although she later found *Sex and the City*). Her best friend is brace-faced Lauren Hutchinson (Amy Linker). They are often ridiculed and cast out by the "cool girls" in school, such as the bossy, take-charge head cheerleader Muffy Tupperman (Jami Gertz); the sophisticated and opinionated African-American LaDonna Fredericks—L. D. for short (Claudette Wells); and the wealthy fashion and boy crazy "valley girl" Jennifer DeNuccio (Tracy Nelson—Rick's daughter), who begins every sentence with the word "like." Jennifer dates the egotistical babe magnet Vinnie Pasetta (Jon Caliri), who always dons the tightest T-shirt imaginable and/or a leather jacket, admiring himself in every mirror, and constantly flexing his biceps. The regular faculty members include Principal Winthrop Dingleman (love the name), played by Basil Hoffman; Mr. Rob "Lovebeads" Donovan (Steven Peterman); Ms. Loomis (Catlin Adams); and drama teacher Mr. Spacek (Craig Richard Nelson). Nelson also directed the final first-run episode, titled "The Arrangement," and Femia said, "The writers used to titter about him, saying that he could have easily been a character on *The Addams Family*. The director's name for each episode is shown written on a school locker during the opening credits. They spray painted 'Directed by Lurch' for his episode. It wasn't used, though. Bummer!" When asked about other behind-the-scenes anecdotes, Femia replied, "I did an impression of Roseanne Rosannadana [one of Gilda Radner's characters on *Saturday Night Live*] in the 'A Cafeteria Line' episode on the day of my sixteenth birthday. All I remember about it is that my friggin' legs were cold." About the baseball-themed episode titled "No Joy in Weemawee," Femia stated, "I wore a pimp coat and there was a joke that was really *not* a joke. As one of his *many* demands, guest star Reggie Jackson wanted fruit to be served in his dressing room. Since he was so difficult to deal with, Jackson was eventually replaced with Steve Sax of the Los Angeles Dodgers."

When asked about censorship on *Square Pegs*, Femia reflected, "There were two censorship issues I remember. In the Devo episode they performed the song 'That's Good.' The video of it had an image of a corncob going through a donut hole. At first, the network wouldn't allow the song for that reason, but once they were assured that the donut would be obscured in the editing, they okayed it. The biggest one, though, was in the pilot. They strongly objected to The Prince Phillip joke:

Lauren: You have to stand behind us at six paces, just like Prince Phillip.
Marshall: Who?
Lauren: Prince Phillip. You know ... he always comes six paces behind the queen.
Marshall: Boy ... they must have a dynamite sex life.

The network cried 'Foul!' over that one, yet somehow it did make it into the show. However, when CBS reran it, those lines were deleted."

Episodes were titled "The Pilot" (with guest stars The Waitresses), "A Cafeteria Line," "Pac-Man Fever" (with guest star Don Novello as Father Guido Sarducci), "Square Pigskins," "Halloween XII," "A Simple Attachment," "Weemaweegate," "Open 24 Hours," "Muffy's Bat Mitzvah" (with guest stars Devo and Dena Dietrich), "Hardly Working," "A Child's Christmas in Weemawee, Parts One and Two," "It's all How You See Things," "Merry Pranksters," "It's Academical," "The Stepanowicz Papers," "To Serve Weemawee All My Days," "No Substitutions" (with guest star Bill Murray), "No Joy in Weemawee" (with guest star Steve Sax), and "The Arrangement."

Femia said, "I deem the 'Child's Christmas at Weemawee' episode to be the worst. Not because I was hardly in it, but because the story is very disjointed and doesn't flow like the others. It was also a half-hour too long. My favorite episode? It's a tie between 'A Simple Attachment (Love Detector)' and 'Muffy's Bat Mitzvah' with guest star Devo. I loved Devo—that was a great week. I had a long conversation with the group's Jerry Casale, who was friendly and genuinely good-natured. Mark Mothersbaugh, on the other hand, kept mostly to himself, but that shouldn't surprise anyone. 'Pac-

Man Fever' was also lots of fun. I loved working with Father Guido Sarducci [Don Novello]. I loved impersonating him, and am glad the writers had the common sense to write that into the show. However, when I was doing publicity pictures for that episode, the photographers got pissed at me because I couldn't stop laughing. Well ... *you* try to play Pac-Man with a straight face when you have Father Guido whispering in your ear, 'C'mon-a Marshall, stop-a dis machine. Save-a-your quarters ... buy a woman.' My biggest disappointment, however, was the week we had Bill Murray, but that had nothing to do with him. To this day, I will never understand why the writers didn't give me a scene with him, seeing that Marshall had a couple of the traits of 'Nick—the lounge singer,' hence Marshall's catch phrase, 'Love ya, you're beautiful, now get outta here.' I'm over it now, but I was bitter about that for years."

The executive producer and creator was Anne Beatts; the writers included Anne Beatts, Janis Hirsch, Marjorie Gross, Andy Borowitz, Susan Silver, Chris Miller, Michael Sutton, David Felton, Deanne Stillman, Rosie Shuster, and Margaret Oberman; the directors included Kim Friedman, Terry Hughes, James Nasella, and Craig Richard Nelson. Musical scores were provided by Tom Scott. The Waitresses performed the theme song, and special musical material was by Paul Shaffer. A DVD box set of *Square Pegs* was released in 2008. Does he still get royalties from the box set? Femia said, "Yes! Thanks for buying it. I got a residual just last week ... for eleven cents. I am not kidding you. Sometimes I wonder how much of a major financial hit Sony takes whenever they have to cut a check for me." Did the DVD box set reunite the cast? Femia stated, "No, we have little or no contact, other than on Facebook. The only exception is Amy Linker, whom I had dinner with the year the DVD came out. That's just the way it is."

Still *Square Pegs* after all these years.

Star of the Family R. J. M. B./Little Andrew Enterprises/Paramount Television. ABC. Thursday nights 8:30 (September 30, 1982–December 23, 1982). Ten episodes were videotaped in front of a live audience.

Thirty years earlier, *Star of the Family* was the title of a CBS series starring Peter Lind Hayes and Mary Healy. Director Joel Zwick said, "We weren't aware of the title having been used before, but back in those days you couldn't protect a title, you couldn't copyright a title." In 1982, *Star of the Family* was a short-lived sitcom starring Brian Dennehy as gruff, burly, and old-fashioned Captain Leslie "Buddy" Krebs, of Fire Company 64, in Southern California. Zwick stated, "Given the right TV vehicle, Dennehy could've been the next Jackie Gleason. He's a great actor and a great guy who possessed all the elements to make comedy magic on TV, but this just wasn't the right vehicle for him. He did go on to a brilliant career on Broadway after this."

Buddy's wife left him for a bellhop several years earlier and he now has his hands full as a single dad there at 7136 LaSalle Drive, with two teenagers in his ward. Son Douggie (Michael Dudikoff) is the stereotypical dumb blond jock—definitely the dullest butter knife in the silverware drawer. Zwick recalled, "He played stupid very well—he added a new dimension to it. He was a very gifted athlete and became an action/adventure hero in several motion pictures in the U. S., and a few in Japan. His martial arts skills are off the charts." Buddy's sixteen-year-old daughter Jennie Lee (Kathy Maisnik) got all the brains and talent in the family. She attends Monroe High School, and garners a recording contract, along with a popular pop/country song called "Daddy, I'm a Woman Now" (complete with lyrics that raise her dad's hackles). Zwick takes great pride in having written one of the funniest lines in the pilot in which Buddy attempts to make people believe that the song was titled "Daddy, I'm a Mormon Now." Maisnik performed her own material on the show, and also sang the theme song. Zwick said, "She was only sixteen and a bit inexperienced as an actress, but grew quickly in her role. After raising a family, she's now looking to get back into the business." Buddy has difficulty letting go of his little girl, and the revealing outfits she is asked to wear at her concerts cause him great discomfort. Jennie Lee also has a manager—the very tall and unfeminine Moose (Judy Pioli), whom Buddy often asks to leave the Krebs household (she has no filter and usually says exactly what she is thinking). About her, Zwick said, "She was a writer on *Laverne and Shirley*, and we threw her six-foot-one inch frame on camera and she was very good." At the fire company, Buddy is surrounded by misfits (or as Zwick calls them "the Three Stooges")—Leo Feldman (Todd Susman) is often seen writing to his mother and perpetuating the lie that he is a chief cardiologist at Cedars-Sinai Medical Center; Max (Danny Mora, who replaced blond, bespectacled Robert Clotworthy from the pilot) is the stereotypical hot-tempered Latino who speaks broken English; and Frank Rosetti (George Deloy) is sexually obsessed. In fact, Frank's verbalized lust for Buddy's sixteen-year-old daughter renders watching this sitcom in the present day an uncomfortable experience (that, and Buddy's penchant for physically abusing his out-of-line co-workers). About that, Zwick shared, "Sensibilities were so different in 1982. There's also a joke about Scientology in the pilot episode that certainly wouldn't fly today. These three things are all part of the sterilized social mores of the present day."

So why did this sitcom ultimately fail? Zwick avers, "It had a very tricky premise with three arenas. The complex concept ate us up. We had a sixteen-year-old girl who was *The Star of the Family*, and yet Brian Dennehy was the star of the show. The strongest and funniest elements of the show occurred at the firehouse with Susman, Mora and Deloy's characters. Had we created a show that focused on the firehouse instead of the teenaged country music singer, it might have caught on. It's interesting to watch this show again after all these years—I definitely shot tighter in those days, tighter on the face. Nowadays, I shoot looser to allow for more body language." After ten episodes, *Star of the Family* flickered and flamed out, never to be seen again.

Episodes were titled "The Pilot," "The Critic," "Save My Life, Please," "Marking Time," "Quiet Kind of Hero" (with guest star Regis Philbin), "Spring Is in the Air," "I Got It Good and That Ain't Good," "The Boy Next Door" (with guest star Vanna White), "Phil," and "Arcade Wars." The executive producers were Charles H. Joffe, Paul Waigner, Jack Seifert, and Larry Brezner; the producer was Stu Silver; the writers included Stu Silver (whom Joel Zwick calls the funniest line-by-line writer in the business), and the directors included Joel Zwick. The program was created by Stu Silver and Rick Mitz. Music was provided by Steve Nelson and Buddy Kaye, and the theme song, "Movin' Along," was performed by Kathy Maisnik. The program was an R. J. M. B. production, which Zwick recalled stood for Jack Rollins, Charles H. Joffe, Buddy Morrow, and Larry Brezner.

Starting from Scratch Syndicated. Saturday nights 6:30 (October 1, 1988–May 27, 1989). Twenty-two episodes were videotaped with a laugh track.

Character actor Bill Daily enjoyed two very successful runs in sitcomland (*I Dream of Jeannie* and *The Bob Newhart Show*), but once the 1980s hit he wasn't quite as successful. *Aloha Paradise*, *Small and Frye*, and the syndicated *Starting from Scratch* were all short-lived. In the latter, Daily played the very nice and well-respected Ohio veterinarian Dr. James "Jamie" Shepherd. After an amicable divorce from his wife, Helen D'Angelo (Connie Stevens), Helen constantly invades his life and his busy practice. She also dabbles in writing poetry. Their two children have issues—nineteen-year-old University of Ohio student Kate (Heidi Helmer) and the younger towheaded Robbie (Jason Marin) necessitate a lot of attention. Others in the cast included sitcom veteran Nita Talbot as the doctor's assistant, Rose (a one-time lion tamer's assistant); Carmine Caridi as Helen's second husband, Frank; Larry Linville as the doctor's brother Brandon; and Helen's mother and father—Miriam (Maxine Miller) and Alfred (Larry Haines). Eclipsing the stellar cast was the vast array of cute furry creatures that wandered through the good doctor's waiting and examination rooms. The program lasted for just one season, and was put down before a second one could begin.

Episodes were titled "The Pilot," "The Contract," "Divorce, American Style," "Double Date," "Helen's Parents," "James' TV Debut," "Blood Relations," "Helen the Receptionist," "James in Love," "Horse Race," "Kate's Broken Heart," "James' Brother," "The Woman Who Came to Dinner," "House for Sale," "Classmates," "Kate Leaves Home" (with guest star Joely Fisher), "Robbie and Friends," "A Matter of Trust," "Confidence Game" (with guest star Sandra Bullock), "Me, the Jury," "Working Gal," and "Nothing but the Tooth." The executive producers were Perry Rosemond and Victor Solnicki; the writers included Brian Cooke, Gordon Farr, Terry Saltsman, Joe Chilco, Eleanor James, Paul Wayne, Ken Steele, Michael P. Williams, Bruce Mohun, Bill Murtagn, and Franelle Selver; the directors included Ari Dikijian, Phil Ramuno, Stan Harris, Perry Rosemond, Tony Singletary, and Jerry Ross.

Steambath Falrose Productions/Pollock Davis, Inc./Warner Bros. Television. Showtime. Air dates and times varied (June 1983). Six episodes were videotaped with a laugh track.

Steambath began as an off-Broadway play by Bruce Jay Friedman, and directed by Anthony Perkins in 1970 at the Truck and Warehouse Theater. Charles Grodin was supposed to play the lead role of Tandy in this original version, but Perkins wound up taking the role for himself. Also featured in this version were Héctor Elizondo and Conrad Bain. Elizondo won an Obie Award for his role as Morty, a Puerto Rican attendant in the play, in which the afterlife is represented as a "steambath." Some of those in attendance in the "steambath" are unaware that they have died, and continue to obsess over the condition of their daily lives. The production featured some nudity and rather coarse language for its day. The play was lampooned in an early episode of *The Odd Couple* titled "What Does a Naked Lady Say to You?" (the play in that episode was titled *Bathtub*).

When a videotaped version of *Steambath* was produced in 1973 for PBS, some of the language was softened considerably. Bill Bixby earned the role of Tandy in this version, allegedly because Friedman's son was a huge fan of Bixby's series *The Courtship of Eddie's Father*. Others cast in this version included Valerie Perrine as Meredith, and Jose Perez as Morty (God). Because Valerie Perrine exposed her breasts, and two characters portraying the gay lovers exposed their bare buttocks, only a handful of PBS affiliates carried the film, and it certainly left a lasting impression and generated a lot of favorable chatter. A decade later, *Steambath* became a Showtime limited-run comedy series (six episodes), with David Pollock and Elias Davis serving as executive producers and writers. Jose Perez once again portrayed Morty, Robert Picardo was Tandy, and Janis Ward was Meredith. It was produced by Warner Bros. Television for the Showtime cable channel. By 1983, the subject matter proved far less provocative. Memorable guest stars included Peter Scolari, Barbara Babcock, Dick Shawn, and Alex Rocco. The episode featuring the latter two, "Madison Avenue Madness," won David Pollock and Elias Davis the 1983 Writers Guild Award for Episodic Comedy. Shawn and Rocco portrayed a Dean Martin and Jerry Lewis–type comedy team in that episode.

Episodes were titled "The Big Bang," "Madison Avenue Madness," "A Visit from Yuri," "In the Beginning," "A Preacher and a Jock," and "Tandy's Legacy." The executive producers were David Pollock, Elias Davis, Joe Byrne, and Jeb Rosebrook; the producer was Jerry Madden; the writers included David Pollock and Elias Davis; the directors included Burt Brinckerhoff and Terry Hughes. Music was provided by Artie Butler and David Frishberg.

Stir Crazy Larry Larry Productions/Columbia Pictures Television. CBS. Wednesday nights 8:00 (September 18, 1985–October 23, 1985), and Tuesday nights 8:00 (December 24, 1985–January 7, 1986). Nine hour-long episodes were filmed single-camera style without a laugh track.

The opening narrative said: "Two escaped convicts wanted for murder—a crime they did not commit. Captain Betty Phillips was under orders from Washington to apprehend them. The real killer, a man with a tattooed hand, still walks free. Two nice guys with a price on their heads, who just want to go home." All of this was loosely based on the hit 1980 motion picture with Richard Pryor and Gene Wilder. Larry Riley played the Richard Pryor part of Harry Fletcher, and Joseph Guzaldo took on the Gene Wilder role of Skip Harrington (in the film Harry's last name was Monroe, and Skip's was Donohue). In the series, Harry and Skip take over Uncle Willy's ice cream business and collect four thousand dollars to buy the building. Harry also drives a taxi, and Skip and he are paid by a man with a tattooed hand to take another man to the airport. When that fare in the backseat turns out to be a dead body, they are mistakenly identified as the murderers. All of that cash found on them make them look even more conspicuous. They are interrogated by no-nonsense Texas police Captain Betty Phillips (in the series it was Jeannie Wilson, but in the pilot it was Polly Holliday, of *Flo* and *Alice* fame). Harry and Skip try to convince her of the existence of the real killer, Crawford, the man with the tattooed hand (played by Royce Applegate in the pilot, but by Marc Silver in the series), but to no avail—they are sentenced to 132 years in prison. They initially thought the tattoo read ULU, but they figured out that it was upside down and was actually two horseshoes with a numeral 7 in the middle. The famous millionaire that Crawford killed was named P. K Hunter. Disguised as members of a Japanese TV film crew making a documentary in the prison, Harry and Skip manage to escape. Their lawyer, Kathryn D'Angelo (Cynthia Sikes), keeps them informed of Captain Betty's whereabouts and intentions. The aforementioned cast changes between the pilot and the series proved to be a waste of time because *Stir Crazy* failed to find an audience, and it was quickly placed on hiatus after only six episodes had aired. It was given another shot in late December of 1985 and early January of 1986, but ratings did not improve one bit, and the entire premise received a lethal injection after nine episodes.

Episodes were titled "The Pilot," "The Ping Pong Caper," "Welcome to the Tribe," "The Magnificent Repossession," "The Football Story," "The Sulky Race," "Love Affair" (with guest star Alice Ghostley), "Where's Mary?," and "Basic Straining." The producers were David J. Latt and Mark Waxman; the writers included Michael Russnow, Mark Waxman, Larry Rosen, and Larry Tucker; the directors included Peter H. Hunt and Christian Nyby. The program was developed for television by Larry Rosen and Larry Tucker. Music was provided by Dennis McCarthy, John E. Davis, and William Goldstein. The theme song, "Stir It Up," was written by Allee Willis and Danny Sembello, and performed by Paulette McWilliams.

The Stockard Channing Show Little Bear Productions. CBS. Monday nights 8:30 (March 24, 1980–April 28, 1980) and Saturday nights 8:30 (June 7, 1980–July 12, 1980). Thirteen episodes were videotaped before a live audience at KTLA Studios in Los Angeles.

Grease was the word, and Stockard Channing was a hot commodity because of it. She earned two shots at eponymous sitcom success on CBS. Stockard and her husband, David, had their own production company, named after their dog, Little Bear. Both of her sitcoms were Little Bear Productions, and were rather similar. Each one starred Stockard as Susan, a newly single girl with a new job, a new apartment, a clean slate. The theme song for each sitcom was identical—written and performed by Delaney Bramlett of Delaney and Bonnie fame (and bearing a striking resemblance to the old Scottish song "The Bonny Banks of Loch Lomond"). In her 1979 sitcom, *Stockard Channing in Just Friends*, she is Susan Hughes, who had left her husband, Frank (Lawrence Pressman), in Boston and boarded an airplane to start anew in Los Angeles. She quickly gets herself an apartment (without a functioning lock on the front door), a used Volkswagen, and employment at an exclusive health spa/gym in Beverly Hills.

This program aired on Sunday nights for most of its run and started strong, but faded quickly in the Nielsens. Only ten episodes of her first sitcom were videotaped before a live audience. The program was then completely retooled, and a few of Stockard's co-stars were to be utilized in *The Stockard Channing Show* almost exactly a year later. However, when they asked for more money, it was viewed as a breach of contract and only Sydney Goldsmith was retained for the new series. Stockard was "suddenly Susan" again in *The Stockard Channing Show*, but now her surname was Goodenow—a surname suggested by Mimi Kennedy, who portrayed Stockard's wealthy, conservative, and stuffy older sister Victoria in the first series (but was one of the cast members let go after requesting a raise). Despite a degree from Radcliffe in Slavic languages, experience as a field hockey player, and the ability to open a beer bottle with her teeth, Susan Goodenow works mostly behind the scenes on a local consumer-advocate TV program called *The Big Rip-off* (but she is occasionally utilized on camera). The program is hosted by her boss, Brad Gabriel (Ron Silver)—a graduate of CCNY, a tofu- and sprout-loving vegan who exposes the public to the unhealthy and unscrupulous. Susan is his guinea pig (she is elected to test all of the products in question), and often samples said products while in a wide array of costumes.

About Silver, head writer John Boni shared, "Ron and I had some really nice conversations between scenes about politics. I was an old school liberal and he had very conservative leanings, which only got stronger in later years. He was very outspoken about his beliefs and, ultimately, his career suffered as a result."

Sydney Goldsmith was back, but now instead of Coral behind the counter of the gym her name is Earline Cunningham, Brad's secretary. Earline also lives in the same apartment complex as Susan (and had recommended Susan for the job opening at the TV station). Max Showalter, (also acted under the name of Casey Adams and played the original Ward Cleaver in the "Leave It to Beaver" pilot called "It's a Small World"), portrayed Gus Clyde, the general manager of the TV station. Clyde has his own parking space, and although rather inept and clueless, has a hands-on approach to his job. Steve Alterman portrayed his son, Todd Clyde, in the "Puppy Love" episode. Jack Somack portrayed a character named Kramer a decade before *Seinfeld* hit the airwaves. Mr. Kramer was Susan and Earline's gruff-but-friendly landlord. He and his rarely seen wife, Eloise (played by the show's fashion coordinator, Valorie Armstrong, formerly of Sandy Duncan's short-lived *Funny Face*) also runs a fast-food falafel stand. Kramer also has aspirations to become a published author, but the program was canceled before his dream was fulfilled. Bruce Baum had a small, recurring role as Alf—a loose cannon jack-of-all-trades who owns a health food store in one episode, but is the building's security guard in numerous others.

The program was pulled from the CBS lineup after the first seven episodes failed to catch on. The remaining six episodes were burned off in June and July of 1980. A DVD box set containing the entire runs of both *Stockard Channing in Just Friends* and *The Stockard Channing Show* was released by VEI in 2006. Channing attempted one more sitcom, in 2005, as Dr. Lydia Barnes on *Out of Practice*, but met with similar results. Recurring roles on the drama programs *The West Wing* and *The Good Wife* finally earned her success on the small screen.

Episodes were titled "A Funny Thing Happened on the Way to the Unemployment Office," "Catch a Falling Star," "Advise and Consume," "A Number Three with Sprouts, Hold the Ptomaine," "You Can't Quit Me, I'm Fired," "Life Begins at 30," "The Threat," "Exclusive: Love Finds Brad Gabriel," "Susan's Big Break," "Puppy Love," "Texas Bob and the Consumer Ranch Gang," "Punt, Pass and Kick," and "Ask Gratis Gus." The producer was George Yanok; the writers included John Boni, Mitzi McCall, George Yanok, Mickey Rose, Anne Convy (Bert's wife), Stephen Nathan and Paul B. Price (both of the short-lived CBS sitcom *Busting*

Loose), Michael Weinberger, John Arthurs, Tom Ruben, and the prolific Aaron Ruben (writer for and producer of *The Andy Griffith Show*, *Gomer Pyle U.S.M.C.*, *Sanford and Son*, and *CPO Sharkey*); the directors included Jeff Bleckner, Aaron Ruben, John Tracy, Will Mackenzie, and the legendary Jay Sandrich and James Burrows. About the amazing list of directors, Boni said, "That was an era when directors really directed. Those directors were very involved and very busy, unlike the modern-day camera pushers. It was a great, creative time in television."

Suzanne Pleshette Is Maggie Briggs Chagrin Productions/Page One Productions/Lorimar. CBS. Sunday nights 8:00 (March 4, 1984–April 15, 1984). Six episodes were videotaped in front of a live audience.

Maggie Briggs is a seasoned news reporter for the *New York Examiner*. She has fifteen years of experience in real news, but she and her longtime boss, Walter Holden (Kenneth McMillan), the man who gave her a start in the newspaper business, are transferred to the feature department. Episodes revolve around Maggie's difficulties making the transition to writing human-interest stories for the Modern Living Section, and her romance with her new boss, Geoff Bennett (John Getz). Bennett uses a board with gold stars next to staff members' names to denote excellence.

Others in the cast included Sherman Milslagle (Stephen Lee), the insecure food critic; Donny Bauer (Roger Bowen), who writes for the Religion Section; columnist Melanie Bitterman (Alison LaPlaca), and fellow feature writer Diana Barstow (Michelle Nicastro). Maggie's bff is a dizzy model named Connie Piscipoli (Shera Danese). The staff's favorite hangout is the Pleaz All Tavern next door. On March 7, 1984, *Variety* reviewed the program this way—"The premise can work if it's productive of enough laughs, but the introductory show fell short in that department. Nevertheless, the focal characters are potentially attractive enough for 'Maggie Briggs' to flourish if it gets its laugh content straightened out."

Episodes were titled "Maggie Meets Jeff," "Wrong Bad Dumb Stinks," "Roman Holiday," "A New Leaf," "Double Date," and "Maggie's Theater Review." The executive producer was Charlie Hauck; the producers were Tom Cherones and Deborah Leschin; the writers included Bob Ellison, Charlie Hauck and Tom Whedon; and the

Sans Bob Newhart, Suzanne Pleshette attempted success on her own in the short-lived, eponymously titled CBS show *Suzanne Pleshette Is Maggie Briggs*.

lone director was Suzanne's former co-star on *The Bob Newhart Show*, Peter Bonerz. The creators were Suzanne Pleshette and Charlie Hauck. The theme song was provided by Patrick Williams.

Sweet Surrender Dahn Tahn Productions/Embassy Television. NBC. Saturday nights 8:30 (April 18, 1987–May 16, 1987), and Wednesday night 9:30 (July 8, 1987). Six episodes were videotaped with a laugh track.

The program's unique opening and closing credits include no faces, but rather mostly torsos of the family and a couple of shots taken from above the kitchen table. The closing credits showed the program's writers at work, again shot from above. Set in Philadelphia, Georgia Macklin Holden (Dana Delany) surrenders her business career to raise her children—son Bart (Edan Gross), whom she affectionately calls "Lima Bean" and "Pumpkin Face," and who often locks himself in the closet; and newborn baby girl Lynnie (Sarah and Rebecca Simms). Because of that decision, Georgia has to rely on her husband, Ken (Mark Blum), to be the lone breadwinner. Ken is a good father, but he has a childish streak and frequently longs for his carefree bachelor days. Both Georgia and Ken, in fact, are experiencing the "seven-year itch." His co-worker and best friend is Vaughn Parker (Christopher Rich). Other friends are the Gafneys—Lyla and Marty (Louise Williams and Thom Sharp, respectively). This sitcom marked the return to "sitcomland" for David Doyle, as Georgia's divorced father, Frank Macklin, and Marjorie Lord (formerly of *Make Room for Daddy*) as Ken's mother, Joyce Holden. Georgia wants her father and his mother to hook up. The Holden's zany teenage babysitter has spiked hair and the unusual name of Cak (Viveka Davis). Episodes focus on Georgia's adjustments to full-time motherhood.

Episodes were titled "The Big Seven," "Where There's a Will," "The Holdens Go to Dinner," "High School Confidential," "I Got Those No Dough No Justice Crazy Dog Blues," and "Sexual Diversity in Philadelphia." The executive producers were Deidre Fay and Stuart Wolpert; the writers included Deidre Fay, Burt Prelutsky, and Stuart Wolpert; the directors included John Bowab, Linda Day, Valentine Mayer, and Jack Shea. The creators were Stuart Wolpert and Deidre Fay. The theme song was provided by Jack Colcord. Marjorie Lord died November 28, 2015 at the age of 97.

Take Five Imagine Entertainment/Empire City Presentations/Tri-Star Television. CBS. Wednesday nights 8:30 (April 1, 1987–April 8, 1987). Six episodes were filmed in front of a studio audience, but only two aired.

The life of Andy Kooper (George Segal) is on a downward spiral—his wife, with whom he had two children, has divorced him, and her father terminated Andy's public-relations job. Here's where the program's title comes in—he then attempts to start life anew with the Lenny Goodman Quartet, a Dixieland jazz band in which he plays the banjo and supplies vocals. Others in the combo are Lenny (Jim Haynie) on sax and drums; Al (Derek McGrath) on piano; and the two-years-divorced Monty (Bruce Jarchow) on drums.

Jarchow recalled, "This was my first 'series regular' role. Though it was shot in Los Angeles at the Radford Lot in Studio City, I was cast out of New York, where I had been living for a few years after my move from Chicago. CBS bundled *Take Five* and *Roxie*, probably hoping one would survive. With George Segal as the draw, I would have hoped ours was the odds-on favorite early on, and they would have done more to ensure success than they did."

It's interesting to note that Jarchow's character, Monty, is in a relationship with Andy's ex-wife, Eleanor, and is briefly replaced in the band with a drum machine when Andy finds out. About the band, Jarchow added, "George could play. We were novices. We didn't play live. There was no pre-condition in the audition process that we had to have musical talents, but it was clear that we were in a band. George had us up to his house before we began shooting to 'jam' with him. He had a room filled with instruments and asked us to choose whichever we felt we could play. I think Derek and Jim found something they could make reasonable noises with, but I was floundering and eventually settled at a drum set where I was totally lost. Eventually, I got an expert tutoring session from Teddy Sarafin, the drummer for the group Chicago, through a mutual friend. I was able to fake it pretty well toward the end. But I was disappointed that my character wasn't flushed out more. I think the writers were trying to find the right 'A' storyline and the band members were the first casualty. Basically, I can't remember much about my character other than he played drums every so often."

Segal's Andy character also found a second source of income with a new public-relations gig at Davis and Son (he had to sell his own blood for cab fare to get to the interview). The elder Max Davis (Eugene Roche) had recently placed his incompetent son, Kevin (Todd Field), in charge (and he is running the company into the ground). Laraine McDermott (Melanie Chartoff) was to be Andy's coworker, and she was bitter that Andy was about to get the position for which she had been vying. Andy often discusses his troubled life with his psychiatrist, Dr. Noah Wolf (Severn Darden). About Darden, Jarchow shared, "He was an original member of *Second City*. He was a genius and one of the funniest men I ever met. We worked together later off-Broadway for Paul Sills' *Sills and Company*. And Eugene Roche, who played Max Davis, was a well-recognized character actor who was known as 'The best half-hour man in the business.'"

Unfortunately, this sitcom could have been titled *Take Two*, because it was canceled after that many episodes had aired. About that, Jarchow reflected, "I was so new to the sitcom world that when we finished taping the sixth episode I went back to New York without telling my agent. Yes, I was disappointed, but I wasn't ready to move out to Los Angeles. I was enjoying New York too much. We eventually did move out a few years later, but I was getting work in both places and preferred the energy where I was. Every actor back then was torn as to where to live to get the most and best work.

A friend of mine once said, 'If the work was in Peoria, we'd all live in Peoria.'" It has been alleged that Segal was so unhappy with some of the scripts for this series, he once lost his patience and spat in writer/creator Lowell Ganz's face. Yet Jarchow stated, "I was impressed with all the writers and crew. They were funny people, but that doesn't always translate into a successful show. Lowell's brother, Jeff, was also involved in the show as was David Misch, who was a few years behind me at the same Chicago-area high school."

Episodes were titled "Kooper with a K," "The Return of Marty," "The Boss Is Back," "George's Dream Girl," "My Friend Dad," and "Men Who Hate Men Who Hate Women." The executive producers were Brian Grazer and Ron Howard; the producers were David Misch and Todd Stevens; the writers included David Misch, Lowell Ganz and Babaloo Mandel; the directors were Barnet Kellman and Michael Lessac. About the directors, Jarchow said, "Michael was great. His father developed the famous 'Lessac Method' of speech therapy. Barnet Kellman was also a fun director on the show." The creators were Lowell Ganz and Babaloo Mandel. Music was provided by Richard Bernard, David Michael Frank, and James Burt. As one would expect, the theme song was a Dixieland jazz piece, and the cast's names were shown one by one on a musical staff.

Tanner '88 Zenith and Darkhorse Productions. HBO. Air dates and times varied (February 15, 1988–August 22, 1988). Eleven episodes were videotaped multiple-camera style without a laugh track.

Doonesbury creator Garry Trudeau and director Robert Altman teamed up for this so-called "mockumentary" miniseries about a presidential campaign. A former United States representative from Michigan, John Quinton "Jack" Tanner (Michael Murphy), is testing the waters for the Democratic Party's nomination for president in 1988. The behind-the-scenes story is told in a pseudo-Rashomon style (from several different perspectives), and lending credence to the campaign's slogan "For Real," many political figures appeared on the series in cameo roles (Bruce Babbitt, Kitty Dukakis, Jesse Jackson, Bob Dole, Gary Hart, Ralph Nader, and Pat Robertson, to name a few). The "For Real" slogan really comes into play when Tanner is filmed (without his knowledge) giving his staff an impassioned motivational speech—a speech later used in his political ads. Jack's no-nonsense campaign manager is Theresa Jean "T. J." Cavanaugh (Pamela Reed); Alex is his astute, well-spoken teenage daughter (played by a young Cynthia Nixon); Andrea Spinelli (Ilana Levine) is his naïve assistant; Stringer Kincaid is his aide (Daniel Jenkins); Deke Connors is his campaign filmmaker (Matt Malloy); the aptly named poll taker is Emile Berkoff (Jim Fyfe); Molly Hark (Veronica Cartwright) is the persistent TV reporter; Joanna Buckley (Wendy Crewson) is Tanner's Republican secret love; and Billy Ridenhour (Harry Anderson, post–*Night Court*) keeps the staff on their toes. Tanner ultimately fails to get his party's nomination, but that isn't the end of the story, as Tanner is revisited in a sequel series, *Tanner on Tanner*, for the Sundance Channel in 2004, with a high percentage of the original cast and crew intact (Trudeau, Altman, Fyfe, Murphy, Nixon, Malloy, and Levine). The "Boiler Room" episode (the penultimate episode) garnered Altman an Emmy Award for his direction. Also in 2004, a DVD box set of *Tanner '88* was made available by Sandcastle Productions.

Episodes were titled "The Dark Horse," "For Real," "The Night of the Twinkies," "Moonwalker and Bookbag," "Bagels with Bruce," "Child's Play," "The Great Escape," "The Girlfriend Factor," "Something Borrowed Something New," "The Boiler Room," and "The Reality Check." The executive producers were Robert Altman and Garry Trudeau; the producers included Matthew Seig, Mark Jaffee, Scott Bushnell, Frank Barhydt, and Zennia M. Barahona; the writer was Garry Trudeau; the director was Robert Altman. The program was created by *Doonesbury*'s Garry Trudeau.

Tattingers The Paltrow Group NYLA/MTM Enterprises. NBC. Wednesday nights 10:00 (October 26, 1988–January 25, 1989), Thursday night 9:30 (April 20, 1989), and Wednesday night 9:30 (April 26, 1989); the latter two as *Nick and Hillary*. Eleven hour-long episodes of *Tattingers* were filmed in New York without a laugh track, but only ten aired, and three half-hour episodes of *Nick and Hillary* were filmed without a laugh track, but only two aired.

Originally sixty minutes in length, the opening credits for this romantic dramedy called *Tattingers* features a series of black-and-white New York City photographs. Nick Tattinger was played by Stephen Collins, and Hillary by Blythe Danner. Even after their divorce, Nick maintains ownership of a swanky Manhattan restaurant called Tattingers. However, after being shot by a narcotics dealer, Nick sells his interest in the restaurant and opts to start life anew in Paris. A second attempt on his life is made in the debut episode, and Nick shows up at a school ceremony for his younger daughter all dirty, bloodied, and sporting a black eye (to which said daughter uttered, "Why can't you be like other dads? They never get shot at.") The restaurant's new owner does such a poor job, however, that Nick decides to give it another go. Although their marriage has ended, both Nick and Hillary still have feelings for each other and are ill at ease when the other is romantically linked with someone else. Others in the cast included Sid (Jerry Stiller), the no-nonsense assistant manager and yes man; Nina (Patrice Colihan), Nick and Hillary's eldest daughter; Winnifred (Chay Lentin), their younger daughter; Norman Asher (Simon Jones), Hillary's new love; Sonny Franks (Zach Grenier), a drug dealer; Sheila Bradley (Mary Beth Hurt), the female chef; Alphonse (Yusef Bulos), the male chef; Louis Chatham (Roderick Cook), the head waiter; Marco (Rob Morrow) a bartender; and Tom Smaraldo (Robert Clohessy), also a bartender. About his character's surname, Clohessy shared, "I think the producers and writers were having problems with clearance on the use of other names and they probably came up with Smaraldo because it sounded funny."

Despite a stream of uniquely New York guest

stars making cameo appearances (Broadway star Elaine Stritch, screenwriter Garson Kanin, cabaret singer Bobby Short, and 100-year-old producer George Abbott), up against *China Beach* and *Wise Guy* on Wednesday nights the program had a hard time gaining a footing in the ratings and was pulled after ten of the eleven filmed episodes had aired. NBC still had faith in the concept however, and the show was retooled as a half-hour sitcom called *Nick and Hillary*. The first few seconds of the opening credits were just like the opening of *Tattingers*, and then the film burns and melts into the new *Nick and Hillary* titles with a new, much more upbeat opening theme song with vocals. This time around, Hillary has the reins and turns the restaurant into an über-trendy establishment while Nick is briefly vacationing in Brazil. A couple of minor cast changes came along with the new version—like Walt Disney's old TV series, this show also has a Spin (Chris Elliott) and Marti (Anna Levine) working in the restaurant. Well, Marti didn't actually work, or for that matter, say anything—her job was to sit at the bar with a deadpan expression. Chris is the son of Bob Elliott, of Bob and Ray fame, and a funny inside joke in the debut episode has Chris's Spin character commenting that he could never remember which one was Bob and which was Ray. Daughter Winnifred was now portrayed by Jessica Prunell.

Clohessy said, "I wasn't utililzed for the half-hour sitcom version of the series, but the executive producers, Bruce Paltrow and Tom Fontana, are responsible for my career. Paltrow had directed me in an off-Broadway musical called *Lucky Lucy and the Fortune Man* in which I co-starred with his wife, Blythe Danner. He then brought me over to do *Tattingers* there in New York." Despite some truly clever *Moonlighting*-esque banter, the retooled *Nick and Hillary* failed to attract an audience, and disappeared after only two of the three filmed episodes had aired. NBC finally got the hint and canceled the whole thing for good.

Episodes were titled (as *Tattingers*) "The Pilot," "The Sonny Also Rises," "Nouvelle York," "Virgin Spring," "Rest in Peas," "Death and Taxis" (with guest star Richard Lewis), "Two Men and a Baby," "Broken Windows" (with guest stars Jane Curtin and Susan St. James), "Wall Street Blues," "Screwball," "Ex-Appeal" (with guest star Robert Klein), (as *Nick and Hillary*) "Half a Loaf," "El Sid" (with guest star Paul Shaffer), and "Tour of Doody." The executive producers were Bruce Paltrow, and Tom Fontana; the producers were Robert DeLaurentis, John Tinker, and Channing Gibson; the writers included Tom Fontana, John Masius, John Tinker, Channing Gibson, Bruce Paltrow, Deborah R. Baron, and Noel Behn; the directors included Mark Tinker, Art Wolff, John Whitesell, Allan Arkush, Bruce Paltrow, Gwen Arner, Don Scardino, and Michael Fresco. The creators were Tom Fontana, John Masius, and Bruce Paltrow. Music was provided by Frank Kulaga and Jonathan Tunick. The theme song for *Nick and Hillary*, "Anybody's Guess," was by Brock Walsh. Many songs of the day, such as "Walk the Dinosaur" and "I Wanna Dance with Somebody" were part of the soundtrack.

Tenspeed and Brown Shoe Stephen J. Cannell Productions/Paramount Television. ABC. Sunday nights 8:00 (January 27, 1980–March 30, 1980), and Friday nights 10:00 (May 20, 1980–June 27, 1980). Fourteen hour-long episodes were filmed without a laugh track.

A crimedy, these two were *The Odd Couple* of detectives. Tenspeed (Ben Vereen) is E. L. ("Early Leroy") Turner (born in a taxi—he arrived earlier than anticipated) who is adept at disguises, quite cunning, and is utilized for detective work to satisfy his parole requirements for stealing money from a safety deposit box. Brown Shoe (Jeff Goldblum) is Lionel Whitney (a black belt in karate and a marksman) who got his nickname from an old term for straight-laced bankers and businessmen. He has a voracious appetite for old novels and motion pictures, and quotes from them liberally. Some episode titles begin with the words "Savage Says," referring to the mythical crime novel series Mark Savage Mysteries by Stephen J. Cannell—favorites of Brown Shoe's. The two first meet on an airplane in the pilot, and then in a limo. Others in the cast included Richard Romanus as Crazy Tommy Tedesco, and Larry Manetti (pre–*Magnum, P.I.*) as Chip Vincent. Guest stars included Jayne Meadows, Joe Spano, John Hillerman, Rene Auberjonois, and even Stephen J. Cannell himself. This program started strong in the Nielsens, but faded quickly. Cannell utilized a similar premise a few years later for the much more successful *Hardcastle and McCormick*. A DVD set of all fourteen episodes was released in 2010 by Mill Creek Entertainment.

Episodes were titled "Tenspeed and Brown Shoe, Parts 1 and 2," "The Robin Tucker Roseland Roof and Ballroom Murder," "Savage Says There's No Free Lunch," "Savage Says What Are Friends For?," "The 16 Byte Data Chip and the Brown-Eyed Fox," "The Millionaire's Life," "Savage Says the Most Dangerous Bird Is the Jailbird," "It's Easier to Pass an Elephant Through the Eye of a Needle than a Bad Check in Bel Air," "Loose Larry's List of Losers," "This One's Gonna Kill Ya," "Untitled," "The Treasure of Sierra Madre Street," and "Diamonds Aren't Forever." The executive producer was Stephen J. Cannell; the producers included Alex Beaton, Juanita Bartlett, and Chuck Bowman; the writers included Stephen J. Cannell, Juanita Bartlett, Shel Willens, Rudolph Bongheri, and Gordon T. Dawson; the directors included Chuck Bowman, Harry Winer, Rod Holcomb, Stephen J. Cannell, Reza Badiyi, Ivan Dixon, Arnold Laven, Georg Stanford Brown, E. W. Swackhamer, and John Patterson. Music was provided by Mike Post and Pete Carpenter.

The Thorns Icarus Productions/Reeves Entertainment Group. ABC. Friday nights 9:00 (January 15, 1988–February 12, 1988) and Friday nights 9:30 (March 4, 1988–March 11, 1988). Twelve episodes were filmed with a laugh track, but only seven aired.

Even the late great Mike Nichols, who had been successful in so many ventures, had an off day now and again. Nichols was the executive producer of this short-lived sitcom. Like *Buffalo Bill*, this is another failed attempt to create a series around really unlikable main characters. At least they were given an apt surname—Thorn. Sloan Thorn (Tony Roberts) and his wife, Ginger (Kelly Bishop), are very wealthy and live in a beautiful New York townhouse. Their main objective in life is to climb to the highest heights of the social stratosphere, and to rake in still more greenbacks. Self-serving Sloan and Ginger rarely show affection for each other, and, in fact, each seeks a little action on the side—Sloan with the kids' babysitter Cricket (Lori Petty), and Ginger with Andre (David Purdham), the man who designed their home.

Their three children are usually tertiary (if that) on their priorities list. Instead of discipline, the kids are usually plied with money (as a result, said offspring become as snobbish, shallow, and superficial as their parents). Chad (Adam Biesk), at sixteen, is the eldest child, and, like his dad, is constantly hitting on Cricket; a tomboy named Joey (Lisa Fieffel), age fourteen, is the middle child, who is constantly seeking attention with new piercings, spiked/pastel-colored hair, and outrageous clothing; and the youngest, Edmund (Jesse Tendler), age seven, is learning to play the piano, and is unwilling to forgive his father for having his dog, Sam, put down (often pretending to be the canine, crawling on the floor, barking incessantly, and eating kibble out of Sam's old bowl). Their dour-faced, put upon, TV-addicted French maid is named Toinette (Mary Louise Wilson). The sole voice of reason and sanity in the household is Rose Thorn (Marilyn Cooper), Sloan's mother, who—much to Ginger's chagrin—had to move in after her Brooklyn apartment was totaled in a fire. Rose was hidden in the deceased dog's old bedroom—that is, until it was discovered that she received a very sizable check for the damage to her apartment (at which point, she was moved into the guest room). She is asked to stay in her room when the Thorns have guests and hold their frequent fundraisers, but she rarely listens. Maureen Stapleton appeared on occasion in a bizarre dual role—that of Mrs. Hamilton, an extremely wealthy widow living next door, and as a maid named Peggy.

Episodes were titled "Death and Transfiguration," "Nothing Happened," "The Girlfriend," "Condolence Call," "The Maid," "The Other Maid," "The Thief," "The First Date," "The Rage," "The Horse," "The Prodigal Son," and "The Dream House." The executive producer was Mike Nichols; the producers were Allan Leicht, Millee Taggart, and Tom King; the writers included Allan Leicht, Tom King, and Millee Taggart; the directors were John Bowab, Valentine Mayer, J. D. Lobue, and Peter Bonerz. The program was created by Allan Leicht. The theme song, "We're All Right," was written by John Kander and Fred Ebb, and performed by Dorothy Loudon. *The Thorns* is not to be confused with *The Thorn Birds*—a popular miniseries also on ABC.

Three's a Crowd NRW Productions. ABC. Tuesday nights 8:30 (September 25, 1984–October 23, 1984), Tuesday nights 8:00 (October 30, 1984–July 30, 1985), and Tuesday nights 8:30 (August 6, 1985–September 10, 1985). Twenty-two episodes were videotaped in front of a live audience.

Reminiscent of the premise of the British series *Robin's Nest*, *Three's a Crowd* picks up where *Three's Company* left off. Jack Tripper (John Ritter) falls head over heels in love, and has designs on marrying a sweet and pretty young flight attendant named Vicky Bradford (Mary Cadorette). Her wealthy father is none too pleased at the prospect, and, frankly, neither is she. Yes, she loves Jack very much, but influenced by her own parents' rocky road to divorce, she suggests that they "live together." This angers her old-fashioned father, James Bradford (Robert Mandan) even more, and he purchases their building, and becomes their landlord (in an effort to split the couple up). He has a tendency to pop in for a visit at the most inopportune moments. Seen less frequently is Vicky's mom, Claudia, portrayed by Jessica Walter (her first appearance on the show is in episode three, "The Maternal Triangle," in which it is revealed that Vicky's parents' special song was "I Wish You Love"). This "new life situation" gives Jack Tripper trepidations about breaking the news to his own family. Much in the manner that he pretended to be gay around the Ropers and Mr. Furley in *Three's Company*, his world now revolves around the ruse that he and Vicky are married.

The couple share an apartment located conveniently over Jack's Bistro, Tripper's new business venture. Jack's new chef is a young, blonde, and totally gnarly surfer dude named E. Z. Taylor (Alan Campbell). E. Z. calls everyone "babe" or "dude," but is inexplicably savvy about international cuisine. Actor Stuart Pankin guest starred as a director named Alex Cummings in the episode titled "A Star Is Born," and recalled, "John Ritter was one of my absolute favorite people. There were only three people in my life who could consistently make me double over with laughter, and John was one of those three. I was actually supposed to become a recurring character on the show for the next season. I would have been doing *Not Necessarily the News* at the same time, but sadly *Three's a Crowd* never got picked up. I must say that doing *Three's a Crowd* and working on-camera with John was truly one of the most fun and memorable moments in my sitcom career. In the episode, I was directing Vicky for a TV commercial, and, when the actor who was supposed to be in the commercial with her took ill, John's Jack Tripper character filled in and it was just hysterical. What a delightful man."

The lovely Teresa Ganzel had a similarly wonderful experience working with Ritter: "My very first time being on TV was playing Greedy Gretchen on the original *Three's Company*. John was the sweetest and most supportive actor you could ever ask for. I was so nervous, but he put me completely at ease. And I was thrilled when they had my character come back on *Three's a Crowd* [in the 'Deeds of Trust' episode]. It's surprising how many people still recognize me from that. It shows how loved that series is and how often people are still watching the reruns."

So why wasn't this sequel series as successful as its predecessor? Producer/writer Joseph Staretski said, "America so loved *Three's Company, and had invested so much time in it, they felt betrayed, in a way, that Jack Tripper had left all of those other great characters behind for this. For the audience to accept the Tripper character moving on, the girl really needed to be someone extremely special. Don't get me wrong: Mary Cadorette is a very good actress, but the chemistry just wasn't there. Ritter was absolutely certain after reading with dozens of actresses up for the part of Vicky that Mary was the one with whom he had the best chemistry, but unfortunately, it just didn't work out that way. Perhaps with a Pam Dawber we might have been more successful, but it wasn't meant to be."

Fellow writer/producer Martin Rips added, "John Ritter had such range to his acting and we wanted America to see more of that. We had designs on making this spinoff series more mature than its predecessor, but NRW really wanted more of the same. Ultimately, the show failed. I'm so glad people finally got to see what John could really do with his amazing role alongside Billy Bob Thornton in the movie *Sling Blade*." *Three's a Crowd* was briefly syndicated as *Three's Company, Too*, and was seen most recently on the Antenna Cable TV channel paired with another *Three's Company* spinoff, *The Ropers* (see entry).

About *Three's Company*'s amazing longevity, Staretski added, "We were told not to be too topical or smart, but rather, relatable, when writing for the show. The powers-that-be were looking for something more in the vein of an *I Love Lucy*—something that would hold up thirty-plus years later. We writers were influenced by the smart comedy of Mort Sahl and Woody Allen, but that's not at all what they were seeking. We rolled our eyes at that, thinking it absurd. The thought of people watching something like this over thirty years later was preposterous. But they were so right. I'm continually amazed at how popular the original show still is today."

Episodes were titled "Family Affair" (with guest star Billie Bird), "The Happy Couple," "The Maternal Triangle," "Daddy's Little Girl," "Jack's Problem," "Vacation from Sex," "A Matter of Money," "The Honeymooners," "A Little Competition," "A Foreign Affair," "James Steps Out," "Father Knows Nothing," "A Friend in Deed," "A Case of Sour Grapes," "Private Lessons," "One Ego to Go," "September Song," "Deeds of Trust" (with guest star Teresa Ganzel), "The New Mr. Bradford," "King for a Day," "Jack Gets Trashed," and "A Star Is Born" (with guest star Stuart Pankin). The executive producers were Don Nicholl, Michael Ross, Bernard West, and George Burditt; the producers were Martin Rips, George Sunga, and Joseph Staretski; the writers included George Burditt, Brian Cooke, Johnnie Mortimer, Martin Rips, Michael Ross, Joseph Staretski, Bernard West, Mark Tuttle, Rich Reinhart, Budd Grossman, Phil Mishkin, Lissa Levin, Karyl Miller, David Mirkin, Korby Siamis, Stan Burns, Marty Farrell, Norman Chandler Fox, and Paul Wayne; the director was Dave Powers. Music was provided by Michael Lloyd.

Together We Stand Sherwood Schwartz Productions/Al Burton Productions/Universal Television. CBS. Monday nights 8:30 (September 22, 1986–September 29, 1986), Wednesday nights 8:00 (October 1, 1986–October 15, 1986), Wednesday night 8:30 (October 29, 1986), Sunday nights 8:30 (February 8, 1987–February 15, 1987), and Friday nights 8:00 (March 27, 1987–April 24, 1987). In the latter two time slots, the show was known as *Nothing Is Easy*. Nineteen total episodes were videotaped in front of a live audience (ten as *Together We Stand*, and nine as *Nothing Is Easy*, but only six of the former, and seven of the latter, aired).

Together We Stand has a rather intricate history. It was a very short-lived Sherwood Schwartz sitcom patterned after an episode of another Schwartz sitcom, *The Brady Bunch*. The "Brady" episode is titled "Kelly's Kids," and even though *Together We Stand* came to fruition more than a decade later, it served as a pilot of sorts. In the series, the very diverse Randall family resides at 37 Brookfall Road, in Portland, Oregon. Lori Randall (Dee Wallace Stone) discovered that she was unable to have children, so she and her husband, David (a former school blackboard monitor and basketball player/coach, played by Elliott Gould), adopt Amy (Katie O'Neill) when she was just an infant. As she matures, Amy acquires a reputation as the goody-goody of the Randall family. Somehow, Lori did manage to get pregnant once, and gave birth to Jack—a mischievous red-headed goldbrick, played to a tee by Scott Grimes. A very persuasive social worker (Edie McClurg) persuades the Randalls to adopt two more children several years after Jack was born—a less-than-confident thirteen-year-old Sam (Ke Huy Quan), who has trouble making new friends; and a six-year-old African American, Sally (Natasha Bobo). Two factors led to the program's short life—ratings, and Elliott Gould. Gould was allegedly unhappy with the show and left after appearing in ten episodes (of which only six aired). Producer Cindy Begel clarified, "Michael Jacobs, one of the executive producers and writers for the show, was leaving, and they needed Lesa Kite and me to take over very quickly. The show's executives pulled us aside and said that they wanted the show to set its focus on the kids. The caveat here was that we were not to tell the adult performers. Like they wouldn't figure it out for themselves? There was also an issue with Elliott Gould. He was a very nice guy, but at the time he seemed to have some issues with focus and coherency. In fact, after a bizarre incident in rehearsal, he had a guest shot on *The Late Show* with Joan Rivers. To our amusement, Rivers said to him something to the effect of 'I don't know what the hell you are talking about.'" A few months later, CBS gave the sitcom another stab at ratings success, this time without Gould. It was retitled *Nothing Is Easy*, and it was explained that Gould's David character had been killed in an automobile accident. Lori then has to go back to secretarial work to support the four children. A new neighbor, Marion Simmons (Julia Migenes), was added. Marion constantly whines about her (unseen) eight-year-old hellion of a son named Chuckie, and her (equally unseen) ex-husband, whom she refers to as a "golfball." She often babysits while Lori is studying to become a court stenographer.

This new configuration lasted only nine episodes (only seven of which aired). Along with the cast changes, *Nothing Is Easy* had a new opening theme song. Begel added, "We were part of the changes, too. There were mostly new writers for the show's second incarnation—almost a total upheaval." At the end of each episode of *Nothing Is Easy*, the cast steps out of character and talks about next week's episode. After this second attempt failed to attract viewers, CBS threw in the towel.

Episodes were titled (as *Together We Stand*) "The Pilot," "Oh, Brother," "It Happened One Night," "Betrothal," "Sock and Bonds," "A Chicken in Every Wok," "Girls Night In," "Against All Odds," "Love Is in the Air," "My Mentor," (as *Nothing Is Easy*) "We're a Family," "I Never Dance with Mother," "A Kiss Is Just a Kiss," "Double Date," "Mother, Can You Spare a Dime?," "That's What Friends Are For?," "Sunday, Monday, and Always," "Little Miracle," and "Jack's Alter Ego." The executive producers were Al Burton, Michael Jacobs, and Sherwood Schwartz; the producers were Don Segall, Mark Warren, Dennis Rinsler, Cindy Begel, and Lesa Kite; the writers included Michael Jacobs, Mark Miller, Dennis Rinsler, Marc Warren, Sam Greenbaum, Paul Haggis, David Lerner, Patt Shea, Harriet Weiss, Stephen Sustarsic, Lesa Kite and Cindy Begel. Begel shared, "Dee Wallace Stone and I had a little falling out one week—she wasn't happy with the script, and I kind of lost my cool over it. Well, the next day there were apologies all around, and recently I ran into Dee and we hugged and apologized to one another all over again—a great reunion." The directors included Will Mackenzie, Lee Miller, Andrew D. Weyman, Herbert Kenwith, Alan Bergmann, Peter Bonerz, John Bowab, Joan Darling, Dolores Ferraro, Jack Shea, and Michael Zinberg. The creators were Al Burton, Michael Jacobs, and Sherwood Schwartz. The theme songs were by Michael Jacobs, Sherwood Schwartz, David Kurtz, Dee Wallace Stone, and Al Burton.

The Tortellis Charles/Burrows/Charles Productions/Paramount Television. NBC. Thursday night 9:30 (January 22, 1987), Wednesday nights 9:30 (January 28, 1987–April 1, 1987), and Tuesday nights 9:30 (April 21, 1987–May 12, 1987). Thirteen episodes were filmed in front of a live audience.

The Tortellis was a spin-off of *Cheers*. Many members of the *Cheers* crew were involved in this spin-off as well. It all sounded so good on paper, but on film—that was another story. In a nutshell, Nick Tortelli (Dan Hedaya), the vile and slippery ex-husband of Carla Tortelli (Rhea Perlman), played a TV repairman at The Tortelli TV Hospital (phone no. 555-4768), complete with a house full of crazies—Loretta (the *t*'s in her name are always emphasized), a bubble-headed blonde trophy wife with show business aspirations (Jean Kasem, Casey Kasem's real-life wife); Loretta's elder sister Charlotte Cooper (Carlene Watkins), who is the only one who sees through Nick's self-serving lies and schemes; Charlotte's wise-cracking young towheaded son, Mark (Aaron Moffatt); Nick's dimwitted son, Anthony (Timothy Williams); and Anthony's sex-obsessed young wife, Annie (Mandy Ingber). Set in Las Vegas, most episodes feature the shattering of Nick's dreams of success, great wealth, and fame (Nick called it being "a day too late and a dollar too short"). The opening credits show a slot machine (like the opening for the 1960s sitcom *Accidental Family*) with pictures of the cast popping up with each pull of the lever; the theme song is an a cappella doo wop number titled "Mr. Nice Guy" (similar in texture and tempo to Billy Joel's "The Longest Time").

Episodes were titled "The Pilot," "An Affair to Remember," "Frankie Comes to Dinner," "Svengali," "The Ad Game," "Viva Las Vegas" (with guest star Fred Travalena), "Coochie Coochie" (with guest star Charo), "Man of the Year," "The Good Life," "Father Knows Best," "The Customer's Always Right," "Innocent as Charged," and "His Girl Friday." The executive producers were Patricia Nardo, James Burrows, Glen Charles, and Les Charles; the producer was Stu Kreisman; the writers were Ken Estin, Jake and Mike Weinberger, Jeff Abugov, Kimberly Hill, Cheri Eichen, Bill Steinkellner, Stuart Silverman, Anne Convy, Tom Moore, Phil Kellard, Chris Cluess, Stu Kreisman, Tom Williams, Ken Levine, Dennis Klein, David Isaacs, and Ray Morton; the directors included James Burrows, Greg Antonacci, Michael Zinberg, Jack Shea, and Charlotte Brown. Music was provided by Perry Botkin.

Tough Cookies Witt/Thomas Productions. CBS. Wednesday nights 8:30 (March 5, 1986–April 23, 1986). Six episodes were videotaped single-camera style without a laugh track.

Actor/director Robby Benson starred in this extremely short-lived Witt-Thomas Production called *Tough Cookies* in the spring of 1986. It was much more of a dramedy than a sitcom, and unlike most Witt-Thomas shows, was *sans* studio audience or laugh track. In an effort to shatter his image as a child actor, Robby jumped head first into this adult role as a plain clothes police detective named Cliff Brady, who resides in a tough neighborhood on Chicago's Southside. When off duty, he is often seen at a local saloon known as The Windbreaker, run by chatty Rita (Lainie Kazan), who simply can't keep a secret. It was here that Cliff often runs into his fellow thirtysomething single boyhood buddies Danny Polchek (Adam Arkin) and bartender Richie Messina (Matt Craven). Cliff's co-workers at the police station included Officer Connie Rivera (Elizabeth Peña), who sits at a desk across from him. It is revealed in the "Unfantasy" episode that she has a crush on Cliff and is quite envious of any other woman earning his attention. Cliff's boss is the tough-as-nails Lieutenant Iverson (Art Metrano), and the police chaplain (who calls him Clifford), Father McCaskey (Alan North, formerly of the short-lived *Police Squad*). Ratings were abysmal and *Tough Cookies* crumbled after only six episodes.

Episodes were titled "Ships in the Night," "Grudge Match," "Naked City," "The Unfantasy," "The Stoolie," and "Temper Fidelis." The executive producers were Paul Junger Witt and Tony Thomas; the producers were Stephen Neigher and Lynn H. Guthrie; the writers included Jan Fisher, Stephen Neigher, Vincent

Even with (left to right) Adam Arkin, Matt Craven, and Robby Benson among its cast, CBS's *Tough Cookies* crumbled.

Patrick, Mark Rosner, and William Weidner; the directors included Georg Stanford Brown, James Frawley, Paul Krasny, Stuart Margolin, John Patterson and Robert Scheerer. The program was created by Hal Dresner. Music was provided by George Aliceson Tipton.

Trial and Error Embassy Television/Columbia Television. CBS. Tuesday nights 8:00 (March 15, 1988–March 29, 1988). Eight episodes were videotaped in front of a live audience, but only three aired.

Poor Paul Rodriguez. Between this series

and *a.k.a. Pablo*, a mere total of nine episodes hit the airwaves. *Trial and Error* was given very little *trial* before CBS cleared the courtroom. The program revolves around the Latino odd couple of Tony Rivera (Rodriguez), a free-spirited buttinski and Pat Boone fan who, as a downtown Los Angeles T-shirt vendor, in his words, "made his nut on James Dean alone," while his roommate in apartment 2B, handsome John Hernandez (Eddie Velez) graduated from law school (one of only three Latinos in his class), and recently joined the respected Century City law firm of Kittle, Barnes, Fletcher and Gray.

About the significance of the law firm's name, creator, writer, and executive producer Jerry Perzigian shared, "I don't think anybody on the writing staff knew or knows—or gives a shit, frankly—but I have been since boyhood a huge Chicago White Sox fan. When it came time to invent a name for the firm, I chose a quartet of '80s Sox sobriquets that I thought had a good sound: the last names of Ron Kittle (1st base), Harold Baines (DH), Scott Fletcher (shortstop), and Carlton Fisk (behind the plate). Stupidly, though, I listened to my idiot younger brother, who told me that that grouping sounded silly and transparent. So, acceding to him, I changed two of the names. On behalf of that quartet of great old White Sox, I'm mad at myself now—and at my brother—for the modification."

Hernandez's office is on the 17th floor—the same office in which a huge new copier is stored. Hernandez is initially quite perturbed to find out that he had been hired by the firm over numerous other applicants only because of his ethnicity, but instead opts to seize the opportunity and become the best at his job. Was there ever any backlash from the Latino community? Perzigian said, "None that I ever knew of. It would not be considered backlash, but a problem for me at the time was that our by-the-book P.C. production company would not permit us to cast any old garden-variety Latino in roles portraying a Mexican or Mexican-American. The actors had to be Mexican. I wonder if we might not have done better had the occasional Venezuelan, Dominican, or Cuban performer been able to be hired."

Hernandez's prestigious new job was not without its challenges, including a condescending co-worker named Bob Adams (John deLancie). However, the big boss, Edmund Kittle, played by Stephen Elliott (Kittle had hired Barnes, Fletcher and Gray), has John's back. John's secretary, a busybody named Rhonda (Debbie Shapiro), has all the dirt on everyone in the building and knows all of the office politics inside and out. Although few in number, each episode deals with John's new white-collar world clashing with Tony's blue-collar presence. Susan Saldivar played Lisa, John's on-again/off-again girlfriend.

When asked about memorable guest stars, Perzigian recalled, "There's one in particular that your readers might enjoy hearing about. Our casting person was—is—a brilliant purveyor of her craft named Denise Chamian. In one episode (I couldn't even tell you whether it was one of the broadcast ones or one that never left the can), the script called for a one-line part for a hotel bellboy. Denise chose a guy, telling me, essentially (and probably not inaccurately), that I was always fighting her about her recommendations and that I was always wrong. For this role, she told me unequivocally, I would not be permitted to challenge her. She, as I told you, is brilliant, and she was right: the kid she hired, who only three days prior had stepped off a plane from Springfield, Missouri, was Brad Pitt. It was his first paid Hollywood gig. As a private joke, for what it's worth, the name we gave the character—which the now-famous movie-star announced as part of his one line—was the name of my college roommate. Or maybe my roommate's dad, I can't quite recall."

Tommy Chong, of Cheech and Chong fame, is listed in the credits as one of the co-executive producers and creators. About his involvement, Perzigian stated, "He was virtually never around, that I can recall. The way I heard it, he lived next door to a high-ranking CBS executive at the time and casually mentioned one morning over the back fence that a sitcom featuring East L.

A. Latinos ought to be on the air. The exec, evidently, agreed. To be honest, I can't even remember whether the odd couple premise—a souvenir salesman on Olvera Street Los Angeles and an attorney-at-law as roommates and friends—was Chong's idea, the network's, or ours, as a staff. But looking back, our writing staff, me included, was young and unsophisticated. The series was sillier than it could've been. Should've been. I would love to have another crack at this premise knowing what I know now!"

About the goings-on behind the scenes, Perzigian remembered, "It was a fun, happy set. Probably too happy, to tell you the truth. I think a little less levity and a little more discipline would've enhanced the product. Also, *Matlock* on NBC kicked our ass." Additionally, it didn't help much that part of the debut episode was interrupted (in certain time zones) by a Dan Rather presidential primary election update.

Asked about one of the most memorable aspects of working on the show, Perzigian smiled and said, "While *Trial and Error* was in production, my partner at the time and I were assigned to an office that used to be Norman Lear's. It was a lovely and large office, but that's not what was best or most memorable about it. It featured some sort of electro-magnetic apparatus that allowed me to close the office door from across the room with a nice, loud, definitive bang just by pushing a button under my desk. That remains about as empowering and big-shot a feeling as Hollywood ever delivered to me."

Episodes were titled "The Pilot," "Bon Appetit," "Man's Best Friend," "Deride and Conquer," "Ring of Truth," "Casino Night," "Strike Three, You're Out," and "Born to Squirm." The executive producers were Donald L. Seigel, Jerry Perzigian, Howard Brown, Tommy Chong, and Michael Moriarty; the producer was Al Aidekman; the writers included Donald L. Seigel, Jerry Perzigian, Steve Kunes, and Al Aidekman; the lone director was Andrew D. Weyman. The creators were Donald L. Seigel, Jerry Perzigian, and Tommy Chong. Music was provided by Ray Colcord, and Sister Sledge performed the theme song (written by Joni Sledge, Kathy Sledge, and Phil Lightfoot). About Sister Sledge, Perzigian reflected, "In 1985, they appeared on an episode of *The Jeffersons* that I worked on. I liked and admired them (then and still do) not just as musicians, but also as people, so when we needed a theme song, that's where I turned."

Tucker's Witch Hill/Mandelker Films. CBS. Wednesday nights 10:00 (October 6, 1982–November 10, 1982, and March 31, 1983–June 9, 1983). Twelve episodes were filmed single-camera style without a laugh track.

The unaired pilot was titled "The Good Witch of Laurel Canyon." The title wasn't the only difference. In the title roles of Rick and Amanda Tucker were Art Hindle and Kim Cattrall, respectively. Kim Cattrall's racy role in *Porky's* at the same time put the kibosh on her getting the part when the series was bought by CBS (it's unclear why the role of Rick was recast). For the series Catherine Hicks got the nod as Amanda, and the by-now-familiar Tim Matheson was chosen for the Rick role. The program, now titled *Tucker's Witch*, was, for all intents and purposes, a modern-day *Bewitched*, set in the Tucker and Tucker Detective Agency, at 7000 Vista del Mar Drive, in Los Angeles. *Tucker's Witch* is what this author likes to call a crimedy—a very light-hearted crime show (the polar opposite of a Quinn Martin Production). Witchcraft runs in Amanda's family (although it sometimes skips a generation). Amanda had inherited powers, but is still perfecting them. Said powers pale in comparison to those of Samantha on *Bewitched*. A spooky pet cat named Dickens often enhances her somewhat spotty psychic abilities. These abilities, while not perfect, aid in solving crimes. Your author was working in Manhattan at the time of the program's premiere, and was one of many enticed right off the streets to view the freshman series in a special viewing room with hand controls to register likes and dislikes during the viewing process. Others in the cast included Barbara Barrie as Amanda's mother, Ellen Hobbes; and Duncan Ross was Stucky, the mortician. Speaking of morticians, up against *Dynasty*, the series was a goner from the get-go and was placed on hiatus after only a month. The remaining unaired episodes were burned off between late March and early June of 1983. It's interesting to note that Ted Danson was the guest star on the debut episode that aired less than a week after his own new series, *Cheers*, made its bow. Reruns aired briefly on the USA Network.

Episodes were titled "The Good Witch of Laurel Canyon," "Big Mouth," "The Corpse Who Knew Too Much," "The Curse of the Toltec Death Mask," "Terminal Case," "Abra Cadaver," "Dye Job," "Psych-Out," "Rock Is a Hard Place," "Formula for Revenge," "Living and Presumed Dead," and "Murder Is the Key." The executive producers were Philip Mandelker and Leonard Hill; the producers were William Bast, Steve Kline, John Thomas Lenox, Mel Efros, and Michael P. Schoenbrun; the writers included William Bast, Paul Huson, Steve Kline, Bernie Kukoff, Lee Sheldon, Maryanne Kasica, Michael Scheff, and Marc Rubin; the directors included Peter H. Hunt, Rod Daniel, Harry Winer, Corey Allen, Victor Lobl, Randa Haines, and Harvey S. Laidman. The creators were William Bast and Paul Huson. Music was provided by Brad Fiedel, and the theme song was composed by Shirley Walker, J. A. C. Redford, and George Kahn.

Under One Roof see *Spencer*

United States O. T. P., Ltd. NBC. Tuesday nights 10:30 (March 11, 1980–April 29, 1980). 13 episodes were videotaped without a laugh track, but only six aired.

This was television's first "dramedy." Well, at least it was the program for which the *term* dramedy was coined. *United States* was supposed to be a landmark program, and the critics loved it, but viewers found it painfully boring. Modern-day marriage and child rearing are explored in depth on this program, and most episodes take place in the financially comfortable Chapin household, set in the suburbs of Los Angeles. No, their last name isn't States—the program's title refers to the rare moments when the hostilities within the Chapins' abode are allayed. They were then in *United States*. Topics included death, infidelity, child molestation, alcoholism, second thoughts about having become parents, and numerous other subjects that categorized this program as more drama than comedy. Richard Chapin was played by Beau Bridges; his wife, Libby, by Helen Shaver; and their offspring, Dylan and Nicky. by Rossie Harris and Justin Dana, respectively. Justin is the son of singer Vic Dana of "Red Roses for a Blue Lady" fame. The program was seen again (including the previously unaired episodes) on the A&E Network in 1986, and many years later as part of the now defunct Trio cable channel's "Brilliant but Canceled" series.

Episodes were titled "All Our Weapons," "Uncle Charlie," "A Touching Story," "Sometimes," "Better than Burning," "Room Service," "Josh," "Windmills," "The Grand Funk," "Slide Area," "Broccoli," "And Baby Makes Two," and "Lysdexia Is No Joek." The executive producer was Larry Gelbart; the producer was Gary Markowitz; the writers included Larry and Cathy Gelbart, Gary Markowitz, Carol Gary, Everett Greenbaum, and Tom Whedon; and the directors included Will Mackenzie and Nick Havinga. Music was provided by Jack Elliott.

The Van Dyke Show GTG Entertainment. CBS. Wednesday nights 8:00 (October 26, 1988–December 7, 1988). Ten episodes were videotaped in front of a live audience but only six aired.

This was Dick's fourth program with Van Dyke in the title. Of course, first came the brilliant and legendary *Dick Van Dyke Show*, then *The New Dick Van Dyke Show*, a variety series called *Van Dyke and Company* (which featured Andy Kauffman in the cast), and this—the forgettable *Van Dyke Show*. In this series, Van Dyke portrayed screen and Broadway star Dick Burgess, who, in the debut episode, is on his way to begin work on the Broadway musical version of *The Hunchback of Notre Dame*, in

New York City. He stops off in Pennsylvania to see his son, Matt (played by Dick's real-life son, Barry Van Dyke), his daughter-in-law, Chris (Kari Lizer), and his grandson, Noah (Billy O'Sullivan), whom Dick occasionally calls Joshua. Matt owns and operates the local Arley Playhouse, where a turkey of a play called *Love for Rent*, written by the town's mayor, is currently being performed. Dick then accidentally enters the theater through a wrong door and suddenly finds himself stumbling on stage in the middle of a performance. His awkward entrance actually makes the bad play better, and ticket sales then improve greatly. After some thought, Dick decides to stay on in the Keystone State and assist his son in running the struggling theatre. Other playhouse employees include sixteen-year-old aspiring actor Eric Olander (Paul Scherrer), Matt's secretary Jillian Ryan (played by Maura Tierney, pre–*E. R.*), and the theatre's technical director Doc Sterling (played by *Sanford and Son*'s Whitman Mayo).

Episodes were titled "Opening Night," "Dick Stops Smoking" (similar to an episode of *The New Dick Van Dyke Show* titled "Smoke Rings"), "My Favorite Person," "Death Can be Catching," "Fatal Condo" (with guest star Lainie Kazan), "The Benefit," "The Revival," "A Dark and Stormy Night," "Chris' Old Flame," and "Dick Burgess between the Sheets." The executive producers were Sam Bobrick and Ron Clark; the producers were Walter Barnett and Jim Geoghan, the writers included Sam Bobrick, Ron Clark, Jim Geoghan, Stephen Langford, Neil Rosen, and George Tricker; the directors included Jay Sandrich, Zane Buzby, Frank Bonner and J. D. Lobue. The creator was Donald Todd. Music was provided by Stewart Levin. Even though this program with Dick and Barry Van Dyke was very short-lived, there is a happy ending—they would go on to work for eight seasons together on CBS in *Diagnosis: Murder*.

Washingtoon Telecom Entertainment, Inc./ Lasterday Productions. Showtime. Usually aired Thursday nights, although air dates and times varied (August 15, 1985–November 27, 1985). Ten episodes were videotaped with a laugh track.

Bob Forehead (Thomas Calloway) works in a mall and hosts a few TV commercials for his business (patio furniture), but wants more out of life. He's always wanted to be a game show host, but aims even higher. Bob is very upbeat and positive (and quite naïve), but through his rose-colored glasses "he wanted to make a better world for every girl and boy." So he runs for a seat in Congress, and, surprisingly, wins. He is woefully inexperienced and ill at ease with the ways of Washington. There, in the District of Columbia, Bob's political backer is the dour Tom Mittleman (Jack Riley), and his secretary is the stern, stone-faced Laura Esterjack (Beverly Archer). In his many attempts to do good things for his constituents, Bob consistently manages to alienate a longtime senator from the Deep South, Hugh "Bunky" Muntner (Barry Corbin). (Bunky's nickname is a result of his golf game, which often finds him in sandtraps.) After a tough day on Capitol Hill, Bob always has the comforts of home and his dutiful wife, Ginger (Hilary Thompson); their sarcastic, spiky-haired daughter, Sally (Christina Applegate), and son Bob, Jr. (Jason Naylor). Young Bob calls his father Bob instead of Dad. After only a short time in Congress, Bob begins to revel in the attention he is receiving as a dogooder on the hill. The sitcom was based upon the *Washingtoon* comic strip by Mark Alan Stamaty, which first appeared in the *Village Voice* and the *Washington Post*. It was developed for television by Neil Cuthbert.

The program's episodes do not appear to have been assigned titles. The executive producers were Michael Lepiner and Kenneth Kaufman; the producer was Tom Patchett; the writers included Gary Jacobs and Gary Markowitz; the directors included John Tracy. Music was provided by Dan Foliart and Howard Pearl. The lyrics for the theme song were written by Tom Patchett.

What a Country Ripstar Productions/Primetime Entertainment/Tribune Entertainment/ Viacom. Syndicated. Air dates and times varied. (September 27, 1986–May 23 1987). Twenty-two episodes were videotaped in front of a live audience.

Borrowing from the manner in which the late great Hal Kanter had fun with the credits on his shows, every episode of this series ends with one member of the cast saying some variation of the following: "*What a Country* was taped in front of a group of very well-dressed people," or "*What a Country* was taped in front of a loud, crazy bunch of people," or even "*What a Country* was taped in front of a most honest studio audience." Reminiscent of the premise of the British series *Mind Your Language* (created by Vince Powell) as well as a book, *The Education of Hyman Kaplan* (by Leo Rosten), *What a Country* is a sitcom about diversity, tolerance, and America—the great melting pot. It is set in Los Angeles, specifically a citizenship class led by Mr. Taylor Brown (Garrett M. Brown), a native of North Dakota, who now resides at 36 Whitney Way. Despite the discomfort caused by the lack of air conditioning in classroom no. 107, this grouping of adult students seems genuinely interested in learning American history, American culture, and the overall American way.

Every ethnic group is represented here—Yakov Smirnoff (a real life Russian immigrant who made the words *What a Country* famous in his stand-up routines) as cab driver Nikolai Rustopovich; Julian Reyes as Victor Ortega, a suave, confident, and handsome Latino ladies' man; Ada Maris as Maria Conchita Lopez, a sexy, young Latino Beverly Hills housekeeper (for a furniture store magnate) with an amazing wardrobe (that she loves to flaunt); Leila Hee Olsen as Yung Hee, a shy, pretty young Asian girl who is very naïve about the opposite sex; Harry Waters, Jr., as Robert Muboto, the smug, ill-humored son of a deposed African king, who works as a waiter in Dani's Diner; the very funny Vijay Amritraj as Pakistani Ali Nadeem, who tends to take everything literally; and George Murdock as Laszlo Garbo, a retired Hungarian doctor who doesn't like people.

About the last two on that list, executive producer/writer Joseph Staretski recalled, "Vijay was a star tennis player and a complete natural as a comedic actor. We wanted him to have an Indian accent much in the manner of a Peter Sellers character, but he really wanted to play it as himself and not a stereotype. He was right and we were wrong. He was extremely funny in that role. Now, George Murdock was a brilliant actor and could play some really dark and chilling characters as well as comedy. The one problem we had was that he never delivered his lines the same way twice, and that made editing quite a nightmare."

A yet unknown Michael Richards guest starred on an episode of the show. Staretski recalled, "We were told about this up-and-coming funny guy, but on our show it just didn't work. When we saw him years later on *Seinfeld*, however, we were blown away by his amazing talent and how savvy Larry David and Jerry Seinfeld were, knowing how to use his considerable comedic skills. We were too green at the time to use him to his fullest potential."

Gail Strickland played Principal Miss Joan Courtney in the first ten episodes. About her, Staretski recalled, "She was a wonderful actress and a fine comedienne, but after ten episodes the program wasn't doing as well in the ratings as was anticipated, so to accommodate The Tribune Company and Viacom, it was suggested we bring in a big, over-the-top comedic talent. I had enjoyed working with Don Knotts previously on *Three's Company*, and so he was brought in as the replacement. After *Three's Company*, we feared that he wouldn't want to do a first-run syndicated series, but he came on board. Don was a great comedian and a very nice guy. He did have a temper, though, but when he lost his cool and shouted in that Barney Fife voice of his, it was very hard to take him seriously and not laugh. It may not be well known, but Don was quite the ladies' man. I was always impressed at his prowess with the guest stars on *Three's Company*. At this time in his career, 1986 on *What a Country*, Don had acquired a degenerative eye disease and had problems memorizing large blocks of dialogue as a result. He got upset one week with what he called 'a monologue.' However, the following week when we heeded his wishes and gave him fewer lines, he said that he felt that his character wasn't even there. We then had to find some kind of balance, some middle ground. It's interesting to note that we got him a UCLA student with whom he could run lines at home. He and the UCLA student really hit it off and, despite the difference in their ages, got married and stayed together until his passing. He'd finally met his soul mate, and he was a great dad, too. He was so gifted, and made anything he touched so much funnier. In his autobiography, *Barney Fife and Other Characters I Have Known*, Don had wonderful things to say about his experiences on *What a Country.*"

Fellow executive producer/writer Martin Rips added, "Joseph and I were now in charge on this show, and when the time came to make the change the onus was on us to let Gail go. That was tough to do, but her contract was bought out and she did alright in the long run. I'm still amazed that this program, in first-run syndication, had a budget almost comparable to the networks. I must admit, the change was a good one. Those episodes with Don were the show's best." Knotts portrayed F. Jerry "Bud" McPherson ("only my wife calls me 'F'") beginning with episode no. 11, titled "Taylor Loses His Cool." McPherson lives at 11 Fairlawn Street, and is an old-fashioned, rather intolerant former marine who makes sure the citizenship class students knows that his forces had invaded many of their native countries.

This almost forgotten sitcom was not without merit, and managed to mine a few moments of comedy gold and many a chuckle. Staretski added, "In today's pc-conscious world, the characters might seem a bit stereotypical. We were asked to write in a middle-of-the-road mode—something to which all of America could relate. Unfortunately, when Sumner Redstone took over as the head of Viacom, he immediately raised the ratings criterion for renewal, and *What a Country* fell short." The series was almost picked up for another season but, after twenty-six episodes, the entire cast was deported. Rips recalled, "After this experience, *Hearts Afire*, and a bunch of great, unsold pilots, I became disillusioned with the suits in Hollywood. For a while, I wrote for sitcoms in Europe, but ultimately decided to get my masters in psychology. It's funny, in my practice I still see quite a few celebrities. The only difference is nowadays they're clients."

Episodes were titled "First Class," "Soul Man," "A Busboy Named Desire," "Don't Leave Home Without It," "My Fair Yung Hee," "Holiday on Ice," "Best Laid Plans," "Chicken à la Prince," "A Birthday with Class," "Ali's Arrangement," "Taylor Loses His Cool," "The Road from Morocco" (with guest star Jack Riley), "Nikolai Speaks," "California Dreamin'," "Moonlighting," "Play It Again, F," "Citizen Pain," "Educating Inga," "Victor at an Exhibition," "What a Tangled Web We Weave," "Love Finds Nikolai," "We're in the Mubotos," "What Are Friends For?," "The Candidate," "The Apartment," and "Old World Charmer." The executive producers were Martin Rips and Joseph Staretski (Ripstar Productions); the producer was Wendy Blair; the writers included Bo Kaprall, Frank Mula, Martin Rips, Leonard Ripps, Mike Scully, Joseph Staretski, and Bernard West; the directors included Peter Baldwin, Howard Storm, Bob Claver, Russ Petranto, Linda Day, and Dolores Ferraro. The theme song, "I Want to Be an American," was performed by Dick DeBenedictis. About the theme, Staretski reflected, "I'd always liked that song. It was a perfect fit." After this series was canceled, Yakov Smirnoff enjoyed a long run as the spokesman for Best Western Hotels.

When the Whistle Blows Daydream Productions. ABC. Friday nights 8:00 (March 14, 1980–April 25, 1980), Saturday nights 10:00 (June 7, 1980–June 14, 1980), and Sunday nights 8:00 (July 13, 1980–July 20, 1980). Nine hour-long episodes were filmed, single-camera style without a laugh track.

When the Whistle Blows was a jiggle-and-flex fest, much in the manner of *The Dukes of Hazzard*. Set somewhere in the Southern United States, this program revolved around a group of construction workers and their search for fun both on and off the job. Norm Jenkins

(Dolph Sweet) is the senior member of the crew, and his nagging wife, Dottie (Alice Hirson), is overly concerned that he is working too hard. She wants him to leave more of the work to the virile young members of the crew, such as the outgoing Buzz Dillard (Doug Barr); college man Randy Hartford (Philip Brown, who years earlier had portrayed Doris's son Billy on *The Doris Day Show*); or former NFL hopeful Martin "Hunk" Kincaid (Tim Rossovich). Hunk has a collection of T-shirts, all with silly messages, such as "I Love Iron," "Post No Bills," and, simply, "Hunk," emblazoned on the front. Noble Willingham had the recurring role of Bulldog, about whom director Michael Preece shared, "I got to work with him again a few years later on *Walker, Texas Ranger*." This horny, testosterone-laden bunch is balanced a bit by the lone female crew member—the lovely Lucy Davis (Susan Buckner).

About Buckner, Preece recalled, "Early on in the series, she ran the lunch wagon. She was beautiful and all of the guys loved flirting with her. She was very effervescent and enthusiastic, and the producers and writers decided to give her more to do on the show. They made her one of the construction workers. Well, about three days after that started, I was told to get her to tone down the bubble—it was too much of a good thing. That put me in a very awkward situation, being the one to have to break this news."

After hours, the gang's favorite hangout is a saloon called Darlene's, run by curly-haired Darlene Ridgeway (sitcom veteran Sue Ane Langdon). Preece said, "The characters spent a lot more time at the bar than on the job. These construction workers loved to party." The series took an interesting turn in the "Miss Hard Hat USA" episode when a young Vietnamese orphan named Tuy (Sally Imamura) is placed under the watchful eye of the construction crew.

Acting was not necessarily the high point in this rowdy hour-long comedy/drama series, and after only six episodes aired, the program was put on hiatus. The three remaining unaired episodes were burned off during the summer of 1980, after which ABC blew the whistle on this series for good. About the series, Preece added, "All in all, *When the Whistle Blows* was probably not a very good idea in hindsight."

Episodes were titled "The Pilot," "Love Is a Four-Letter Word," "Macho Man," "Wildcatters," "God's Country," "Beauty Pageant," "Miss Hard Hat USA" (with guest stars Barbi Benton and Dave Madden), "Love in the Fast Lane," "Episode Eight," and "Run for the Roses." The producers were Gerald Sanford and Carroll Newman. Preece said, "This was one of her [Carroll's] first producing jobs. Universal was a tough place for women at that time, but she held her own. She is my son-in-law Randy's cousin." The writers were Robert Sherman, Chuck Gordon, and Tom Kartozian; the directors included Christian I. Nyby II, Edward Parone, and Michael Preece. The creators were Chuck Gordon and Tom Kartozian. The theme song, "When the Whistle Blows," was written by Molly-Ann Leikin and Mark Snow, and performed by Jerry Whitman and the Sweet Inspirations.

Women in Prison Embassy Television. FOX. Sunday night 8:30 (October 11, 1987), and Saturday nights 8:30 (October 24, 1987–April 2, 1988). Thirteen episodes were videotaped with a laugh track. Sponsors included Duracell batteries and Kentucky Fried Chicken.

Even though a sitcom set in a men's prison called *On the Rocks*, on ABC in 1975, was a flop, the upstart FOX Network attempted one in 1987, set in Bass Women's Prison in Wisconsin. Those incarcerated in Cellblock J include no. 659142 Vicki Springer (Julia Campbell), who had been framed for shoplifting a bracelet by her cheating husband; Dawn Murphy (C. C. H. Pounder), an African American inmate who had murdered her abusive husband; Eve Shipley (Peggy Cass), an elderly and senile thief who is doing time for standing by her man (while he mowed down four bank guards on their honeymoon); Pam Norwell (Wendy Jo Sperber), a sarcasm-hurling embezzler and organ player; and Bonnie Harper (Antoinette Byron), a British lipstick lesbian hooker. Minding these reprobates are Meg Bando (Denny Dillon), a nasty, diminutive guard, and surly Assistant Warden Clint Rafferty (Blake Clark). Vicki is put to work as his secretary, and he develops an attraction to her. The theme song ends with the lyrics, "While other girls make dates, you make license plates. You're in jail." Like its predecessor, *On the Rocks*, this program failed to find an audience and was sent to the chair after only thirteen episodes. Turns out, being in prison is no laughing matter—who knew? Even a 1987 drama series called *Mariah*, on ABC, failed to catch on. However, in recent years, a dramedy series about the subject called *Orange Is the New Black* succeeded with flying orange colors.

Episodes were titled "Vickie Does Prison," "Goldfinger," "Hello, I Must Be Going," "Nell's Bells," "Walk This Way," "Skirts on Ice," "The Hole Story," "Veni Vidi Vickie," "Prisoner of Love," "52 Pick Up," "One Hero with Relish," "I Do, I Don't," and "The Triangle." The executive producers were Katherine Green, Ron Leavitt, Michael G. Moye, and Richard Gurman; the writers included Katherine Green; the directors included Gerren Keith, Shelley Jensen, Tony Singletary, Dick Martin, John Sgueglia, Phil Ramuno, and Linda Day. The creators were Katherine Green, Michael G. Moye and Ron Leavitt. Music and the theme song were provided by Ray Colcord and Phyllis Katz.

You Can't Take It With You Harps Productions/Procter and Gamble Productions/LBS Communications. Syndicated. Air dates varied. 7:30 p.m. (September 1, 1987–February 26, 1988). Twenty episodes were videotaped in front of a live audience.

You Can't Take It with You, a classic comedy play written by George S. Kaufman and Moss Hart, made its Broadway debut in 1936, first at Booth Theatre, and later, the Imperial Theatre, with a run of 838 performances. It won a Pulitzer Prize, and the film adaptation, directed by Frank Capra and starring Lionel Barrymore, garnered two Oscars. A 1979 television version also received great notices and an Emmy nomination, and consisted of an amazing array of TV sitcom veterans, such as Jean Stapleton, Howard Hesseman, Polly Holliday, Robert Mandan, Tim Reid, Art Carney, Barry Bostwick, Marla Gibbs, Kenneth Mars, Joyce Van Patten, Paul Sand, Blythe Danner, Harry Morgan, and Beth Howland. It's interesting to note that Harry Morgan later starred in, and Beth Howland later guest starred on, an episode of Hal Kanter's TV sitcom adaptation of *You Can't Take It with You*.

The eccentric Staten Island, New York, family in this version was headed by Morgan as the income tax-evading, circus-loving, stamp-collecting Grandpa Martin Vanderhof. He often addresses the audience directly. Showrunner Cindy Begel recalled, "Harry was very funny and so professional. Going into the project, I'd heard that he'd previously had a minor stroke and had some difficulty remembering lines, so cue cards were necessary. Personally, it wasn't noticeable at all."

His only daughter on the show, Penny Sycamore (Lois Nettleton), thinks of herself as a very talented artist and musician, and is humored by the family; and Penny's child-like husband, Paul Sycamore (Richard Sanders, post–*WKRP in Cincinnati*), invents toys and loves playing with his creations, such as the talking dartboard (in the original play, Paul is a fireworks manufacturer, but that was updated for the series). Paul's African American friend Darwood Pinner (Teddy Wilson)—an updated bit of ethnic casting for 1987 to show some diversity—helps manufacture the toys (coincidentally, Pinner is the role played by Harry Morgan in the much-lauded 1979 TV version). Penny and Paul have two daughters—Essie (Heather Blodgett), a teenager, but as Grandpa says in the opening credits, "We love her anyway" (Essie is a candy maker who, in the original play, dreams of being a ballerina)—her grandpa calls her "sweet potato"; and the family's lone non-loon, Alice (Lisa Aliff), who has a really good job with a Manhattan brokerage firm.

Begel recalled, "All in all, it was not a very good show, despite this group of immensely talented people. Most of the writers on this show were of the vintage variety, and the jokes were almost vaudevillian and I had difficulty relating, although I did like one episode [largely] set in a jail." The opening credits of the syndicated sitcom version begin with some thorough expository information about the characters from Morgan's Grandpa character, in true Hal Kanter fashion (Kanter's opening credits for *Valentine's Day*, *Julia*, *The Jimmy Stewart Show*, and *The George Gobel Show* were equally unique).

About Kanter, Begel said, "There was one script he wrote that the network didn't like and he walked out, insulted, and left everything in our hands and said, 'You girls fix it.' It was the night before the shoot, and we stayed up until all hours doing the rewrite. However, the next day when we handed out the new scripts, poor Teddy Wilson started crying. He was so upset about having to learn all new lines in such a short amount of time. Well, to accommodate him and the rest of the cast, we just went back to the script the network rejected. There was no time to do anything else."

Titles for only a small handful of the twenty-six episodes seem to exist—"Like Mother Like Son," "The Trial of Martin Vanderhof," "For Whom the Phone Rings," and "Grandpa's Two Suits." The executive producers were Pamela Rosser, Sid O. Smith, Larry Patterson, Lesa Kite, and Cindy Begel; the producer was Chris Hart (Moss Hart's son); the writers included Doug Molitor, Gail Roch, Cindy Begel, Lesa Kite, Steve Barker (and Moss Hart and George S. Kaufman are credited, too); the director was Bob LaHendro.

Zorro and Son Gertz Larson Productions/Walt Disney Productions. CBS. Wednesday nights 8:00 (April 6, 1983–June 1, 1983). Five episodes were filmed with a laugh track.

Zorro and Son is a humorous and often quite funny take on the original, played for laughs and set over twenty years after the original. Don Diego de la Vega, a.k.a. Zorro, Sr. (Henry Darrow) is now fifty-three years old, has bursitis, has to be helped onto his horse, has difficulty swinging from chandeliers, and is much less adventurous than he was in his prime. Because he is slowing down, his servant Bernardo (Bill Dana) sends for Zorro, Jr. (Paul Regina), in Spain. Surprisingly, the suave young playboy only discovers in the program's debut episode that his father is, in fact, the legendary Zorro. Realizing that his dad needs some assistance, he too dons a cape and mask, but initially experiences some difficulty with his sword when it comes to making the trademarked letter Z. Junior prefers employing more effective, modern methods for capturing bad guys, such as the use of onion gas and guns along with the traditional sword (against his father's wishes). Zorro has a bevy of nicknames (more nicknames than episodes, in fact)—"The Very Spirit of Freedom," "The Saver of the Oppressed," "The Friend of the Friendless," "The Curse of Capistrano," "The Scourge of El Camino," "The Black Fox," and "The Black Blight of San Bernardino." Many of the program's gags had a Mel Brooks' feel to them—a character named Corporal Cassette (John Moschitta), is a human recording device, and local citizens are strung up and imprisoned for "selling wine before its time" (a quote from a series of 1970s TV commercials featuring Orson Welles for Paul Masson wines). Others in the cast included Gregory Sierra as the evil Commandante Paco Pico (people were constantly calling him Pico Paco, much to his dismay); Richard Beauchamp as Sergeant Sepulveda; Catherine Parks as Senorita Anita; and Barney Martin as Brothers Napa and Sonoma.

Episodes were titled "Zorro and Son," "Beauty and the Mask," "A Fistful of Pesos," "Wash Day," and "The Butcher of Barcelona." The executive producer was William Robert Yates; the producer was Kevin Corcoran; the writers included Eric Cohen and Nick Arnold; the directors included Peter Baldwin, Gabrielle Beaumont, and Alan Myerson. Music was provided by George Duning.

Appendix A: Shows Invited Back for a Truncated or Vastly Different Second Season

Aftermash 20th Century Television. CBS. Monday nights 9:00 (September 26, 1983–March 12, 1984), Sunday nights 8:00 (April 1, 1984–June 24, 1984), Tuesday nights 8:00 (July 5, 1984–October 30, 1984), and Tuesday night 8:30 (December 4, 1984). Thirty-one episodes were filmed single-camera style with a laugh track, but only twenty-nine aired.

The finale of *M*A*S*H* (titled "Goodbye, Farewell, and Amen") was such a ratings bonanza that CBS kept the story going with *Aftermash*, which took place immediately after the Korean War (or police action) came to an end. The first ten seconds of the opening theme song was still "Suicide Is Painless," but it then quickly dissolves into a new theme song by the prolific Patrick Williams.

Sherman Potter (Harry Morgan) has returned to civilian life in Missouri with his wife, Mildred (played by both Barbara Townsend, and, later, Ann Pitoniak). After getting out one day early, Sherman returns to private practice, but he isn't happy—there is too little action. Mildred then recommends that he get a job at The General Pershing Veterans Administration Hospital (better known as General General), in the town of River Bend. The hospital has its drawbacks—the building shakes every time a train goes by, but after the conditions Sherman encountered in Korea, this is paradise by comparison. Getting the job necessitates that the Potters move closer to the hospital (actually on the hospital grounds), but Mildred just wants Sherman to be happy, so she makes the big sacrifice of giving up the house she loves. Sherman is named the chief of staff, although he is frequently at odds with his by-the-books administrator, Mike D'Angelo (John Chappell). D'Angelo's bossy and conniving secretary, Alma Cox, was played by Brandis Kemp. Up to this point, the story was plausible, but then comes the stretch—Corporal Maxwell Klinger (Jamie Farr) is arrested for bookmaking, but when Sherman vouches for him in court, Klinger is allowed to work at General General (if Sherman keeps a close eye on him). Klinger is married to a Korean girl named Soon-Lee (Rosaline Chao), and the viewer occasionally catches a glimpse of the Klingers at home. Sherman then learns that Father Francis Mulcahy (William Christopher) has gone deaf, is depressed, and is suffering from alcoholism. Potter urges him to come to General General for an operation to restore his hearing. Fortunately, the operation is a success, and Mulcahy stays on as the hospital's chaplain and miraculously achieves instant sobriety. Also on staff are Dr. Gene Pfeiffer (Jay O. Sanders), a brilliant surgeon who is known to steal food from his co-workers' plates in the cafeteria, and even from patients with a small appetite.

The program did just well enough to get a renewal for a second season. The Klingers had a baby, and several new doctors and nurses were added to the fray for that very short second season, but ratings were abysmal and Potter, Klinger, and Mulcahy said "Goodbye, Farewell, and Amen" for good in December of 1984. Two of the thirty-one produced episodes were left in the can and didn't air. A pilot titled "W*A*L*T*E*R," starring Gary Burghoff as Corporal Walter "Radar" O'Reilly in the post-war period, was not picked up, but was shown as a special on CBS on July 17, 1984. It was only seen, however, in Eastern and Central Time Zones. It was preempted elsewhere because of CBS's coverage of the Democratic National Convention. Burghoff also guest starred in two episodes of *Aftermash*, and Edward Winter (Colonel Flagg) in one. The only other remnant of *M*A*S*H* after the cancellation of *Aftermash* was *Trapper John, M. D.* starring Pernell Roberts. It ran until September 4, 1986.

Episodes were titled (*Season One*) "September of '53/Together Again" (the hour-long debut), "Klinger vs. Klinger," "Snap, Crackle, and Plop," "Staph Infection," "Night Shift," "Shall We Dance?," "Little Broadcast of '53," "Sunday Cruddy Sunday," "Thanksgiving of '53," "Fallout," "The Bladder Day Saints," "All About Christmas Eve," "Chief of Staff," "C. Y. A.," "Yours Truly, Max Klinger" (with guest star Gary Burghoff), "It Had to Be You" (with guest star Gary Burghoff), "Odds and Ends," "Another Saturday Night," "Fever Pitch," "By the Book," and "Up and Down Payments"; (*Season Two*) "Less Miserables," "Calling Doctor Habibi," "Strangers and Other Lovers," "Trials" (with guest star Edward Winter), "Madness to His Method," "The Recovery Room," "Ward Is Hell," "Saturday's Heroes," and "Wet Feet." The executive producer was Burt Metcalfe; the producer was Dennis Koenig; the writers included Larry Gelbart, Ken Levine, David Isaacs, Everett Greenbaum, Elliott Reid, Gordon "Whitey" Mitchell, Janis Hirsch, Larry Balmagia, Richard Hooker, Tom Straw, and Jay Folb; the directors included Burt Metcalfe, Nick Havinga, Will Mackenzie, Edward H. Feldman, Burt Brinckerhoff, Peter Levin, Gabrielle Beaumont, Hy Averback, Charles S. Dubin, and even Jamie Farr. Music was provided by Lionel Newman, and orchestration by Billy May. The theme song was by Patrick Williams.

Angie Miller-Milkis Productions/Paramount Television. ABC. Thursday nights 8:30 (February 8, 1979–May 17, 1979), Tuesday nights 8:30 (September 11, 1979–December 18, 1979), Monday nights 8:30 (January 14, 1980–February 11, 1980), Saturday nights 8:00 (April 12, 1980–April 26, 1980), and Thursday nights 8:30 (July 31, 1980–September 4, 1980). Thirty-six episodes were filmed in front of a live audience, and all but one aired.

Angie might be considered Garry Marshall's take on *Rhoda* and/or *Bridget Loves Bernie*. However, instead of being star-crossed lovers, Angie and Brad come from vastly different socio-economic backgrounds. The program started out like gangbusters, debuting at a time when ABC and Marshall could seemingly do no wrong. The action takes place in Philadelphia.

Angela "Angie" Falco (Donna Pescow) is a waitress in a diner (The Liberty Coffee Shop), and she hits it off instantly with one of her steady customers—Dr. Bradley Benson (Robert Hays), a pediatrician who works at the medical center across the street. His family is extremely well-to-do, and his romance with and eventual marriage into the earthy Italian-American Falco family causes much consternation for the blue-blooded Bensons. Initially, it was a show about a clash of the classes, and that made it funny (that aspect of the show was softened in Season Two, likely causing its downfall). Angie and Brad opt to elope, thinking it the easy way around family tensions. That decision, however, actually exacerbates family strife, and a small wedding ceremony was finally agreed upon. Angie's mother, Theresa Falco (the ubiquitous Doris Roberts), runs a newsstand to support the family after her husband abandoned them years earlier (despite this, she still sets a place at the table for him each night). Angie's younger sister, the kindly-but-klutzy Marie (Debralee Scott), still lives at home with Mom, at 421 Vernon Street. On the Benson side of the family is Joyce (Sharon Spelman), Brad's snooty older sister who has been married and divorced three times; Joyce's daughter, Hilary (Tammy Lauren), one of the few Bensons who like Angie and make her feel welcome in the family; and Brad's father, Randall (John Randolph). After the ceremony, the couple moves into a huge new home at 76 Clinton Street. When the series returned for a second season, a few changes were afoot—Angie sold the coffee shop so that her mother could open a beauty salon (Rose's House of Beauty); Deidre "DiDi" Malloy (Diane Robin), who had helped out at the diner, was never seen again; Hilary Benson was written out of the show; Angie and Brad moved into a smaller, more manageable house, with Brad's medical practice set up on the ground floor; the program moved from Thursday nights on ABC to Tuesday nights; and a few cast members were added—Tim Thomerson as the self-indulgent hairstylist Gianni, Tessa Richards as another hairstylist named Connie, and the always-funny Florence Halop as a regular customer named Ceil. Other recurring characters include Phipps the Butler (Emory Bass), and Angie's old friends Mary Mary (Valri Bromfield), Mary Grace (Susan Duvall), and Mary Katherine (Nancy Lane). One of the most popular episodes of the series is the one in which the Bensons go head to head with the Falcos on the ABC game show *Family Feud*.

The show was moved around several more times on ABC's schedule in Season Two, but nothing seemed to help, and it disappeared after thirty-five of its thirty-six episodes had aired. That lone unaired episode finally saw the light of day when *Angie* was briefly seen in reruns on ABC's daytime schedule during the summer of 1985. Doris Roberts, who had won a well-deserved Supporting Actress Emmy for her unforgettable portrayal of Marie Barone on the long-running CBS sitcom, *Everybody Loves Raymond*, was seen most recently on an Internet series called *The 4 to 9ers: The Day Crew*, with co-stars Ted McGinley and Amy Yasbeck. *Angie* was released on DVD by VEI in 2015.

Episodes were titled (*Season One*) "The Proposal," "Wedding Wings," "The Elopement," "The Morning After," "The Adjustment," "Theresa's Date," "The House Guests," "The Opportunity," "Joyce's Job," "The First Fight," "Angie's Good Deed," and "The Checkup"; (*Season Two*) "Angie's Old Friends," "The First Separation," "Moving Day," "Marie's Crush," "The Gift," "The Thief" (with guest star Peter Scolari), "Vinnie's Return," "Uncle Cheech" (with guest star Danny DeVito), "Family Feud" (with guest stars Richard Dawson and Gene Wood), "Harvey's Brother," "Mary Mary Marries," "The Gambler," "Coffee Wars," "Angie and Brad's Close Encounter" (with guest stars Michael Tucci and Rhea Perlman), "The Beauty Shop," "Theresa's Gigolo," "Marie Moves Out," "Brad's Best Buddy," "February Fever," "The President's Coming! The President's Coming!," "The Kid Down the Block," "Friends in Need," "Angie and Joyce Go to Jail," and "Angie and the Doctor." The executive producers were Leonora Thuna, Dale McRaven and Bob Ellison; the producers were Larry Mintz, Bruce Johnson, and Alan Eisenstock; the writers included Garry Marshall, Dave McRaven, Alan Eisenstock, Larry Mintz, Sheldon Bull, Emily Levine, Leonard Ripps, Thad Mumford, David Barlow, Dan Wilcox, Louis Del Grande, Kenneth Berg, Jeff Franklin, Richard B. Eckhaus, Terry Grossman, Gary H. Miller, Gary Kott, Ellen Guylas, Simon Muntner, Bruce A. Taylor, Kathy Speer, Diane Asselin, Leonora Thuna, Harry Cauley, Gloria Banta, Pamela Morrison, Carmen Finestra, and Gideon Farr; the directors included John Tracy, Lowell Ganz, Jeff Chambers, Tony Mordente, Robert Drivas, Howard Storm, Doris Roberts, Harvey Medlinsky, and Norman Abbott. Music was provided by Dan Foliart, and the theme song titled "Different Worlds" was written by Charles Fox and Norman Gimbel, and performed by Maureen McGovern of "The Morning After" fame (the Oscar-winning song from the 1972 blockbuster film *The Poseiden Adventure*). Cyndi Grecco was the first choice to sing the theme, but Fox and Gimbel were unable to get her on the telephone at the time, and she didn't have an answering service. Talk about opportunity knocking (or ringing)! Doris Roberts died on April 17, 2016 at the age of 90.

The Bad News Bears Huk, Inc./Frog Productions/Paramount Television. CBS. Saturday nights 8:00 (March 24, 1979–June 23, 1979), Saturday nights 8:30 (September 15, 1979–October 6, 1979) Saturday nights 8:00 (June 7, 1980–June 28, 1980), and Saturday nights 8:30 (July 12, 1980–July 26, 1980). Twenty-six

The cast and crew members of CBS's *Bad News Bears* crew: (top, left to right) Teri McCoy, Paul Diamond, Jeff Ganz, Al Aidekman; (middle, left to right) Brian Levant, Cindy Begel, Jack Warden, Miss Nancy, Lesa Kite, Ron Leavitt; (front row) Richard Rosenstock, David Lerner, and Richard Gurman (photograph courtesy Cindy Begel).

episodes were filmed with a laugh track, but only twenty-three aired.

The Bad News Bears was a hit 1976 motion picture starring Walter Matthau and Tatum O'Neal. It spawned two movie sequels—*The Bad News Bears in Breaking Training* (1977) and *The Bad News Bears Go to Japan* (1978). It also became a CBS TV series, albeit briefly. In the small-screen incarnation, Jack Warden took on the Morris Buttermaker role. Writer Cindy Begel remembered, "He had an amazing photographic memory, learning his lines at almost the last minute before we started shooting. He was always called simply Buttermaker. His first name, Morris, was rarely used."

The character of Buttermaker was a notorious quitter. His marriage ended in divorce, he was ousted from college, he had quite a temper, and he was an avid gambler. He was down on his luck and cleaning pools for a living. When one of the regular customers for his pool cleaning service declared bankruptcy and couldn't pay what he owed, Morris retaliated by driving the man's Cadillac into the pool—a crime that subjects him to legal action. Morris is presented with a choice—he can do jail time for his actions, or he can coach, on a volunteer basis, a ragtag baseball team called The Bears at Hoover Junior High School; he is urged by Principal Emily Rappant (Catherine Hicks) to take the latter sentence. After a short stint with the hapless team, Morris is again a quitter. However, when he realizes that the powers-that-be meant business and his only other option is the lockup, he gives coaching another shot. Producer and head writer John Boni recalled, "Warden was great. We had some wonderful talks between scenes. He was a regular guy. I started my career as an actor, and I loved discussing acting with him. He was a very nice man."

Some of the members of his sorry team of misfits went on to even bigger things—Corey Feldman played Regi Tower; Meeno Peluce was Tanner Boyle; Kristoff St. John was Ahmad Abdul Rahim; Billy Jacoby (later Billy Jayne) was Rudi Stein; and Tricia Cast was ace pitcher Amanda Whirlitzer. It's interesting to note that Morris used to date Amanda's mother, and Amanda made numerous attempts to get the couple back together. Boni ran into Cast again years later, and shared, "They have these weekend film-making contests in Durham, North Carolina, where I settled after retiring. The film I was to produce was to be done in Nashville and a mature blond actress was required for the lead role. By sheer coincidence, Tricia Cast was chosen. I didn't even realize it was her, having not seen her since she was a child. She recognized me and we had a great little reunion all those years later. It's a small world." The coach of the very proficient rival team called The Lions was Roy Turner (Phillip R. Allen), who was a very poor winner. Boni remembered, "All of the actual game sequences were filmed in a stadium in the proximity of the studio, but all of the dugout and locker room scenes were conveniently done back at the studio."

The episodes from Season One did just well enough to warrant a second season. Added to the team in that sophomore year was Rad Daly as Josh Matthews, who was transferred to Hoover Junior High. Frequently heard in the soundtrack of this series was "The Toreador Song" by Georges Bizet from the opera *Carmen*. Season Two was a real strike out in the Nielsen Ratings, and *The Bad News Bears* was placed on hiatus after only four new episodes had aired. Numerous previously unaired episodes were shown during June and July of 1980. Three episodes remained unaired until the program was rerun on Comedy Central in the early 1990s. Writer Cindy Begel shared, "This was my first job in the business—I was an apprentice writer. It was so exciting driving under the Paramount sign every day. I loved working on this show, it was all very exciting and new. Not long ago, I ran into Corey Feldman. We shared a good long hug. He had such a sad and abusive childhood and had absolutely no pictures from that era. I got him a few, and he was very grateful. That was quite a moving experience."

Episodes were titled (*Season One*) "Here Comes the Coach," "Amanda Joins the Bears," "Nakedness Is Next to Godliness," "The Kelly Story," "Tanner's Bird," "Emily Loves Morris," "The Food Caper," "Men Will Be Boys," "Three's a Crowd," "Save the Bears," "Dance Fever," and "Fielder's Choice"; (*Season Two*) "Run Down," "Buttermaker Rides Again," "First Base," "Wedding Bells, Part One," "The Birds and the Bees and the Bears," "Lights Out," "Wedding Bells, Part Two," "Matched Set," "Old Timers' Day," "Scrambled Eggs," "Double Play," "The Good Life," "The Pride of the Bears," and "The Headless Ghost of MacIntosh Manor." The executive producers were Bob Brunner and Arthur Silver; the producers were John Boni, Ron Leavitt, Brian Levant, and Norman Stiles; the writers included John Boni, Bill Lancaster, Bob Brunner, Arthur Silver, Sam Greenbaum, Tom Moore, Jeremy Stevens, Richard Rosenstock, Paul Diamond, Jeff Franklin, Al Aidekman, Ron Leavitt, Brian Levant, John Boni, Jim Brecher, Jeffrey Ganz, Hap Schlein, Betty Steck, Norman Stiles, Roy Teicher, Elliot Werber, Fred Fox, Jr., Allen Goldstein, Richard Gurman, David Lerner, Judy Olstein, Levi Taylor, Stephen Fischer, Lesa Kite, and Cindy Begel; the directors included several legends—Bruce Bilson, William Asher, Norman Abbott, Gene Nelson, John Tracy, Jeffrey Ganz, Lowell Ganz, Alan Myerson, and Jeffrey Hayden. Music was provided by David Michael Frank.

About Huk and Frog Productions, Boni recalled, "Huk was Arthur Silver's and Frog was Bob Brunner's production company. They were great to work with and really inspired creativity in their crew. Unlike another show for which I wrote called *The Practice* with Danny Thomas where practically every word was rewritten (I even had them take my name off of one of the scripts for that show), Silver and Brunner really trusted their writers, and that was wonderful."

The Baxters BBI Communications/T. A. T. Communications/Field Communications (*Season One*)/Wilkes and Close Communications (*Season Two*). Syndicated. Air dates and times varied. Fifty episodes were videotaped—some episodes (1979–1981) with a laugh track. The original 1977 WCVB version used a laugh track on several, but not all episodes. All three versions utilized the unique audience participation segment at the end.

The sitcom called *The Baxters* was a show like no other—it was interactive. The second half of the program was a question-and-answer session with the small studio audience that had just viewed that week's segment. Created by a divinity student named Hubert Jessup, it began locally in the Boston area on WCVB-TV in 1977. It was aired as a Sunday morning public affairs program, with Jessup was the host. The Baxter family at that time consisted of Harriet Rogers as Grandma Lizzie, Scott Evans as Dennis, Frank Dolan as Stan, Anita Sangiolo as Susan, and Tiki Fuhro as Amy. The writer at that time in the show's infancy was Henry David Abraham, and the director was Karl Nurse. This version, shot on videotape, employed a laugh track (for most episodes).

The show garnered such a following, it got the attention of producer Norman Lear, who then wanted to try the concept on a national level. His T. A. T. Communications produced the program for the 1979–1980 season in Hollywood. The program was quite a bit more serious in tone in Season One and, like the original WCVB version, every episode began with a segment involving the Baxter family, with audience participation in the second half. Lear's national version consists of Fred Baxter (Larry Keith), a St. Louis insurance salesman; his wife, Nancy (Anita Gillette); their nineteen-year-old adopted daughter Naomi (Derin Altay), and their biological children fourteen-year-old Jonah (Chris Petersen) and ten-year-old Rachel (Terri Lynn Wood). Many controversial issues of the day were addressed in that first segment each week—women's lib, homosexuality, whether to place one's parents in a nursing home, getting married vs. living together, etc. Season One granted each station that had opted to carry the show the opportunity to air the question-and-answer segment conducted by the show's producers, or produce their own. The second season was produced at Toronto, Ontario's, CHCH-TV, but still set in St. Louis. Because of poor ratings, Lear abandoned the project after one season, but, surprisingly, a Canadian company, called Wilks and Close Communications, opted to take the reins and attempted another season of episodes in Toronto. Wendell Wilks hosted the audience segment for this version. The cast and crew were completely overhauled. The patriarch of the family was now schoolteacher Jim Baxter (Sean McCann); his working wife, Susan (Terry Tweed); and their kids: nineteen-year-old Allison (Marianne McIsaac), fourteen-year-old Greg (Sammy Snyders), and ten-year-old Lucy (Megan Follows). This new version of the show had a very small budget, and many flubs and stumbles were left in. Edits and retakes were expensive.

The episodes don't seem to have been assigned titles. The executive producer was Norman Lear (*Season One*) and Chet Collier (*Season Two*); the producers were Fern Field (*Season One*) and Wendell Wilks (*Season Two*); the writers for the Lear version included Ann Gibbs, Joel Kimmel, and Harry Cauley, and for the Chet Collier version Jeanne Lucas and Phyllis Rossen Sewall; the director for the Lear version was Don Shannon, and, for the Collier version, Ray Arsenault. The creator was Hubert Jessup. Music for the Lear version was provided by Marvin Laird (uncredited for Collier's).

Buffalo Bill Stampede Productions. NBC. Wednesday nights 9:30 (May 31, 1983–August

24, 1983) and Thursday nights 9:30 (December 22, 1983–April 5, 1984). Twenty-six episodes were filmed. Thirteen used a laugh track; the other thirteen, a live audience.

Buffalo Bill was the on-air name for Bill Bittinger (Dabney Coleman), who resides in the Timon Towers apartments. Originally from Truckee, California, he became a popular TV talk show host on Buffalo, New York's WBFL Channel 12. It has always been an article of faith in network TV that the main character of a series, however flawed, still has to be likeable. That golden rule was shattered here. Bittinger had no redeeming qualities—he had a bad temper, he was politically incorrect, impatient, condescending, shallow, cocky, insensitive, self-serving, conniving, bigoted, and quite the horn dog. He freely used terms such as chick, broad, and bimbo to describe his latest sexual conquests. Anything that went awry in his personal life or with the TV program was someone else's fault.

Director/head writer/producer/showrunner Dennis Klein recalled, "NBC Entertainment President Brandon Tartikoff called putting *Buffalo Bill* on the air like playing Russian roulette with all six chambers loaded." Bill didn't "buffalo" anyone around him, however. Everyone who knows him is aware he is extremely insecure, petrified of growing old, and disappointed his talents only took him as far as Buffalo. A running gag on the show has Bill always calling audio stagehand Stan (Claude Earl Jones) by the wrong name. Viewers felt pity for Stan and for Bill's other co-workers, such as the Mozart-loving station manager Karl Shub (Max Wright), whose nervous tics make Don Knotts appear calm, cool, and collected (Shub was constantly putting out fires set by Bill's inflammatory on-air comments and rants); Wendy Killian (Geena Davis), the show's smart and feisty research assistant, is always resisting Bill's advances; straightforward, no-nonsense, brutally honest African American makeup man Newdell (Charles Robinson); the assistant director Tony Fitipaldi (Meshach Taylor, pre–*Designing Women*); and prop girl (and Bill's tomboy daughter) Melanie (Pippa Pearthree) who, in one episode, is dangled by Bill from his dressing room window during one of his fits

Dabney Coleman was the hopelessly self-centered Bill Bittinger on NBC's *Buffalo Bill*.

of rage (at one point she is actually let go; thankfully, she is caught by Woody, the stage manager). Jo Jo White (Joanna Cassidy), the director, thinks Bill is a complete jerk and yet is inexplicably attracted to him They have a tempestuous, on-again/off-again romance (even coming close to getting hitched at one point). Stage manager Woody Deschler (John Fiedler) ignores Bill's caustic personality and feels a kind of hero worship for the man. Bill's nicknames for him are Woodpile and Man of Wood.

After a thirteen-episode first season, the show did well in reruns and was therefore brought back. Too late for a fall launch of Season Two, *Buffalo Bill* returned midseason. The series never really did find an audience in its sophomore year, but its return did delight the critics (and the cast). Years later, NBC's Brandon Tartikoff came to rue the day he opted to cancel this series, but the low ratings left him with little choice in the matter. Among the best episodes: "Have Yourself a Degrading Christmas," provides the viewer with a true glimpse of the pathetic and vulnerable Bill; in "The Interview," Bill's co-workers are asked—on camera—their honest opinions about Bill; and "Jerry Lewis Week," with a young, yet-unknown Jim Carrey as one of several dozen annoying Jerry Lewis impersonators who add a surreal comic presence to the already off-kilter backstage goings-on.

Episodes were titled (Season One) "The Pilot," "Buffalo Beat," "Woody Quits," "Buffalo Bill and the Movies," "Mrs. Buffalo Bill?," "Wilkinson's Sword," "Guess Who's Coming to Buffalo?," "Below the Belt," "Ratings," "True Love," "The Fan," "Hackles," "Hit the Road, Newdell" (with guest star R&B great Little Esther Phillips), (Season Two) "Jerry Lewis Week," "The Interview," "Company Ink," "Jo Jo's Problem, Parts One and Two," "Miss WBFL," "Nuclear Freeze," "The Girl on the Jetty," "Buffalo Bill Versus the Kremlin," "A Hero," "The Tap Dancer," "Have Yourself a Degrading Christmas," and "Church of the Poisoned Mind." The executive producers were Tom Patchett, Jay Tarses, and Bernie Brillstein; the producer was Dennis Klein; the writers included Tom Patchett, Jay Tarses, Dennis Klein, Mitch Markowitz, Gary Markowitz, Merrill Markoe, and Carol Gary; the directors included Tom Patchett, Jim Drake, and Dennis Klein. Klein noted, "*Buffalo Bill* was very unusual in that we had no staff writers, story editors or script consultants." The program was created by Tom Patchett and Jay Tarses. Music was provided by Tom Wells. In 2005, all twenty-six episodes were issued in a DVD box set from Lionsgate Entertainment. However, because of exorbitant royalties being demanded by the Ray Charles estate, the "Hit the Road, Jack" sequence in the "Hit the Road, Newdell" episode had to be cut (and the DVD set has a humorous disclaimer by one Jay Tarses).

The Cavanaughs Mandy Films/Paramount Television. CBS. Monday nights 9:30 (December 1, 1986–March 9, 1987), Monday nights 8:30 (August 8, 1988–October 3, 1988), and Thursday nights 9:00 (June 29, 1989–July 27, 1989). Twenty-six episodes were videotaped in front of a live audience.

Francis Patrick Cavanaugh (Barnard Hughes) is the patriarch of an Irish-Catholic family from South Boston, and the eldest Cavanaugh. Much like the Red Sox, who broke the curse of the Bambino in the year 2004 by winning The World Series, Francis breaks the family curse by reaching the age of seventy-two (no other Cavanaugh had accomplished that feat). However, his eyesight is failing him and he has to give up his driver's license and his beloved 1941 light blue Plymouth convertible as a result. He is a Democrat, and his brother, James (Art Carney in a recurring role), is a staunch Republican (Francis's nickname for him is "Weasel"). A lot of their hostility dates back to a girl they both loved named Bridget. Carney and Barnard, with their gray/white hair and glasses, look as though they could be brothers in real life.

Christine Ebersole, who played the thrice-married Kit (short for Kathleen, at one time married to TV actor Tom Elgin, played by John Getz) on the show recalled, "They loved one another as brothers, too. Two great Broadway veterans. Truthfully, I believe they were both Democrats in real life. Art's role was recurring, but he fit right in and was like family. He came out of retirement for our show. He was a fan of the show and watched it even when he wasn't on. And Barney Hughes was so much fun—a very funny man. Some of the stories about their relationship as brothers on the show were based on real events from the Moloney brothers, Bill and Bob, behind the scenes."

The elder brother, Francis, is a widower and owns The Cavanaugh Construction Company. The company is now run by Francis's son, Charles (Peter Michael Goetz), usually called Chuck and sometimes Cluck or Chunk—also a widower. Charles's daughter is cute Mary Margaret (Mary Tanner); she calls Francis "Poppy." Charles is also the father of John (Parker Jacobs), Kevin (Danny Cooksey), and Charles Cavanaugh, Jr. (John Short)—the latter is a priest, and was given some of the show's funniest lines. Kit Cavanaugh (Christine Ebersole) is Francis's only daughter and a former Golddigger (The Golddiggers were a group of sexy singers and dancers on *The Dean Martin*

Show) on TV; (she also danced on *Hullabaloo* and *Shindig*), and Ebersole added, "She was a June Taylor Dancer [The June Taylor Dancers were a group of shapely women who danced Busby Berkeley–style production numbers on *The Jackie Gleason Show*]. The character of Kit, despite the vast age difference, was loosely based upon the Moloney brothers' mother—a larger-than-life character, presence, and dancer. Kit was a divorcee with the last name of Elgin, but reverted to her maiden name." In her checkered past, the Kit character had also appeared nude in one low-budget movie as actress Ensalada Verde. In her character's words, "It was scale, it was four weeks' work, and it wasn't my body."

The Cavanaughs all lived under one roof at 36 Brookhaven Street. The opening credits feature music reminiscent of an Irish jig, and occur inside of a picture frame as the entire Cavanaugh family assembles for a group photograph (Season One). In Season Two, the same theme played as a series of still photographs of the cast are shown. Ebersole said, "That opening theme was written by my husband, Bill Moloney, along with his partners Denny Polen and Paul Pilger. That was the best thing to come of that wonderful experience doing *The Cavanaughs*. We've been married some twenty-seven years now. That show was among my happiest times on TV. The cast was just darling. Barney Hughes and Peter Michael Goetz used to always joke about sex on the set—not in a disgusting manner, but more of a PG way. Barney used to say that a happy cast is one that talks and jokes about sex, and he was right. I was friends with Barney until his passing. I think he and Art Carney stayed in touch, too. I heard that Art went to see one of Barney's shows on Broadway, and was very embarrassed to discover he'd forgotten to bring his hearing aid along with him."

There was one other cast member that viewers didn't know about. Ebersole elaborated, "I had a pet Chihuahua named Chichi that I'd gotten on the beach in Puerto Rico in 1986. It was frowned upon to bring pets to the studio, so I always had Chichi hide when I drove through the Paramount gate every day. I only got caught once, but I was able to convince the guard at the gate that she was part of the show. She was always with me, and was present at every curtain call."

Asked about her favorite guest star, Ebersole said, "Besides Art Carney was Frances Bay. She played the recurring role of the widow Kelsey, and was always seeking the affections of Barney's character Francis. She'd bring him casseroles, but his character wanted none of it. She was adorable and a delight."

The 1980s were a busy time on the Paramount lot, and Ebersole reflected, "Michael J. Fox, and also members of the casts of *Happy Days* and *Cheers* wandered in to see our tapings. It was also alleged that our show was Steve Allen's personal favorite. Our ratings were good for both half seasons on Monday nights, but when CBS's programming chief, Bud Grant, left, Kim LeMasters was hired and CBS opted to cancel our show. The same thing happened to me recently on a sitcom called *Sullivan and Son*." Reruns of *The Cavanaughs* were aired, briefly, during the summer of 1989.

Episodes were titled (*Season One*) "Member of the Wake-Ing," "Not So Gently into the Night," "Love with an Improper Stranger," "Yes, Virginia There Is a Pop," "Bishop's Back," "Angst a Lot," "Strike Too," "The Arrangement," "The Eyes Have Had It," "A Chorus Malign" (with guest star Caroline McWilliams), "Banned in Boston," "He Ain't Heavy, Father …," and "Aunt Mom"; (*Season Two*) "Weasel Waltz," "Coastal Disturbance," "Careers," "Smoke Gets in Your Eyes and Up Your Nose," "Many Happy Returns," "Gimme Shelter," "Fair Weather Friend," "Last Temptation of Chuck," "Cavanaugh Curse," and "Just Weaseled." The executive producer was Robert Moloney; the producers were Seth Pearlman and Leonard Goldberg. About Goldberg, Ebersole recalled, "Mandy Films was his production company. It was named for his daughter, Amanda." The writers included Robert Moloney, Trish Soodik, and Robert Griffard; the directors included Andrew D. Weyman, Ginger Gregg, Robert Moloney, John Pasquin, Jack Shea, and Matthew Diamond.

The creator was Robert Moloney. Music was provided by Paul Pilger, Dennis Polen, and William Moloney.

Charles in Charge Scholastic Productions/Al Burton Productions/Universal Television. CBS. Wednesday nights 8:00 (October 3, 1984–April 3, 1985). Twenty-one episodes were videotaped in front of a live audience; one episode used a laugh track. After a long absence, a total of 104 episodes, with a mostly different cast, were later videotaped for syndication.

Season one of *Charles in Charge* was rather different from the later syndicated series, even though the show's title remained the same. The pilot episode is strong, and its focus is on a nineteen-year-old college student named Charles—just plain Charles. The program employed a running gag in which every time Charles is about to reveal his surname, he is interrupted. He takes a job as a live-in helper for the Pembroke family, at 10 Barrington Court, in New Brunswick, New Jersey.

Jill Pembroke (Julie Cobb) is a theater critic; her husband, Stan (James Widdoes), is a company vice president (however, the company's name is never revealed). They have three "interesting" children—a little hellion named Douglas (Jonathan Ward); an obnoxious genius named Jason (Michael Pearlman); and a boy-crazy teenage daughter named Lila (April Lerman). Charles's dim bulb of a best friend, Buddence "Buddy" Lembeck (Willie Aames), is nicknamed "Goon Machine." If one looked up the word "horny" in the dictionary, Buddy's picture would be next to it as a definition. He alone is responsible for most of Charles's ridiculous predicaments. Jennifer Runyon (Jennifer Corman, nowadays) portrayed Charles's dream girl, Gwendolyn Pierce, in Season One.

This original setup lasted for a solitary season on CBS, and the program was canceled after twenty-two episodes had aired. About the syndicated episodes, Julie Cobb recalled, "When it was picked up for syndication later the budget was smaller and they couldn't afford to relocate the kids who lived in New York, so they recast the whole family. It was very disappointing because the show was a lot of fun to work on. We basically went to work and laughed all day." Runyon concurred: "I do think the syndicated show was very fun. Scott Baio and Willie Aames were amazing together. I was busy doing other things at the time, but it would have been so cool to do it all again with the original cast." Asked about her memories of the show's star, Cobb said, "The thing I most remember about Scott is his youth. He was our star, yes, but his parents were ever-present. I believe his father managed him and so was on set quite often. His mother, Rose, was a very sweet presence. Scott was young, not sure how old he was, but he was quite the ladies' man. Scott was always very dear but I also felt his mischief, like maybe he and Willie [Aames] were laughing at me when I wasn't looking."

When the program was resurrected for first-run syndication (1987–1990), there were a slew of changes. With almost a *Twilight Zone* feel to it, Charles returned with Buddy from a two-week camping trip to find that the Pembrokes had up and left for a new home in Seattle. Charles's key still worked, but the house is now occupied by an entirely new family, the Powells. The Pembrokes had tried to contact Charles while he was away, but the message "We have something to tell you about your life" is relayed to him thusly: "We have something to tell you about your wife," which he promptly ignores. The Powells had gotten a glowing report from the Pembrokes about Charles and they want to keep him on in their employ, but Charles needs some convincing. Charles weighs his options—live with the Powells, or share an apartment (with a hot tub) with Buddy. After much consideration, Charles decides to stay on with the new family; the group consists of Ellen (Sandy Kerns), whose husband, Robert, is away in the navy; Ellen's father-in-law and former naval officer, Walter (sitcom veteran James Callahan); and Ellen's children—Sarah (Josie Davis), Jamie (Nicole Eggert), and Adam (Alexander Polinsky).

Only Charles and Buddy remained from the original series, although Jennifer Runyon got to return for a two-parter called "Twice upon a Time" in the new format. "I was so happy to return for that," she said. "I loved being part of the show. The new cast was wonderful, but it was strange not having my original cast mates around." In that episode, Runyon, as Gwendolyn, returned because she'd become engaged to another man but still had feelings for Charles and wanted to make sure she was doing the right thing by marrying her fiancé. Regarding the romantic scenes on camera with Baio, Runyon said, "Scott and I sure did have a lot of kissing scenes, but we were just friends. I got along very well with Scott—he was like an obnoxious brother, always teasing me. I think we had great chemistry together. The best memory I have of the show is all of the laughter—it never stopped. Julie [Cobb] and I loved to tease James Widdoes, and Scott [Baio] and Willie [Aames] were very mischievous. I have five brothers, so I enjoy that male energy. I'm still very close to Willie Aames—he's one of my best friends. We actually do a show together now called F. L. U. I. D. for WBAR [FM] in New York with our other co-star, Susan Olsen [of *The Brady Bunch*]. I'm in touch with Julie [Cobb], Michael [Pearlman] and Jonathan [Ward], but I haven't spoken to April [Lerman] since the show ended. I loved this show. I learned a lot about working on a sitcom. I worked with the most wonderful cast and it was such a great experience."

Actor Renny Temple guest starred in the first-season episode "Mr. Brilliant": "I got the call after they fired an actor for that week. After a few days, he just wasn't working out and they needed someone on quick notice. I knew Scott because my wife, Caren Kaye, had worked with him on the series *Who's Watching the Kids?* I came in, learned the part fast, and with Alan Rafkin's direction and no audience that week, we got it done. Even though it was only a couple of days out of my life, I recall it being a lot of fun."

In the new syndicated format, even the name of the guys' favorite hangout had changed from The Lamplight to The Yesterday Café. This new syndicated version of the show was connected to *Happy Days* and *Joanie Loves Chachi* in two ways—in all of those series, Baio's character was named Charles, and Ellen Travolta played his mother. She owned The Yesterday Café. Actor/comedian/producer/writer Paul Provenza guest starred on the episode "Second Banana," from the syndicated version of the series. He recalled, "That show was like a family, and Scott Baio was extremely warm and fun. It was a very pleasant experience. I played a director for a commercial in the episode. Someone, I think Scott, had to wear a banana suit." The Season one DVD set from Universal Home Entertainment was released in 2006.

All told, there were 126 episodes. The twenty-two from the first season (and first format) were titled "The Pilot," "Extracurricular Activity," "Another Saturday Night," "War," "Cousin Elliot," "Slumber Party" (with guest star Christina Applegate), "Discipline," "Trick or Treat," "A Date with Enid," "Friends and Lovers," "Home for the Holidays" (with guest star Rue McClanahan), "Accidental Puppy," "The Commotion," "Mr. President," "Jill's Dream," "Pressure for Grandma," "Snowed In," "Charles R Us," "Charles' Spring Break" "The Wrong Guy" (with guest star Matthew Perry), "Mr. Brilliant," and "Meet Grandpa." The executive producer was Al Burton; the producers included Michael Jacobs and Roseanne Leto; the writers included Michael Jacobs, Barbara Weisberg, Peter Gethers, David Handler, Al Jean, Craig Kellem, Mike Reiss, David Simon, Shelley Zellman, Larry Balmagia, Mitchell Wayne Cohen, Eugene Lebowitz, and George Tibbles; the directors included Alan Rafkin and Tony Singletary. The creators were Barbara Weisberg and Michael Jacobs. Music was provided by Timothy Thompson and Todd Hayes. The theme song was written by Michael Jacobs, Al Burton and David Kurtz, and performed by Shandi Sinnamon. Baid was seen most recently in an ad for avocados during Super Bowl 50.

The Charmings Sternin and Fraser Ink/Embassy Television. ABC. Friday nights 8:00 (March 20, 1987–April 17, 1987), Thursday nights 8:30 (September 17, 1987–December 17, 1987) and Thursday nights 8:00 (January 7, 1988–February 11, 1988). Twenty-one episodes were videotaped before a live audience, only twenty aired.

The setup for this series takes longer to explain than the program lasted in prime-time. Every episode begins with the traditional "Once upon a time"—after all, it *is* a fairy-tale-cum-sitcom. Once upon a time, a wicked, vengeful queen was insanely jealous of her lovely stepdaughter, Snow White. So much so, that she poisoned her with an apple on which a spell was cast. Luckily, however, a handsome prince happened by, kissed Snow White, and broke the spell. That charming prince named Prince Charming aided Snow White in tossing the spiteful queen into a bottomless pit (talk about your dysfunctional family). The only problem was that the pit wasn't bottomless at all, but just very, very deep. The angry queen then cast a spell upon Prince Charming and his bride and they all slept for a thousand years. Eventually, the spell wears off and they find themselves, like fish out of water, in modern-day Van Oaks, California (near Los Angeles), attempting to adjust and conform. Much like when the cave people were brought back to the present day in the 1960s sitcom *It's About Time*, the Charmings are puzzled by technological wonders, such as lamps, television sets, and telephones. Early on, the prince wears tights and a suit of armor, and rides off to work each day on his mighty steed that lives in the garage. Stories of the slaying of dragons frighten the neighbors, the neighbors' children, and school faculty.

The program debuted on ABC in the spring of 1987 and had a six-episode run. Caitlin O'Heaney played the naïve and demure Snow White Charming; Christopher Rich portrayed her noble husband, the prince, Eric Charming; their children, Thomas and Cory, were played by Brandon Call and Garette Ratliffe, respectively; diminutive Cork Hubbert portrayed their housekeeper, Luther (one of the seven dwarfs); Dori Brenner and Paul Eiding played the perplexed next-door neighbors Sally and Don Miller, respectively (much in the manner of the Kravitzes on *Bewitched*); Judy Parfitt played the evil Queen Lillian White (and lives upstairs and possesses her own laugh-track machine), and Paul Winfield portrayed the sarcastic African American Magic Mirror in queen's bedroom. The Charmings eventually don modern clothing and acquire horsepower of the four-wheel variety, but never fully make the adjustment to the 20th century. The prince finds work as both a writer and a carpenter, and Snow discovers that she is a natural when it comes to fashion designing. In a couple of episodes, the Charmings reconnected with fellow fairy-tale characters, such as Cinderella and the giant from *Jack and the Beanstalk*.

Did the program's original Snow White have to audition for the role? Caitlin O'Heaney shared, "Yes, I auditioned, received a callback to read with Christopher [Rich] and then received an offer. I was well known from my previous work ... *Tales of The Gold Monkey*, *3 O'Clock High*, *He Knows You're Alone*, and all my guest star work. I was thrilled to get it! I really felt like I knew Snow White!"

The program's original run was six episodes in the spring of 1987, and it fared well enough to warrant a return for a second season (albeit, a truncated one). There were a couple of big differences, however—gone was O'Heaney as Snow White, replaced by Carol Huston, and also gone was the original Friday nightime slot. O'Heaney explained, "The night that the pilot aired, we were all watching it at a Chinese Restaurant in Universal City. Throughout the filming of the pilot everyone got along well ... specifically because no one knew who was going to get star billing ... that was at the producer's discretion. The moment that the credits rolled and 'Starring Caitlin O'Heaney' came on screen, Christopher Rich's face went white with anger. I was shocked and even more shocked when he no longer looked in my eyes when we acted, only at my forehead. The next morning I told my agents that I would be fired ... they laughed it off and told me how wonderful I was and that it would never happen. Judy Parfitt and Paul Winfield joined Christopher in his anger, jealousy, and verbal abuse toward me. It was *not fun*! And not long after, I *was* fired! The reason given by Robert Sternin was that 'my interpretation of Snow was not theirs,' which was not true. As I was cleaning out my dressing room, Robert appeared and told me the truth ... that Christopher, who was his and Prudence's good friend, was very angry with them because he had helped them come up with this idea [for] *The Charmings* ... and always assumed that he would get star billing. Now that I had received it he demanded that I be fired and star billing be given to him. Prudence was standing behind Robert this entire time telling him to be quiet! This is the truth. It hurt me very much because I couldn't care less about my billing, I care only about my work, and the wonderful fact that I have work. They all should have just asked me. The show would have most likely stayed on the air! How do I feel now? Well, that's showbiz! I have even more shocking stories about my time in Hollywood that will come out in my own memoir. For years all my fans have wondered why I was fired ... well, this was my experience!"

The program now aired on Thursday nights against *A Different World* on NBC's big *Cosby Show* night, and it was pulled from the lineup on February 11, 1988, with one episode still in the can (an episode that ran only in the UK). Surprisingly, in the early 1990s the reruns aired in syndication briefly on the short-lived "Ha" cable channel.

Episodes were titled (*Season One*) "The Charmings," "The Mirror Cracked," "Modern Romance" (with guest star Rip Taylor), "The Charmings Buy a Car," "The Incredible Shrinking Prince," and "An '80s Kind of Prince"; (*Season Two*) "Lillian Loses the Kids," "The Charmings Go Plastic," "The Witch Is of Van Oaks" (with guest star John Astin), "The Fish Story," "Cindy's Back in Town," "A Charming Halloween," "Trading Places," "Lillian Loses Her Powers" (with guest star Bernie Kopell), "The Charmings and the Beanstalk" (with guest star Teresa Ganzel), "Yes, Lillian, There Is a Santa Claus," "The Charmings Get Robbed," "Birth of a Salesman" (with guest star Robin Leach), "The Man Who Came to Dinner," "The Woman of His Dreams," and the unaired "Lillian's Protégé." The creators and executive producers were Robert Sternin and Prudence Fraser; the producers were Mark Fink, Al Lowenstein, and Roxie Wenk Evans; the writers included Robert Sternin, Prudence Fraser, Christopher Ames, Doug Bernstein, Mark Fink, Jay Folb, Jeff Greenstein, Ellen Guylas, Carrie Honigblum, Danny Kallis, Dennis Markel, Bob Myer, Lan O'Kun, Dan O'Shannon, Renee Phillips, Richard Reinhardt, Carolyn Shelby, Jeff Strauss, and Bob Young; and the directors included Mark Cullingham, Bill Foster, Gerren Keith, Will Mackenzie, Howard Murray, Mark Shea, and Phil Squyers. The program's theme song was by Ray Colcord. Things you may not have known about Caitlin O'Heaney—her great-great-great grandfather was the founder of what became the Pabst Brewing Company (his beer won many blue ribbons, hence the name); and she marketed her own cruelty-free fragrance called "Caitlin" from 1997 to 2005. She is a vegan and an active spokesperson for animal rights, seen most recently in the 2014 motion picture titled *Late Phases*.

Coming of Age Bungalow 78 Productions, Universal. CBS. Tuesday nights 9:00 (March 15, 1988–March 29, 1988), Monday nights 8:30 (October 24, 1988–November 21, 1988), and Thursday nights 9:30 (June 29, 1989–July 27, 1989). Fifteen episodes were filmed before a live audience, but only eleven aired.

This sitcom's credo was a quote from Russian theorist Leon Trotsky, who said, "Old age is the most unexpected of all things that happen to a man." Trotsky, however, didn't get to experience old age—he was murdered with an ice pick at the age of sixty. Pittsburgh native and retired pilot Dick Hale (who has just turned sixty), played by Broadway great Paul Dooley, is wishing for a similar fate after he and his bride, Judy (Phyllis Newman), take up residence in the Dunes Retirement Community (part of The Walnut Corporation) in condo 9C in the Arizona desert. Judy is thrilled with the area, but Dick views it as a waiting room for St. Peter, with its four-hole golf course, its casserole parade, and its sea of gray heads. He takes an instant dislike to the development's social director—the self-serving Brian Brinker (Kevin Pollak); the widow Birdy, who bangs pots and pans whenever he blocks her view of the sand dunes; and the daft Colonel Peck, who shoots skeet all day.

Even though Peck was not seen in the pilot episode, he was portrayed by Ray Goulding, of the famed Bob and Ray comedy team, in a later story, "Hale to the Chief," which also features his partner, Bob Elliott, as the colonel's brother, Peter, the association's sergeant-at-arms. It was "arguably the best" of the entire series, executive producer Barry Kemp told David Pollock, author of *Bob and Ray, Keener Than Most Persons*. It was plain to see, as Kemp pointed out in Pollock's book, that Ray was "having a very difficult time trying not to laugh because Bob is cracking him up.... They were just flat out funny.... Everybody from the writing staff to the cast was very excited to have them on.... Had the show survived, we undoubtedly would have brought them back because they would have been part of that community."

The terminally perky and positive Peppers live next-door—Trudy (Glynis Johns) and Ed (Alan Young). Ed is a retired chiropractor, and Trudy was his nurse. A running joke on the show is that his professional name was Dr. Pepper. Ed also picked out all of Trudy's clothing, sewed, cooked, made jewelry and shelf paper. Others in the complex include Wilma Salzgaber (Lenore Woodward); Marvel Whitsett (Pearl Shear), who has a pampered dog named Crystal; and the sexy blonde temptress Pauline Spencer (Ruta Lee), who takes an immediately liking to Dick Hale, leading Judy to incessantly remind her of his marital status.

Episodes were titled "Pilot," "Sopwith Pup" (with guest star Jerry Van Dyke), "A Wife in the Theatre," "Boy Meets Girl," "The Kids Are Coming, The Kids Are Coming," "Fever," "All I Wanted Was a New Car" (Parts One and Two), "Hale to the Chief" (with guest stars Bob and Ray), "Pauline et Rouge," "Todd Is My Co-Pilot," "Cindy Flies the Coop," "Christmas at the Dunes," "Daddy's Girl," and "Dick's Back." The executive producer was the prolific Barry Kemp; the producers were Penny Adams and Emily Marshall; the writers included Emily Marshall, Jeffrey Duteil, Sheree Guitar, Miriam Trogdon, and Michael Zinberg; the directors included Matthew Diamond, James Gardner, Michael Lembeck, and Tony Mordente. The creator was Emily Marshall. The show opened with a big-band number performed by Doc Severinsen and a bevy of old photos of the cast.

Day by Day Ubu Productions/Paramount Television. NBC. Monday night 8:30 (February 29, 1988), Thursday night 8:30 (March 3, 1988), and Sunday nights 8:30 (March 6, 1988–June 25, 1989). Thirty-three episodes were videotaped before a live audience.

Day by Day ran for two abbreviated seasons on NBC. Apparently, NBC had a lot of faith in the program's success, airing three episodes in its first week on the air. After debuting on Leap Day 1988, it eventually settled into its Sunday nightime slot for the rest of its stay in prime-time. Set in St. Louis, it focuses on Brian Harper (Douglas Sheehan), a very successful stockbroker and his wife, Kate Harper (*Lou Grant's* Linda Kelsey), a big-time attorney, and their decision to give up their lucrative-but-time-consuming careers to be with their children. They decide to open a daycare center in their spacious home. Their awkward, girl crazy, dedicated Bon Jovi fan and classic TV sitcom–obsessed teenaged son, Ross (Christopher Daniel Barnes), has his life suddenly turned upside-down with his mom and dad now constantly underfoot. The Harpers also had a new addition to the family—young Emily Harper (played by both Catherine and Mary Donahue).

Two of the program's co-stars went on to bigger and better things—Julia Louis-Dreyfus (later of the wildly successful *Seinfeld*, *Veep*, and *The New Adventures of Old Christine*) portrayed Brian's old business colleague and neighbor, Eileen Swift (not in the least a "kid person," she is perplexed by Brian's new career direction), and Courtney Thorne-Smith (later of the long-running *According to Jim*) played the Harpers' hot young daycare assistant, Kristin Carlson (much to the pleasure of young Ross). Thora Birch portrayed the Harpers' brightest ward, Molly. Actor Jack Blessing, who guest starred in several episodes, said, "You had to know then that Julia Louis-Dreyfus was going to be a big star, really obvious. Same was true for Courtney Thorne-Smith and Thora Birch, who played my daughter. Linda [Kelsey], if I remember correctly, was living in Ojai and commuting in." The program's most famous and fondly remembered episode reunited most of the cast of *The Brady Bunch* in one of Ross's dreams. Incidentally, Christopher Daniel Barnes later went on to play Greg Brady in the motion pictures *The Brady Bunch Movie* and *A Very Brady Sequel*. *Day by Day* had ties to *Family Ties*, and the crossover episode titled "Trading Places" was included in the *Family Ties* DVD box set.

About the experience, Meldrum said, "I recall Julia Louis-Dreyfus on this show as always being present and engaged—wonderfully brimming with love of the work. I also worked with her on *Seinfeld* years later, and I think her work is stellar on *Veep*. *Day by Day* was a real heart project for Gary David Goldberg. He had been the force behind getting daycare at Paramount. He also produced a pilot for me called *Morning Glory* that Henry Winkler had directed. It was a buddy comedy with an actress named Gayle Herd. ABC thought it was great, but it didn't go."

The executive producer was Andy Borowitz; the producers were June Galas, Janis Hirsch, and Werner Walian; writers included Philip LaZebnik, Janis Hirsch, Bruce Rasmussen, Matt Ember, Ben Cardinale, Katie Ford, Jeffrey J. Sachs, Peter Schneider, Susan Stevenson, Lloyd Garver, Judi Lampert, Susan Strauss, Andy Borowitz, and Gary David Goldberg. About Goldberg, Blessing shared, "Great guy, super supportive of every one of his cast and crew members. Maybe the best exec I have ever worked for. He was completely his own man, did things his way, and always seemed to ignore (actively) the network people. As I recall, Andy Borowitz ran this show and did a great job keeping the Goldberg/UBU vibe going."

The directors included Will Mackenzie, Matthew Diamond, Asaad Kelada, Sam Weisman, Carol Englehart Scott, Art Dielhenn, and Tony Mordente. Music and lyrics for the classic theme song were provided by Sammy Cahn, Axel Stordahl, and Paul Weston. Robert Kraft provided other music for the program.

Episodes were titled (*Season One*) "Birthday Presence," "How to Succeed in Day Care," "One Big Happy Family," "That Saturday Feeling," "Community Service," "Birth Wait," "What I Did for Love," "Great Expectations," "How Now, Dow Jones?," "Life at a Glance," "The Age of Dinosaurs," "Do You Think I'm Sexy?," and "Field Trip"; (*Season Two*) "My World and Welcome to It," "Won't You Be My Neighbor?," "Trading Places" (with guest stars Michael Gross and Bob Keeshan), "Girl Wars," "Harper and Son" (with guest star Leslie Nielsen), "Merry Kristin," "You Gotta Be a Football Hero," "Smart Women—Nice Refreshments," "Out for a Stretch," "The Music Man," "A Very Brady Episode" (with guest stars from the cast of *The Brady Bunch*), "My Momma Done Tol' Me," "Fraternity" (with guest star George Wendt), "Tears of a Clown," "Hairless Harper," "Three Men and a Babe," "Foul Play," "The Reunion," "Lost Weekend," and "Father Knows Best" (with guest star Wendel Meldrum).

Double Trouble Embassy Television. NBC. Wednesday nights 9:30 (April 4, 1984–May 30, 1984), Saturday nights 8:30 (December 1, 1984–March 30, 1985). Twenty-three episodes were videotaped before a live audience.

Double Trouble was a modern-day version of *The Patty Duke Show,* but with *two* sixteen-year-old actresses (real twins Liz and Jean Sagal) instead of just one playing both parts. Real twins also rendered *Double Trouble* a lot more credible than "identical cousins" Patty and Cathy Lane. Set in Des Moines, Iowa, Liz portrayed Allison—the anal-retentive twin who follows all the rules to the letter. Jean portrayed Kate—the one on Santa Claus's naughty list. Kate, a big fan of the rock group The Police, sometimes gets them in trouble with the real police. Kate has failed her driving test countless times, but Allison passed on the first try. Donnelly Rhodes portrayed their gray-haired, but very physically fit, widowed father, Art Foster. Conveniently, he owns a combination gym and dance studio, allowing the girls to show off their dancing chops. One of the instructors at the studio, Beth McConnell, was played by Patricia Richardson—the future Jill Taylor on *Home Improvement*. Kate briefly has a boyfriend, named Michael Gillette (Jon Caliri). This short first season consists of a mere eight episodes. The program wasn't a huge success, but fared just well enough to warrant a second season—a short second season with a few changes in format. The twins now reside in New York City. Allison is seeking a degree in fashion design, and Kate is attempting to find work as an actress. Gone were Art, Beth, and Michael. The twins now share part of a town house with their very odd aunt Margo (the ubiquitous Barbara Barrie), a writer of children's books. Adding a little spice to the show, two young men also rent part of the town house. Like Kate, they (Billy Batalato, played by Jonathan Schmock, and Charles Kincaid, played by James Vallely) are seeking work as actors. Michael D. Roberts played Mr. Arrechia—the stone-faced and demanding instructor at the fashion institute (a true Scrooge at Christmas), and Anne-Marie Johnson played Jamaican fashion student (and Allison's friend) Aileen Lewis.

Episodes were titled (*Season One*) "One Drives, the Other Doesn't," "Lust," "First Day," "Bad Chemistry," "Dueling Feet," "Separate Birthdays," "Hearthache," and "Bombshell"; (*Season Two*) "If We Can Make It Here," "Do You Believe in Magic?," "Dream Girls," "O Come All Ye Faithful," "Man for Margo," "The Boy Next Door," "Memories," "Two Girls for Every Boy," "The Write Stuff," "Commercial Break," "Old Movies," "September Song," "Funny Girl," "The Day of the Rose," and "Where's Poppa?" The executive producers were Saul Turteltaub and Bernie Orenstein; the producer was Janis Hirsch; the writers included Saul Turteltaub, Bernie Orenstein, Deidre Fay, James R. Stein, Bill Richmond, Don Reo, Ellen Potter, Lissa Levin, Susan Jane Lindner, Robert Illes, Janis Hirsch, Jill Gordon, Judith D. Allison, and David W. Duclon; the directors included Marlene Laird, Saul Turteltaub, Bernie Orenstein, Robert Illes, James R. Stein, John Pasquin, Ellen Falcon, Jim Drake, and John Bowab. The show's creators were David W. Duclon, Robert Illes, and James R. Stein. The theme song was written by Tom Snow and the lyrics by Dean Pitchford. Reruns of both truncated seasons were shown on the USA Network in the late 1980s and early 1990s.

Filthy Rich L. J. Bloodworth Productions/Larry White Productions/Columbia Pictures Television. CBS. Monday nights 9:30 (August 9, 1982–August 23, 1982), Wednes-

Real-life sisters Jean and Liz Sagal experienced *Double Trouble* and two short TV seasons on NBC.

day nights 9:30 (October 6, 1982–November 10, 1982), Monday nights 8:30 (January 17, 1983–February 14, 1983), and Wednesday nights 8:30 (June 8, 1983–June 15, 1983). Fifteen episodes were videotaped in front of a live audience.

The opening credits said it all—"A fact is a fact, you gotta clean up your act if you wanna be *Filthy Rich*." Spoofing *Dallas* and its ilk, *Filthy Rich* is an apt description of Big Guy Beck (played first in flashback sequences by Slim Pickens, and then Forrest Tucker). Beck has amassed amazing wealth and shortly before kicking the solid gold bucket (and being cryogenically frozen), he videotaped a series of stipulations that needed to be followed for his heirs to inherit his estate (each ending with a painful rendition of "Happy Trails to You"). The conditions to be met include his eldest, snootiest, and greediest son, Marshall (Michael Lombard); Marshall's equally materialistic wife, Carlotta (Dixie Carter); and Beck's own conniving second wife (many years his junior), Kathleen (Delta Burke)—none can collect on the will until they welcome Beck's illegitimate son, Wild Bill Westchester (Jerry Hardin), who sells used RVs for a living, and his daft-but-kindly aspiring-singer wife, Bootsie (Ann Wedgeworth), with open arms. All of them are to live under one roof and all have to get along at Beck's mansion, Toad Hall, in Memphis, Tennessee (no easy task). The setup is similar to a British series about inheritance, called *Nearest and Dearest*.

Others in the cast include Beck's senile first wife, Winona (Nedra Volz), nicknamed Mother B, who repeatedly escapes the nursing home in which she was placed; Beck's youngest son, the handsome, Dr. Pepper–loving Stanley (Charles Frank), who is independently wealthy and not vying for his father's fortune (he is also the nicest and most sane of the bunch). Stanley is Kathleen's stepson, and she finds him irresistible, but he consistently thwarts her unwelcome advances. His biological mother, Mother B, nicknamed him Skippy. The lawyer overseeing this mess is George Wilhoit (played by both David Healy and Vernon Weddle). It's interesting to note that Dixie Carter originally auditioned for the role of Bootsie, but the casting director just knew she'd make the ideal Carlotta.

At first CBS was on the fence about placing the sitcom on its schedule and three episodes were aired in a "limited run" capacity during the summer of 1982. The ratings for each of those Monday night airings were huge and it was invited back, but CBS had nowhere to put it. With a potential hit show on its hands, the network shelved *Mama Malone* (see entry) for a couple of seasons and quickly added *Filthy Rich* to its Wednesday night lineup. Surprisingly, now on Wednesday nights, the ratings instantaneously tanked and the show was yanked a month later. It was given yet another opportunity to prove itself on Monday nights in January and February, but the Nielsens were anemic and *Filthy Rich* was canceled. A couple of previously unaired episodes were burned off during June of that year. However, this was not the end of the line for Delta Burke, Dixie Carter and Linda Bloodworth-Thomason—just three short years later they all got to work together again on another sitcom about eccentric Southerners, this one called *Designing Women*, and after a very shaky start, enjoyed a seven-season run (and all three became "filthy rich").

Episodes were titled (*Season One*) "Pilot, Parts One and Two," and "Town and Garden"; (*Season Two*) "Some Like It Not," "Kidnapping of Stanley," "Real Men," "Happy Medium," "Take This Job and Love It, Parts One and Two," "The Country Club," "A Beck Goes Back," "Treasure off Toad Hall," "The Blue and the Gray for the Green," "First Heir," and "The Best Revenge Is Stealing Your Ex-Husband's Second Wife's Fiance." The executive producers were Linda Bloodworth-Thomason and Larry White; the producer was E. Jack Kaplan; the writers included Linda Bloodworth-Thomas, E. Jack Kaplan, Barry E. Blitzer, and Jim Brecher; the directors included Rod Daniel, Wes Kenney, and Bill Persky. Music was provided by Bucky Jones, and the theme song was performed by Ronnie McDowell.

Flo Warner Bros. Television. CBS. Monday nights 9:30 (March 24, 1980–April 28, 1980),

Monday nights 8:00 (October 27, 1980–January 26, 1981), Saturday nights 9:00 (February 7, 1981–February 28, 1981), Saturday nights 8:30 (March 14, 1981–April 18, 1981), and Tuesday nights 8:30 (June 23, 1981–June 30, 1981). Twenty-nine episodes were videotaped in front of a live audience.

Flo seemed like a permanent fixture on *Alice*, but many will be surprised to learn she was really only a part of that series for the first four of its nine seasons on CBS. In 1980, Florence Jean Castleberry (Polly Holliday), the sassy waitress at Mel's Diner (catchphrase: "Kiss my grits!") got her own spinoff, called simply *Flo*. Wanting to be closer to home, Flo leaves Mel's Diner in Phoenix, Arizona, for a waitressing job that has opened up in Houston, Texas. As if by divine intervention, she gets a flat tire while passing through her native Cowtown, Texas.

A lot had changed since she'd last been there, but the garage that worked on her car was next door to a favorite old hangout of hers—a broken down saloon called The Prairie Dog (with a sign on the wall that reads, "You have to work like a dog to live like a dog"). Flo had some of the best times of her life in that old watering hole, and, on a whim, decides to buy the establishment and puts down roots on her old stamping grounds. Even without any prior managerial experience, Flo believes she can still turn a profit. She meets with a lot of resistance from the bartender, Earl Tucker (Geoffrey Lewis), who doesn't cotton to the idea of working for a woman, but he eventually caves and opts to stay on at what is renamed Flo's Yellow Rose (with a big, gaudy yellow neon sign). The rest rooms bear the respective signs "Dudes" and "Darlins." Farley Waters (Jim B. Baker), the saloon's previous owner, is holding the deed until Flo is able to pay in full. Les Kincaid (Stephen Keep) is the chain-smoking piano player for the bar. Rusty Stumphill (Leo Burmester) is the mechanic next door who fixes Flo's flat tire, and also develops a healthy crush on her.

At home, Flo reconnects with her rowdy but very religious mother, Velma (Sudie Bond), and her refined, anal-retentive, bossy, and snooty sister Fran (Lucy Lee Flippin). Fran is an employee with the DMV, and has a steady boyfriend, Wendell (Terry Wills), of Tubbs Feed and Grain. The character of Wendell was written out in the sitcom's abbreviated second season, along with Flo's childhood friend Miriam (Joyce Bulifant). Bulifant recalled, "I asked to leave the show because Polly had creative control. I feel it is dangerous for leading actors to have control of a show. It is difficult when the star has control to be objective. After one show, a story that revolved around me, she asked the writers not to write any more story lines for me. That was all right except that Polly seemed not to be pleased with me. She was quite a task master and wanted the show to run just as she wanted it to. Because of this my perception was that of a very unhappy cast, myself included. Everyone in the cast had a theatre background and we all respected each other's work. The guest actors on the show may not have been aware of the underlying unhappiness on the set. I think Polly is an excellent actress and I would hope she would continue to perform."

Flippin, who portrayed Flo's snooty sister, added, "The program had two problems—the wonderful character of Flo was overused in the series, she was in almost every scene, as opposed to her brilliant showings in *Alice*. Also, Polly and Sudie Bond, who played Mama, did not get along, so domestic scenes were few compared to [those in] the bar locale. There was ongoing tension with Polly and Sudie. Additionally, there were too many main characters. I admired Polly's talent and discipline. She was wound a little tight, but it was her show! She was very gracious to me after a *Little House on the Prairie* episode I did and sent me an amazing telegram. And I adored Sudie. It was fun working with her." One of the program's writers, John Boni, added, "We writers heard all the rumblings of unhappiness on the set, but I must admit we writers had a great time writing for the show. If we had an idea, we pitched it. If it worked, we came up with the script. One might think that it would be difficult to write for a spinoff, but it really wasn't."

How difficult was it to deliver Miriam's lines with a Southern accent? Bulifant shared, "I was born in Virginia, but left at about age two. I was raised up and down the east coast in Southern states until age twelve when my mother and I moved to New York City. It was very easy for me to do a Southern accent, and I did one in the play *Vanities* as well." After twenty-nine episodes, *Flo* was gone from CBS's prime-time schedule, and Flo Castleberry did not return to *Alice*. Bulifant added, "I really liked Vic Tayback, who played Mel on *Alice*. He did a guest shot on *Flo* and I adored Vic, what a great guy he was." Boni concurred saying, "Tayback was just a big teddy bear. He was a joy to work with. *Alice* had both Linda Lavin and Tayback to carry it. I don't think *Flo* had legs as a spinoff. It's very hard for second bananas to suddenly become the main focus. Sometimes it works, but most times it doesn't." Flippin, who had a guest starring role on *Alice* (as a totally different character) several years after *Flo* was canceled, said, "I recall Vic Tayback and myself, standing in line in a bank, being very cranky and trying not to giggle." About another member of the cast of *Flo*, Flippin recalled, "Geoffrey Lewis was such a unique, laid-back character with a wry, slippery sense of humor. He and his wife had a pool party where we met a very young Juliette Lewis, his daughter." Regarding a few memorable guest stars, she added, "It was super exciting to have Hoyt Axton as a guest star, and Forrest Tucker as our father was thrilling and very emotional." Cast member Geoffrey Lewis died at the age of seventy-nine on April 7, 2015.

Episodes were titled (*Season One*) "Homecoming," "Showdown at the Yellow Rose," "Happy Birthday, Mama," "Take My Sister, Please," "The Hero of Flo's Yellow Rose," and "The Reunion"; (*Season Two*) "The Enemy Below," "Farley, the People's Choice," "Bull Is Back in Town," "A Castleberry Thanksgiving, Parts One and Two," (with guest star Forrest Tucker) "Willoughby vs. Willoughby," "So Long, Shorty," "Deserted Islands," "The Miracle of Casa de Huevos," "Grey Escape," "Pretty Baby," "Not with My Sister, You Don't," "The Price of Avocados, Parts One and Two," "Welcome to the Club," "Gunsmoke at the Yellow Rose," "What Are Friends For?" (with guest star Vic Tayback), "Just What the Doctor Ordered," "Footsie," "You Gotta Have Hoyt" (with guest star Hoyt Axton), "Flo's Encounter of the Third Kind," "No Men's Land," and "The Daynce." The executive producer was Jim Mulligan; the producers were Tom Biener, George Geiger, Bob Illes, and James R. Stein; the writers included Tom Biener, John Boni, David Brown, Dick Clair, Jenna McMahon, George Geiger, Robert Getchell, Bob Illes, Phillip Harrison Hahn, Ron Landry, Stephen A. Miller, Richard Orloff, and James R. Stein; the directors included Marc Daniels, Dick Martin, and Bob LaHendro. Music was provided by Susan Glicksman and Fred Werner. The theme song, "Flo's Yellow Rose," was performed by Hoyt Axton. A DVD box set of the series including all twenty-nine episodes was made available by Warner Bros. late in 2013.

FM MTM Productions. NBC. Thursday night 9:30 (August 17, 1989), Wednesday nights 9:30 (August 23, 1989–September 14, 1989, and March 28, 1990–April 18, 1990), Saturday nights 10:30 (May 26, 1990–June 9, 1990), and Thursday night 9:30 (June 28, 1990). Thirteen episodes were videotaped in front of a live audience.

Mythical 91.6 WGEO-FM, "Radio Free D.C." is the setting for the action in this short-lived situation comedy. Ted Costas (Robert Hays) is the program director, and he also hosts a daily music-intensive program titled *Long Day's Journey into Lunch*. Ted is neither the most patient nor diplomatic boss—qualities that are amplified by the return of his ex-wife, Lee Ann Plunkett (Patricia Richardson). After her divorce from Ted, she left the radio station for three years, but was suddenly back to co-host a talk show called *Toe-to-Toe* with the pompous and condescending Harrison Green (Fred Applegate). Right from the get-go, it is obvious that Ted and Lee Ann will soon come to loggerheads. Even though this was an FM radio station and not a TV news show, the 2007 sitcom set in a TV newsroom, *Back to You*, bore a strong resemblance. Ted and Lee Ann still care about each other, and while both have moved on with their lives after the divorce, some small part of each of them wants to be a couple again. Their fifteen-year-old daughter, Maude (Nicole Huntington), also wants them to reunite. However, there is always something standing in their way—like a gorgeous new blond assistant named Gretchen Schreck (DeLane Matthews), for whom both Ted and the station's longtime volunteer Jay Edgar (Leo Geter) have the hots. It's interesting to note that Lawrence Pressman's actor son, David, was originally up for the role of Jay Edgar, but at the last minute it went to Geter (although Pressman still got a small role in the debut episode). Others on the staff included Quentin Lamoreaux (James Avery), who has double duty as both a classical and reggae music show host (under the alias of "The Mighty Doctor Q"); station manager Naomi Sayers (Naomi Thigpen), one of the few sane members of this radio asylum; Daryl Tarses (Rainbow Harvest), the knockout female computer wizard who is also a nude model and a barmaid; and Don "the voice man" Baumgartner (John Kassir) who can imitate anybody and anything. Most of the show's action takes place on the job, but there is an occasional scene at the staff's favorite D.C. hangout, a bar called P. J's. After a short late-summer run in 1989, the program returned midseason in 1990 with more new episodes. The program bounced around on the schedule quite a bit, attempting to find an audience, and was soon modulating with very little frequency.

Episodes were titled (*Season One*) "Love or Money," "Play Laura for Me," "Ultimate Aphrodisiac," "Kiss and Tell," and "If a Man Answers"; (*Season Two*) "Doing It Again," "Leave It to Me," "Two Taxing Women," "No Fool like an April Fool," "Let's Spend the Night Together," "The Last Virgin," "Sex, Lies, and 35mm Slides," and "Off the Record." The executive producers were Allan Burns and Dan Wilcox; the producer was Andy Cadiff; the writers included Allan Burns, Dan Wilcox, Shelley Zellman, and Howard Michael Gould; the directors included Andy Cadiff, Dan Wilcox, David Trainer, and Burt Metcalfe. The creators were Allan Burns, Dan Wilcox, and Shelley Zellman. Music was supplied by Eddie Karam, and the theme song by Patrick Williams.

Good Morning, Miss Bliss Peter Engel Productions/NBC Productions. The Disney Channel. Air dates and times varied (November 30, 1988–March 18, 1989). Fourteen episodes were videotaped with a laugh track.

In the original *Good Morning, Miss Bliss* pilot, Miss Carrie Bliss (Hayley Mills) is a newlywed—she'd gotten married to a man named Charles Davis over summer vacation. Even though she is officially Mrs. Davis, she still has her students call her Miss Bliss. In said pilot, the unnmamed grammar school is in Indianapolis, and the students (Jaleel White as Bobby Wilson; Brian Austin Green as Adam, Matt Shakman as Georgie) and faculty (Oliver Clark as Principal Gerald Belding; Maria O'Brien as Tina Paladrino) are very different from the cast that made it into the actual series (the pilot also contains heavier subject matter than did the much lighter series). The pilot was almost completely overhauled and Hayley's character became a widow, now teaching eighth grade history in room 103 at John F. Kennedy Junior High (still in Indianapolis). The one constant is that she cares almost too deeply about her students, and her meddling in their affairs sometimes leads to even bigger problems.

The young actors portraying the students were the nucleus of what would later be called *Saved by the Bell*—Mark-Paul Gosselaar was Zack Morris, the girl-crazy dreamer/schemer; Lark Voorhies was wealthy fashion plate Lisa Turtle; Dustin Diamond was Screech Powers, the dweeb with the distinguished title of "glue monitor"; and Heather Hopper was the outspoken, cause-driven Nikki Coleman. The faculty consisted of T. K. Carter as Mylo Williams; a different actress playing Tina Paladrino (Joan Ryan); and a different actor playing Principal

Richard (no longer Gerald) Belding (Dennis Haskins). It's interesting to note that one of the episodes (no. ten) was titled "Let's Get Together"—a title that paid homage to Hayley Mills' Top Ten hit record from the movie *The Parent Trap*.

Writer R. J. Colleary recalled, "I started as of episode five. Hayley Mills is lovely and one of the nicest people I've ever worked with, but she was not terribly funny. It's rare that overhauled shows succeed, but when this series was retooled, apparently everything was done right. It was almost like the dream sequence on *Dallas*—we started over as if none of the previous shows had occurred. We kept most of the same writers, but the only consistent cast members were Screech, Zack, and Belding. Even the school and its location was different."

After fourteen episodes, Hayley Mills was dropped from the cast, the title of the show became *Saved by the Bell*, the program moved over as a live-action Saturday morning program on NBC, the setting was now Bayside High School in Pacific Palisades, California, and both Mario Lopez and Tiffani-Amber Thiessen joined the cast. The series became immensely popular and ran for four seasons, and led to sequels. Colleary said, "The *Good Morning, Miss Bliss* episodes became part of the *Saved by the Bell* syndication package without the original opening credits, with Zack introducing each episode as being 'from our junior high days,' even though it was set in a different school in a very different city."

About the cast, Colleary said, "Everyone was very nice. Dennis Haskins truly embraced his character, and still does countless appearances as Belding—award ceremonies, openings, autograph shows. Dustin Diamond was always different. He was an odd kid, as was his dad, who also appeared in a few episodes of the series. He really was Screech and a true teenage drama. He participated in the entire run and all of the sequels. Things got weirder in the *Saved by the Bell* days."

Episodes were titled "The Pilot," "Summer Love," "Love Letters," "Wall Street," "Leaping to Conclusions," "Parents and Teachers," "Showdown," "Save the Last Dance for Me," "The Boy Who Cried Rat," "Let's Get Together," "Practical Jokes," "Stevie," "Clubs and Cliques," and "The Mentor." The executive producer was Peter Engel; the producers were Sam Bobrick, Marica Govons, and Bennett Tramer; the writers included Michael Poryes, Sam Bobrick, Peter Engel, Diana Ayers, Susan Sebastian, Lawrence H. Levy, Skip Frank, Jim Carlson, Terrence McDonnell, Gwyn Gurian, Jack and Mike Weinberger, Howard Ostroff, and Jeffrey J. Sachs; the directors included Burt Brinckerhoff, Gary Shimokawa, and Peter Bonerz. The creator was Sam Bobrick. Music was provided by Scott Gale and Charles Fox.

Goodnight, Beantown Bixby-Brandon Productions/Warner Bros. Television. CBS. Sunday nights 8:00 (April 3, 1983–April 30, 1983), Sunday nights 9:30 (October 1, 1983–January 18, 1984). 18 episodes were filmed single-camera style with a laugh track.

Matt Cassidy (Bill Bixby), a bachelor, has been the lone nightly newscaster for WYN-TV Channel 11 in Boston ever since the days of Nehru jackets in the 1960s. He ends every broadcast with the words "Goodnight, Beantown," hence the title. However, after ratings began to slip on his *Six O'Clock Report* (to no. three in a three-station market), management decides to add a female co-anchor because "team newscasts" are all the rage in town. The news program airs immediately after reruns of *Gomer Pyle, U.S.M.C.* on WYN. Management—egged on by the station's owner, a character nicknamed "The Colonel"—made this monumental decision, however, without first notifying or consulting Cassidy. In a major metropolis such as Boston, the odds of his new co-host living next door to him were astronomical, and yet it happened. In fact, they meet as she (Mariette Hartley, as Jennifer Barnes, formerly of Sacramento) is moving into the apartment building (with the number 321 on its edifice) even before they realize that they will soon be co-workers. Her armoire gets stuck in the doorway and he has to climb through her apartment window to get to his apartment (and, in the process, he

Mariette Hartley and Bill Bixby portrayed newscasters, neighbors, and (eventual) romantic partners in CBS's *Goodnight, Beantown*.

tears his pants). Barnes's teenage daughter Susan was played by Tracey Gold (pre–*Growing Pains*). Gold's Susan character immediately notices a chemistry between her mom and Matt, and quickly engages in trying to get them engaged. Their initial TV newscasts are icy and uncomfortable, but a huge positive reaction from viewers thaws things out considerably. They, in fact, become friends, and then more-than-friends off the air. His nickname for her is "Red." Dick Novak (George Coe) is their harried program director; Sam Holliday (Charles Levin) is their news director, formerly of Cleveland (he made his first appearance on the program's second episode). Added in the show's abbreviated second season were Albert Adelson (G. W. Bailey), Valerie (Stephanie Faracy), and Frank Fletcher (Jim Staahl).

The program's first season consists of only six trial episodes. It did well enough to warrant a second season on CBS, but much like Cassidy's newscasts, the ratings were down, and after twelve episodes in Season Two, *everyone* said "Goodnight, Beantown" for good. Mariette Hartley was nominated for an Emmy for "Outstanding Lead Actress in a Comedy Series" for her work as Barnes, but did not win.

Episodes were titled (*Season One*) "The Pilot," "The Out-of-Towner," "The Source" (with guest star Jean Smart), "Custody" (with guest star Jim MacKrell), and "Please Stand By"; (*Season Two*) "Hooking for Mr. Goodbar," "What's Good for the Goose," "A Felon Needs a Girl," "Invasions of Privacy," "Popsicle," "Our Man in the Slammer," "Looking Forward to the Past" (with guest star James Hampton), "Happy Medium," "Valerie's Fan," "An Old Flame Flickers," "Peace on Earth" (with guest star Richard Sanders), "The Consumer's Best Friend" (with guest star Dick Gautier), and "Lost and

Foundering" (with guest star Ron Masak). The executive producers were Bill Bixby, Paul Treva Brandon, and A. J. Carothers; the producers included Charles B. Fitzsimmons and Steve Kline; the writers included Bill and Kathy Greer, A. J. and Gibson Carothers, Ron Osborn, Jeff Reno, Steve Kline, Elias Davis, and David Pollock; the directors included Harry Winer, Bill Bixby, Bob Sweeney, Peter Baldwin, Kim Friedman, Alan Bergmann, Will Mackenzie, Dick Martin, and David Nelson. Music was provided by Dennis McCarthy.

Harper Valley see ***Harper Valley P. T. A.***

Harper Valley, P.T.A. Redwood Productions (*Season One*)/Ten-Four Productions (*Season Two*)/Universal Television. NBC. Friday nights 8:00 (January 16, 1981–May 1, 1981), Thursday nights 8:00 (October 29, 1981–November 19, 1981), Saturday nights 8:00 (December 12, 1981–January 2, 1982), Saturday nights 8:30 (January 23, 1982–February 27, 1982), Saturday nights 8:00 (April 10, 1982–May 1, 1982). Thirty episodes were filmed with a laugh track.

Initially considered as an hour-long sitcom, but halved before filming began, *Harper Valley P.T.A.* was based on the classic 1968 number-one pop hit, written by Tom T. Hall and recorded by Jeannie C. Riley for Plantation Records. The lyrics tell the tale of Stella Johnson (Barbara Eden)—a widowed mother who moves to Harper Valley, Ohio, with her thirteen-year-old daughter, Dee (Jenn Thompson); the number on their mailbox is 769. Stella sells Angel Glow cosmetics, door to door. She isn't accepted by the women in town, who accuse her of having loose morals and of being a bad influence upon her own daughter. In reality, they are envious of her youth and beauty, and how much attention she is receiving from their husbands. It doesn't help matters any that Stella often wears miniskirts and is a women's libber.

Barbara Eden first played Stella in the 1978 movie version. The movie did extremely well in the ratings when it aired on NBC, and the network execs quickly decided to turn it into a series. One of the program's producers and writers, Dave Hackel, shared, "Barbara Eden was, as you might guess, just charming and set a nice tone for the work environment of the stage." The Season One title for the series was *Harper Valley P. T. A.*, and while Stella is a board member of Harper Valley Junior High's P.T.A., said board try everything to remove her and drum her out of town. The only person in town who is in Stella's corner is Cassie Bowman (Fannie Flagg), who operates La Moderne Beauty Shop in Season One, and the local *Sentinel* newspaper in Season Two. Together, Stella and Cassie scheme (much like Lucy Ricardo and Ethel Mertz on *I Love Lucy*) to "sock it to" the Harper Valley P.T.A.

At the top of the heap of adversaries and gossips is one Flora Simpson Reilly (Anne Francine)—the snooty head of Harper Valley society; following very closely in her footsteps is her daughter, Wanda (Bridget Hanley); her attorney son-in-law, Bobby (Rod McCary); her granddaughter, Scarlett Taylor (Suzi Dean); and the egotistical junior high school coach Cliff Willoughby (Robert Gray), to name but a few. Harper Valley was named for the Harper family. A member of that family is the town's mayor—the oft-intoxicated Otis Harper (Lonesome George Gobel).

The first season of the series did just well enough to warrant a second, but changes were afoot. The P.T.A. part of the show (and the show's title) was eliminated. The focus shifted to Stella's home life, and a new character was added to the fray—Winslow "Uncle Buster" Smith (Mills Watson), an inventor with great ideas but not-so-great follow through. About one particular episode from that second season, titled "Grizzly Gap," writer/producer Dave Hackel recalled, "Steve Hattman and I wrote that episode and Neville Brand was the guest star in one of his last performances. Everyone was quite excited to work with him because we'd known him from many of the classic westerns of our youth, as well as his portrayal of Al Capone on *The Untouchables*. I do remember that everyone was a bit nervous to have him on the set because I think we all confused him with his convincing villainous performances." For whatever reason, the series began to falter in the ratings in its second season, even with numerous different time slots. So after two short seasons and a total of thirty episodes, NBC socked it to *Harper Valley*. The program was briefly rerun on the TV Land cable network. It should be noted that Barbara Eden donned a costume almost identical to that of her *I Dream of Jeannie* character in this program's third episode in Season One, titled "Mail and Female." Even though it was well over a decade since she and Major Nelson left prime-time, it still fit like a glove.

Episodes were titled (*Season One*) "To Dunk or Not to Dunk," "A Husband for Sale," "Mail and Female," "Don Juan and Two," "The Life of Reilly," "Moonlighting Becomes You," "A Tree Grows in Harper Valley," "Dirty Tricks," "Stella and Howard," "Mayor Bobby," "Bad Day at Harper Valley," and "My Fair Stella"; (*Season Two*) "Make Room for Buster," "Good for the Goose," "Reunion Fever," "$500 Misunderstanding," "Stella's Scam" (with guest star Abe Vigoda), "Harper Valley Christmas" (with guest star Stubby Kaye), "Low Noon," "Flora's Dinner Party," "The Show Must Go On" (with guest star Larry Storch), "Firechief Follies," "Svengali of the Valley," "Stella Della," "Stella Rae," "Harper Valley Hoedown," "Grizzly Gap" (with guest star Neville Brand), "Return of Charlie's Chow Palace" (with guest star Joyce Bulifant), and "Harper Valley Sentinel." The executive producers were Sherwood Schwartz, Greg Strangis, Sam Strangis, and Lloyd J. Schwartz; the producers were Dave Hackel, Steve Hattman, Les Sheldon, Jerry Ross, Arthur E. McLaird, Gordon "Whitey" Mitchell, and Edward Montagne; the writers included Dave Hackel, Steve Hattman, Judy Gabriel, Phil Mishkin, Jordan Moffet, Lloyd J. Schwartz, Sherwood Schwartz, Jerry Davis, Jerry Rannow, Joan Brooker, Bill Dial, Richard Freiman, Ron Friedman, David P. Harmon, Charles Isaacs, Lou Messina, Jackie McKane, Warren S. Murray, Gordon "Whitey" Mitchell, Brad Radnitz, Jerry Ross, Missy Stewart Taggart, Diane Messina Stanley, Alexandra Stoddart, Amy and Malcolm Webb, Joel Tappis, Donald Ross, Greg Strangis, and Mike Weinberger; the directors included Alan Cooke, William Asher, Nick Havinga, George Tyne, Leslie H. Martinson, Rod Daniel, Alan Myerson, Claudio Guzman, Bruce Bilson, Sigmund Neufeld, Jr., and Richard C. Bennett. Music used was by Nelson Riddle and Arthur Rubinstein.

Hello, Larry TAT Communications/Columbia Pictures Television. NBC. Friday nights 9:30 (January 26, 1979–February 9, 1979), Friday nights 8:30 (February 16, 1979–October 19, 1979), and Wednesday nights 9:30 (October 24, 1979–April 30, 1980). Thirty-eight episodes were videotaped in front of a live audience.

This was McLean Stevenson's third attempt (there were still two more to come) to make a splash after unwisely leaving *M*A*S*H*. *Hello, Larry* lasted longer than any of the others—a season and a half. Here he portrayed Larry Alder, a radio talk show host who left Los Angeles after his divorce from his wife, Marion (Shelley Fabares). He then relocates with his two daughters, Diane (first played by Donna Wilkes and then Krista Errickson), and Ruthie (Kim Richards). Larry is now working full time in Portland, Oregon, at KLOW-AM, and his boss (also his neighbor) is the lovely Morgan Winslow (Joanna Gleason, Monty Hall's daughter). Morgan also resides in the same apartment building as Larry, as does a snarky twelve-year-old named Tommy Roscini (John Femia); Tommy's mother, Marie (Rita Taggart); schoolteacher Leona Wilson (played by legendary R&B singer Ruth Brown); and Harlem Globetrotter and sporting goods store owner Meadowlark Lemon as himself. In Season Two, Larry's father, Henry (Fred Stuthman), comes to live with the Alder family in Portland. Henry's favorite phrase is "bull pucky." Also working at the radio station (in Season One) Earl (George Memmoli), a morbidly obese engineer.

About McLean Stevenson's reputation for being difficult to work with, John Femia shared, "McLean was one of the funniest men I've ever met. He made me laugh constantly. Yes, he was extremely difficult to work with. However, in light of the bad to mediocre scripts, I felt he was right. Had they given him more control over the writing (which he took over anyway, after a while), the show could have been much funnier. Off the set, he was a funny, sweet and generous man. On the set, he ranged from being difficult to extremely horrid. From a quality standpoint, he was absolutely right. But sometimes his mood would upset other cast members. I remember he yelled at Kim [Richards] once over something which I can't remember. He also yelled at me once, but he did apologize afterwards. In fact, *Hello, Larry* became funnier as a result of his control-freak nature as the second season progressed, so his behavior was justified. NBC, however, did not see it that way. The show had mediocre ratings, which actually improved over time. When *The Facts of Life* premiered that year, their ratings were in the cellar. At the end of the year, the network had one slot left to fill for the next season, and because of McLean's behavior, it fell to *Facts* by default. The rest is history."

Hello, Larry was often a crossover show with the hit NBC sitcom *Diff'rent Strokes*, about which Femia reflected, "The story went that Phillip Drummond [Conrad Bain] and Larry Alder were Korean War buddies, which to my knowledge was the first ever melding of two different shows into one, as opposed to a spinoff of characters from a separate show. This became my first big show-biz disappointment, because at the time it was my dream to work with Gary Coleman, the biggest star NBC had, next to Bob Hope. I almost had my chance during the crossover when the Alders came to New York. There was one scene solely between Gary and me, but either Gary or his parents resented anyone who was funnier than he was, and they had the power of veto. So, the scene was cut and I never did the taping."

Femia remembered a funny behind-the-scenes story about the crossover shows: "McLean once told me that Gary Coleman had a pet mouse, which he kept in the schoolroom next to the rehearsal halls. Somehow, the mouse was left there after the first season of *Diff'rent Strokes*. It was a female mouse, and it was pregnant. When everyone returned for the next season, the schoolroom had not been opened all throughout the hiatus. When the door was finally opened, it became a scene from the movie *Willard*. Hundreds of mice ran out of the room and all throughout Metromedia Square! The exterminator they hired obviously walked into a gold mine."

Asked to describe his own character of Tommy Roscini on the show, Femia chuckled and said, "Tommy Roscini was a horny twelve-year-old kid looking to rub himself against the Alder sisters, especially Ruthie. He moved out of Brooklyn to Portland with his mother, who raised Tommy by herself after his father had abandoned him. So, he took to the Alders as the family he never had, as his mom evidently was too busy to look after him, either. Shortly after *Hello, Larry* ended, I got a call from executive producer Perry Grant. He said he wanted to reprise my character, but make him slightly different from Tommy, for the hit show *One Day at a Time*. Would I be interested? Absolutely! However, I had previously worked with Danny Wilson and his production company—they produced the show *Here's Boomer*. Danny cast me as the lead in one of the *Boomer* episodes. As it turned out, I was shooting that episode when it was time for *One Day at a Time* to go into production, and since I was unavailable, they cast Glenn Scarpelli, who is one of my good friends. Not really a disappointment as it turned out, because if not for that, I wouldn't have been available for *Square Pegs* [see entry]."

About his co-star singer Ruth Brown, Femia said, "Ruth was a dear woman, and one of my favorite singers of all time now, and before I met her. My father had a collection of her records, both 45s and 78s, which I listened to constantly. She was astounded by my knowledge of her catalog and we became very close. She had an amazing voice and was one of the more underappreciated blues singers in history."

About the disappearance of George Memmoli after Season One, Femia shared, "While it can be argued that it was impossible for George to disappear, I think McLean resented all the old, stupid fat jokes, which were *very* old, *very* stupid, and *very* unfunny. The first season was basically ignorant fat and sex jokes. When Meadowlark, Fred, and I joined in Season Two, all our characters improved the dynamics greatly. I liked George also, so while I felt bad about it at the time, it really was for the greater good."

There was one other noticeable change in Season Two—the elder of the two Alder daughters, Diane, was played by Krista Errickson instead of Donna Wilkes. About that personnel change, Femia recalled, "It's a bit weird, actually. I really liked Donna, so it's kind of a shame. I know that she and McLean had a major disagreement, so McLean had her fired. We did a taping of the first episode of Season Two with Donna ["Hello Marion, Part One"] and I don't know if NBC kept the footage. Then, believe it or not, there was *another* Diane—I only remember her first name was Wendy. We did a second taping of that episode, and NBC felt she wasn't right for it. Krista was the third choice for Diane, and I guess the network liked the chemistry between her and Kim Richards."

Hello, Larry employed numerous seasoned sitcom-writing veterans. According to Femia, "Most of Larry's writers, except for Woody Kling, Dick Bensfield and Perry Grant, were all throwbacks to famous 1960s sitcoms, and it showed in the writing. Its sensibilities were rehashings of old family-style sitcoms, mixed with cheap sex and fat jokes. I guess if I had to pick my favorite writers, it would be George Tibbles and Woody Kling, both of whom were always very nice to me."

On *Square Pegs*, Femia worked single-camera style with a laugh track, but *Hello, Larry* was videotaped in front of a live audience. "I've always loved live audiences. I love doing theater and stand-up comedy for that reason, and it's my biggest regret about Larry being canceled, because I had the time of my life performing. I'm not a fan of the one-camera shoot, although it is good training if you do a movie. I've always hated laugh tracks, and I've always felt *Square Pegs* would have worked better without one. To my knowledge, it was one of the very last sitcoms that had one."

Hello, Larry was a TAT Communications show, so how involved was Norman Lear in its production? Femia: "Not at all. In fact, I've never met the man. I know Tandem was a mutual partnership between Lear and Bud Yorkin, but the main producers who had hands-on were Alan Horn and Al Burton, also of *The Facts of Life*."

The writers for this series loved multiple part episodes. Episodes were titled (*Season One*) "How to Not to," "The New Kid," "The Final Papers," "The Hitchhiker," "Mother Morgan," "Ruthie's First Crush," "Larry's First Date," "Peer Pressure," "Leona, the New Neighbor," "The Trip Part Two" (a crossover with *Diff'rent Strokes*, with guest star Edie McClurg), "The Triangle," "Larry's Bad Back," "Rap with Ruthie," and "My Sister, the Criminal"; (*Season Two*) "Feudin' and Fussin,' Part Two (a crossover with *Diff'rent Strokes*), "Hello, Marion, Parts One, Two, and Three," "Ruthie Grows Up, Parts One and Two," "The Thanksgiving Crossover, Part Two" (with *Diff'rent Strokes* cast), "The Nude Emcee," "Morgan, the Boss," "Marion's Fiance," "Diane Drinks" (with guest star Frank Aletter), "Tommy, the Houseguest," "Larry's Father," "The Blind Friend," "Love around the Corner," "The Neighbor Dies," "Money from Home," "Larry's Midlife Crisis, Parts One, Two, and Three" (with guest star Parley Baer), "The Rock Star, Parts One and Two," "The Protégé" (with guest star Gloria DeHaven), and "Yearning." The executive producers were Dick Bensfield, Perry Grant, and Howard Leeds; the producers were Alan Horn, Al Burton, Heywood "Woody" Kling, Ben Starr, Herbert Kenwith, and Martin Cohan; the writers included Dick Bensfield, Perry Grant, George Tibbles, Barbara Tibbles, Doug Tibbles, Woody Kling, Al Gordon, Jack Mendelsohn, Dick Chevillat, Jay Sommers, Milt Rosen, Norman Paul, Wayne Kline, Lois Hire, Howard Albrecht, Celia Bonaduce, Martin Cohan, Earle Doud, Mark Fink, Sol Weinstein, Bambi Burton, Mitchell Wayne Cohen, Michael Endler,

Elaine Newman, Glenn Padnick, and Ralph Phillips; the directors were Doug Rogers and Art Dielhenn. The theme song was by John LaSalle and Tom Smith. The program was very loosely based upon a film titled *Wednesday* by Marvin Kupfer and Barbara Witus. Meadowlark Lemon died on December 27, 2015 at the age of 83.

Joanie Loves Chachi Paramount Television. ABC. Tuesday nights 8:30 (March 23, 1982–April 13, 1982), Thursday nights 8:00 (September 30, 1982–December 16, 1982), and Tuesday nights 8:30 (May 17, 1983–September 13, 1983). Seventeen episodes were filmed in front of a live audience.

This *Happy Days* spinoff started strong on its four-week trial run in the spring of 1982, and earned a spot on ABC's fall lineup that year as a result. However, the ratings for the second season were far from spectacular, and the show was placed on hiatus shortly before Christmas of that same year. The premise was a bit of a stretch. Al Delvecchio (Al Molinaro) had married Chachi Arcola's (Scott Baio's) mom, Louisa (Ellen Travolta), and moved to Chicago to open Delvecchio's Family Restaurant at 1632 Palmer Avenue (and he and his new bride lived in the apartment directly above their place of business). Al, a new member of the Chicago Leopard Lodge, was now Chachi's stepfather. Chachi then gets a job singing in Al's new establishment, and a grown-up Joanie Cunningham (Erin Moran), now a college student, is his romantic interest. She also becomes a vocalist in the band. The only issue Chachi has with Joanie is her cooking. Two other bandmates are cousins of the Arcola family—the food-obsessed, insecure, and eternally dateless Annette (Winifred Freedman), and her skinny brother Mario Mastorelli (Derrel Maury), who always seems to be in the wrong place at the wrong time. (Mario rarely had more than one or two lines per show.) The band's drummer, Bingo (Robert Peirce), is the exception—he

Joanie Loves Chachi **takes the stage. Pictured (left to right): Derrel Maury, Scott Baio, Erin Moran, Robert Peirce and Winifred Freedman (photograph courtesy Joel Zwick).**

isn't family, and he seems to have come from Mars. He usually wears shorts and sandals with his sports jacket on stage, and is utterly oblivious to all goings-on, including the endings of songs. Louisa's older brother, the very frugal Rico Mastorelli (Art Metrano), also Annette and Mario's dad, is ostensibly the band's manager, exhibiting many old Chicago gangster-esque traits (but down deep, he is a big softy).

Athough the program was set in the 1960s, the music created by Joanie and Chachi had much more of a 1980s feel. Director Joel Zwick called it "upgrading. Viewers for this series were likely to be of a younger demographic, so the music reflected that somewhat." There were many visits from Milwaukee's *Happy Days* cast—Howard and Marion Cunningham (Tom Bosley and Marion Ross) guest starred in the debut episode, "Chicago," and in "Joanie's Roommate." Fonzie (Henry Winkler) appropriately guest starred in the episode titled "Fonzie's Visit." Winkler also directed the "Best Foot Forward" episode.

Actor/comedian Bill Kirchenbauer guest starred in the episode titled "Goodbye Delvecchio's, Hello World" and recalled, "It took us two weeks to shoot it. Joanie [Erin] was sick the first week. They also celebrated Scott Baio's birthday on the set during that time. Pamela Anderson, before she was famous, had flown in for the occasion, and I remember thinking what a lucky guy he was."

Director Joel Zwick said, "Perhaps, as an actor, Scott Baio, who is a dear, sweet man, was not yet ready to be the center of attention with his own show—but he certainly grew to be a leading man. Although they were both troopers and true professionals, Erin and Scott weren't exactly the best of friends at this time in their relationship. They reportedly had dated while still on *Happy Days*, but had broken up by the time they were spun off into their own show. However, in later years Erin claimed that she had been pressured into a romance with Scott. Whatever the situation, on camera it appeared that Joanie did indeed love Chachi, and vice versa. It was probably a stipulation in their contracts that if the spinoff failed, they would be able to return to *Happy Days*, unlike *The Ropers* of *Three's Company* or *Flo* of *Alice*. Al Molinaro apparently had the same deal. They all rejoined the *Happy Days* fray."

The live studio audience was very raucous and rambunctious on *Joanie Loves Chachi*, making editing the show somewhat difficult, Zwick said. "We recorded the audience's responses and laughter on a separate track. Sure, there was still some bleed through, but the track separation made it easier to smooth out necessary edits."

Episodes were titled "Chicago" (with guest stars Tom Bosley and Marion Ross), "The Performance," "I Do, I Don't, I Do," "College Days," "Fonzie's Visit" (with guest star Henry Winkler), "Joanie's Roommate" (with guest stars Tom Bosley and Marion Ross), "One-On-One," "No Nudes Is Good Nudes," "Everybody Loves Aunt Vanessa" (with guest star Jessica Walter), "Beatlemania," "Best Foot Forward," "Goodbye Delvecchio's, Hello World" (with guest star Bill Kirchenbauer), "Term Paper," "My Dinner with Chachi," "Christmas Show," "First Love Last Love," and "The Elopement." The executive producers were Garry Marshall, Lowell Ganz, Ronny Hallin (Garry Marshall's sister), Thomas L. Miller, and Robert L. Boyett; the producers included James Patrick Dunne and Fred Fox, Jr.; the writers included Lowell Ganz, Terry Hart, James P. Dunne, Cheryl Alu, George Tricker, Neil Rosen, William Bickley, Cindy Begel, Lesa Kite, Nancy Churnin, Nancy Eddo, Joan Brooker, Steve Granat, Fred Fox, Jr., Barry O'Brien, Larry Levinson, Dana Olsen, Gary Menteer, Paula A. Roth, Michael Warren, Millee Taggart, and Mel Sherer; the directors included Joel Zwick, Tom Trbovich, Howard Storm, Lowell Ganz, Henry Winkler, and John Tracy. Kirchenbauer shared, "John Tracy was a really good director. He loved to hear himself talk, but he was a really good director. He directed *Growing Pains*, and the pilot for my show *Just the Ten of Us*. He used a lot of football analogies in his direction." The creators were Lowell Ganz and Garry Marshall. Music was provided by Dan Foliart and Howard Pearl. The theme song, "You Look at Me," was written by James P. Dunne and Pamela Phillips. A DVD box set of all seventeen episodes was made available by CBS Entertainment just in time for Valentine's Day 2014.

***Laverne and Shirley* (animated).** Hanna-Barbera Productions/Paramount Television. ABC. Saturday mornings 11:00 (*Season One*) and 10:00 (*Season Two*) (October 10, 1981–September 3, 1983). Twenty-one animated episodes were filmed without a laugh track—thirteen as *Laverne and Shirley*, and eight as *Laverne and Shirley with the Fonz*.

Often referred to as *Laverne and Shirley in the Army*, the words "in the army" never actually appeared in the title. An episode of the live-action series that aired as a two-parter on November 15, 1979, titled "You're in the Army Now" served as a model for the animated series. Penny Marshall and Cindy Williams provided the voices for their respective characters. Added were Kenneth Mars as Sergeant Turnbuckle, and Ron Palillo as Sergeant Squealy. After the first season, the animated *Laverne and Shirley* was joined by the already established *Fonz and the Happy Days Gang* and cartoon newcomer *Mork and Mindy* as *The Mork and Mindy/Laverne and Shirley/Fonz Hour*. The Fonz was now a motor pool army mechanic in the *Laverne and Shirley* segment, joined by his pooch, Mr. Cool. Both Mork's and Fonz's dogs were "voiced" by Frank Welker. There was a lot of well-publicized strife on the live-action *Laverne and Shirley* set, and Cindy Williams quit that show—occurring during this second season of animation, wherein only eight episodes were completed. Despite the setback, the program continued intact, with numerous reruns, until September of 1983 when ABC finally said, "That's All, Folks."

Episodes were titled (*Season One*) "Invasion of the Booby Hatchers," "Jungle Jumpers," "Naval Fluff," "April Fools in Paris," "I Only Have Ice for You," "When the Moon Comes Over the Werewolf," "Bigfoot," "Two Mini Cooks," "Super Wacs," "Meanie Genie," "Tokyo Ho Ho," "Dark Knight," and "Super Duper Trooper"; (*Season Two*) "The Speed Demon Getaway Caper," "Swamp Monsters Speak with Forked Face," "Movie Madness," "One Million Laughs, B. C.," "The Robot Recruit," "All the President's Girls," "Laverne and Shirley and the Beanstalk," and "Raiders of the Lost Pork." The executive producers were William Hanna, Joe Barbera, Joe Ruby, and Ken Spears; the producers were Duane Poole, Tom Swale, and Art Scott; the writers included Duane Poole and Tom Swale; the directors included George Gordon, Bob Hathcock, Carl Urbano, Rudy Zamora, Rudy Larriva, and John Kimball. Music was provided by Hoyt Curtin.

Me and Mrs. C. Scomi Productions/MMC Productions. NBC. Saturday nights 9:30 (June 21, 1986–July 26, 1986, and April 11, 1987–May 30, 1987), and Saturday nights 8:30 (June 6, 1987–July 4, 1987). Nineteen episodes were videotaped (some with a laugh track; some in front of a live audience).

No, this show was not a *Happy Days* spinoff, as the title might lead one to believe. Mrs. C. was Mrs. Ethel Conklin (Peg Murray), a widow who has suffered a considerable reversal of fortune. The last thing she wants to do was move in with her goofy efficiency-expert son Ethan (Gary Bayer) and her pompous daughter-in-law Kathleen (Ellen Regan), so she opts to take in a boarder to help with expenses. That boarder, twenty-two-year-old Gerri Kilgore (Misha McK) was the "me" in the show's title. She is brash, bold, beautiful, and black (Ethan and Kathleen are quite taken aback by the latter). She is also unemployed and unlikely to be able to pay the monthly rent of eighty-seven dollars. She has also done some hard time in prison for armed robbery.

Were one to ask why the sixtyish Mrs. C. would take in such a boarder, she would likely reply that it was still better than moving in with her son and daughter-in-law and their two little monsters she nicknamed Rambo and Rocky (really, Ricky and Rodney). Wayne Powers, later of *13 East*, had a recurring role as Mr. Barton: "I actually portrayed two different characters on this series. It's also important to note that Misha's character was set up—she wasn't actually guilty of anything. Misha was discovered by Scoey Mitchlll (Yes, there really are three *l*'s in the correct spelling of his name)—she had very little prior experience, but a natural appeal and it worked. Peg Murray is a Tony Award–winning Broadway star and a total joy to work with. She had done some work in New York–based daytime dramas, but this was, sadly, I believe, her only foray into network television. Scoey and I are still great friends. He is one of a group of African American stand-up comedy pioneers, and in the 1980s started his own TV production comedy called Scomi TVP, blazing a trail for African Americans in network TV production. He wasn't afraid to deal with issues related to race, and his shows had a lot of heart. Some cast members and staff found him difficult to work with, but I adore the man." Mitchlll also guest starred on the sitcom as Reverend Kilgore in two episodes. Several episodes ended with Gerri writing a letter to her folks. The sitcom did well enough during its short summer run in 1986 to be invited back in the spring of 1987. It didn't quite have the legs NBC thought, however, and the second season was its last.

Episodes were titled (*Season One*) "Moving in and Moving Out," "Ladies Choice, Parts One and Two," "Checks Are in the Mail," "Lottery," and "Let's Have a Party"; (*Season Two*) "It's My Party," "Jailbird," "Happy Birthday to You," "Hero for a Day," "Last Rites, Parts One and Two," "Ethan, Go Home," "Coming to Terms," "Dear Ether," "Give Till It Hurts," "It's the Thought That Counts," "Bump in the Night," and "Smarty Pants." The executive producer was Scoey Mitchlll; the writers included Scoey Mitchlll, Anne Anderson, Jennie Blackton, Migdia Chinea, Ray Combs, Philip Whitehill, Kevin White, George Vallejo, Jim Tisdale, Chuck Tately, Donna Schwartz, Joe Restivo, Jim Parker, Tracy Morgan, Gordon "Whitey" Mitchell, Brenda McAdams Minge, Dana Klosner, Bill Kenny, Victoria Hochberg, and Joanne Greenberg; the directors included Scoey Mitchlll, Lee Lochhead, Tony Singletary, Pat Fischer-Doak, Whitney J. LeBlanc, Ron Troutman, and Howard Storm. About the latter, Powers recalled, "Howard Storm was a wonderful director, and in one episode Howie wanted an extreme close-up, and the only way to get the shot he wanted was to cut a hole behind a desk. Well, when Scoey saw the hole in his set he went absolutely ballistic and Storm was never brought back to direct the show again. Scoey was very hands-on, very protective of his shows." The creator was Scoey Mitchlll. The theme song, "Side by Side," was written by Harry Middlebrooks, and performed by La Vonne Rucker.

The Misadventures of Sheriff Lobo Glen Larson Productions/Universal Television. NBC. Tuesday nights 8:00 (September 18, 1979–May 6, 1980, and December 30, 1980–May 5, 1981). Thirty-seven hour-long episodes were filmed without a laugh track (twenty-two in Season One; fifteen in Season Two, as *Lobo*).

The Misadventures of Sheriff Lobo was, for all intents, a spinoff of *B. J. and the Bear*. The series was occasionally referred to as a "police comedy." Elroy P. Lobo (Claude Akins) is the less-than-honest sheriff of Orly County, Georgia. His money-making schemes are abundant and borderline larcenous, but somehow he always ends up on the right side of the law. His ideas of justice clash with most of his superiors.

The program's first season aired under the title of *The Misadventures of Sheriff Lobo*. Actress Caren Kaye guest starred in the debut episode: "The Universal lot was unlike any other. Tour buses came through regularly, and we occasionally had to stop filming to allow them through and to wave and smile as they went by. Tourism was the main focus there and actors were considered secondary supply. I also recall that we had quite a few outdoor scenes, and there was a pool into which I was to fall. Mind you, that pool was not cleaned very regularly. It was recommended that I get a tetanus shot afterwards—LOL."

However, when the series returned for the 1980–1981 season, its sitcom elements were toned down a bit, and aired under the shortened title of *Lobo*. Both incarnations featured countless buxom babes and crazy car chases.

Cast members of NBC's misstep *The Misadventures of Sheriff Lobo*: (left to right) Mills Watson, Claude Akins, and Brian Kerwin. In season two, the show was retooled and its title shortened to *Lobo*.

Season One co-stars included Mills Watson as Lobo's gray-matter-challenged brother-in-law, Deputy Perkins; Brian Kerwin as the mayor's son, Birdwell "Birdie" Hawkins; and William Schallert as Mayor Hawkins. Other Season One characters Rose Perkins, the deputy's wife (Cydney Crampton); Birdie's girlfriend, Sarah Cumberland (Leann Hunley); Oscar Gorley (J. D. Cannon); and the sheriff's mom (played by veteran actress Rosemary DeCamp) didn't return for Season Two. B. J. (Greg Evigan) guest starred in three episodes in Season One. Under the *Lobo* banner, the show was set in Atlanta, and Lobo was assigned to a special police task force. New characters included Chief of Detectives John E. Carson (Nicholas Coster); Sergeant Hildy Jones (Nell Carter, listed in the credits as Nell Ruth Carter); Officer Brandy Ames (Tara Buckman); Officer Peaches McLain (Amy Botwinick); and George (Dudley Knight). Season Two's debut was midseason and consists of only fifteen episodes, as opposed to Season One's twenty-two. Episodes were filmed without a laugh track.

Episodes were titled (*Season One*) "The Day That Shark Ate Lobo," "Dean Martin and the Moonshiners" (with guest star Dean Martin), "Panhandle Pussycats Come to Orly," "Disco Fever Comes to Orly," "The Mob Comes to Orly" (with guest star Raymond Burr), "Run for the Money, Parts One, Two, and Three" (with guest star Glen Campbell), "Buttercup Birdie and Buried Bucks," "The Senator Votes Absentee," "The Boom Boom Lady," "First to Finish, Last to Show," "Hail, Hail, the Gang's All Here," "The Luck of the Irish," "Double Take Double Take," "Police Escort," "Who's the Sexiest Girl in the World?," "The Martians Are Coming, The Martians Are Coming," "Treasure of Nature Beach," "Perkins Bombs Out," "Birdie's Hot Wheels," "The Haunting of Olry Manor" (with guest star Delta Burke), "Murder on the Orly Express," and "Orly's Hot Skates"; (*Season Two*) "The Dirtiest Girls in Town," "The Girls with the Stolen Bodies," "The Fastest Women Around," "Macho Man," "Airsick 1981," "Co-eds with Sticky Fingers," "Sex and the Single Cop," "Another Day, Another Bomb" (with guest star Sid Caesar), "The French Follies Caper," "Bang Bang … You're Dead," "The Cowboy Connection" (with guest stars Bobby Sherman, Dr. Joyce Brothers, and Barbi Benton), "What're Girls Like You Doing in a Bank Like This?," "Lobo and the Pirates," "The Roller Disco Karate Kaper" (with guest star Pat Morita), and "Keep on Buckin'." The executive producers were Glen A. Larson and Lou Shaw; the producers were Robert F. O'Neill, Frank Lupo, Joe

Boston, Norm Liebmann, Bill Dial, and Richard M. Bluel; the writers included Glen A. Larson, Frank Lupo, Mark Jones, Paul M. Belous, Stephen A. Miller, Michael Sloan, Robert Wolterstorff, Howard Liebling, Robert E. Feinberg, Chris Bunch, Lou Shaw, Sidney Ellis, Allan Cole, John Peyser, Robert McCullough, Bill Dial, Mark Fink, Bob Baublitz, Jeffrey Scott, Harvey Bullock, Christopher Crowe, Chris Lucky, Richard H. Landau, Richard Christian Matheson, Richard M. Bluel, Thomas E. Szollosi, Tom Chehak, David Chase, Pat Fielder, David Ketchum, Thomas Joachim, Eugene A. Fournier, Michael Russnow, Richard Lindheim, Bruce Shelly, Lloyd Turner, Warren Douglas, G. J. Young, Elana Lesser, David P. Harmon, Sy Salkowitz, and Cliff Ruby; the directors included James Sheldon, Dick Harwood, Daniel Haller, Sidney Hayers, Bruce Bilson, Jack Arnold, Christian I Nyby II, Nicholas Colasanto, Leslie H. Martinson, Mel Ferber, William P. D'Angelo, Gene Levitt, Harvey S. Laidman, Corey Allen, Bruce Kessler, and Charles R. Rondeau. Music was provided by Stu Phillips, William Broughton, Jimmie Haskell, and John Andrew Tartaglia. Frankie Laine, who had performed the theme songs for TV's *Rawhide* and *Rango*, also sang the "Sheriff Lobo Theme." For Season Two, the theme was "Georgia on My Mind."

Mr. President Carson Productions. FOX. Sunday nights 9:00 (May 3, 1987–July 26, 1987), Sunday nights 9:30 (September 27, 1987–October 18, 1987), Saturday nights 8:00 (October 24, 1987–January 2, 1988), and Saturday nights 9:30 (January 16–April 2, 1988). Twenty-four episodes were produced—the first ten filmed single-camera style with a laugh track, and the last fourteen videotaped in front of a live audience.

This program served as George C. Scott's return to television after the much-lauded but short-lived *East Side, West Side* drama series in 1963. The two shows couldn't be more different. *Mr. President* was a situation comedy from Johnny Carson's Carson Productions. In fact, Carson is credited as having contributed to the writing of a couple of the episodes. Here, Scott portrays the cranky, brusque, and curmudgeonly former Wisconsin governor Samuel Arthur Tresch, who threw his hat into the presidential race and won.

When the program debuted midseason in 1986, Tresch's wife was First Lady Meg (Carlin Glynn). However, when the program was renewed for what became a truncated second season, Meg, unable to deal with the pressures of life in the political fishbowl, had left the president to fend for himself. Much in the manner of an earlier sitcom titled *The Governor and J. J.*, with a widowed governor and his daughter serving as a surrogate first lady, President Tresch is in search of someone to accompany him to the Washington functions, banquets and fundraisers that come with the position. The person who should fill that void becomes very obvious when Meg's sister Lois Gullickson (Madeline Kahn) moves into the White House to help care for the kids. We are also made privy to the fact that Lois has a mad, longtime crush on her brother-in-law.

Tresch has one married daughter, the rarely seen Jennifer Hayes (Susan Duff Wheeler). Jennifer's husband, Fred (Daniel McDonald), is seemingly always getting under the president's skin. Also living with President Tresch at 1600 Pennsylvania Avenue are his sixteen-year-old daughter Cynthia (Maddie Corman), and his twelve-year-old son Nick (Andre Gower). Both of them find it very confining having the Secret Service following them everywhere. They also have a hard time adjusting to their parents' separation.

Jack Blessing, who had the recurring role of Brian on the show, said, "I did a bunch of episodes, maybe ten or so. I only left because I was offered a steadier gig on *Moonlighting*. I did love being on the show, especially when it was a filmed show, before they retooled it and went to four-camera, live audience. I was pretty darn sick during this time. I had lost thirty or so pounds during the course of making it. Wardrobe literally had to tailor my suits every week, to everyone's concern. Turns out I had type 1, then known as 'juvenile diabetes.' All worked out well, though, and thirty years later, no complications."

About the show's star, Blessing added, "What can you say about getting to work with George C. Scott? It's an actor's dream come true. He loved acting and he loved actors. Generous to a fault. He would do a table read before we filmed each episode. As was my way, I would always make overly broad comedy choices at the table read to see if I could make the jokes work in a way that was unexpected, and then would simplify and make real the performance as the week went on. Usually, not surprisingly, my choices would fail. Spectacularly. But George always knew what I was doing, and would burst out in hysterical laughter and say 'Jesus, Jacky, you make me laugh!' I always loved him for that. He was pretty much of a loner, always holed up in his dressing room, playing electronic chess by himself. But when he was on the set, he always made you feel that it was about you.

However, he hated writers. At least TV writers. Uncomfortably so. Towards the end of the run, he actually had Ed. Weinberger, the exec and head writer, banned from the set, never to return. He also hated the network folk who would show up. My wife came to the stage one day dressed in a corporate suit, as she had come from an audition on the lot. He started berating her for being there, assuming that she was a network person. After finding out who she was and that she was an actor, of course, he was incredibly kind to her."

Conrad Bain, post–*Maude* and *Diff'rent Strokes*, played presidential aide and longtime friend Charlie Ross. According to Blessing, "Bain was exactly as he appeared. Comically so. Would have bought insurance from him, if he was selling it. Impossible not to like." Other White House staffers included Daniel Cummings (Allen Williams) and Dave (Earl Boen). On a regular basis, the president was presented with pressing dilemmas, such as whether to hire a pretty, blonde, immensely capable translator, fearing a public outcry of an ulterior motive. The opening credits feature video snippets of former Presidents Nixon, Reagan, and Carter. Another sitcom about the White House occupant, *Hail to the Chief* (see entry), aired that same year, with similar ratings results. There was a big difference with *Hail to the Chief*, however. The president on that series was portrayed by Patty Duke, leading many to consider the program to be way ahead of its time.

Episodes were titled (*Season One*) "The Pilot" (with guest star Alley Mills), "Magnetic Presidency," "Cabin Fever," "Freedom of Speech," "Meet the People" (with guest star Barry Corbin), "Private Moments," "First Son-in-Law," "Uncle Sam," "Strange Bedfellows," and "Love's Labor Last" (the last two with guest star Barbara Barrie); (*Season Two*) "Dear Sam, Parts One and Two," "Armageddon Kinda Sore," "He'll Have to Go," "Language Barrier," "Loisgate," "Yes, Mr. President," "Lois Gets Lucky" (with guest star Steve Landesberg), "The President's Brother," "The Christmas Story," "Insecurity," "The Royal Send-Off," "All About Jean," and "Get a Job." The executive producers were Johnny Carson, Gene Reynolds, and Ed. Weinberger; the producer was Peter Noah; the writers included Johnny Carson, David Lloyd, Gene Reynolds, Ed. Weinberger, Martin Sage, Bill Kenny, Craig Heller, Sybil Adelman, Roger S. H. Schulman, Arthur and Mady Julian, David Steven Cohen, and Peter Noah; the directors included Marc Daniels, Greg Antonacci, and Gene Reynolds. The creators were Ed. Weinberger and Johnny Carson. Music was provided by Pat Williams.

My Sister Sam Pony Productions/Warner Bros. Television. CBS. Monday nights 8:30 (October 6, 1986–May 4, 1987), Saturday nights 8:00 (October 3, 1987–November 7, 1987), and Tuesday night 9:00 (March 15, 1988–April 12, 1988). Forty-four episodes were filmed in front of a live audience, but only thirty-two aired.

Twenty-nine-year-old San Francisco photographer Samantha Russell (Pam Dawber) is enjoying single life. Business is good and her studio is based in her spacious apartment that came with a winding staircase, a loft, and some unique sliding bedroom doors. That huge apartment suddenly seems a lot smaller when Patti (Rebecca Schaeffer), a sister thirteen years her junior, relocates from Oregon and moves in, cramping Sam's style. Sam's romantic interests and "sleepovers" suddenly become awkward and an issue to be sorted out. The two sisters have little in common—Patti likes contemporary music, while Sam is a fan of oldies, such as the Crystals' 1963 pop hit "Da Doo Ron Ron." A female *Odd Couple* is in play—Sam is very tidy (she even combs the throw rugs) and follows "all the rules." Patti is only an average student, not quite an over-achiever, not very tidy, and quite a free spirit. They love each other like sisters, but they also fight like sisters (they hadn't lived under the same roof together since they were both very young). Because of the difference in their ages, their relationship frequently takes on a "mother-daughter" feel, even though Patti had been raised by an aunt. There was also a sense of rivalry between the siblings—especially noticeable in the debut episode, "Sam Russell, Man Stealer."

Pam Dawber (right) and Rebecca Schaeffer (left), of CBS's *My Sister Sam*, played siblings who share an apartment but little else, due to a thirteen-year age difference.

Young actor Dean Cameron portrayed Brandon in that episode: "They had originally shot a pilot about which the network wasn't thrilled. Well, Pam Dawber is married to Mark Harmon, and I had been cast in a movie called *Summer School* with him. I read for the part of Brandon—a real 'out there' punk rocker with spiked hair, leather and studs galore. I got the part and instantly fell in love with Rebecca Schaeffer. It's interesting that, in the episode, I was Rebecca's date, but I made a pass at her older sister, Sam, and this led to a big fight between siblings in the episode. I'm very proud of the fact that I also ad-libbed a line about 'squidballs' in the episode. Ad-libbing is generally a no no, but they liked it and kept it in. Everyone was very nice on that show. David Naughton was a great guy. It was a very smooth and fun experience."

Naughton played Jack Kincaid, who lives across the hall, in apartment 3D. Jack is a photojournalist who spends most of his time on the road. He and Sam have a one-night fling, but discover that they were meant to be just very good friends with available shoulders on which to lean. There is, however, an on-going and palpable sexual tension between them, which keeps their relationship interesting. Sam's photography assistant is the brash and funny Dixie Randazzo (Jenny O'Hara), who is married to a guy named Vic. They have six kids. She lied on her résumé and had absolutely no prior photography experience before being hired for this job. Sam's agent is the pushy, emotional, and slippery-but-kindhearted J. D. Lucas (Joel Brooks), who is married to the never-seen-on-camera Lorraine.

The program does contain some very good one-liners and did well enough in its freshman season to become a sophomore, but a move to Saturday nights at 8 P.M. proved to be its undoing. It was gone from the prime-time schedule by early November, and a few unaired episodes were burned off in the spring of 1988, but still only thirty-two of forty-four filmed episodes were aired. All forty-four episodes ran in syndication on the USA Network, albeit briefly. Sadly, only a year after *My Sister Sam* was canceled, Rebecca Schaeffer was killed by a crazed stalker at her West Hollywood apartment on July 18, 1989. She was only twenty-one years old. The show was nominated for a "Best Costuming" Emmy Award, but did not win.

Episodes were titled (*Season One*) "Samantha Russell, Man Stealer," "Patti's Party" (with guest star Kathleen Freeman), "Shooting Stars," "What Makes Samantha Run?," "Roomies," "The Aunt Elsie Crisis: Day One," "Teacher's Pet" (with guest star Scott Bakula), "Mirror, Mirror on the Wall," "Babes in the Woods," "Jingle Bell Rock Bottom," "Club Dread," "Anything for a Friend," "Almost-in-Laws," "Go Crazy," "Another Saturday Night," "Family Business," "Making Up Is Hard to Do," "If You Knew Suzy," "Sister, Can You Spare a Fifty?," "Exposed," "Campaign Contributions," and "Fog Bound"; (*Season Two*) "Goodbye, Steve," "And They Said It Would Never Last," "Deep Throat," "Never a Bridesmaid," "Who's Afraid of Virginia Schultz?," "Drive, She Said," "Revenge of the Russell Sisters," "Play It Again, Sam," "Old Green Eyes Is Back," "Life, Death, and Admiral Andy," "It's My Party and I'll Kill if I Want To" (with guest star Robert Pastorelli), "Good Neighbor Sam," "Patti, I Have a Feeling We're Not in Kansas Anymore," "The Art of Love" (with guest star Richard Kind), "Camp Burnout," "The Grand Prize," "Walk a While in My Shoes," "The Wrong Stuff," "The Thrill of Agony, the Victory of Defeat" (with guest star Ed Marinaro), "The Good, The Bad, and The Auditor," "Earthquake," and "A Day in the Lives." The executive producer was Diane English; the producers were Karyl Miller and Korby Siamis; the writers included Danny Jacobson, Stephen Fischer, Diane English, Korby Siamis, Karyl Miller, Tom Palmer, Gary Murphy, Lisa Albert, Larry Strawther, Ramona Schindelheim, Dennis Danzinger, Susan Beavers, Ellen Sandler, Sy Dukane, Deborah Zoe Dawson, Duncan Scott McGibbon, Victoria Johns, Denise Moss, Tom Spezialy, and Irene Mecchi; the directors included Ellen Falcon, Matthew Diamond, Peter Bonerz, Zane Buzby, Barnet Kellman, Steve Zuckerman, James Gardner, Burt Metcalfe, Peter Baldwin, and Tom Cherones. Music was provided by Steve Dorff, and the theme song, "Room Enough for Two," was performed by Kim Carnes.

The New Leave It to Beaver (see *Still the Beaver*)

Rags to Riches Leonard Hill Films/New World Television. NBC. Monday night 8:00 (March 9, 1987), Sunday nights 8:00 (March 15, 1987–April 26, 1987), Friday nights 8:00 (September 18, 1987–January 15, 1988). Nineteen hour-long episodes and a two-hour pilot were filmed without a laugh track.

John Clapper (Douglas Seale), a British butler, narrated this show, which was set in 1962. "Clap" works for multi-millionaire Nick Foley (Joseph Bologna), a nouveau riche resident of Bel Air, California, with an image problem. The son of a bricklayer who only spoke a few words of English, Nick (real last name Folatini) is rough around the edges, but managed to build the small Foley's Frozen Foods Company into a huge conglomerate. He is a compulsive gambler, and a womanizing cold fish—traits that proved polarizing in his business dealings. To soften his image, he takes in five street-savvy orphan girls after reading a newspaper item about the closing of the Margaret Keating Home. He isn't especially fond of children, and only plans to keep them around until a particular business deal, the Baldwin merger, goes through. His girlfriend isn't too thrilled about the situation, either. Said merger does indeed go through, but it is suggested that, to keep up appearances, Foley should allow the girls to stay. Being single and used to being alone, this really cramps Nick's style, but he slowly begins to warm to the idea of having them around.

In the pilot, there are six girls, but the role of shy Nina (Heather McAdam) was eliminated when her mother reclaimed her. Nina's boyfriend, Tommy (Billy Warlock), a Fonzie lookalike, rides a motorcycle and belongs to a gang called The Roadhogs. The remaining five include the very outgoing Rose (Kimiko Gelman); Diane (Bridget Michele); business-minded Marva (Tisha Campbell); reading-challenged Patti (Blanca DeGarr); and young

Mickey (Heidi Zeigler), who plays saxophone and is always in search of a restroom. Each hour-long episode is akin to a Broadway musical comedy, with lots of familiar songs from the 1950s and '60s. After a short first season, consisting of eight episodes, the program was invited back for a short second season of twelve episodes. The ratings in Season Two slipped and the program got the axe after the "Sweet 16" episode. Image Entertainment released the entire series in a DVD box set in 2012.

Episodes were titled (*Season One*) "The Pilot" (with guest star Bill Maher), "High Society," "Foley vs. Foley," "First Love," "Business Is Business," "Patty's Mom," "Bad Blood," and "Born to Ride"; (*Season Two*) "Vegas Rock," "Once in a Lifeguard," "That's Cheating," "Wilderness Blues," "Dear Diary" (with guest star Dick Van Patten), "Hunk in the House," "Marva in the Key of Cee" (with guest star Sid Melton), "Beauty and the Babe" (with guest star Edd "Kookie" Byrnes), "Russian Holiday," "A Very Foley Christmas" (with guest star Wolfman Jack), "Guess Who's Coming to Slumber" (with guest star Danny Bonaduce), and "Sweet 16." The executive producers were Leonard Hill and Bernie Kukoff; the producer was Ronald H. Gilbert, the writers included Bernie Kukoff, Andrew Schneider, Steven Baum, Robin Schiff, Chris Carter, Neil Alan Levy, Susan Goldberg, Diane Frolov, Deborah R. Baron, David Garber, Bill Daley, Steve Johnson, Bruce Kalish, David Garber, Molly-Ann Leikin, Sharon Spelman, and Renee and Harry Longstreet. The creator was Bernie Kukoff. Music was provided by J. Peter Robinson. Lyrics for original oldies songs were cleverly altered to fit the subject matter in each episode.

The Ropers The Ropers Company/The NRW Company/T. T. C. Productions, Inc. ABC. Tuesday nights 10:00 (March 13, 1979–April 17, 1979), Saturday nights 8:00 (September 15, 1979–December 15, 1979), Saturday nights 8:30 (January 26, 1980–May 8, 1980), and Thursday night 9:30 (May 18, 1980). Twenty-eight episodes were videotaped in front of a live audience.

Helen and Stanley Roper (Audra Lindley and Norman Fell, respectively) had been funny fixtures as the landlords on *Three's Company* from March of 1977 until March of 1979, when they were spun off into their own series. Norman Fell wasn't exactly overjoyed at Fred Silverman's and the network's decision to create the spinoff. After a long career and countless short-lived TV roles, Fell was finally in a hit series and leery about going it alone. Unlike Joanie, Chachi, and Al on *Happy Days* (who were all allowed to return after *Joanie Loves Chachi* was canceled), once Helen and Stanley Roper moved into their new condo, there was no going back.

One of the show's head writers, Martin Rips, recalled, "I'd constantly see Norman in his dressing room, looking at the ratings and one could see how despondent he was. Fell's trepidation was warranted. The show was pretty well doomed from the get-go—it was never a home run. It lacked something. However, it was a very pleasant experience. We were brought in to write for the show by friends of ours. They were seeking young writers, and Joseph Staretski and I got that lucky break. After *The Ropers* was canceled, Joseph and I were brought over to write for *Three's Company*, and that was great."

After a decent start in Season One, consisting of only six episodes, *The Ropers* faltered in Season Two. The ratings were so low, in fact, even Mr. Roper's plunger, seen in the opening credits, couldn't save the day. The program was moved around a lot on the ABC schedule, but nothing seemed to work. Fellow headwriter Joseph Staretski explained, "In hindsight, the characters of Helen and Stanley were great in a recurring capacity on *Three's Company*, but probably not strong enough to carry a series of their own. The spinoff probably worked better in the English version, *George and Mildred*, because the class difference there is so much more palpable. The concept of placing a middle-class couple like the Ropers into an upper-class scenario would play funnier there and mean more."

The program has a simple premise—the middle-aged, unhappily married couple sell their apartment building to a Mr. Furley (Don Knotts), and move into a condo at 46 Peacock Drive in Cheviot Hills' Royal Dale Condominium Town Houses, in an upscale neighborhood in California. Helen is still sex-starved, and constantly attempting to fit in among the neighbors in this new, upwardly mobile community. Stanley is still his same sarcastic, unsociable, boorish self. He finds himself immediately at odds with the snooty realtor next-door, named Jeffrey P. Brookes III (Jeffrey Tambor). Helen befriends Jeffrey's wife, Anne Brookes (Patricia McCormack), and her coy seven-year-old son, David (Evan Cohen), much to Stanley's dismay. Other recurring roles included Helen's sisters—the snobbish and condescending Ethel (Dena Dietrich), and the serially-pregnant Hilda (played by both Lucy Lee Flippin and Darcy Pulliam), with five children and a sixth on the way.

About the experience, Flippin shared, "That was an easy and fun show to do. I vividly remember Norman's Fell's very expressive hang-dog eyes. Patricia McCormack was lovely, and it was so hard to picture her as *The Bad Seed* girl. [*The Bad Seed*, Maxwell Anderson's Broadway play, was adapted for the big screen in 1956, with McCormack reprising her stage role of an inherently evil child.] I was so happy for Jeffrey Tambor's career trajectory. They wanted to have me back again on the show, but I was taping *Flo* at the time and couldn't because of scheduling conflicts."

Helen's mother, played by Lucille Benson, also drops in from time to time, and always has difficulty remembering people's names. The Ropers briefly had a boarder, Jenny Ballinger (Louise Vallance). The phone number for The Ropers was 555-3099, and Helen's dog was named Muffin. Brian Cooke and Johnnie Mortimer, the creators of *George and Mildred*, on which the program was very loosely based, are credited with writing the first few episodes of *The Ropers*.

Episodes were titled (*Season One*) "Moving On," "Friends and Neighbors," "Your Money or Your Life" (with guest star John Fiedler), "The Doris Letters," "The Family Planning," and "Opportunity Knocks" (with guest star Richard Kline); (*Season Two*) "The Party" (with guest stars John Ritter, Suzanne Somers, and Joyce DeWitt), "The Days of Beer and Rosie," "Power Play," "Baby Talk," "Two for the Road," "Puppy Love," "All Around the Clock," "Odd Couples," "Pal Joey," "Helen Makes Music," "The Skeleton" (with guest star Barry Nelson), "The Other Man," "And Who's Been Sleeping in My…?," "Jenny's Date," "Of Mice and Horses," "Family Feud," "The Other Woman," "Men About the House," "Old Flames," "The Rummage Sale," "Four-Letter Word," and "Mother's Wake." The executive producers were Don Nicholl, Michael Ross, and Bernie West; the producer was George Sunga; the writers included Brian Cooke, Johnnie Mortimer, Joseph Staretski, Martin Rips, George Burditt, Wayne Kline, Mark Fink, Stephen Neigher, Neil Rosen, George Tricker, Don Nicholl, Michael Ross, Bernie West, Katherine Green, Barbara Allyn, and Alan Hackney. About Hackney, Staretski recalled, "We were all very excited when he was brought in. He was a very good and successful writer in the UK and had written a classic British Peter Sellers film called *I'm All Right Jack* [1959, based on Hackney's novel *Private Life*]. However, he just didn't have the right sensibility for writing thirty-minute American sitcoms." The directors were Dave Powers and Jack Shea. Music was provided by Joe Raposo.

Sanford Redd Foxx Productions/Tandem Productions, Inc. NBC. Saturday nights 9:00 (March 15, 1980–May 31, 1980), Friday nights 8:30 (January 9, 1981–January 30, 1981, and May 29, 1981–July 10, 1981). Twenty-six episodes were videotaped in front of a live audience.

The character of Fred Sanford (Redd Foxx) was already well known to audiences following the success of *Sanford and Son* from 1972–1977. Fred, the sly, cranky, widowed junk dealer, resided at 4707 South Central Avenue in Watts. In the series' first spinoff, however, the audience was supposed to believe that Fred's property had been turned into *The Sanford Arms*, a residential hotel. Featuring neither Sanford, nor Son (Demond Wilson), *The San-*

ford Arms flopped and disappeared from the NBC lineup within a month of its debut.

In *Sanford*, Fred resides in his old digs as if *The Sanford Arms* never happened (much like the dream sequence on *Dallas*). Lamont is said to be away, working on the Alaskan pipeline, and one of his co-workers—the calorically challenged Cal Pettie (Dennis Burkley)—shows up at Fred's door with some long underwear, a gift from Lamont. Fresh from the job, Cal has a pocketful of money and Fred cons his new pigeon into investing that money into "The Sanford Empire." Rollo Larson (Nathaniel Taylor) was still around from the original series, but Fred now has a new love interest—an extremely wealthy widow, Evelyn "Eve" Lewis (Marguerite Ray), who resides at 77 Kantwell Drive in Beverly Hills and buys numerous items at Fred's advertised junk sale (most viewers likely missed the Kantwell Drive pun). The two quickly become an item (and Fred frequently invokes the name of his deceased wife, Elizabeth, for approval), much to the chagrin of both Eve's brother Winston (Percy Rodriguez) and acerbic housekeeper Clara (Cathy Cooper). Clara was Aunt Esther and *The Jeffersons*' Florence rolled into one. Eve's pretty young daughter, Cissy (Suzanne Stone), bonds quickly with Fred and approves of her mother dating him.

The program did well enough in its truncated first season to be brought back as a midseason replacement on NBC. Fred's sister-in-law, Aunt Esther (LaWanda Page), came back for a visit to kick off the second season, and her college student son Cliff Anderson (Clinton Derricks-Carroll), Fred's nephew, became a resident in The Sanford Empire as of the "Cissy and the Nephew" episode from Season One. The ratings for Season Two paled in comparison to Season One, and, now seen on Friday nights, *Sanford* was quickly placed on hiatus. It returned in the late spring, when the remaining videotaped episodes were burned off. Fred and Eve became engaged during the run of this show, but never did get to tie the knot. Cliff and Cissy were also romantically linked during the run of the series.

Episodes were titled (*Season One*) "The Meeting, Parts One, Two and Three," "In the Still of the Night," "Dinner at George's" (with guest star Tom Dreesen), "Younger than Springtime Am I," "Retrospective, Parts One and Two," "Perfect Husband," "The Ring," "Cissy and the Nephew," "Cal's Diet, Parts One and Two," and "The Benefit" (with guest star Sammy Davis, Jr.); (*Season Two*) "Here Comes the Bride, Parts One and Two," "Fred Has the Big One," "Cal the Coward," "Love Is Blind," "Cal's Mom," "Gaslight," "Freeway," "Jury Duty," "Cal's Illegal Alien," "Private Lives," and "To Keep a Thief." The executive producer was Mort Lachman; the producers were Sy Rosen, Mel Tolkin, and Larry Rhine; the writers included Ted Bergman, Sy Rosen, Bill Box, John Donley, Ken Hecht, Jim Gagan, Chip and Doug Keyes, Judi Ann Mason, Neil Lebowitz, Michael Morris, Winston Moss, Dick Westerschulte, Bob Weiskopf, Harriet Weiss, Warren S. Murray, Michael G. Moye, Mark Sheffler, Patt Shea, Bob Schiller, J. Standford Parker, Phil Doran, and Douglas Arango; the directors included Jim Drake and Sammy Davis, Jr. The program's theme song was the identical version of the theme by Quincy Jones utilized in the original *Sanford and Son* series. Reruns of this short-lived sitcom ran on the BET cable network.

Sledge Hammer Spencer Productions/New World Television. ABC. Tuesday night 8:30 (September 23, 1986), Friday nights 9:30 (September 26, 1986–November 13, 1986), Saturday nights 8:30 (November 22, 1986–February 21, 1987), Tuesday nights 8:30 (April 21, 1987–April 28, 1987), Thursday nights 8:00 (September 17, 1987–January 7, 1988), Friday nights 9:30 (January 15, 1988–February 12, 1988). Forty-one episodes were filmed with a laugh track.

Spoofs of police and detective shows were abundant in the 1980s, and this one was somewhat more successful than *Police Squad*, *Nobody's Perfect*, or *Last Precinct*, and survived for almost two full seasons. The creation of Alan Spencer, *Sledge Hammer* was *Dirty Harry* played for laughs. It was said that Hammer (David Rasche) made Rambo look like Pee

Wee Herman. He was a loose cannon who slept with, showered with, and talked to, his prized Smith and Wesson .44 magnum revolver, on which a sledge hammer is engraved. He calls it (somewhat unimaginatively) "Gun." His car has an "I Love Violence" sticker on it, and his nicknames for perps in his path include "scum-sucking creep," "pizza face," "sea urchin," "yogurt sucker," "genetic mistake," "ragweed," and "brain-dead mutant." He truly believes that *all* perps—from jaywalkers to serial murderers—should be dealt with in the same harsh manner. Despite his unorthodox methodology, his destructive tendencies, and his clumsiness, he manages to luck into a solution for every crime, and frequently utters the phrase, "Trust me, I know what I'm doing." He wears cheap sport jackets and loud ties. His partner, Dori Doreau (Anne-Marie Martin), is everything he is not—intelligent, agile, sensitive, and sophisticated. She is very adept at deflecting his male chauvinistic comments (not surprisingly, Hammer is divorced—his wife left him for a sensitive man who works for the Peace Corps).

By the end of the debut episode, Hammer and Doreau bond; she has even taken to saying, "Trust me, I know what I'm doing." Guest star Robin Leach uttered that same phrase in "The Spa Who Loved Me," the final episode of the first season. Leach opens that episode, stating immodestly that he is there to boost the ratings to ensure a second season. Hammer's harried supervisor is Captain Trunk (Harrison Page). Early on, the program struggled on ABC's Friday night schedule (a matter that was addressed in one episode, on which competing shows *Dallas* and *Miami Vice* were mentioned) but it did just well enough after being moved to Saturday nights to be welcomed back for what became a truncated second season. In that second season, the program had a smaller budget and, except for a few erratically scheduled reruns, was gone before spring of 1988. There were twenty-two episodes in Season One, but only nineteen in Season Two. All forty-one episodes have been issued on DVD by Anchor Bay Entertainment, but the laugh track was removed. Especially in Season Two, this series boasted numerous high-profile actors as directors (Dick Martin, Bill Bixby, and Jackie Cooper).

Many episode titles were plays on movie titles (*Season One*) "Under the Gun," "Hammer Gets Nailed," "Witless," "They Shoot Hammers, Don't They," "Doris Day Afternoon," "To Sledge, with Love," "All Shook Up," "Over My Dead Bodyguard," "Magnum Farce," "If I Had a Little Hammer," "To Live and Die on TV," "Miss of the Spider Woman," "The Old Man and the Sledge," "State of Sledge," "Haven't Gun, Will Travel," "The Color of Hammer," "Brother, Can You Spare a Crime?," "Desperately Seeking Dori," "Sledgepoo," "Comrade Hammer," "Jagged Sledge," and "The Spa Who Loved Me"; (*Season Two*) "A Clockwork Hammer," "Big Nazi on Campus," "Play It Again, Sledge," "Wild about Hammer," "Death of a Few Salesmen," "Vertical," "Dressed to Call," "Hammer Hits the Rock," "Last of the Red Hot Vampires," "Hammeroid," "Sledge in Toyland," "Icebreaker," "They Call Me Mr. Trunk," "Model Dearest," "Sledge, Rattle and Roll," "Suppose They Gave a War and Sledge Came," "The Secret of My Excess," "It Happened What Night?," and "Here's to You, Mrs. Hammer." The executive producers were Alan Spencer, William P. D'Angelo, and Robert Lovenheim; the producer was Thomas John Kane; the writers included Alan Spencer, Al Jean, Mike Reiss, Diana Ayers, Susan Sebastian, Mert Rich, Brian Pollack, Jim Staahl, Jim Fisher, Deborah Raznick, Daniel Benton, Gerald Gardner, Alan Mandel, Tony DiMarco, Dave Ketchum, Chris Ruppenthal, Tino Insana, Robert Wuhl, Rod Ash, Mark Curtiss, Ron Friedman, and Alicia Marie Schudt; the directors included Bill Bixby, Jackie Cooper, Dick Martin, Seymour Robbie, Gary Walkow, Reza Badiyi, Chuck Braverman, Bruce Bilson, Bob Sweeney, Thomas Schlamme, Dan Attias, David Wechter, Kim Manners, James Sheldon, Charles S. Dubin, and Martha Coolidge. Music was provided by Danny Elfman.

Still the Beaver Sprocket/Telvan Productions/Universal Television. The Disney Channel. Wednesday nights 8:00 (November 7, 1984–October 12, 1985). Twenty-seven episodes were filmed, single-camera style, with a laugh track, and aired every two weeks.

This *Leave It to Beaver* reunion began with a CBS TV movie that aired on March 19, 1983, called *Still the Beaver*—twenty years after the original series wrapped up its sixth and final season in prime-time (before entering into eternal reruns). About the TV movie, producer Nick Abdo recalled, "Brian Levant and I took the idea for the movie to Universal. We then pitched the idea to CBS, who bought it. They wouldn't let Brian write it because he wasn't on their list and insisted we hire someone else. The writers didn't share our passion for the show and the script was not of the quality we wanted, so we convinced them to let Brian do the rewrite, and he did a great job. After the movie aired, we made a twenty-minute series presentation from the footage as a sales piece to sell the series. CBS passed on it and then it was taken to Disney, who bought the show."

The original *Leave It to Beaver* began on CBS in 1957, but jumped to ABC in its second through sixth seasons. Twenty-seven episodes of the new series, *Still the Beaver*, were produced, and under this title it had a single-season run on Wednesday nights. The setting was still Mayfield, USA, population 18,240. Well, make that 18,243—Theodore Cleaver (Jerry Mathers) is now in his mid-thirties, newly divorced with two sons, Kip (Kipp Marcus) and Oliver (John Snee). He and the boys move back in with Mom (and, now, Grandmother) June Cleaver (Barbara Billingsley), who still resides at 211 Pine Street. Abdo said, "We tried to get the Kip character to appeal to the girls by having him wear button shirts that were open to the chest, but Disney nixed that right away, saying that it was too much." Also back for the reunion was Beaver's older brother, Wally (Tony Dow), now a successful attorney, married, and living right next door. Of course, he married his childhood sweetheart, the former Mary Ellen Rogers (now played by Janice Kent, but by Pamela Baird in the original series) and they have a daughter named Kelly (Kaleena Kiff). Mischievous old friend Eddie Haskell (Ken Osmond) still lives in the neighborhood. It is revealed that he likes to bet on professional sports, and collects ashtrays and Dallas Cowboys Christmas ornaments. Eddie now has two sons, Freddie and Bomber, who were played by his real-life sons Eric and Christian Osmond, respectively. They not only sound like their dad, they have also inherited his mannerisms and slippery ways. Abdo recalled, "It wasn't natural in Eric's case. He was taught to be that way. He was talented enough to pick up the attitude and inflections." Frank Bank was also back in the goofy recurring role of Clarence "Lumpy" Rutherford, and on a few occasions viewers once again got to see some of the original show's characters: Miss Canfield (Diane Brewster), one of the Cleaver boys' teachers; Larry Mondello (Rusty Stevens); and Richard Rickover (Richard Correll). Of course, Ward (Hugh Beaumont), the Cleaver family patriarch, had died in May of 1982, but he is remembered in photographs in the opening credits and mentioned reverently quite often.

The program was still filmed and still utilized a laugh track, but was now in color (all six seasons of the original were in black and white). Was the use of a live audience instead of a laugh track ever considered for *Still the Beaver*? Abdo stated, "No, it wouldn't have been true to the original series." The program was still very G-Rated, but there were subtle differences—June Cleaver frequently wears slacks (duly noted by Eddie Haskell) and she is no longer afraid to tell Eddie to "put a sock in it" when he attempts to schmooze her with his false flattery. She also has taken up the game of golf. Likely, the most interesting difference is seeing both Wally and The Beaver, now in the role of disciplinarian, raising kids of their own (while still remembering their own hijinks from the original 234 episodes). About that, Abdo added, "We always intended for the show to be true to the original series and its characters."

After completing a single season as *Still the Beaver* on the Disney Channel, production was halted for an entire year, only to have it surface again in 1986 as *The New Leave It to Beaver* on the TBS cable channel, where it enjoyed a three-season run. Although Nick Abdo didn't stay with the program in that transitional period, he recalled, "After going off at Disney, it took time to sell the show and negotiate a license fee with TBS. Once the fee was negotiated, they had to design the show to shoot for a smaller budget than we had for the Disney version—a budget that was already lower than any other show on the Universal lot." As a result, the original 211 Pine Street house was not used in the TBS series. Even though the cast was pretty much intact, the TBS version of the series noticeably shifted its focus from Wally and "The Beav" to the mischief and mishaps of their children. For viewers of a certain age, however, it was fun to catch up with our old friends; the Cleavers, after all, were like our extended family. Seventy-four episodes were produced for TBS, including one titled "Scrapbook II"—a follow-up to the final episode of the original black-and-white series in 1963. In recent years, Barbara Billingsley (2010) and Frank Bank (2013) have left us for that big Mayfield treehouse in the sky.

Episodes were titled "Growing Pains," "Supply and Demand," "Thanksgiving Day," "The Gladiators," "Girl Talk," "Pet Peeves," "Haskells vs. Cleavers," "Dear Pen Pal," "No Free Lunch," "Paper Tiger," "Our Big Girl," "The Piano Lesson," "Slumber Party," "Escape from the Salt Mines," "Steppin' Out," "Father's Day," "Give and Take," "String of Pearls," "Movin' On," "Carried Away," "Violet Rutherford Returns," "Sink or Swim," "Punching In," "Wow," "A Boy and His Snake," "While the Beav's Away," and "Dear Pen Pal II." The executive producers were Nick Abdo and Brian Levant; the producers were Richard Gurman, Al Aidekman, Fred Fox, Jr., Peter Ware, Cindy Begel and Lesa Kite; the writers included Brian Levant, Richard Gurman, Dennis Snee, Michael J. DiGaetano, Lawrence Gay, Paul Diamond, Al Aidekman, Lesa Kite, and Cindy Begel. Begel shared, "This was Brian Levant's dream. He loved the original series, knew every episode forwards and backwards, and sold the concept by having Barbara Billingsley show up at the meeting with a tray of cookies and milk. That nailed it. It was a great, fun experience, and Billingsley was a great, saucy, and very funny lady. By the way, Brian Levant still holds reunions for everyone who worked on the show—there is always a great turnout." The directors included Nick Abdo, Brian Levant, Roger Duchowny, Bob Claver, Steven Hilliard Stern, and Jeffrey Ganz. Music was provided by David Michael Frank. *Still the Beaver* was a Telvan and Sprocket Production, about which Abdo stated, "Telvan is Brian Levant's Company [Telvan is Levant scrambled], and Sprocket was mine."

Teachers Only Carson Productions. NBC. Wednesday nights 9:30 (April 14, 1982–June 9, 1982), and Saturday nights 9:30 (February 2, 1983–May 21, 1983). Twenty-one episodes were videotaped in front of a live audience.

Teachers Only was based in a Los Angeles high school in Season One, and in Brooklyn in Season Two. Two somewhat different groupings of faculty members were also used—neither received an A on the Nielsen report card. Even the name of the high school changed from Millard Fillmore to Woodrow Wilson High in Season Two. The only constant was Norman Fell, as Principal Ben Cooper. Lynn Redgrave, as Diana Swanson, was there in both incarnations, too, but she changed from an English teacher to a guidance counselor in the second season. In Season Two she rented an apartment with the words *Seven C* emblazoned in very large lettering on the front door. Those who didn't graduate to Season Two were Adam Arkin, as Michael Dreyfuss (biology teacher); Van Nessa Clarke, as Gwen Edwards (teacher); Norman Bartold, as Brody (assistant principal); Kit McDonough, as Lois (the busybody clerk); and Richard Karron, as Mr. Pafko (janitor). Only eight episodes were videotaped for that first season. Changes in Season Two, which yielded thirteen episodes, included Jean Smart as Shari (the principal's secretary); Joel Brooks, as Barney Baker (teacher); Tim Reid, as Michael Horne (teacher); Steve Ryan, as Spud LaBoone (the coach); and Teresa Ganzel, as "Sam" Keating (history teacher, and Diana's best friend).

The opening credits for that second season said, "Introducing Teresa Ganzel," about which she recalled, "Yes, this was my first time being a series regular. I had a great manager named Rodney Sheldon who got me an audition to go straight to the network test. I had only done one TV job prior to this—a guest spot on *Three's Company* [as Greedy Gretchen]. So, it was really amazing that he was able to sell me like that. I had an advantage because the other actresses had already been through the grind of auditions and callbacks, etc. I remember when I got there Sandra Bernhardt, Lorna Luft, and a couple of other actresses were up for the same part. So I don't think they had a clear idea who the character of Sam was. It was more about the actress bringing her own personality to the role. I remember walking in the room when it was my turn and I couldn't believe how many people were there. Not only the producers but the network [executives]. And Lynn Redgrave, herself, who cared enough to read with each actress. Reading with another actor makes a huge difference as opposed to reading with a casting director. And someone like Lynn Redgrave understood that. I was so sure I wouldn't get it, I was loose and just played with her. It went great, with big laughs. But it was such a fluke that someone so unknown and inexperienced as I would be that confident. They had me come back the next day and read. I was still sure they wouldn't give it to me, so once again I just had fun. Next thing you know I had a great job for thirteen weeks, with a fabulous cast that was easygoing—no divas, no conflicts. We played cards and laughed all day. And we socialized. Norman Fell had a wonderful home in the Colony in Malibu, and Lynn had a wonderful home in Topanga Canyon, and they threw some wonderful brunches. I wish it had lasted for years. I remember one episode where they had my character make an entrance with a huge, real boa constrictor wrapped around my waist. I am not afraid of snakes, so I was fine with it. But I remember the producers warning me that I would get a long, long laugh on my entrance, and to make sure that I held it for as long as possible before my line. On show night, I entered with the studio audience reacting in complete silence. Actually, there were some gasps of horror. The audience remained in terror throughout the rest of the scene. Lesson to be learned ... live audiences don't think live snakes are funny!"

Teachers Only was a Carson Production. Was Johnny very active behind the scenes? Ganzel said, "I never saw Johnny Carson at rehearsals, but Jean Smart and I shared a dressing room since this was her first series as well. And during one taping I came back to the dressing room and Jean said, 'You will never believe it but Johnny Carson came to our dressing room! He introduced himself and said he would like to meet you. I told him you always stayed backstage during the shows, but he stayed around for a bit just in case you did come back.' I was *so* mad I had missed meeting the King of Late Night—and my boss. But a few days later I got a call to be a guest on *The Tonight Show*! I was so freaked out I told the woman who called from Carson Productions that I was very flattered but I was too nervous, so I would have to say no. Two minutes later she called back and explained to me how that was not a wise choice. So, trembling, I made my first appearance as a guest. Johnny knew I was terrified and held my hand and made me funnier than I was. Our chemistry was cute. I think [the fact] that we are both Midwesterners helped. He *got* me. Of course one of his many talents was his ability to *get* all his guests so quickly. And I showed a clip from *Teachers Only* to promote the show. Weeks later, the show was canceled, but I got a call to come on as a guest again. I said I had nothing to promote and was told that Johnny didn't care, he just thought I was funny to talk to. He had me on many times more as a guest and never cared if I had something to promote or not. And then one day during a commercial break of one of my appearances he asked me if I would like to do sketches with him. I said yes and I loved each and every sketch we did. What amazed me was how much Johnny loved doing those sketches. You have to remember, I did the show for the last ten years. He had already been doing sketches for twenty years but he acted like an enthusiastic newcomer each time. I loved that playful joy he had. My agents told me I should stop doing the sketches with him because I was getting known as a sketch actress because of it. And it was getting harder to sell me for what I really wanted, a television series as an actress. Sometimes I fear they were right. Maybe if I hadn't done them I would have gotten more times up at bat for a sitcom. I guess I'll never know. But I do know the sketch work with Johnny was a joy and a privilege that I will always cherish."

Episodes were titled (*Season One*) "Diana the Substitute Mother," "The Dreyfuss Affair," "Cooper's Grab for Gusto," "Quote Unquote," "The Make-Up Test" (with guest star Michael J. Fox), "I've Got a Crush on You," "Once and Future Teacher," and "Guns and Butter"; (*Season Two*) "The Rose," "Cooper's Arrangement," "Take This Job and Shove It," "Praise the Lord and Pasta Ammunition," "Rex the Wonder Husband," "Teacher's Pet," "Take the Money and Run," "Otherwise Engaged," "Beetlemania," "Leather and Lace," "It's My Party and I'll Cry If I Want To," "Dead Mice Don't Wear Plaid," and "Loss of Innocence." The executive producers were Aaron Ruben, Larry Rosen, and Larry Tucker; the producers were George Yanok and April Kelly; the writers included Aaron Ruben, April Kelly, George Yanok, Mike Weinberger, Larry Rosen, Larry Spencer, Larry Tucker, Tom Chehak, Joel Kimmel, Ann Gibbs, Julie Kirgo, Dinah Kirgo, and Ann Martin; the directors included Peter Baldwin, John Bowab, Rod Daniel, Charles S. Dubin, Linda Day, Mel Ferber, Alan Bergmann, and Tony Singletary. The theme song, "Reach High," was composed and performed by The Commodores.

13 East Scomi Productions—Scoey Mitchlll Organizations, Inc./Pieratt Productions, Ltd.

Wayne Powers and Diana Bellamy filled a prescription for laughter on NBC's *13 East* (photograph courtesy Wayne Powers).

NBC. Saturday night 9:30 (July 29, 1989), Saturday nights 8:30 (August 5, 1989–September 2, 1989, and April 14, 1990–May 5, 1990), Saturday nights 8:00 (May 12, 1990–May 26, 1990) and Saturday nights 8:30 (August 4, 1990–August 25, 1990). Sixteen episodes were videotaped in front of a live audience.

13 East was a ward at a large hospital run with a heavy hand by a taskmaster head nurse named Maggie Poole (Diana Bellamy). In the original, unaired pilot for the series, called "Ward 13," that character's name was Etta Mae Jones, and she was played by *That's My Mama*'s Theresa Merritt. Co-star Wayne Powers recalled, "Theresa Merritt was great, but I guess because of her age at that time in her life she had great difficulty remembering her lines, so Scoey Mitchelll had to replace her and brought in the great Diana Bellamy. Well, Merritt was still under contract and, in order to honor her contract and keep her starring-role paychecks coming, she showed up for work each and every day. There was nothing for her to do, but she never missed a day. Scoey tried everything to discourage her from showing up every day. She had the equivalent of a broom closet for a dressing room. Nothing worked. Theresa was quite content to clock in and out with the stage manager and spend her days reading and getting paid for it. Finally, after many weeks of this, Scoey had had enough and asked NBC to please buy out her contract, and Brandon Tartikoff did."

In Season One, Bellamy's Poole character is the boss of the following—man-crazy Nurse Monique Roberts (Jan Cobler); introverted Nurse Kelly (Barbara Isenberg); worthy cause–champion Nurse Janet Tom (Ellen Regan); sex-obsessed Dr. Warren Newman (Timothy Wade); daft senior volunteer Gertrude Boynton (Marie Denn); and the hard-to-please, cheapskate hospital administrator Wayne Frazier (Wayne Powers). Powers said, "I had worked with Ellen Regan previously in a McDonald's commercial and on another Scoey Mitchlll show called *Me and Mrs. C*. Ellen is a very talented actress. Her character on that earlier show was very well defined by the writers, and her portrayal was spot-on hilarious. Not so, on *13 East*. Scoey cast her because she was good, but her character was never really fleshed out by the writers and, thus, she was one of the casualties in Season Two. The show really started to find itself near the end of Season One. However, Scoey was fed up with constant interference from the network. The suits were meddling too much, so for Season Two, Scoey moved the entire production to the Dallas, Texas, area. What a wonderful experience that was. We were treated like royalty there and the suits were forced to leave us alone."

Only Poole, Frazier, and Monique remained for Season Two. Powers said, "Diana Bellamy and I had developed a special comic chemistry on the show. In fact, in one episode with an *Odd Couple* flavor, I briefly moved in with Diana's Poole character. Poole grew upset with me as her new messy couch-potato roommate when I played my trumpet in the middle of the night. That particular scene received maybe one of the biggest laughs in the history of television, when Poole sprung a line on me, which she and Scoey had secretly planned. She screamed at me to take the trumpet and blow it out my ass. Well, the audience went hysterical for an unbelievable amount of time. The stunned look on my face was priceless. We both held and held for the laugh. The longer we held, the longer they laughed. A comedian's dream moment, for sure. The editors had to cut at least about 75 percent of the audience reaction, lest the show run way over with what home audiences might think was a very long laugh track. It wasn't. They also bleeped out the word ass, totally destroying this hilarious moment for broadcast. Diana and I were also great friends off camera. She died in 2001, and I still miss her terribly.

"I looked a little bit different for Season Two—I grew a pencil-thin moustache, and put on sixty-eight pounds, intentionally. I didn't enjoy having to deliver so many fat jokes aimed at Bellamy's character, so I saw this as a way around it. If I was overweight, the fat jokes would be funny instead of mean or hurtful. It worked. However, I almost didn't make the move to the Lone Star State for Season Two.

Scoey and I had a business-oriented falling out, contractually. I had an out clause in my contract and when negotiations fell apart I exercised it and left the show. Scoey was suddenly left with only two returning original cast member [Bellamy and Cobler]. Well, during the season's hiatus, I was coincidentally cast as a guest star on an episode of *Alf* on the week NBC president Brandon Tartikoff was cast to play himself in the same episode [titled 'Make 'em Laugh']. During a rehearsal break, Brandon pulled me aside for a little chat about the situation on *13 East*, and, lo and behold, a very short time later the contractual disagreement was suddenly totally resolved. Tartikoff was a truly one of a kind. I liked him immensely and respected him greatly."

Added to the second season fray were wannabe comic and disorderly orderly Sidney Cooper (Eric Glenn); ditsy Nurse A. J. Gilroy (Rosemarie Jackson), with an extremely messy apartment; and the ward's priest, Father Frankie (Philip Proctor). Powers added, "Rose was one of the genuinely funniest comic actresses I've ever worked with. The audiences absolutely loved her A. J. character and our scenes together were riotous great fun. She should have been a huge star, but retired from performing to raise a family. The Father Frankie role was very problematic. A hip priest. We had several different actors in the role, and no one really nailed it. Wonderfully gifted Philip Proctor (of *Firesign Theatre* fame) did the best job with it, and Father Frankie continued as a recurring character."

The program was produced and directed by actor/comedian Scoey Mitchlll for his Scomi Production Company. Powers stated, "Scoey always referred to it as our 'little show' as in we have a nice 'little show' to do here." Powers added, "Despite a really lousy lead-in, *A Family for Joe* with aging big screen bad boy Robert Mitchum in a sitcom with children, and despite excellent ratings, our show was canceled when Warren Littlefield took the helm at NBC. Littlefield replaced Tartikoff's show with *Nurses*, a near carbon copy of *13 East*. But, it was his show, not Tartikoff's." So, after a total of sixteen episodes, unfortunately, *13 East* went south.

Episodes were titled (*Season One*) "Where's the Ticket?," "I've Got a Loan to Pick with You," "A Day in the Life," "The Switch," "Tabloid Time," and "Poppa's Coming"; (*Season Two*) "Second Time Around," "Hallelujah Amen," "The Affair," "Maggie's Special Friend," "The Ledge," "So This Is How It's Gonna Be?," "Detrimental Reliance," "Welcome Sidney," "Monique Turns 40," and "Bullseye." The producers were Scoey Mitchlll, Paul Pieratt, Sr., and Walter Glover; the writers included Ray Hoese, David Ankrum, Mara Lideks, Patricia Rust, Lesa Kite, and Cindy Begel. Begel said, "Our office had a door with a most unusual feature—a hole obviously made by a fist. Also, Scoey often requested that we insert more racist jokes into the scripts, and that made us all very uncomfortable, almost to the point of writing the scripts under an alias." The director was Scoey Mitchlll. The theme song was written by Harry Middlebrooks, and performed by Marie Cain (*Season One*) and Benita Arterberry (*Season Two*).

Trying Times KCET Productions. PBS. Sunday nights in some markets, but Monday nights in others (October 18, 1987–November 22, 1987), and Thursday nights (October 12, 1989–November 16, 1989). Air dates and times varied. Twelve episodes were filmed single-camera style without a laugh track.

Trying Times was a PBS sitcom anthology series with two very short seasons, two seasons apart. Both the 1987 and 1989 fall season consisted of six episodes each, and a lot of famous guest stars—most notably Candice Bergen, Peter Scolari, Robert Klein, Rosanna Arquette, Hope Lange, Stockard Channing, Steven Wright, Teri Garr, Jean Stapleton, Geena Davis, Carrie Fisher, and Keanu Reeves. Each episode dealt with the comedic struggles of daily life: meeting one's in-laws for the first time; deciding whether or not to have a baby because of a ticking biological clock; a thirty-year-old student opting to get his first job; a divorcee moving into her own home; and attending a disastrous high school reunion. Producer Jon S. Denny admitted that some of the subject matter was drawn from his own psychotherapy sessions. It was the first PBS sitcom series without a British accent.

Episodes were titled (*Season One*) "A Family Tree," "Driver, She Said," "Get a Job," "Bedtime Story," "The Visit," and "Moving Day"; (*Season Two*) "Hunger Chic," "Hit List," "Death and Taxes," "Sad Confession," "The Boss," and "A Good Life." The executive producers were Phylis Geller and Philip Keatley; the producers were Jon S. Denny and Ed Richardson; the writers were Christopher Duran, Spalding Gray, George C. Wolfe, Wendy Wasserstein, Budge Threlkeld, Richard Greenberg, A. R. Gurney, Albert Innaurato, Beth Henley, Marilyn Suzanne Miller, Terrence McNally, Renee Shafransky, Bernard Slade, and Earl Pomerantz; and the directors included Alan Arkin, Buck Henry, Jon S. Denny, Sheldon Larry, Jonathan Demme, Michael Lindsay-Hogg, Sandy Wilson, and Christopher Guest. Music was provided by Brian Tate and Robert Kraft.

The Two of Us Marble Arch Productions. CBS. Monday nights 8:30 (April 6, 1981–April 27, 1981, October 12, 1981–January 4, 1982), Wednesday nights 8:30 (January 13, 1982–February 24, 1982). Twenty episodes were videotaped in front of a live audience.

Inspired by characters created by Bill Macilwraith for the London Weekend Television series *Two's Company*, *The Two of Us* was an American sitcom that aired for two truncated TV seasons on CBS. Nan Gallagher (Mimi Kennedy) is a divorced mother and career woman who works for a New York TV station, co-hosting a program called *Mid-Morning Manhattan*—a program very much like the old *Live with Regis and Kathie Lee* program. In fact, her co-host was at first the unseen and egotistical Reggie Philbis (an obvious takeoff on Regis Philbin), but was later renamed Reggie Cavanaugh (and portrayed by the ubiquitous Tim Thomerson). Were she to be cast in *The Odd Couple*, Nan could take on the sloppy Oscar Madison role (she is anything but domestic). Nan has the added onus of a teenage daughter named Gabby (Dana Hill), so this called for a little help around the house. A reluctant Robert Brentwood (Peter Cook) is hired to take on the monumental task of creating order at the Gallaghers' residence. Initially, he is appalled at the idea of working for a woman with a child, but takes on the task anyway. Though sarcastic, overbearing, pompous and overtly proper, Brentwood gets the Gallaghers' home running liked a well-oiled machine. It also helps that he is a gourmet chef, as Nan entertains some rather important guests. Nan's agent is the insecure and hypochondriacal Cubby Royce (Oliver Clark).

The program fared well in its limited four-episode run in Season One, and was invited back in the fall. The program's premise, however, wore thin very quickly in Season Two and the ratings took a nosedive. After sixteen new episodes in Season Two and a move from Mondays to Wednesdays, CBS pulled the plug. Select episodes were rerun in prime-time during the summer of 1982. Mimi Kennedy is, as of this writing, enjoying great success on the CBS sitcom *Mom*.

Episodes were titled (*Season One*) "Nan Meets Brentwood," "Slumber Party," "Old Alf," and "Weekend Away"; (*Season Two*) "Nan's Fan," "Brentwood's Agony," "Upstairs, Downstairs," "Duke of Lawford," "A Big Hand for Brentwood," "Chicken Marengo," "A Family Counseled," "German Lesson," "A Man from Brentwood's Past," "The Christmas Thief" (with guest star Helen Hunt), "Basketball Gabby," "Butler of the Year," "Gabby's Birthday Party," "Odd Couples," "Torch Song" (with guest star Joyce Bulifant), and "Brentwood Goes on Strike." The producers were Charlie Hauck and Tom Cherones; the writers included Bill Davenport, Eric Cohen, Charlie Hauck, Katherine Green, Arthur Julian, and Tom Whedon; the directors included Asaad Kelada and Peter Bonerz.

We Got It Made Intermedia Entertainment/The Farr Organization, Inc./Twenty Paws Productions/The Fred Silverman Company/MGM/United Artists. NBC (*Season One*), and Syndicated (*Season Two*). Thursday nights 9:00 (September 8, 1983–December 8, 1983), Saturday

Teri Copley was the maid on both seasons of NBC's *We Got It Made*. She is pictured here, sandwiched between co-stars Tom Villard and Matt McCoy.

nights 9:00 (January 7, 1984–March 10, 1984), and Syndicated at 7:30 P.M., air dates varied (September 11, 1987–March 30, 1988). Forty-six episodes were videotaped in front of a live audience.

This rather forgettable sitcom, lambasted by the critics at the time, featured two young slovenly Manhattan bachelors who use the classified ads to hire a hot maid. David Tucker (Matt McCoy) is a straight-laced lawyer, with a creative, but bizarre, child-like importer roommate named Jay Bostwick (Tom Villard). With two Oscar Madisons under one roof (Apartment 9A at 1054 West 61st Street), the sexy young woman who answers their ad certainly has her hands full. Mickey McKenzie (Teri Copley) had just arrived in New York, and is the stereotypical blonde bombshell, much in the mode of Marilyn Monroe. Her previous job was with The American Flag Company, but they moved their plant to Japan. She had also previously been a dancer and an usherette. Up until this point, Mickey had led a very safe life, but now she channels her more adventurous side and takes the job. Even though the situation was totally innocent, David and Jay's girlfriends, Claudia and kindergarten teacher Beth (Stephanie Kramer and Bonnie Urseth, respectively) are understandably suspicious and a wee bit jealous. NBC gave the program a shot in two different time slots, but it failed to "clean up" in the ratings and was gone from the lineup by the spring of 1984.

This program has a most unique history in that, over three years later after it had been pretty well forgotten, it was resurrected for first-run syndication (in the 7:30 P.M. time slot with competition from reruns and game shows on the other channels). Some members of the original cast were unavailable (Stephanie Kramer had found success on *Hunter*), and others—Matt McCoy and Bonnie Urseth—just weren't interested in recreating their respective roles. Only Teri Copley and Tom Villard returned from the original. David Tucker was now played by John Hillner, and two new cast members—neighbors Max Papavailios, Sr., and Jr. (Ron Karabatsos and Lance Wilson-White, respectively) joined the fray. Max Sr., is a policeman, and Max Jr., falls head over heels for Mickey. Not surprisingly, the second version of the show didn't fare much better than the first, and after March of 1988, no more episodes of *We Got It Made* got made.

Episodes were titled (*Season One*) "The Pilot," "Mickey Sleepwalks," "The Boyfriend," "Mickey Goes Topless," "David's Birthday," "Mickey the Shoplifter," "Mickey's Mom" (with guest star Elaine Joyce), "Mickey Gets Married, Parts One and Two," "The Super," "Am I Blue?" (with guest star Edie McClurg), "Mickey's Tee Shirt," "Sexiest Bachelor," "Mickey's Misconception," "Mickey's Poster," "The Other Tucker," "The Break-Up, Parts One and Two," "Miss Mom," "The Fight," "A Paige in David's Life," and "Mickey Makes the Grade" (with guest star Scatman Crothers); (*Season Two*) "Instant Family," "Three Faces of Mickey," "And David Makes Three," "Mickey Meets Mr. Right?," "Hello, Dolly," "Prisoner of Love," "On the Ropes," "The Naked Truth," "Man Around the House," "Upstairs, Downstairs," "A Dog's Life," "Save the Last Dance for Me," "Mickey Times Two" (Teri Copley has a dual role as her identical twin, Lucy Ann—shades of *The Patty Duke Show*), "Fatal Distraction," "Jay's on the Roof," "Centerfold Mickey" (with guest star Dick Gautier), "Confidence Man," "Not for Love or Money," "La Vie En Jay, Parts One and Two," "Four Loves Have I," "Crime Busters," "Temporary Mickey," and "Video Mickey." The executive producer was Fred Silverman; the producers were Lynn Farr Brao, Gordon Farr, Gene Marcione, Casey Keller, Richard Albrecht, and Alan Rafkin; the writers included Lynn Farr Brao, Michael S. Baser, Bob Brunner, David Chambers, Chet Dowling, Ken Kuta, Jeffrey Ferro, Gordon Farr, Arnold Kane, Ken Hecht, Susan H. Lee, Sandy Krinski, C. M. Leon, Bowie Lennon, Coleman "Chick" Mitchell, Laura Levine, Kim Weiskopf, Geoffrey Neigher, Fredric Weiss, and Margaret Weisman; the directors included Alan Rafkin, Stan Harris, and Jim Drake. Music was provided by Tom Wells.

You Again? Taft Entertainment Television/The Lawson Group/Sweater Productions. NBC. Thursday night 8:30 (February 27, 1986), Monday nights 8:00 (March 3, 1986–June 9, 1986), Wednesday nights 9:30 (October 1, 1986–January 7, 1987). Twenty-six episodes were videotaped in front of a live audience (13 each season).

You Again? was based upon a British series *Home to Roost*, by Eric Chappell. In fact, it's interesting to note that Elizabeth Bennett, who played the housekeeper Enid Tompkins on the UK version, simultaneously played the role on the American show (imagine the frequent flyer miles she accumulated!). *You Again?* takes place ten years after the main character's contentious divorce. Henry Willows (Jack Klugman) has long since adjusted to single life and his position as the purchasing manager for Global Markets grocery stores. His very conservative world is suddenly turned upside down when his seventeen-year-old son, Matt (John Stamos) shows up at his door. Matt (who calls almost everyone "dude" or "babe") is unhappy living with his mother and new stepfather and seeks out his biological father, whom he hasn't seen in seven years. Matt, a handsome young girl-crazy drummer, is Henry's exact opposite. Their opinions are also at opposite ends of the spectrum, and yet they love and respect each other very much. After a rocky start, Henry grows fond of having Matt around on a full-time basis.

Recurring characters include the hilarious Guy Marks, as Harry; Barbara Rhoades, as Henry's secretary, Maggie; and Valerie Landsburg, as Henry's surly assistant, Pam. Pam is needed because Henry is simply not computer savvy. The sitcom started strong in its short first season, but was unable to maintain those ratings in its truncated second season, despite boasting a Beach Boys' reunion (Mike Love, Brian Wilson, Carl Wilson, Al Jardine) in an episode titled "The Audition," on which Matt gets the opportunity of a lifetime—to fill in for the group's regular drummer. It's interesting to note that all these years later, Stamos still plays and even records with the group on occasion.

Episodes were titled (*Season One*) "All You Need Is Love," "Dating Henry," "Small Change," "Henry and Matt Get Sick," "Plastic Dream World," "Bad Apples," "Enid Quits," "A New Life," "Suspect," "The Wake," "Uncle Randy," "Marry Me a Little," and "The Strike"; (*Season Two*) "The Grad, "Quit Is a Four-Letter Word," "The Audition" (with guest stars The Beach Boys), "Life, Liberty, and the Pursuit of Traffic Lights," "Sports Fantasy" (with guest star Willie Shoemaker), "Lush Life" (with guest star Robert Morse), "The D. J.," "Social Insecurity," "Personals" (with guest star Marion Ross), "Enid Moves In," "Good Neighbors," "Henry the Kissinger" (with guest star Anita Gillette, Klugman's former *Quincy M. E.* co-star), and "Where the Sun Don't Shine" (with guest star Frank Aletter). The executive producers were Ronny Hallin, Sarah Lawson, Bernie Orenstein, and Saul Turteltaub; the producers included Al Aidekman, Liz Sage and Rick Mitz; the writers included Jay Abramowitz, Al Aidekman, Eric Chappell, Gary Jacobs, Doug McIntyre, Tom Musca, Zachary D. Wechsler, Jerry Stahl, James Kearns, Sam Greenbaum, Vivian Rhodes, Jay Wolf, Sally Wade, Bernie Orenstein, and Saul Turteltaub; the directors included Peter Bonerz, Jerry Paris, Bill Foster, Gerren Keith, Barbara Schultz, and Howard Murray. The program was created by Eric Chappell. Music was provided by Chris Boardman, Rik Howard, and Bob Wirth.

Appendix B:
Sitcom Topical Index

Addresses on short-lived 1980s sitcoms— *Angie* (76 Clinton Street [Angie] and 421 Vernon Street [Theresa Falco]); *The Cavanaughs* (36 Brookhaven Street); *Domestic Life* (106 Liberty Lane); *Easy Street* (4163 Hillcrest Drive); *Hail to the Chief* (1600 Pennsylvania Avenue); *Jennifer Slept Here* (32 Rexford Drive); *Joanie Loves Chachi* (1632 Palmer Avenue—Delvecchio's Restaurant); *Just in Time* (133 Wilshire Boulevard—*West Coast Review Magazine* offices); *Learning the Ropes* (34 Hampton Street); *Me and Mom* (2936 Hampton Boulevard—Garfield and Hunnicutt Detective Agency); *Melba* (623 Bleecker Street); *Mr. President* (1600 Pennsylvania Avenue); *Open House* (7150 Beverly Glen [work] and 13205 Ocean Avenue [Laura Kelly]); *Raising Miranda* (863 Fairview Lane); *Report to Murphy* (832 Church Street), *The Ropers* (46 Peacock Drive); *Sanford* (4707 South Central [Fred Sanford], 77 Kantwell Drive [Eve]); *Shirley* (602 Kingsbeach Road); *Snoops* (30th Street); *Star of the Family* (7136 La Salle Drive), *Still the Beaver* (211 Pine Street); *Together We Stand/Nothing Is Easy* (37 Brookfall Road); *Tucker's Witch* (7000 Vista del Mar Drive [Tucker and Tucker Detective Agency]); *We Got It Made* (1054 West 61st Street, Apartment 9A); *What a Country* (11 Fairlawn Street [Bud McPherson], 36 Whitney Way [Taylor Brown])

Animated short-lived 1980s sitcoms— *The California Raisin Show, The Completely Mental Misadventures of Ed Grimley, Drak Pack, The Dukes, Galaxy High, The Gary Coleman Show, Gilligan's Planet, Laverne and Shirley, Meatballs and Spaghetti, Mork and Mindy*

Beverly Hills/Bel Air–based short-lived 1980s sitcoms— *Beverly Hills Buntz, Brand New Life, Down and Out in Beverly Hills, Easy Street, Jennifer Slept Here, Leo and Liz in Beverly Hills, Open House, Rags to Riches, Sanchez of Bel Air*

Big name stars of short-lived 1980s sitcoms— Lucille Ball (*Life with Lucy*), George Burns (*George Burns Comedy Week*), Brian Keith (*Heartland, Pursuit of Happiness*), Mary Tyler Moore (*Annie McGuire, Mary*), Debbie Reynolds (*Aloha Paradise*), Mickey Rooney (*One of the Boys*), Danny Thomas (*I'm a Big Girl Now, One Big Family*), Dick Van Dyke (*The Van Dyke Show*), Ellen Burstyn (*The Ellen Burstyn Show*)

Eponymous titles of short-lived 1980s sitcoms— *Ann Jillian, The Dom DeLuise Show, The Ellen Burstyn Show, The Gary Coleman Show, George Burns Comedy Week, The Lucie Arnaz Show, Mary, Melba, The Redd Foxx Show, The Robert Guillaume Show, The Stockard Channing Show, Suzanne Pleshette Is Maggie Briggs, The Van Dyke Show*

Ethnic-oriented short-lived 1980s sitcoms— *a.k.a. Pablo, Angie, Bustin' Loose, The Cavanaughs, Charlie and Company, Checking In, Chicken Soup, Condo, Gung Ho, I Married Dora, The New Odd Couple, One of the Boys* [1989], *Phyl and Mikhy, The Redd Foxx Show, Sanchez of Bel Air, Sanford, Steambath, Trial and Error, What a Country*

Fantasy-based short-lived 1980s sitcoms— *Free Spirit, Herbie the Love Bug, Jennifer Slept*

Here, Just Our Luck, Madame's Place, Misfits of Science, Mr. Merlin, Mr. Smith, Nearly Departed, Once a Hero, The People Next Door, Probe, Reggie, Second Chance, Small and Frye, Steambath, Tucker's Witch

Fish-out-of-water themed short-lived 1980s sitcoms—*Better Days, Beverly Hills Buntz, Down and Out in Beverly Hills, Easy Street, Leo and Liz in Beverly Hills, Lewis and Clark, Phyl and Mikhy, Rags to Riches, Sanchez of Bel Air*

Hotel/Restaurant/Saloon themed short-lived 1980s sitcoms—*Aloha Paradise, Amanda's, Checking In, Flo, Frank's Place, Isabel Sanford's Honeymoon Hotel, Lewis and Clark, Marblehead Manor, Nick and Hillary, No Soap Radio, The Nutt House, Tattingers*

Large family themed short-lived 1980s sitcoms—*Baby Makes Five, Brand New Life, The Cavanaughs, Charlie and Company, Together We Stand/Nothing Is Easy, You Can't Take It with You*

Law themed short-lived 1980s sitcoms—*Day by Day, Eisenhower and Lutz, Foley Square, Free Spirit, It Takes Two, Park Place, Sara, Trial and Error*

Legal problem themed short-lived 1980s sitcoms—*The Bad News Bears, Bustin' Loose, Me and Mrs. C., Report to Murphy, Stir Crazy, Women in Prison*

Living arrangements in the spotlight in short-lived 1980s sitcoms—*The Brady Brides, Brand New Life, Charles in Charge, Dads, Down and Out in Beverly Hills, Easy Street, Foot in the Door, Goodtime Girls, Heartland, Life with Lucy, Live In, Living Dolls, Mama's Boy, Me and Mrs. C., My Sister Sam, One of the Boys* [1982]*, Rags to Riches, Roomies, Seven Brides for Seven Brothers, Sister Kate, Three's a Crowd, Together We Stand/Nothing Is Easy, The Two of Us, Under One Roof, We Got It Made, You Again?*

Medical themed short-lived 1980s sitcoms—*Aftermash, Angie, E/R, Gloria, Harry, It Takes Two, The Robert Guillaume Show, Starting from Scratch, 13 East*

Movie or play–based short-lived 1980s sitcoms—*Baby Boom, Breaking Away, Dirty Dancing, Down and Out in Beverly Hills, Fast Times (at Ridgemont High), Foul Play, The Four Seasons, Freebie and the Bean, Gung Ho, Herbie the Love Bug, Nothing in Common, Steambath, You Can't Take It with You*

Period piece short-lived 1980s sitcoms—*Aftermash, Best of the West, The Charmings, Goodtime Girls, Gun Shy, Joanie Loves Chachi, Laverne and Shirley* (animated)*, Rags to Riches, Six O'Clock Follies, Zorro and Son*

Pets on short-lived 1980s sitcoms—Ramon the parrot (*a.k.a.* Pablo), Ace (*At Ease*), Crystal (*Coming of Age*), Mike (*Down and Out in Beverly Hills*), Flash (*The Dukes*), Godiva (*E/R*), Angie (*The Ellen Burstyn Show*), Hunk (*Half Nelson*), Waldo (*The Last Precinct*), Woofer (*Meatballs and Spaghetti*), Furball (*Reggie*), Muffin (*The Ropers*), Oregano (*Shirley*), Sam (*The Thorns*)

Politically themed short-lived 1980s sitcoms—*Annie McGuire, The Cavanaughs, Hail to the Chief, He's the Mayor, Mr. President, Tanner '88, Washingtoon*

Private Eye/Crimefighter/Police themed short-lived 1980s sitcoms—*Ace Crawford Private Eye, Baker's Dozen, Beverly Hills Buntz, A Fine Romance, Fitz and Bones, Foul Play, Freebie and the Bean, Half Nelson, Hard Knocks, I Had Three Wives, Jack and Mike, Joe Bash, The Last Precinct, Legmen, Me and Mom, The Misadventures of Sheriff Lobo, Nobody's Perfect, Partners in Crime, Police Squad, Probe, Shadow Chasers, Shell Game, Sledge Hammer, Small and Frye, Snoops, Tenspeed and Brown Shoe, Tough Cookies, Tucker's Witch, Zorro and Son*

Rags-to-riches short-lived 1980s sitcoms—*Down and Out in Beverly Hills, Easy Street, Filthy Rich, Rags to Riches*

School-based short-lived 1980s sitcoms—*The Bad News Bears; Better Days; Fast Times; Fathers and Sons; Good Morning, Miss Bliss; Harper Valley P.T.A.; Homeroom; Learning the Ropes; The Life and Times of Eddie Roberts; Living Dolls; Maggie; Making the Grade; One of the Boys* (1982); *The Pursuit of Happiness; Roomies; Spencer/Under One Roof; Square Pegs; Teachers Only*

Show business themed short-lived 1980s sitcoms—*a.k.a. Pablo; All Is Forgiven; Buffalo Bill; The California Raisin Show; Domestic Life; Dreams; The Duck Factory; FM; The Famous Teddy Z; A Fine Romance; First Impressions; Fitz and Bones; Foul Play; Good Time Harry; Goodnight, Beantown; Hello, Larry; Joanie Loves Chachi; Just Our Luck; Knight and Daye; The Lucie Arnaz Show; Madame's Place; Mama Malone; Roxie; Shell Game; Six O'Clock Follies; Star of the Family; The Stockard Channing Show; Take Five; The Two of Us; The Van Dyke Show*

Single dads in short-lived 1980s sitcoms—*Buffalo Bill; Dads; Hello, Larry; I'm a Big Girl Now; Me and Maxx; Raising Miranda; The Robert Guillaume Show; Star of the Family; Still the Beaver; You Again?*

Single moms in short-lived 1980s sitcoms—*Ann Jillian, Baby Boom, Brand New Life, The Ellen Burstyn Show, Gloria, Harper Valley P. T. A., I'm a Big Girl Now, It's Your Move, Nothing Is Easy, Second Chance, Shirley, The Two of Us, Under One Roof*

Spinoff/sequel short-lived 1980s sitcoms—*Beverly Hills Buntz, The Brady Brides, Checking In, The Dukes, Flo, Gilligan's Planet, Gloria, Joanie Loves Chachi, The Misadventures of Sheriff Lobo, Living Dolls, The New Love American Style, The New Monkees, The New Odd Couple, Open House, The Ropers, Sanford, Still the Beaver/The New Leave It to Beaver, Three's a Crowd, The Tortellis*

Sports themed short-lived 1980s sitcoms—*The Bad News Bears, Fathers and Sons, Good Time Harry, Learning the Ropes, Phyl and Mikhy, Semi Tough, Shaping Up*

Stars with the most short-lived 1980s sitcoms—Barbara Barrie, Bill Daily, Patty Duke, Héctor Elizondo, Norman Fell, Harold Gould, Andre Gower, Dan Hedaya, Mimi Kennedy, Rod McCary, Tim Reid, McLean Stevenson, Christopher Rich, Tony Roberts, Tim Thomerson, Carlene Watkins

Teen-focused short-lived 1980s sitcoms—*Better Days; Breaking Away; Charles in Charge; Fast Times; Good Morning, Miss Bliss; It's Your Move; The New Adventures of Beans Baxter; The Popcorn Kid; Second Chance; Spencer/Under One Roof; Square Pegs; Together We Stand/Nothing Is Easy*

Working women themed short-lived 1980s sitcoms—*Amanda's, Ann Jillian, Annie McGuire, Baby Boom, Checking In, The Ellen Burstyn Show, Foley Square, It's Your Move, Ladies' Man, Live-in, Mary, Me and Mom, One in a Million, Partners in Crime, Sara*

Writers in short-lived 1980s sitcoms—*The Ellen Burstyn Show, Family Man, Good Time Harry, It's Your Move, Jack and Mike, Just in Time, Ladies Man, Mama's Boy, Mary, The Slap Maxwell Story, Suzanne Pleshette Is Maggie Briggs*

Index

Numbers in ***bold italics*** refer to pages with photographs.

The A-Team 4
Aal, Deborah 134
Aames, Angela 28
Abbott, Kevin 51
Abbott, Norman 114, 185, 187
Abdo, Nick 115, 222–23
Abdul-Samad, Hakeem 44
Abraham, Henry David 188
Abrahams, Jim 129, 130
Abramowitz, Jay 231
Abrell, Sarah 45
Abugov, Jeff 172
Accidental Family 172
According to Jim 43, 196
Ace Crawford, Private Eye 3–4, ***3***, 233
Adams, Bryan 44
Adams, Caitlin 157
Adams, Casey 162
Adams, Fletcher 147
Adams, Mason 79
Adams, Penny 196
Addams, Gomez 97
The Addams Family 157
Adell, Ilunga 66
Adelman, Sybil 140, 155, 215
Aftermash 183–4, 233
Agony 91
Aidekman, Al 74, 115, 175, 186–7, ***186***, 223, 231
Aidem, Monty 24, 28
Airplane 129
Aitkens, Michael 45
a.k.a. Pablo 4–5, ***5***, 142, 174, 232, 233, 234
Akerling, Mya 75
Akins, Claude 83, 212–13, ***213***
Akune, Shuko 39
Alan, Sylvia 137
Albert, Eddie 106
Albert, Lisa 11, 217
Albrecht, Howard 28, 208
Albrecht, Richard 72, 230
Albright, Lola 3
Alcott, Louisa May 152
Alda, Alan 49, 50
Alda, Beatrice 49, 50
Alda, Elizabeth 49, 50
Alderson, Brooke 26
Aletter, Frank 208, 231
Alexander, Jason 1, 39, 40, ***40***
Alexander, Les 114
Alf 100, 227
Alfred Hitchcock Presents 74
Alice 91, 161, 200–201, 210
Alice Doesn't Live Here Anymore 36
Aliff, Lisa 181
All in the Family 24, 26, 55, 106

All Is Forgiven 5–7, ***6***, 234
Allen, Corey 84, 176, 214
Allen, Gracie 53, 72
Allen, Phillip R. 187
Allen, Rae 128
Allen, Rex 15
Allen, Steve 127, 191
Allen, Woody 170
Allison, Judith D. 65, 198
All's Fair 138
Allyn, Barbara 219
Aloha Paradise 7–8, ***8***, 159, 232, 233
Alonso, Maria Conchita 122
Alsberg, Arthur 66
Altay, Derin 188
Alterman, Steve 162
Altier, Jackie 61
Altman, Robert 165–6
Alu, Cheryl 145, 210
Alzado, Lyle 71, 82–3
Amanda's 9–10, ***9***, 233, 234
Amanda's by the Sea 9
Amateau, Rod 38
The Amazing Race 16
Ameche, Don 102
Amelio, Phillip J. II 88
Amendolia, Don 95
Ames, Christopher 195
Ames, Morgan 137
Amico, David 65
Amodeo, John 45
Amritraj, Vijay 82, 178
Amsterdam, Morey 61
Anders, Lauren 53
Andersen, Bridgette 58
Anderson, Anne 212
Anderson, Harry 166
Anderson, Jane 134, 135
Anderson, John Maxwell 74
Anderson, Josef 146
Anderson, Lauren Eve 127
Anderson, Loni 33–5, ***34***, 126
Anderson, Maxwell 219
Anderson, Pamela 210
Anderson, Richard Dean 146
Anderson, Sam 95
Anderson, Sheila 111, ***111***, 112
The Andrews Sisters 58
The Andy Griffith Show 128, 163
Angell, David 26, 29
Angie 1, 184–5, 232, 233
Ankrum, David 227
Ann Jillian 10–11, 232, 234
The Ann Jillian Show 11
Annie McGuire 11, 232, 233, 234
Another Day 98
Anspach, Susan 151
"Answers" 139

Antoinette, Marie 101
Antonacci, Greg 73, 96, 137, 172, 215
Antonio, Lou 52, 148
Antoniou, John 145
Any Which Way You Can 102
Anything but Love 64
Appel, Leah 146
The Apple Dumpling Gang 58
The Apple Dumpling Gang Rides Again 58
Applebaum, Bill 115
Appleby, Shiri 79
Applegate, Christina 7, 177, 193
Applegate, Fred 201
Applegate, Royce 161
Aquino, Amy 123
Arango, Douglas 13, 76, 220
Arbus, Allan 49
Archer, Beverly 154, 177
Archie Bunker's Place 55
Argo, Allison 80, ***80***, 81
Arkin, Adam 7, 20, 172–3, ***173***, 223
Arkin, Alan 52, 62–3, 228
Arkush, Allan 167
Armstrong, Bess 5–6, ***6***
Armstrong, Louis 50
Armstrong, R.B. 111
Armstrong, Valorie 162
Arnaz, Lucie 91–2, ***91***, 232, 234
Arndt, Denis 11
Arner, Gwen 18, 167
Arnie 12
Arnold, Buddy 129
Arnold, Danny 76
Arnold, Jack 214
Arnold, Nick 14, 44, 76, 153, 182
Aronsohn, Lee 127
Aronson, Judie 132
Arquette, Rosanna 148, 149, 227
Arrested Development 103
Arsenault, Ray 188
Arterberry, Benita 227
Arthur, Bea 5, ***5***, 9, ***9***
Arthur, Maureen 37
Arthurs, John 163
Ash, Rod 117, 221
Ashby, Hal 17
Asimov, Isaac 131, 132
Asner, Ed 117, 130, 131
Asselin, Diane 185
The Associates 1, 69
Astin, John 77, 97, 102, 195
At Ease 11–12, 233
"At This Moment" 139
Atari, Scott 59
Atkinson, Buddy 110
Attias, Daniel 44, 221

235

Index

Attila the Hun 101
Auberjonois, Rene 97, 168
Auerbach, David 154
Austin, Ray 45
Avalon, Frankie 93
Avalos, Luis 26, 39
The Avengers 37, 96
Averback, Hy 12, 50, 52, 82, 184
Avery, James 202
Axelrod, David 54, 63, 84
Axton, Hoyt 29, 140, 201
Ayers, Diana 203, 221
Aykroyd, Peter 84
Aylesworth, Aggie 32
Aylesworth, John 110
Azrialy, Barbara 97
Azzara, Candy 39

Babbitt, Bruce 166
Babbitt, Karin 28, 120
Babcock, Barbara 15, 49, 98, 103, 160
Babers, Christopher 154
Baby Boom 12–13, 233, 234
"Baby It's You" 28
Baby Makes Five 13–14, 176, 233
Bacarr, Jina 52
Bach, Catherine 33
Back to You 202
Backus, Jim 54
"Bad, Bad Leroy Brown" 82
The Bad News Bears 185–8, **186**, 233, 234
The Bad News Bears Go to Japan 186
The Bad News Bears in Breaking Training 186
The Bad Seed 219
Badalato, Bill 75
Baddeley, Hermione 147
Badiyi, Reza 45, 130, 168, 221
Baer, Donald A. 46, 68
Baer, Parley 208
Baer, Richard 26, 50
Baggetta, Vincent 17, 75
Bagni, Gwen 149
Bailey, G.W. 204
Bailey, Hillary 113
Bain, Conrad 160, 207, 215
Baines, Harold 174
Baio, Scott 58, 192–3, 209–10, **209**
Baird, Pamela 222
Baker, Jim B. 200
Baker, Joby 150
Baker's Dozen 14, 233
Bakula, Scott 35, 59, 217
Baldwin, Gerard 52
Baldwin, Peter 19, 33, 35, 44, 48, 58, 78, 88, 92, 98, 121, 122, 152, 179, 182, 205, 217, 225
Ball, Lucille 87–8, 92, 232
Ball, Sue 84
Ballantine, Carl 121
Ballard, Glen 66
Balmagia, Larry 76, 100, 118, 184, 193
Balson, Allison 86
Baltzell, Deborah 71
Banfield, Bever-Leigh 123
The Bangles 139

Bank, Frank 222, 223
Banks, Ernie 72
Banks, Jonathan 138
Bannick, Lisa A. 29, 119
Banta, Gloria 185
Barasch, Norman 113, 114, 122, 145
Barbera, Joseph 25, 30, 33, 52, 53, 104, 211
Bardol, Daniel 13
Barimo, George 40
Barker, Steve 182
Barlow, David 185
Barnes, Christopher Daniel 196, 197
Barnette, Neema 51
Barney Fife and Other Characters I Have Known 179
Barney Miller 14, 63, 65, 112, 125
Barnhart, Don 62, 93
Baron, Allen 92
Baron, Deborah R. 167, 218
Barr, Douglas 145
Barrie, Barbara 20, 45, 137, 175, 198, 215, 234
Barron, Fred 77
Barry, Gene 8
Barry, Jack 95
Barrymore, John 117
Bartlett, Juanita 168
Bartold, Norman 223
Barton, Peter 148
Barty, Billy 3
Basanese, Manny 25, 145
Basehart, Richard 101
Baser, Michael S. 100, 230
Basinger, Kim 52
Baskin, Jerry 29
Baskin, John 104, 105, **105**, 106
Bass, Emory 185
Bassett, Skye 27
Bast, William 176
Bate, Jeremy 111
Bateman, Jason 1, 74, 89
Bateman, Justine 74
Bates, John 53
Bates, Rhonda 72
Bathtub 160
Batman 82, 119
"The Batman Theme" 82
Baublitz, Bob 86, 151, 214
Baum, Bruce 162
Baum, Steven 218
Baxter, Benjamin, Sr. 108
Baxter, Clayton 10
The Baxters 188
Bay, Frances 191
Baywatch 145
The Beach Boys 231
Beacham, Stephanie 63, 149–50, **149**
Beal, John 58, 84
Beasley, Allyce 147
Beasley, John 91, 125
The Beatles 28, 154
Beaton, Alex 84, 148, 168
Beatts, Anne 156, 158
Beauchamp, Richard 182
Beaumont, Gabrielle 17, 28, 45, 182, 184
Beaumont, Hugh 222

Beaumont, Rex 137
Beavers, Susan 217
Becker 7
Beckerman, George 62
Beers, Francine 121
Begel, Cindy 21–2, 24, 30, 118–9, 171, 181–2, 186–7, **186**, 210, 223, 227
Behar, Joy 13
Behn, Noel 167
Behr, Ira Steven 119, 146
Beimler, Hans 147
Belack, Doris 14
Belford, Christine 37, 73
Bellamy, Diana 225–7, **225**
Bellamy, Earl 24
Belous, Paul M. 214
Belson, Jerry 113
Belushi, John 129
Belyeu, Faye Oshima 64
Benben, Brian 103
Bender, Jack 20, 75
Bendetson, Bob 24, 155
Bendetson, Howard 24, 155
Benedek, Barbara 26, 71
Benedek, Edgar Benny 146
Bening, Annette 76
Benjamin, Richard 145
Bennett, Elizabeth 115, 230
Bennett, Jahary 68
Bennett, Richard C. 38, 206
Bennett, Ruth 125, 144
Bensfield, Dick 11, 113, 208
Benson 26, 45, 71, 105, 138
Benson, Bradley 184
Benson, Hillary 185
Benson, Lucille 219
Benson, Robby 172–3, **173**
Benton, Barbi 180, 213
Benton, Daniel 221
Berg, James 60, 77, 155
Berg, Kenneth 185
Bergan, Judith-Marie 6–7, **6**, 29, 62, 94
Bergen, Candice 227
Bergman, Ted 220
Bergmann, Alan 13, 35, 77, 171, 205
Bergstein, Eleanor 27
Berkowitz, Myles 44
Berlinger, Warren 152
Berman, Ron 39
Bernard, Richard 165
Bernardi, Herschel 60
Bernhardi, Lee 91, 122, 137
Bernhardt, Sandra 224
Bernstein, Doug 195
Bernstein, Jaclyn 127
Bernstein, Jonathan 125
Bernstein, Nat 13
Berres, Richard 106
Berry, Chuck 100
Berry, Halle 90
Berry, Tim 7
Bessell, Ted 56, 60
Best, James 33
Best of the West 14–15, 58, 233
Better Days 15–16, 233, 234
Bettis, John 37, 51
Betts, Harry 151
The Beverly Hillbillies 15, 16, 36, 84

Beverly Hills Buntz 16–17, 96, 232, 233, 234
Beverly Hills 90210 149
Bewitched 51, 175, 194
Bickley, William 58, 210
"A Bicycle Built for Two" 3
Bielak, Robert 132
Biener, Tom 12, 201
Biesk, Adam 168
Big Business 116
Big John, Little John 152
The Big Rip-Off 162
Billingsley, Barbara 13, 222, 223
Bilson, Bruce 61, 77, 88, 117, 187, 206, 214, 221
Bingham, Charlotte 45, 118, 119
Bingham, Nicolette 7
Birch, Thora 196, 197
Bird, Billie 72, 170
Birk, Raye 131
Birnbaum, Robert 149
Bishop, Kelly 168
Bisoglio, Val 76
Bisson, Yannick 83
Bixby, Bill 16, 31, 58, 66, 102, 117, 160, 203–205, *204*, 221
Bizet, Georges 187
B.J. and the Bear 212
Black, Karen 39
Black, Royana 134
Blackton, Jennie 212
Blair, Wendy 70, 179
Blake, Josh 42
Blakely, Susan 96
Blakeney, Eric 16
Blanchard, Tully 83
Blankfield, Mark 116, 117
Blansky's Beauties 96
Blauner, Steve 111
Bleckner, Jeff 20, 99, 163
Blecktman, Marshall 156, 157
Blessing, Jack 54, 57, 90, 152, 196, 214
Blitzer, Barry E. 199
Block, Bruce A. 13
Blodgett, Heather 181
Blomquist, Tom 126
Blondie 65
Bloodworth-Thomason, Linda 199
Bloom, George 26, 111
Blu, Susan 52
Blue Skies 17–18
"Blue Suede Shoes" 82
Blue Thunder 61
Bluel, Richard M. 214
Blum, Mark 164
Blythe, Cheryl 36
Boardman, Chris 231
Bob 14
Bob and Ray 167, 196
Bob and Ray, Keener than Most Persons 196
The Bob Crane Show 65
The Bob Newhart Show 40, 72, 159, 164
Bobo, Natasha 171
Bobrick, Sam 120, 177, 203
Boen, Earl 72, 215
Bogart, Paul 56, 95
Bohrer, Corinne 39

Bole, Cliff 147
Bolger, John 40–1, *40*
Bolger, Ray 8
Bologna, Joseph 217
Bombeck, Erma 93–4
Bon Jovi 196
Bonaduce, Celia 208
Bonaduce, Danny 218
Bond, Polly 200
Bond, Sudie 200
Bonerz, Peter 40, 48, 54, 74, 126, 164, 169, 171, 203, 217, 228, 231
Bones 155
Bongheri, Rudolph 168
Boni, John 109, 110, 162, 187, 200, 201
Bonner, Frank 42, 51, 83, 177
"The Bonny Banks of Loch Lomond" 161
Boone, Pat 174
Booth, Doug 30
"Bop Shop" 142
Borowitz, Andy 31, 35, 156, 158, 197
Bosley, Tom 210
Bosom Buddies 13, 57
Boston, Joe 213–4
The Boston Globe 56
Bostwick, Barry 27, 49, 181
Bostwick, Jay 229
Botkin, Perry 24, 76, 142, 172
Botwinick, Amy 213
Bougie, Garin 94
Boulware, Bill 66
Bourne, Larz 30
Boustead, Ron 22
Bowab, John 11, 41, 49, 60, 71, 73, 76, 132, 137, 153, 164, 169, 171, 198, 225
Bowen, Roger 12, 163
Bowie, David 92
Bowman, Cassie 205
Bowman, Chuck 147, 168
Bowman, Rob 132
Box, Bill 121, 220
Boyett, Robert L. 49, 58, 210
Boyle, Donald R. 52
Boyle, Peter 76
Boyle, Tanner 187
The Boys 18
"Boys Like You" 36
Boys Will Be Boys 18, 144–5
Brackett-Zika, Christian 29
Bradford, Hank 13, 86, 120
Bradford, John 33
Bradford, Vicky 169
Brady, Mike 19
Brady, Terence 45, 118, 119
The Brady Brides 18–19, 233, 234
The Brady Bunch 18, 19, 170, 193, 197
The Brady Bunch Hour 18
The Brady Bunch Movie 197
The Brady Girls Get Married 18, 19
The Bradys 18
Bramlett, Delaney 161
Brammer, Shelby 20
Brand, Neville 205, 206
Brand New Life 19–20, 232, 233, 234
Brando, Marlon 42
Brandon, Clark 101

Brandon, Paul Treva 205
Brandstein, Eve 39
Brandt, Victor 114
Brao, Lynn Farr 230
Braverman, Bart 111–13, *111*
Braverman, Charles "Chuck" 147, 221
Bray, Thom 20, 62
Brayfield, Douglas 99
Breaking Away 20, 62, 233, 234
Breaking Bad 134
Brecher, Jim 187, 199
Breeding, Larry 73
Bregman, Martin 50
Bremner, Scott 107–9, *107*
Brennan, Eileen 117
Brenner, Dori 194
Brenner, Mary 97–8
Brenner, Ray 38
Brentwood, Michael 146
Brentwood, Robert 228
Brewster, Diane 222
Brezner, Larry 56, 159
The Brian Keith Show 12
Bridges, Beau 176
Bridget Loves Bernie 24, 184
Brill, Betty 81
Brill, Marty 121
Brillstein, Bernie 18, 124, 152, 190
Brinckerhoff, Burt 33, 101, 160, 184, 203
Broadside 12
Brock, Stanley 66
Brody, Adrien 11
Brody, Lawrence 46, 126
Bromfield, Valri 14, 91, 185
Brooke, Sorrell 33
Brooker, Joan 206, 210
Brookes, Anne 219
Brookes, Jacqueline 75
Brookner, Howard 132
Brooks, Claude 68
Brooks, Joel 60, 216, 223
Brooks, Mel 114, 116, 117, 182
Brooks, Norman 56
Brooks, Randi 82
Brothers 94
Brothers, Dr. Joyce 93, 127, 129, 213
Broughton, Cecil 33
Broughton, William 214
Brown, Carlos 145
Brown, Charlotte 45, 73, 172
Brown, David 201
Brown, Dennis C. 22
Brown, Garrett R. 178
Brown, Gary 120
Brown, Georg Stanford 129, 130, 140, 168, 173
Brown, Howard 175
Brown, James 132
Brown, James H. 146
Brown, Jeffrey 13
Brown, Leonard 131
Brown, Pendleton 95
Brown, Philip 180
Brown, Ross 90, 91
Brown, Ruth 24, 206, 207
Bruce, Barry 22
Bruce, Carol 96
Bruce, Robert 30, 37

Index

Brull, Pamela 118
Brunner, Bob 117, 187, 188, 230
Brush, Bob 152
Bryant, Lee 92
Buck, Craig 147
Buckman, Tara 213
Buckner, Susan 180
Buffalo Bill 188–90, *189*
Buford, Gordon 66
Bulifant, Joyce 152, 200, 206, 228
Bull, Sheldon 26, 35, 58, 185
Bullock, Harvey 214
Bullock, Sandra 160
Bulos, Yusef 166
Bunch, Chris 214
Burditt, George 170, 219
Burghoff, Gary 183, 184
Burke, Delta 58, 199, 213
Burke, Sonny 137
Burkley, Dennis 220
Burleigh, Janette 143
Burmester, Leo 200
Burns, Allan 33, 35, 36, 202
Burns, George 53–4, *53*, 84, 125, 232
Burns, John 150
Burns, Jonathan 121
Burns, Peter 36
Burns, Stan 28, 121, 170
Burns, Timothy 132
Burr, Courtney 97
Burr, Raymond 213
Burrows, James 5, 7, 15, 56, 163, 171, 172
Burstyn, Ellen 1, 36, 232, 233, 234
Burt, James 84, 165
Burton, Al 170, 171, 192, 193, 208
Burton, Bambi 208
Burton, James 139
Burton, Rod 28
Burton, Tony 50
Busfield, Timothy 137
Bustin' Loose 20–22, *21*, 232, 233
Busting Loose 20, 162, 163
Butkus, Dick 61
Butler, Artie 37, 151, 160
Butler, Rudey 21
Butrick, Merritt 156
Butterworth, Kent 22
Buttons, Red 8
Buzby, Zane 27, 65, 177, 217
Buzzi, Ruth 54, 58, 88
"By the Time I Get to Phoenix" 146
Byrd, David 97
Byrne, Joe 160
Byrnes, Edd "Kookie" 218
Byron, Antoinette 180

Caan, James 52
Cacavas, John 50
Cadiff, Andy 36, 65, 91, 202
Cadorette, Mary 169–70
Caesar, Sid 213
Caffrey, Michael 38, 52
Cage, Nicholas 41
Cahn, Sammy 197
Cain, Marie 227
Caldwell, Stephen 131
Calfa, Don 83, 125
The California Raisin Show 22, 232, 234

Caliri, Jon 156–8, *156*, 198
Call, Brandon 194
Callahan, Gene 102
Callahan, James 192
Callahan, Margaret 132
Callas, Charlie 28, 73
Callaway, William 30
Calloway, Thomas 177
Calvert, Bill 152
Cameron, Dean 43–4, 154–5, 216
Campanella, Frank 129
Campanella, Roy II 51
Campanelli, Linda 101, 147
Campbell, Alan 169
Campbell, Glen 213
Campbell, Julia 79, 180
Campbell, Tisha 217
Cannell, Stephen J. 81–2, 140, 167–8
Cannon 129
Cannon, Hughie 4
Cannon, J.D. 213
Canova, Diana 48, 70–1, *70*
Canova, Judy 70
Caper, John, Jr. 82
Capers, Virginia 50
Capone, Al 205
Carbone, Joey 45
Cardinale, Ben 197
Carew, Alyce S. 22
Carew, Topper 21–2, 68
Carey, Ron 63, 65
Caridi, Carmine 159
Carlson, Jim 140, 203
Carmel, Roger C. 46
Carmen 187
Carmen, Julie 26
Carnes, Kim 217
Carney, Art 181, 190–1
The Carol Burnett Show 3
Caron, Glenn Gordon 20, 56
Carothers, A.J. 205
Carothers, Gibson 205
Carpenter, Pete 168
Carr, Darleen 131
Carradine, David 126
Carrerow, Jack 29
Carrey, Jim 1, 31–3, *31*, 190
Carroll, Bob, Jr. 88
Carroll, Janet 18
Carroll, Pat 52
Carroll, Victoria 152
The Cars 139
Carsey, Marcy 24, 118, 119
Carson, Johnny 32, 67, 85, 214, 215, 223, 224
Carter, Chris 19, 20, 218
Carter, Dixie 15, 199
Carter, Jimmy 127, 151
Carter, Lynda 126
Carter, Nell 1, 213
Carter, Randy 60
Carter, T.K. 77, 202
Carter Country 85, 121
Cartwright, Amanda 9
Cartwright, Nancy 52
Cartwright, Veronica 166
Carver, Randall 150–1
Carvey, Dana 121–2, *122*
Carville, James 97
Casablanca 94

Casale, Jerry 157
Case, Allen 86
Cass, Peggy 40, 180
Cassidy, Diana 71
Cassidy, Joanna 189
Cassidy, Mark 203
Cassidy, Patrick 27
Cassidy, Shaun 20
Cassutt, Michael 56, 73, 101
Cast, Tricia 74, 187
Castle 148
Castle, Johnny 27
Castle, Mickey 131
Castrodad, Eddie 27
Catlett, Mary Jo 49
Cattrall, Kim 175
Cauley, Harry 185, 188
Cavanaugh, Reggie 228
Cavanaugh, T.J. 166
The Cavanaughs 101, 190–2, 232, 233
Cazenove, Christopher 44
Cey, Ron 39
Chais, Pamela 155
Chambers, David 31, 51, 230
Chambers, Everett 126
Chambers, Jeff 7, 15, 56, 60, 98, 120, 185
Chambers, Michael 28
Chamian, Denise 174
"Chances Are" 119
Chandler, Gene 66
Chandler, Jared 110
Channing, Stockard 81, 161–3
Chao, Rosaline 183
Chapman, Richard 84
Chappell, Eric 230, 231
Chappell, John 183
Charles, Glen 172
Charles, Les 172
Charles, Ray 154, 190
Charles in Charge 1, 192–3, 233, 234
Charlie and Company 22–24, *23*, 54, 232, 233
Charlie's Angels 12
The Charmings 193–5, 233
Charo 96, 172
Chartoff, Melanie 165
Chase, Chevy 49
Chase, David 214
Chase, Sydney 8
Checking In 24, 232, 233, 234
Cheech and Chong 174
Cheers 1, 17, 59, 94, 95, 97, 115, 131, 172, 176, 191
Chehak, Tom 13, 68, 76, 102, 214
Cherones, Tom 11, 77, 163, 217, 228
Cherry, Byron 33
Cherry, Marc 68
Cheung, George Kee 150
Chevillat, Bruce 16
Chevillat, Dick 208
The Chicago Bears 82
The Chicago Eagle 97
Chicago Magazine 76
The Chicago Teddy Bears 65
Chicago White Sox 174
Chicken Soup 24–5, 232
Chico and the Man 98, 142
Chihara, Paul 84

Chilco, Joe 160
China Beach 151, 167
Chinea, Migdia 212
Chong, Tommy 174, 175
A Chorus Line 127
Christie, Dick 3
Christopher, A.J. 38
Christopher, Dennis 20
Christopher, William 183
Chulack, Christopher 75
Churnin, Nancy 210
The Cincinnati Reds 79
Cinderella 194
Cioffi, Rebecca Parr 51
Civita, Diane 100
Clair, Dick 201
Clark, Blake 181
Clark, Dick 127, 129
Clark, Elizabeth 146
Clark, Oliver 202, 228
Clark, Ron 4, 39, 177
Clark, Roscoe 84–6
Clarke, Cam 22
Clarke, Van Nessa 223
Clausen, Alf 27, 63
Claver, Bob 56, 72, 110, 143, 179, 223
Claxton, William F. 149
Clayburgh, Jill 145
Cleary, Patrick 11
Cleese, John 9
Clennon, David 125
Cleopatra 77
The Cleveland Browns 82
Clohessy, Robert 122–3, 166–7
Clooney, George 1, 39
Clooney, Harry 15
Clotworthy, Robert 159
Cluess, Chris 70, 172
Coach 64
Cobb, Julie 79, 81, 192
Cobbs, Bill 68, 152
Cobler, Jan 226–7
Coca, Richard 142
Coe, George 204
Coe, Liz 75
Cohan, Martin 90, 123, 208
Cohen, David Steven 37, 44, 54, 215
Cohen, Eric 58, 136, 182, 228
Cohen, Evan 73, 219
Cohen, Lawrence J. 38, 45
Cohen, Mitchell Wayne 193, 208
Colasanto, Nicholas 46, 214
The Colbys 149
Colcord, Jack 164
Colcord, Ray 11, 89, 175, 181, 195
Cole, Allan 214
Cole, Marie 21, *21*
Cole, Olivia 138
Coleman, Dabney 151, 189, **189**
Coleman, Gary 52–3, 207, 232
Coleman, Sally 63
Colihan, Patrice 166
Colin, Margaret 46–7, *47*
Colleary, R.J. 70–1, 90, 91–2, 134–5, 203
Collier, Chet 188
Collins, Patrick 24
Collins, Stephen 54, 166
Collis, Alan 31
Collucci, Jill 20

Colombier, Michel 148
Colomby, Harry 138
Columbo 61
Columbus, Chris 52
Colvin, Tony 77
Combs, Ray 212
Coming of Age 195–6, 233
The Commodores 225
Community 152
Company 71
The Completely Mental Misadventures of Ed Grimley 25–6, 232
Condo 26, 232
Conlan, Joseph 77
Connolly, Marie 62
Connor, Kevin 126
Connors, Chuck 15
Connors, Deke 166
Conrad, William 129
Conreid, Hans 30
Constantine, Michael 9, 51, 131
Conti, Bill 68
Convy, Anne 11, 73, 162, 172
Convy, Bert 73, 81
Conway, Tim 3–4, **3**, 58
Cook, Peter 228
Cook, Roderick 166
Cooke, Alan 61, 126, 206
Cooke, Brian 49, 160, 170, 219
Cooke, Sam 74, 155
Cooking with Mama Malone 95
Cooksey, Danny 25, 190
Coolidge, George 57
Coolidge, Irma 57
Coolidge, Martha 221
Coolidge, Rita 37
Cooper, Cathy 220
Cooper, Hal 128, 129
Cooper, Jackie 221
Cooper, Maggie 68
Cooper, Marilyn 168
Cooper, Mason 150
Copley, Lisa 30
Copley, Teri 68, 228–30, **229**
Corbin, Barry 177, 215
Corcoran, Kevin 66, 182
Corday, Barbara 137
Core, Natalie 66
Corley, Pat 66
Corman, Jennifer 192
Corman, Maddie 214
Cornelius, Don 77
Correll, Charlie 18
Correll, Richard 222
Cosby, Bill 10, 131
The Cosby Show 1, 10, 22, 118, 131, 147, 195
Costanzo, Robert 24
Coster, Nicholas 213
Cote, Chris 121
The Cotton Club 112
"The Couch" 54, 84
Cougar Town 78
Coulier, Dave 51, 104
The Courtship of Eddie's Father 45, 98, 160
Cox, Courteney 1, 100
Cox, Jim 145
Cox, Neil 84
Cox, Ronny 154–5

CPO Sharkey 163
Cragg, Stephen 146
Cramer, Douglas S. 9, 12, 88
Crampton, Cydney 213
Crane, Barry 140, 146
Crane, Candy 29
Crane, David 40
Crane, Peter 18, 75
Cranston, Bryan 1, 134
Craven, Matt 62, 172–3, **173**
Craven, Wes 126–7
The Crazy Ones 45
Crenna, Richard 72
Crewson, Wendy 166
Croft, Alyson 17
Cromwell, James 34, 96
Crosby, George E. 54
Crosby, Norm 18, 109
Cross, Harley 150
Cross, Murphy 127–9, 143
Crothers, Scatman 121, 230
Crow, Ashley 131
Crowe, Cameron 44
Crowe, Christopher 214
Cryer, Jon 1, 41–2, **42**
The Crystals 216
CSI 148
Cuddington, Chris 30
Cuervo, Alma 4
Cullingham, Mark 195
Culp, Robert 42
Culp, Roland 32
Cummings, Quinn 60
Curiale, Joe 100
"Curiosity" 154
Curran, William Brian 118
Curtin, Hoyt 30, 33, 53, 211
Curtin, Jane 167
Curtis, Jamie Lee 64
Curtis, Keene 9, 121
Curtiss, Mark 117, 221
Curvey, Troy, Jr. 153
Cuthbert, Neil 177
Cutler, Stan 98
Cutrona, Hannah 150
Cypher, Jon 131

Da 101
"Da Doo Ron Ron" 216
"Da Ya Think I'm Sexy?" 155
"Daddy, I'm a Mormon Now" 158
"Daddy, I'm a Woman Now" 158
Dads 26–7, 233, 234
Dahl, Charbie 125
Daily, Bill 8, 152, 159, 234
Daley, Bill 66, 218
Daley, Madelyn 129
Dallas 37, 59, 100, 199, 203, 220, 221
The Dallas Cowboys 222
Dalton, Wally 145
Daly, Rad 187
Dames, Rob 62, 97, 129
Damon, Gabriel 120
Damone, Mike 43
Damone, Vic 131
Damski, Mel 95
Dana, Barbara 62
Dana, Bill 113, 182
Dana, Justin 176
Dana, Vic 176

240 Index

Dancing with the Stars 23
D'Andrea, John 98
Danese, Shera 3, 163
D'Angelo, Helen 159
D'Angelo, William P. 214, 221
Daniel, Rod 33, 98, 126, 176, 199, 206, 225
Daniels, Dari 102
Daniels, Marc 10, 88, 201, 215
Daniels, Stan 15, 102
Daniels, William 52
Danner, Blythe 166-7, 181
The Danny Thomas Show 71, 120
Danson, Ted 176
Dante, Joe 130
Danton, Ray 17
Danza, Tony 89, 90
Danzinger, Dennis 38, 48, 100, 124, 127, 217
Darden, Severn 165
Darin, Bobby 77
Darling, Jennifer 53
Darling, Joan 5, 171
Darrow, Henry 99, 182
Davenport, Bill 10, 94, 228
David, Bruce 104
David, Larry 178
Davidson, Sara 75
Davies, Gareth 36, 56
Davis, Ann B. 18, 19
Davis, Elias 120, 160, 205
Davis, Geena 54, 143-4, *143*, 189, 227
Davis, John E. 161
Davis, Josie 192
Davis, Madelyn 88
Davis, Mark 66
Davis, Sammy, Jr. 125, 220
Davis, Vincent 22
Davis, Viveka 164
Dawber, Pam 104, 170, 215-7, *216*
Dawson, Deborah Zoe 217
Dawson, George T. 168
Dawson, Richard 185
Day, Linda 68, 74, 100, 164, 179, 181, 225
Day, Richard 117
Day by Day 1, 196-7, 233
Dean, Barton 119
Dean, James 174
Dean, Suzi 205
Dear Abby 63
The Debbie Reynolds Show 7
DeBenedictis, Richard "Dick" 99, 179
Debin, David 40
Debussy, Claude 54
DeCamp, Rosemary 213
DeCaro, Denise 93
Dees, Julie McWhirter 30, 53, 104
DeGarr, Blanca 217
DeGeneres, Ellen 1, 124-5, *124*
Degrassi Junior High 83
DeHaven, Gloria 208
Dehner, John 38
DeJesus, Wanda 133
DeKay, Colman 132
DeKorte, Paul 33
Delaney and Bonnie 161
Delany, Dana 164

Del Grande, Louis 185
Del Mar, Marcia 142
Deloy, George 159
Del Regno, John 14
Delta House 12, 43
DeLuise, Dom 28, 35, 232
DeLuise, Michael 120, 123
Demme, Jonathan 228
Dempsey, Patrick 1, 43
Dench, Judi 44
Dendy, LaShana 53
Denn, Marie 226
Dennehy, Brian 158-9
Denny, Jon S. 227-8
Denoff, Sam 91, 92
Denver, Bob 54
The Denver Broncos 82
DePatie, David H. 99
DePatie, Steven 99
Derricks-Carroll, Clinton 220
Designing Women 81, 189, 199
DeSouza, Steven E. 49
Desperate Housewives 78
Despotovich, Nada 76
Deutsch, Patti 21
DeVito, Danny 98, 185
Devo 157
DeVol, Frank 19, 66
Devore, Cain 30
DeWitt, Joyce 219
Dexler, Jerry 30
Diagnosis: Murder 177
Dial, Bill 84, 206, 214
Diamond, Dustin 202-3
Diamond, Janis 53
Diamond, Matthew 41, 191, 196, 197, 217
Diamond, Paul 186-7, *186*
Diamond, Steve 72
The Dick Van Dyke Show 41, 176, 177
Dielhenn, Art 51, 60, 143, 197, 209
Dietrich, Dena 88, 157, 219
A Different World 1, 118, 195
"Different Worlds" 185
Diff'rent Strokes 207, 208, 215
DiGaetano, Michael 123, 223
Digging a Ditch 139
Dikijian, Ari 160
Dilbert, Bernard 95
Diller, Barry 108, 109
Diller, Phyllis 93
Dillon, Denny 181
Dillon, Rita 11
DiMarco, Tony 221
Dimitri, Richard 151
Di Muci, Dion 65
Dini, Paul 53
Dirty Dancing 26, 27-8, 233
Dirty Harry 220
Disney, Walt 19, 58, 62, 66, 152, 167, 182, 222, 223
DiTillio, Lawrence G. 22
Dixon, Dianne 53
Dixon, Ivan 168
Dixon, Peter L. 53
"Do You Know What It Means to Miss New Orleans?" 50
Dobkin, Lawrence 52
Doc 101

Doctor, Doctor 2
Dodson, Jack 128
Doering, Charles 45
Dog and Cat 52
Dolan, Frank 188
Dole, Bob 166
The Dom DeLuise Show 28, 232
Domestic Life 28-9, 232, 234
Donahue, Catherine 196
Donahue, Elinor 81, 107-9, *107*
Donahue, Mary 196
Donley, John 136, 220
Donnelly, Dennis 38
Donovan, Russell 58
Don't F#k My Mother* 74
"Don't Sit Under the Apple Tree" 58
Doogie Howser, M.D. 81, 134
Dooley, Paul 195
Doonesbury 165, 166
DoQui, Robert 83
Doran, Ann 148
Doran, Phil 13, 51, 76, 220
Dore, Bonny 45
Dorff, Steve 51, 217
Dorfman, Sid 95, 121
The Doris Day Show 180
Dotto 78
Double Trouble 197-8, *198*
Doucette, Jeff 39
Doud, Earle 208
Douglas, Pamela 51
Douglas, Robert 114
Douglas, Ronalda 111-13, *111*
Douglas, Warren 214
Dow, Tony 222
Dowling, Chet 155, 230
Down and Out in Beverly Hills 29-30, 232, 233, 234
Doyle, David 11, 164
The Drak Pack 30, 232
Drake, Jim 7, 14, 26, 29, 33, 74, 140, 145, 190, 198, 220, 230
"Dream On" 134
Dreams 1, 30-1, 234
Dreesen, Tom 220
Dreith, Dennis 119
Dresner, Hal 173
Dreyfuss, Lorin 137
Dreyfuss, Richard 29
The Drifters 74
Driskill, William 126
Drivas, Robert 185
Dryer, Fred 140
Dubin, Charles S. 10, 50, 66, 76, 126, 143, 153, 184, 221, 225
Dubin, Richard 35, 42, 51
Dubin, Steve 153
Dubov, Paul 149
Duchowny, Roger 117, 223
The Duck Factory 1, 31-3, *31*, 142, 234
Duclon, David W. 145, 198
Ducommon, Rick 82
Dudikoff, Michael 158
Duell, William 129
Duet 124, 125
Dufau, Oscar 33
Duffy, Patrick 54
Dugan, Dennis 39, 146

Dugan, Jessie Ward 17
Dukakis, Kitty 166
Dukakis, Olympia 122
Dukane, Sy 106, 217
Duke, Maurice 40
"The Duke of Earl" 66
The Dukes 33, 232, 233, 234
The Dukes of Hazzard 33, 38, 140, 179
Duncan, Bob 86
Duncan, Sandy 162
Dungan, Frank 150
Dunigan, Tim 102
Duning, George 182
Dunne, Dominique 20
Dunne, James P. 115, 210, 211
Duran, Christopher 228
Durrell, Michael 71, 114
Dusenberry, Ann 88
Duteil, Jeffrey 113, 196
Dynasty 37, 74, 176
Dzundza, George 123

Earp, Wyatt 140
Earth, Wind and Fire 22
East Side, West Side 214
Eastwood, Clint 102
Easy Street 33–5, **34**, 84, 232, 233, 234
Eaton, Anthony 109
Ebb, Fred 95, 169
Ebersole, Christine 190–2
Eckhaus, Richard B. 185
Eddo, Nancy 210
Edelman, Herb 81, 152
Edelman, Randy 104
Eden, Barbara 19, 205–6
The Education of Hyman Kaplan 178
Edwards, Anthony 72
Edwards, Rob 16
Edwards, Ronnie Claire 76, 143
Eek the Cat 109
Efros, Mel 176
Egan, Mark 36, 129, 131
Egan, Richard 37
Eggert, Nicole 192
Ehrlich, Alan 83
Ehrlich, Jayne C. 126
Ehrmann, Paul L. 146
Eichen, Cheri 172
Eiding, Paul 194
Eight Is Enough 148
Eilbacher, Cindy 148
Eilbacher, Lisa 99
Eisenberg, Jerry 99
Eisenberg, Ned 59
Eisenhower and Lutz 35–6, 233
Eisenstock, Alan 49, 185
Eisner, Michael 129
Elam, Jack 33–4, **34**
Elfman, Danny 44, 221
Elias, Caroline 20
Eliasberg, Jan 28, 75
Elikann, Larry 102
Elinson, Jack 5, 11
Elizondo, Hector 5, 29, 46–8, **47**, 52, 160, 234
The Ellen Burstyn Show 1, 36–7, 232, 233, 234

Elliott, Alison 90
Elliott, Bob 167, 196
Elliott, Chris 167
Elliott, Jack 12, 76, 81, 92, 114, 126, 176
Elliott, Lang 145
Elliott, Nick 45
Elliott, Patricia 37
Elliott, Stephen 174
Ellis, Joseph M. 44
Ellis, Sidney 214
Ellison, Bob 104, 163, 185
Ember, Matt 197
Emerson, Douglas 66, **67**
Empire 37–8
Empty Nest 1, 26
Endler, Michael 208
Engel, Georgia 57, 75
Engel, Peter 202–3
English, Diane 47–8, 217
Enos 38, 140
Enright, Dan 95
Ensign O'Toole 12, 65
Espinoza, Rollin 93
E/R 1, 33–4, 233
ER 39
Erbe, Kathryn 25
Erdman, Richard 83
Errickson, Krista 206–8
Essinger, Mark 19
Essman, Susie 13
Estin, Ken 147, 172
Eubanks, Bob 19
Eulo, Ken 97
Evans, Denny 98
Evans, Roxie Wenk 195
Evans, Scott 188
Eve, Trevor 146
Everett, Chad 140
The Everly Brothers 155
Every Which Way but Loose 102
Everybody Loves Raymond 45, 76, 185
Everything's Relative 1, 40–1, **40**
Ewell, Tom 15
Exercise with the Plotniks 141
The Exorcist 36
Ezrin, Bob 123

F Troop 15
Fabares, Shelley 206
Fabian 110
The Facts of Life 90, 132, 134, 207, 208
Falcon, Ellen 40, 41, 48, 98, 137, 198, 217
Falk, Peter 3
The Fall and Rise of Reginald Perrin 137
Falzon, Charles 83
Fame 130
Family 17
Family Feud 185
A Family for Joe 227
Family Guy 41
Family Man 41, **41**, 234
Family Matters 16, 22
Family Ties 1, 26, 29, 95, 139, 197
The Famous Teddy Z 1, 41–2, **42**, 234

Fanaro, Barry 61
Fann, Al 66
Fantasy Island 8
Faracy, Stephanie 204
Farentino, James 97
Farid, Zaid 39
Farquhar, Ralph 16, 113
Farr, Gideon 185
Farr, Gordon 72, 110, 160, 230
Farr, Jamie 110, 183–4
Farr, Kimberly 89
Farrell, Marty 170
Farrell, Mary 133
Farrell, Richard 83
Fassberg, Matt 111
Fast Times 1, 42–4, 233, 234
Fast Times at Ridgemont High 43
Father Knows Best 13, 109
Father Murphy 44
Fathers and Sons 44, 234
Faustino, David 39, 68
Fawlty Towers 9, 10
Fay, Deidre 11, 81, 164, 198
Feemster, Nikki 12
Feig, Paul 27
Feinberg, Robert E. 214
Felder, Don 52
Feldman, Corey 49, 71, 93, **93**, 139, 187
Feldman, Edward H. 12, 14, 92, 153, 184
Fell, Norman 18, 218, 223–4, 234
Felton, David 158
Femia, John 156–8, 206–8
Ferber, Bruce 60, 76, 119, 125
Ferber, Mel 16, 49, 100, 149, 153, 214, 225
Ferguson, Maynard 109
Ferman, Benny 33
Ferman, Clive 33
Ferraro, Dolores 37, 98, 171, 179
Ferrell, Conchata 39, 51, 94
Ferrell, Will 69
Ferrier, Gerry 24
Ferris Bueller's Day Off 89, 127, 154
Ferro, Jeffrey 230
Fiedel, Brad 75, 176
Fiedler, John 189, 219
Fieffel, Lisa 168
Field, Fern 188
Field, Sally 116, 134
Field, Todd 165
Fielder, Pat 214
Fielder, Richard 146
Fielding, Anastasia 120
Fielding, Dorothy 121
Fields, Greg 93
Fields, Ronald J. 97
Fields, W.C. 56
Filipi, Carmen 52
Fillmore, Millard 223
Filthy Rich 198–200, 234
A Fine Romance 44–5, 233, 234
Finestra, Carmen 73, 81, 185
Fink, Mark 51, 66, 195, 208, 214, 219
Finkelman, Ken 63
Fire, Richard 39
Firesign Theatre 227
First Impressions 45, 65, 125, 234
"First Impressions" 45

Fisch, Joe 7
Fischer, Jan 70
Fischer, Stephen 187, 217
Fischer-Doak, Pat 212
Fishburne, Lawrence 150
Fisher, Bob 88
Fisher, Carrie 84, 227
Fisher, Gail 66
Fisher, Jackie 25
Fisher, Joely 160
Fisk, Carlton 174
Fitz and Bones 45-6, 233, 234
Fitzgerald, Geraldine 118
Fitzsimmons, Charles B. 205
Flagg, Fannie 205
Flaherty, Joe 25
Flair, Ric 83
The Flamingos 154
Fleischer, Charles 8
Fletcher, Aaron 85
Fletcher, Harry 161
Fletcher, Scott 174
Fligg, Emma 72
Flippin, Lucy Lee 82, 200-201, 219
Flo 1, 58, 161, 199-201, 210, 219, 233, 234
"Flo's Yellow Rose" 201
Florea, John 76, 146
Flowers, Wayland 93, 103
F.L.U.I.D. 193
The Flying Nun 63
Flynn, Don 122
Flynn, Miriam 93, 134
FM 201-2, 234
Folb, Jay 49, 51, 52, 120, 184, 195
Foley Square 46-8, *47*, 233, 234
Follows, Megan 29, 188
Fontaine, Joan 9
Fontaine, Michael 147
Fonz and the Happy Days Gang 211
Foot in the Door 48-9, 233
"For Better or Worse" 72
Foraker, Lois 17, 28
Forbes, Douglas C. 109
Forbes, John 66
Ford, Faith 130
Ford, Katie 197
Forrester, Blaze 101
Forster, Robert 119
Forsythe, Henderson 35, 105-106, *105*
Forsythe, John 28
Forte, Ken 138
Foster, Bill 30, 35, 97, 137, 195, 231
Foster, Eric 19
Foul Play 49, 233, 234
The Four Seasons 49, 233
The 4 to 9ers: The Day Crew 185
The Four Tops 22
Fournier, Eugene A. 214
Fox, Charles 9, 49, 58, 73, 84, 149, 185, 203
Fox, Fred, Jr. 66, 74, 187, 210, 223
Fox, John 54
Fox, Michael J. 13, 146, 191
Fox, Norman Chandler 170
Fox, Vivica 90
Foxx, Redd 135-7, *135*, 219, 232
Fraley, Pat 52
Francine, Anne 205

Francis, Anne 126
Frank, Charles 199
Frank, David Michael 29, 30, 51, 54, 60, 79, 84, 165, 187, 223
Frank, Skip 203
Frankel, David 37
Frankie Lymon and the Teenagers 32
Franklin, Aretha 44
Franklin, Jeff 185, 187
Franklin, Richard 45
Frank's Place 50-1, 233
Franz, Dennis 16, 39, 96
Fraser, Bob 62, 96, 97, 129
Fraser, Prudence 73, 89, 119, 195
Frasier 28
Fratkin, Stuart 108
Frawley, James 102, 173
Frazier, Joe 51
Frazier, Ronald E. 15, 31, 37, 77
Freberg, Stan 104
Frederick, Jesse 16
Free Spirit 51, 232, 233
Freebie and the Bean 51-2, 233
Freedman, Winifred 209-11, *209*
Freeman, Fred 37-8
Freeman, Kathleen 217
Freeman, Sandy 31
Freeway of Love 44
Freilich, Jeff 16
Freiman, Richard 61, 73, 95, 206
Fremin, Jourdan 12
Fresco, Michael 28, 167
Fresco, Victor 111
Fresher Pastures 17
Frey, Leonard 14, 102-3
Fried, Ian 44
Friedberg, Rick 111
Friedlander, Leonard 87
Friedman, Bruce Jay 160
Friedman, Kim 20, 33, 158, 205
Friedman, Ron 4, 153, 206, 221
Friends 100
Fries, Sandy 53
Frishberg, David 160
Froelich, Bill 45
Frolov, Diane 147, 218
Frontiere, Dominic 20, 52
Frye, Drake 26
Fuhro, Tiki 188
Fujioka, Yutaka 52
Fulger, Holly 75
Full House 30
Fuller, Parmer 35
Funny Face 162
Furst, Stephen 63
Fyfe, Jim 166

Gabor, Zsa Zsa 28
Gabriel, Judy 206
Gaddafi, Muammar 145
Gagan, Jim 220
Galas, June 197
Galaxy High 52, 232
Gale, Scott 61, 96, 203
Gallagher, Farnsworth 58
Gallagher, Keeley Mari 41
Gallagher, Megan 151
Gallay, Peter 114
Gallery, James 123

Gallo, Lew 9, 114
Gallo, William 144
Galloway, Don 39
"Galveston" 146
Gannon, Joe 56
Gans, Danny 124-5, *124*
Ganz, Jeffrey 79, 187, 223
Ganz, Lowell 58, 60, 79, 112, 165, 185, 187, 210
Ganzel, Mark 131
Ganzel, Teresa 31-3, *31*, 142, 169, 170, 195, 223-4
Garber, David 218
Garber, Terri 102
Garber, Victor 68
Garcia, Andy 48
Gard, Cheryl 37
Gardenia, Vincent 20
Gardner, Gerald 117, 221
Gardner, James 13, 41, 131, 196, 217
Garfield, Allen, 18
Garland, Beverly 38
Garlington, Lee 134
Garman, Stephanie 12, 102
Garofalo, Tony 93
Garr, Teri 227
Garrett, Brad 45, 125, 132
Garrett, Lila 14, 155
Garrison, David 74
Garrison, Greg 28
Garth, Jennie 19
Garver, Lloyd 95, 197
Garvin, Jimmy 83
Gary, Carol 124, 176, 190
The Gary Coleman Show 52-3, 232
Gass, Marc 145
Gautier, Dick 88, 204, 230
Gay, Lawrence 123, 223
Gaye, Marvin 28
Gayle, Crystal 73
Gayle, Jackie 18
"Gee Whiz" 28
Geiger, George 102, 201
Gelbart, Cathy 176
Gelbart, Larry 176, 184
Geller, Phylis 228
Gelman, Kimiko 217
Gelman, Laurie 100, 119
"Gents" 64
Geoghan, Jim 38, 117, 145, 177
George and Mildred 218-19
The George Burns and Gracie Allen Show 53
George Burns Comedy Week 53-4, *53*, 84, 232
The George Burns Show 53
The George Gobel Show 182
Gerard, Danny 17
Gerber, David 75, 145, 146
Gertz, Jami 30, 156-7
Getchell, Robert 201
Geter, Leo 35, 202
Gethers, Peter 193
Getty, Estelle 14
Getz, John 163, 190
Gewirtz, Howard 7, 29, 36, 37, 145
Geyer, Stephen 140
Ghostbusters 146
Ghostley, Alice 95, 161
G.I. Joe 64

Giambalvo, Louis 118
Gibbs, Ann 188, 225
Gibbs, Jordan 24
Gibbs, Marla 24, 181
Gibbs, Timothy 140
Gibson, Cal 126
Gibson, Channing 167
Gibson, Henry 52, 153
Gibson, Judy 92
Gidget 134
Gilbert, Gary 14, 23, 24, 39, 68
Gilbert, Ronald H. 218
Gilford, Jack 32, 36, 76
Gillespie, Dizzy 51
Gillette, Anita 188, 231
Gilley, Mickey 83
Gilligan's Island 19, 54
Gilligan's Planet 54-5, 232, 234
Gilliland, Eric 91
Gilliland, Richard 65, 77
Gillingham, Kim 120
Gilman, Kenneth 48
Gilmore, Doug 145
Gilmore Girls 120
Gilutin, Jon 145
Gilyard, Clarence, Jr. 32
Gimbel, Norman 9, 49, 58, 149, 185
Gimbel, Roger 137, 138
Girardin, Ray 22
Gittelsohn, Ellen 73, 137
Glass, Ron 111-13, ***111***
Glasser, Barry 52
Gleason, Jackie 115, 158, 191
Gleason, Joanna 206
Glenn, Eric 227
Glick, Phyllis 90
Glicksman, Susan 201
Gloria 55-6, 233, 234
Glover, Walter 227
Glucksman, Marge 127
Glynn, Carlin 214
Gobel, George 93, 182, 205
"God Bless the Domestic Life" 29
Godfrey, Lynne 110
Goe, Bob 26
Goetz, Peter Michael 190-1
Gold, Barry 143
Gold, Brandy 13, 45
Gold, Jeff 46
Gold, Tracey 148, 204
Goldberg, Barry 44, 155
Goldberg, Danny 52
Goldberg, Gary David 94, 95, 144, 197
Goldberg, Leonard 191
Goldberg, Marshall 50
Goldberg, Susan 147, 218
Goldblum, Jeff 167
The Golddiggers 190
The Golden Girls 1, 9, 26, 71
Goldin, Ricky Paul 60
Goldman, Gina 36, 126
Goldman, Peggy 147
Goldman, Wendy 77
Goldrich, Zina 122
Goldsmith, Merwin 57
Goldsmith, Sydney 162
Goldstein, Allen 187
Goldstein, Josh 11
Goldstein, Shelly 66

Goldstein, William 161
Gomer Pyle, U.S.M.C. 163, 203
Good Morning, Miss Bliss 202-203, 234
Good Morning, Vietnam 151
Good Morning, World 150
Good Time Harry 56, 234
Good Times 12, 20, 21
The Good Wife 162
"The Good Witch of Laurel Canyon" 175
Goodman, Dody 21, 77
Goodman, Miles 99
Goodnight Beantown 203-205, ***204***, 234
Goodtime Girls 56-8, 233
Gordon, Al 208
Gordon, Barry 56, 99
Gordon, Chuck 180
Gordon, Gale 88
Gordon, Geoffrey 53
Gordon, George 33, 53, 211
Gordon, Jill 198
Gordon, Lawrence 77
Gordon, Leo 38
Gordon, Mark 56
Gordon, Scott Spencer 77
Gordon, Steve 56
Gordon, Stuart 39
Gordy, O. 33
Gore, Nick 97, 145
Goren, Rowby 22
Gorman, Mari 66
Gorme, Eydie 88, 123
Gosselaar, Mark-Paul 202
Gotham Magazine 92
Gottlieb, Carl 54, 84
Gould, Elliott 38, 171
Gould, Harold 48, 125, 155, 234
Gould, Howard Michael 202
Goulding, Ray 176
Goulet, Robert 129-130
The Governor and J.J. 214
Govons, Marica 203
Gower, Andre 13, 44, 214, 234
Graf, David 66
Graff, Ilene 85
Grafton, Sue 146
Graham, Clay 136
Graham, John T. 33, 53
Granat, Steve 88, 210
Grant, Amy 150
Grant, Barra 28
Grant, Bud 191
Grant, David S. 148
Grant, Perry 113, 207, 208
Grau, Doris 7
Graves, Peter 88
Gray, John 17
Gray, Robert 205
Gray, Spalding 228
Grazer, Brian 146-7, 165
Grease 161
Great Day 4
The Greatest Show on Earth 17
Grecco, Cyndi 149, 185
Green, Brian Austin 202
Green, James 75
Green, Katherine 33, 74, 181, 219, 228
Green, Patricia 149

Green Acres 17, 85
Greenbaum, Everett 176, 184
Greenbaum, Sam 10, 171, 187, 231
Greenberg, Ed 111
Greenberg, Joanne 212
Greenberg, Richard 228
Greene, Lorne 8, ***8***, 9, 129
Greene, Tom 9
Greenland, Seth 5
Greenspan, Michael 91
Greenstein, Jeff 195
Greenwood, Bruce 83
Greer, Bill 114, 205
Greer, Dabbs 11, 45
Greer, Kathy 114, 205
Gregg, Ginger 42, 191
Greif, Leslie 45
Grenier, Zach 166
Grey, Brad 18
Greyhosky, Babs 140
Grey's Anatomy 43
Grier, David Alan 6-7, ***6***
Griffard, Robert 191
Griffeth, Simone 9, 80-1, ***80***
Griffin, Merv 5
Griffith, Andy 14, 15, 110, 128, 163
Grimes, Scott 171
Grippo, Joelyn 133-4
Gross, Edan 51, 164
Gross, Marjorie 62, 158
Gross, Mary 127
Gross, Michael 197
Grossman, Budd 170
Grossman, Terry 61, 92, 185
Grosso, Sonny 14
Group, Mitchell 95
Growing Pains 1, 204, 210
Grubbs, Gary 61
Guber, Peter 31
Guest, Christopher 228
Guestward Ho 85
Guillaume, Kevin 139, 232, 233, 234
Guillaume, Robert 138-9
Guitar, Sheree 196
Gun Shy 58, 233
Gung Ho 58-60, 232, 233
Guntzelman, Dan 56, 118
Gunzenhauser, Norm 7
Gurian, Gwyn 203
Gurman, Richard 19, 51, 86, 181, 186, ***186***, 187, 223
Gurney, A.R. 228
Gurvitz, Ian 45
Gustafson, Mark 22
Guthrie, Lynn H. 172
Guttenberg, Steve 113
Guylas, Ellen 50, 51, 89, 185, 195
Guzaldo, Joseph 161
Guzman, Claudio 206

Haas-Mull, Wendy 29
Hack, Shelley 75
Hackel, Dave 142-3, 149, 205-6
Hackney, Alan 219
Hadley, Michael W. 83
Hagan, Molly 103, 116
Haggis, Paul 102, 171
Hahn, Phillip Harrison 201
Hail to the Chief 60-1, 78, 215, 232, 233

244   Index

Haim, Corey 139
Haines, Larry 128, 159
Haines, Randa 176
Hale, Alan, Jr. 54
Haley, Jackie Earle 20
Half Nelson 61, 233
Hall, Arsenio 109
Hall, Barbara 11, 26, 31, 33
Hall, Kevin Peter 100
Hall, Monty 76, 206
Hall, Tom T. 205
Hall and Oates 41
Haller, Daniel 214
Hallin, Ronny 115, 210, 231
Halmi, Robert, Jr. 83
Halop, Florence 26, 73, 185
Hamilton, Alexa 60
Hamilton, Ann 17
Hamilton, Frank 63
Hamilton, Lee 130
Hamilton, Murray 60
Hamner, Robert 17
Hampton, James 94, 204
Hampton-Cain, Brenda 150
Handler, David 193
Hankin, Larry 76
Hanks, Tom 57, 115
Hanley, Bridget 205
Hanley, David 132–4
Hanna, William 25, 30, 33, 53, 104, 211
Hannigan, Alyson 51
Happy Days 56, 57, 110, 144, 191, 193, 209, 210, 211, 218
"Happy Together" 89
"Happy Trails to You" 199
Hard Knocks 61–2, 233
Hardcastle and McCormick 65, 168
Hardin, Jerry 199
Hardin, Melora 27
Harewood, Dorian 22
Hargrave, Dean 99
Harman, Barry 100, 122
Harmon, David P. 84, 206, 214
Harmon, Deborah 84
Harmon, Mark 216
Harnell, Joe 147
Harpaz, Udi 68
Harper, Robert 50
Harper Valley 205–206
Harper Valley P.T.A. 19, 205–206, 234
Harris, Cynthia 10
Harris, Glenn Walker, Jr. 79
Harris, Harry 45
Harris, Jeff 27
Harris, Johnny 126
Harris, Ross 155
Harris, Sam 11
Harris, Stan 160, 230
Harris, Susan 61, 70, 71, 73
Harrison, Gracie 62, 99
Harrison, Gregory 41
Harrison, Ken 102, 126
Harrison, Lindsay 27
Harry 62–3, 233
Hart, Bobby 52
Hart, Cecilia 103
Hart, Corey 43
Hart, Don 97

Hart, Gary 166
Hart, James C. 45
Hart, Mary 42
Hart, Moss 181–2
Hart, Terry 66, 76, 98, 149, 210
Hart, Trisha 65
Hart in San Francisco 114
Hart of Dixie 81
Hart of the Yard 114
Hart to Hart 18, 114
Hart-Angelo, Judy 97, 131
Hartley, Mariette 203–205, **204**
Hartman, Phil 150
Harty, Patricia 65–7, **67**
Harvest, Rainbow 202
Harwood, Dick 214
Hashimoto, Saburo 52
Haskell, Eddie 222
Haskell, Jimmie 214
Haskins, Dennis 203
Hasselhoff, David 1, 145
Hatcher, Teri 1, 78
The Hathaways 102
Hathcock, Bob 53, 211
Hattman, Steve 11, 68, 149, 205–206
Hauser, Kim 17
Hauser, Wings 82
Have Faith 63–5, **63**
"Have Faith" 65
Havinga, Nick 98, 176, 184, 206
Hawn, Goldie 49
Hayden, Jeffrey 84, 101, 102, 187
Hayers, Sidney 214
Hayes, Cathy Lind 25
Hayes, Chip 62, 97
Hayes, Peter Lind 25, 158
Hayes, Steve 146
Hayes, Todd 193
Haymer, Johnny 93
Haynie, Jim 164
Hays, John 25
Hays, Robert 184, 201
Haysbert, Dennis 118, 139
Hayward, Chris 76, 114
He Knows You're Alone 194
Head, Helaine 11
Head of the Class 95
Healy, David 199
Healy, Mary 25, 158
"Heart of the City" 137
Heartland 65–6, 89, 232, 233
Hearts Afire 81, 179
"Heat Wave" 28
Hecht, Gina 40, 114
Hecht, Ken 137, 220, 230
Heckart, Eileen 11, 36, 56, 126
Heckerling, Amy 44
Hedaya, Dan 56, 96, 123, 138, 172, 234
Hedren, Tippi 13
Hefti, Neal 113
Hegyes, Robert 86
Heifer, Ralph 102
Heim, Teena 143
Heine, Frances 126
Heinz, James 38
Helford, Allan 53
Helford, Bruce 104
Helgenberger, Marg 148
Heller, Craig 215

Heller, Ken 126
Heller, Randee 16, 95, 144
Hello, Larry 24, 26, 206–209, 234
Helmer, Heidi 159
Hemphill, Shirley 120–1
Hemsley, Sherman 39
Henderson, Bill 3
Henderson, Florence 18–19, 51, 129
Henderson, Ty 93
Hendler, Janis 126
Hendricks, Bruce 99
Hendricks, Paula 65
Henley, Beth 228
Henry, Bob 23
Henry, Buck 228
Herbie Goes to Monte Carlo 65
"Herbie, My Best Friend" 66–7
Herbie the Love Bug 65–6, **67**
Herd, Gayle 197
"Here at Madame's Place" 93
"Here Comes the Bride" 66, 87, 220
"Here Is Where the Love Is" 149
Here We Go Again 73
Here's Boomer 207
Here's Lucy 91
Herford, Whitby 41
Herman, Pee Wee 221
Herskovitz, Marshall 146
Hervey, Jason 43, 58
Hervey-Stallworth, Winifred 13
He's the Mayor 66, 233
Heslov, Grant 154
Hesseman, Howard 54, 181
Hey, Mulligan 121
Heydorn, Nancy 143
Hickox, S. Bryan 99
Hicks, Catherine 175, 186
Higgins, Joel 63–5, **63**, 88, 135
Highway to Heaven 46
Hiken, Nat 12
Hilberman, David 52
Hill, Dana 228
Hill, Kimberly 7, 172
Hill, Leonard 176, 217, 218
Hill Street Blues 16, 17, 96
Hillerman, John 168
Hillner, John 230
Hillshafer, Beth 36
Hilton-Jacobs, Lawrence 86, 136
Hindle, Art 175
Hingle, Pat 17, 61
Hinkley, Tommy 61
Hire, Lois 208
Hirsch, Janis 31, 35, 158, 184, 197, 198
Hirschfeld, Gerald 102
Hirson, Alice 180
Hiruma, Toshiyuki 52
"Hit the Road, Jack" 28, 40, 190
Hobin, Bill 114
Hochberg, Victoria 212
Hoese, Ray 227
Hoffman, Alphy 110
Hoffman, Basil 101, 157
Hoffman, Frederick 56
Hogan, William 149
Hogan's Heroes 15
Hogestyn, Drake 146
Holcomb, Rod 168
Holcombe, Wendy 85

Holland, Amy 99
Holland, Savage Steve 108–109
Hollander, David 85
Holliday, Polly 161, 181, 200–202
Holmes, Clint 76
Holmes, Jennifer 100
Holmes, Sherlock 131
Holt, Robert J. 38
Holznagel, Ryan 22
Home Improvement 198
Home to Roost 230
Homeroom 67–8, 234
Honeymoon Hotel 71–2, 233
Honigberg, Gail 121
Honigblum, Carrie 13, 195
Hooker, Richard 184
Hooks, Kevin 45, 66, 119, 132
Hope, Bob 207
Hopkins, Telma 112
Hopper, Heather 202
Horn, Alan 208
Horowitz, David 41
Horst, Jason 69
Horton, Peter 146
"Hot Properties" 124
Hotchkis, Joan 86
Houser, Jerry 18
Houston, Gary 39
Houston, Thelma 67
Howard, Bob 93
Howard, Clint 59–60
Howard, Ken 73
Howard, Rik 75, 145, 231
Howard, Ron 59, 165
Howard, Terrence 37
Howland, Beth 181
Hubbert, Cork 194
Hubley, Season 17
Hudson, Ernie 82
Hudson, Mark 143
The Hudson Brothers 143
Hughes, Barnard 101–102, 190–2
Hughes, John 12
Hughes, Miko 150
Hughes, Susan 161
Hughes, Terry 25, 38, 45, 66, 120, 138, 158, 160
Hullaballoo 191
Humperdinck, Engelbert 77
Humphrey, Steven 146
The Hunchback of Notre Dame 176
Hunley, Leann 213
Hunt, Gordon 45
Hunt, Helen 72, 228
Hunt, Mie 29
Hunt, Peter H. 70, 161, 176
Hunter 230
Hunter, Blake 90, 123
Hunter, Paul Robinson 50
Hunter, Tab 77, 93
Huntington, Nicole 202
Hurst, Rick 9
Hurt, Mary Beth 166
Hurwitz, Harry 119
Hurwitz, Mitchell 65
Huson, Paul 176
Huston, Carol 194
Huston, Jimmy 49, 133
Hyde-White, Wilfrid 69

I Dream of Jeannie 77, 159, 206
"I Fought the Law" 19, 82
"I Gotta Go Back" 144–5
I Had Three Wives 58, 233
"I Heard It through the Grapevine" 22
I Love Lucy 88, 118, 142, 170, 205
I Married Dora 68–70, 232
I Married Joan 68
"I Only Have Eyes for You" 154
"I Wanna Dance with Somebody" 167
"I Want to Be an American" 179
"I Wish I Was Eighteen Again'" 54
"I Wish You Love" 169
Idle, Eric 104–106, **105**
If You Knew Sushi 141
Iger, Bob 64
Illes, Robert 198, 201
Ilson, Saul 99, 100
I'm All Right, Jack 219
Imamura, Sally 180
Impert, Margie 94
In the Beginning 26
Inch, Kevin 45, 119
Ingber, Mandy 27, 172
Innaurato, Albert 228
Insana, Tino 130, 221
INXS 139
Irsay, Robert 13
Irving, Patricia 13
Irving, Robert 106
"Is It Because of Love?" 98
Isaacs, Charles 206
Isaacs, David 98, 124, 172, 184
Isabel Sanford's Honeymoon Hotel 71–2, **72**
Iscove, Robert 132
Isenberg, Barbara 226
Ishiodori, Hiroshi 52
Israel, Neal 44, 54
"It Had to Be You" 40, 76, 184
It Takes Two 72–3, 78, 233
"It's a Grand Life" 97
It's a Living 10
"It's a Small World" 162, 187
It's About Time 194
It's Garry Shandling's Show 62
It's Not Easy 14, 723
It's Your Move 1, 73–5, 234
Itzin, Gregory 116–7
Ivens, Terry 144
Ivey, Dana 34
Ivey, Lela 79

Jabbar, Kareem Abdul 21
Jablons-Alexander, Loretta 92
Jack and Mike 75, 233, 234
Jack and the Beanstalk 194
Jackson, Anne 40–1, **40**
Jackson, Jesse 166
Jackson, Kate 12
Jackson, Reggie 157
Jackson, Rosemarie 227
Jackson, Victoria 61
Jacobi, Lou 99
Jacobius, Jerry 97, 145
Jacobs, Christian 55, 94
Jacobs, Gary 49, 63, 177, 231
Jacobs, Michael 114, 171, 193

Jacobs, Parker 190
Jacobs, Rachel 73, 94
Jacobson, Danny 77, 217
Jacobson, Larry 14
Jacoby, Billy 73, 94, 187
Jacoby, Laura 102
Jaeckel, Richard 12
Jaffe, Taliesin 60
Jaffee, Mark 166
James, Clifton 85
James, Dennis 119
James, Eleanor 160
James, Ralph 104
James, Timothy 118
Jarchow, Bruce 164–5
Jardine, Al 231
Jarvis, Graham 94
Jason, Robert 60, 61
Jayson, Robert 53
Jean, Al 193, 221
Jefferson, Thomas 132, 134
The Jeffersons 24, 72, 127, 138, 175, 220
Jenkins, Dan 145
Jenner, Bruce 99
Jennifer Slept Here 10, 75–6, 103, 232
Jensen, Sanford 46, 69
Jensen, Shelley 62, 97, 181
Jessup, Hubert 188
Jillian, Ann 10–11, 75–6, 232, 234
The Jimmy Stewart Show 182
Joachim, Thomas 214
Joanie Loves Chachi 1, 193, 209–11, **209**, 218, 232, 233, 234
Joe Bash 76, 233
Joel, Billy 172
Joens, Michael 99
Joffe, Charles H. 56, 159
"Johnny B. Goode" 100
Johns, Glynis 196
Johns, Tracy Camilla 154
Johnson, Anne-Marie 198
Johnson, Bruce 113, 127, 185
Johnson, Jean 66
Johnson, Kenneth 146, 147
Johnson, Lyndon Baines 150
Johnson, Magic 132–3
Johnson, Mark 63
Johnson, Penny 68
Johnson, Russell 54
Johnson, Steve 218
Johnson, Tyrone 145
Johnson, Van 8
Johnstone, Tom 145
Jones, Bucky 199
Jones, Claude Earl 189
Jones, Dean 65–6, **67**
Jones, Henry 58, 69
Jones, James Earl 99
Jones, Jeffrey 127
Jones, John Christopher 130
Jones, Mark 101, 140, 214
Jones, Mickey 100
Jones, Patricia 138
Jones, Quincy 220
Jones, Renee 72
Jones, Shirley 148–9
Jones, Simon 166
Jordan, Glenn 70

Jordan, Leslie 127
Joseph, Bryan 49
Joseph, Jeffrey 130
Joseph, Marc 138
Joy, Christopher 111–12, *111*
Joyce, Elaine 101, 230
Juarbe, Israel 46–8, 146
Juber, Hope 19
Judd, Chris 28
Julia 182
Julian, Arthur 12, 215, 228
Julian, Mady 145, 215
Julian, Sally 99
Jump, Gordon 110, 150
The June Taylor Dancers 191
Jupiter, Joey 95
Jurado, Katy 4
Jurasik, Peter 16, 138
Just in Time 76–7, 232, 234
"Just One Look" 28
Just Our Luck 77, 233, 234
Just the Ten of Us 210
"Just to See Her" 77
"Just You and Me" 45

Kaatz, Wayne 26
Kadish, Ben 46
Kagan, Mike 24, 26
Kahn, George 176
Kahn, Madeline 118–19, 214
Kalcheim, Lee 113
Kalember, Patricia 76
Kaline, Al 151
Kalish, Austin 119
Kalish, Bruce 218
Kalish, Irma 49, 119
Kallis, Danny 195
Kander, John 95, 169
Kane, Arnold 121, 230
Kane, Carol 5–7, *6*
Kane, Thomas John 221
Kanter, Hal 100, 178, 181, 182
Kantor, Jay 42
Kaplan, Barry Jay 17
Kaplan, E. Jack 199
Kaplan, Ed 28
Kaplan, Gabe 85–6
Kaprall, Bo 36–7, 151, 179
Karabatsos, Ron 31, 230
Karam, Eddie 36, 202
Karen's Song 1, 78, *78*
Karin, Rita 25
Karlen, John 154
Karlin, Fred 118
Karp, Marshall 40, 41, 100
Karron, Richard 22, 56, 223
Kartozian, Tom 180
Kasem, Casey 54, 72, 127, 172
Kasem, Jean 172
Kasica, Mary Ann 147, 176
Kassir, John 202
Kate and Allie 1, 140
Katlin, Mitchel 13
Katselas, Milton 103, 142
Katt, Nicky 66, *67*
Katz, Allan 23–4, 142
Katz, Andrew 109
Katz, Phyllis 181
Katzin, Lee H. 126
Kauffman, Marta 41

Kaufman, Andy 176
Kaufman, George S. 181, 182
Kaufman, Kenneth 177
Kaufman, Leonard B. 38
Kay, Dianne 137
Kay, Dusty 119, 149
Kaye, Buddy 159
Kaye, Caren 37–8, 74–5, 86, 110, 193, 212
Kaye, Lila 95
Kaye, Peter D. 111
Kaye, Stubby 206
Kazan, Lainie 78, 172, 177
Keach, Stacy 101
Kean, Jane 11
Kearns, James 231
Keatley, Philip 228
Keaton, Diane 12
Keaton, Michael 59, 105, 137–8
Keel, Howard 146
Keenan, Walter J. 102
Keep, Stephen 200
Keeshan, Bob 197
Keiser, Kris 66
Keith, Brian 12, 65, 89, 132–4, 232
Keith, Daisy 65
Keith, Gerren 145, 181, 195, 231
Keith, Larry 188
Kelada, Asaad 51, 78, 126, 138, 197, 228
Kellard, Phil 16, 172
Kellard, Rick 77, 136
Kellaway, Roger 137
Kellem, Craig 29, 193
Keller, Casey 72, 88, 230
Keller, Mary Page 124–5
Kelley, William 38
Kellin, Mike 46
Kellman, Barnet 7, 17, 77, 165, 217
Kelly, April 51, 84, 126, 142, 143, 225
Kelly, Daniel Hugh 68–70
Kelsey, Linda 196
Kemp, Barry 130, 131, 196
Kemp, Brandis 183
Kennedy, Betty 79–81, *80*
Kennedy, Burt 146, 154
Kennedy, George 129
Kennedy, Kristina 13
Kennedy, Michelle 13
Kennedy, Mimi 41, *41*, 154, 162, 228, 234
Kenney, Anne 133
Kenney, Wes 81, 199
Kenny, Bill 212, 215
Kenny, William C. 150
Kent, Janice 222
The Kentucky Fried Movie 129
Kenwith, Herbert 19, 75, 98, 102, 171, 208
Kerns, Joanna 49
Kerns, Sandy 192
Kerwin, Brian 212–14, *213*
Kessler, Bruce 38, 52, 140, 214
Ketchum, David 214, 221
Keyes, Chip 15, 81, 220
Keyes, Doug 15, 81, 220
The Kid with the Broken Halo 53
Kidder, Margot 148
Kiff, Kaleena 222
Kiger, Robert 94

Kilbourne, Wendy 115
Killum, Guy 16
Kilpatrick, Lincoln 50
Kimball, John 104, 211
Kimmel, Joel 13, 188
Kimmel, Peter 87
Kimmons, Ken 84
Kind, Richard 217
King, Cynthia Marie 11
King, Don 51
King, Freeman 145
King, Kip 22
King, Rori 71
King, Tom 115, 169
King Arthur 77, 101
King of Queens 90
Kiraly, Sherwood 39
Kirby, Bruce 10
Kirchenbauer, Bill 210
Kirgo, Dinah 102, 122, 137, 225
Kirgo, George 102
Kirgo, Julie 102, 122, 137, 225
Kirschenbaum, Alan 40
Kite, Lesa 22, 24, 30, 118–19, 171, 182, 185–7, *186*, 210, 223, 227
Kittle, Ron 174
Kleckner, Jay 131
Klein, Dennis 14, 15, 60, 138, 172, 189, 190
Klein, Robert 167, 227
Kline, Richard 144, 147, 219
Kline, Steve 33, 95, 176, 205
Kline, Wayne 208, 219
Kling, Heywood "Woody" 208
Klosner, Dana 212
Klous, Pat 8
Kluge, John 63
Klugman, Jack 111–12, 231
Klynn, Herbert 33
Knell, David 103
Knight, Christopher 18
Knight, Dudley 213
Knight, Gladys 22–4, *23*
Knight and Daye 78–9, 234
Knight Rider 145
Knotts, Don 3, 54, 58, 178–9, 189, 219
Knox, Terence 5–7, *6*
Knudson, Kurt 62
Kobart, Ruth 45
Koenig, Dennis 98, 184
Koock, Guich 85
Kool and the Gang 137
Koonce, Ken 52
Kopell, Bernie 83, 195
Korman, Harvey 9, 54, 84, 116
Korty, John 54
Kostmayer, John 50
Kott, Gary 73, 185
Kovacs, Ernie 129
Kovas, Dino 110
Kowal, Staffin 50
Kowalski, Bernard L. 99, 146
Kowalski, Stanley 110
Kraft, Robert 7, 197, 228
Kramer, Stephanie 230
Kramer, Susan 63
Krasny, Paul 75, 130, 148, 173
Kreinberg, Steve 98
Kreisman, Stu 70, 172

Krinski, Sandy 155, 230
Kristofer, Jason 65
Kristofferson, Kris 145
Kubiak, Walt 22
Kuentz, Xavier 45
Kuhlman, Ron 18
Kukoff, Bernie 137, 176, 218
Kulaga, Frank 167
Kunes, Steven 5, 97, 175
Kupfer, Martin 151, 209
Kuroda, Emily K. 59
Kurtz, David 171, 193
Kuta, Ken 110, 143, 230

"L.A. Is My Home" 61
"L.A. You Belong to Me" 61
Lachman, Mort 13, 220, 92–3, 113–14, 154, 155
Ladies' Man 79–81, **80**, 234
Ladies of the Corridor 109
Lagomarsino, Ron 13
La Grua, Tom 18, 42
LaHendro, Bob 182, 201
Laidman, Harvey S. 146, 176, 214
Laine, Frankie 214
Laird, Marlene 22, 198
Laird, Marvin 188
Lala, Joe 79
Lally, Bob 22, 74, 75, 110
Lambert, Jay 104–106, **105**
Lampert, Judi 197
Lampkin, Charles 50
Lancaster, Bill 187
Landau, Richard H. 214
Lander, David L. 52, 72
Landers, Audrey 8–9
Landers, Judy 93
Landesberg, Steve 215
Landis, John 54
Landry, Ron 12, 201
Landsberg, David 137
Landsburg, Alan 13, 113, 154
Landsburg, Valerie 5–7, **6**, 231
Lane, Charles 128
Lane, Jeffrey 126
Lane, Nancy 32, 185
Lane, Nathan 121–2, **122**
Laneuville, Eric 17, 19
Langdon, Sue Ane 180
Lange, Henry J., Jr. 143
Lange, Hope 79, 227
Lange, Michael 82
Lange, Ted 22
Langen, Todd W. 134
Langford, Stephen 145, 177
Langhams, Bob 53
LaPlaca, Alison 124–5, **124**, 163
Larkin, Bill 14
Larriva, Rudy 104, 211
Larroquette, John 10
Larry, Sheldon 142, 228
The Larry the Lizard Show 142
Larson, Glen A. 45, 46, 61, 213, 214
LaSalle, John 209
Lasorda, Tommy 18, 129
The Last Picture Show 36, 116
The Last Precinct 81–2, 220, 233
"The Last Train to Clarksville" 110
Late, Jason 44
Late Phases 195

The Late Show 171
Latham, Lynn Marie 95
Lathan, Stan 16, 20, 45, 51, 137, 149
Latimer, Jack 61
Latt, David J. 161
Laurance, Mitchell 140–2, **141**
Lauren, Tammy 184
Laurence, Paul 146
Laven, Arnold 52, 140, 168
Laverne and Shirley 5, 57, 72, 104, 159, 211, 232, 233
Laverne and Shirley in the Army 104, 211
Laverne and Shirley with the Fonz 104, 211
Lavin, Linda 201
Lawlor, John 72
Lawrence, Matthew 143
Lawson, Sarah 231
Layman, Kathleen 65
LaZebnik, Philip 197
Leach, Robin 195, 221
Leachman, Cloris 116
Leahy, Janet 7
Lear, Norman 4, 5, 24, 55, 175, 188, 208
Learned, Michael 90
Learning the Ropes 82–3, 232, 234
Leave It to Beaver 1, 13, 162, 222, 234
Leavitt, Ron 74, 181, 186, **186**
LeBlanc, Whitney J. 97, 212
Lebowitz, Eugene 193
Lebowitz, Neil 220
Lechowick, Bernard 95
Lee, Mendy 134
Lee, Ruta 196
Lee, Stephen 59, 163
Lee, Susan H. 230
Leeson, Michael 14–5, 69–70
Leetch, Tom 58
Lefcourt, Peter 68
Legmen 83–4, 233
Leicht, Allan 169
Leiken, Molly-Ann 180, 218
Leisure, David 96
Leitch, Christopher 101, 148
LeMasters, Kim 191
Lembeck, Michael 47–8, 57, 196
Lemmon, Chris 125
Lemmon, Jack 81
Lemon, Meadowlark 206
Lemon, Wayne 42
Lenney, Dinah 45
Lennon, Bowie 230
Lennon, Thomas 113
Leno, Jay 93
Lenox, John Thomas 19, 176
Lenski, Robert W. 52
Lentin, Chay 166
Lenz, Rick 108
Leo and Liz in Beverly Hills 33, 54, 84, 232, 233
Leon, C.M. 230
Leonard, Herbert B. 20, 79, 81
Leonard, Sheldon 71
Leopold, Glenn 30
Lepiner, Michael 177
Lerman, April 192, 193
Lerner, David 76, 119, 171, 186, **186**, 187

Leschin, Deborah 26, 71, 125, 163
Lessac, Michael 15, 29, 147, 165
Lesser, Elana 214
Lester, Jeff 119
"Let the Good Times Roll" 155
Leto, Roseanne 193
"Let's Get Together" 203
Letterman, David 124
Levant, Brian 186–7, **186**, 222, 223
Levay, Sylvester 68, 132
Levi, Alan J. 101, 131, 132
Levin, Charles 78, 204
Levin, Larry 18, 40
Levin, Lissa 56, 118, 170, 198
Levin, Peter 146, 184
Levin, Stewart 177
Levine, Anna 167
Levine, Emily 185
Levine, Ilana 166
Levine, Ken 98, 124, 172, 184
Levine, Laura 86, 88, 92, 230
Levinson, Barry 63
Levinson, Bill 96
Levinson, Larry 210
Levitt, Gene 214
Levy, Eugene 54
Levy, Lawrence H. 203
Levy, Lew 56
Levy, Neil Alan 106, 218
Lew, Jeremy 65
Lew, Jerome 64, 65
Lewald, Eric 52
Lewis, Al 15
Lewis, Bobby 28
Lewis, C.E. 146
Lewis, Geoffrey 58, 200–201
Lewis, Jeffrey 17
Lewis, Jenny 88
Lewis, Jerry 160, 190
Lewis, Juliette 69, 201
Lewis, Lightfield 89
Lewis, Marcia 57
Lewis, Richard 62, 95, 167
Lewis and Clark 84–6, 233
Liberace 84
Libertini, Richard 41, **41**
Lichtman, Jules 62, 115
Liddy, G. Gordon 61, 109
Lideks, Mara 19, 227
Liebling, Howard 214
Liebmann, Norm 214
The Life and Times of Eddie Roberts (L.A.T.E.R.) 86–7, 110, 234
Life Goes On 155
Life with Lucy 87–8, 232, 233
Lightfoot, Phil 175
Lincoln, Abraham 68, 130
Lindbergh, Charles 44
Lindheim, Richard 214
Lindley, Audra 218–19
Lindner, Susan Jane 198
Lindsay, Allison 89
Lindsay, Melissa 89
Lindsay-Hogg, Michael 228
Lindsey, George 66
Link, William 132
Linker, Amy 85, 157–8
Lintz, Paula 102
Linville, Larry 24, 65, 101, 159
"The Lion Sleeps Tonight" 139, 156

Index

Lisson, Mark 45
Little, Cleavon 122
Little Eva 28
Little House on the Prairie 200
Little Men 152
Little Richard 21
Littlefield, Warren 227
"Live and Love It Up" 26
Live-In 88–9, **89**, 234
Live with Regis and Kathie Lee 228
Living Dolls 89–90, 233, 234
Livingston, Alan 121
Livingston, Harold 126
Lizer, Kari 177
Lloyd, Christopher 14
Lloyd, David 15, 102, 104, 215
Lloyd, Michael 28, 98, 170
Lobl, Victor 20, 33, 75, 147, 176
Lobo 1, 91, 212–14, **213**, 233, 234
Lobue, J.D. 10, 35, 49, 61, 78, 96, 119, 127, 169, 177
Locane, Amy 154–5
Lochhead, Lee 212
"The Locomotion" 28
Lofaro, Thomas 60
LoGuidice, Jack 28
Lohman, Rick 55, 127–9
Lohr, Aaron 21
Loman, Michael 10, 81
Lombard, Carole 126
Lombard, Michael 199
London, Robby 55
The Long Day's Journey into Lunch 201
"The Longest Time" 172
Longstreet, Harry 218
Longstreet, Renee 147
Lookinland, Mike 18
Lopez, Mario 4, 203
Lord, Marjorie 164
Lorre, Chuck 22
Lorre, Peter 30
The Los Angeles Chronicle 68
The Los Angeles Dodgers 39, 78, 157
The Los Angeles Raiders 82
The Lost Boys 139
Lou Grant 196
Loudon, Dick 130
Loudon, Dorothy 169
Louis-Dreyfus, Julia 1, 196–7
Louise, Tina 54
Love, Keland 19
Love, Mike 231
Love American Style 109–10, 234
The Love and Lucas Show 92
The Love Boat 7, 8, 52, 140
Love for Rent 177
"Love Spends the Night" 73
Lovenheim, Robert 28, 221
Loverboy 109
Lovitz, Jon 47
Lovy, Alex 99
Lowe, Chad 154–5
Lowenstein, Al 27, 195
Loy, John 26
Lucas, Jeanne 188
The Lucie Arnaz Show 91–2, **91**, 232, 234
Luckinbill, Laurence 92

Lucky, Chris 31, 214
The Lucy Show 88
Ludin, John 26
Luft, Lorna 224
Luger, Lex 83
Lupo, Frank 82, 140, 213–14
Lupus, Peter 129
Lusk, Don 26
Lustig, Gordon 25, 65, 134
Luz, Frank 51
Lyden, Mona 115
Lynch, Paul 17
Lynley, Carol 14
Lynne, Amy 10, 134

M Squad 129
"MacArthur Park" 146
MacGyver 104, 106, 146
Macilwraith, Bill 228
MacKenzie, Patch 38
MacKenzie, Philip Charles 71, 94, 124–5, **124**, **150**
Mackenzie, Will 15, 29, 31, 44, 86, 89, 98, 123, 124, 131, 144, 163, 171, 176, 184, 195, 197, 205
Macklin, Albert 30
MacKrell, Jim 145, 204
Macnee, Patrick 37–8, 97
MacRae, Sheila 110
Macy, Bill 42, 115, 119–20
Mad About You 72
Mad Magazine 129
Madame's Place 92–3, **93**, 233, 234
The Madame's Place All-Divorced Orchestra 93
Madden, Dave 88, 180
Madden, Jerry 160
Madonna 32
Madrid, Lance, III 149
Maffeo, Gayle S. 124
Magar, Guy 126, 140
Maggart, Brandon 25, 75
Maggie 93–4, 234
Magnum, P.I. 85, 130, 168
Maguire, Hugh 89
Maher, Bill 61, 143, 218
Maher, Joseph 144–5
Mahon, Jacqueline 83
Mahoney, John 28
Maisnik, Kathy 158–9
Make Room for Daddy 71, 120, 164
Make Room for Granddaddy 120
Making the Grade 1, 94–5, 234
Malick, Wendie 121
Malloy, Matt 166
Mama Malone 95, 199, 234
"Mama Said" 155
Mama's Boy 95–6, 233, 234
Manasseri, Mike 134
Mancini, Ray "Boom Boom" 111
Mandan, Robert 169, 181
Mandel, Alan 13, 77, 221
Mandel, Babaloo 60, 79, 165
Mandelker, Philip 175, 176
Manetti, Larry 168
The Manhattan Examiner 96
Manheim, Chris 149
Manilow, Barry 49, 119
Manings, Allan 22

Mann, Danny 52
Mann, Terrence 91
Manners, Kim 221
Manning, Richard 147
Manning, Ruth 56
Mantegna, Joe 124
Manza, Ralph 95
Marblehead Manor 1, 96–7, 233
March, Alex 52
Marcione, Gene 230
Marcus, Ann 86, 87
Marcus, Kipp 222
Marcus, Richard 45, 140
Marcus, Russell 70
Marcus, Sparky 57
Maren, Jerry 113
Margo, Phil 50, 139
Margolin, Arnold 120
Margolin, Stuart 102, 173
Marguiles, Donald 13
Mariah 181
Marie, Constance 27
Marie, Rose 61
Marin, Jason 159
Marinaro, Ed 13, 217
Maris, Ada 178
Marko-Sanders, Marilynn 42
Markoe, Merrill 95, 98, 124, 147, 190
Markowitz, Gary 176, 177, 190
Markowitz, Mitch 15, 138, 190
Markowitz, Peachy 45
Marks, Guy 231
Markus, John 10
Marlens, Neal 10, 119
Marmer, Mike 145
Married People 5
Married with Children 74, 97
Mars, Kenneth 152–3, 191, 211
Marsh, Linda 78
Marshall, Anthony W. 113
Marshall, Emily 104, 131, 196
Marshall, Garry 56, 58, 112, 113, 115, 184, 185, 210
Marshall, Lew 99
Marshall, Penny 211
Marshall, Steve 56, 118
Martha and the Vandellas 28
Martin, Andrea 25, 140–2, **141**
Martin, Ann 13
Martin, Anne-Marie 221
Martin, Barney 120, 122, 153, 182
Martin, Dean 28, 61, 100, 160, 190, 213
Martin, Dean Paul 100
Martin, Dick 60, 135–7, **135**, 145, 181, 201, 205, 221
Martin, Joe 39
Martin, Kiel 144
Martin, Nan 103
Martin, Quinn 129, 175
Martin, Steve 29, 54, 84
Martindale, Wink 77
Martinson, Leslie H. 153, 206, 214
Marvin, Lee 129
Marvin, Mitzi 146
Marx, Arthur 88
The Marx Brothers 129
Mary 1, 46–8, 97–8, 232, 234
Mary Hartman, Mary Hartman 86

The Mary Tyler Moore Show 11, 32, 46, 79, 97
Masak, Ron 21, 39, 99, 205
Maschler, Tim 102, 146
M*A*S*H 12, 15, 24, 26, 28, 32, 39, 62, 91, 150, 183–4, 206
Masius, John 167
Mason, Calvin 53
Mason, Jackie 24–5
Mason, Judi Ann 220
Mason, Tom 52, 75
Masuoka, Mark 39, 70, 127
Masur, Richard 37
Matalin, Mary 97
Mathers, Jerry 222
Matheson, Ali Marie 26
Matheson, Richard Christian 38, 214
Matheson, Tim 76–7, 175
Mathews, DeLane 35, 76, 202
Mathis, Johnny 119
Matlock 175
Matthau, Walter 186
Mattison, Mark 134
Matz, Peter 4, 10, 56
Maude 9, 115, 147, 215
Mauer, Michael 102
Mauldin, Nat 63–5, 73
Maurer, Norman 104
Maury, Derrel 209–11, **209**
Maxted, Ellen 77
Maxwell, Bill 127
May, Billy 184
"Maybe an Angel" 150
Mayer, Christopher 33
Mayer, Gerald 149
Mayer, Jim 145
Mayer, Valentine 41, 78, 89, 91, 164, 169
Mayo, Whitman 177
McAdam, Heather 212, 217
McAllister, Chip 16
McBroom, Amanda 36
McCall, Mitzi 73, 81, 162
McCann, Chuck 145
McCann, Sean 188
McCarren, Fred 9
McCarthy, Dennis 38, 58, 161, 205
McCary, Rod 148, 205, 234
"McCaskey" 96
McClafferty, Mark 61
McClanahan, Rue 153, 193
McClurg, Edie 113, 128, 171, 208, 230
McConnell, Thomas 5, 75, 124
McCoo, Marilyn 110
McCormack, Patricia 219
McCormick, Kathy 45
McCormick, Maureen 18
McCormick, Pat 58
McCoy, Matt 229–30, **229**
McCullough, Robert 44, 214
McDonald, Daniel 214
McDonnell, Mary 39
McDonnell, Terrence 140, 203
McDonough, Kit 43, 223
McDougall, Donald 38, 40
McDowall, Roddy 152–3
McDowell, Ronnie 199
McEveety, Bernard 38, 61, 101

McEveety, Vincent 66, 132, 146
McGavin, Darren 152
McGee, Vonetta 21
McGeorge, Jim 145
McGibbon, Duncan Scott 217
McGill, Bruce 145
McGinley, Ted 185
McGovern, Maureen 185
McGovern, Terry 22
McGrath, Derek 164
McGuire, Michael 37
McHale's Navy 3, 12
McIsaac, Marianne 188
McIntyre, Doug 231
McK, Misha 211–2
McKane, Jackie 149, 206
McKean, Michael 58
McKeand, Carol 17
McKeand, Nigel Evan 17
McKenzie, Richard 72
McLaird, Arthur E. 206
McLarty, Rod 91
McLean, Michael S. 68
The McLean Stevenson Show 26
McMahon, Jenna 201
McMahon, John 85
McManus, Michael 85
McMillan, Alison 120
McMillan, Kenneth 120, 163
McMurray, Sam 14, 27
McNair, Barbara 136
McNally, Terrence 228
McNamara, Brian 116–7
McNeely, Jerry 20
McRae, Ellen 36
McRaney, Gerald 73
McRaven, Dale 106, 185
McWhirter-Dees, Julie 30, 53, 104
McWilliams, Caroline 104–106, **105**, 191
McWilliams, Paulette 161
Me and Maxx 98, 234
Me and Mom 98–9, 232, 233, 234
Me and Mrs. C. 211–12, 226, 233
Me and the Chimp 56, 102
Meadow, Barry 121
Meadows, Audrey 88
Meadows, Jayne 8, **8**, 73, 168
Meatballs and Spaghetti 99, 232, 233
Mecchi, Irene 131, 217
Medlinsky, Harvey 185
Medway, Lisa 22
Meek, Barbara 99
Meet the Raisins 22
The Megan Mullally Show 36
Melba 99–100, 232
Meldrum, Wendel 70, 132–4, 197
Melfi, Leonard 95
Melman, Jeffrey L. 95, 126, 150
Meloni, Christopher 18
Melrose, Barrie 45
Melton, Sid 42, 218
Melville, J.W. 13
Melvin, Allan 104
Memmoli, George 206–209
Mendelsohn, Jack 99, 208
Menteer, Gary 145, 210
Mercer, Marian 49, 128
Meredith, Burgess 55

Merl, Judy 155
Merritt, Theresa 226
Merson, Marc 68, 118
Messick, Don 30, 32
Messina, Lou 206
Metcalfe, Burt 184, 202, 217
Metrano, Art 172, 210
Meyers, Nancy 12–13
Meyers, Susan 51
Miami Vice 221
Michaelsen, Melissa 98
Michele, Bridget 217
Mickey 121
The Mickey Rooney Show 121
Mid-Morning Manhattan 228
The Middle 152
Middlebrooks, Harry 212, 227
Midler, Bette 29
Migenes, Julia 171
Mike Hammer 152
Mike the Dog 29
Milano, Alyssa 89–90
Milch, David 17
Milford, John 38
Miller, Chris 158
Miller, Gary H. 185
Miller, Gene 16
Miller, Joanne 26
Miller, Karyl Geld 10, 48, 94, 170, 217
Miller, Lee 171
Miller, Marilyn Suzanne 228
Miller, Mark 171
Miller, Mark C. 91
Miller, Mark Thomas 100
Miller, Marsha 99
Miller, Mary Cory 113
Miller, Maxine 159
Miller, Michael K. 93
Miller, Paul 93
Miller, Penelope Ann 130
Miller, Randall 70
Miller, Sidney 53
Miller, Stephen A. 201, 214
Miller, Thomas L. 49, 58, 210
Milli Vanilli 150
Milligan, Mike 24, 100
Mills, Alley 69, 94, 215
Mills, Hayley 202–203
Milsap, Ronnie 140
Mind Your Language 178
Minge, Brenda McAdams 212
Mintz, Larry 49, 185
The Miracles 155
Mirand, Evan 99
Mirisch, Andrew 84
Mirkin, David 170
The Mirror 75
The Misadventures of Sheriff Lobo 91, 212–14, **213**, 233, 234
Misch, David 165
Misfits of Science 1, 100–101, 233
Mishkin, Phil 170, 206
Mission: Impossible 129
Mistal, Karen 108
Mr. Merlin 101–102, 233
"Mr. Nice Guy" 172
Mr. Potato Head 113
Mr. President 214–15, 232, 233
Mister Roberts 12, 98

Index

"Mister Sandman" 84
Mr. Smith 102, 233
Mr. Sunshine 102–104
Mr. T. and Tina 98
Mitchell, Brian Stokes 22
Mitchell, Coleman "Chick" 140, 230
Mitchell, Gordon "Whitey" 184, 206, 212
Mitchell, Keith 58
Mitchell, Scoey 212, 225–7
Mitchum, Robert 227
Mittleman, Rick 38, 52, 76
Mitty, Walter 137
Mitz, Rick 5, 159, 231
Mitzubi, Samuro 115
Modern Family 92, 152
Moffatt, Aaron 172
Moffet, Jordan 33, 73, 114, 206
Mohun, Bruce 160
Mokihana 8
Molinaro, Al 209–10
Molitor, Doug 182
Moll, Richard 15
Moloney, Bill 190–2
Moloney, Bob 190–2
Mom 228
Monaghan, Greg 114
Monnickendam, Freddy 25
Monroe, Marilyn 230
Montagne, Edward 114, 206
Monti, Mary Elaine 126
Monty Python's Flying Circus 105, 113
Moody, Lynne 39
Moody, Ron 114, **114**
Moon, Guy 42, 154
Moonlighting 48, 75, 148, 167, 214
Moonves, Les 105
Moore, Mary Tyler 11, 32, 46, 79, 97, 232
Moore, Melba 99–100
Moore, M.M. Shelly 101, 147
Moore, Terry 33
Moore, Tom 16, 93, 136, 172, 187
Mora, Danny 159
Moran, Erin 209–11, **209**
Mordente, Tony 14, 19, 35, 56, 58, 71, 114, 185, 196, 197
Moreno, Rita 49
Morgan, Christopher 28
Morgan, Harry 106, 181, 183–4
Morgan, Tracy 212
Moriana, Rocky 88
Moriarty, Jay 24, 100
Moriarty, Michael 175
Morita, Pat 213
Mork and Mindy 85, 104, 211, 232
The Mork and Mindy/Laverne and Shirley/Fonz Hour 104, 211
"The Morning After" 185
Morning Glory 197
Morrill, Priscilla 13
Morris, Anita 29
Morris, Garrett 74, 110
Morris, Howard 52
Morris, Linda 70, 77, 88, 110, 140
Morris, Michael 220
Morris, Phil 96
Morrisette, Billy 123

Morrison, Pamela 185
Morrow, Buddy 159
Morrow, Karen 79–81, **80**
Morrow, Rob 40, 166
Morse, Hollingsworth 38
Morse, Robert 231
Mortimer, Johnnie 170, 219
Morton, Gary 88
Morton, Ray 172
Moschitta, John 182
Moscow, David 89–90
Mosely, Roger E. 145
Moss, Denise 106, 217
Moss, Winston 66, 220
Mostel, Joshua 12
The Mothers-in-Law 46
Mothersbaugh, Mark 157
Motta, Bess 110
Moultrie, Emily 13
Mount, Michael 13
"Movin' Along" 159
Moxey, John Llewellyn 84
Moye, Michael G. 24, 74, 181, 220
Mula, Frank 70, 93, 179
Muldaur, Diana 46
Mull, Martin 28–9, 44, 54
Mullally, Megan 1, 36
Mullavey, Greg 88
Mulligan, Jim 12, 37, 82, 201
Mulligan, Richard 137
Mulligan's Stew 81
Mumford, Thad 33, 124, 185
Muntner, Simon 38, 61, 72, 126, 185
Murcia, Joey 11, 76
Murder She Wrote 68
Murdock, George 178
Murphy, Eddie 138
Murphy, Gary 24, 217
Murphy, Maureen 28
Murphy, Michael 165
Murphy Brown 3, 66, 130
Murray, Bill 157, 158
Murray, Don 19
Murray, Howard 195, 231
Murray, Jan 83
Murray, Peg 211, 212
Murray, Warren S. 19, 206, 220
Murtagn, Bill 160
Musca, Tom 231
My Life Story 134
My Sister Sam 215–17, **216**, 233
My Two Dads 134
My World and Welcome to It 32
Myer, Bob 195
Myerson, Alan 19, 22, 54, 86, 102, 147, 149, 182, 187, 206
Myman, Robert M. 64
Myrick, Ryan 22

Nabors, Jim 8
Nader, Ralph 166
Nadler, Holly 37
Nadler, Marty 16, 115
Naked Gun 130
Naked Gun 2 1/2: The Smell of Fear 130
Namba, Keiko 52
The Nancy Walker Show 96
Napoleon 77
Nardini, James 43

Nardino, Gary 61, 62, 97
Nardo, Patricia 73, 172
Narz, Jack 78
Nasella, James 158
Nathan, A.J. 68
Nathan, Mort 61
Nathan, Stephen 56, 137, 162
Nation, Terry 45
The National Enquirer 146
National Lampoon's Animal House 43, 63, 145
The National Register 146
Naughton, David 12, 216
Naughton, James 94, 134
Navin, John P., Jr. 75, 103
Naylor, Jason 27, 177
The NBC Monday Night Movie 19
Nearest and Dearest 199
Nearly Departed 104–106, **105**, 137, 233
Neary, Brian 81
The Neighbors 30
Neigher, Geoffrey 140, 230
Neigher, Rick 121
Neigher, Stephen 11, 73, 172, 219
Nelson, Barry 219
Nelson, Craig 42, 51
Nelson, Craig Richard 157, 158
Nelson, David 205
Nelson, Dick 52
Nelson, Don 66
Nelson, Gary 117, 146
Nelson, Rick 139
Nelson, Steve 159
Nelson, Tracy 156–8, **156**
Nepus, Ria 77
Nettleton, Lois 181
Neufeld, Sigmund, Jr. 126, 140, 206
Neuwirth, Bebe 42
The New Adventures of Beans Baxter 106–9, **107**, 234
The New Adventures of Old Christine 196
The New Andy Griffith Show 110
The New Dick Van Dyke Show 176, 177
The New England Patriots 82
The New Gidget 1
The New Leave It to Beaver 1, 217, 222, 234
The New Loretta Young Show 110
The New Love American Style 109–10, 234
The New Monkees 110–11, 234
The New Odd Couple 110, 111–13, **111**, 232, 234
The New Phil Silvers Show 110
The New York Examiner 163
The New York Giants 68
The New York Mets 86, 95
Newbound, Laurie 122
Newhart 1, 13, 57, 130
Newman, Carroll 180
Newman, Elaine 209
Newman, Julie 131
Newman, Lionel 20, 24, 184
Newman, Phyllis 195
Newmar, Julie 61
Nicastro, Michelle 163
Nicholl, Don 170, 219

Nichols, David 16, 35, 89
Nichols, Mike 168, 169
Nicholson, Sam 52
Nicholson and Muir 40
Nick and Hillary 113, 166–7, 233
Nieber, Linda 22, 125
Nielsen, Leslie 129–30, 147, 197
Nierman, Greg 15
"Night and Day" 58, 79
Night Court 1, 17, 145, 166
Nightmare on Elm Street 127
Nilsson, Harry 45
Nirvana, Yana 82
Nittoli, Tony Deacon 40
Nixon, Cynthia 1, 166
Nixon, Richard 215
No Soap Radio 113–14, 116, 233
No Time for Sergeants 13
Noah, Peter 104, 215
Nobbs, David 137
Noble, James 45
Nobody's Perfect 114, **114**, 220, 233
Nolte, Nick 29
Noone, Peter 35
Noonoo, Bob 110
Norell, Michael 9
Norris, Bruce 130
Norris, Pamela 37, 74, 101
North, Alan 129, 172
North, Sheree 70–1, **70**
North of Hollywood 109
Not Necessarily the News 113, 169
Nothing in Common 45, 114–15
"Nothing in the World like Love" 37
Nothing Is Easy 115, 170–1, 232, 233, 234
Novack, James L. 132
Novak, Kim 126
Novello, Don 157–8
Nurse, Karl 188
Nurses 227
The Nutt House 114, 115–17, 233
Nyby, Christian 161
Nyby, Christian, II 180, 214

Oakley, Annie 14
Oas-Heim, Gordon 110
Oberman, Margaret 158
O'Brien, Barry 113, 210
O'Brien, Maria 202
Occasional Wife 65
O'Connor, Carroll 55, 136–7
O'Connor, Donald 61, 106
The Odd Couple 26, 40, 52, 79, 110, 111, 112, 144, 147, 160, 167, 175, 216, 226, 228
O'Donnell, Tim 56
Off the Rack 117–18
Oh, God 54
Oh, Madeline 118–19
"Oh, Yeah" 89
O'Hara, Catherine 25
O'Hara, Jenny 89, 216
O'Heany, Caitlin 193–5
O'Herlihy, Michael 146
Oingo Boingo 44
O'Kun, Lan 129, 195
O'Leary, Jack 138
Oliver, John E. 31

Oliver, Lyla 11
Olkewicz, Walter 126
Olsen, Dana 210
Olsen, Leila Hee 178
Olsen, Merlin 44
Olsen, Susan 18, 193
Olson, Martin 109
Olstein, Judy 187
O'Malley, Leonore 37, 98
On Our Own 5
"On the Homefront" 57
On the Rocks 180, 181
Once a Hero 119, 233
One Big Family 119–20, 232
One Day at a Time 207
One Froggy Evening 77
One in a Million 120–1, 234
One More Try 92
One of the Boys (1982) 121–2, **122**, 232, 233, 234
One of the Boys (1989) 122–3, 232
O'Neal, Ryan 37, 186
O'Neal, Tatum 186
O'Neil, Danny 121
O'Neill, Dennis 82
O'Neill, Dick 15, 37
O'Neill, Katie 171
O'Neill, Robert F. 213
"Only the Lonely" 155
Open All Hours 123
Open All Night 123–4
Open House 1, 124–5, **124**, 232, 234
Oppenheimer, Alan 30
Orange Is the New Black 181
Orbison, Roy 77, 155
Orenstein, Bernie 25, 26, 39, 48, 120, 121, 122, 198, 231
Orloff, Richard 95, 138, 201
Ortelli, Dyana 96
Ortiz, April 29
Ortiz, Humberto 96
Orton, Peter 17
Osborn, Ron 68, 205
O'Shannon, Dan 195
O'Shea, Milo 119
Osmond, Christian 222
Osmond, Eric 222
Osmond, Ken 222
Ostroff, Howard 203
O'Sullivan, Billy 177
Otto, Linda 128
"Our Kind of Town" 75
Out of Practice 162
Out of the Blue 101
Overton, Rick 59, 109
Owen, John Steven 33, 81, 134, 145, 151

Pace, Evan 72
Padnick, Glenn 209
Page, Harrison 221
Page, LaWanda 76, 220
Pagliaro, Joanne 138
Paige, Janis 13, 58, 85–6
Paige, Sam 150
The Pajama Game 85
Palermo, Tony 109
Paley, William 127
Palillo, Ron 211
Palladino, Daniel 106, 120

Palmer, Betsy 94
Palmer, Patricia Fass 24
Palmer, Tom 123, 217
Paltrow, Bruce 167
Pankin, Stuart 19, 104–106, **105**, 113–14, 144, 169–70
Pardini, Lou 127
Parent, Kevin 44
The Parent Trap 203
Parfitt, Judy 194
Park Place 125–6, 233
Parker, J. Standford 220
Parker, Jim 212
Parker, Rod 128, 129
Parker, Sarah Jessica 1, 156
Parks, Catherine 182
Parks and Recreation 152
Parone, Edward 180
Parr, Larry 53
Parr, Stephen 86
Parriott, James D. 46, 100, 101
Parriott, Sara 101
Partners in Crime 126, 233, 234
Pasko, Martin 51
Pasquin, John 27, 74, 191, 198
Pastorelli, Robert 97, 217
Pataki, Michael 94, 128
Patchett, Tom 124, 177, 190
Paterson, Doug 30
Patrick, Lisa 89, **89**
Patterson, John 17, 94, 146, 168, 173
Patterson, Larry 182
Patterson, Lorna 57
Patterson, Ray 33, 53
The Patty Duke Show 106, 197, 230
Paul, Norman 208
Paul, Richard 60, 65, 122
Paul, Rod 127
Pavlon, Jerry 142
Paxton, Bill 150
Payne 10
Payne, Bill 76
Payne, Julie 32, 84
Payton, Jo Marie 112
Peaker, E.J. 93
Pearl, Barry 109
Pearl, Howard 25, 62, 84, 97, 98, 110, 113, 119, 177, 210
Pearlberg, Irving 49
Pearlman, Michael 192
Pearlman, Seth 191
Pearthree, Pippa 189
Peck, Ed 145
Peete, Bob 66, 100
Pierce, Gwendolyn 192
Pierce, Hawkeye 62
Peluce, Meeno 14, 187
Peluso, Florence 97
Pena, Elizabeth 69–70, 172
Penn, Leo 102
Penn, Richard 153
Penn, Sean 43
Penn and Teller 134
The People Next Door 126–7, 233
Perez, Jose 160
Perfect Strangers 128
Perine, Parke 49, 102, 149
Perlman, Rhea 172, 185
Perlove, Paul 25, 54, 84
Perpich, Jonathan 82

Perrine, Valerie 54, 84, 160
Perry, Jamilla 99
Perry, John Bennett 58
Perry, Matthew 58, 103, 113, 144, 193
Perry, Tyren 21, *21*
Pershing, Diane 110
Persky, Bill 14, 79, 155, 199
Perzigian, Jerry 136, 174–5
Pesci, Joe 61
Pescow, Donna 184–5
Peter Gunn 3
Peterman, Steve 56, 94, 157
Peters, Barbara 101, 147
Peters, Jon 31
Peters, Margie 78
Petersen, Chris 188
Petersen, Randy 105, 106
Peterson, Robyn 13
Petlock, John 133
Petranto, Russ 14, 179
Petryni, Michael 146
Petteway, Jane 45
Pettler, Pam 84
Petty, Lori 168
Pevney, Joseph 140
Peyser, John 214
The Phil Silvers Show 12, 48, 62, 74
Philbin, Regis 110, 159, 228
Philips, Lee 18
Phillips, Little Esther 190
Phillips, Pamela 211
Phillips, Renee 13, 195
Phillips, Stu 46, 61, 214
Phillips, Wendy 138
Phillips, William F. 82
Phoenix, River 146
Phyl and Mikhy 127–9, 232, 233, 234
Picard, Paul R. 39
Picardo, Robert 160
Pickens, Slim 199
Pickles, Christina 127
Pieratt, Paul, Sr. 225, 227
Pig in the Middle 118
Pilger, Paul 191, 192
Piller, Michael 131, 132
Pinchot, Bronson 143
The Pink Panther 114
Pinto, Johnny 25
Pioli, Judy 71, 159
Pitchford, Dean 198
Pitlik, Noam 63, 65, 71, 118, 150
Pitoniak, Ann 183
Pitt, Brad 174
Place, Mary Kay 13
Plana, Tony 146
Platt, Howard 37
Pleshette, Suzanne 78, 163–4, **163**, 232, 234
Plumb, Eve 18
Poledouris, Basil 101
Polen, Denny 191
Police Squad 81, 129–30, 172, 220, 233
Polinsky, Alexander 192
Pollack, Brian 221
Pollak, Kevin 195
Pollard, Michael J. 84
Pollock, David 120, 160, 196, 205
Pomerantz, Earl 15, 41, 228
Pompian, Paul 119

Ponterotto, Donna 138
Poole, Duane 211
The Popcorn Kid 130–1, 234
Poree, Greg 22
Porky's 175
Porter, Alisan 25
Portillo, Rose 35
Portnoy, Gary 97, 131
Poryes, Michael 203
Post, Markie 145
Post, Mike 17, 140, 168
Poston, Tom 56
Potter, Carol 75
Potter, Ellen 198
Potter, Sherman 183
Potts, Annie 57
Pounder, C.C.H. 180
Powell, Jane 146
Powell, Vince 178
Power, Udana 86, 87
Powers, Dave 137, 170, 219
Powers, Wayne 211–12, 225–7, **225**
The Practice 120, 188
Praiser, Ian 7, 29, 145
Pratt, Deborah 128
Preece, Michael 3, 4, 52, 149, 180
Prelutsky, Burt 36, 164
Pressman, David 81, 202
Pressman, Lawrence 79–81, **80**, 161, 202
Prestia, Shirley 39
Pretty Little Liars 155
Price, Marc 26
Price, Paul B. 137, 162
"Pride and Joy" 28
Priestly, Jason 1, 109, 149
Prince, Jonathan 11, 101
Prince Charming 194
Prince Phillip 157
Prinze, Freddie 4
Pritchard, Mary Jo 109
Pritzker, Steve 20
The Prizefighter 3
Probe 131–2, 233
"Problems" 155
Proctor, Philip 227
Profft, Pat 130
Props, Babette 62
Provenza, Paul 132–4, 193
Prunell, Jessica 167
Pryor, Richard 20, 21, 161
Pugh, Willard E. 22
Pulliam, Darcy 219
Purdham, David 168
Purdum, E.J. 58
Purdy-Gordon, Carolyn 39
The Pursuit of Happiness 132–4, 232, 234
Pyle, Denver 33

Quan, Ke Huy 171
Que Pasa, U.S.A.? 142
Quincy, M.E. 231
Quinn, Chance 127
Quinn, Kevin 105, 106
Quinn, Thomas 14
quiz show scandals 95

Rabinowitz, Robert 28, 70
Rackauskas, Giedra 109

Radin, Roy 112
Radler, Robert 111
Radner, Gilda 157
Radnitz, Brad 206
Raeburn, Anna 91
Raffin, Deborah 49
Rafkin, Alan 18, 23, 24, 25, 45, 193, 230
Rags to Riches 1, 217–18, 232, 233, 234
"Ragtime Cowboy Joe" 140
Raising Miranda 1, 134–5, 232, 234
Raisins: Sold Out—The California Raisins II 22
Ramuno, Phil 45, 150, 160, 181
Randall, Bob 118, 142
Randall, Tony 111, 112
Randolph, John 11, 184
Rango 3, 214
Rannow, Jerry 206
Ransome, Preston 146
Raposo, Joe 219
Rappaport, John 59–60
Rappaport, Michele 148
Rasche, David 220–1
Raskin, Bonnie 127
Raskin, Richard 10, 31, 39
Rasmussen, Bruce 35, 197
Ratliffe, Garette 194
Ratray, Devin 65
Rauseo, Vic 70, 77, 88, 110, 140
Rawhide 214
Rawlings, Brian 150
Rawls, Lou 40, 110
Ray, Jeff 140
Ray, Leslie 51
Ray, Marguerite 220
Rayburn, Gene 9
Rayle, Hal 52
Raynor, William 38
Raznick, Deborah 221
"Ready to Take a Chance Again" 49
Reagan, Ronald 215
"The Real Me" 137
"Red Roses for a Blue Lady" 176
The Redd Foxx Comedy Hour 135
The Redd Foxx Show 135–7, **135**, 232
Redford, J.A.C. 11, 176
Redgrave, Lynn 24–5, 223–4
Redigo 38
Redstone, Sumner 179
Reed, Erin 149
Reed, John 147
Reed, Pamela 166
Reed, Philip 132
Reed, Robert 18, 51, 61
Reed, Shanna 68
Reeder, Tom 126, 129
Reese, Della 22
Reeves, K.C. 43
Reeves, Keanu 43, 227
Regalbuto, Joe 3, 7, 15, 69, 71, 119
Regan, Ellen 211, 226
Reggie 137, 233
Regina, Paul 182
Rehwaldt, Frank 97
Reid, Daphne Maxwell 50, 153
Reid, Elliott 184
Reid, Tim 50–1, 153–4, 181, 223, 234

Reid, Tim, II 154
Reiker, Donald 137, 138
Reilly, John 93
Reinhart, Rich 56, 145, 170, 195
Reinhold, Judge 124
Reiser, Paul 54
Reisner, Allen 84, 126
Reiss, Mike 193, 221
Remick, Lee 128
Remini, Leah 90
Reno, Jeff W. 68
Reno, Mike 109
Reo, Don 62, 65, 96, 198
Report to Murphy 137–8, 232, 233
Ress, Gary 50
Restivo, Joe 212
Reyes, Julian 178
Reynolds, Burt 28, 145
Reynolds, Debbie 7–9, **8**, 76, 93, 232
Reynolds, Gene 33, 45, 104, 215
Rezyka, Mark 31
Rhine, Larry 220
Rhoades, Barbara 231
Rhoda 184
Rhodes, Donnelly 138, 197
Rhodes, Vivian 231
Rice, Ernie 126
Rice, Greg 49
Rice, John 49
Rich, Adam 58
Rich, Christopher 51, 164, 194
Rich, Hollis 140
Rich, John 10, 26, 102, 104, 105, **105**, 106
Rich, Mert 221
Richards, Evan 29, 95
Richards, Kim 206, 208
Richards, Lou 55
Richards, Michael 1, 96, 178
Richards, Ron 114
Richards, Tessa 185
Richardson, Bob 99
Richardson, Ed 228
Richardson, Patricia 35, 201
Richdale, Jace 70
Richmond, Bill 23, 24, 142, 198
Richmond, Len 91
Richwood, Patrick 115
Rickey, Patricia 150
Rickles, Don 54
Riddle, Nelson 206
Ridgely, Robert 29
Rieffel, Lisa 10
The Righteous Apples 2
Riley, Jack 26, 29, 45, 142, 177, 179
Riley, Jeannie C. 205
Riley, Larry 161
Rinsler, Dennis 44, 93, 171
Riordan, Monica 93
Ripps, Leonard 58, 153, 179, 185
Rips, Martin 170, 179, 218, 219
Ritter, John 64, 88, 169–70, 219
Rivera, Jose 5
Rivers, Joan 171
Robbins, Tim 83, 147
The Robert Guillaume Show 138–9, 232, 233, 234
Roberts, Cliff 30, 53
Roberts, Doris 94, 184–5

Roberts, Francesca P. 50, 63, 64
Roberts, Jonathan 44
Roberts, Michael D. 198
Roberts, Pernell 184
Roberts, Tony 49, 91–2, 168, 234
Roberts, Tracey 87
Robertson, Pat 166
Robin, Diane 185
Robins, John 114
Robin's Nest 169
Robinson, Charles 189
Robinson, Fran 22–3, **23**
Robinson, J. Peter 218
Robinson, Joel 149–50, **149**
Robinson, Phil Alden 54
Robinson, Sally 45
Robinson, Smokey 77
Robman, Steve 13, 20, 41, 63
Rocco, Alex 42, 160
Roch, Gail 182
Roche, Eugene 56, 165
Rodd, Marcia 49, 94
Rodriguez, Paul 4–5, **5**, 56, 173–5
Rodriguez, Percy 220
Rogers, Doug 15, 71, 100, 122, 209
Rogers, Harriet 188
Rogers, Jim 38
Rogers, Mimi 140
Rogosin, Joel 101
Roker, Renny 114
Roley, Sutton 126
Rolike, Hank 82, 138
Roll Out 12
Rolle, Esther 113
Rolling Stone 156
Rollins, Jack 159
Romanus, Richard 49, 168
Romero, Cesar 61
Rondeau, Charles R. 214
"Room Enough for Two" 217
Roomies 139–40, 233, 234
Rooney, Mickey 121–2, **122**, 232
The Ropers 73, 169–70, 218–19, 232, 233, 234
Rosannadanna, Roseanne 157
Rosario, Bert 4, 44
Rosato, Tony 9
Rose, Alexandra 115
Rose, Margot 138
Rose, Mickey 4, 56, 162
Roseanne 1, 25, 64, 118
Rosebrook, Jeb 160
Rosemond, Perry 160
Rosen, Larry 76, 101, 102, 161, 225
Rosen, Milt 38, 208
Rosen, Neil 83, 98, 177, 210, 219
Rosen, Sy 13, 14, 15, 124, 130, 140, 155, 220
Rosenberg, Len 10
Rosenberg, Phil 14
Rosenberg, Stuart 14
Rosenblum, Ralph 20
Rosencrantz, Zachary 10
Rosenfarb, Bob 7, 37, 51, 147
Rosenstock, Richard 30, 119, 185, **185**, 187
Rosin, Charles 20
Rosner, Mark 173
Ross, Chuck 37, 42
Ross, Donald 114, 121, 126, 206

Ross, Duncan 175
Ross, Jerry 86, 113, 155, 160, 206
Ross, Marion 90, 150, 210, 231
Ross, Marty 110
Ross, Michael 170, 219
Rosser, Pamela 182
Rossi, Leo 126
Rossovich, Tim 180
Rosten, Leo 178
Roth, Paula A. 71, 210
Rothman, Mark 58, 112–13
Rothstein, Barbara 100
The Rousters 140
Rowan and Martin's Laugh-In 113, 137
Rowland, Melody 56
Roxie 140–2, 164, 234
The Royal Family 135
Ruben, Aaron 13, 163, 225
Ruben, Joe 20
Ruben, Tom 163
Rubin, Andrew 76
Rubin, Fred 66
Rubin, Lance 117
Rubin, Marc 176
Rubin, Ronald 16
Rubini, Michel 28
Rubinstein, Arthur 206
Ruby, Cliff 214
Ruby, Joe 104, 211
Rucker, Allen 44
Rucker, La Vonne 212
Ruegger, Tom 33, 53
Rugolo, Pete 56
Runyon, Jennifer 192–3
Ruppenthal, Chris 221
Rushing, Jerry 33, 221
Russnow, Michael 77, 161, 214
Rust, Patricia 227
Ruttan, Susan 37
Ruvinsky, Morrie 101
Ryan, Fran 113
Ryan, Joan 202
Ryan, Meg 121
Ryan, Natasha 80–1, **80**
Ryan, Steve 223

Sabella, Ernie 45, 74, 142
Sachs, Jeffrey J. 197, 203
Sadowsky, Adam 74, 144
Sagal, Jean 197–8, **198**
Sagal, Katey 1, 97
Sagal, Liz 197–8, **198**
Sage, Liz 24, 142, 231
Sage, Martin 140, 155, 215
Sahl, Mort 170
St. Germaine, Mark 17
St. James, Susan 167
St. John, Kristoff 22–4, **23**, 187
Saldana, Teresa 146
Saldivar, Susan 174
Salkowitz, Sy 214
Sallan, Bruce J. 45
Saltis, Larry 110
Saltsman, Terry 160
Saltzan, Terry 83
Salvay, Bennett 16
Salzman, Linda 17
Sanchez of Bel Air 142–3, 232, 233
Sand, Bob 93

Sand, Paul 29, 56, 68, 181
Sandefur, B.W. 38
Sanders, Jay O. 183
Sanders, Kelly 44
Sanders, Richard 36, 42, 154, 181, 204
Sandler, Ellen 38, 48, 100, 124, 127, 217
Sandrich, Jay 50, 73, 118, 163, 177
Sanford 135, 219–20, 232, 233, 234
Sanford, Arlene 11, 36, 37, 125
Sanford, Gerald 38, 180
Sanford and Son 104, 112, 135, 163, 177, 219, 220
The Sanford Arms 219, 220
Sangiolo, Anita 188
Santana, Arnaldo 4
Santoni, Reni 142
Santos, Joe 4, 98
Sara 143–4, ***143***, 233, 234
Sarafin, Teddy 165
Sassover, Nathan 126
"Satin Doll" 130
Satlof, Ron 140
Saturday Night Live 25, 47, 157
Savalas, Telly 54
Saved by the Bell 90, 202–203
Savel, Dava 36, 123
Saviola, Camille 13
Sawyer, Connie 83
Sax, Steve 157
Sbarge, Raphael 15–16
Scannell, Kevin 132
Scarbury, Joey 76
Scarpelli, Glenn 75, 207
Schaal, Wendy 104–106, ***105***
Schaefer, Mark 39
Schaeffer, Rebecca 215–17, ***216***
Schafer, Natalie 54
Schallert, William 39, 213
Scharfman, Mort 121
Scharlach, Ed 84–6
Schatzberg, Andy 45
Scheerer, Robert 173
Scheff, Michael 147, 176
Scheimer, Lou 55
Scheinman, Andrew 68
Schenck, George 153
Schenck, Rocky 111
Scherrer, Paul 51, 177
Schiavelli, Vincent 43
Schiff, Robin 218
Schiller, Bob 18, 24, 66, 96, 220
Schiller, Craig 147
Schiller, Tom 13
Schilling, William G. 39
Schindelheim, Ramona 217
Schlamme, Thomas 221
Schlein, Hap 187
Schmock, Jonathan 198
Schneider, Andrew 218
Schneider, John 33
Schneider, Peter 197
Schneider, Sascha 154
Schock, Harriet 14
Schoenbrun, Michael P. 176
Schubb, Mark 26
Schuck, John 39, 111–13, ***111***, 126
Schudt, Alicia Marie 117, 221
Schulman, Emily 79

Schulman, Roger S.H. 37, 44, 54, 68, 215
Schultz, Barbara 231
Schulze, Larry 109
Schwab, Lana 72
Schwartz, Donna 212
Schwartz, Elroy 38
Schwartz, Lloyd J. 19, 206
Schwartz, Nan 75
Schwartz, Sherwood 19, 54, 170, 171, 206
Scolari, Peter 13, 57, 160, 185, 227
Scott, Art 30, 53, 211
Scott, Carol Englehart 197
Scott, Debralee 184
Scott, George C. 215–15
Scott, Harry Lee 137
Scott, Jeffrey 102, 214
Scott, Jud 146
Scott, Kelsey 138
Scott, Marc 52
Scott, Oz 28, 66, 139
Scott, Tom 95, 114, 158
Scott-Hudson, Rodney 96
Scrubs 43
Scudder, Billy 28
Scully, Mike 179
Scully, Vin 72
Seale, Douglas 217
Search for Tomorrow 128
Sebastian, Susan 203, 221
Second Chance 18, 144–5, 233, 234
Second City 25, 165
Seeger, Efrem 11
Seeger, Susan 71, 92, 125
Seeley, Tom 7
Seely, Eileen 29
Segal, George 164–5
Segal, Misha 14
Segall, Don 50, 171
Segall, Pamela 135
Segall, Penina 150
Seidelman, Arthur Allan 61
Seifert, Jack 105–106, ***105***, 135–7, ***135***, 159
Seigel, Donald L. 136, 175
Seinfeld 34, 40, 85, 96, 162, 178, 196, 197
Seinfeld, Jerry 178
Selbo, July 135
Self, Ed 82, 83
Sellers, Peter 178, 219
Selver, Franelle 160
Selzer, Milton 42
Semel, David 125
Semi-Tough 1, 145, 234
Senensky, Ralph 17–18
The Sentinel 205
Serafian, Richard C. 47
Serra, Deborah 145
Seven Brides for Seven Brothers 145–6, 233
Severinsen, Doc 196
Sex and the City 157
Sgueglia, John 91, 150, 181
Shadow Chasers 146–7, 233
Shaffer, Paul 158, 167
Shafransky, Renee 228
Shakman, Matt 202
Shalamar 77

Shallat, Lee 70, 97, 125
Shannon, Don 188
Shaping Up 147, 234
Shapiro, Debbie 174
Shapiro, George 85, 86
Sharp, Jon 71
Sharp, Thom 45, 164
Shatner, William 93, 129
Shaver, Helen 176
Shaw, Lou 46, 61, 213, 214
Shaw, Scott 25
Shawn, Dick 60, 83, 160
Shayne, Bob 49, 126
Shea, Jack 24, 45, 78, 145, 164, 171, 172, 191, 219
Shea, Mark 195
Shea, Patt 56, 70, 95, 97, 171, 220
Shear, Pearl 196
Sheehan, Douglas 196
Sheehan, Tony 65, 150
Sheffler, Mark 220
Sheiner, Mary-David 149
Shelby, Carolyn 195
Sheldon, James 61, 126, 146, 153, 214, 221
Sheldon, Lee 132, 176
Sheldon, Les 206
Sheldon, Rodney 224
Shell Game 147–8, 233, 234
Shelly, Bruce 214
Sherer, Mel 210
"The Sheriff Lobo Theme" 214
Sherman, Bobby 142, 213
Sherman, Robert 180
"She's a Free Spirit" 51
She's the Sheriff 1
Sheslow, Stuart 16, 136
Shields, Brooke 94
Shimokawa, Gary 143, 203
Shimono, Sab 59
Shindig 191
Shiney, Mark 53
The Shirelles 28, 46, 55
Shirley 148–9, 232, 233, 234
Shirley and Lee 155
Shoemaker, Willie 231
Shoenman, Elliot 10, 11
Shore, Howard 115
Short, Bobby 100, 167
Short, John 190
Short, Martin 25–6, 69, 71
Shortridge, Stephen 8
Showalter, Max 162
Shroyer, Sonny 38
Shryer, Bret 148
Shubb, Jason 79, 139, 140
Shuster, Rosie 158
Shyer, Charles 12–13
Siamis, Korby 48, 94, 170, 217
Sibbett, Jane 42
Sidney, Sylvia 29, 126
Siegel, Bugsy 32
Siegel, Sandra Kay 149
Siegelman, Jan 89
Sierra, Gregory 56, 182
Silas, Phil 146
Silbar, Adam 154
Silberman, Harvey 10
Sills, Paul 165
Sills and Company 165

Silver, Marc 161
Silver, Ron 14, 162
Silver, Stu 113, 159
Silver, Susan 158
Silver Spoons 14, 63
Silverman, Fred 72, 99, 122, 123, 148, 218, 228, 230
Silverman, Jonathan 39
Silverman, Peter 17
Silverman, Stuart 11, 33, 172
Silvers, Cathy 46, 47, 48
Silvestri, Martin 88, 135
Simmon, Alexaundra 150
Simms, Hank 129
Simms, Rebecca 164
Simms, Sarah 164
Simon, David 193
Simon, Joel 127
Simon, Leonard 77
Simon, Neil 112
Simon, Sam 15, 147
Simon, Suzy 122
Simon and Simon 73
Simpson, O.J. 129
Simpson, Sandy 118
Sinatra, Frank 79
Sinbad 136
Singer, Alexander 18
Singer, Carla 68
Singer, Raymond 95
Singletary, Tony 35, 68, 73, 74, 124, 137, 160, 181, 193, 212, 225
Sinnamon, Shandi 193
Sister Kate 1, 63, 65, 149–50, **149**, 233
Sister Sledge 175
Sitowitz, Hal 49, 98–9
Sivad, Darryl 67–8
Six O'Clock Follies 150–1, 233, 234
The Six O'Clock Report 203
Slade, Bernard 228
Slade, Demian 144
The Slap Maxwell Story 151–2, 234
Sledge, Joni 175
Sledge, Kathy 175
Sledge Hammer 1, 220–1, 233
Sling Blade 170
Sloan, Michael 214
Sloyan, James 118
Small and Frye 152–3, 159, 233
Smart, Doug 120
Smart, Jean 137, 204, 223, 224
Smiar, Brian 151
Smirnoff, Yakov 178–9
Smith, Arlando 68, 75
Smith, Bubba 61, 98, 123, 145
Smith, Dick 114
Smith, Kurtwood 108
Smith, Lewis 78, **78**
Smith, Lionel 126
Smith, Shawnee 6–7, **6**, 19
Smith, Shelly 69
Smith, Sid O. 42, 182
Smith, Tom 209
The Smith Family 76
Smithee, Allan 78
Smithers, Jan 83
Smothers, Dick 46
Smothers, Tom 46
The Smothers Brothers Comedy Hour 46

The Smothers Brothers Show 46
Snavely's 9
Snee, Dennis 222, 223
Snee, John 222
Sneider, Caryn 119
Snider, Dee 109
Snyders, Sammy 188
Snoops 153–4, 232, 233
Snow, Mark 180
Snow, Tom 198
Soap 26, 70, 113, 138
Sobel, Barry 36
Solnicki, Victor 160
Solomon, Aubrey 61
Solomon, Mark 36, 129, 131
Solutions 148
Somack, Jack 162
Somers, Suzanne 219
Sommer, Paul 26
Sommers, Jay 208
Sons and Daughters 92
Soodik, Trish 89, 191
Sorel, Louise 80–1, **80**
Soria, Mireille 28
Sotkin, Marc 71
Soul, David 126
Spears, Ken 104, 211
Speer, Kathy 26, 61, 92, 185
Spelling, Aaron 7–9, 11–12, 87–8
Spelman, Sharon 184, 218
Spencer 154–5, 176, 234
Spencer, Alan 115–17, 220–1
Spencer, Larry 66, 76, 143, 225
Spencer, Peter 45
Spenser for Hire 154
Sperber, Wendy Jo 180
Die Spezialisten Unterwegs 101
Spezialy, Tom 217
Spiroff, Tom 62
Sprung, Sandy 74, 100
Square Pegs 1, 44, 156–8, **156**, 207, 208, 234
"Squeezy Easy" 84
Squyres, Phil 51, 195
Staahl, Jim 204, 221
Stack, Timothy 137
Stahl, Jerry 231
Stahl, Richard 57
Stairway to Paradise 75
Staley, James 130
Stamaty, Mark Alan 177
Stamos, John 1, 30, 231
"Stand by Me" 139
Stander, Lionel 18
Stanis, BernNadette 21
Stanley, Diane Messina 206
Stanley, Florence 126
Stanley, Kim 73
Stanley, Paul 75
Stanwyck, Barbara 126
Stapleton, Jean 181, 227
Stapleton, Maureen 168
Star of the Family 158–9, 232, 234
Star Wars 136
Staretski, Joseph 169–70, 178–9, 218–19
Stark, James 126
Stark, Ray 115
Starke, Anthony 120
Starr, Ben 208

Starting from Scratch 159–60, 233
Steambath 160, 232, 233
Steck, Betty 187
Steele, Ken 160
Steen, Mark 84
Steen, Nancy 31, 130
Steiger, Joel 99, 146
Stein, James R. 198, 201
Steinberg, David 11, 36, 41, 120, 131, 151
Steinberg, Norman 36, 38, 151
Steinfeld, Jake 7, 147
Steinhauer, Robert Bennett 84
Steinkellner, Bill 172
Steinman, Roger 15, 41
Steinmetz, Dennis 72
Stern, John 126
Stern, Leonard 126
Stern, Sandor 132
Stern, Steven Hilliard 223
Sternin, Robert 73, 88, 89, 119, 193–5
Stevens, Barry 83
Stevens, Bob 33
Stevens, Connie 9, 53, 159
Stevens, Craig 3
Stevens, Jeremy 187
Stevens, Rusty 222
Stevenson, Alvin "Bully" 36
Stevenson, McLean 26–8, 63, 206–209, 234
Stevenson, Parker 131
Stevenson, Susan 10, 31, 39, 197
Stevenson, Valerie 30
Stewart, Mel 52, 121
Stewart, Rod 155
Stiles, Norman 187
Still Standing 30
Still the Beaver 1, 217, 221–3, 232, 234
Stiller, Jerry 10, 166
Stillman, Deanne 158
Stir Crazy 54, 160–1, 233
"Stir It Up" 161
Stockard Channing in Just Friends 81, 161–3
The Stockard Channing Show 1, 161–3, 232, 234
Stoddard, Brandon 69
Stoddart, Alexandra 206
Stoffman, Nicole 83
Stolfi, Robert F. 49
Stone, Dee Wallace 170–1
Stone, Jeremy 88, 135
Stone, Leonard 10
Stone, Ron 52, 121
Stone, Suzanne 220
Storch, Larry 104, 128, 152, 153, 206
Stordahl, Axel 197
Storm, Howard 10, 15, 16, 45, 59, 102, 137, 179, 185, 210, 212
Straight, Beatrice 75
"Straight from the Heart," 44
Strangis, Greg 149, 206
Strangis, Sam 206
Strassman, Marcia 39, 56
Stratton, Charles 27
Strauss, Jeff 195
Strauss, Susan 197
Straw, Tom 11, 98, 184

Strawther, Larry 217
A Streetcar Named Desire 110
Strickland, Gail 178
Stritch, Elaine 36, 167
Struthers, Sally 55, 150
Stuart, Maxine 60, 140
Stuthman, Fred 206
Suddenly Susan 94
Sue Thomas, F.B. Eye 83
Sues, Alan 19
Sugartime 98
"Suicide Is Painless" 183
Sullivan, Jenny 98
Sullivan, Kevin Rodney 51
Sullivan and Son 191
Sultan, Arne 114
Sultan, Rick 50
Summer School 43, 216
Sunga, George 60, 136, 170, 219
Sunshine, Madelyn 113, 126–7
Sunshine, Steven 113, 126–7
The Sunshine Boys 54, 120
Superman 148
The Supremes 46
Surnow, Joel 84
Susman, Todd 63, 159
Sustarsic, Stephen 110, 171
Sutherland, Hal 55
Sutton, Michael 158
Suzanne Pleshette Is Maggie Briggs 163–4, **163**, 232, 234
Swackhamer, E.W. 140, 168
Swale, Tom 211
Swayze, Patrick 27
Sweeney, Allison 19, 41
Sweeney, Bob 12, 68, 77, 101, 120, 147, 150, 151, 205, 221
Sweet, Dolph 71, 180
The Sweet Inspirations 180
Sweet Surrender 164
Swerling, Jo, Jr. 82, 140
Swit, Loretta 52
Switzer, Michael 101
Sylvan, Paul 48
Sylvester, Harold 96
Szollosi, Thomas 38, 214
Szysznyk 138

Tacker, Francine 57, 118
Tadman, Aubrey 24
Taggart, Millee 113, 115, 169, 210
Taggart, Missy Stewart 206
Taggart, Rita 206
Tait, Don 66, 102
Take Five 140, 164–5, 234
Talbot, Nita 159
"Tales of the Apple Dumpling Gang" 58
Tales of the Gold Monkey 194
Tambor, Jeffrey 15, 40, 56, 103–104, 119, 218–19
Tanasescu, Gino 13, 152
Tanner, Mark 147
Tanner, Mary 190
Tanner '88 1, 165–6, 233
Tanner on Tanner 166
Tanz, Bernie 121
Tappis, Joel 149, 206
Tarses, Jay 32, 123, 124, 151, 152, 190
Tartaglia, John Andrew 214

Tartikoff, Brandon 17, 96, 100, 189, 226, 227
Tash, Max 13, 35, 42, 51, 56
Tate, Brian 228
Tate, Nick 125
Tately, Chuck 22, 212
Tattinger's 113, 166–7, 233
Taub, Bill 52
Tavera, Michael 26, 123
Taxi 15, 125, 150
Tayback, Vic 201
Taylor, Bruce A. 185
Taylor, C.D. 111
Taylor, Chip 139
Taylor, Holland 62, 98
Taylor, Josh 145
Taylor, Kurt 113
Taylor, Levi 187
Taylor, Mark L. 104
Taylor, Meshach 189
Taylor, Nathaniel 220
Taylor, Paul K. 97
Taylor, Philip John 19
Taylor, Ronald 129
Teachers Only 223–5, 234
Teicher, Roy 119, 187
Temple, Renny 39, 86, 110, 193
Tendler, Jesse 36, 168
Tenowich, Tom 85, 86
Tenspeed and Brown Shoe 1, 167–8, 233
Terlesky, J.T. 83
Terwilliger, Wayne 13
Tesich, Steve 20
Thames, Byron 19
That 70s Show 118
"That's All Right Mama" 82
"That's Good" 157
That's My Mama 226
"They're Playing Our Song" 91
Thiel, Nick 68, 148
Thiessen, Tiffany-Amber 203
Thigpen, Naomi 202
Thin Man 153
Third Rock from the Sun 118
13 East 211, 225–7, **225**, 233
Thirtysomething 137
Thomas, Carla 28
Thomas, Jay 125
Thomas, Tony 26, 61, 65, 70, 71, 73, 120, 172
Thomas, William, Jr. 50
Thomerson, Tim 29, 58, 69, 98, 185, 228, 234
Thomopoulos, Tony 130
Thompson, Chris 58, 61, 62
Thompson, Hilary 177
Thompson, Jenn 205
Thompson, Neil 31, 130
Thompson, Robert C. 146
Thompson, Timothy 193
Thompson, Wesley 67, 132
Thorne-Smith, Courtney 43, 196–7
The Thorn Birds 169
Thornley, Stephen 38
The Thorns 168–9, 233
Thornton, Billy Bob 170
Thornton, Brittany 79
Thorson, Linda 96
3 O'Clock High 194

The Three Stooges 159
Three's a Crowd 169–70, 233, 234
Three's Company 15, 18, 169, 170, 178, 210, 218, 224
Three's Company, Too 170
Threlkeld, Budge 228
Thuna, Leonora 58, 185
Tibbles, Barbara 208
Tibbles, George 193, 208
Ticket to Ride 44
Tierney, Maura 177
Tierra 5
Tilly, Jennifer 119, 147
The Tim Conway Comedy Hour 3
The Tim Conway Show 3
Timm, Doug 78
Tinker, Grant 32
Tinker, John 167
Tinker, Mark 95, 167
Tipton, George Aliceson 26, 61, 65, 71, 73, 96, 120, 173
Tisch, Steve 27, 28
Tischler, Bob 127
Tisdale, Jim 212
Todd, Beverly 136
Todd, Donald 101, 177
Toddman, David R. 33
Todman, Bill, Jr. 127
Toe-to-Toe 201
"Together" 5
Together We Stand 115, 170–1, 232, 233, 234
Tolkan, James 97
Tolkin, Mel 220
Toll, Judy 77
Tolsky, Susan 93
Tom, David 19
Tom, Dick and Harriet 49
Tomarken, Peter 26
Tomizawa, Nobuo 52
Tomlin, Lily 116, 152
The Tonight Show 32, 67, 224
Too Close for Comfort 72
Topper 75, 105–106
Topper, Tim 146
"The Toreador Song" 187
Torn Between Two Lovers 128
Torp, Jonathan 110
Torres, Liz 22, 24, 111–12, **111**
The Tortellis 14, 171–2, 234
"Tossin' and Turnin'" 28
Totten, Robert 38
Tough Cookies 62, 172–3, **173**, 233
"Tough Enough" 140
Tour of Duty 151
Towbin, Fredi 121
Towles, Tom 39
Townsend, Barbara 183
Tracy, John 37, 73, 74, 81, 94, 101, 113, 140, 145, 155, 163, 177, 185, 187, 210
Trainer, David 41, 202
Tramer, Bennett 203
Trampler, Bruce 110
Transparent 15, 81, 103
Trapper John, M.D. 127, 184
Travalena, Fred 150, 172
Travolta, Ellen 193, 209
Trbovich, Tom 14, 15, 31, 117, 210
Treas, Terri 146

Trial and Error 142, 173–5, 232, 233
Tricker, George 98, 155, 177, 210, 219
Trikonis, Gus 75
Trogdon, Miriam 7, 196
Trotsky, Leon 195
Trout Fishing with Earl 141
Troutman, Ron 212
Troy, Doris 28
Trudeau, Garry 165–6
Truman, Tim 131
Trying Times 227–8
Tucci, Michael 185
Tucker, David 45, 229, 230
Tucker, Deborah 90
Tucker, Forrest 199, 201
Tucker's Witch 175–6, 232, 233
Tunick, Jonathan 167
Turman, Glynn 60
Turn On 3
Turner, Janine 83
Turner, Lloyd 214
Turteltaub, Jonathan 122
Turteltaub, Saul 25, 26, 39, 48, 120, 121, 122, 198, 231
The Turtles 89
Tuttle, Mark 88, 170
Tweed, Terry 188
12 O'Clock High 17
20/20 72
The Twilight Zone 192
Twisted Sister 109
Two-and-a-Half Men 39, 41, 42
The Two of Us 228, 233, 234
Tyne, George 22, 206
Tyrell, Stephanie 20, 42, 154
Tyrell, Steve 13, 42
Tyrrell, Susan 123

Uger, Alan 26
Ugly Betty 146
Ulrich, Alicia 63–5
Under One Roof 154–5, 176, 233, 234
United States 176
The Untouchables 205
"Up, Up and Away" 146
Urbano, Carl 33, 53, 211
Urseth, Bonnie 230
Utman, Brian 146
Utt, Kenneth 14

Vaccaro, Brenda 143
Vail, Steven A. 51
Valentine's Day 182
Vallance, Louise 210
Vallejo, George 212
Vallely, James 62, 198
Van Atta, Don 63, 93
Van Buren, Abigail 63
Van Cleef, Lee 14
Van Dusen, Granville 78
Van Dyke, Barry 58, 177
Van Dyke, Dick 4, 11, 41, 176–7, 232
Van Dyke, Jerry 196
Van Dyke and Company 176
The Van Dyke Show 11, 176–7, 232, 234
Vanities 201
Van Lowe, Ehrich 66

Vannelli, Ross 22
Van Patten, Dick 218
Van Patten, Joyce 181
Van Scoyk, Robert 13, 95, 126
Vargas, John 12
Variety 163
Varney, Jim 140
Veep 196, 197
Veitch, Trevor 31
Veith, Sandy 121
Vela, Norma Safford 18, 152
Velez, Eddie 22, 173–5
Velez, Martha 4
The Velvelettes 46
Vennera, Chick 60
Vera, Billy 62, 139–40
Verdon, Gwen 7
Vereen, Ben 167
Vernon, John 60
A Very Brady Sequel 197
Vester, John 91, 125
Victor, James 26
Vieha, Mark 33
Vieth, Alessandro 66
Vigoda, Abe 206
Vigon, Barry 77, 125
The Village Voice 177
Villaire, David 53
Villard, Tom 229, 230
Vincent, E. Duke 88
Vincent, Ed 124
Vinovich, Steve 134
Vinton, Will 22
Viola, Joe 146
Viscuso, Sal 44
Vitarelli, Joseph 109
Vittes, Michael 17
Vogel, Virgil W. 132
Volz, Nedra 199
Voorhees, Lark 202
Vosburgh, Marcy 74, 100
Vrandenburg, Trish 40

Wackiest Ship in the Army 12
Wade, Sally 39, 121, 231
Wade, Timothy 226
Waggoner, Lyle 58
Wagner, Bruce 109, 127
Wagner, Carla Jean 148
Wagner, Michael J. 131, 132
Waigner, Paul 159
The Waitresses 157, 158
Waldron, Gy 33, 38
Walian, Werner 197
"Walk Like an Egyptian" 139
"Walk the Dinosaur" 167
Walker, Jimmie 12, 20–2, *21*
Walker, John 33
Walker, Nancy 96
Walker, Shirley 176
Walker, Texas Ranger 180
Walkow, Gary 221
Walla, Tom 37, 125
Wallace, Dee 170–1
Wallace, Earl W. 146
Wallace, George 28
Wallace, Marcia 72, 109
Walston, Ray 43, 118–19
Walter, Jessica 62, 169, 210
Walter, Tracey 14

The Waltons 17, 18, 90
Wanamaker, Sam 13
Wapner, Judge 127
War Babies 86
Ward, Janis 160
Ward, John H. 139
Ward, Kelly 26
Ward, Sela 68
"Ward 13" 226
Warden, Bradley 11
Warden, Jack 63, 79, 185–8, **186**
Ware, Peter 223
Waring, Todd 91, 92, 114–15
Warlock, Billy 217
Waronov, Mary 128
Warren, Marc 44, 93, 171
Warren, Michael 58, 210
Warren, Richard Lewis 126, 148
The Washington Post 177
Washingtoon 177, 233
Wasserman, Jerry 108
Wasserstein, Wendy 228
Watanabe, Gedde 59
Waters, Harry, Jr. 178
Watkins, Carlene 14, 73, 97, 172
Watson, Mills 205, 213, **213**
Watson-Johnson, Vernee 46, 48
Waxman, Mark 27, 161
Wayman, Andrew D. 89
Wayne, Mitchell 193, 208
Wayne, Patrick 148
Wayne, Paul 160, 170
We Got It Made 228–30, **229**, 232, 233
Weatherly, Shawn 147
Weaver, Lee 33–4, **34**
Webb, Amy 206
Webb, Jimmy 40, 146
Webb, Malcolm 206
Weber, Chris 52
Wechsler, Zachary 231
Wechter, David 221
Weddle, Vernon 199
Wedgeworth, Ann 199
Wednesday 209
Weege, Reinhold 126, 145
Weeks, Alan 14
Weidner, William 173
Weill, Claudia 44, 119
Weimers, David 52
Weinberger, Ed. 14, 15, 102, 163, 215
Weinberger, Jake 172
Weinberger, Mike 81, 172, 203, 206, 225
Weiner, Alitzah 142
Weinstein, E. Michael 13
Weinstein, Sol 28, 208
Weintraub, Carl 27
Weintraub, Cindy 14
Weis, Don 19, 126, 150, 151
Weisberg, Barbara 193
Weisberg, Sheila Judis 149
Weiskopf, Bob 24, 66, 96, 220
Weiskopf, Kim 100, 230
Weisman, Margaret 230
Weisman, Sam 29, 35, 37, 125, 134, 197
Weiss, Harriet 13, 56, 70, 95, 97, 171, 220
Weiss, Jonathan 91

Weiss, Martin 30, 37
Weiss, Robert K. 130
Weithorn, Michael J. 95, 132–4
Weitz, Bruce 96
Weitzman, Harvey 95, 121
Welcome Back, Kotter 85, 86, 95, 156
"Welcome to the Club" 147
Weldon, Ann 121
Welker, Frank 33, 99, 211
Weller, Mary Louise 145
Welles, Jesse 56, 118
Welles, Joan 71
Welles, Orson 182
Wells, Aarika 150
Wells, Claudette 156, 157
Wells, Claudia 43, 66, **67**, 117
Wells, Danny 114
Wells, Dawn 54–5
Wells, Tom 33, 124, 190, 230
Weltman, Philip 4
Wendt, George 1, 56, 59, 94–5, 197
Wendy and Me 53
Werber, Elliot 187
"We're All Right" 169
Werner, Fred 201
Werner, Martin 53
Werner, Tom 118, 119
Wesley, John 27
West, Adam 81–2, 119
West, Bernard 170, 179, 219
West, Howard 85, 86
West, Valerie 17
The West Coast Review 76, 232
The West Wing 162
Westerschulte, Dick 121, 220
Weston, Jack 49
Weston, Jim 98
Weston, Paul 197
Westside Medical 17
Weyman, Andrew D. 41, 171, 175, 191
Whalin, Justin 123
What a Country 36, 177–9, 232
"What I Want" 110
"What You Need" 139
What's Happening? 120
What's It All About, World? 65
"What's So Good About Goodbye?" 155
Whedon, Tom 94, 163, 176, 228
Wheeler, Susan Duff 214
Wheeler-Nicholson, Dana 16
"When Everyone Cared" 58
When the Whistle Blows 179–80
"Where Everybody Knows Your Name" 131
Whipple, Sam 123
Whipple, Shonda 51
Whitaker, Forest 95
White, Betty 9, 15, 93
White, David 72
White, Hollace 12, 102
White, Jaleel 22–4, **23**, 202
White, Kevin 22, 212
White, Larry 199
White, Snow 194
White, Vanna 159
Whitehead, Paxton 96
Whitehill, Philip 212

Whitesell, John 13, 123, 135, 167
Whitlow, Jill 12
Whitman, Jerry 180
Whitman, John 29, 44
Whitmore, James 54
Whitton, Margaret 44
Who's the Boss? 89, 90
Who's Watching the Kids? 57, 193
"Wichita Lineman" 146
Widdoes, James 91, 126, 192, 193
Wiggin, Tom 20
Wiggins, Bud 127
Wiggins, Mrs. 4
Wilcox, Dan 33, 36, 124, 185, 202
Wilcox, Ralph 121
Wilcox, Robert 42
"Wild About Harry" 56
Wilder, Gene 161
Wilder, Myles 38
Wilder, Yvonne 26
Wiley, Bill 6–7, **6**
Wilk, Diane 10, 73
Wilkes, Donna 206, 208
Wilks, Wendell 188
Will and Grace 36
Willard 207
Willard, Fred 44, 54, 110
Willcox, Pete 82
Willens, Shel 168
William the Conqueror 101
Williams, Allen 215
Williams, Barry 18
Williams, Christian 17
Williams, Ed 129
Williams, Francis E. 50
Williams, Jan 153
Williams, Larry O., Jr. 21
Williams, Louise 13, 164
Williams, Maiya 136
Williams, Marsha Posner 61, 120
Williams, Michael P. 160
Williams, Patrick 36, 38, 44, 102, 152, 164, 183, 184, 202
Williams, Paul 26, 73
Williams, R.J. 117, 118
Williams, Robin 104
Williams, Samm-Art 51
Williams, Steve "Dr. Death" 83
Williams, Timothy 172
Williams, Tom 114, 172
Williams, Vanessa 66, 136
Williamson, Fred 61
Williamson, Martha 91, 134, 135
Willingham, Noble 10, 180
Willis, Billy Dee 68
Willis, Melissa 90
Wills, Terry 200
Willson, Karen 52
Wilson, Brian 231
Wilson, Carl 231
Wilson, Cheryl 83
Wilson, Danny 207
Wilson, Demond 111–13, **111**, 219
Wilson, Flip 22–4, **23**
Wilson, Hugh 35, 41, 42, 51
Wilson, Jeannie 161
Wilson, Mary Louise 168
Wilson, Rita 83
Wilson, Roger 146
Wilson, Sandy 228

Wilson, Teddy 181–2
Wilson, Woodrow 223
Wilson-White, Lance 230
Wiltse, David 81
Winans, Sam 51
Windom, William 49, 64
Winer, Harry 33, 75, 102, 168, 176, 205
Winfield, Paul 194
Winkler, Henry 102, 104, 197, 210
Winnick, Jerry 121
Winter, Edward 37, 184
Winters, Jonathan 8, 25
Wirth, Billy 115
Wirth, Bob 75, 231
Wise, Marie Lynn 21
Wise Guy 167
"With a Little Help from My Friends" 150
Witt, Paul Junger 26, 61, 65, 70, 71, 73, 120, 172
Witus, Barbara 209
The Wizard of Oz 108, 113
WKRP in Cincinnati 32, 42, 51, 113, 138, 181
Wolf, Jay 231
Wolfe, George C. 228
Wolfert, Jonathan 138
Wolff, Art 54, 68, 91, 117, 134, 167
Wolff, Jon 31
Wolff, Jurgen 76, 131
Wolff, Paul 11
Wolfman Jack 218
Wollert, David 37
Wolpert, Stuart 11, 81, 164
Wolterstorff, Robert 214
A Woman on Top 37
Women in Prison 180, 233
Women's Digest Magazine 97
Women's Life 79, 81
The Wonder Years 43, 58, 94, 150
"Wonderful World" 22, 165, 233
Wood, Gene 185
Wood, Terri Lynn 188
Woodall, Ann 102
Woodard, Alfre 143
Woodland, Lauren 28
Woodward, Lenore 196
Woolvett, Gordon 83
Wopat, Tom 17, 33
Working Stiffs 138
Worrall, Tom 66
"Worst That Could Happen" 146
Worthington, Jan 68
Wright, Kay 33
Wright, Max 100, 189
Wright, Samuel E. 38
Wright, Stephen 227
Wright, Thomas J. 109, 114
Wuhl, Robert 45, 130, 221
Wyatt, Jane 13, 109, 140
Wyman, Douglas 98, 102
Wyner, George 12, 61
Wynn, Keenan 82

Yanok, George 162, 225
Yarnell, David 72, 110
Yasbeck, Amy 109, 185
Yasutake, Patti 59, 60
Yates, Cassie 114, **114**

Yates, Peter 20
Yates, William Robert 58, 66, 182
A Year at the Top 121
Yello 89
Yesso, Don 50, 51
Yniguez, Richard 95
Yohn, Erica 41
Yothers, Corey 117
Yothers, Tina 29
You Again? 230–1
"You and Me, Babe" 52
You Can't Take It with You 181–2
"You Look at Me" 210
"You Might Think" 139
Young, Alan 104, 196
Young, Bob 195
Young, Bruce A. 39
Young, Burt 139
Young, Chris 89, **89**
Young, G.J. 214
Young, Mark 25, 26
Young, Roger 84
Youngman, Henny 127

Zabriskie, Grace 96
Zamora, Rudy 33, 53, 211
Zanetos, Dean 39, 46
Zappa, Moon Unit 44
Zateslo, George 38
Zaylor, Judy 136
Zeigler, Heidi 21
Zellman, Shelley 11, 36, 145, 155, 193, 195, 202
Zicree, Mark Scott 52
Zien, Chip 91, 137, 148
Ziffren, John 148
Zimbalist, Efrem, Jr. 126
Zimmer, Jeff 28
Zimmerman, Stan 60, 77, 155
Zinberg, Michael 44, 125, 171, 172, 196
Zipp, Debbie 152
Zisk, Randall 44
Zlotoff Lee David 75
Zmed, Adrian 57, 71
Zorro and Son 182, 233
Zucker, David 129, 130
Zucker, Jerry 129, 130
Zuckerman, Steve 65, 134, 217
Zweibel, Alan 18

www.ingramcontent.com/pod-product-compliance
Lightning Source LLC
Chambersburg PA
CBHW080802300426
44114CB00020B/2798